NATIONAL GEOGRAPHIC

TRAVELER

The Caribbean

NATIONAL GEOGRAPHIC

TRAVELER

The Caribbean

Nick Hanna & Emma Stanford

National Geographic
Washington, D.C.

Contents

Page 1: Conch shell
Pages 2–3: Walking on the sand, Bonaire
Page 4: Girl dancing, Antigua

How to use this guide

See back flap for keys to text and map symbols.

The *National Geographic Traveler* brings you the best of the Caribbean in text, pictures, and maps. Divided into three main sections, the guide begins with an overview of history and culture. Following are 12 regional chapters with sites selected by the authors for their particular interest; each is treated in depth. Each chapter opens with its own contents list for easy reference.

The islands or island groups, and sites within them, are arranged geographically. Some island groups are further divided into two or three smaller areas. A map introduces each region, highlighting the featured sites. Walks and drives, all plotted on their own maps, suggest routes for discovering an area. Features and sidebars offer detail on history, culture, or contemporary life. A more places to visit page rounds off some island chapters.

The final section, Travelwise, lists essential information for the traveler—pre-trip planning, getting around, useful websites, and what to do in emergencies—plus a selection of hotels, restaurants, and shops.

To the best of our knowledge, site information is accurate as of the press date. However, it's always advisable to call ahead.

62

Color coding

Each region is color coded for easy reference. Find the region you want on the map on the front flap, and look for the color flash at the top of the pages of the relevant chapter. Information in **Travelwise** is also color coded to each region.

Bob Marley Museum
26 B3
56 Hope Rd.
876/927-9152
Closed Sun.
$$$

Visitor information

Practical information is given in the side column by each major site (see key to symbols on back flap). The map reference gives the page number where the site is shown on a map, followed by the grid reference.

Further details include the site's address, telephone number, days closed, and entrance charge in a range from $ (under $2) to $$$$$ (over $15). Other sites have visitor information in italics and parentheses in the text.

TRAVELWISE

JAMAICA — Color-coded region name

KINGSTON — Town name

HOTEL FOUR SEASONS
$$-$$$ — Hotel name, price range

18 RUTHVEN RD.,
KINGSTON 10
TEL 876/926-8805
FAX 876/929-5964 — Address, telephone & fax numbers

Within walking distance of the uptown entertainment areas, the hotel has a section converted from an Edwardian house and a new annex. — Brief description of hotel

76
All major cards — Hotel facilities and credit card details

STRAWBERRY HILL
$$$$ — Restaurant name & price range

IRISH TOWN
TEL 876/944-8400 — Address & telephone number

High up in the Blue Mountains, this excellent restaurant specializes in "new Jamaican cuisine" with dishes such as sweet potato gnocci. — Brief description of restaurant

All major cards — Restaurant facilities and credit card details

Hotel and restaurant prices

An explanation of the price ranges used in entries is given in the Hotels & Restaurants section (beginning on p. 353).

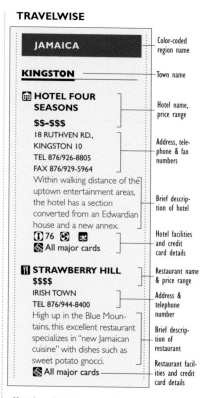

REGIONAL MAPS

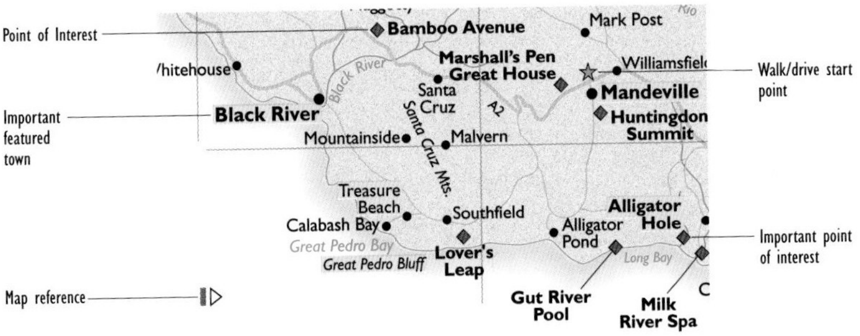

- A locator map accompanies each regional map and shows the location of that region in the Caribbean.

WALKING TOURS

- An information box gives the starting and finishing points, time and length of walk, and places not to be missed along the route.

DRIVING TOURS

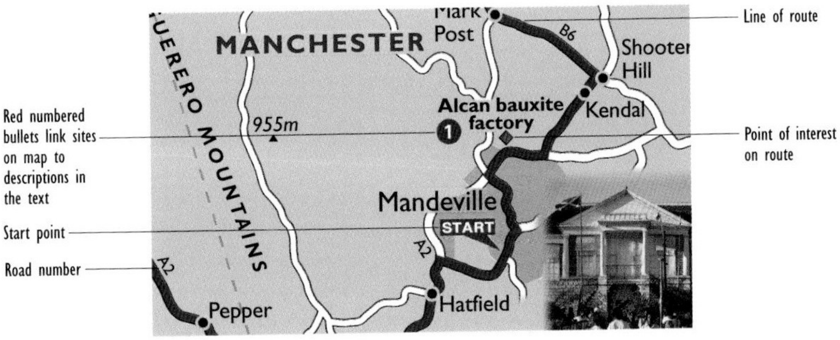

- An information box provides details that include starting and finishing points, places not to be missed along the route, the time and length of drive, or tips on terrain.

NATIONAL GEOGRAPHIC

TRAVELER The Caribbean

About the authors

Nick Hanna is a graduate in Social Anthropology from Sussex University and has been a professional travel writer and photographer for 25 years. He has worked as a freelance writer for numerous national and international newspapers and magazines and has written nine guidebooks, including one that covered more than 200 tropical beaches around the world. He has also co-authored a book on the conservation of coral reefs and written extensively on the marine environment and scuba diving.

Being a seasoned island-hopper and experienced travel writer ensures that Emma Stanford is frequently drawn toward the Caribbean. She has, however, also written and edited numerous other works covering destinations as diverse as Hawaii, Florida, and Los Angeles, Morocco, the Himalayas and New Zealand during her 20-plus years on the road, boat, train, and (occasionally) horse.

History & culture

Churchgoers in Christchurch, St. Kitts

The Caribbean today

"A CARIBBEAN VACATION" IS ONE OF THE MOST EVOCATIVE PHRASES IN THE English language. The merest suggestion can unleash a stream of dreamy images featuring golden beaches, coconut palms, limpid azure seas, and hibiscus blooms accompanied by a sound track of tinkling steel-pan music or the rhythmic beat of reggae. The extended Caribbean show reel might incorporate coral-reef diving and rain forest trails, exploring colonial relics, and sailing through the Virgin Islands archipelago or the Grenadines. But however satisfying this momentary daydream may be, it cannot beat the reality, the feel of powder-soft coral sand between your toes, the squawk and colorful flash of a rare parrot in the rain forest, the taste of a fresh mango plucked straight from the tree.

The Caribbean is the quintessential escape from the grim, gray northern winter, an island paradise with guaranteed blue skies, sun-soaked lazy days, and the option of a lively, reggae-fueled nightlife. If your idea of a perfect vacation involves succumbing body and soul to the languor of the tropics, relaxing by the pool or on a crescent of manicured sand with a frosted glass of planter's punch in hand, the Caribbean can deliver, no problem. Fortunately for more adventurous visitors, there is plenty more to the region than two-dimensional travel-poster imagery. To get a real feel for the islands and experience their third dimension—the varied landscapes, exotic flora and fauna, bustling waterfront towns, and friendly laid-back people—venture beyond the limited confines of the beach, resort, or cruise ship and dig a little deeper. In no time at all it will become apparent that there is no such thing as a homogeneous Caribbean entity. Each island has its own particular style shaped by a unique combination of geology, historical influences, and attitudes that can vary dramatically between neighbors separated by a few nautical miles.

CHOOSING AN ISLAND

Selecting the right combination of ingredients for a perfect Caribbean vacation needs a little research. Accommodations are a prime consideration: Should it be a romantic plantation hotel in St. Kitts and Nevis or a family-friendly beach resort offering a wide range of activities and water sports? As a rule of thumb, the better the beaches the more developed the island, so expect a greater choice of accommodations and easy access to top beach destinations. Favorites with beach lovers include Aruba in the Netherlands Antilles; the Leeward Islands of Antigua and Anguilla; Barbados; the U.S. Virgin Islands; and Jamaica and the Dominican Republic, which both score highly on beaches and fabulous mountain scenery, as does Puerto Rico.

Caribbean activity holidays have taken off in a big way, with diving representing a major attraction for many visitors. The Cayman Islands are famously positioned on the brink of the Cayman Trench, offering dramatic wall diving. In the Netherlands Antilles, Bonaire, Saba, and Sint Eustatius forgo beaches for spectacular dive sites; or head to the Windward Islands for St. Lucia and up-and-coming Dominica.

The Windwards, which include Grenada and St. Vincent, are also celebrated for their lush rain forest highlands, which offer terrific hiking, while Trinidad and Tobago at the tail end of the island chain are an ornithologist's paradise. Interspersed with the Windwards are the French Caribbean islands of Guadeloupe and Martinique: These share many of the same physical characteristics and are the crucible for the eastern Caribbean's vibrant Creole culture. True Francophiles, on the other hand, might find themselves gravitating towards tiny St. Barthélemy, a distinctly European-style jet-set haunt reminiscent of the French Riviera.

Perfect Caribbean vacations come in all shapes and sizes, and this brief overview can only hint at the wealth of options available.

Snorkelers explore the translucent waters below a trimaran in the Netherlands Antilles.

WHEN TO GO

The Caribbean region lies in the tropics, so temperatures are fairly consistent all year. Temperatures on the coast average 78–86°F (26–30°C) in the day and 59–64°F (15–18°C) at night, often tempered by cooling trade winds. At higher elevations, around 1,000 feet (300 m) above sea level or more, the temperature will drop a few degrees and may warrant packing a sweater for the evening or a light waterproof jacket for hikers heading into the mountains.

High season in the Caribbean is the generally cooler and drier period between December and April, when hotels charge their top rates. The humidity increases in the build-up to the rainy season, which lasts from June to November, though showers occur throughout the year and on a daily basis in the rainforest highlands. For years this has been a winter-only destination, but now the early part of the wet season is becoming increasingly popular with visitors who want to sample a

Caribbean vacation at more affordable prices. However, expect high humidity, as well as short, sharp downpours and a fair amount of cloudiness.

Though the Caribbean experiences few climatic extremes, the region is in the hurricane zone. These violent tropical storms rise off the coast of West Africa and gather strength as they cross the Atlantic, smashing into the islands with devastating force. In recent years, hurricanes have wreaked widespread destruction across the north of the region, while Hurricane Ivan in 2004 caused considerable damage as far south as Grenada, formerly thought to be safely below the Hurricane Belt with Trinidad, Aruba, Bonaire, and Curaçao off the coast of Venezuela. The official hurricane season runs from June to November, though a

Churches such as this one in Christchurch, St. Kitts, are part of the fabric of Caribbean society.

View of Carriacou, one of the Grenadines. It lies about 23 miles (37 km) north of Grenada.

traditional rhyme advises "June, too soon; July, stand by; September, remember; October, all over." Statistically, mid-September is the most likely time for a hurricane to pass through.

LAND & LANDSCAPES

The Caribbean islands form a 2,500-mile (4,000-km) arc from Cuba, which lies 90 miles (145 km) south of Key West on the southern tip of Florida, to Trinidad, just 7 miles (11 km) off the coast of Venezuela. The 50-plus islands, which do not include the Bahamas or far-flung Bermuda to the north of the region, and several thousand uninhabited cays, rocks, and reefs, encircle the million-square-mile (2.6-million-sq-km) Caribbean Sea. They are buffeted on their windward sides by the Atlantic Ocean, and the more sheltered leeward sides of the islands face the gentle Caribbean.

Early explorers christened the entire archipelago the Antilles, but today the islands are grouped into the Greater Antilles, or western Caribbean, consisting of Cuba (not included in this guide), the Cayman Islands, Jamaica, Hispaniola (the Dominican Republic/Haiti; Haiti is not included in this guide), Puerto Rico, and the Virgin Islands; and the Lesser Antilles, or eastern Caribbean.

The Lesser Antilles chain is further divided into the Leeward Islands and Windward Islands, interspersed with the French Antilles, the Dutch Windwards group of the Netherlands Antilles islands (Saba, Sint Eustatius, Sint Maarten/St. Martin), and Trinidad and Tobago. Barbados stands on its own to the east of the Windward Islands. The Dutch Leewards, or ABCs (Aruba, Bonaire, and Curaçao), lie west of Trinidad along the Venezuelan coast.

GEOLOGY

The islands are poised on the brink of the Caribbean and Atlantic tectonic plates. The majority are volcanic in origin, though there are a few low-lying coral atolls such as the Cayman Islands and Anguilla, and the arid, desertlike Dutch Leewards. The oldest islands in the region lie to the north, where Jamaica, Hispaniola, and Puerto Rico were formed around 70 million years ago.

In the eastern Caribbean, Montserrat, Guadeloupe, Martinique, Dominica, St. Lucia, St. Vincent, and Grenada remain volcanically active with bubbling mud pools and oozing, foul-smelling sulfur pits. Off the coast of Grenada, the submarine volcano Kick 'em Jenny is currently around 500 feet (150 m) below the surface and rising.

Giant philodendrons blanket the floor of the rain forests in St. Kitts.

FLORA & FAUNA

The Caribbean's mountain ranges are cloaked in dense rain forest, which grows with explosive rapidity in the fertile volcanic soil. True rain forest is the richest natural habitat on the planet and requires an annual rainfall in excess of 70 inches (178 cm), which the Caribbean islands receive courtesy of the Atlantic trade winds. In the hothouse atmosphere beneath the rain forest canopy, dozens of ferns, creepers, and bamboo flourish at the feet of giant buttress-trunked santinay trees, mahogany, gommier, and mahoe.

At higher elevations, in the montane or cloud forest, tree branches play host to a variety of bromeliads (which gain nutrients from the air) and orchids, while higher still the lichen-encrusted elfin forest opens onto grasslands frequently visited by cool, hazy drizzle and wisps of cloud.

Few mammals live in the rain forest, and indigenous species such as armadillos, opossums, and agoutis are rarely spotted. Reptiles, including tree frogs, iguanas, and dozens of species of small lizards, are a constant presence, as are winged insects such as butterflies and predatory mosquitoes. Though there are occasional sightings of nonvenomous tree snakes, the sole poisonous snake is the fer de lance, found only on Martinique and St. Lucia.

Bird lovers are in for a treat in the Caribbean. Several species of rare indigenous parrot live in the Windward Islands, and the woodlands are also home to numerous varieties of hummingbirds, honeycreepers, tanagers, and cheeky bananaquits, which frequently leave the rain forest to feed on the brilliant tropical blooms in gardens.

Many species of herons, waders, ducks, and other wetland birds gather in the coastal mangrove swamps of Jamaica and Trinidad, while flamingo colonies can be found in Bonaire and Lago Enriquillo in the Dominican Republic. Seabirds, including boobies, magnificent frigatebirds, pelicans, and elegant scissor-tailed tropic birds, colonize rocky outcrops visible from the shore.

Just as the rain forest flourishes, so does the myriad variety of other plants and trees. While many islanders cultivate colorful flower gardens, botanical gardens are the best place to see a whole range of eye-catching heliconias and gingers, spice trees such as nutmeg and cinnamon, and flowering trees such as the yellow- or pink-blossomed poui, scarlet poinciana, and spreading immortelle, which flowers in January and February. ■

History & culture

CHRISTOPHER COLUMBUS FIRST SIGHTED THE ISLAND OF SAN SALVADOR IN the Bahamas on October 12, 1492, and sailed on into the Caribbean Sea intent on discovering a westward passage to the East Indian spice islands. The arrival of European explorers opened the book on the recorded history of the region, and the islands were named the Antilles after the legendary island of Antillia, once thought to lie between Europe and the Americas. However, the Caribbean's first settlers had arrived several thousand years earlier—Amerindian tribes who paddled their canoes to the islands from Central America, or possibly Florida.

PRE-COLUMBIAN CARIBBEAN

The Stone Age Ciboney people (or Archaic Indians) were the earliest inhabitants of the Greater Antilles islands. Archaeological digs in Cuba have uncovered Ciboney sites about 6,000 years old, while relics in Hispaniola are reckoned to be about 4,000 years old. These nomadic hunter-gatherers lived off a nourishing and varied diet of fish and shellfish, birds, iguanas, and snakes, supplemented by roots and wild fruits, and they crafted tools and utensils from stone, wood, bone, and shell.

About 300 B.C. the first Arawak migrated to the islands. They are thought to have originated in the Amazon Basin, and then they pushed north to make the sea crossing from northeastern South America (present-day Venezuela and Guyana) to the southernmost of the Lesser Antilles. Gradually they moved up the island chain, and by the time Columbus appeared on the scene, the three major Arawak groups were populating the Greater Antilles islands and Bahamas: the Taino (Cuba, Jamaica, and Hispaniola), the Borequio or Borinquen (Puerto Rico), and the Lucayan (Bahamas).

The Arawak were more sophisticated than the Ciboney. They were farmers, cultivating cassava (for flour), yams, corn, beans, cocoa, peanuts, tobacco, and cotton. Skilled hunters and fishermen, they were also potters capable of producing earthenware for domestic and religious purposes.

Arawak society was well organized. Villages were generally built close to the shore, and each community was presided over by a *cacique*, or village chieftain, who was responsible for both the temporal and religious life of the villagers. At the center of the village was a large open-sided *carbet* (thatched shelter) where the cacique and men held council: It was out-of-bounds to women and children except by invitation to attend special ceremonies. Unmarried men could sleep here or in a separate carbet, stringing maybe a hundred hammocks from the roof. Religion played an important part in Arawak daily life. There were gods associated with food crops, fertility, and weather, and benevolent spirits that inhabited plants and animals. Religious ceremonies included snorting trance-inducing narcotics and dancing, as well as the worship of *zemi*, simple shapes or human and animal figures made of wood, bone, or stone. Arawak believed in the afterlife and took great care with burial rituals. The dead were placed in a squatting position and were equipped with personal belongings (the wives of important chieftains were buried alive), and food for the journey to Coyaba, a plentiful land of nonstop dancing and feasting.

ARRIVAL OF THE CARIB

After a thousand years, the Arawak's peaceful existence came to an abrupt end with the arrival of the Carib. Also from South America, the warlike Carib progressed northward through the Lesser Antilles, slaughtering Arawak men and assimilating women and children into their tribes. Though the proof is somewhat sketchy, the Carib had a reputation for cannibalism and were said to barbecue (a Carib word) their male victims, which included Europeans as they began to explore the region. The Carib were excellent marksmen with bows and arrows and fearlessly attacked

The mountainous island of Dominica was given its name by Christopher Columbus who made landfall here on a Sunday.

J7036-SHD

Spanish sailing ships from their wooden war canoes, or *piragua* (from which the simple pirogue fishing boats still used in the Windward Islands take their name). The Europeans pushed the Carib back into the rugged terrain of the Windward Islands, where they managed to hold out for more than 200 years, and a few mixed-blood survivors still live on Dominica and St. Vincent.

A resident of Jamaica's Cockpit Country holds a copy of the original constitution, dating back to the British colonial era.

EUROPEAN INVASION

Columbus made five voyages to the Caribbean in his attempt to discover a western route to the East Indies, stubbornly naming his finds the West Indies despite all the evidence to the contrary. On his fourth voyage, in 1502, he located the South American mainland and secured its vast mineral wealth for the Roman Catholic kings of Spain.

During the early 16th century, Spanish settlements sprang up in the Greater Antilles, first in Hispaniola, then Cuba, Jamaica, and Puerto Rico. The Arawak were enslaved, and within 50 years the indigenous population of these northern islands had been eradicated through warfare, disease, and transportation to work the mainland gold mines.

The Spanish treasure fleets making their way home to Europe acted as a magnet for pirates and privateers. Throughout the 16th and 17th centuries, French, English, and Dutch vessels preyed mercilessly on heavily laden armadas, lurking in the isolated cays of the Virgin Islands. The next logical step for the interlopers was to claim colonies of their own in the region, which became easier as Spanish influence declined in Europe during the 17th century. The English and French moved in on the Lesser Antilles, commencing a 250-year struggle for dominance in the eastern Caribbean, and the Dutch cannily selected islands with a view to their strategic importance on the trading routes used by their rivals.

COLONIAL ERA

Sugarcane was introduced to the Caribbean by Dutch planters from Brazil in the 1630s (see p. 308). From small-scale beginnings in Barbados, the enormously profitable trade in "white gold" triggered the rapid expansion of European colonialism in the region, and its labor-intensive cultivation brought an immediate demand for a cheap and inexhaustible workforce. Spanish settlers had imported small numbers of West African slaves to work their Caribbean plantations since the early days, but the sugar trade boosted numbers to unprecedented levels. Untold millions of Africans were sold into slavery and shipped across the Atlantic to work the plantations; many thousands died en route (see p. 248).

By the start of the 19th century, the importance of the Caribbean sugar trade dwindled as sugar beet production in Europe rose to satisfy local demand. The planters' profits decreased, and in 1808, the antislavery movement in Britain succeeded in banning the slave trade to the colonies. This was followed in 1834 by the Emancipation Act, which outlawed the ownership of slaves. The other European nations followed suit, and the former sugar colonies fell into a decline.

As the freed slaves abandoned the plantations, major producers such as Jamaica and Trinidad imported East Indian indentured laborers, but most islands slipped quietly into the doldrums, largely forgotten by their erstwhile colonial masters.

THE MODERN ERA

The Spanish-American War of 1898 introduced U.S. influence to the region. The U.S. claimed its first territory with the capture of Puerto Rico from Spain. It followed up this belated foray into Caribbean empire-building with the purchase of the U.S. Virgin Islands from Denmark in 1917. The Caribbean islands experienced the trickle-down effect of the 1930s Great Depression, which deepened the region's economic problems and heralded the rise of grassroots labor movements. These in turn spearheaded the transition toward greater independence from Europe.

In 1962, Jamaica was the first British colony to achieve full independence, and Britain divested most of its colonies during the 1970s and 1980s. Several smaller islands opted to remain Crown Colonies, while others have joined the British Commonwealth as independent states. The Dutch and French retain closer ties with their colonies.

The region has 24 separate political entities and a stable though deeply fragmented political scene. Tourism is the economic mainstay, although sugar production in the Dominican Republic, Barbados, and Jamaica, bananas in the Windward Islands, and oil in Trinidad all contribute to individual national economies.

COLONIAL LEGACY

As European colonists staked their claims to the Caribbean islands, each nation attempted in some degree to re-create a miniature home away from home in the sun. Thus, the Spanish Catholic heritage is readily apparent in the historic cities and churches of the Dominican Republic and Puerto Rico; the ex-British colonies in the Leeward and Windward Islands are rich in four-square stone Georgian architecture; the French islands retain an inimitable savoir faire combined with gastronomic flair; and in the Dutch Leewards, Curaçao's elegantly gabled buildings have been designated a World Heritage site.

Language is another legacy from colonial days. English is spoken in Jamaica, the Cayman Islands, the Virgin Islands, the Leeward and Windward Islands (Dominica and St. Lucia islanders traditionally speak a form of French patois among themselves), and Trinidad and Tobago. The Netherlands Antilles are bilingual in Dutch and English, while visitors to the French Antilles should be aware that little English is spoken outside

A French flag flies above the stone walls of Marigot's St. Louis Fort, built on St. Martin in 1767.

more expensive hotels. Most Spanish-speaking Puerto Ricans also speak English, while a Spanish phrase book will prove essential in the nontourist areas of the Dominican Republic.

The majority of Caribbean people are of African origin, and although African culture was subjugated by European customs during the colonial era, it did not disappear altogether. Freed from Old World dominance, the African heritage is now the strongest element of pan-Caribbean cultural trends. Its influence is unmistakable in music, traditional cooking, and the common animist superstitions that operate alongside traditional European religions in a very typically Caribbean compromise.

MUSIC

Music is, so they say, the heartbeat of the Caribbean, and it is certainly hard to ignore. The strains of calypso, reggae, soca (soul-calypso), and steel pan, throbbing bass dub

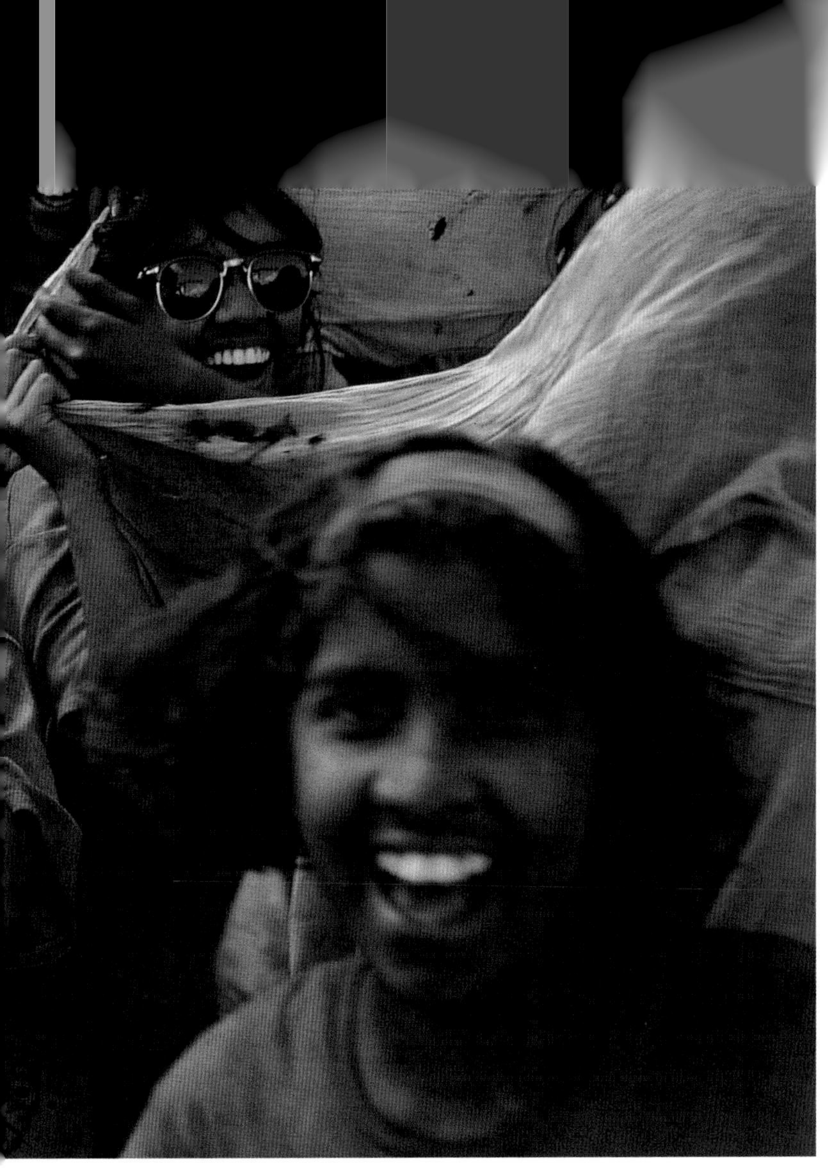

music booming out from dollar buses, and the dance rhythms of Puerto Rican salsa, merengue from the Dominican Republic, and zouk from the French Antilles, provide a catchy backdrop to the Caribbean experience.

Calypso is the grandfather of the music scene, with its origins buried way back in West African slave traditions. Forbidden to speak their native languages, slaves were, however, permitted to sing; the planters believed it helped them work faster. Yet unbeknownst to their employers, the slaves used song to keep alive the West African storytelling tradition and to pass along information and messages of protest concealed in allegorical terms. Today's calypsonians (calypso singers) are still judged not only on the music but also on the message they put across.

Residents of multicultural Trinidad celebrate the Hindu festival of Phagwa in the San Juan district.

Trinidad is the home of calypso and steel-pan music, which originated in the dockyards of Port of Spain during World War II when oil drums were recycled for makeshift drums. Reggae emerged from the Kingston ghetto of Trenchtown, Jamaica with its most famous exponent, Bob Marley, in the 1970s.

Live music performances in clubs and bars are easy to find throughout the islands. Music festivals are also well worth tracking down. The most famous events include Jamaica's Reggae Sunfest (July–Aug.), the St. Lucia International Jazz Festival (May), and the St. Kitts Music Festival (June).

CARNIVAL

Carnival is a magnificent explosion of elaborate costumes, music, singing, and dance that captures the creativity and natural exuberance of the Caribbean people. The date varies from island to island, but most carnivals take place before Lent (Feb.–March), while others celebrate the end of the sugar harvest (July–Aug.) or the anniversary of emancipation.

Europeans introduced carnival to the Caribbean, marking the approach of Lent, a traditional period of Christian abstinence, with a hectic round of feasting and parties ("carnival" is derived from the Italian *carnevale*, meaning the removal of meat). After emancipation, former slaves hijacked the party season by introducing their own processions featuring folkloric characters, dancing, and African drumming, which, once banned by the authorities, became the core of the new Caribbean-style carnival.

The buildup to Lenten carnivals, such as the famous one in Trinidad (see p. 321), begins soon after Christmas, when musicians take part in the hotly contested qualifying heats, and band members and dancers participating in the main carnival processions put the final touches to their costumes.

Carnival begins in earnest on the Friday before Lent, and competitions held over the weekend decide the winners of the various calypso, steel-pan, and costume prizes. The main processions begin before dawn on Monday with a wild jump-up known as Jouvert (*jour ouvert* or daybreak in French Creole), followed by Tuesday's dazzling Mardi Gras parade.

FOOD & DRINK

Traditional Caribbean cooking is simple, nutritious, and filling, using plentiful local ingredients from fresh fish and seafood to a wide variety of tropical fruits and vegetables, supplemented with chicken and a little red meat. Staple foods such as rice 'n' peas (the "peas" are red kidney beans), fried plantains (a variety of banana that is inedible raw), spinachlike callaloo, starchy breadfruit, and root vegetables (yam, eddoe, cassava) known as "ground provision" are found throughout the islands. Adventurous visitors should sample soursop, sugar and golden apples, tart tamarinds, and tiny plums. Markets are the best place to find and taste what is in season.

Guadeloupe and Martinique are renowned for Creole cuisine (see p. 238), while Puerto Rican specialties such as *lechón asao* (roast suckling pig), and *locrio* (a variation on paella), served in the Dominican Republic, show a distinctive Spanish influence. The Indian influence is unmistakable in Trinidad's curries and *rotis* (chapati envelopes filled with curried meat, seafood, or vegetables) that have now become a popular snack food in neighboring islands. Jamaican jerk is said to have been invented by runaway slaves who cooked in earth pits covered with branches.

RUM & BEER

Rum has been produced in the Caribbean since the 17th century, when sugar planters first distilled a spirit from molasses. Still made throughout the region, the best quality rums traditionally come from Barbados, Jamaica, Guadeloupe, and Martinique. While most islanders prefer their rum neat, visitors are more attracted to the long list of rum cocktails available, including piña coladas (flavored with pineapple and coconut), Cuba libre (with cola), fruit daiquiris, and planters punch (the original only has lime and cane juice, but added fruit juices are popular today). There are also delicious nonalcoholic fruit punches.

Wine is not produced in the Caribbean, so it is expensive. Local breweries, on the other hand, turn out some good lager-type beers. Particularly good are Banks from Barbados, Carib from Trinidad and franchises on several islands, Presidente from the Dominican Republic, and Red Stripe from Jamaica. ■

The third largest island in the Caribbean after Cuba and Hispaniola, Jamaica offers a staggering display of magnificent waterfalls and mountain landscapes, fascinating historic sites, and a vibrant cultural life.

Jamaica

A Jamaican Rastafarian

Jamaica

THE TAINO INDIANS WHO SETTLED JAMAICAN NAMED IT XAYMACA (LAND of Wood and Water). Despite the island's bigger population today, the description is still largely accurate. The Spanish occupation from 1510 onward led to the decimation of the native population and the arrival of the first slaves. Most Jamaicans can trace their ancestry to those slaves, as well as those brought over under later British rule. Jamaican culture is a vibrant fusion of African and European influence.

Under British rule the slave trade boomed, providing a labor force for the sugar plantations. Jamaica also served as a haven for pirates and buccaneers, encouraged by the British to make Kingston's Port Royal their base for harassing the Spanish fleets. Slave rebellions were also a prominent feature of Jamaica's history until British-implemented emancipation in 1834, four years after the British parliament had abolished the slave trade.

The island became a British Crown Colony in 1866, and during the 1890s the first tourists arrived on banana boats from North America. The Depression of the 1930s led to bloodshed and riots as the economy faltered, giving birth to the country's first labor union and the socialistic People's National Party (P.N.P.) led by Norman Manley (1893–1969). Universal suffrage was granted in 1944, and in 1962 Jamaica won full independence.

Jamaica's culture is a potent brew of fierce national pride, reggae and Rastafarians, sassy attitudes, and snatches of the local dialect (known as Jamaican patois). The poverty and absence of opportunity that led to the political unrest and occasional riots of the past still affect much of the island.

With over one million visitors a year, Jamaica has one of the largest tourism industries in the Caribbean—and that means it has one of the widest selections of accommodations, from luxury villas or budget cottages on the beach to private mountain retreats.

Jamaica's 4,244 square miles (10,992 sq km) embrace an enormous variety of landscapes. Like many of its neighbors, the island evolved from a broad arc of volcanoes

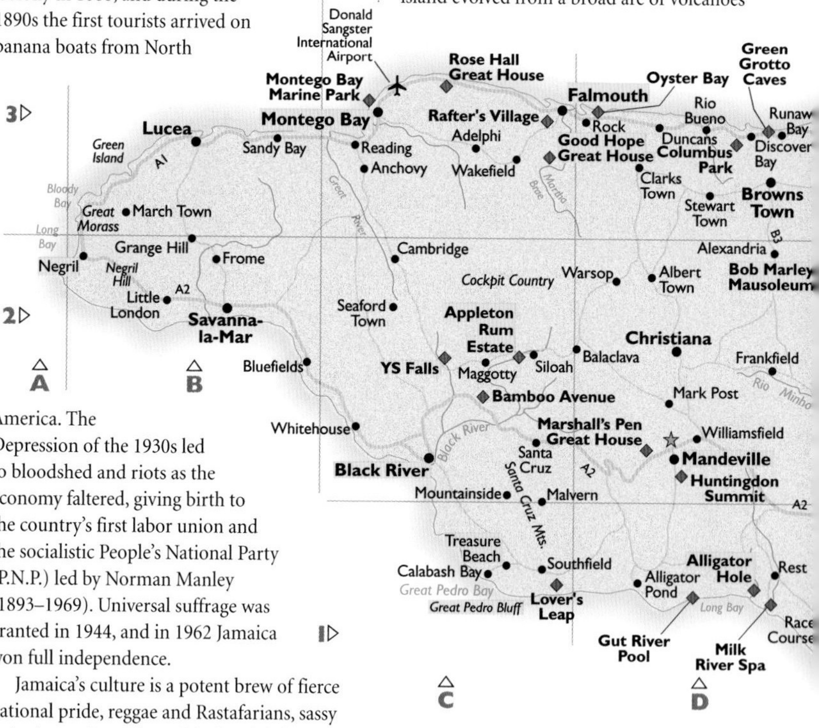

rising from the seabed billions of years ago. This igneous rock forms the Blue Mountains, which traverse the eastern third of the island and reach their summit at the 7,402-foot (2,256 m) Blue Mountain Peak. The land surrounding the Blue Mountains is capped by limestone plateaus that cover about two-thirds of the island. Over the centuries, rivers have carved sinkholes, caves, and deeply rutted gullies in the limestone—most visible in the Cockpit Country region.

An offshore coral reef shields the white, sandy beaches of Jamaica's north shore, where there are many resorts. The eastern coastline, unprotected from ocean swells, is far more rugged and dramatic. With a few exceptions, the south and west coasts are typified by volcanic black-sand beaches.

Jamaica's mist-shrouded mountains are the source of more than a hundred rivers. The longest, the 44-mile (71 km) Black River, flows to sea on the southwest coast.

The island's lush vegetation includes more than 3,000 species of trees and plants. Of these, about 800 are indigenous, including 200 species of orchids, 550 types of ferns, and 60 species of bromeliads.

Almost half of Jamaica is under cultivation. Before Europeans arrived, the only native fruits were guava, pineapple, and soursop. Successive colonists introduced breadfruit, sugarcane, coconuts, and ackee, a yellow fruit that, when combined with saltfish (cod), is a national dish. Today, huge plantations cloak the landscape with sugarcane, bananas, cocoa, coffee, rice, tobacco, and citrus fruits.

Besides agriculture and tourism the other mainstay of Jamaica's economy is bauxite, which has provided towns such as Mandeville (see pp. 54–59) with considerable wealth. The "red gold" is extracted from the earth and then converted into aluminum.

Jamaica has a population of about 2.6 million, around a quarter of whom live in the capital, Kingston. ■

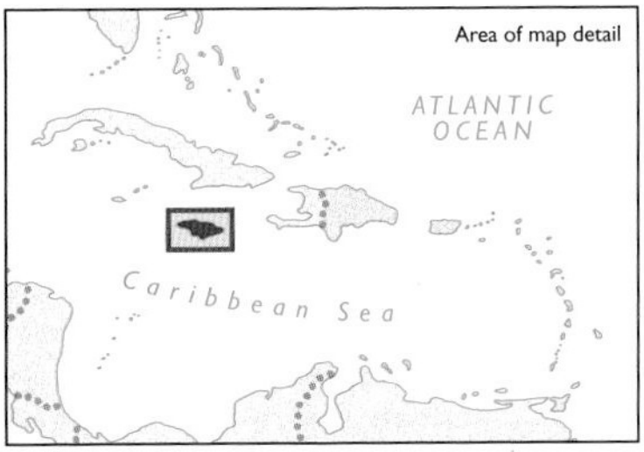

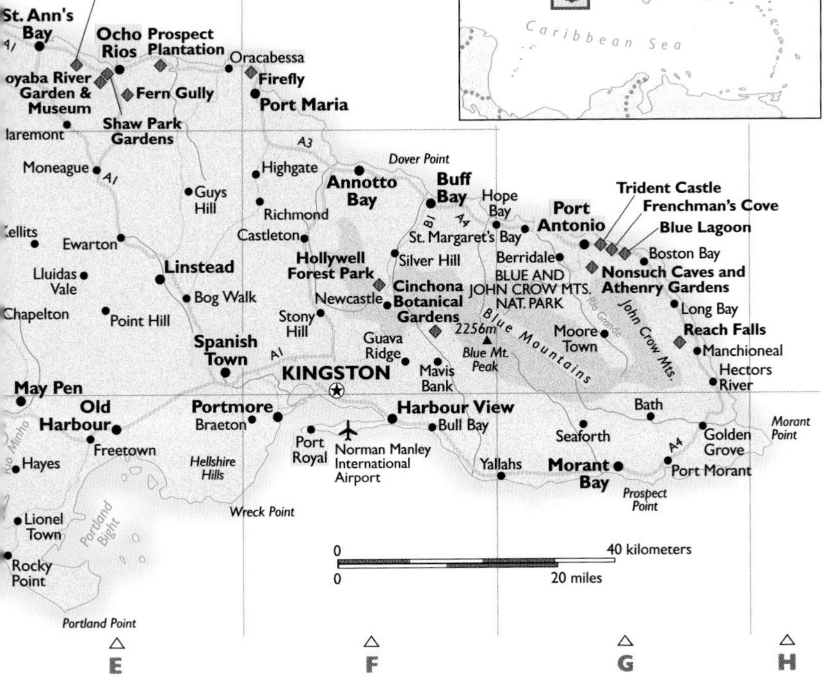

Kingston

Kingston
25 F2
Visitor information
www.visitjamaica.com
64 Knutsford Blvd.
876/929-9200
Closed weekends

THROBBING WITH ENERGY AND SPIRIT, THE DYNAMIC capital of Jamaica is home to more than half a million people. The largest English-speaking city in the Caribbean, it is also one of the most important cultural and political hubs in the region.

Kingston owes its growth to its magnificent natural harbor, the seventh largest in the world. The English recognized its strategic importance, building no fewer than five forts on the sandspit of Port Royal (see pp. 30–31) in the 17th century. When an earthquake destroyed Port Royal on June 7, 1692, its inhabitants fled to Kingston, and the concentration of economic and political power in the city eventually led to the capital being transferred here from Spanish Town in 1872. The city kept on growing, and today it spreads into the foothills of the Blue Mountains.

The heart of Kingston is the downtown area, which embraces the waterfront, historic sites, and to the west some of the city's most notorious slums. In the center is the **Parade,** once the British army's parade ground. Today it reverberates with the sound of reggae as vendors of cane juice, cassettes, bus tickets, and baubles ply their wares. The green heart of the Parade is **Sir William Grant Park,** a

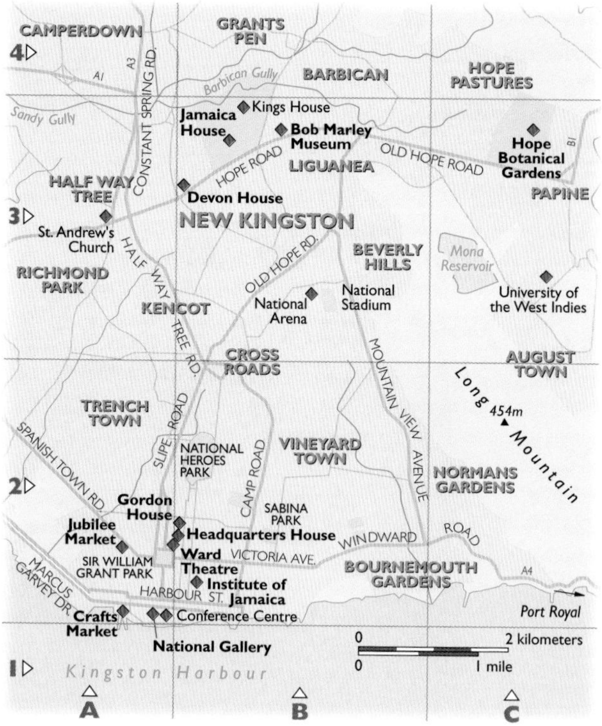

leafy square with a fountain and statues of Queen Victoria, Norman Manley (see p. 24), and Alexander Bustamante (1884–1977), founder of the country's first trade union. On the north side of the Parade is the **Ward Theatre** *(Tel 876/922-3213)*, an elegant building completed in 1911, which hosts performances by amateur dramatic groups as well as the National Dance Theater Company. To the west of the Parade is the colorful **Jubilee Market,** a good place to sample some of the country's exotic fruits and vegetables.

A few minutes' stroll east from here on Duke Street is Headquarters House, which was built in 1755 by a wealthy local merchant, Thomas Hibbert, as part of a wager with three other rich friends to see who could construct the most elegant building to win the attentions of a local beauty. Hibbert lost, but the winning house is no longer in existence. Headquarters House, with its handsome white facade and graceful fan window, has served as both a military headquarters and as home to Jamaica's legislative assembly, which met here between 1872 and 1960. Today it houses the offices of the **National Heritage Trust,** but you can visit the rest of the building, which includes the debating chamber and a lookout on the roof with splendid views of Kingston, the mountains, and the harbor. Next door stands **Gordon House** *(Corner of Beeston & Duke Sts., tel 876/922-0200)*, where the House of Representatives and the Senate meet. *(Entrance to the public gallery is free during debates.)*

Jubilee Market

- 26 A2
- Spanish Town Rd.
- Closed weekends

National Heritage Trust

- 26 B2
- 79 Duke St.
- 876/922-1287
- Closed weekends

The ornate Ward Theatre was built on the site of the former Theatre Royal.

Allow an hour to explore the Bob Marley Museum.

National Gallery
- 26 A2
- Roy West Bldg.
- 876/922-1561
- Closed Sun.–Mon.
- $

Institute of Jamaica
- 26 B2
- 12 East St.
- 876/922-0620
- Closed weekends

National Heroes Park
- 26 B2
- Duke St.

Bob Marley Museum
- 26 B3
- 56 Hope Rd.
- 876/927-9152
- Closed Sun.
- $$$

Fronting Kingston Harbour, the waterfront was once embellished with fingerlike piers jutting into the sea, but these were swept away when the area was redeveloped in the 1960s and a new shipping port was created farther west. **Ocean Boulevard** along the waterfront is lined with high-rise office buildings, shops, hotels, and apartments. About midway you'll find the bronze sculpture "Negro Aroused," a famous work by Edna Manley (1900–1987), the former wife of politician Norman Manley. It captures the spirit of the 1930s labor movement in its depiction of a bowed worker uncoiling from the chains of bondage. The original bronze is in the **National Gallery,** the highlight of the waterfront area. Its impressive permanent collection includes numerous wood carvings (particularly noteworthy are those by Edna Manley), African-style and Rastafarian paintings, landscapes, and contemporary photography covering a variety of Jamaican themes.

Walk two blocks west to the **Crafts Market** *(Ocean Blvd., closed Sun.)*, a good place to hunt for carvings, souvenirs, T-shirts, and jewelry. In the other direction on East Street is the **Institute of Jamaica,** which was founded in 1879 for the "encouragement of literature, science and art." The institute houses the **National Library,** which holds one of the largest collections of historical documents in the Caribbean, as well as the **Museum of Natural History,** which chronicles the arrival on the island of coconuts, bananas, sugarcane, and other plants that now form the backbone of Jamaica's agricultural sector.

NATIONAL HEROES PARK

Poised midway between downtown and the city's uptown area, New Kingston, is the National Heroes Park, a 75-acre (30-ha) open space that was once the city's race track. It now honors the country's national heroes, including Norman Manley and Alexander Bustamante (the founders of modern Jamaican politics); Sam Sharpe (1801–1832) and Paul Bogle (died 1865), both Baptist preachers involved in slave rebellions; Marcus Garvey (1887–1940), father of the Black Power movement; and Nanny, a legendary 18th-century leader of the Maroons. Norman Manley, Alexander Bustamante, and Marcus Garvey are buried here. Simón Bolívar (1783–1830) and Antoneo Maceo (1845–1896), independence leaders in South America and Cuba, are also honored in the park.

NEW KINGSTON

New Kingston extends from the busy crossroads of Half Way Tree Road up to Vale Royal. Wealthy merchants settled this district in the 18th century, when they fled the noise and squalor of downtown to build large residences surrounded by grazing land for their horses and cattle. Today this relatively gentrified zone has both businesses and residences, and most visitors to the capital choose to stay in hotels around here.

Many people make a pilgrimage to this part of Kingston to visit the **Bob Marley Museum,** the most popular attraction in the city. The house was a recording studio for Marley's Tuff Gong record label, as well as his home from 1975 until his death from cancer in 1981. A statue of Marley with his favorite guitar and soccer ball stands at the entrance. (This is the only thing that may be photographed; cameras are prohibited elsewhere in the house.) The one-hour guided tour leads you through the grounds and house, which

contains memorabilia of Marley's life, including his gold and platinum records, his favorite denim stage shirt, and several unusual guitars. There's also a re-creation of Wail'n'Soul—the shack in the poor Trenchtown area that was Marley's first house in Kingston. Two rooms are wall-papered with Marley's international press clippings, and another still has bullet holes in the wall from a failed assassination attempt in 1976. The tour ends with a film about his life, screened in the room that once housed the Tuff Gong studio. The complex also houses a photo gallery, restaurant, and souvenir shops.

The other main draw in New Kingston is **Devon House.** The house was built in 1881 by Jamaica's first black millionaire, George Stiebel (1820–1896), who made his fortune in gold mining in South America. He lived here until his death. This fine Georgian-style mansion has been refurbished with four-poster beds, chandeliers, Chippendale cabinets, and other original antiques. The courtyard, which was formerly slaves' quarters, houses an upscale craft souvenir shop, and an excellent bakery and ice cream shop. A restaurant occupies the former stables.

Also along Hope Road you can take a look through the gates of **Jamaica House—**the prime minister's office—which stands amid expansive lawns, manicured shrubbery, and graceful palms.

The **Hope Botanical Gardens,** said to be the largest botanical gardens in the Caribbean, stretch along the outskirts of New Kingston. Located on the former estate of Maj. Richard Hope, who arrived in Jamaica with Oliver Cromwell's army in 1655, the 200-acre (81-ha) gardens feature pathways meandering between pond and lakes, greenhouses, and numerous flowering trees and shrubs. The grounds also contain diversions to keep children amused (an aquarium, small zoo, and playground) as well as a coconut museum, orchid house, maze, and palm avenue. The gardens are popular with Kingstonians escaping the heat of the city on weekends. ■

Coco palms grace the elegant gardens of Devon House.

Devon House

- Map: 26 B3
- Address: 26 Hope Rd.
- Phone: 876/929-6602
- Hours: Closed Sun.–Mon.
- Price: $$

Hope Botanical Gardens

- Map: 26 C3
- Address: Old Hope Rd.
- Phone: 876/927-1257

Originally known as Fort Cromwell, Fort Charles was renamed on the restoration of King Charles II of England in 1660.

Port Royal

IN THE 17TH CENTURY PORT ROYAL WAS AMONG THE wealthiest ports in the Caribbean. Built on a small island in Kingston Harbour and connected to the mainland by a causeway (the Palisadoes), it was first used by the Spanish to repair their ships. When the English captured Jamaica in 1655, they strengthened its defenses by building five forts. The combined nautical and military legacies create a powerful atmosphere in the present-day fishing village.

Port Royal
25 F1

Traders took advantage of this safe haven, and Port Royal grew to a settlement of some 6,000 people. The wealth from trade and pirate booty turned it into one of the richest ports in the Caribbean, with fine brick houses, piped water—and innumerable brothels, gambling dens, and taverns.

The Roman Catholic Church condemned it as "the wickedest city in Christendom," and for many people it must have seemed like judgment day when a massive earthquake on June 7, 1692, sent most of the city to the watery depths, killing 2,000 people and sinking all the ships in the harbor. Most of the survivors fled to Kingston. Port Royal suffered further from a major fire in 1702 and another earthquake in 1907.

Today Port Royal is a quiet fishing village and the home base of the

Jamaican Coast Guard. You can reach Port Royal by car or ferry from Kingston *(For ferry details contact Kingston visitor information, tel 876/929-9200)*, and it is easily navigable on foot *(allow 2–3 hours)*. Of the buildings that survive, one of the most impressive is **Fort Charles,** the first of the five forts built around the port. Although it is now landlocked, due to the 1692 earthquake, its embrasures still feature cannon pointing out to sea. Within the fort is the **Maritime Museum,** which depicts the history of Port Royal with artifacts dredged up from the sunken city. To one side of the fort's parade ground stands a raised wooden platform known as Nelson's Quarterdeck. The young commander kept watch here against the threat of a French invasion fleet in 1779–1780. Between the fort and the water is Giddy House, a former ammunition store that now tilts at an alarming angle. Next to it is a massive gun emplacement, the Victoria and Albert Battery, which was also pitched earthward by the severe earthquake of 1692.

Other places of interest in Port Royal include the **Old Naval Hospital,** a stone-and-cast-iron building dating from 1819 and now in disrepair. **St. Peter's Church** is noteworthy for the tombstone in its graveyard inscribed with the tale of Frenchman Lewis Gaddy, who was swallowed up by the earthquake but was then spat out by an aftershock into the sea.

The submerged portion of Port Royal, covering 33 acres (13 ha), now lies in depths of up to 40 feet (12 m). Excavations by Texas A&M University's Institute of Nautical Archaeology have turned up a watch whose hands stopped at 11:43 a.m. on June 7, 1692, thus giving a precise time for the earthquake. Port Royal belongs to an elite group of archaeological sites that have stayed undisturbed over the centuries: Everyday items such as furniture, tableware, pots and pans, tools, and shoes remain more or less in place as they were left—except, of course, that they are now underwater.

Plans are now under way to develop the sunken city as an attraction for divers and to redevelop the entire Port Royal area as a port of call for cruise ships, with actors in period costumes interpreting life in this 17th-century pirate stronghold. The ambitious project will include a new pier, a renovated museum, and restaurants and shops. The aim is to create one of the most exciting historical and cultural attractions in the Caribbean—with a service industry to match. ■

A tombstone commemorates Lewis Gaddy, who died in the earthquake of 1692.

Fort Charles

✉ Off Elizabeth Ave.

☎ 876/967-8438

$ $$

Named after the hazy blue mist that can envelop the peaks, this wilderness is the most biologically diverse area in the country.

Blue & John Crow Mountains National Park
25 G2
876/920-8278

Blue Mountains

ONE OF THE LONGEST CONTINUOUS MOUNTAIN RANGES in the Caribbean, the majestic Blue Mountains dominate the eastern third of Jamaica, rising to a height of 7,402 feet (2,256 m) at Blue Mountain Peak. On these slopes some of the world's finest coffee is grown—sharing space with a profusion of verdant forest.

Bordering Kingston's eastern edges, the Blue Mountains form a cooling contrast with the sprawling metropolis below. High rainfall feeds the lush vegetation, which includes towering trees shrouded in a green veil of epiphytic lichens, mosses and bromeliads, prolific bamboo and ferns, and more than 500 species of flowering plants. The mountains are also home to the largest butterfly in the Americas (the giant swallowtail with a wingspan of six inches), coneys (a type of rabbit), several non-poisonous snakes, tree frogs, and glorious native birdlife including orioles, tangers, and the rare Streamer-tailed hummingbird (or Doctor Bird, whose tailfeathers are thought to resemble the tailcoats once worn by doctors).

The **Blue and John Crow Mountains National Park** was established in 1993 to protect 193,000 acres (78,100 ha) of this area. The most accessible parts are toward the park's western end, reached via Rte. B1, which runs

from Kingston to Buff Bay in the north. The **Cinchona Botanical Gardens** *(Tel 876/927-1257)* were established in 1886 to provide quinine from cinchona trees. The project failed, but the gardens then became a botanical research center. The 10-acre (4-ha) grounds, clinging to the ridge at an elevation of 5,000 feet (1,524 m), contain a wide range of imported and endemic trees, shrubs, and flowering plants. The road is tortuous, and it isn't an easy drive.

More easily accessible is the **Hollywell National Recreational Park** *(Tel 876/920-8278)* 2 miles (3 km) north of Newcastle, which covers 300 acres (121 ha) of magical montane forest with pines, eucalyptus, soapwood, and dogwood trees, often shrouded in mist and alive with birdsong.

The area is also famed for its coffee, introduced to the Blue Mountains in the 18th century. The high-quality beans grown here soon commanded top prices in Europe, but the industry suffered a setback with the abolition of slavery in 1834, and hurricanes took their toll in the following century. In the 1950s the government stepped in to save the plantations; it established guidelines ensuring that only coffee grown just below 5,000 feet (1,525 m) could use the Blue Mountain label.

At the **Mavis Bank Coffee Factory** a tour of the plant is rounded off with a cup of the country's finest brew. In operation for over a century, Mavis Bank is the biggest processor of Blue Mountain coffee and handles around 70,000 bushels of beans annually. ■

Connoisseurs consider Blue Mountain coffee the finest in the world.

Sports & activities

Hiking and Biking: The Blue and John Crow Mountains National Park has more than 30 hiking trails, many of which follow old mule tracks. The most spectacular views are from the 7-mile (11-km) track that leads from the village of Mavis Bank to Blue Mountain Peak. Guides are recommended, contact the Jamaica Tourism Board *(876/929-9200)* or the Jamaica Conservation and Development Trust *(29 Dumbarton Ave., Kingston 10, tel 876/920-8278)* which manages the park. The most popular biking and hiking tours are run by Blue Mountain Bicycle Tours *(121 Main St., Ocho Rios, tel 876/974-7075, www.bmtoursja.com)*. The biking tours involve an 18-mile downhill run. ■

Mavis Bank Coffee Factory

- N 25 F2
- ✉ Mavis Bank, St. Andrew
- ☎ 876/977-8013
- ⏲ Closed weekends; Mon.–Fri. by appt. only
- $ $$$

Port Antonio

Port Antonio
25 G2
Visitor information
City Center Plaza
876/993-3051

PORT ANTONIO'S GLORY DAYS, BOTH AS A BANANA PORT and an upscale resort, are well behind it, and this quiet backwater is now mostly frequented by independent travelers who use it as a base for exploring the natural attractions in the area. However, there are ambitious plans for a revival of its fortunes through the creation of a marina complex and renovation of the historic Titchfield district.

Boundbrook Wharf, on Port Antonio's western harbor, was once Jamaica's main transshipment port for bananas and the inspiration for the "Banana Boat Song," better known as "Day-O" ("Work all night for a drink of rum, daylight come and me wanna go home"). Nowadays fruit is loaded mechanically.

Opposite the wharf is the **Marina at Port Antonio** mega-yacht complex with 32 ships, and plans to add a cruise pier and terminal building, duty-free shops, dockside restaurants and bars, and customs facilities.

The downtown area is easy to navigate, centering as it does on a central square and clock tower; alongside the square you'll find the busy Musgrave Market. From here it is a short stroll up to **Titchfield Peninsula,** which bisects the two harbors. At the end of this you'll find the crumbling remains of **Fort George** *(Fort George St.)*, dating back to 1791 and now part of Titchfield High School. The fort was once one of the most powerful

Panorama of Port Antonio, with Navy Island offshore

in the region, but little remains except for a few cannon and parts of its 10-foot-thick (3 m) walls. This historic Georgian and Victorian residential area is scheduled for restoration. While here, you might like to look in at the venerable **DeMontevin Lodge** *(21 Fort George St., tel 876/993-2604)*, an ornate colonial relic dating from 1881 that has seen better days but retains its elegant Victorian gingerbread architecture and wood-paneled interior. Arrangements for a walking tour of the historic downtown district can be made through local hotels.

Back in the town center you can turn your attention toward an unusual building on the waterfront known as **St. George's Village** *(Gideon Ave.)*. Conceived and built by local architect Ziggy Fahmi, this striking structure resembles a complex of town houses from different eras in history. Its interior conceals two levels of shops, one of the best art galleries in Jamaica (representing the works of well-known Jamaican artists, such as locally born Ken Adendana Spencer), a café, and an imaginatively designed restaurant upstairs with views over the bay. Its success depends, alas, on cruise ships, which may never return.

Across from St. George's Village is the redbrick **Christ Church** *(Gideon Ave.)*, a neo-Romanesque structure built on the site of an earlier church in the mid-19th century. It has some impressive memorials dating back to the 17th century.

Just offshore from Port Antonio (reached via a five-minute boat ride from West Pier) is **Navy Island,** which was a barracks for the British Navy in the 18th century. Errol Flynn bought the 60-acre (24-ha) property when he arrived in Port Antonio and allegedly used it as a hideaway to court Hollywood starlets. There are beaches (owned by a resort but open to non-residents), snorkeling, a restaurant, and a nature trail winding its way through verdant vegetation.

Four miles (6.5 km) south of Port Antonio and most easily reached by car are the **Nonsuch Caves and Athenry Gardens.** Your guide will first take you through the caves themselves, which feature impressive formations (including shapes resembling various figures and animals that have been given names) and caverns, as well as a bat colony hanging from the ceiling in the lofty Cathedral Cavern.

Well-lit concrete paths and steps lead through the caves and out into the 3-acre (1-ha) gardens of well-tended tropical plants and flowers. The café on the promontory, 600 feet (183 m) above sea level, commands a breathtaking view of the coastline and Port Antonio. ■

Nonsuch Caves & Athenry Gardens

- Map: 25 G2
- Address: Nonsuch, Portland
- Tel: 876/993-3740
- Price: $$$

The dramatic Nonsuch Caves are a popular excursion from Port Antonio.

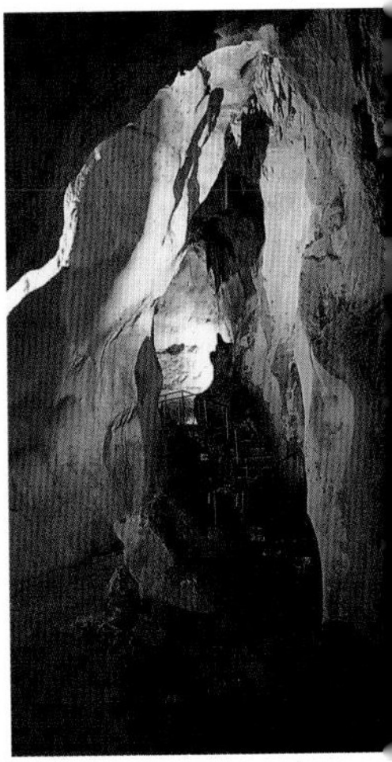

Around Port Antonio

Frenchman's Cove
25 G2

San San Beach
$

THE COASTLINE TO THE EAST OF PORT ANTONIO EMbraces some of the prettiest coastal scenery in the country, with rugged headlands interspersed with golden beaches and some fine hotels in choice locations. (Day visitors usually must pay a small charge, which also includes use of the hotel facilities.)

Heading east from town on Rte. A4, the first major landmark is extraordinary **Trident Castle,** a fantasy creation that is part of the neighboring Trident Hotel *(P.O. Box 119, Port Antonio, tel 876/993-2602)*. About a mile (1.5 km) from here you come to **Frenchman's Cove,** a gorgeous little beach framed by rocky headlands and skirted by a cool mountain stream. Another 0.75 mile (1 km) along is **San San Beach,** a narrow strip fronting a broad bay with reasonable snorkeling on the reef, and it is an easy swim across to a small beach on jewel-like Pelew Island, on the east side of the bay.

Rafting on the Rio Grande, a popular pastime

Just past San San Beach is the **Blue Lagoon** (*Tel 876/993-7791*). Surrounded by forest foliage, the lagoon is a limestone sinkhole fed by underground streams. This scenic spot was indeed the setting for the Brooke Shields movie *Blue Lagoon* (1980), as well as *Club Paradise* (1986), which was filmed in the restaurant/bar hanging over the water's edge. It is a lovely spot for a swim and lunch.

Two miles (3 km) east is **Dragon Bay** (*P.O. Box 176, Port Antonio, tel 876/993-8751*). At the hotel you can have a drink at the beach bar where Tom Cruise displayed his bartending talents in the film *Cocktail* (1988).

Continuing on, you then reach **Boston Bay,** a big public beach famous for its jerk cooking (see p. 38). This is primarily a fishing beach, but in rough weather the incoming swells can create good conditions for surfing. The main road and the beach are lined with stands selling authentic, sizzling jerk chicken, pork, or seafood.

It is 2 miles (3 km) to the next major stopping point of **Long Bay,** a broad expanse of sand that is considered to be Jamaica's top surfing spot. A few beach bars, guesthouses, and discos have sprung up along the road to cater to independent travelers, creating a laid-back atmosphere. The beach, however, is not in the same league as the surf. Unless you're a surfer, or you just like the rollers, there is little reason to linger.

One of the highlights of this part of the coast is lovely **Reach Falls,** accessible via a well-paved road from Manchioneal on the coast. The falls are part of the Driver River, which tumbles down from the John Crow Mountains into a series of cascades and crystal-clear pools where you can swim. The entrance fee includes a guided walk up to the falls. Although not as spectacular as Dunn's River Falls (see p. 42), there are far fewer people here, and it is a lovely spot to while away an hour or two.

Extending deep into Portland behind Port Antonio is the **Rio Grande Valley,** a lush wilderness overlooked by the splendor of the Blue Mountains. The main attraction is **rafting** along the Rio

Frenchman's Cove is ideal for picnics.

RIO GRANDE RAFTING

You can book a trip on the Rio Grande from your resort or drive yourself to the put-in point at Berridale and buy your ticket there (*Rio Grande Rafting, tel 876/993-2778*). Arrange for an insured driver to deliver your car to the finishing point at the Rafter's Rest restaurant in St. Margaret's Bay. Do not under any circumstances hire unofficial drivers.

Blue Lagoon, Dragon Bay, Reach Falls

Ⓝ 25 G2

$ $

Grande, one of Jamaica's largest rivers. Originally the bamboo rafts were used by local farmers to carry their bananas to Port Antonio, but when Errol Flynn arrived here, he started organizing raft races for his friends; the ride has now become one of the area's most popular attractions. The two-hour trip from Berridale to the coast passes through some delightfully unspoiled scenery—riverside villages, gorges, and shoals. The 30-foot-long (9 m) rafts are built from lengths of bamboo lashed together, with a seat for two at the back, and poled along by a raft captain standing at the front. There are stops for swimming and to buy snacks or drinks from vendors. ■

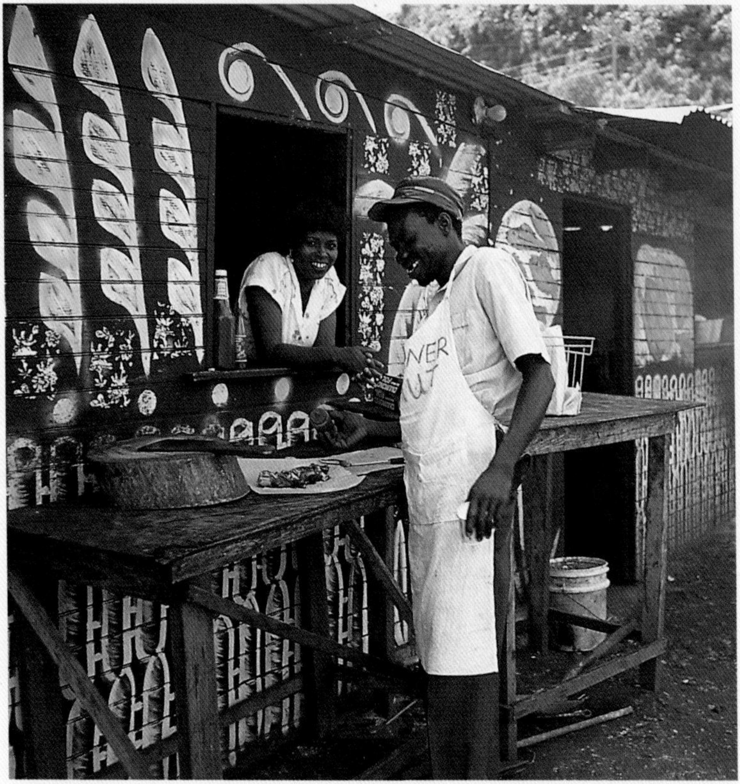

Jerk chicken makes a tasty lunchtime or evening meal.

Jerk cooking

Jerk cooking may have originated in the 17th century with the Maroons (see p. 48), who hunted wild boar in the mountains and then marinated the meat in a spicy sauce to preserve it. Today jerk cuisine is found all over the island and is one of Jamaica's most distinctive styles of cooking. The meat (usually chicken or pork) is marinated in a special blend of spices (including peppers, cinnamon, and nutmeg) and then slowly grilled over a pimento wood fire. Boston Beach is a good place to buy a few bottles of the marinade to take home. ■

Oracabessa

AS YOU PASS THROUGH THIS TRANQUIL VILLAGE, 15 MILES (24 km) east of Ocho Rios on Rte. A3, it is hard to imagine anything much happening. Oracabessa (from the Spanish for "golden head") was a busy port at the beginning of the 1900s, but since the demise of Jamaica's banana exporting industry in the late 1960s it has slumbered peacefully, with life revolving around its daily market. In its heyday Oracabessa attracted royalty, literati, and politicians.

Oracabessa
25 E3

Oracabessa has an interesting literary heritage, and it can thank two famous writers for this. The first is the English playwright Sir Noël Coward (1899–1973), who built a house in the hills midway between Oracabessa and neighboring Port Maria in the 1950s. His home until his death, **Firefly** has now been restored to look as it did when he lived here, with his paintings on easels in the studio, two grand pianos back to back in the music room, and the table set for lunch as it was on the day the Queen Mother visited on February 28, 1965. Coward's simple grave on the hillside overlooks one of the most stupendous views on the island, taking in the Blue Mountains to the south and the coastline to the north, which stretches into the Caribbean Sea.

The second writer is Ian Fleming (1908–1964), who wrote most of the James Bond novels in **Goldeneye,** the house he built on the outskirts of Oracabessa. Fleming wintered here every year from 1946 to 1964, and his guests included such notables as Graham Greene (1904–1991) and Truman Capote (1924–1984). The house now belongs to the Island Outpost hotel group, and although not open to visitors, it can be rented.

In Oracabessa Bay itself, Island Outpost has created **James Bond Beach,** a seafront development with three beach areas, outdoor performance areas (several major concerts have been held here), and sports facilities. There are also plans for a hotel on the Outer Bank below Goldeneye's headland. ■

Noël Coward entertained royalty and celebrities at his home, Firefly.

Firefly
25 F3
www.islandjamaica.com
Grants Pen
St. Mary
876/725-0920
Closed Fri. & Sun.
$$$$

Ocho Rios

Ocho Rios
25 E3
Visitor information
Ocean Village Shopping Centre
876/974-2582

SITUATED MIDWAY ALONG JAMAICA'S NORTH SHORE, OCHO Rios is the country's second largest resort, after Montego Bay. The town, which lies at the intersection of the main north coast route and Rte. A3 to Kingston, is a popular getaway spot for residents of the capital, just a 90-minute drive away. But far more visitors disembark from the cruise ships that moor at the dock at the western end of the bay. And, like many of Jamaica's coastal resorts, Ocho Rios has some superb hotels (such as the long-standing Jamaica Inn) tucked away in quiet coves on either side of town.

A bathing suit is essential garb for climbing the Dunn's River Falls.

Turtle Beach
25 E3
$

The Spanish who settled here christened the area Las Chorreras, referring to the "gushing water" of Dunn's River Falls (see p. 42). The British mistook the name as Ocho Rios, or "eight rivers," even though no such rivers existed. Today its name is usually shortened to Ochi.

Despite the wide sweep of the bay and the mountain backdrop, Ocho Rios is not the most attractive of resorts—or indeed a place where you can expect to find the real Jamaica. The town sprawls around the bay, which is also home to a bauxite-loading terminal looming above the cruise ship dock.

In the 19th century, Ocho Rios was surrounded by plantations, principally for sugarcane and pimentos. In the 1920s an old plantation house at Shaw Park became the country's first upscale hotel, and it was soon followed by several others—but although the resort's mountainous backdrop was lovely, development was held back by the absence of an accessible beach. Meanwhile high levels of the valuable mineral bauxite, used to produce aluminum, were found in the local soil, which led to the construction of a deepwater terminal. By the 1960s a cruise ship terminal was in place, the swamps behind the town had been drained, and thousands of tons of white sand imported to create a beach.

Today **Turtle Beach** buzzes with activity and water sports. Around and behind the beach, you'll find plenty of opportunities for eating out and enjoying the varied nightlife, and you can easily stroll around Ocho Rios in an hour or two. The main daytime activity is shopping, with several malls and dozens of stalls providing an outlet for all manner of handmade crafts as well as duty-free items for cruise ship passengers. The only reminders of the town's history are the remains of its fort. Built by the English in the 17th century, it is now dwarfed by the adjoining bauxite works. Two rather forlorn cannon point out to sea from the surviving stonework ramparts.

Modern industry and the potent colonial military heritage would seem to overwhelm Ocho Rios, but the surrounding natural wonders dispel any sense of

You can sail and fish, as well as snorkel, in Ocho Rios.

overdevelopment. Foremost among these attractions is **Dunn's River Falls** *(Map 25 E3, off Rte. A1 between St. Ann's & Ocho Rios, tel 876/974-2857, $$$$)*. The spectacular falls cascade down 600 feet (183 m) of slippery rocks and ledges before spilling out onto the beach below. All day, long daisy chains of tourists wend their way up the falls, getting thoroughly drenched (a bathing suit is essential) in the process. The sure-footed guides carry dozens of cameras around their necks as they lead the hand-holding climbers upward. The whole process is as entertaining to watch from the wooden steps running alongside the falls as it is to do. Adjacent to Dunn's River Falls is **Dolphin Cove** *(P.O. Box 21, Ocho Rios, tel 876/974-5335, www.dolphincovejamaica.com; advance reservations recommended, $$$$$)*, where you can swim and interact with captive dolphins. There are several interactive dolphin programs daily, with varying degrees of contact. (See sidebar p. 114.) Dolphin Cove also has a jungle trail, where you will be introduced to native birds and reptiles, and a beach grill and bar. ■

Sports & activities

Adventure tours: Chukka Cove Adventure Tours *(Tel 876/972-2506, www.chukkacove.com)*, based in Ocho Rios, is Jamaica's leading provider of soft adventures—beach horseback rides, mountain bike tours, jeep safaris, hiking, gliding, polo, and river tubing.

Water sports: Ocho Rios offers a wide range of options for water sports. Among the most popular are yacht and catamaran cruises to nearby Dunn's River Falls. A reliable operator is Red Stripe *(Tel 876/974-2446)*.

Tours: Guided horseback tours are available through Hooves Ltd. *(Tel 876/972-0905, www.hoovesjamaica.com)* or Prospect Plantation *(Tel 876/994-1058)*. ■

A sweetly fragrant frangipani

Around Ocho Rios

COYABA RIVER GARDEN & MUSEUM

Near Shaw Park Gardens, the wooden walkways of these landscaped gardens traverse well-tended beds, miniature waterfalls, and ponds. The site was once an Arawak settlement (*coyaba* means "heaven" in Arawak), and the small museum concentrates on pre-Columbian Jamaica as well as its more recent history. There is also a café-bar and craft shop.
25 E3 Shaw Park Rd. 876/974-6235, www.coyabagardens.com $$

FERN GULLEY

Heading south from Ocho Rios on Milford Road (Rte. A3 to Kingston) is the famous 3-mile (5 km) stretch overhung with a canopy of dense vegetation said to include more than 500 varieties of native ferns. First planted in the late 19th century, this deep gully would be a remarkable beauty spot were it not for the heavy traffic now threatening to wipe out many of the plants with noxious fumes.

PROSPECT PLANTATION

Two miles (3 km) east of Ocho Rios, and signposted off Rte. A3, the attraction offers tours in open-top buses to a working plantation, growing crops such as cocoa, soursop, ackee, pimentos, and limes. This popular tour takes you around the farm in a tractor-drawn jitney (open trailer) and provides a commentary on the crops. You are given the chance to stop occasionally and sample them. Horseback rides are also offered.
25 E3 Prospect 876/994-1058
$$$$

SHAW PARK GARDENS

Within a few minutes' drive of Ocho Rios, in the hills high above the town, lies Shaw Park Gardens. Once the grounds of the original Shaw Park Hotel, which burned down in 1937, the 25-acre (10 ha) gardens overflow with frangipani, bougainvillea, crotons, bamboo, and many other glorious tropical plants. A lovely cascade drops almost vertically from the rock face and a magnificent 80-year-old banyan tree arches its massive branches over a large pond that was the original hotel swimming pool. The lawns where the hotel once stood command superb views of the coast from 550 feet (168 m) above. The site has a bar and a gift shop.
25 E3 Shaw Park Rd. 876/974-2723
$$$ ■

Rafters get ready for the hour-long trip down the Martha Brae.

Falmouth & around

THE TOWN OF FALMOUTH, 23 MILES (37 KM) EAST OF Montego Bay, was once one of the busiest ports in Jamaica, exporting sugar from nearby plantations and importing slaves and goods. Today Falmouth wears a down-at-the-heel air, but the riches accumulated are reflected in the many elegant, Georgian-style town houses erected here. Providing a contrast is the town of Nine Miles, where Jamaican legend Bob Marley grew up. Sugar, slavery, and reggae provide a shorthand view of Jamaican history.

Falmouth
24 C3

Good Hope Great House
See map p. 24/5
South of Falmouth
876/610-5798

The town centers on **Water Square** (so named because Falmouth was Jamaica's first town to provide piped water) and nearby **Market Street.** Here you'll find the old courthouse, the Baptist Manse, Barrett House, Tharp House, the William Knibb Memorial Baptist Church (named after an antislavery campaigner), and other reminders of the glory days, such as St. Peter's Anglican Church (1791), which is said to be an almost exact copy of the local church in Falmouth, England.

East of Falmouth on Rte. A1 is **Oyster Bay,** also known as the Luminous Lagoon, and believed to contain one of the world's largest concentrations of bioluminescent microorganisms. After dark, the water lights up with bright green phosphorescence when disturbed. You can rent a boat and a local guide for a mini-cruise—or indeed for a dip—through the Fisherman's Inn *(Tel 876/954-3427)*. Tours are also available from Glistening Waters *(Tel 876/954-3229)*, a restaurant and marina on the lagoon's shoreline.

South of Falmouth is the **Good Hope Great House,** one of the most impressive of the remaining plantation houses. Built in 1755, it commanded a sugar estate of 10,000 acres (4,050 ha) and 3,000 slaves. Today the Georgian-style house is a deluxe guesthouse offering tours with lunch, horse rid-

ing, and a private beach on a 2,000-acre (810-ha) estate.

Running through the estate is the Martha Brae River, which rises in Cockpit Country and reaches the sea east of Falmouth. Rafting trips start at the **Rafter's Village,** signposted from Martha Brae (*Tel 876/952-0889*) 3 miles (5 km) inland, coasting downstream for just over an hour through dense tropical vegetation and limpid pools.

BAYSIDE SITES

The town of **Discovery Bay** is a major port for bauxite exports, and the orange-stained facilities dominate the landscape. Just outside town, on Rte. A1, is **Columbus Park,** an open-air museum with historical artifacts as well as a mural depicting Columbus's landing nearby in 1494.

Runaway Bay is a major center for all-inclusive hotels, several of which line the beachfront. Golfers are also drawn here to the excellent PGA-quality 18-hole **SuperClubs Golf Club** (*Tel 876/973-7319*), which is open to non-residents.

Between Discovery Bay and Runaway Bay are the **Green Grotto Caves** (signposted by the side of Rte. A1), an impressive and extensive cave system once inhabited by Taino. During the turbulent 17th century, Spanish troops fleeing the English hid here. The 45-minute tour includes a boat ride on an underground lake.

Rte. B3 heading inland to Alexandria is the best road to take to reach the **Bob Marley Mausoleum** in his hometown of Nine Miles. Surrounded by high fences topped with characteristic flags of red, gold, and green, the compound is revered by Rastafarians and visited by fans from all over the world. At its center is the hut where Marley was brought up, complete with the small bed he sang of in "Is This Love." Behind the hut is the meditation stone where he rested his head to sleep or contemplate.

The mausoleum itself is housed in a small chapel of Ethiopian design, which also contains his guitars, favorite soccer ball, a Bible, and other items. Sadly, a multistory building rising up behind the mausoleum now blights this revered spot. ■

The Bob Marley Mausoleum is in Nine Miles, Marley's hometown.

Columbus Park
Map: 24 D3
$: $

Green Grotto Caves
Map: 24 D3
www.greengrottocavesja.com
Tel: 876/973-2841
$: $$$$$

Bob Marley Mausoleum
Map: 24 D2
www.bobmarley.com
Address: Nine Miles
Tel: 876/995-1763
$: $$$

The fountain at the center of Sam Sharpe Square is dedicated to John Edward Kerr (1840–1903), who pioneered the local banana trade.

Montego Bay

MONTEGO BAY IS THE COUNTRY'S SECOND LARGEST CITY and its biggest resort stretching 15 miles (24 km) along the north coast. It is Jamaica's tourism capital, with a wider range of accommodations and amenities than anywhere else on the island. Although its beaches cannot compare with Negril, it has an undeniably attractive setting in a sweeping natural harbor backed up by a fringe of gently sloping hills. This feisty resort also hosts the Reggae Sumfest (July-Aug.), which pulls in devotees from all around the world.

Montego Bay
24 C3
Visitor information
Cornwall Beach
876/952-4425
Closed Sun.

Reggae Sumfest
www.reggaesumfest.com
876/953-2933

When Columbus anchored here in 1494, he christened it El Golfo de Buen Tempo (The Bay of Good Weather), but its modern name derives from the days when the Spanish hunted wild boars in the surrounding hills. They called it Manteca Bahia, the Bay of Lard. The English interpreted this as Montego Bay; now most people just call it Mo'Bay.

Montego Bay became a sugar and banana town during the 19th century, but with the decline in these trades its fortunes revived only when it gained international recognition as a spa. In the late 19th century, a local physician, Alexander McCatty, began to extol the virtues of swimming in salt water at his Sanatorium Caribee.

He donated the land to the community as a bathing club in 1906, and in the 1920s it was discovered by an English doctor, Sir Herbert Baker, whose articles about the mineral springs at what had become known as Doctor's Cave Beach marked the beginning of tourism at the resort.

Today **Doctor's Cave Beach** forms part of the tourist stretch of the town, along Gloucester Avenue, now known as the Hip Strip. The beach club has good swimming and all the necessary facilities (changing rooms, lifeguards, etc.). Nearby, rival **Aquasol Theme Park,** Walter Fletcher Beach, combines activities such as tennis and go-karting with watersports and a beachfront restaurant. Both beaches are open 9 a.m.–sunset daily and charge a nominal usage fee. Most of the other beaches along here belong to individual hotels.

Encircling these beaches is an extensive fringing reef that forms part of the **Montego Bay Marine Park,** covering some 9 square miles (23 sq km) of coral reef, sea-grass beds, and mangroves. Snorkeling, diving, and glass-bottom boat tours are readily available if you want to experience the reef at closer quarters. Other water activities include jet skiing, parasailing, and a 110-foot-long (33-m) water slide that ejects you into the ocean from the deck above the busy waterfront bar of Margueritaville—just the chance to make a big splash.

Around one mile (1.5 km) south of the Gloucester Avenue hotel zone is the downtown, a lively, typically Caribbean area. Its focal point is **Sam Sharpe Square,** named after a black slave who led the Christmas Slave Rebellion in 1831 and died on the gibbet in this square. There is a small local history museum in the Old Courthouse, and in the northwest corner you can also see the **Cage,** a lock-up that was once used to house drunken

At Doctor's Cave Beach, a private swimming club, nonmembers can enter for a small fee.

The room in Rose Hall where Annie Palmer is said to have murdered her third husband

Rose Hall Great House
24 C3
www.rosehall.com
Rose Hall
876/953-2323
$$$$

sailors or slaves who were out past the Sunday curfew of 3 p.m. Nearby is a tableau of five bronze statues, the **Sam Sharpe Memorial,** which depicts him alongside fellow martyrs who shared the credit for hastening the abolition of slavery. A short walk away is the **Crafts Market** with about 200 artisan stalls *(Harbour St., 7 a.m.–7 p.m.).*

Also worth a look is the 18th-century parish church of **St. James,** a handsome white limestone building in the shape of a Greek cross. Considered to be one of Jamaica's finest churches, it was extensively restored after an earthquake in 1957 caused considerable damage.

Eight miles (13 km) east of Mo'Bay is one of Jamaica's most famous plantation houses, **Rose Hall Great House.** Occupying a commanding position on the hillside with lawns sweeping downward toward the sea, it was built between 1770 and 1780 at the heyday of the sugar plantation era.

Local legend says that this splendid Georgian house is haunted by the ghost of a wicked mistress, Annie Palmer, who ruled over it for 13 years and murdered several husbands. Supposedly a voodoo practitioner, she is said to have been strangled in her bed by one of her slave lovers: The story was fictionalized in Herbert Lisser's 1958 book, *The White Witch of Rose Hall.* The house was abandoned in the 19th century, and sympathetically restored in the 1960s; it contains beautiful original antiques and is well worth a visit. ■

Cockpit Country

South of Montego Bay is an area known as Cockpit Country, a 500-square-mile (1,300 sq km) region of strange limestone formations riddled with caves and sinkholes. This jungle-covered landscape was one of the main refuges for runaway slaves. They became known as Maroons (from the Spanish *cimarrón,* wild or unbroken), and their intimate knowledge of the terrain and guerrilla tactics meant that few missions to track them down succeeded. Also known as the District of Look Behind (which the pursuing British soldiers were obliged to do frequently), the region is peppered with peculiar and evocative place-names such as Me No Sen You No Come, Rest and Be Thankful District, and Quick Step. For more than a century the Maroons lived in this isolated area, developing their own culture and harassing the British until a peace treaty was signed in 1739.

Several became folk heroes, such as Nanny, a female Maroon leader, whose statue can be seen in Kingston's National Heroes Park. (Cockpit Country Tour, *tel 876/610-0818).* ■

Negril

Watching the sunset from Rick's Café

LYING AT JAMAICA'S FAR WESTERN TIP, NEGRIL IS OFTEN regarded as Jamaica's most permissive and hedonistic resort. The truth is perhaps somewhat more prosaic, but nonetheless Negril has traded on its laid-back, indulgent image for two decades or more.

Like so many others, the resort started out as a simple fishing village. Cut off from the rest of the country by swampland, it received its first trickle of visitors when the road to Montego Bay (52 miles/84 km to the east) was completed in 1965. Soon afterward its glorious 7-mile-long (11-km) beach was discovered by hippies, who descended en masse to live in simple huts beneath the coconut palms and while away their days smoking marijuana (ganja) and experiencing sunsets enhanced by readily available hallucinogenics. ("Mushroom tea" is still a specialty you can find on the beach.)

In the late 1970s one of Jamaica's first all-inclusive resorts, Hedonism II (there was no Hedonism I), opened at the eastern end of Long Bay, Negril's main beach. Tales of unlimited alcohol, nudity, and sex soon cemented Negril's reputation as a center for uninhibited bacchanalia. A building boom that began in the 1980s marked the beginning of mass tourism, inevitably quashing the freewheeling spirit it tried so hard to emulate. Today Negril offers a full range of hotels and guesthouses, several of which are all-inclusive.

The bay is a nonstop parade of jet skis, parasail boats, day-trip catamarans, glass-bottom boats, and dive boats, and you have to be careful now where you plunge into its once pristine waters. There is even a water and theme park for family fun seekers.

For all the new elements, Negril retains a certain insouciant attitude, and the traditional ingredients—beach bars where reggae plays nonstop, ganja and Red Stripe beer circulating freely—are still there. It

Negril
Map 24 B2
Visitor information
Coral Seas Plaza
876/957-9314

Sports & activities

Adventure tours: Chukka Blue Adventure Tours *(Tel 876/953-5619)* features horseback riding, river tubing, mountain-to-river bike tours, and jeep and ATV safaris.

Horseback riding: Rides are available through Rhodes Hall Plantation *(Tel 876/957-6883)*, a five to ten minute drive east of Negril.

Diving & water sports: Negril Scuba Centre *(Tel 876-957-4425)* offers trips to protected off-shore reefs. Aqua Nova Watersports *(Tel 876/957-4323)* offers other cruises. ■

has a great reputation for live music too, and big-name bands visit the resort regularly.

Most of the action takes place along the sandy swath of **Long Bay.** Here you'll find most of the hotels, beach bars, discos, and vendors offering everything from aloe massages to hair braiding. To the north of Long Bay is **Bloody Bay,** a perfect crescent-shaped beach that takes its name from the days when whales were once butchered here. Offshore lies a small island, **Booby Cay,** named for the booby birds (sooty terns) that nest here.

Behind both beaches runs Norman Manley Boulevard, a long straight road that separates the hotels from an area of swampland known as the **Great Morass.** Jamaica's second largest wetland, this 6,000-acre (2,300-ha) refuge

protects crocodiles, land crabs, and numerous species of birds, including egrets, parakeets, jacanas, and Jamaican euphonias. Within the Great Morass is the **Royal Palm Reserve** *(Sheffield, tel 876/364-7407, www.royalpalmreserve.com, $$$)*, a 300-acre (120-ha) site that boasts 114 plant species and over 300 species of birds, butterflies, and reptiles. This beautiful spot can be visited for walks, nature tours, bird watching, and fishing. Norman Manley Boulevard continues on into Negril town; there are a couple of shopping malls and a craft market in the small town center but little else to detain you.

Beyond Negril is **West End,** a 3-mile (5-km) stretch of coastal road peppered with guesthouses and hotels. This area is now undergoing a resurgence in popularity as an alternative to the mass tourism that has taken hold on the beaches, and some of Negril's most imaginatively designed resorts (such as the Rockhouse and The Caves, see p. 354) can be found here. There are no beaches, but you can reach the waters below the cliffs via stone steps, iron ladders, and diving boards. Cliff diving is one of the West End's hallmarks, particularly at Rick's Café. Every evening, busloads of tourists watch the sun sink beneath the horizon here. The West End terminates at **Negril Point,** where there is a historic lighthouse, built in 1894. A popular excursion from Negril is to the **Mayfield Falls** *(Glenbrook, Westmoreland, tel 876/971-6580, www.mayfieldfalls.com, $$)*, a 5-acre (2-ha) property with natural pools and waterfalls. ■

The Caves resort occupies one of the choicest stretches of Negril's waterfront.

Rastafarianism

The characteristic colors of Rastafarianism—red, black, green, and gold—are highly visible in Jamaica, adorning everything from bar fronts to bus stops and braided belts. The Rastas themselves, with their dreadlocks piled high under tall hats or knitted tams, have come to symbolize the face of Jamaica—even though for mainstream society they are still cultural rebels.

Looking to Africa

The Rastafarian movement has its roots in the teachings of the black activist Marcus Garvey (1887–1940), a national hero who prophetically advised his followers to "look to Africa, where a Black King shall be crowned." In 1930 Ras Tafari Makonnen (Ras is an honorific given to royalty, Tafari his family name) was crowned Negus of Ethiopia, taking the title Emperor Haile Selassie, King of Kings, Lord of Lords, Conquering Lion of the Tribe of Judah. The Scriptures seemed to support his claims to divinity, and Selassie was elevated to the role of the messiah who would redeem black people from suffering and white oppression.

In its early days Rastafarianism provoked considerable antagonism as it developed support in the poorer parts of Kingston, and police consistently harassed Rasta communities that they believed were drug-crazed and planning to undermine white society. In the 1970s Rastafarianism gained a degree of respectability when the politician Norman Manley visited Haile Selassie in Ethiopia and was presented with a sacred rod, which he employed with great effect in political rallies back home. Casting himself as the people's savior, he swept to power in the 1972 elections with the support of Rastas and their allies.

Musical breakthrough

But the real turning point for Rastafarianism came in the 1970s with the huge success of Bob Marley and the Wailers, whose music spread the word about Rasta beliefs worldwide. Reggae and Rastas became Jamaica's trendiest cultural export, but inevitably a certain commercialization set in, affecting the credibility of the movement.

The Rastafarian faith is based on the belief that Rastas are one of the lost tribes of Israel, and that eventually they will be delivered from Babylon (the corrupt white world) and returned to the promised land in Ethiopia, or Zion. Rastas let their hair grow until it mats together into dreadlocks, following the directive in Leviticus (21:5): "They shall not make baldness upon their heads, neither shall they shave off the corner of their beard, nor make cuttings in the flesh." Following the injunction not to make "cuttings in the flesh," Rastas believe in herbal bush medicine, and many are also strict vegetarians following a regime of natural and unprocessed foods, known as I-tal. Salt, meat, dairy products, and alcohol are eschewed in favor of pulses and vegetables.

Rastas are renowned for their copious consumption of marijuana ("ganja" or "herb"), which was introduced to Jamaica by Indian plantation workers in the late 19th century. Smoking it is a religious sacrament, as outlined in Psalm 104:14: "He causeth the grass to grow for the cattle, and the herb for the service of man." Smoking the sacred herb is believed to provide access to a higher level of spirituality and is often accompanied by recitations of prayers or poems at "reasonings," when the communal pipe or chalice is passed round the group counterclockwise.

Many latter-day Rastas don't follow all these precepts and smoke ganja whenever they wish, eat meat, drink, and allow their dreadlocks to hang loose. The 100,000 Rastas in Jamaica today are split into different sects, and many have gravitated toward the more Christian-based Ethiopian Orthodox Church. The more traditional still remain in rural communes (called camps), venturing out only to secure supplies they cannot produce themselves.

Finally, what do those vibrant Rasta colors represent? Red stands for the blood spilled in Jamaica's history, black represents the skin color of the majority of the population, gold stands for the victory over oppression, and green symbolizes the fertility of both Jamaica and Ethiopia. ■

Above: Bob Marley's music spread the word about Rasta beliefs worldwide.

The belief in letting the hair grow until it mats into dreadlocks can lead to some spectacular results (above). The Rasta faith has adherents throughout the Caribbean; this young woman (right) is from Montserrat.

Mandeville

JAMAICA'S FIFTH LARGEST TOWN, MANDEVILLE (LOCATED 2,000 feet/600 m above sea level), was established in the early 19th century and once served as a hill station for British soldiers recuperating from the heat of the coastal areas. The landscape around Mandeville has been shaped—and in places, marred—by large-scale bauxite mining. Yet the surrounding hills are scented with a heady aroma of coffee, chocolate, and spices. The town is the capital of the parish of Manchester, created in 1816.

Left: The bauxite industry is an important export earner for Jamaica.

Mandeville is the center of Jamaica's bauxite industry. As you approach, you cannot fail to notice the massive, red-stained bauxite factories and the huge scars on the landscape caused by the extraction of Jamaica's "red gold," a major industry here since the 1950s. The bauxite companies built housing suburbs for their employees on the undulating hillsides outside the town center, which combined with Mandeville's air of prosperous tranquility, has turned it into one of the main centers for expatriate Jamaicans returning to their homeland from Britain. Many are snapping up the large homes built for ex-pat Americans and Canadians who once managed the bauxite industry.

The oldest buildings in the town cluster around Mandeville Square, recently renamed **Cecil Charlton Park** after a former mayor. On the south side of the square is the parish church of **St. Mark,** built in 1819. Opposite the church is the Georgian-style **courthouse,** constructed a year later next to the market. The venerable **Mandeville Hotel,** just to the east, was established as an officers' quarters and mess in 1875. It claims to be the oldest hotel in Jamaica; the entrance is shaded by three equally old sandbox trees. To the east is the Manchester Golf Club, one of the oldest in the Caribbean founded

Mandeville
N 24 D2

Mrs. Stephenson's Garden
✉ 25 New Green Rd.
$ $

in 1868. A more recent Mandeville landmark is **Mrs. Stephenson's Garden.** The owner is a regular winner at the town's annual flower show, and her garden is a riot of orchids, anthuriums, and other beautiful plants *(Tel 876/962-2328, tours by appointment).*

Northwest of Mandeville is **Marshall's Pen Great House.** Built in 1795, the house was once used as a "factory" for preparing

The tranquil rural landscapes provide a striking contrast to the bauxite mines.

The parish church of St. Mark, at the heart of Mandeville

Marshall's Pen Great House

- 24 D2
- Winston Jones Hwy.
- 876/877-7335
- By appt. only; minimum 6 people
- $$$$

Community tours show Jamaican life in the countryside.

Huntingdon Summit
George's Valley Rd.
876/962-0585

Kirkvine Works
876/962-3141
By appt. only. One day's notice required

My Jamaica

Tourism in the Caribbean often leads to a gulf between the local people and visitors, particularly when the latter are isolated in all-inclusive compounds that don't give them any real opportunities to get out and explore the destination or meet the people. In view of this, the Jamaica Tourism Board created "My Jamaica," a program that aims to offer intimate experiences of the island for small groups and individual travelers. The Jamaica Tourist Board says: "Our mission is to provide experiences and insights that capture the authentic Jamaica—our Jamaica. At the heart of our programs is a commitment to responsible tourism that supports our local communities and conserves our precious natural resources." A wide range of tours allow guests to tailor their travels, creating personal itineraries and programs which aim to "reveal the soul of the nation." As well as unique and unusual places to stay, the scheme encompasses "Tastes of Jamaica," "Roots Jamaica," Jamaica Naturally," and "Happenings in Jamaica." For further information, visit www.visitjamaica.com. ■

coffee beans. It has since become a home filled with artifacts, including shell and stamp collections, Oriental objets d'art, and antiques. The grounds serve as a bird sanctuary and nature reserve. (Owner Arthur Sutton's son, Robert, has written the definitive guide to birds of Jamaica.)

Another mansion, to the south of town, is **Huntingdon Summit,** home of Cecil C. Charlton, a self-made millionaire who was also mayor of Mandeville for more than 20 years. The pagoda-like house is renowned for its ostentatious interior, esoteric furnishings, and trophy-filled library. An indoor swimming pool

One of Jamaica's excellent liqueurs

is connected to another one outdoors by an underground tunnel.

If you want to see what made Mandeville so wealthy in the early 1950s, you can tour Alcan Jamaica's **Kirkvine Works** to the north-east of town. This is the largest alumina plant in Jamaica. Alcan owns more than 30,000 acres (12,000 ha) in the surrounding area that are either not yet mined or under rehabilitation.

You can also visit the **High Mountain Coffee Factory,** Williamsfield, where producers JSP roast, grind, and package some of the finest coffee in Jamaica. There is another olfactory treat next door and one chocoholics won't want to miss: a tour of the delectably scented **Pioneer Chocolate Factory.** This miniature gourmet experience can be rounded off at the **Pickapeppa Factory,** Shooter's Hill, which produces spicy Pickapeppa sauce. ■

High Mountain Coffee Factory
✉ Williamsfield
☎ 876/963-4211
🕒 By appt. only. Closed weekends

Pickapeppa Factory
✉ Shooter's Hill
☎ 876/603-3441
🕒 By appt. only. Closed weekends

Mandeville drive

This drive from Mandeville into the neighboring parish of St. Elizabeth passes through lovely stretches of countryside. The road is in reasonably good repair, and driving conditions are relatively easy.

North From Mandeville, follow signs out of town toward Christiana, and then turn left at a sign marked Kendall. After 2 miles (3 km) you'll see the massive **Alcan bauxite factory ❶.** This is the biggest mining operation in Jamaica, scouring the "red gold" from vast pits in the surrounding area and leaving a fine red film of bauxite powder over the countryside. Some of the unused pits on either side of the road are being rehabilitated as farmland.

Follow the road for about a mile (1.6 km), and turn left toward Christiana. At Shooter's Hill turn left onto Rte. B6 past the abandoned Orchid Sanctuary.

The stretch of road between here and **Balaclava ❷** is an idyllic farming region reminiscent of the English countryside. Sheep and cattle graze in well-tended pastures surrounded by low stone walls, presided over by towering tropical trees like the silk cotton. Occasionally these majestic specimens are found on their own in the middle of a field—shrouded sentinels with a green mantle of luxuriant bromeliads and hanging lichens.

About 21 miles (34 km) from the start, the road opens out to reveal a panorama of hills stretching into the distance to the south. To the north rise the higher peaks of Cockpit Country (see p. 48), forest-clad and almost impenetrable.

From Balaclava Rte. B6 gently drops to the valley floor, where a good, wide road bisects the massive sugarcane fields on either side, rolling off into the distance like a vast green carpet.

Two miles (3 km) beyond the ramshackle little town of Siloah is the **Appleton Rum Estate ❸** (see p. 62). After visiting the estate, drive to the town of **Maggotty** and then head south to the junction with Rte. A2 (8 miles/13 km). Turn right and soon you find yourself driving along **Bamboo Avenue ❹,** a 2-mile (3 km) stretch completely overshadowed by giant bamboo, which arches over it to create a photogenic tunnel of foliage.

One mile (1.6 km) farther west, take a right signposted to reach **YS Falls ❺** (see p. 61), on an upcountry cattle ranch. There's a shortcut from Maggotty to YS Falls, on Rte. B6, but the poor road means that it is only recommended for experienced drivers.

From YS Falls return to Rte. A2 and turn left to head back to Mandeville. This is a big busy road, but the driving conditions are good. ■

YS Falls

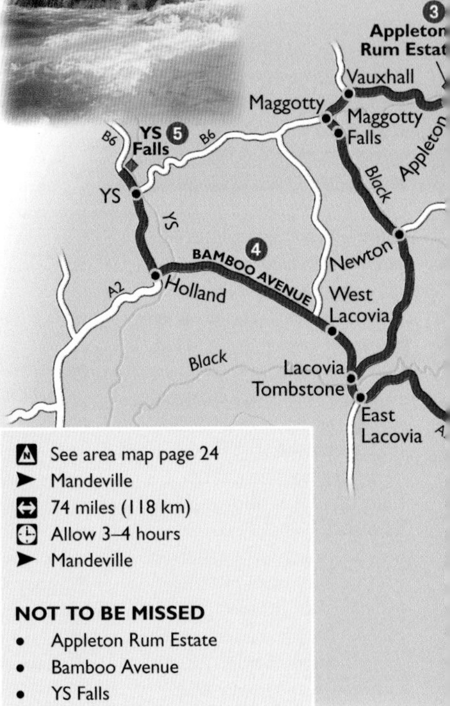

- See area map page 24
- ➤ Mandeville
- 74 miles (118 km)
- Allow 3–4 hours
- ➤ Mandeville

NOT TO BE MISSED

- Appleton Rum Estate
- Bamboo Avenue
- YS Falls

Bamboo Avenue

Mandeville parish church

Mandeville courthouse

Black River was once a thriving port shipping logwood.

South coast

THOUGH JAMAICA'S SOUTH COAST IS OFF THE TOURIST track, it repays adventurous travelers with mountain scenery, busy coastal fishing villages, hidden beauty spots, and discreet resorts tucked away in tranquil coves.

Black River
24 C2
Visitor information
2 High St.
876/965-2074

The landscapes of the southern parishes range from arid, cactus-strewn savannas to lush cattle pastures and vast swamplands. In the easternmost parish, St. Elizabeth, the main town is **Black River,** a peaceful port facing Black River Bay. Its main street has several colonnaded timber houses harking back to Black River's heyday in the mid-19th century when the town was a thriving depot for the export of logwood, which was used to produce textile dyes. Black River claims to have been the first town in Jamaica to introduce electricity, telephones, and the automobile. The invention of synthetic dyes killed off the logwood industry, and the town reverted to its earlier existence as a quiet backwater.

Most of the activity in Black River centers on the wharfside and the main street, where you'll find such faded gems as the Waterloo Guesthouse, the Invercauld Great House & Hotel with its ornate Victorian fretwork, bay windows and gabled roofs, and the yellow-brick parish church of St. John's. Alongside the town's bridge, where the river cruise boats depart, is the

Hendrick's Building, dating from 1813.

The majority of visitors come here for a **boat safari** (see p. 62) on the Black River itself, one of the few easily accessible waterways in Jamaica for spotting wildlife. The 44-mile (71 km) river, Jamaica's longest, is named for the inky black color of its waters (an appearance due to the peat moss lining the riverbed). The river is the main source for a vast swampland known as the Great Morass, which covers about 125 square miles (324 sq km) on either side of the lower reaches of the river as it descends from its source in Cockpit Country (see p. 48) south of Montego Bay. In the course of its relatively short route—compared with rivers in North America, for example—the Black River empties an area of astonishingly varied landscape.

The boats travel about 6 miles (10 km) through swaths of water hyacinths and beneath the boughs of venerable mangrove trees. You're likely to see flocks of roosting cattle egrets and possibly whistling ducks, herons, ospreys, and jacanas—just some of the hundred or so species of birds that live here. The main attractions, however, are the crocodiles. Once abundant around Jamaica's coastline, their numbers are now depleted due to loss of habitat and hunting. There are now around 400 of the reptiles; 12 of which are regularly spotted on the boat safaris. They all have names (albeit a different name depending on which boat you take!) and are used to being approached by the boats and fed scraps. Don't, however, be lulled into complacency.

YS Falls is 10 miles (16 km) to the north of Black River, signposted off Rte. A2. This scenic cascade lies at the heart of the 2,500-acre (1,000 ha) **YS Estate,** where the owners raise pedigree Red Poll cattle and thoroughbred racehorses. The origin of the name YS has been debated for decades. One version is that it derives from the Gaelic word *wyess*, meaning "winding" or "twisting," to describe the river; another is that it comes from the original 17th-century owners, John Yates and Richard Scott, who branded their cattle with the first letter of each of their surnames.

The tour starts at the visitor center, where a tractor-drawn jitney takes you on the 10-minute ride across farmland to the falls. This is a well-maintained area, with grassy spots for picnics and shaded gazebos alongside the riverbank. A wooden stairway leads up the highest and most spectacular waterfall, and there are caves behind some of the cascades to explore and cool pools where you can swim. ■

A refreshing sense of informality attracts visitors to some of the more out-of-the-way sights, such as Windsor Caves.

YS Estate & Falls

- 24 C2
- Off Rte. A2
- 876/634-2454
- Closed Mon.
- $$$$

A roadside shack on the south coast

More places to visit in the south

ALLIGATOR HOLE

Just beyond Gut River Pool, near Milk River Spa, is a small nature park, Alligator Hole, which is home to rare and endangered manatees. The manatees live in a maze of reeds in the river delta and come in close to the jetty to be fed. You can rent a boat at the jetty with a guide to take you out to look for them, but don't expect too much. Manatees are reclusive creatures, and the most you might see is a shadowy form gliding past underwater near the riverbank or telltale bubbles rising from the reeds as you silently drift by. You can also rent kayaks here.

24 D1

APPLETON ESTATE RUM TOUR

Three miles (5 km) east of YS Falls, beyond the small junction town of Maggotty, lies the Appleton Estate. Set amid the rolling sugarcane fields of the Black River Valley, this 250-year-old institution is the oldest rum-producing factory in the English-speaking Caribbean, and its products are among the most popular on the island. Most of the process is now mechanized, although some of the copper distillation pots are over a century old. An aging donkey demonstrates the old-fashioned method of squeezing the juice out of the cane by turning a grinder. You can peek into the warehouse where more than 8,400 barrels of maturing rum rise up in tiers to the ceiling. The tour ends in the visitor center, where you can sample some of the assorted rums and other liquors produced here.

24 C2 876/963-9215 Closed Sun.
$$$$ or $$$$$ for tour with lunch

Black River safaris

Boat journeys up the Black River, which last about 90 minutes, are available. One of the most experienced operators is St. Elizabeth Safaris *(Tel 876/965-2374)*. Also J. Charles Swaby's Black River Safari Tours *(Tel 876/965-2513)*. ■

AROUND GREAT PEDRO BLUFF

At the far end of Great Pedro Bay is Great Pedro Bluff, which is one of the few places in the Caribbean where a dry savanna exists in the coastal zone; efforts are under way to give it protected status. Beyond here (signposted from Southfield) are the sheer cliffs and lighthouse *(Tel 876/965-6634)* of

Lover's Leap, where, legend has it, two slaves who were forbidden to meet each other leaped to their deaths rather than be separated. Entrance to the clifftop is through a café-restaurant complex. The view is spectacular, with the sheer bluff of the Santa Cruz Mountains dropping 1,700 feet (518 m) almost straight down to the ocean; the panorama extends down the coastline to Rocky Point and Clarendon in one direction, and back toward Great Pedro Bluff and Treasure Beach in the other.

Ten miles (16 km) east of Treasure Beach is the fishing village of Alligator Pond. From here a scenic drive winds (18 miles/29 km) along the south coast toward Alligator Hole and Milk River Spa. This wild, unspoiled part of the country embraces dry savanna as well as the extensive swamplands of the Long Bay Morass. Midway along is an exquisite little spot known as the **Gut River Pool.** The river flows under the road and emerges in an oasis of palm trees, bulrushes, and water lilies, with crystal-clear pools that you can jump into from the surrounding rocks: It's very popular with local lads cooling off on weekends.

The Gut River banks are an oasis of cool greenery on a mostly arid coastline.

24 C1

TREASURE BEACH

The main resort area on the south coast is picturesque Treasure Beach, 19 miles (30 km) east of Black River. In fact, Treasure Beach is not just one beach, but a series of connected bays including Billy's Bay, Frenchman's Bay, Calabash Bay, and Great Pedro Bay. Most of the accommodations are based in Calabash Bay, where a series of guesthouses and small hotels provide simple lodging for those wanting to get away from it all. The pace of life follows a rural rhythm and the coming and going of the brightly colored fishing boats.

24 C1 ■

Spanish Town

Spanish Town
25 E2

JAMAICA'S CAPITAL FOR MORE THAN 300 YEARS, SPANISH Town is today a large industrial city with few traces of its past prominence. Called St. Jago de la Vega by the Spanish who founded the first capital here in 1523, the city was later razed by British soldiers during the invasions in 1596 and 1643. It remained the capital under the British until 1872, when Kingston took over the role. Nestled within the modern cityscape are fascinating reminders of Spanish Town's past—and of the European powers that shaped Jamaica.

Visitor at Rodney Memorial

People's Museum of Craft & Technology
King's House, Parade Sq.
876/907-0322
Closed weekends
$

At the heart of the city is **Parade Square,** a park surrounded by the faded grandeur of Georgian buildings. On the north side is the **Rodney Memorial,** built to commemorate Admiral Rodney's defeat of the French fleet off Guadeloupe in 1782. Sculptured by John Bacon, the marble statue depicts Rodney in classical attire and is flanked by two rare cannon captured from the French flagship. The cupola housing the statue is adorned with friezes depicting the battle itself. The buildings that flank the memorial, linked by a porticoed walkway, house the **National Archives** *(closed weekends).*

The redbrick Georgian facade on the west side of the square is all that remains of the **King's House,** built in 1762 as the governor's residence but largely destroyed by fire in 1925. The stables now house the **People's Museum of Craft and Technology,** which features industrial and agricultural equipment (including an ancient sugar press, coffee huskers, and corn grinders) and other items relating to the country's industrial heritage. They provide a snapshot of Jamaican history. Opposite the King's House is the former House of Assembly, now occupied by local government offices.

To the south of Parade Square stands the **Cathedral of St. Jago de la Vega** *(White Church St.).* The oldest Anglican cathedral outside England, it was built in 1714 on the site of a 16th-century Spanish church. The black-and-white checkered floor tiles in the aisle belonged to the original Catholic church. The elaborate interior contains many important monuments from the colonial era and elaborately carved pews and choir stalls. ■

Enjoying a location almost in the center of the Caribbean, the Cayman Islands is one of the most prosperous enclaves in the region. The principal industries are offshore finance and tourism, with visitors lured to the pristine waters.

Cayman Islands

A pufferfish inflates itself when threatened.

Cayman Islands

THE LOW-LYING CAYMAN ISLANDS GROUP IS SITUATED ALMOST IN THE middle of the Caribbean, 480 miles (772 km) southwest of Miami. There are three islands in this British Crown Colony, each different in character. The biggest island, Grand Cayman, is the home of the capital, George Town, as well as Seven Mile Beach, one of the most famous in the Caribbean. Tourism and offshore finance have given the island's 36,600 inhabitants one of the highest per capita incomes in the region. About 90 miles (145 km) to the northeast lie the two sister islands of Cayman Brac and Little Cayman, both comparatively undeveloped and the perfect antidote to life in the fast lane.

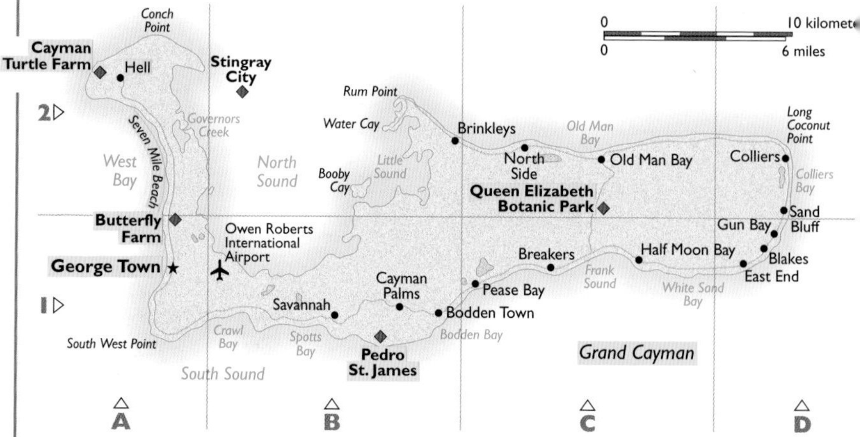

The three islands share a similar appearance—relatively flat, mostly covered with dry scrub. The Caymans sit on the edge of the Cayman Trench, a massive trough that drops some 25,000 feet (7,620 m) into the deepest part of the Caribbean Sea. The reef walls that surround the islands descend into the depths and attract scuba divers from all over the world. The Caymans have become one of the Caribbean's top diving destinations thanks largely to marine park regulations introduced in 1979.

There are over 100 moored dive sites around Grand Cayman alone and all types of diving courses are available, from beginner level through to technical specialities. Stingray City, the Caymans' most popular underwater attraction, is home to more than 100 friendly stingrays, which can be handled and stroked in open water. Because it takes place in depths of 3-12 feet (1-4 m), it is also accessible to snorkelers. Several types of tourist submarines—including one which descends 1,000 feet (305 m) into the Cayman Trench—allow even non-divers to experience the thrills of the underwater world.

The first European sighting of the islands was by Columbus on May 10, 1503, when he was blown off course on his way to Hispaniola. The explorer spotted the two smaller islands, Cayman Brac and Little Cayman. Although he didn't stop to explore, Columbus noted the enormous numbers of turtles in the surrounding waters and named the islands Las Tortugas. Over the next hundred years or so they came to be known as Las Caymanas, from the Carib name for the saltwater crocodiles that were also abundant around the islands.

In the 16th century, Dutch, French, English, and Spanish sailors used the islands as places to take on water and capture sea turtles, an abundant source of fresh meat for the long sea voyage back to Europe. Even though Sir Francis Drake visited Grand Cayman in 1586 and reported that the

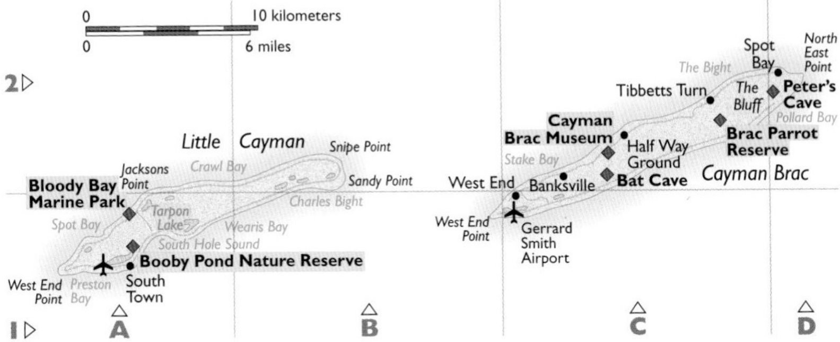

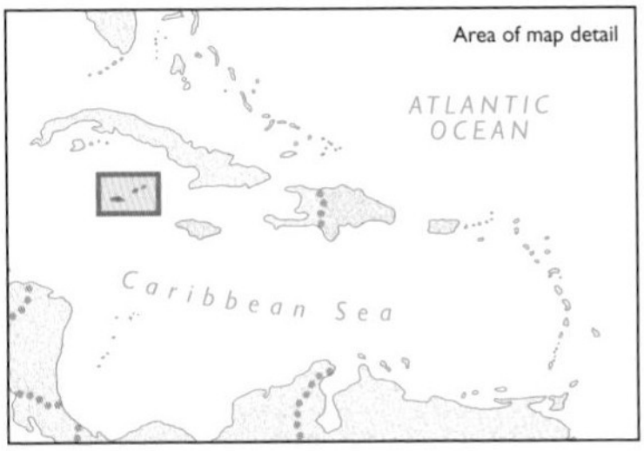

caimans were edible, the islands remained unclaimed and uninhabited.

The Cayman Islands came under English jurisdiction in 1655, when England took Jamaica and neighboring islands from the Spanish; they were formally recognized as English territory in 1670. In the mid-1660s the first settlers arrived from Jamaica, setting up semipermanent habitations on Little Cayman and Cayman Brac to trade turtles, vegetables, water, wood, and coconuts with passing ships. Grand Cayman, which offered better protection from pirate attacks, was settled beginning in 1700.

The Caymans developed a maritime economy. By the late 1800s up to one-third of the population was employed as merchant sailors, fishermen, or turtle catchers. The islanders rescued numerous mariners shipwrecked on the offshore reefs and salvaged lumber and cargo to build their houses and supply other needs. Over the course of time, however, a growing sense of self-sufficiency began to take hold among the islanders. They turned from salvage to construction. By the 1780s the Caymanians were building their own schooners and becoming renowned throughout the Caribbean as master boatbuilders. Shipbuilding prospered for more than 150 years, until the final launching of a traditional Caymanian ship in January 1967.

Although the first legislative assembly was formed in 1832, the islands remained a dependency of Jamaica until 1959. Following Jamaica's independence from Britain in 1962, the Caymans chose to remain a British Crown Colony. In 1966 they introduced landmark legislation to encourage growth of the offshore banking industry, today one of the mainstays of the economy; and recognized in 2000 as the world's fifth largest.

The first tourists arrived on board the cruise ship *Atlantis* in 1937, and in 1953 the first airfield opened on Grand Cayman. Today the islands, while protective of their coral reefs, receive more than 300,000 overnight visitors, and nearly two million day-trippers arrive by boat every year. ■

The tax-free myth

According to accepted wisdom the Cayman Islands' tax-free status is due to the Wreck of the Ten Sails. In 1794 a convoy of ten merchant ships from Jamaica was wrecked on the reefs of Grand Cayman's east end, but thanks to the brave efforts of the local settlers, everybody was saved. Legend has it that a member of the British royal family was on board and in gratitude King George III proclaimed that the islanders should never be taxed. This is a colorful tale—but untrue. In fact, income tax was abolished in 1971 by the Finance Ministry in order to kick-start a sluggish economy. The policy eventually paid off, transforming the Caymans into one of the world's largest offshore banking centers. ■

George Town enjoys a protected harbor.

Grand Cayman

THE LARGEST OF THE THREE CAYMAN ISLANDS, GRAND Cayman is 22 miles (35.4 km) long and 4 to 8 miles (6–13 km) wide. The most prosperous of the islands, it is home to 96 percent of the country's population. A busy coastal fringe gives way to an interior of mangroves, lakes, and native woodlands.

George Town
66 C1
Visitor information
www.caymanislands.ky
Regatta Office Park, Leeward Two, West Bay Road
345/949-0623

National Museum
www.museum.ky
Harbour Dr. George Town
345/949-8368
Closed Sun.
$$

Most of the development on Grand Cayman is concentrated along **Seven Mile Beach** (which is actually just 5.5 miles/8.8 km long), a glorious stretch of powdery sand on the west side of the island sloping into the shallow waters of West Bay. A ribbon of hotels and condominiums lines the beach, while behind it lies a strip of shopping malls, fast-food outlets, restaurants, and bars.

Grand Cayman's capital, **George Town,** is primarily a business center clustered around a protected harbor. The harbor is a popular stop for cruise ships, which disgorge their passengers by the thousands into the duty-free souvenir and jewelry shops on the surrounding streets. One of the few remaining 19th-century structures has been converted into the commendable **National Museum.** Displays here chronicle the natural and seafaring history of the islands.

Just outside of George Town is the **Butterfly Farm,** a 10,000 sq foot (929 sq m) facility with 46

Hawksbill turtles are now rarely seen around the islands.

species of butterflies from around the world. A guided tour of the tropical gardens with commentary on butterflies and their life-cycles is included in the entry fee.

To the north of Seven Mile Beach, **Boatswain's Beach** is the island's latest tourist magnet. The 23-acre marine park has incorporated the hurricane-damaged former Cayman Island Turtle Farm and added a whole raft of attractions including a saltwater snorkel lagoon with tropical fish, a 300,000 gallon swimming pool with views of the predator tank, an aviary, iguana sanctuary, and research facility. You can still see the famous green sea turtles, indeed there are thousands of them, ranging in size from hatchlings to 600-pound adults. When you are done with wildlife, there's a Caymanian heritage street with craft vendors, a couple of restaurants, and a nature trail.

A short distance east of the farm, however, you can go to **Hell.** In the 1930s, so the story goes, a British commissioner shot at a bird and missed. His exclamation, "Oh hell," was adopted as a place-name. The

Sports & activities

Diving & snorkeling:

Grand Cayman has more than 40 dive operations, reflecting its enormous popularity with sports divers. Many specialize in particular areas such as the North Wall, East End, and South and West Sides. For an overview of the island's 200-plus dive and snorkel sites, diving conditions, marine life, video footage, and details of local operators, check out the dedicated dive website: www.divecayman.ky or contact DiveTech *(Tel 345/946-5658, www.divetech.com)*, or Ocean Frontiers *(Tel 345/947-0000, www.oceanfrontiers.com)*; or Peter Milburn *(Tel 345/945-5770; www.petermilburndivecayman.com)*. ■

Butterfly Farm
66 A1
www.thebutterflyfarm.com
Harquail Bypass
345/946-3411
$$$

Boatswain's Beach
66 A2
www.boatswainsbeach.ky
North West Point
345/949-3894
$$$$$

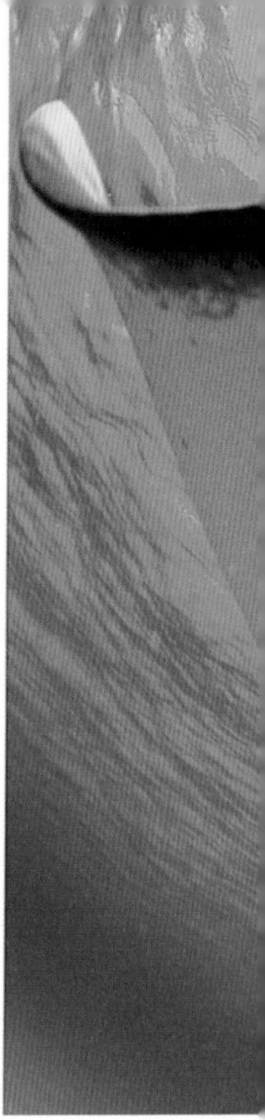

small area of phytokarst rocks is supported by the **Hell post office** and souvenir shop.

The south coast features two major attractions. The first of these is **Pedro St. James,** just outside the township of Savannah. Built about 1780, this historic building is the oldest surviving structure on the Grand Cayman island. It has had a colorful history: The solid stone house was built using slave labor and was originally referred to as St. James Castle. It was in the dining room here that judges held court and Caymanians decided to form an elected legislature.

Recently Pedro St. James has been extensively restored, and the complex now includes a visitor center and audiovisual theater, oceanfront restaurant, and other amenities. But the real strength of Pedro St. James is its depiction of the lives of the early settlers, the realities of slavery, and the re-creation of times past. In the mansion's upstairs dining room, the island's first elected assembly convened on December 10, 1831, and from the Palladian staircase here the Proclamation of Emancipation abolishing slavery was read in 1835.

Eight miles (13 km) farther east, just outside the township of Breakers on Frank Sound, is the **Queen Elizabeth II Botanic Park.** This 65-acre (26-ha) park, jointly managed by the National Trust for the Cayman Islands and the government, features colorful gardens, a trail through native woodlands, and a lakeside nature reserve. Halfway around the woodland trail is an iguana enclosure with several specimens of Grand Cayman's endangered blue iguana (see below). Highlights of the park include the excellent Heritage Garden, with native Caymanian home and sand garden, and the Colour Garden—one of Grand Cayman's most underrated attractions. ■

Blue iguanas

The Cayman blue iguana *(Cyclura nubila lewisi)* is the most endangered rock iguana in the West Indies. These gentle blue giants can grow up to 5 ft (1.8m) in length, and are primarily herbivorous, though destruction of their natural habitat and predation by dogs and cats has brought the species to the brink of extinction. Fortunately, help is at hand in the form of the Blue Iguana Recovery Program, which offers tours of its captive breeding facility in the Queen Elizabeth II Botanic Park *(Tel 345/925-7599 for advance reservations, $$$$$, www.blueiguana.ky).* ■

Pedro St. James

66 B1

www.pedrostjames.ky

Savannah, off coast road

345/947-3329

$$$$

Queen Elizabeth II Botanic Park

66 C2

www.botanic-park.ky

North Side

345/947-9462

$$$

Despite its fierce appearance, the blue iguana is a peaceful vegetarian.

A diver strokes one of the 100 stingrays at Stingray City.

Little Cayman

THE SMALLEST AND LEAST DEVELOPED OF THE CAYMAN Islands, Little Cayman is a far cry from the commercial frenzy of Grand Cayman's Seven Mile Beach. Nine miles (15 km) long and just one mile (1.5 km) across at its widest point, the island is predominantly flat scrub in the interior and fringed with palm trees and sea grapes along its shoreline.

Little Cayman
67 A1

Carin and Arawak peoples may have visited the island from Cuba and Jamaica, drawn by supplies of fresh turtle, but the first permanent settlers were a ragged band of escaped slaves and shipwrecked sailors who set up a turtling station here in the 1660s. By 1900 there were still only 200 people on the island, making a living from phosphate mining, shipbuilding, and turtle catching. A hurricane destroyed most of the houses in 1932, and the inhabitants migrated to Cayman Brac or Grand Cayman in search of work.

Isolated for decades, Little Cayman (population 70) has remained comparatively undeveloped, and it is the peace, quiet, and wilderness that now attract tourists. Diving, bird-watching, and fishing are the main activities.

The diving is superb. Extending along the north shore of the island is **Bloody Bay Marine Park,**

Booby Pond interpretive center

67 A1

Outside Blossom Village

Closed Sun.

CAYMANITE

Caymanite is a rare, semiprecious rock that is found only in Cayman Brac and on the eastern end of Grand Cayman. A hard dolomite, formed during the Oligocene-Miocene epoch (between 16–25 million years ago), it has a composition similar to manganese nodules found on the ocean floor. The stone's colored layers are formed by its various metallic contents, with manganese dominating in the black layers, iron in the red layers, and nickel, titanium, and copper among the others. When polished, the stone is made into jewelry. ■

Sports & activities

Diving & snorkeling:

There are dive centers at all the main resorts on Little Cayman. Southern Cross Club (*Tel 345/948-1099, fax 345/948-1098, www.southerncrossclub.com);* Reef Divers *(Tel 345/948-1070, fax 345/948-1040, www.littlecayman.com);* Pirate's Point *(Tel 345/948-1010, fax 345/948-1011, www.piratespointresort.com);* Paradise Divers *(Paradise Villas, tel 345/948-0001, fax 345/948-0002, www. paradisevillas.com).* ■

one of the Caribbean's most spectacular dive locations. The reef wall here starts in just 20 feet (6 m) of water and plunges some 6,000 feet (1,830 m) to the ocean floor. These pristine walls feature an abundance of marine life, including giant barrel and elephant ear sponges, massive elkhorn corals, lush forests of sea fans, and reef fish of all sizes and descriptions. Eagle rays and turtles flip lazily past in the deep blue, and the coral canyons and crevices harbor a mass of gobies, blennies, basslets, wrasses, and other brilliantly colored fish (see above for dive operators).

Little Cayman is also an important reserve for birdlife. The **Booby Pond Nature Reserve** *(National Trust for the Cayman Islands, tel 345/948-1010),* just outside Blossom Village, is home to the largest colony of red-footed boobies in the Western Hemisphere. Some 20,000 of these pelagic seabirds nest here, wandering the oceans in search of food by day and returning to roost at night. The Caymans' only breeding colony of magnificent frigatebirds also nests here, and you'll often see them engaged

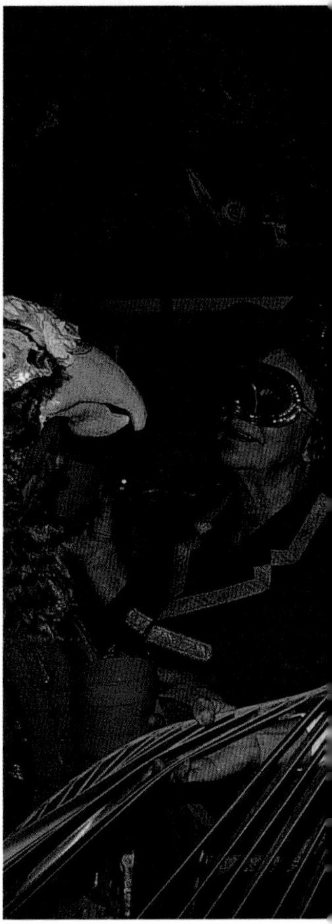

in aerial battles with the boobies as they return at sundown, trying to get them to disgorge their catch. The reserve has been designated a Wetland of International Importance under the 1971 RAMSAR convention. An **interpretive center** and a bird-watching tower are beside the road. The islands are also home to a significant iguana population: The lizards can often be seen sunning themselves beside the road.

Tarpon Lake, a large, brackish pond in the middle of the island, is a curiosity: During Hurricane Gilbert, in 1988, the

lake was flooded with seawater, and the tarpon now found in the lake have since developed into a subspecies of those out in the ocean. There are nature trails around the lake, and you can fish from the jetty.

For fishing fanatics the main attractions are spectacular bonefishing on the flats of **South Hole Sound** and deep-sea fishing for marlin, tuna, and wahoo. ■

"Booby" (with blue beak) leads revelers at a fund-raiser for the Booby Pond Nature Reserve.

How Bloody Bay got its name

Legend has it that Little Cayman was once settled by pirates and buccaneers who anchored their ships on the north shore and made forays out to attack passing ships. The British finally dispatched a squadron to deal with this problem by using the element of surprise. As the British vessels sailed into view, the pirates raced for their ships but were cut off and attacked as they attempted to board. The subsequent massacre was how Bloody Bay gained its name. ■

Coral reefs of the Caribbean

Beneath Caribbean waters lies the complex and colorful environment of coral reefs. This mysterious, enchantingly beautiful world more than matches the terrestrial flora and fauna of the islands. It is second only to the rain forests in terms of biological diversity.

The coral reef

Coral reefs have existed for 450 million years, making them among the oldest ecosystems on the planet. These remarkable structures have been built up over the centuries by tiny coral animals, or polyps, which convert sunlight and the carbon dioxide from seawater into calcium carbonate with the help of captive partners known as zooxanthellae plants that live within their tissues. The polyps use this calcium carbonate (or limestone) to build the stony structure in which they live. This symbiotic relationship only functions in warm, clear tropical waters where there is enough sunlight for the zooxanthellae to perform.

Like reefs all over the world, Caribbean reefs are subject to numerous stresses including anchor damage, pollution, sedimentation, and coral bleaching caused by ocean warming.

Opposite: School of blue-striped grunts
Below: Yellow tube sponge and snappers

Marine tourism can help to preserve coral reefs, but snorkellers and divers must play their part by not touching the corals while underwater and not buying marine souvenirs.

The Caribbean is home to around 50 species of hard corals; each builds its own unique structure. Among the more familiar are the brain corals, which can grow up to 6 feet (1.8 m) across and resemble a human brain; staghorn corals, which branch out like deer antlers; elkhorn corals, which form dense patches in the surf zone; star corals, which are important reef builders; pillar corals, whose distinctive pillars can grow up to 10 feet (3 m) high; and boulder corals, which are found almost everywhere.

There are also about 20 species of soft corals, the most prominent of which are large sea fans or gorgonians. Others include black corals, sea whips, sea plumes, and sea rods. Colorful sponges of all descriptions—delicate azure vase sponges, blood-red barrel sponges, and bright yellow tube sponges—are another important component in the dynamic reef environment, playing host to tiny invertebrates or providing hiding places for fish.

Reef fish

The Caribbean is home to about a thousand species of fish belonging to more than 140 families. Many of them display a dazzling array of colors as they school around the reef. Among the most common are butterfly fish, particularly the four-eyed and banded butterfly fish, and angelfish, such as the magnificent queen angelfish, the yellow-and-gray French angelfish, and the black-and-yellow rock beauty. Damselfish are at home on the shallow reefs, darting out from their hiding places in the coral to graze on algae; one species, the striped sergeant major, lays its eggs in round patches and defends them aggressively against all comers.

The wrasse family are prime scavengers on the reef, and their behavior is full of surprises. The males rule a harem of females, but should the dominant male get eaten, then one of the females changes sex to take his place. Closely related to the wrasses are the brightly colored

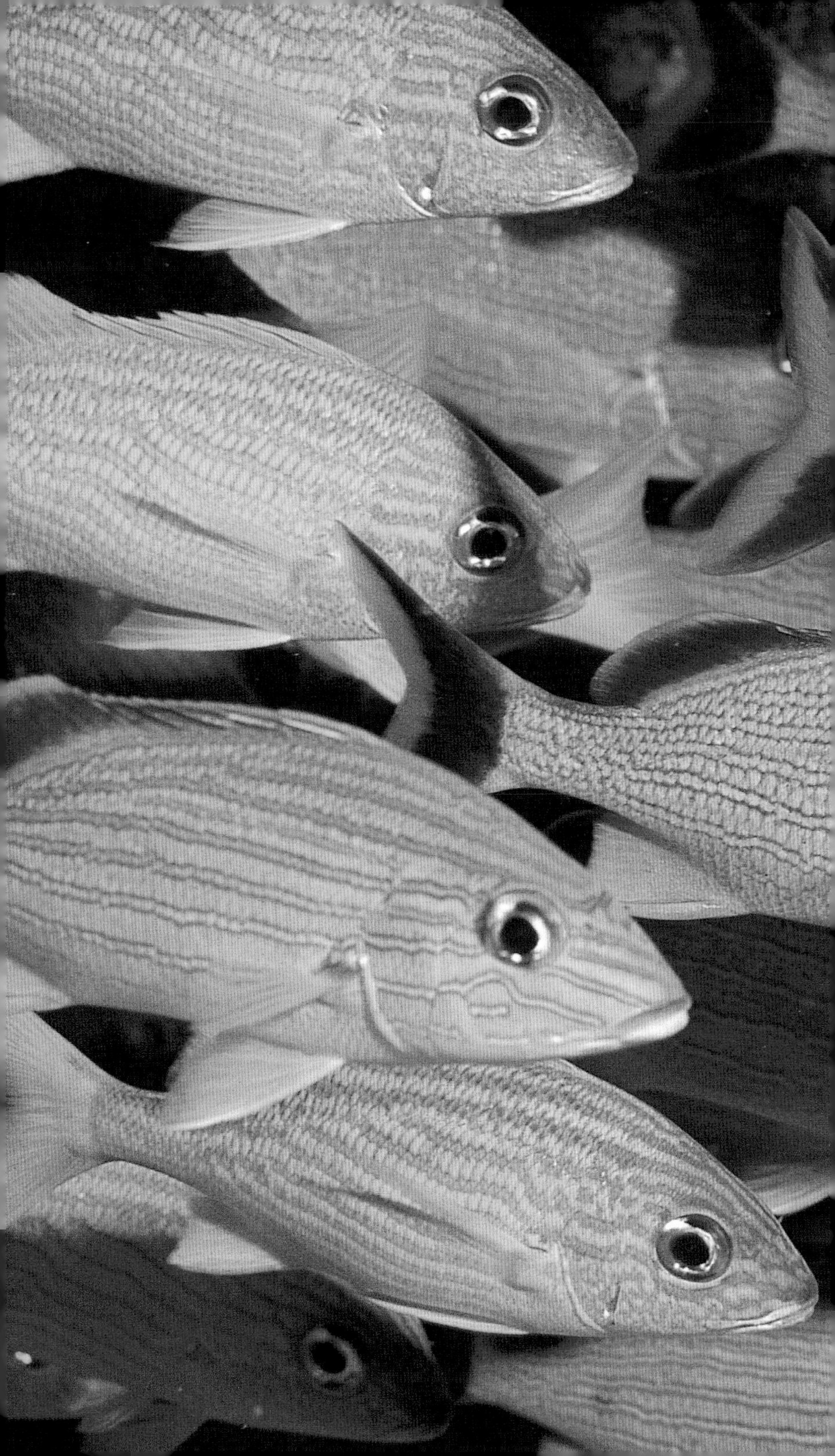

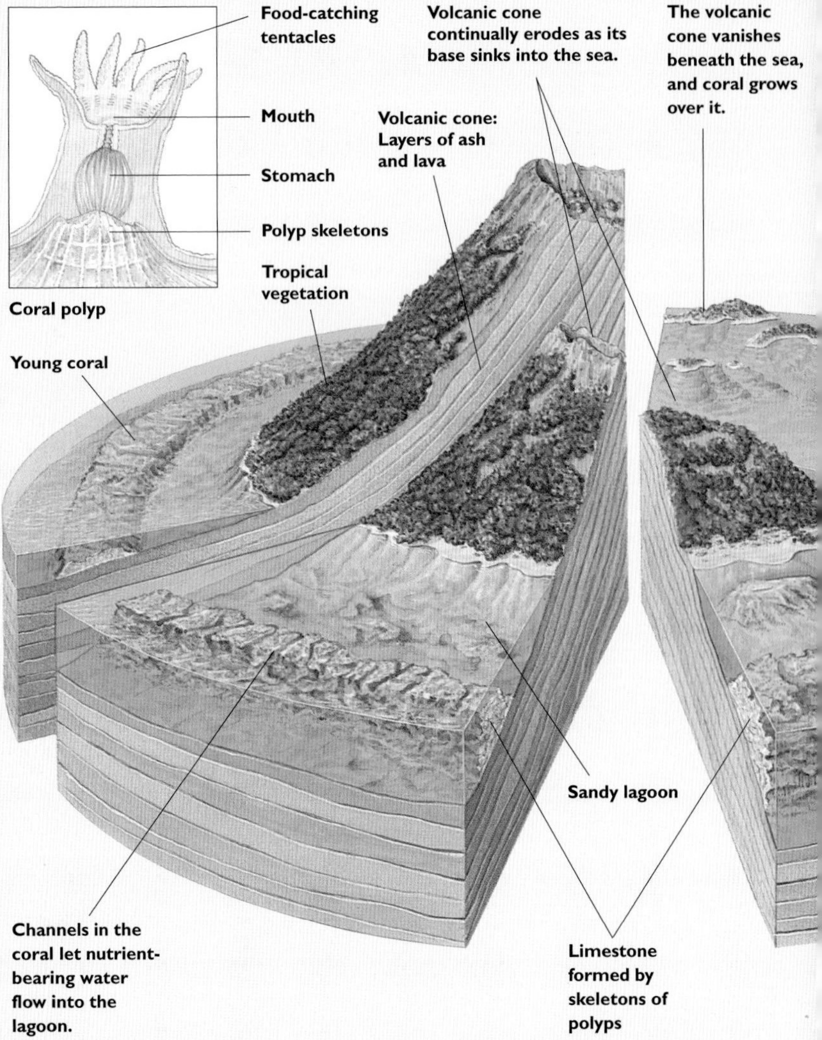

Reefs are formed by accumulated limestone that has been created by the hard, outer skeletons of tiny coral polyps.

parrotfish, 14 species of which live in the Caribbean. Parrotfish feed off algae on the coral rock, grinding up surprisingly large quantities of coral with their powerful jaws and expelling it as coral sand.

Predators often seen hovering near the reef include jacks, pompano, and scads, as well as the ubiquitous snappers, of which there are 19 species. Snappers usually school facing into the current, maintaining the same position in the water column and grabbing anything that comes their way. Groupers, like snappers, are prime food fish and not as common as they once were. Groupers can grow up to 8 feet (2.5 m) in length and weigh more than 650 pounds (295 kg). The great

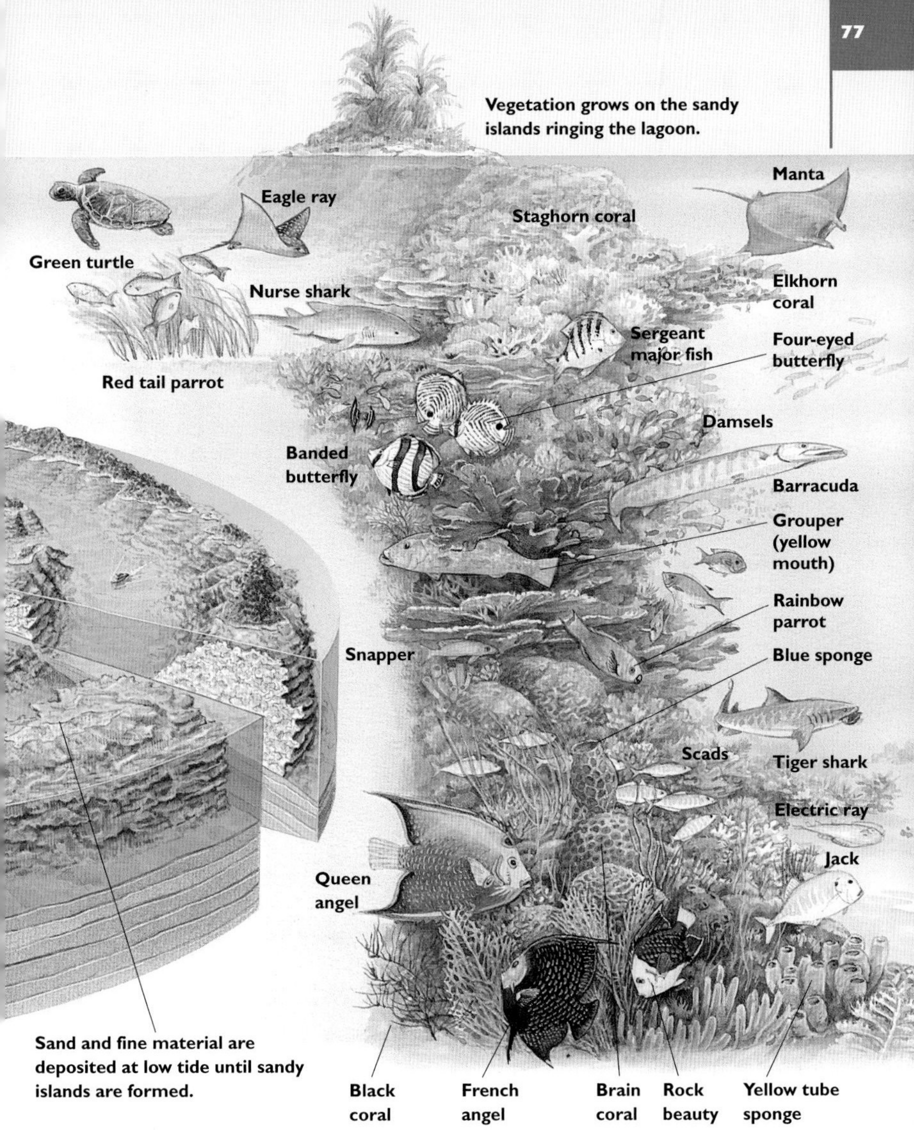

barracuda usually hunts on its own, often around a chosen reef or wreck site; the three smaller species of reef barracuda are more often seen in schools.

Sharks, rays, & turtles

The Caribbean has 44 recorded species of sharks, although most of these stay away from areas with people. The most common is the harmless nurse shark, often found resting on the seabed. There are 22 species of rays, among them the southern stingray (which inhabits Grand Cayman's famous Stingray City), the majestic eagle ray, and the electric ray. Probably the most awe-inspiring ray is the Atlantic manta, also known as the devilfish or giant devil ray, but it is rare to encounter these graceful creatures. Other Caribbean residents include hawksbill and green turtles, although their numbers are now much reduced because of human predation for their meat and shells. ■

Cayman Brac

Cayman Brac
67 C2

ALTHOUGH IT'S JUST 90 MILES (145 KM) TO THE NORTHEAST of Grand Cayman, Cayman Brac seems a world away from the frenetic atmosphere of the main island. Quiet, easygoing, and laid-back are some of the adjectives used to describe this little island, which is usually referred to as "the Brac."

The island supports a thriving community of about 1,200 people. Residents (known as Brackers) are renowned for their hospitality and friendliness.

The Brac is 12 miles (19 km) long and just a mile (1.5 km) wide. The western portion is flat, whereas the eastern half is dominated by a central bluff, which rises to dramatic cliffs some 140 feet high (42 m) at the shoreline. This bluff gives the island its name (*brac* is Gaelic for bluff). The bluff supports a wide variety of plant life, most notably saguaro cactuses and century plants, and bird species including boobies, frigatebirds, white tropic birds, herons, egrets, and bananaquits.

Other island inhabitants include a small population of endangered Brac parrots. The best place to look for them is in the **Brac Parrot Reserve,** which covers 180 acres (73 ha) of rocky woodland on the bluff. The reserve is reached by taking the main cross-island route, and turning down Major Donald Drive (also known as Lighthouse Road), toward the lighthouse at North East Point.

You can explore limestone caves around the bluff (most are marked as turns off the main road). Naturally, **Bat Cave** houses a small bat colony, and **Peter's Cave** is famous as a hurricane shelter. For more information about the island's natural history, check out the dedicated website, *www.naturecayman.com.*

The main attraction on Brac is **scuba diving.** The island is surrounded by pristine reefs teeming with fish and has around 45 registered dive sites. Of particular note is the spectacular wreck of a former Soviet warship sunk here in September 1996. The 330-foot-long (100-m) frigate, originally known as *Patrol Vessel no. 356,* was part of the Soviet fleet stationed in Cuba during the Cold War and was purchased from the Russians with the express intent of sinking it as an artificial reef. Renamed the ***M.V. Captain Keith Tibbets*** in honor of a local personality, it now lies in 55 to 110 feet (17–33 m) of water just off the island's north shore. ■

BRAC BOAT-BUILDING

The first settlers were a random assortment of people including Jamaican planters, shipwrecked mariners, and adventurers. In 1833 slaves from Africa arrived on Cayman Brac and quickly established the island's reputation for boatbuilding, which remained one of its principal activities until the 1960s, when sail was superseded by motor yachts. Small boats used for turtle catching, known as "catboats" (because they could silently sneak up on unsuspecting turtles), were also built here. The story of the Brac's early days is related in the quaint Cayman Brac Museum *(Stake Bay, tel 345/948-2622, closed Sun., $).* ■

Sports & activities

Diving & Water sports: For scuba diving contact Dive Tiara *(Tel 345/948-1553, fax 345/948-1316 or 800/801-5550, www.diviresorts.com);* or Reef Divers *(Tel: 345/948-1642, fax 345/948-1270; www.brac reef.com).*

Fishing: Sportfishing is often called the unofficial "national sport" in the Cayman Islands. Contact Condor Watersports *(Tel: 345/949-1344)* for fishing off both Cayman Brac and Little Cayman. ■

Scattered across nearly 250 square miles (650 sq km) of ocean to the southeast of the Bahamas, the Turks and Caicos group counts some 40 low-lying islands and cays. This remote British dependency is an unspoiled natural gem.

Turks & Caicos Islands

The pink flamingo thrives among the mangroves of Turks & Caicos.

Turks & Caicos Islands

THE TURKS & CAICOS ISLANDS LIE ABOUT 575 MILES (926 KM) SOUTHEAST of Miami and consist of two island groups separated by the 22-mile-wide (35-km) Columbus Passage. To the west is the Caicos group: West Caicos, Providenciales, North Caicos, Middle Caicos, East Caicos, and South Caicos. To the east is the Turks group: Grand Turk and Salt Cay. The country's eight islands and assorted small cays translate to just 166 square miles (430 sq km) of dry land, 80 percent of which is uninhabited.

The Turks & Caicos are more sea than land. They are located on two shallow, sand-covered limestone banks that cover nearly 13 times that of the land area. These huge banks provide important habitats for marine life. Many are covered with sea-grass meadows, where burrowing sea urchins, sea cucumbers, bivalves, and mollusks live in abundance. The banks are a rich fishing ground, and the 8,000 foot deep passage that divides them is popular with migrating humpback whales, rays, turtles and dolphins. The breathtaking underwater scenery has propelled the islands into the top five rankings of the world's best dive destinations.

The first inhabitants of these islands were Lucayan migrating from Haiti; they arrived in the Bahamas chain around 1,200 years ago. After making landfall on Sand Cay or the Seal Cays, the Lucayan established themselves on the northwest corner of Grand Turk. This site, which has been extensively excavated, is the oldest known settlement in the Bahamas chain and was occupied from around A.D. 705 to 1170. Analysis of bones at the site reveals that the inhabitants ate mostly sea turtles. Artifacts recovered include shell beads, a mother-of-pearl pendant, a nearly complete greenstone ax, and conch-shell tools. The most important find from pre-Columbian times on Grand Turk has been a wooden paddle, dating from A.D. 1100. It is now on display in the Turks & Caicos National Museum (see p. 83).

No one lived on the islands when the first Europeans arrived. Controversy surrounds the issue of whether Columbus made his landfall here or on San Salvador in the Bahamas; the evidence points to the latter. In the 17th century, Bermudians settled Grand Turk, Salt Cay, and South Caicos, using slave labor to rake the *salinas* (salt pans) for the salt trade. They also deforested the islands in order to speed up the evaporation process.

During the American Revolution, Loyalists fleeing the conflict set up plantations here for sisal and cotton, again using slave labor. With the abolition of slavery in 1834 the plantation system collapsed, and the Loyalists left the islands. The slaves remained and relied on subsistence farming and fishing. The old plantations eventually returned to wilderness.

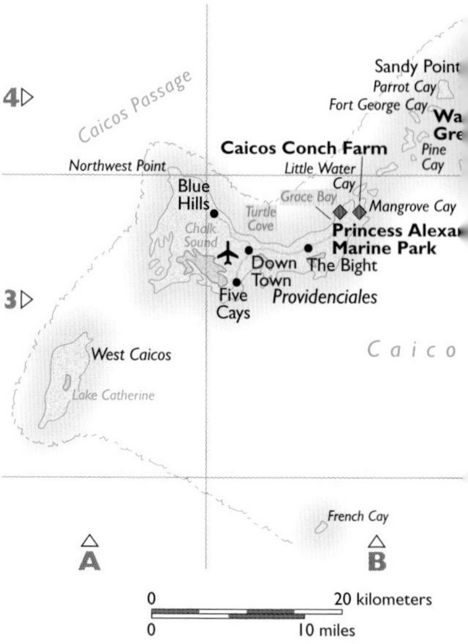

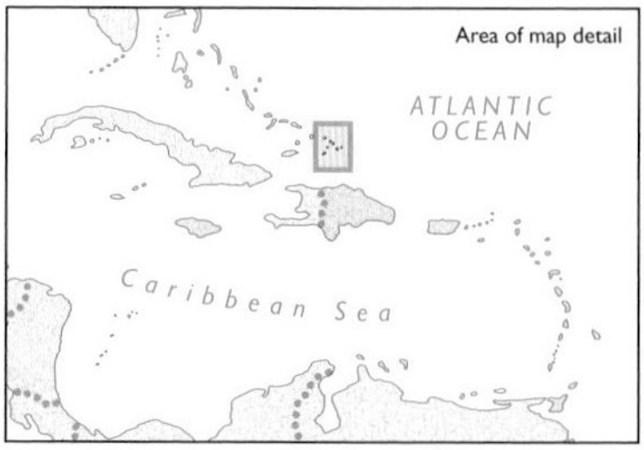

Despite their connections with the Bermudian salt rakers, the islands were under the jurisdiction of the Bahamas from the 18th century until annexed to Jamaica in 1873. After Jamaican independence in 1962, the salt industry foundered and the Turks & Caicos opted to become a British Crown Colony. Tourism on the islands has exploded in recent years, but it is carefully controlled and there is a strong element of eco-awareness as the local industry strives to avoid the pitfalls of over-development. Opinion is still divided over the merits of Grand Turk's cruise ship berth and hotel developments on Providenciales, but TCI can still boast dozens of stunning untouched beaches and dive sites, and a choice of luxurious boltholes on quiet cays, so nobody needs to worry quite yet. ■

Local boys hand-line fishing, Grand Turk

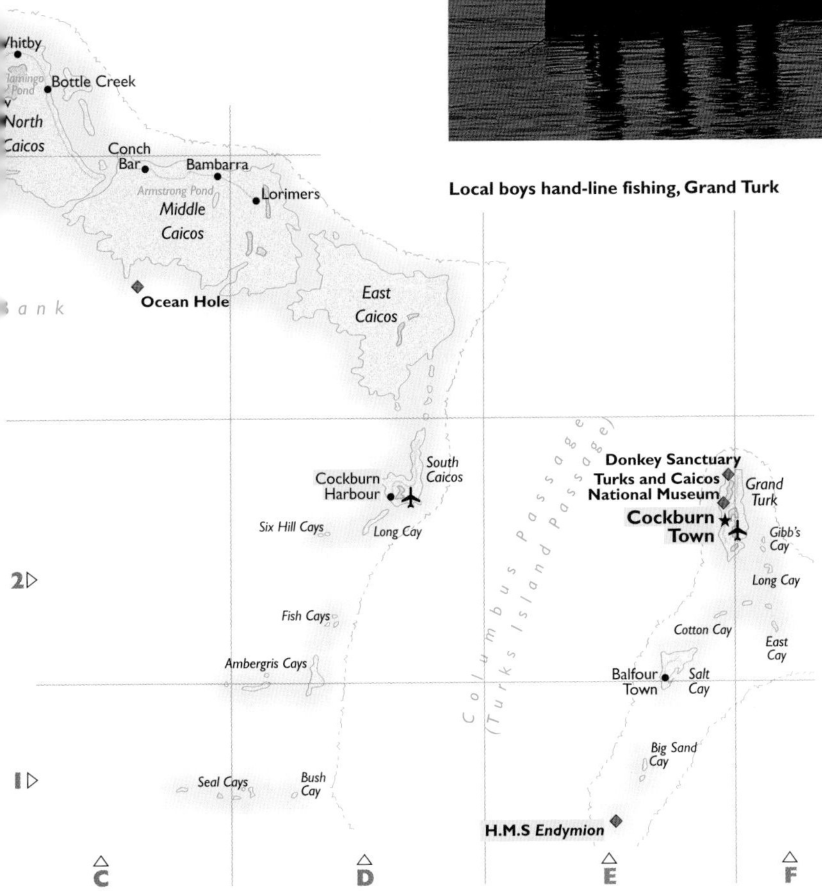

Interacting with stingrays at Gibb's Cay

Grand Turk

GRAND TURK COVERS ONLY 7 SQUARE MILES (18 SQ KM) but it is the second most populous island in the group and home to Cockburn Town, an attractive old colonial port and the seat of government. As with other islands in the Turks & Caicos, the vegetation is chiefly scrub and cactus, interspersed with flat expanses of unused salt pans and crumbling windmills. Wild donkeys and horses wander freely, descended from ancestors who once played a vital role in the salt industry (see page 84).

Grand Turk

81 E2

Visitor information

Front St., Cockburn Town

649/946-2321

What Grand Turk lacks in natural beauty on land is more than made up for by the glorious, exuberant world of its coral reefs. Just a stone's throw offshore on the west side of the island, a sheer wall drops away from about 40 to 7,000 feet (12–2,134 m) in one fell swoop, providing some of the most thrilling reef diving in the Caribbean. All diving off Grand Turk is within 10 to 15 minutes of the shoreline, so operators simply pick up clients from the beach outside their hotels and whisk them straight to the dive sites. All the operators use small boats, carrying around six people, and offer a personal service.

One of the best excursions is Sea Eye's half-day barbecue trip to **Gibb's Cay,** an uninhabited island

The government complex in Cockburn Town

where you can hand feed and snorkel with stingrays and free dive to the seabed for conch, which the crew will then use in a conch salad (see box page 84).

Don't come to Grand Turk if you're looking for shopping or sophisticated nightlife. Who needs them when you can watch Atlantic humpback whales migrating from an observation point up by the old lighthouse? The island is perfect for those who appreciate quirky, out-of-the-way places, friendly "belongers", and a relaxed pace. You can cycle the entire length of the island in a couple of hours.

Grand Turk's hub is **Cockburn Town,** with a pretty, historic heart around Duke Street and Front Street, which is ideal for a gentle stroll and a cool drink in one of the old inns. The government offices reside in a series of brightly painted buildings surrounding a small square where old cannon still face out to sea. Slightly to the north, you'll see the blue-trimmed **Odd Fellows Lodge,** one of the oldest buildings on the island. Folklore has it that the emancipation of the slaves was announced here in 1832.

Grand Turk's unexpected jewel is the superb **Turks & Caicos National Museum.** It is housed in the pre-1825 stone Guinep House on the island, which is thought to have been built by a former shipwright who named it after the magnificent guinep tree outside its door.

The museum's centerpiece is its extensive display on the Molasses Reef Wreck, the oldest European shipwreck so far discovered in the Caribbean. The early 16th-century Spanish caravel foundered on the rim of the Caicos Bank, and numerous items from the ship are on display. Remains of the hull and rigging, as well as cannon, crossbows, tools, and the crew's personal possessions, provide a fascinating time capsule of the

Turks & Caicos National Museum

www.tcmuseum.org

✉ Guinep House, Front St.

☎ 649/946-2160

🕘 Closed Sun.

$ $$

The Turks head cactus thrives in the sunbaked soils of Grand Turk island.

ISLAND DONKEYS

Grand Turk was once famous for its donkeys, which were found all over the island, roaming the scrub, foraging in gardens, standing quietly in the shade, or even holding up traffic on the roads. They were introduced by settlers in the 17th century to haul cartloads of salt to waiting ships. By the 1800s more than 800 of the long-eared beasts were on the island, but after the salt trade collapsed in 1964, the donkeys came to be viewed as a nuisance rather than an asset. Some were exported to islands that needed them, such as Jamaica. Many now live in a donkey sanctuary on the north shore. About 50 animals, however, still roam free, causing mischief, as they have always done. ■

daily life of early Hispanics. The upper floor of the museum is devoted to natural history, the salt trade, the Lucayan, and other aspects of the islands' history.

If you continue on down front street, passing the Governor's office, **Waterloo** *(Front St., tel 649/946-2309)*, built as a private residence in 1815, you'll reach **South Base,** a former U.S. Air Force missile tracking base that had its moment of fame in 1962 when the first U.S. astronaut to go into orbit around the Earth, John Glenn, was brought ashore here after his Mercury capsule splashed down just offshore. ■

Sports & activities

Diving & snorkeling: Sea Eye Diving *(Grand Turk, tel 649/946-1407, e-mail ci@tciway.tc,www.seaeyediving.com)* Oasis Divers *(Grand Turk, tel 649/946-1128, e-mail oasisdiv@tciway.tc, www.oasisdivers.com)* Blue Water Divers *(Salt Raker Inn, Grand Turk, tel 649/946-2432, e-mail info@grandturkscuba.com, www.grandturkscuba.com)*

Sportfishing: Deepsea fishing charters are widely available from local marinas. Bonefishing trips to South Caicos from Beyond the Blue *(tel 649/231-1703 or US 321/795-3136, e-mail bonefishbtb@aol.com, www.beyondtheblue.com)*. ■

Islands around Grand Turk

EAST CAICOS

Covering some 18 square miles (47 sq km), East Caicos is one of the largest islands in the archipelago. **Flamingo Hill,** on its north side, is the highest point (156 feet/ 48 m) in the Turks & Caicos, but most of the island consists of swamps, mangroves, and tidal mudflats.

At the beginning of the 20th century, the settlement of Jacksonville administered a 50,000-acre (20,000-ha) sisal plantation and cattle farm, but the island is now uninhabited. In fact, it is the largest uninhabited island in the Caribbean. Near Jacksonville are several caves with evidence of Lucayan occupation, including petroglyphs carved on the walls.

81 D3 Information 649/946-2321

SALT CAY

The only other inhabited island in the Turks group, Salt Cay lies 7 miles (11 km) to the south of Grand Turk. Bermudians first landed here in 1645, and salt production began in 1673, lasting for almost 300 years until the collapse of the industry in the 1960s. The old windmills and other tools of the trade were literally abandoned where they dropped.

Recently declared a UNESCO World Heritage site, Salt Cay has a landscape dominated by reminders of its age-old industry. Miles of intricate low stone walls and canals (used to speed up evaporation) are still visible, as are numerous derelict windmills. Bermudian architecture predominates, most noticeably in the form of the White House in **Balfour Town,** which was built in the 1830s from stone ballast carried in ships' holds and then unloaded to be replaced with salt.

In the 19th century, Salt Cay was also a major center for whaling. Nowadays the whales are more valuable alive than dead. Visitors may be lucky enough to spot migrating humpbacks from January through March.

Like Grand Turk, Salt Cay was deforested long ago, but the lack of terrestrial flora is more than compensated for by a flourishing underwater environment. The island has many buoyed dive sites and offers virgin diving on its reef walls with their tunnels, undercuts, and caverns. A diving highlight is the wreck of the H.M.S. *Endymion,* a British warship dating from 1790; it was armed with 18 enormous cannon to protect British maritime trade and lies in about 25 feet of water.

Whatever your reason for being here, Salt Cay's residents (there are just 60 of them) will welcome you with open arms and—as the sign at the airport states—urge you to "return by any means."

81 E2 Information 649/946-2321

SOUTH CAICOS

Tourists very seldom visit South Caicos, once a major commercial center for the islands, but this was not always the case. In fact, the island had the first hotel in the Turks & Caicos Islands, the Admiral's Arms Inn; it opened in the 19th century to serve the Brazilian pilots who stopped here en route between Miami and South America.

During the 19th century, South Caicos was a major player in the salt trade when the salinas of Grand Turk and Salt Cay could not meet the demand for salt from the North American market. The salinas here were fed by a unique boiling hole, a subterranean passage that allowed salt water to naturally flow into the pans, where windmills pumped it into a series of reservoirs. The hot, dry climate, in combination with the boiling hole, enabled the island to export more salt than any of the other islands and even to set up three steam-driven salt mills.

Today South Caicos still claims the best anchorage in the archipelago at **Cockburn Harbour,** a busy fishing port and the center of the export trade in queen conch, spiny lobster, and bonefish. The tourism potential of the island is as yet unrealized, even though it has some superb beaches (particularly Long Beach), excellent diving on the breathtaking coral walls which drop off from its eastern shoreline, and beautiful, uninhabited cays nearby (Long Cay, Ambergris Cays, Fish Cays, and Bush Cay) that can be visited on day trips. Accessible only by boat, none of the cays have any accommodations.

81 D2 Information 649/946-2321 ■

Middle Caicos

Middle Caicos
81 C3
Visitor information
Front St., Cockburn Town, Grand Turk
649/946-2321

WITH AN AREA OF 48 SQUARE MILES (124 SQ KM), THIS IS THE largest island in the Turks & Caicos archipelago. Its 275 inhabitants live mainly in the three settlements of Conch Bar, Lorimers, and Bambarra and depend on fishing and small-scale tourism.

Middle or Grand Caicos was occupied by the Taino between A.D. 750 and 1500, who called it Aniyana.

Armstrong Pond, south of Bambarra, is an important Taino settlement (one of 38 on the island). It features the only ceremonial ball court in the region and an arrangement of stones that may have had astrological significance. In **Conch Bar** you can explore a series of imposing limestone caves decorated with stalagmites and stalactites and home to bats and saltwater lagoons (guided tours included in day trip itineraries from Grand Turk and Providenciales).

The island's northwest coast is characterized by dramatic limestone cliffs (unique in the archipelago) interspersed with beautiful, deserted beaches. A trail along the coastline, known as the **Crossing Place Trail,** was the main highway on the island for centuries. It runs for 12 glorious miles through some of the most memorable scenery in the TCI, ending up at the ferry crossing to North Caicos. At low tide there is a sand bar here and you can walk

across to the neighboring island. The National Trust is developing the site for hiking and mountain biking.

Another unusual feature is the **Ocean Hole,** on the south side of the island, which is 1,200 feet (366 m) wide and about 200 feet (60 m) deep. It is thought to have been a land cave before being flooded many thousands of years ago and losing its roof. This marine sinkhole is home to bonefish, sharks, and other pelagic fish, and it can only be reached by boat. ■

Bottlenose dolphins are sometimes seen in Middle Caicos waters.

Island wildlife

Middle Caicos is one of the main nesting sites in the islands for the impressive ocean-going frigatebird, which also nests on Penniston Cay and other uninhabited islands. The pristine cays are important nesting areas for the sooty and roseate tern, Audubon's shearwater, and brown noddy. Four species of turtles (hawksbill, green, loggerhead, and leatherback) live in the surrounding waters, although local consumption of these endangered species is still common. The islands have a flourishing population of bottlenose dolphins, including the semitame JoJo, which frequents Grace Bay on Providenciales. In winter, humpback whales pass by on their way from cold northern seas to their breeding grounds southeast of Grand Turk. Divers often hear their haunting songs under water. ■

North Caicos

North Caicos
81 C4
Visitor information
Front St., Cockburn Town, Grand Turk
649/946-2321

North Caicos is a get-away-from-it-all retreat with superb beaches.

IN CONTRAST TO THE ARIDITY OF MOST ISLANDS IN THE group, North Caicos is comparatively lush and is considered the garden center of the country. It does have a higher rainfall (for reasons not fully understood) and its fertile soil produces abundant crops of tomatoes, corn, papaya, yam, pumpkin, lime, and avocado on farms tucked away in the interior.

Like its sister islands Middle and East Caicos (see p. 85), its southern reaches consist mostly of mangrove lagoons and swamps. On the north coast, powdery sand beaches slope into a shimmering lagoon that leads out to a line of breakers crashing onto the offshore reef.

Most of the 1,400-strong population live in a handful of modest settlements. **Bottle Creek** is the commercial center, while hotels and guesthouses are found on the north coast at Whitby.

North Caicos is just a 10-minute flight from Providenciales;

EXPLORING THE ISLAND
It can be difficult to drag yourself away from the beach, but North Caicos is well worth exploring. Several beach hotels at Whitby rent bicycles, kayaks and snorkel gear. Or check out the day trip options from Grand Turk and Provo with the tourist office. ■

boats take 30 minutes.

Place-names echo the North Caicos idiosyncratic history: Hungry Hole (a hidden lagoon); Ready Money (a plot of land that changed hands swiftly because the buyer had just that); Pumpkin Bluff Pond; and Laughland. **Wade's Green** commemorates a Loyalist refugee from Florida, who was granted 860 acres (340 ha) for a cotton plantation near Belleville. By the time of his death in 1821 Wade Stubbs had nearly 400 slaves working on his plantation, now one of the best preserved ruins in the Caicos Islands from the Loyalist period *(Tel 649/941-5710, tours daily by arrangement, $$).*

Birdwatching is a major attraction. North Caicos has the second largest population of flamingos in the Caribbean, but depending on where they are in the extensive **Flamingo Pond Nature Reserve,** you may only see them as pink dots in the distance, so take binoculars. Flamingos can also be spotted at Three Mary's Cays Sanctuary, where ospreys nest. Indigenous rock iguanas inhabit East Bay Cays.

Protected under the international RAMSAR convention, the **Caicos Nature Reserve** (see below) supports substantial numbers of West Indian flamingos and other waterbirds, including West Indian whistling ducks and breeding colonies of magnificent frigatebirds. ■

Caicos Nature Reserve

Stretching over 210 square miles (544 sq km), the North, Grand, and East Caicos Nature Reserve is one of the Caribbean's largest protected areas. A wilderness of tidal sloughs, mangroves, mudflats, and saline ponds, this important wetland zone links the dry uplands of the islands with the turquoise coastal shallows. Submerged banks, creeks, and lagoons provide critical nursery habitat for flamingos, lobsters (sculptured slipper lobster, *above*), conchs, turtles, and other marine species. ■

Diver goes face-to-face with a huge Nassau Grouper.

Providenciales (Provo)

ON A CLOUDY DAY YOU CAN SOMETIMES SEE A GREEN sheen on the underside of the cloud banks over Providenciales. This unique phenomenon is caused by reflections from shallow inland lagoons such as Chalk Sound.

Providenciales
80 B3
Visitor information
Stubbs Diamond Plaza, Le Deck Rd., The Bight
649/946-4970

About 25 miles (40 km) long and 3 miles (5 km) wide, Providenciales is the most developed of the islands in terms of tourism and commerce, and the main airport gateway to the TCI. Commonly called Provo, the island has wide sandy beaches and dramatic offshore diving sites, and makes an excellent jumping-off point for exploring further afield.

Along the north shore **Grace Bay**'s superb sweep of fine, powdery white sand ranks among the top beaches in the Caribbean and has attracted most of Provo's hotel and condominium development. Bordering the bay is the **Princess Alexandra Marine Park,** a vast area of offshore patch reefs, walls, and lagoons. There is excellent diving here and along the coast at **Northwest Point.**

Behind the south coast, the **Chalk Sound National Park** encompasses a huge expanse of shallow turquoise water dotted with green rocky cays popular with a variety of bird species. In the eastern corner, **Sapodilla Bay** has a lovely secluded beach and on the cliffs

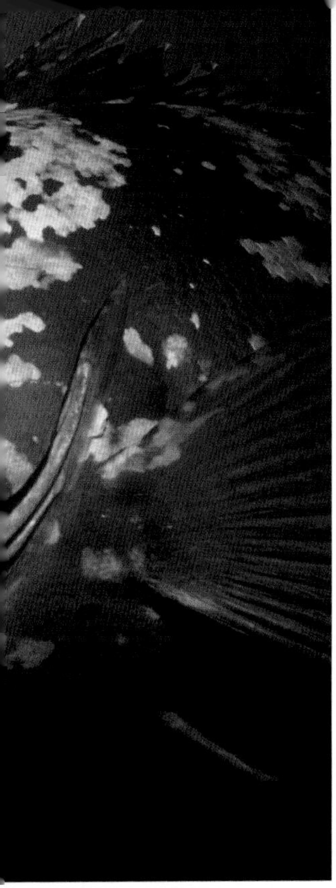

behind the bay shipwrecked sailors once carved their names in the rock.

Heading back towards the north coast, the ruins of **Cheshire Hall** can be seen just off the Leeward Highway. This was one of the three large cotton and sisal plantations started by Loyalists fleeing the American Revolution.

Of Provo's three original settlements—Five Cays, Blue Hills, and The Bight (meaning "the Bay")—the most scenic is **Blue Hills,** a small fishing port on the north coast. Government offices and other businesses are located in downtown, near the airport, but in general the island lacks a focal point. Shopping malls and other facilities have sprung up haphazardly along

Sports & activities

Diving & snorkeling: Art Pickering's Provo Turtle Divers *(Turtle Cove, Providenciales, tel 649/946-4232, fax 649/941-5296, e-mail info@provoturtledivers.com, www.provoturtledivers.com);* Flamingo Divers *(Turtle Cove, Providenciales, tel/fax 649/946-4193 or 800/204-9282, e-mail greatdiving@flamingodivers.com, www.flamingodivers.com);* Caicos Adventures *(Grace Bay, Providenciales, tel/fax 649/941-3346, e-mail divucrzy@tciway.tc, www.caicosadventures.com.*

Golf: Provo Golf Club *(Tel 649/946-5991, fax 649/946-5992, e-mail: provogolf@tciway.tc, www.provogolf.com).* ■

OUT ON THE WATER

A visit to some of the surrounding uninhabited cays (particularly Little Water Cay—see p. 94) is a must during a stay on Provo. The biggest water sports operator is J&B Tours *(Tel 649/946-5047, www.jbtours.com).* A fleet of 11 fast powerboats takes visitors on half- or full-day excursions to the cays, on beach cruises, on snorkel trips, and on beach barbecues. Another recommended operator is Silver Deep *(Tel 649/946-5612, www.silverdeep.com).* ■

Dive boats moor up between dives at Northwest Point.

The queen conch (above and below right) has distinctive eyes.

Island conchs

The beautiful, pink-lipped shellfish known as the queen conch *(Strombus gigas)* has been a staple of the Caribbean diet since long before Columbus arrived in the New World. Today more than 40 million conchs are harvested annually in the shallow waters surrounding the Bahamas, Bermuda, Florida, and the Turks & Caicos. The waters of the Caicos Bank have supplied some four million of these but, as elsewhere in the region, the harvest is declining due to overfishing. Conchs are now listed as an endangered species. The Caicos Conch Farm, which employs more than 20 workers, is the only facility of its kind in the world. Its current target is to export a million conchs a year from their inventory of five million conchs at various stages of development. The farm has recently developed new markets in Florida and elsewhere with the introduction of live-in-the-shell conchs, which are sweeter and more tender than frozen conch. ■

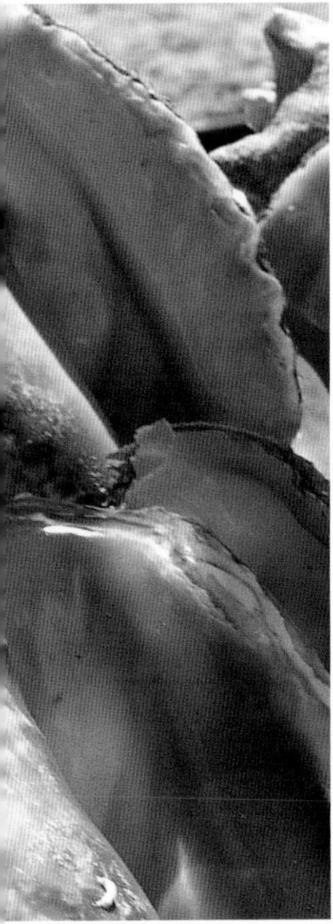

the main road, the Leeward Highway. The closest the island has to a central focus is **Turtle Cove,** where you'll find hotels, a few restaurants, and a tourist office clustered around the yacht basin.

At the eastern end of the island, the 6,560-yard (6,000-m), par 72 championship golf course designed by Karl Litton is one of the best in the Caribbean (see box page 91).

Continue on until the road runs out and you will reach the deep channel that separates Provo from adjacent Mangrove Cay. This natural harbor, known as **Leeward Going Through,** is currently being developed as a marina.

Alongside the marina is the **Caicos Conch Farm.** The only one of its kind in the world, the farm was set up in 1984 to develop techniques for conch farming on a commercial scale. The educational tour of the farm embraces the various stages the conchs move through, from the hatchery to the subsea pasture (where they grow to maturity). The conch farm exports live conchs to Florida and also sells them to local restaurants. ■

A Provo fisherman skillfully removes the flesh from a conch shell.

Caicos Conch Farm

- ✉ At the Marina, Leeward Going Through
- ☎ 649/946-5643
- 🕒 Closed Sun.
- $ $$

The rock iguana has become one of Little Water Cay's main attractions.

Islands around Providenciales

LITTLE WATER CAY

This uninhabited cay close to Provo, now a protected area under the Turks & Caicos National Trust *(Tel 649/941-5710)*, is popular with day-trippers who come to see its iguanas. Sail Provo runs boat excursions to Little Water Cay *(Tel 649/946-4783, e-mail sail provo@tciway.tc, www.sailprovo.com)*.

81 B3

PARROT CAY

Originally known as Pirate Cay, this 1,300-acre (526-ha) luxury resort island was once run as a plantation. Between 1718 and 1720 it was home to the notorious pirate Anne Bonny and her lover, Calico Jack Rackham. Today, you are more likely to encounter "A" list celebrities enjoying a little down time. *(Parrot Cay Resort, tel 649/946-7788.)*

81 B4

Island iguanas

The rock iguana species *(Cyclura carinata)* seen on Little Water Cay is unique to these islands. This long-lived, territorial reptile mates but once a year, producing 7 to 12 eggs per clutch. Rock iguanas have disappeared from many inhabited islands due to predation by humans, cats, and dogs. About 50,000 rock iguanas remain in the Turks & Caicos, the largest population in the world, with about 1,000 on Little Water Cay and the rest on Ambergris Cay, at Fort George, and in other island reserves. ■

WEST CAICOS

Isolated and uninhabited, West Caicos is renowned for its excellent diving *(Visited by day boats from Providenciales, see p. 91)*. During the mid 18th century the island was used as a base by the French corsair, Jean Thomas Dulaien. Later, when known as Yankee Town, it was cleared for salinas (salt ponds) and sisal plantations in the 1890s. Today, ruins of the sisal plant, railroad tracks, and steam engines can still be seen. At the island's center is Lake Catherine a nature reserve that is home to ospreys, herons and pink flamingoes.

West Caicos has 6 miles (10 km) of reefs along its leeward shoreline, with a reef wall which starts in around 35-45 feet (11-14 m) dropping away to depths of 6,000 feet (18,000 m). The dive sites here are renowned for their enormous, colorful sponges, beautiful coral formations, black corals, and gorgonia. Fish life includes jacks, Nassau grouper, moray eels, and French angelfish, while out in the blue there is always the chance of spotting pelagics such as sharks, eagle and manta rays, turtles, and possibly even hammerhead or whalesharks.

81 A3 ■

Site of the first Spanish colony in the Americas, the Dominican Republic encompasses virtually everything from colonial architecture to a lush, mountainous interior and some of the best beaches in the Caribbean.

Dominican Republic

Island color as captured by a local painter

Dominican Republic

OCCUPYING THE EASTERN TWO-THIRDS OF THE ISLAND OF HISPANIOLA (the remaining third is Haiti), the Dominican Republic was home to the first European colony in the New World. It has the Caribbean's highest peak, largest lake, and biggest city. But above all it is known for its extensive white sand beaches, around 1,000 miles (1,500 km) of them, which together with world-class sporting opportunities and value for money provide the cornerstones of a substantial tourist industry. Beyond the beach resorts, however, tourism has had minimal impact. If you're adventurous you will discover an enormously diverse country. If you travel beyond the tourist spots, you'll need to know some Spanish.

This fertile island was heavily populated by Taino Indians when Columbus first arrived on these shores in 1492. He named it Isla Española (or Hispaniola) and decided it would be an ideal place for a colony, especially since gold deposits were also discovered.

The first settlement was built on the north coast at La Isabela, but it was a bad choice—difficult to defend, hot, and disease-ridden. The present-day capital, Santo Domingo, was established on a much more promising site at the mouth of the Ozama River in 1496. During the early years of Spanish rule, the economy was fueled by gold, but by 1515 the gold had run out and the Spanish began to ignore Hispaniola in favor of the more lucrative mines of South America and the prospect of wealth in Mexico.

By the 17th century the northwestern part of the island was occupied by pirates and French buccaneers, who managed to resist attempts by the Spanish to drive them out. France took advantage of this to claim the western third of the island, which was then ceded to them under the Treaty of Ryswick in 1697. Over the next century Saint Domingue, as the French portion was known, became one of the richest colonies in the Caribbean thanks to sugarcane plantations. The eastern part of the island languished under the Spanish, whose attentions had moved elsewhere.

In the 1790s Toussaint L'Ouverture (1743–1803) led a slave uprising in Saint Domingue. The Spaniards supported Toussaint, forcing the French to abolish slavery. In 1794 Toussaint suddenly switched sides and joined forces to oust the Spanish from the island. Toussaint gained control in 1795 and held on until 1802, when Napoleon Bonaparte sent an expeditionary force to arrest him. Meanwhile, rebels had driven the French forces out of the western part of the island, and the Republic of Haiti was declared on January 1, 1804. The Spanish recaptured the eastern part of the

island in 1809, but they were driven out by settlers intent on independence, which was won in 1821. But independence was not to last. The Haitians invaded in 1822 and controlled the whole island for the next 22 years. The occupation fostered an underground opposition movement, La Trinitaria, which seized control in 1844 and declared the independence of the new country, known as the Dominican Republic.

Since independence, politics in the Dominican Republic have swung between democracy and dictatorship. The dark years under Gen. Rafael Leonidas Trujillo (1891–1961), from 1930 until 1961, are still remembered with horror by many.

The country's economy today is based on tourism, agriculture, and mineral exports. Concentrated on the north coast beaches, tourism is the big breadwinner, far outweighing the contribution of the agricultural sector. However, farmers have been encouraged to diversify and traditional crops, such as sugar cane, coffee, cocoa and tobacco, have been augmented by fruits and vegetables, live plants and cut flowers. One major growth area is the tobacco industry, which now rivals that of Cuba, while gold and silver mining is of considerable importance, and the deposits of ferro-nickels are estimated at 10 percent of world reserves. ■

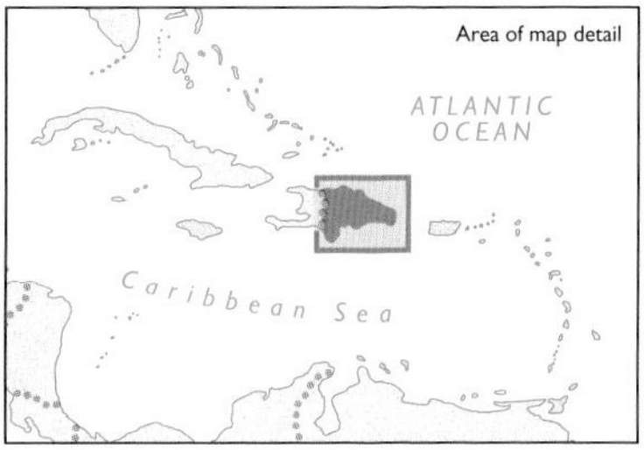

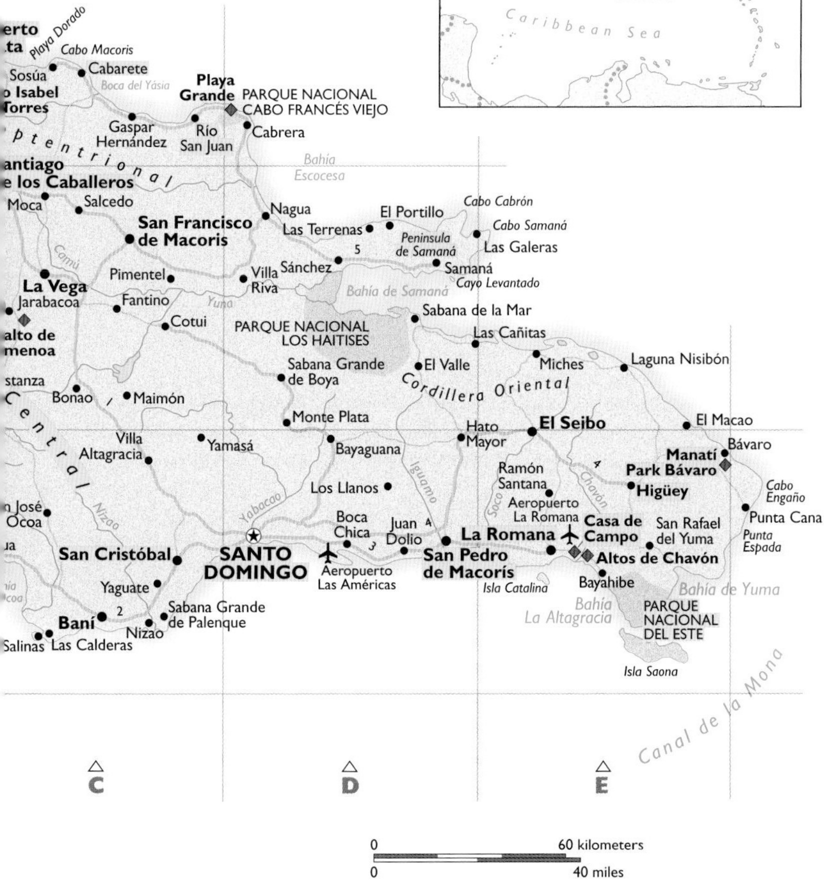

Santo Domingo's Catedral Basilica Santa María la Menor

Santo Domingo

THE CAPITAL AND CHIEF PORT OF THE DOMINICAN Republic, Santo Domingo is the oldest city in the New World and can lay claim to the first university, cathedral, and hospital in the Americas. The city was founded by Christopher Columbus's brother Bartoloméo in 1498, after the Spanish abandoned their attempts to found a colony on the north coast. Santo Domingo has become the hub of life in the Dominican Republic and a magnet for commerce from neighboring islands.

Santo Domingo
97 D2
Visitor information
Calle Isabel La Catolica 103, Zona Colonial
809/686-3858

Built on the east bank of the Río Ozama, the city was christened Nueva Isabel. The name changed to Santo Domingo when the city was moved to the west bank after a hurricane in 1502. It flourished as a port, and from here the Spanish launched major expeditions to Mexico, Puerto Rico, Cuba, and the Pacific. As the riches of the Spanish Main were revealed, Santo Domingo lost its preeminent position in the Caribbean. It suffered a further blow in 1562, when an earthquake destroyed much of the city. English privateer Sir Francis Drake (circa 1540–1596) also caused considerable damage when he attacked the city in 1586.

Despite its decline, Santo Domingo continued to play a major role as the political and commercial center of the country. During the regime of Rafael Trujillo, Santo Domingo was known for 25 years as Ciudad Trujillo, but with the death of the dictator it reverted.

Today Santo Domingo is the industrial, financial, and commercial heart of the Dominican Republic and home to some 3 million people. The restored colonial city is a World Heritage site. The colonial zone is the most attractive part of the city, with pleasant squares, outdoor cafés, and a wealth of historic buildings.

Opposite: Interesting perspectives inside the Faro a Colón

The tomb inside the Faro a Colón is said to hold the remains of Columbus.

EASTERN QUARTERS

Santo Domingo's eastern quarters are the home of one of the city's most extravagant showcases, the **Faro a Colón** *(Tel 809/591-1492)*, which was built as part of the 500th anniversary of Columbus's landfall in 1492. A dramatic series of caves near the monument offer a natural counterpoint to the controversial monument.

Without doubt, the monumental Faro a Colón is a talking point both within the Dominican Republic and beyond. Despite the fact that from the exterior it resembles a shoddy, concrete apartment complex (appropriately enough, since many slum houses were bulldozed to clear the site), the interior is well worth a visit. The idea of a monument to Columbus was first proposed in the 1920s, and a design competition was won by a British architectural student, J. Cleave. The structure, in the shape of a recumbent cross, was eventually built in 1992.

The building covers an area of 107,500 square feet (10,000 sq m), its outer walls featuring plaques bearing the names of every Latin American state. At the center of the cross is the marble **tomb of Columbus,** guarded by uniformed sentries. A sarcophagus said to hold his remains was moved here from the city's cathedral on the opening day—October 6, 1992. The corridors on either side of the tail of the cross contain some rather uninspiring cultural displays contributed by 50 countries around the world. One highlight, however, is an original **Mayan almanac** (one of only four known) dating back to the 14th century. Another precious artifact is

The enigma of Columbus's ashes

The Faro a Colón claims to hold the remains of Christopher Columbus, but is this true? When the explorer died in 1506, he was buried in Valladolid, Spain. Three years later his body was moved to Seville and in the 1540s sent back to Santo Domingo. His remains were then shipped to Cuba when France gained control of Santo Domingo in 1795, and from there back to Seville in 1898. However, in 1877 renovations in the cathedral revealed a casket beneath the altar bearing the inscription "Almirante Cristobal Colón," and it is these ashes that now lie in state in the Faro a Colón. Whether the ashes are those of Columbus can probably never be proved. ■

the original anchor of the *Santa María*, Columbus's flagship, salvaged from the north coast of Haiti, where the ship sank in 1492. The opening of the monument was marred by several explosions in the city, protesting the extravagance in a country with much poverty. Critics also point to the huge cost in electricity for the lasers that occasionally beam a cross shape into the clouds when most of the urban population is still suffering continual power cuts.

A few minutes' drive down the Avenida de las Américas from the Faro a Colón are a series of caves known as **Los Tres Ojos** (The Three Eyes). This spectacular series of collapsed caves contains dramatic formations and underground lakes, the last of which is reached via a rope-winched raft. Luxuriant tropical vegetation adds

Los Tres Ojos is an unusual sight to find in a city.

Los Tres Ojos

Parque Los Tres Ojos, Ave. de las Américas

$

Plaza de Cultura
✉ Ave. Cesar Nicolas Penson

Museo del Hombre Dominicano
✉ Plaza de la Cultura
☎ 809/687-3622
🕒 Closed Mon.
$ $

A colorful version of the Washington Monument soars above the Malecón.

a lost world atmosphere to this unusual location—all the more striking because it's so close to a major city center.

THE MODERN CITY

The modern center of Santo Domingo extends north and west of the colonial zone, down to the seafront and Avenida George Washington, usually referred to simply as **El Malecón.** This seafront avenue is at its liveliest in the evenings, when Dominicans stroll or even dance to the sounds of merengue (see below) blasting out from portable stereos. The annual Merengue Festival takes place here.

In the heart of downtown is the **Plaza de la Cultura,** a large park that includes four major museums *(Tel 809/686-2145, all closed Mon.)*, the **Teatro Nacional** *(Tel 809/687-3191)*, and **Biblioteca Nacional** *(Tel 809/688-4086)*. The best of the museums is the excellent **Museo del Hombre Dominicano,** the largest archaeological and anthropological museum in the Caribbean. It contains a wealth of material relating to pre-Columbian civilizations. The museum occupies the third and fourth floors of a large building, and the best exhibits are found on the third floor. Here you'll see the fossil remains of an extinct bear, *Megatorio,* once hunted by the prehistoric Taino, as well as ceremonial axes dating from 2000 B.C. Comparative displays of South

Merengue

Throughout the Dominican Republic you'll hear the sound of merengue, the national music. Traditionally this fast music has been played by a three-man combo performing on either a *tres* or *cuatro* (both are similar to a guitar), a *tambora* (double drum), and a *guiro* (calabash). The country's exuberant annual Merengue Festival is held between late July and early August. Most of the action takes place on Santo Domingo's Malecón, transformed into a vast open-air disco for the occasion. ■

American indigenous cultures place Taino history in context. Hundreds of prehistoric pieces include necklaces and jewelry, shaped stones used to grate the staple food, yucca, dozens of examples of the three-headed god of agriculture *(Trigonolito)*, heart-shaped pots with phallic necks (fertility symbols), artistically decorated conch shells that were used as trumpets for communicating across a distance, and elaborately carved stone rings whose purpose is unknown. A burial display shows skeletons in a fetal position (the Taino believed in reincarnation, and therefore buried corpses in the fetal position so that they were ready for rebirth); one's jaws are open in a grimace of suffocation (Taino chiefs were polygamous, and when they died their wives were buried with them—alive). The fourth floor, which documents the influences that have shaped today's culture in the Dominican Republic, will take less of your time.

Next door is the **Museo Nacional de Historia y Geografía,** which contains a mountain of memorabilia from the Trujillo era (including the briefcase, wallet, comb, photos, and other items that belonged to the former dictator), and model ships relating to the Haiti-Dominican conflicts in the 19th century. However, the presentation of the displays is old-fashioned and rather dull. The **Museo de Historia Natural** contains a few mounted birds and is equally missable.

On the other hand, the **Galería de Arte Moderno** is well worth a visit, displaying a broad range of contemporary works by both Dominican and foreign artists in the permanent collection.

Go east from the Plaza de Cultura to see the **Palacio Nacional,** an imposing neoclassic building constructed in 1947. It once housed the congress, but it is now the home of the president.

A welcome retreat from the heat and bustle of Santo Domingo can be found on the city's northwest outskirts at the **Jardín Botánico.** Established in 1976, the gardens cover 0.75 square miles (2 sq km). You could easily pass half a day here. A "road train" takes visitors around the broad perimeter track, but a leisurely walk will give you more chance to appreciate the tropical plants and trees. There are separate areas for orchids, water plants, bromeliads, palms, cactuses and other succulents, medicinal plants, and a wide variety of endemic Caribbean species. The Japanese garden, with its bamboo groves and ornamental ponds, is a particular highlight. Although

The neoclassic Palacio Nacional, built from rose-colored marble

Galería de Arte Moderno
- ☎ 809/685-2154
- Closed Mon.
- $ $

Palacio Nacional
- ✉ Calle Dr. Delgado
- ☎ 809/686-4771
- By appt. only

Jardín Botánico
www.jbn-sdq.org
- ✉ Ave. República de Colombia
- ☎ 809/385-0860
- Closed Mon.
- $ $

The 18th-century gateway to the Fortaleza Ozama recalls Spanish colonial might.

labeling is haphazard, these lovely gardens are a delight.

East from the botanic gardens is the **Parque Zoológico** *(Nacional Avenida, Los Arroyos, tel 809/562-3149, closed Mon.).* Located in an unused limestone quarry across the road from an extensive slum area, the zoo covers 24 acres (9.5 ha). Most animals are in open enclosures, but many (including cheetahs, hyenas, and others used to roaming the African plains) are imprisoned in small cages. On a more humane note, the zoo is attempting to nurture a dwindling population of the rare solenodon, a small, insectivorous indigenous mammal that looks a bit like a rat. There are only 500 left in the country, but so far two-thirds of the captive population has died.

Fortaleza Ozama
✉ Calle Las Damas
$ $

Alcázar de Colón
✉ Plaza Espana
$ $

COLONIAL ZONE

The historic colonial zone lies on the western banks of the Río Ozama, overlooking the cruise ship terminal and Puerto Ozama. You should certainly allow at least a day to visit its sights; come equipped with a map and comfortable shoes (see also pp. 106–107).

Among the key historic buildings in this area is the **Fortaleza Ozama.** Built by Governor Nicolas de Ovando in 1503 on a steep bank overlooking the mouth of the Río Ozama, the fortress was Santo Domingo's principal defense from the 16th century on and was occupied by the military until the 1970s. The last fort to be built by the Spanish as they moved from north to south across the island, it guarded the harbor throughout the colonial period. You enter via a neoclassic gateway added in 1787.

Directly ahead is the impressive **Torre del Homenaje** (Tower of Homage), a solid structure with 7-foot-thick (2 m) walls whose clean lines and battlements give it the semblance of a medieval castle: Its design is unique in the New World. You can climb to the top of the turret to gain some idea of the strategic importance of the fort, which guarded every major Spanish flotilla as it left the harbor for the conquest of the Americas—although the historical illusion is hard to conjure up in the face of the giant cement factory looming on the opposite side of the river.

To one side of the tower is an 18th-century armory, beyond which can be seen the remnants of a temporary fort built before the tower was erected. The statue on the grounds is of Gonzalo Fernandez de Oviedo, the fort's governor from 1533 to 1557.

Another major building in the colonial zone is the **Alcázar de Colón.** Built between 1511 and 1516 by Diego de Colón (Columbus's son, who became the first viceroy of the New World), this impressive building has a beautiful Renaissance facade with graceful arcades and is a copy (on a slightly smaller scale) of a castle in Toledo, Spain. Most of the superb furnishings and artworks are genuine

16th-century. They were a gift from the Spanish government when the palace was restored in the 1950s and are not the originals that were once here. Note the wooden ceilings, particularly the one in the entrance hall decorated with 42 sculptured animal heads—a Spanish custom to ward off evil spirits.

For an overview of the history of the Dominican Republic, you can look into the **Museo de las Casas Reales.** The collection covers the country's history from displays on the Taino through Columbus's arrival, colonization, the plantations, and slavery. There's a highly credible reconstruction of an 18th-century pharmacy (the brightly colored ceramics are, however, reproductions), but the highlight is an extraordinary collection of ancient armaments, including a bronze Roman legionnaire's helmet dating from A.D. 1, elaborately decorated Turkish and Moroccan muskets, a Ceylonese executioner's scimitar, Japanese samurai swords, and English crossbows. Between the court rooms you'll see a carved elephant's tusk dating from 1552.

Take time to go to the **Panteón Nacional** at the northern end of the Calle Las Damas. Originally built in the mid-18th century as a Jesuit convent, the pantheon was used as a tobacco warehouse and, later, as a theater after the Jesuits left the island. In the 1950s Trujillo converted it into a memorial to the heroes of Dominican history; the huge candelabra was a gift from the Spanish dictator Gen. Francisco Franco. Every two hours you can see the changing of the guard. ■

Traders size up the day's selection at the central market of Santo Domingo.

Museo de las Casas Reales

- Calle las Damas
- 809/682-4202
- Closed Mon.
- $

Panteón Nacional

- Calle las Damas
- Closed Mon. a.m.

The impressive double archway of the northern portal of the Catedral Basilica Santa María la Menor

Colonial zone walk

The walk starts and ends in the Plaza Colón (Columbus Square), a busy meeting place surrounded by old stone buildings and arched walkways, with a statue of the explorer at its center. On the way you have a chance to savor the pride of Santo Domingo's colonial legacy, an ensemble of handsome buildings and monuments that mirror the country's sometimes turbulent history.

On the south side of the square is the **Catedral Basilica Santa María la Menor** ❶ *(no shorts or short skirts allowed).* Built between 1514 and 1540, it was the first cathedral in the New World—as well as the oldest church of any description in the Caribbean—and the remains of Columbus were supposedly uncovered here during restoration work in 1877 (see p. 100). The tranquil interior features a 17th-century mahogany throne as well as stained-glass windows. The cathedral was fully restored in 1992.

Palacio de Borgella ❷ flanks the east side of the square. Built during the Haitian occupation in the mid-19th century, the building has a graceful, porticoed facade on two levels. It served as the seat of congress until 1947 and now houses administrative offices and a post office.

From here make your way to El Conde, a lively pedestrian street lined with shops and cafés that bisects the heart of the colonial zone. El Conde leads down toward the seafront and the Calle las Damas, a pleasant, tree-lined street where the ladies of the court would take their evening stroll in colonial days. Most of the oldest and loveliest buildings in the colonial zone are located on this street.

See area map page 97
Plaza Colón
3 miles (5 km)
Allow 2–3 hours
Plaza Colón

NOT TO BE MISSED
- Palacio de Borgella
- Casas Reales
- Monasterio de San Francisco

Turn right onto the Calle las Damas to visit the **Fortaleza Ozama** (see p. 104), then double back toward the north: On your right is the **Hostal Palacio Nicolás de Ovando 3,** built in 1502 as the residence of the governor after whom it is named. This beautiful building has been restored as the five-star Sofitel Nicolás de Ovando *(53 Calle las Damas)*. Opposite is the **Pantéon Nacional** (see p. 105).

Continue on to the end of Calle las Damas, where you'll find the imposing palace of the **Casas Reales 4** *(Corner of Calle las Mercedes and Calle las Damas)*, which once housed the governor's office, the royal court of justice (Real Audiencia), treasury, and military administration. Built in the early 16th century, it now houses the excellent **Museo de las Casas Reales** (see p. 105). Opposite is a sundial, dating from 1753, on a site with fine views over the port.

Beyond here the street opens out into a large plaza. On the east side is the imposing **Alcázar de Colón** (see pp. 104–105). Opposite the Alcázar is **La Atarazana 5,** a series of eight buildings that housed the royal armory, customs house, and warehouses; today they are shops, restaurants, and bars.

From La Atarazana turn left onto Calle Isabel la Católica to see the **Casa del Cordón** **6** *(Corner of Calle Emiliano Tejera)*. Built in 1509, it was one of the first stone buildings on the island; it is named after the cord the Franciscan order wore around their robes and which is carved in stone above the doorway. Today it is a branch of the Banco Popular.

Follow Calle Tejera across Calle Arzobispo Merino and then onto Calle Hostos: Here you will find the ruins of the **Monasterio de San Francisco 7,** the first monastery in the New World. Built in the early 16th century, it was sacked by Sir Francis Drake and then further damaged by earthquakes in 1673 and 1751. Take Arzobispo Merino back to the Plaza Colón. ■

Alcázar de Colón overlooks Plaza de María Toledo.

Bananas are divided into "hands" at the base of the tree at harvesttime.

West of Santo Domingo

THE SOUTHWESTERN CORNER OF THE REPUBLIC IS AN ARID region with some unusual coastal landscapes. This is an area scarcely touched by tourism, although the opening of a new international airport in Barahona and a new highway from the capital means that access is now getting easier.

San Cristóbal
97 C2

Casa Las Caobas & Castillo del Cerro
809/528-3553
$

Some 15 miles (24 km) to the west of Santo Domingo is the town of **San Cristóbal,** where the country's first constitution was signed (on November 6, 1844), but it is better known as the birthplace of the dictator Rafael Trujillo. His main residence, **Casa Las Caobas,** sits in ruins on a hilltop just outside the town; there are plans to restore it. Trujillo also built the **Castillo del Cerro,** once a grandiose, six-story house on another hilltop nearby. Today, this abandoned structure is little more than a wreck.

From San Cristóbal the main road (Rte. 2) leads to Baní, to the southwest of which is **Las Salinas** Just outside this fishing village on the Bahía Las Calderas are the largest sand dunes in the Caribbean. From Baní, Barahona is just over 60 miles (100 km) to the west.

Located on the Bahía de Neiba, **Barahona** has a population of more than 80,000. Its airport, the Aeropuerto María Montés

Barahona
96 B2
Visitor information
Carretera Batey Central, Edificio Defrimpo
809/524-3650

Parque Nacional Jaragua
96 A1

Isla Cabritos
96 A2

(named after a Dominican actress who starred in Hollywood movies in the 1940s and 1950s), is intended to promote tourist development in this relatively remote part of the country. One of the main attractions is the coastal scenery south of Barahona. Here the Sierra de Baoruco reach almost down to the Caribbean, and small fishing villages are interspersed with coves and inviting sandy beaches (although swimming is not always possible because these are surfing beaches). After the fishing village of Enriquillo, the route turns inland, toward the town of Pedernales on the border with Haiti.

NATURAL WONDERS

The **Parque Nacional Jaragua** covers 189 square miles (500 sq km) on the southwesterly tip of the island. The park is distinguished by its dry climate, limestone formations, lagoons, and saltwater lakes. You need to be well prepared to visit this area, with its rough terrain and lack of water and decent maps. The largest protected area in the Dominican Republic, Jaragua park is known for its pelicans, terns, and iguanas, and includes two uninhabited offshore islands, **Isla Beata** and **Alto Velo.**

Inland 36 miles (58 km) on Rte. 46 from Barahona, lies **Lago Enriquillo,** a massive saltwater lake that is said to the biggest in the Caribbean. Lying between 100 and 130 feet (30–40 m) below sea level, the lake is fed by streams from the Sierra de Neiba and the Sierra de Baoruco, but it has no outlet to the sea. Water loss is purely by evaporation, leading to a salt content in the lake three times higher than that of the Caribbean Sea. The lake is home to an abundance of wildlife, including crocodiles, iguanas, and flamingos.

Of the three islands in the lake, the biggest is the 5-mile-long (8-km) **Isla Cabritos** (Goat Island), the only one protected as a national park. Home to goats, the island also holds crocodiles and many resident and migratory birds, including flamingos, clapper rails, and roseate spoonbills. The two smaller islands are known as **La Islita** and **Barbarita.** You can drive all the way around the lake, and at the western end you can cross over the border to Haiti. Boat tours of Lago Enriquillo leave from the park entrance, some 2.5 miles (4 km) to the east of the sleepy desert outpost of La Descubierta. (Departures are at 7:30 a.m., 8:30 a.m., and 1:00 p.m.; the earlier ones are better for viewing the crocodiles.)

About 0.5 mile (800 m) to the east of **La Descubierta** at the western end of the lake is a series of pre-Columbian petroglyphs carved into the rock face. These are marked by signs from the Carretera Enriquillo. ■

Visiting Parque Nacional Jaragua Islands

These remote islands are hard to reach, but among the scrubland and rocky terrain of Isla Beata are a series of Taino caves adorned with ancient rock carvings. Alto Vera has recently become famous for a different reason: biologists have discovered the world's smallest reptile—the dwarf gecko measuring just 1.6 cm.

Information and permits for visiting the islands can be obtained from visitor information in Barahona, or from the park office east of Oviedo (no phone). ■

Boats moored up in the lagoon at Bayahibe

Southeast coast

THE SOUTHEAST COAST HAS SOME OF THE COUNTRY'S white sand beaches, lapped by the azure waters of the Caribbean and backed up by swaying palms. In recent years large, luxurious all-inclusive hotels have sprung up on many of the better beaches. Wealthy Dominicans have also built luxury villas here to escape the pollution and overcrowding of Santo Domingo.

Parque Nacional del Este
97 E2

Boca Chica
97 D2
Visitor information
Calle Duarte, esq. Caracol, 2da, Plaza Boca Chica
809/523-5106

The countryside is mostly flat plains in the center and south, carpeted by extensive sugarcane plantations, with a low range of mountains—the Cordillera Oriental—to the north. Much of the wealth of the major towns in this region, such as San Pedro de Macorís and La Romana, comes from the sugar industry.

The region also has its natural attractions, in the form of dazzling offshore islands and the Parque Nacional del Este (see p. 113), and man-made ones, in the form of a mock Italianate village, the Altos de Chavón.

Heading east from Santo Domingo along the Autopista de las Américas, you pass some fine stretches of coastline before arriving at the main international gateway to the island, Las Américas airport. A short distance past here is **Boca Chica,** a beach resort on a shallow bay not more than 5 feet (1.5 m) deep. It was one of the first

A fruit vendor plies his wares on Boca Chica beach.

areas to be developed for tourism on the island under the Trujillo regime. Now it's a busy resort that fills up rapidly with residents from the capital on weekends; it has a genuinely local atmosphere.

The beaches at **Juan Dolio,** 25 miles (40 km) east of Santo Domingo on Rte. 3, are a better choice, although they can also be noisy and crowded on weekends. The main beaches along here are **Embassy Beach** (a small cove popular with body surfers), **Playa Guayacanes** (calmer and more extensive), and **Playa de Juan Dolio** (also a reasonable beach). There is a small mall with restaurants and shops in the village of Juan Dolio, but you'll find little else to visit in the vicinity.

One of the biggest towns on the south coast, **San Pedro de Macorís,** lies at the mouth of the Río Higuama, 9 miles (14.5 km) east of Juan Dolio. This town was the center of the Dominican sugar industry at the turn of the 20th century, and remnants of its glory days can be seen in its houses, fire station, and the neoclassic church of **San Pedro Apostol** on the banks of the river. The town is unusual in that it shows a marked cultural influence from the Leeward and Windward Islands. In the 19th century, skilled craftsmen and builders were brought in from the smaller British islands to help build the Victorian-style wooden houses that can still be seen on Avenida Independencia. They brought with them their own dances (called *guyolas)* and music *(cainanés).* You can see both performed during the annual **Fiestas Patronales** (June).

San Pedro de Macorís
97 D2

LA ROMANA

The provincial capital, La Romana, is also a sugar town, and the noise of diesel engines pulling carloads of cane to the Central Romana Corporation factory, which forms much of the skyline, is a familiar

La Romana
97 E2

Visitor information

Calle Teniente Amado Garcia (Governacion Principal)

809/550-6922

The main plaza at Altos de Chavón, an Italianate village high in the hills

Casa de Campo, Altos de Chavón, & Museo Arqueológico
97 E2
www.casadecampo.com
809/523-3333

Dirección Nacional de Parques (National Parks Office)
Ave. Independencia 539, esquina Cervantes, Santo Domingo
809/472-4204

Higüey
97 E2
Visitor information
Calle de la Altagracia
809/554-2672

sound during the cutting season (Nov.–July). The factory's name comes from *la balanza romana*, the Roman scales once used to weigh the sugar exports. The privately-owned sugar company is one of the largest cane sugar producers in the world.

A drop in sugar prices in the 1970s led to the development of the deserted area of scrub, east of La Romana, into a tourist complex that has since grown into the gigantic **Casa de Campo** (Country House).The biggest resort in the region, it boasts its own international airport, with direct flights from the United States. Its 11 square miles (28 sq km) of grounds include four golf courses (the Pete Dye-designed Teeth of the Dog is ranked as one of the finest in the Caribbean), a 245-acre (100-ha) shooting center, stables with more than 100 riding horses and polo ponies, 19 swimming pools, a private beach and marina, 13 tennis courts, 10 restaurants, and much more (see p. 360). The resort is so big that people get around it on golf carts.

Under the same ownership and on the same site as Casa de Campo is the **Altos de Chavón.** Anyone may visit this mock Italianate village built in the 1970s and 1980s. It is a re-creation of a 16th-century medieval village and constructed entirely from coral rock and stone, with attractive cobbled alleyways festooned with hibiscus and bougainvillea and a huge amphitheater, which seats 5,000 people. It was inaugurated with a concert by Frank Sinatra in 1982. The village overlooks the deep cleft that the Río Chavón has carved through the landscape and features several art galleries, a school of design, craft shops, a church, and numerous restaurants. Prices here are undeniably high, but the best reason to visit is the superb **Museo Arqueológico Regional,** which contains an excellent collection of Taino art and ceremonial objects. Only the capital's Museo de l'Hombre Dominicano can rival it. Although the collection here is not as comprehensive, it is extremely well presented and well lit, with adequate labeling and information. The centerpiece is a rare, carved wooden idol, but the museum is also strong on artistic pieces, amulets, jewelry, ceremonial objects and axes, and household items *(closed Mon.)*.

Offshore from La Romana is the uninhabited **Isla Catalina,** which has beautiful white sand beaches on the coastline facing the mainland. The interior is arid, but the reefs on the leeward shore are excellent for diving. There are some good shallow reefs and also a wall that drops 165 feet (50 m). For information on dive trips, contact Casa de Campo. Excursions are also run from dive operations at Punta Cana.

The fishing village of **Bayahibe,** popular with independent travelers and divers, is about 15 miles (25 km) southeast of La Romana on Rte. 3, turning south at Los Cinco Caminos. A number of budget hotels are dotted among the small wooden houses and cafés in the village. Bayahibe also has a mile-long (1.6-km) sandy beach fringed with coconut palms and is a popular spot for catamaran tours hopping-off to Isla Saona offshore.

Isla Saona forms part of the **Parque Nacional del Este,** which includes the island itself and a stretch of coastline from Bayahibe to the Bahía de Yuma. The 53-square-mile (137-sq-km) Isla Saona has only two small fishing villages—Adamanay on the southwest coast and Punta Gorda on the west coast—but hundreds of people visit each day, drawn to its fantastic white sand beaches, where Columbus is said to have put ashore.

About 20 miles (32 km) inland from La Romana is the town of **Higüey,** one of the oldest on the island, founded in 1502. It holds little of interest to the visitor apart from being a major center of pilgrimage; in the heart of the town is the **Basilica de Nuestra Señora de la Merced,** a 16th-century Spanish church.

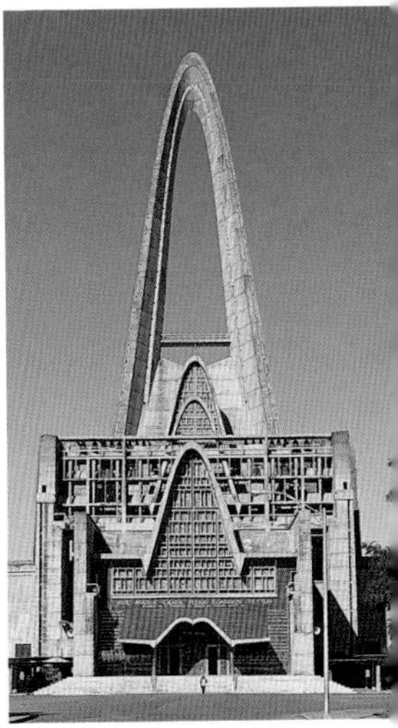

The Basilica de Nuestra Señora de Altagracia, Higüey

Bayahibe

Carnival

In the Dominican Republic the carnival tradition has become associated with the historic dates of February 27, 1844, when national leader Juan Pablo Duarte re-took Santo Domingo from the Spanish, and August 16, 1865, when the Dominican Republic became a fully independent country. Carnival is celebrated on these days irrespective of when Lent is. The days preceding these dates are animated with street dancing, parades, and parties. The highlight, however, is the carnival costumes of the *diablos cojuelos,* or lame devils, which chase people around the streets. They're known as *lechones* in Santiago, *cachuas* (horned devils) in Cabral, *toros* (bulls) in Montecristi, *papeluses* (paper devils) in Cotuí, *diablos de hojas de platano* (plantain leaf devils) in Barahona, and *mascaros* (masked devils) in Bonao. Each of these forms is represented by suitably decorated masks. Some of the best examples can be seen in the Santiago Museo Folklórico de Tomás Morel (see p. 116). ■

The *diablos cojuelos* (lame devils) are the highlight of the carnival festivities.

Manatí Park Bávaro
97 E2
www.manatipark.com
Plaza Bávaro
809/552-6100
$$$$$

DOLPHINS IN CAPTIVITY
Dolphins are sensitive mammals who suffer in captivity. On average a dolphin lives 45 years in the wild, yet half of all captives die within their first two years. For a dolphin used to roaming free for up to 40 miles a day, any enclosure is like a concrete prison. ■

Just 550 yards (500 m) to the north of this is the massive **Basilica de Nuestra Señora de Altagracia,** which is dedicated to the country's patron saint. This huge concrete structure was built in the 1950s and is intended to resemble a 200-foot-high (60-m) pair of hands praying. An annual pilgrimage is made to the site each year on January 21.

COASTAL ATTRACTIONS

Due east from Higüey is the **Coconut Coast,** an uninterrupted stretch of some of the most gorgeous beaches on the island stretching from **Punta Espada** through **Punta Cana** and **Bávaro** almost all the way to **Punta Sabaneta.** Fine white sand, backed by coconut plantations, slopes off into a reef-protected lagoon that offers excellent swimming and water sports. There are scuba diving and snorkeling opportunities offshore. This area has become one of the most intensively developed in the country, with a string of all-inclusive hotels, many with first-class facilities, spread out along different stretches of the beach.

Behind the beach hotels is the **Manatí Park Bávaro.** The park has enclosures with iguanas, parrots, vultures, butterflies, storks, an aquarium with sharks and rays, plus regular performances by parrots, dancing horses, seals, and dolphins. (There are concerns about the welfare of the dolphins in captivity, see side panel.) Also included is a re-creation of a Taino village, with a cultural show depicting the Taino way of life. ■

Horse-drawn carriages await tourists in Santiago de Los Caballeros.

Santiago de Los Caballeros

THE SECOND LARGEST CITY IN THE DOMINICAN REPUBLIC (population 750,000), Santiago de Los Caballeros is the major industrial and agricultural center in the fertile Valle de Cibao. Any industrial smoke, however, can probably be linked to the main crop, tobacco; Santiago is a major producer of hand-rolled cigars and mass-produced cigarettes. The city's name derives from the 30 Spanish nobles *(caballeros)* who founded the town on Columbus's orders in 1495.

A sprawling, prosperous metropolis, Santiago has built its fortunes on tobacco and rum. The huge Martinez factory still turns out tens of thousands of cigars a day—all made by hand—and machinery also produces 18 million cigarettes in the same period. The cigarmaking process is fascinating to watch, as the skilled workers roll the leaves and bind them into the familiar tubular shape. More than 20 factories are still in operation, and the local tourist office can provide details about tours: A popular choice is E. Leon Jiménes Tabacalera *(Tel 809/535-5555, tours every 90 minutes)*. Next to the factory is the **Centro Cultural Léon** *(Tel 809/582-2315, www.centroleon.org.do)*, opened in 2003 to commemorate the tobacco group's centenary. Exhibits showcase

Santiago de Los Caballeros
97 C3
Visitor information
Ayuntamiento Municipal
809/582-5885

Museo Folklórico de Tomás Morel

- 174 Calle Restauracion
- 809/582-6787
- Closed weekends
- Donation

Dominican arts and anthropology in a stunning post-modern building.

On the northeast corner of Santiago's central square is the **Parque Duarte,** whose shady confines are alive with shoe-shine boys, vendors of shaved ice, and picnicking office workers, though it is remarkably small for a city of this size. On the west side you'll find the **Centro de Recreo,** built in 1894. Inside it houses a private billiards club. The splendid facade has been painstakingly restored. Next door is the privately owned **Palacio Consistorial,** a more sober edifice from the same period. Santiago has a plethora of fine Victorian architecture, much of it built by local merchants who profited handsomely from the agricultural wealth of the Cibao Valley in the late 19th century. The style is predominantly Spanish Colonial, and many of the buildings are attractively decorated with painted tiles, ornate wrought iron, and lacy gingerbread work.

A few minutes' walk from the Parque Duarte is the **Museo Folklórico de Tomás Morel.** This quaint museum is a treasure trove of curiosities, from Taino pottery to early calculators and cameras, but the main draw is a priceless collection of hundreds of carnival masks (see p. 114). Santiago is famous for carnival masks, and those presented here range from the grotesque and surreal to the humorous. Worth noting are the masks from the Hoya district of Santiago, characterized by forests of spiky protuberances on the horns.

One monument you can't miss—

Cigarmaking

Cigarmaking has a long tradition in the Dominican Republic and plays an important role in the culture and economy of the country.

The prime tobacco-growing area is along the Yaque Valley, which borders the Río Yaque del Norte for some 15 miles (25 km) from the outskirts of Santiago northwest to the town of Esperanza. Despite a period of decline in the 1960s, the recent upsurge in demand for premium cigars around the world has generated a welcome boom in this area.

The Dominican Republic currently exports about 140 million hand-rolled cigars to the United States annually, making it the top exporter in the region, ahead of Honduras and Cuba. Internationally known brands such as Dunhill, Partaga's, and H. Upmann are produced here. ■

even if only by virtue of its commanding position above the city—is the **Monumento a los Héroes de la Restauración** on Avenida Monumental, which rises some 220 feet (67 m) from a hilltop in the center of Santiago. Made of white marble, this huge monument was constructed during the Trujillo era and honors the heroes of 1844 who helped expel the Haitians and restore self-government to the Dominican Republic (in fact, Trujillo intended it as a monument to himself).

The interior houses displays about the creation of the republic. An elevator (often not working) and steps take you to a platform with panoramic views over Santiago, the Valle de Cibao, and the mountains. Note the frescoes at the top of the stairs, which are by the well-known contemporary Spanish painter Vela Zanetti.

The city's main thoroughfare, **Calle del Sol,** runs from the monument down to Parque Duarte, where most of the better shops in the city are found. ■

Hand rolling a cigar is a labor-intensive job.

Entry sign for folklore museum

Cordillera Central

Jarabacoa
97 C3

Salto de Jimenoa
97 C3
$

INHOSPITABLE AND REMOTE, THE MOUNTAINS OF THE Cordillera Central (Central Highlands) run diagonally across the western half of the Dominican Republic, culminating in the island's highest point—Pico Duarte (10,410 feet/3,175 m). There is no easy access to this wilderness area, which includes two major national parks (the Parque Nacional Armando Bermúdez and the Parque Nacional José del Carmen Ramírez) and the sources of some of the country's major rivers (such as the Río Yaque del Norte and the Río Yaque del Sur).

One of the most easily accessible of the hill stations is **Jarabacoa.** You can reach it on Rte. 28, winding up from the central highway (Rte. 1) through pine forests that have earned this region the title of the Dominican Alps. The alpine-style chalets in the wood-lands are popular with vacationers.

Set in a broad valley and surrounded by the foothills of the Cordillera Central, Jarabacoa is a cool retreat with equable year-round temperatures. Many wealthy Santiago residents have weekend homes here, scattered around the outskirts of town amid fields of cultivated flowers, strawberries, pimentos, and manioc.

There is little to see in Jarabacoa itself, although the charming park at its center, shaded by a magnificent tree whose branches arch over the entire square, is typical of small Dominican towns. A church, which adjoins the park, contains modern frescoes by a well-known local artist, Roberto Flores.

Rafting is popular on the upper reaches of the Río Jimenoa.

Jarabacoa's appeal lies mostly in its proximity to mountainous terrain, rushing rivers, and unspoiled countryside. One of the most popular places to visit is the impressive **Salto de Jimenoa** waterfall; it is easily reached via a turnoff 2.5 miles (6.5 km) from the town center on the La Vega road and a 4-mile (6-km) drive along a dirt track to a hydroelectric station below the falls. The falls themselves are an easy 10-to-15-minute walk from here across a series of swinging bridges. Set in a jungle-filled, natural amphitheater, the cascade tumbles down an 80-foot-high (24-m) rock face into a huge pool where you can swim.

The Río Jimenoa converges on the other side of the town with the Río Yaque del Norte at a spot 2 miles (3 km) from Jarabacoa known as the **Balneario La Confluencia.** This spot is popular with locals for weekend picnics and swimming.

The countryside around Jimenoa is perfect for exploration and adventure sports, with a network of paths and dirt tracks winding through remote hamlets and small farms. On the fringes of town (1 mile/1.6 km to the south) is the busy **Rancho Baiguate** *(Tel 809/574-4940, www.ranchobaiguate.com)*. This multiactivity adventure center offers a wide range of things to do, including horseback riding, quad biking, mountain biking, parapente (descending from hill or mountaintops beneath a specially designed canopy), rafting, trekking, canyoning (rappelling into canyons), tubing, jeep safaris, and expeditions to the top of the Pico Duarte. Within a short distance of Rancho Baiguate are the **Baiguate Falls,** which can be reached on quad bikes from the ranch down several dirt tracks (journey time is around 20–30 minutes) and then a short walk. Here you'll find another natural swimming pool. Rafting takes place on the upper section of the Río Jimenoa, an 8-mile (13-km) ride downstream with Class III rapids. The ranch also provides accommodations and can arrange visits to a local coffee factory and excursions to watch the making of Indian bread *(casabe)* and view other local activities.

Continuing beyond Jarabacoa on the same badly potholed road (Rte. 28) brings you to the town of **Constanza,** set in a high valley surrounded by the peaks of the Cordillera Central. Like Jarabacoa, it is a prime growing area for soft fruit crops such as strawberries, raspberries, peaches, pears, and apples. The town itself is very peaceful, with just a handful of restaurants and hotels, and in December and January temperatures drop below freezing. The main activities are walking and visits to the 100-foot-high (30-m) **Agua Blanca** waterfalls, 6 miles (10 km) to the south. These are much less visited than the falls around Jarabacoa. ■

Cordillera Central is the Republic's largest mountain range.

CLIMBING PICO DUARTE

Climbing Pico Duarte, the highest mountain in the Caribbean, is usually undertaken as part of an organized trip because it's a three-day round-trip from the village of La Ciénega to the peak itself. Outfitters include the Rancho Baiguate *(Tel 809/574-4940)* and Iguana Mama in Cabarete *(Tel 809/571-0908, www.iguanamama.com)*. ■

The cannon of the Fortaleza de San Felipe, with the Pico Isabel de Torres in the background

North coast: around Puerto Plata

THE ATLANTIC COAST OF THE DOMINICAN REPUBLIC extends for some 150 miles (241 km) from Monte Cristi on the Haitian border in the west to the Peninsula de Samaná in the east. In the scenic hinterland a patchwork of canefields lies beneath the rugged Cordillera Septentrional. The coast has some excellent beaches, but because they border the Atlantic the sea can be rougher here, and some of these beaches are more suited to bodysurfing than snorkeling.

Puerto Plata
97 C4
Visitor information
Calle Harmanas, Mirabel 8
809/586-3676

Fortaleza de San Felipe
End of the Malecón
$

The coast's main town is **Puerto Plata** (Silver Port), founded in the early 16th century. Above it towers the dramatic **Pico Isabel de Torres** (2,554 feet/779 m), which bears the scars of a landslide on its seaward slopes. Part of the mountain forms a nature reserve, the Reserva Cientifica Isabel de Torres. At the top of the mountain is a restaurant-café with superb views. You can either drive up or take the cable car, the only one of its kind in the Caribbean.

Puerto Plata has an attractive and very long seafront promenade, the Malecón, at the western end of which lies the **Fortaleza de San Felipe.** The fortress is one of the oldest in the Caribbean, built between 1564 and 1577 to deter pirate attacks. But in 1659 three shiploads of buccaneers captured it. The fort was partially

destroyed when the pirates were eventually forced out, and then it was rebuilt on the orders of King Philip II of Spain, after whom it is now named.

Restored in the 1970s, the fortress has small lookout towers facing the sea and a massive keep at its center, where you'll find the small museum. The exhibits, mostly remnants of 16th-century armaments, are not as compelling as the interior of the keep itself.

Puerto Plata's town square, the **Parque Central,** has several turn-of-the-20th-century wooden houses with characteristic gingerbread style fretwork on the balconies and windows. At the center of the square is a typical pavilion, known as **La Glorieta,** and on its southern side is the modern **Catedral de San Felipe,** built in imitation art deco style.

Apart from the fort, the town's star attraction is the excellent but highly commercialized **Museo del Ambar Dominicano** (Dominican Amber Museum), just a short stroll from the Parque Central. You'll find some fascinating exhibits in this well-presented museum, mostly of insects and small creatures frozen in time since they got stuck on a resinous tree some 50 million years ago.

TOWARD HAITI

Westward from Puerto Plata, Rtes. 1, 5, and 29 pass through arid, cactus-strewn landscapes toward the Haitian border. At Cofresí, **Ocean World Park** *(Tel 809/291-1000, www.ocean-park.info, $$$$$)* is a popular family attraction. Visitors can swim with dolphins and sea lions (see page 114), handle sharks and rays, watch shows and stroll through aviaries and a rainforest exhibit. East of **Luperón** is the site of the first European town in the New World, **La Isabela,** which is now the **Parque Nacional Histórico La Isabela.** Columbus founded the settlement on January 1, 1494, and named it in honor of the Spanish queen. Excavations have revealed the stone foundations of the church and Columbus's house.

The last town before the border is **Monte Cristi.** Faded Victorian buildings hark back to its heyday in the 19th century when it flourished as a major port for the export of timber and agricultural produce.

Of more interest is the nearby **Parque Nacional Monte Cristi,** which covers 204 square miles (528 sq km) of coastline and offshore islands, known collectively as the Cayos Siete Hermanos. This important sanctuary is home to alligators and several rare species of birds, such as the wood stork and the American oystercatcher. ■

THE AMBER COAST

The northern coastline is sometimes called the Amber Coast, thanks to the amazing discoveries in amber deposits that form the basis of Puerto Plata's amber museum. The title is something of a misnomer, though, because the amber actually comes from 15 or so mines in the shale and sandstone sediments between Puerto Plata and Santiago in the interior. ■

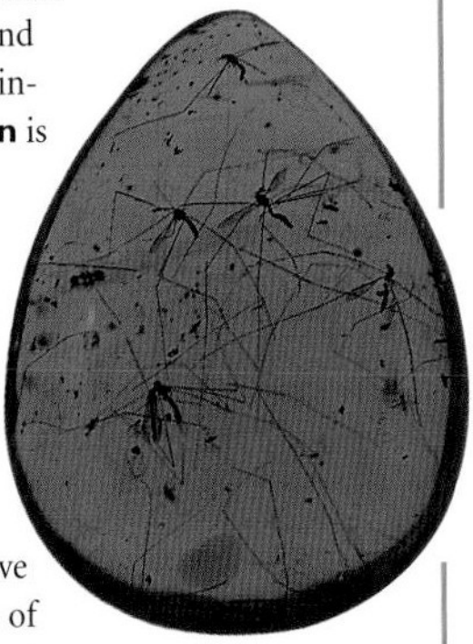

Crane flies caught in amber

Museo del Ambar Dominicano
www.ambermuseum.com
✉ Calle Duarte 61
☎ 809/586-2848,
🕒 Closed Sun.
$ $

Sosúa offers a wide variety of water sports.

Puerto Plata to Playa Grande

SOME 3 MILES (5 KM) TO THE EAST OF PUERTO PLATA IS THE resort complex of Playa Dorada, with a fringe of hotels along its sandy bay. The complex also has a first-class golf course and a commercial center with a good selection of shops, restaurants, cafés, and other facilities. Continuing east, you encounter a less built-up coastline, and the lovely lagoon by Río San Juan is a highlight for many visitors.

Sosúa
97 C4
Visitor information
Edificio Gel Brown, 2da, Planta, Autopista Luperón
809/571-3433

Cabarete
97 C4
Visitor information
809/571-0962

Sosúa (17 miles/27 km east of Puerto Plata) has a big, lively beach and an extensive beach market. Most water sports, including scuba diving and snorkeling excursions, are available from operators at the beach. The town is divided into two sections. To the west of the beach is **Los Charamicos,** a fishing community. The district known as **El Batey,** where most of the hotels, restaurants, shops, and tourist facilities are located, flanks the eastern side. El Batey was settled by about 600 Jewish refugees fleeing from Nazi Germany in 1941. The settlers developed a thriving dairy industry, and although many moved away after the war, their legacy remains in the form of memorial plaques, a synagogue, and bakeries.

Cabarete, which is 7 miles (11 km) east of Sosúa, is one of the top windsurfing resorts in the Caribbean and frequently hosts world championship events. It's a very safe destination, thanks to the sideshore winds that bring tired windsurfers back to the beach. From December through September, the tradewinds generally blow at 15–25 knots in the afternoon, with the strongest winds from late spring through summer. The constant play of the trade winds has also brought kiteboarding to Cabarete. A young, lively and international crowd of kiteboarders and windsurfers gathers here in force every June for top-class competitions and serious partying in the beachside bars. But, even if you're not a windsurfer, you can enjoy an excellent beach that stretches around the bay. Not surprisingly, the resort boasts the highest concentration of budget guesthouses and small hotels on the island.

Cabarete is also a major center for mountain biking and hiking tours of the surrounding countryside, thanks to the presence of **Iguana Mama** *(Tel 809/571-0908 or US 800/849-4720, www.iguanamama.com)*. Founded in 1993 this innovative company offers well-organized, fully guided tours and also plows a percentage of its profits back into local environmental and educational programs.

Some 39 miles (63 km) east of Sosúa is the small fishing village of **Río San Juan,** a picturesque jumping-off point for trips on the nearby Laguna Grí Grí. Boats set off from the jetty at the end of the main street, Calle Duarte, for a two-hour trip through a mangrove-lined canal that eventually opens out to the sea. The excursion continues along the coastline and enters one or two sea caves before stopping for a swim in a natural pool *(piscina natural).*

Continuing on some 7 miles (11 km) past Río San Juan, you'll come to **Playa Grande,** an impressive ribbon of sand that curves more than 0.5 mile (1 km) around a lovely bay. But the riptides can be strong.

Just past here is the **Parque Nacional Cabo Francés Viejo,** a protected coastal rain forest with dirt tracks leading off the road to deserted beaches and bays. Finally, there is the provincial capital of **Nagau** on the Bahía Escocesa, but it has very little to offer tourists. ■

Río San Juan
97 C4
Visitor information
Calle Duarte
809/598-2831

Playa Grande
97 C4

Parque Nacional Cabo Francés Viejo
97 D4

Cabarete is the place to go for some of the best windsurfing in the Caribbean.

Sports & activities

Among the well-equipped **windsurfing** schools in Cabarete are: Happy Surf-pool *(Tel 809/571-0784, www.happycabarete.com)*, the Club Mistral *(Tel 809/571-0770; www.clubmistral.com)*, and Vela/Spinout *(Tel 809/571-0805, www.velacaberete.com)*. Wind-surfing competitors meet here each June for Cabarete Race Week.

For the kiteboarding fraternity, there are rentals and tuition from Kite Club *(Tel 809/571-9748, www.kiteclubcabarete.com)*, and Laurel Eastman Kiteboarding *(Tel 809/571-0564, www.laureleastman.com)*. ■

Peninsula de Samaná

Samaná
97 D3
Visitor information
Calle Santa Bárbara, Edificio Gubernamental
809/538-2332

Parque Nacional Los Haitises
97 D3

Las Terrenas
97 D3

ONE OF THE MOST BEAUTIFUL REGIONS OF THE DOMINican Republic, the Peninsula de Samaná juts out from the northeastern corner of the island. The peninsula is bisected by the Cordillera de Samaná (Samaná Highlands). The cordillera's slopes, luxuriant with coconut palms and pines, plunge into the azure waters of the Bahía de Samaná on one side and the Caribbean on the other. Fine beaches and tropical islands provide sea-level attractions.

When Columbus made landfall here in January 1493, he met with a hostile reception from the Taino, who showered him with arrows. This prompted him to name the bay **Golfo de las Flechas** (Gulf of Arrows). White settlers arrived from the Canary Islands in 1756 and founded the town of Santa Bárbara de Samaná, usually called simply **Samaná.** Most of the town was rebuilt after a serious fire in 1946 and is not particularly attractive. But it is the departure point for boat trips to view humpback whales: Up to 3,000 arrive in the bay to mate and give birth between January and March. Contact whale-watching pioneer Kim Beddall at Whale Samana *(Tel 809/538-2494, www.whalesamana.com).* Samaná is also one of the jumping-off points for trips to the offshore island of **Cayo Levantado,** with its superb beaches.

You can also make day trips from Sánchez over to **Parque Nacional Los Haitises** on the south side of the bay, a protected area of coastal mangroves and small cays that is a haven for birdlife. Its inland section includes several caves with petroglyphs and shards of pottery. Trips to the park can be arranged by tour operators from resorts in Puerto Plata, Sosúa, and Cabarete.

On the north coast is the resort of **Las Terrenas.** It boasts some of the country's best beaches, which run for around 7.5 miles (12 km) eastward and westward. ■

Coconut palms and banana plants (foreground) thrive on the Peninsula de Samaná, which covers an area of nearly 400 square miles (1,036 sq km).

Puerto Rico has been a commonwealth territory of the United States since 1952. This has conferred several advantages, including U.S.-style communications and highways, but beneath this veneer beats a Spanish heart.

Puerto Rico

An evocative silhouette at sunset in San Juan

Puerto Rico

THE MOST EASTERLY OF THE GREATER ANTILLES, PUERTO RICO LIES 1,000 miles (1,600 km) southeast of Miami between the Virgin Islands and the island of Hispaniola. Almost rectangular in shape, it measures 100 miles (161 km) from east to west and 36 miles (58 km) from north to south. A range of mountains, the Cordillera Central, runs across the center of the island from east to west, reaching its highest point at the Cerro de Punta (4,387 feet/1,338 m).

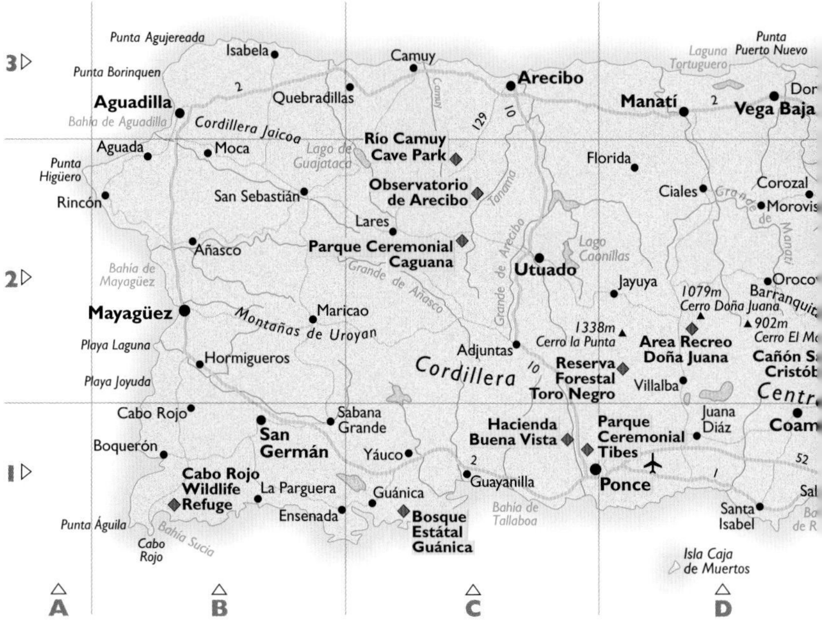

Puerto Rico is unusual in that it is the first Overseas Commonwealth Territory of the United States, and although Spanish is the island's first language, English is widely spoken and Puerto Ricans are U.S. citizens. Puerto Rican culture, music, and dance are Latin American in inspiration, but commercial life is organized with American efficiency. The island has wonderful four-lane highways, but turn off into the countryside and you can find yourself on a potholed rural road.

Puerto Rico's interior is partially clad in dense tropical rain forest, although just one percent of the island's original forest now remains. Huge clumps of bamboo grow alongside the roads and river valleys, and tree ferns, lianas, hibiscus, bougainvillea, and flame trees flourish almost everywhere.

The central mountains are ringed by coastal plains. In the northwest the landscape is shaped by the strange hillocks and caves of limestone karst formations, while in the drier southwest the land is dominated by cactus and other drought-resistant plants.

To the native Taino, the island was known as Boriquen, which meant "land of the noble lord" and referred to their belief that the god Juracan lived atop the highest mountain. From this vantage point he controlled the weather (the word "hurricane" is derived from his name). When Columbus arrived here on his second voyage to the Americas in 1493, he named it San Juan Bautista. With Columbus was Juan Ponce de Léon, who returned to settle the island in 1508; he soon renamed it Puerto Rico or "rich port."

The Spanish enslaved the island's 30,000 Taino and set them to work in the gold mines, but inevitably there was conflict and the Indians were decimated. Ponce de Léon himself was wounded in Florida in 1521 and died in Cuba; his bones were brought back to lie in San Juan's cathedral.

Once the gold was exhausted in the late 16th century, Puerto Rico was neglected by Spain, and the few settlers who remained fought an almost constant battle against diseases, hurricanes, and invasions from Carib, pirates, and European privateers.

In 1765 the Spanish king Carlos III sent an envoy to develop the island's sugar plantations, and trade began to pick up; coffee and tobacco were also exported. In 1809 Puerto Ricans were given Spanish citizenship, but as the century progressed, the independence movement grew in strength and the Spanish appointed a series of military governors (known as the Little Caesars) who ruthlessly repressed any hint of revolution. The first serious uprising took place on September 23, 1868, and the Republic of Puerto Rico was declared. The authorities acted swiftly, however, crushing the revolt at San Sebastian, which came to symbolize the island's struggle for independence.

In 1897 autonomy for Puerto Rico was finally granted, but it did not last long because in 1898 the United States, then at war with Spain, invaded the island. Puerto Rico was ceded to the United States in December 1898, and U.S. citizenship granted to islanders in 1917. In 1952 the island became a commonwealth, but its status is a matter of constant debate. Many politicians in Puerto Rico would like to see it become the 51st state of the Union. In December 1998, however, the Puerto Rican electorate rejected a proposal to do just that.

Nearly a third of Puerto Rico's 3.9 million residents live in and around the capital, San Juan. Over the last 50 or so years the economy has shifted from a rural to an industrial base, and the island now has a well-developed tourist infrastructure with first-rate hotels and good communications. ■

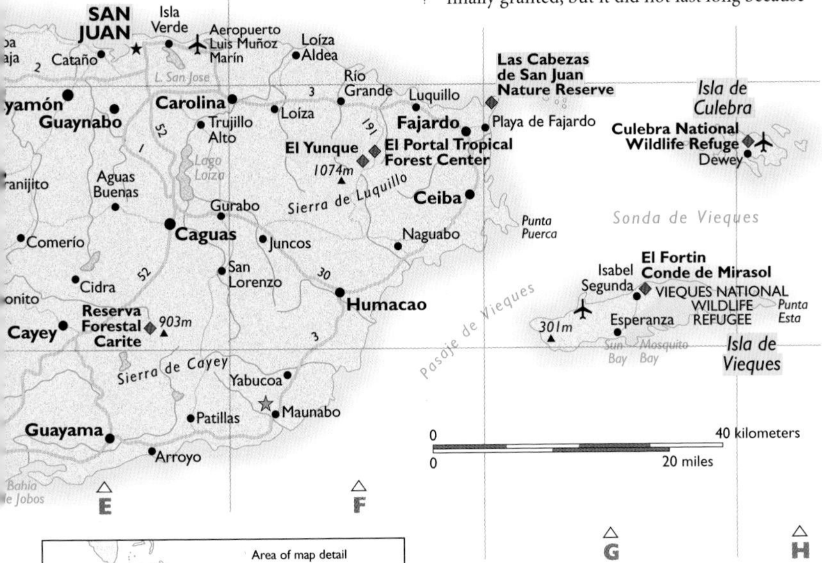

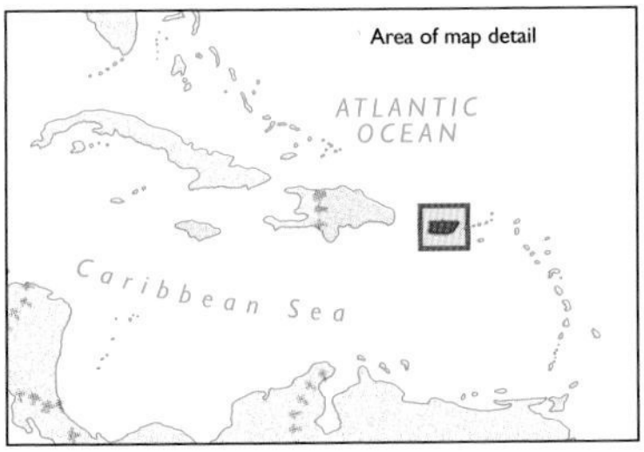

San Juan

San Juan
127 E3
Visitor information
La Casita, Plaza de la Dársena
787/722-1709

FOUNDED IN 1510, PUERTO RICO'S CAPITAL CITY OF SAN Juan has grown from a small town into one of the biggest metropolitan areas in the Caribbean, with a population of more than a million. The island's cultural, political, and economic center, it is also an important air and sea hub for the region. From its initial location at the entrance to the Bahía de San Juan, over the centuries it has spread across to the mainland, enveloped the Laguna San José, and sprouted industrial suburbs crisscrossed with highways and canals.

***Garitas*, sentry boxes, on the huge Castillo de San Felipe del Morro in Old San Juan**

Public transportation information
787/767-7979

El Capitolio
Ave. Ponce de Léon
787/721-6040

Opposite: Hato Rey, the city's main financial district

If the outskirts of San Juan appear unappetizing, the center, by contrast, is a real delight. Old San Juan covers just seven blocks on a long, narrow islet at the northeast entrance to the bay; four causeways connect it to the mainland.

SAN JUAN (NEW CITY)

Unlike Old San Juan, where everything is within walking distance, in the city proper you'll need to use public transportation, taxis, or a rental car to get around. Make the effort, though, since the rewards range from lively stretches of beachfront to bustling merchant districts, and a chance to see Puerto Rico's famous Bacardí rum being made.

Within 550 yards (500 m) of the confines of Old San Juan is **El Capitolio,** a white marble building built in the 1920s as the seat of the island government (Senate and House of Representatives). A guided tour will take you inside the rotunda, where friezes depicting the country's history decorate the elaborate dome.

On the Atlantic seafront, immediately beyond where Old San Juan is connected to the mainland, is **Condado,** a beach strip of high-rise resort hotels behind which are streets full of restaurants, designer stores, fast-food outlets, and souvenir shops. This hotel strip continues along the coast as far as **Isla Verde** (6 miles/10 km), another major beach resort area.

Inland from Condado is the downtown district of **Santurce** and, beyond here, the financial district of **Hato Rey,** where glass-fronted skyscrapers line the street known as the Golden Mile.

Three miles (5 km) farther south still is the suburb of Río Piedras, home to the University of Puerto Rico. The **University Museum** *(Ave. Ponce de Léon, tel 787/764-0000 ext. 2452, closed Sat.-Sun.)* features displays on Puerto Rican history and archaeology as well as contemporary art exhibitions. To the south and east of the university campus are the **Botanical Gardens** *(Corner of Rtes. 1 and 847, tel 787/763-4408)*, a tranquil retreat with numerous walks and waterways meandering among some 200 acres (80 ha) of lush tropical vegetation. The palm garden is particularly appealing.

Another attraction outside Old San Juan is the **Bacardí Rum Distillery** *(Rte. 165, Catano, tel 787/788-8400)*, which you can reach by a short ferry ride from Pier Two in Old San Juan. The 45-minute conducted tour takes in the bottling plant, a museum, and the distillery itself.

OLD SAN JUAN

An area of considerable charm, much of Old San Juan has recently been restored to its original 18th-century character. The streets are paved with cobblestones, originally

BANCO POPULAR

Castillo de San Felipe del Morro
- Calle del Morro
- 787/729-6777
- $$

Museo Casa Blanca
- 1 Calle San Sebastián
- 787/725-1454
- Closed Sun.-Mon.
- $

Museo de las Américas
- Calle Norzagaray
- 787/724-5052
- Closed Mon.

Museo de San Juan
- 150 Calle Norzagaray
- 787/724-1875
- Closed Mon.

El Morro has been massively fortified over the centuries.

brought over from the mainland as ships' ballast, and lined with pastel-painted houses with wrought-iron balconies and shuttered windows.

The entire old town is surrounded by more than 6 miles (10 km) of walls, 50 feet (15 m) high and 20 feet (6 m) thick, studded with small stone sentry boxes known as *garitas.* San Juan has two massive and formidable forts, built to protect the city in the days when buccaneers and pirates were a constant threat.

Today the only invasion the old town faces is by armies of cruise ship passengers. Two piers lie at the very foot of the town, and when both berths are occupied it can seem overrun with day-trippers. Nevertheless, Old San Juan is clearly a community with a life that isn't solely defined by tourism, and locals go about their business, play dominoes in the cafés, and promenade in the evenings, much as they would anywhere else in Puerto Rico.

Old San Juan is a fascinating storehouse of the island's treasures, from colonial fortresses and civic buildings that underpinned Spanish rule to the wealth of historical artifacts on display in its museums.

The most prominent feature of the old town—it dominates the approach by sea and is easily visible from the air—is the massive **Castillo de San Felipe del Morro,** or El Morro as it's known. Sprawling over a rocky promontory at the northwestern tip of the old town, El Morro was begun in 1540 and gradually added to over two centuries until it achieved its present form in 1783. Built on six different levels, the fort's interior is a fascinating complex of tunnels, labyrinths, dungeons, turrets, and ramps. A small museum traces the fort's history, and a reconstruction of an 18th-century military barracks evokes the soldiers' lives. The courtyard here was used in the filming of Steven Spielberg's slave epic, *Amistad* (1997).

Old San Juan's second fort is the **Fuerte San Cristóbal** *(Blvd. del Valle, tel 787/729-6777),* although not as well known as El Morro, it is much bigger, covering some 27 acres (11 ha). Completed in 1678, it was designed to protect the landward side of the town and has five separate bastions linked by underground tunnels, each of which had to fall for the fort to be overrun.

The downtown area has many restored historic buildings of interest. The foremost is **La Fortaleza** *(Calle Recinto Oeste, tel 787/722-5834, closed weekends),* built between 1533 and 1540 but later considerably modified. Today it houses the governor's residence and is believed to be the oldest executive residence in continuous use in the Western Hemisphere. Various ceremonial rooms and the gardens are open to visitors *(Contact the Conservation Trust of Puerto Rico).*

Another reminder of the Spanish establishment is the **Museo Casa Blanca,** originally built as a

home for Ponce de Léon in 1521. The explorer died before he could move in, and the original frame house was destroyed by a fire. Ponce de León's son-in-law built the present house in 1523, making it the oldest of about 800 Spanish colonial buildings in Old San Juan, and his descendants occupied it for some 250 years. It's now a museum of domestic life, with some fine examples of colonial furniture. It also has three lovely courtyards: The Italian courtyard, with fountains and brickwork; the classical courtyard, a wild area leading down to the sea; and the Spanish courtyard, modeled on the Alhambra in Granada, Spain.

One of the most fascinating of the old town's museums is the **Museo de las Américas.** The exhibits trace the evolution of the cultures of the New World over the centuries, including pre-Columbian, and features a comprehensive collection of carnival costumes from Peru, Guatemala, Mexico, Venezuela, Cuba, and the Dominican Republic. Another interesting museum is the **Museo de San Juan,** which houses exhibitions of Puerto Rican art and offers an audiovisual presentation on the history of the city. There are also fascinating exhibits at the **Museo de la Farmacia,** which has displays on 19th-century pharmacies, and at the **Casa del Libro** *(225 Calle Cristo, tel 787/723-0354, closed Sun.–Mon.)*, which is housed in an 18th-century building and features exhibits related to books and bookbinding. Its 5,000 volumes include many rare editions. For exhibits on a lighter note, visit the enjoyable **Museo del Niño.** It contains a wide variety of exhibits relating to childhood, such as large collections of dolls and other toys.

A popular exhibition in the central old town is that of **The Butterfly People,** who have created a gallery of mounted butterfly art in a sympathetically restored 18th-century building. It's purely a commercial venture, with no educational value. To find out more about the flora and fauna of Puerto Rico, visit the **Conservation Trust of Puerto Rico,** which has informative displays and a short film on the island's ecology. ■

The Fuerte San Cristóbal looms above a cruise ship in San Juan's harbor.

Museo de la Farmacia
- 319 Calle Fortaleza
- 787/977-2700
- Closed Sun.–Mon.
- $

Museo del Niño
- 150 Calle Cristo
- 787/722-3791
- $

The Butterfly People
www.butterflypeople.com
- 257 Calle de la Cruz
- 787/723-2432

Conservation Trust of Puerto Rico
- Calle Tetuen 155 San Juan
- 787/722-5834

Old San Juan walk

This lovely walk through Old San Juan traces a roughly circular path, beginning and ending at the Plaza de Colón, one of the many elements of San Juan that play up the Columbus connection. Along the way you can appreciate the disparate components—fortresses, churches, museums, and monuments—that combine so harmoniously in this colonial district.

The triumphal statue of Columbus in Plaza de Colón, originally a fountain

Start in the **Plaza de Colón** at the entrance to the old city, where a statue commemorates the explorer. Follow Avenida Muñoz Rivera uphill to the **Fuerte San Cristóbal** ❶ (see p. 130). After a look at the fort, take Boulevard del Valle along the seafront. On your right you'll see a sprawling collection of closely packed houses clinging to the seashore beneath the city walls. This is the **Barrio La Perla,** originally a village that sprang up to serve the military establishment; it is now home to some 10,000 people who form a tight knit community. La Perla is considered to be quite distinct from other areas of the city, and for safety reasons it is not recommended to venture down here unaccompanied.

As you continue toward Calle Norzagaray and the **Museo de San Juan** (see p. 131), the **Convento de los Dominicos** ❷ is on your left. Built in the early 16th century, it was later used as a headquarters for the U.S. Army. It has now been fully restored and houses the Puerto Rican Institute of Culture *(Tel 787/721-6866)*, which features a chapel with an ornate altar, religious manuscripts, and an art gallery *(Closed Sun.)*. Just past here is the **Plaza del Quinto Centenario**. One of the highest points in San Juan, it was built as part of the 500th anniversary of the discovery of the New World. Its centerpiece, Totem Telúrico, is a 40-foot-high (12-m) sculpture in black granite and ceramics, referred to locally simply as "the totem" due to its tall, cylindrical shape. It's the work of Jaimé Suarez, one of the country's foremost artists. From its southern end two columns point skyward to the North Star, the guiding light for maritime explorers.

On the west side of the square stands the **Museo de las Américas** ❸ (see p. 131). This handsome, three-story neoclassic building has porticoed galleries overlooking the courtyard, and it used to house the military barracks. It was constructed in the mid-19th century and was the largest building erected in the Americas by Spanish engineers.

Continue on toward the broad expanse of park that leads across the headland to the impressive **Castillo de San Felipe del Morro** ❹ (see p. 130). Then return across the park and follow the road down to the **Casa Blanca** ❺ (see pp. 130–31). From the Casa Blanca take Calle San Sebastian to the Plaza de San José, in one corner of which is the **Iglesia de San José** ❻ *(Tel 787/725-7501)*, the family church of the Ponce de Léon family. A statue of the city's founding father, Juan Ponce de León, strikes a dashing pose on the plaza complete with plumed hat and armor. It is made from melted-down cannon. The Spanish explorer was originally laid to rest here, but his ashes were moved to the Catedral de San Juan in 1971. The simple 16th-century church has a particularly ornate altarpiece, and note the fresco (1550) on the far left.

In one corner of the Plaza San José is the **Museo Pablo Casals** *(Tel 787/723-9185, closed Sun.-Mon.)*, dedicated to the memory of this famous Spanish cellist who founded the Casals Festival, held on the island every year since 1957 at the Luis A Ferré Performing Arts Center *(Tel 787/725-7334)*. The museum is a collection of memorabilia from the cellist's career, with videotapes of the Festival concerts.

Follow Calle Cristo downhill, passing the archbishop's residence (No. 50) on your right, to reach the **Catedral de San Juan ❼,** a grandiose structure topped with three cupolas. Inside, a marble tomb holds the remains of Ponce de León *(Tel 787/722-0861)*.

Turn right and walk down the Caleta de San Juan, one of the prettiest little streets in Old San Juan, to reach the **Puerta de San Juan ❽,** once the city's main entrance. Go through the gateway and turn left, following the attractive promenade running alongside the harbor and past **La Fortaleza** (see p. 130).

Turn east past the fountain, continuing on past **Presidio de la Princesa** (now housing the tourist board offices) down the Paseo de la Princesa back toward the docks. Follow Calle Recinto Sur back to the Plaza de Colón. ■

See area map pages 126–27
- Plaza de Colón
- 1.5–2 miles (2.5–3 km)
- Allow 2–3 hours
- Plaza de Colón

NOT TO BE MISSED
- Convento de los Dominicos
- Museo Pablo Casals
- Catedral de San Juan

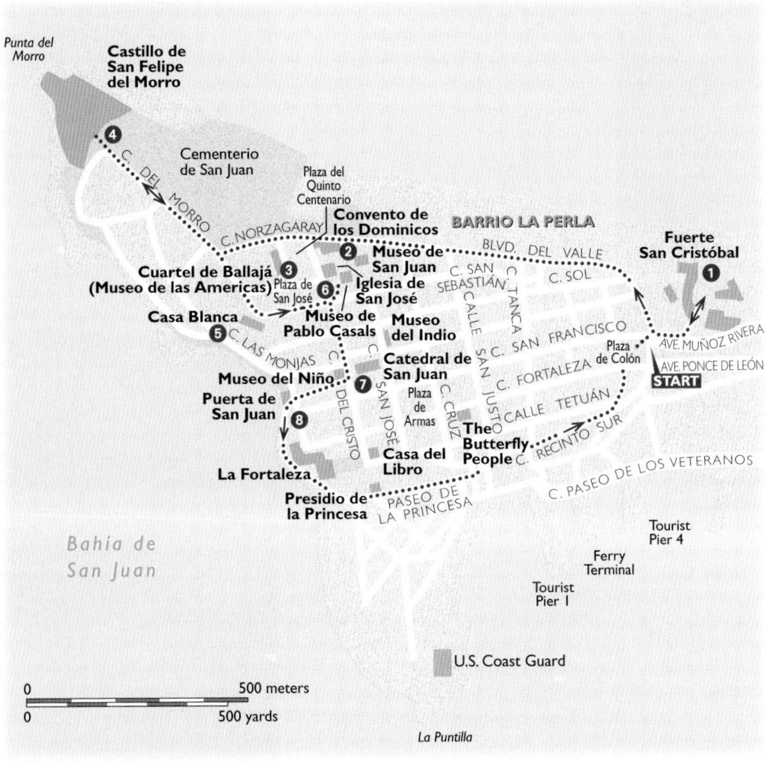

The east

EASILY ACCESSIBLE FROM SAN JUAN, THE EASTERN END OF the island is the area most frequently visited by day-trippers and has several important nature reserves, including El Yunque rain forest. This 28,000-acre (11,210-ha) reserve is by far the most popular attraction in Puerto Rico, with around a million visitors each year.

El Yunque
127 F2

El Portal Tropical Forest Center
127 F2
www.southernregion.fs.fed.us/caribbean
787/888-1810
$$

El Yunque is home to the endangered Puerto Rican parrot.

The largest forested area on the island, **El Yunque** harbors many spectacular waterfalls, thousand-year-old trees, brightly colored flowering plants, and a wealth of bird species. Although much can be seen from the road, the best way to experience the forest is to set off on any of the 13 hiking trails, which cover 23 miles (37 km) of varied terrain throughout the park.

The forest is located in the Sierra de Luquillo, 25 miles (40 km) east of San Juan. Take Rte. 3 from the capital, and near Luquillo turn south into the mountains on Rte. 191. About 3 miles (5 km) along this road is the **El Portal Tropical Forest Center.** Approached via an elevated walkway through the forest canopy, this excellent visitor center has more than 10,000 square feet (930 sq m) of exhibits. These relate to fauna such as the national emblem, the *coqui* frog, the different types of forest within the park (which include tabonuco, colorado, palm, and cloud), and the management of tropical forests worldwide. A film on El Yunque is shown every half hour, alternating between Spanish (9 a.m.–4 p.m.) and English (9:30 a.m.–4:30 p.m.).

Although known as El Yunque in Puerto Rico, the park's official name is the **Caribbean National Forest.** The area was sacred to the Taino Indians, hence the name Yunque, from "Yuke" or white land, and petroglyphs carved on rocks within the riverbeds are evidence of the Taino presence. In 1876 King Alfonso XII of Spain declared 12,000 acres (4,800 ha) of mountainous land in the Sierra de Luquillo as a forest reserve, making it one of the oldest forest reserves in the Western Hemisphere. After the Spanish-American War in 1898, the Spanish crown lands became U.S. property, and in 1903 the area became the Luquillo Forest Reserve, making it the only tropical rain forest in the U.S. national forest system.

From El Portal the road (Rte. 191) leads up toward **La Coca Falls** (alongside the road at 5 miles/8 km), which has an 85-foot (26-m) drop. The **Yokahu Tower** (5.5 miles/9 km), one of several observation towers within the park, affords magnificent views across the mountains. About 0.5 mile (1 km) past here you'll see signs for the **Big Tree Trail.** This lovely mile-long (1.6 km) route, which leads past some of the largest trees in the forest, also passes **La Mina Falls,** probably the most spectacular in the park. At 7 miles (11 km) is the **Sierra Palm Information Center,** which has a picnic area and ranger service, and slightly farther on is the **Palo Colorado Information Center.** Here a trail winds up to the **Mount Britton Lookout Tower** and the peak of El Yunque itself, at 3,496 feet (1,065 m). Allow two hours for the round-trip to the summit.

On the island's northeastern tip, beyond the port of Fajardo, is **Las Cabezas de San Juan Nature Reserve.** This 316-acre (128-ha) reserve is renowned for its unusual range of different ecological communities—sandy beaches, rock escarpments, coral reefs, offshore cays, dry forest, mangroves, and lagoons. The site's most significant natural feature is the **Laguna Grande,** one of three bioluminescent lagoons on the island. At its eastern end a lighthouse, **El Faro,** built in 1880 (the second oldest on the island), houses a nature center and an observation tower. ■

Las Cabezas de San Juan Nature Reserve & El Faro

- Map: 127 G2
- Address: Rte. 987
- Phone: 787/722-5882
- Hours: By appt. only
- Price: $$$

Hiking is a good way to explore El Yunque.

Vieques & Culebra

Isla de Vieques
127 G2
Visitor information
www.vieques-island.com
Mayoral Bldg., 449 Carlos Lebrón St., Isabel Segunda
787/741-5000

El Fortín Conde del Mirasol
787/741-1717
Closed Mon.–Tues.
$

Vieques National Wildlife Refuge
www.fws.gov/southeast/vieques
P.O. Box 1527 Vieques
787/741-2138

Isla de Culebra
127 H2
Visitor information
www.culebra.org
Pedro Márquez St., Rte. 250, Dewey
787/742-3291

Culebra National Wildlife Refuge
www.fws.gov/southeast/culebra
El Campamento, Culebra
787/742-0115

LOCATED 7 MILES (11 KM) OFF THE PORT OF FAJARDO, ISLA de Vieques is the largest of Puerto Rico's offshore islands, covering about 55 square miles (88 sq km). Until recently most of the island was owned by the U.S. Navy and used for training and bombing ranges. In May 2003 the Navy pulled out after 60 years of occupation. Its legacy is a largely undeveloped island, with its dry, rolling hills mostly occupied by roaming wild horses, while spectacular beaches and excellent snorkeling and diving abound. With the Navy gone, tourism is on the increase and upscale hotels are planned, but for the moment Vieques remains a delightful escape.

Most of the 10,000 residents of Vieques live in the main town of **Isabel Segunda,** where the ferries arrive from the mainland. The town has an attractive central square (with a bust of South American revolutionary, Simón Bolívar, who came here in 1816), where you'll find the tourist information center.

On the hill above the town is a restored fort, **El Fortín Conde del Mirasol,** which was one of the last forts to be built by the Spanish.

The other main settlement on the island is lively **Esperanza,** on the south coast, which has a string of bars and restaurants along its seafront.

To the south of Esperanza is **Sun Bay,** one of the island's biggest and most popular beaches, with picnic and camping areas.

Vieques's best known natural attraction, **Mosquito Bay** (also known as Phosphorescent Bay), lies just beyond Sun Bay. This large, shallow bay is surrounded by mangroves and is full of bioluminescent organisms (dinoflagellates), which glow eerily when disturbed by a boat paddle, prop, or your hand dangling in the water.

The former Navy base of Camp Garcia is now part of the **Vieques National Wildlife Refuge** under the control of the U.S. Fish & Wildlife Service. It is the largest wildlife refuge in the Caribbean. Some areas of the former Naval site are closed to the public, but you can visit the beaches at **Bahía Corcho** (formerly Red Beach) and **Bahía de la Chiva** (Blue Beach).

Vieques can be reached either on the frequent ferries from Fajardo *(75-minute crossing, tel 787/863-0705, reservations advisable on weekends)* or by flying from either San Juan or Fajardo (*Contact Vieques Air Link, tel 787/741-8331*). Once there, you can get around by *publicos* (shared public taxis), or you can rent a car from Island Car Rentals *(Tel 787/741-1666)* or Vieques Car Rental *(Tel 787/741-1037).*

ISLA DE CULEBRA

Even more unspoiled than Vieques is the island of Culebra, measuring about 7 miles by 3 miles (11 by 5 km) and surrounded by a series of rocky cays and islets. The landscape is hilly, with tropical rain forest. This peaceful island is home to just 2,000 people, most of whom live in and around the main settlement, **Dewey** (known locally as Pueblo).

About 40 percent of the island forms part of the **Culebra National Wildlife Refuge,** which includes 23 offshore islets and four reserves on Culebra itself. The most important nesting

beaches for birds such as terns and boobies are Playa Resaca and Playa Brava. Contact the refuge for information on guided nighttime walks to watch the leatherback turtles nesting.

The island's best known beach is the mile-long (1.5 km) **Playa Flamenco** on the north coast. This gorgeous stretch of white sand is best visited during the week, because on weekends it fills up with day-trippers. Other good beaches include **Playa Soni** and **Playa Resaca,** on the east coast.

You can reach Culebra from San Juan or Fajardo on Air Culebra *(Tel 787/268-6951)* or by ferry from Fajardo (*90-minute crossing, tel 787/863-0705, reservations advisable on weekends*). You can get around the island by bicycle, or you can rent a car from Jerry's Jeep Rentals (*Tel 787/742-0587)* or Willy's Jeep Rentals (*Tel 787/742-3537)*. The municipal tourist office is located in the City Hall.

Diving can be arranged through Culebra Divers *(Tel 787/742-0803, www.culebradivers.com)*. ■

The offshore reefs around Culebra offer fine diving and snorkeling.

Ponce

PUERTO RICO'S SECOND LARGEST CITY, PONCE LIES MIDWAY along the island's southern coastline. Established in 1692, the city flourished during the late 19th century when it was a major exporter of sugar and rum. The architectural gems from this period benefited from extensive renovations as part of the Columbus quincentennial celebrations; more than 600 of its 1,000 historic buildings have now been restored. Ponce's turn-of-the-20th-century charm is accentuated by the horse-drawn carriages rolling sedately down tree-lined avenues still lit by gas lamps (albeit reconstructions).

Ponce's Plaza Las Delicias (above) is also home to the gaudy Parque de Bombas (above left), the old fire station.

At the heart of the city is the aptly named **Plaza Las Delicias** (Square of Delights), where fountains and shady trees provide a cool atmosphere in which to sit and watch the world go by. At its center is the 17th-century Spanish Creole-style **Catedral de Nuestra Señora de Guadalupe** *(Tel 787/842-0134)*, while immediately behind the church is Ponce's most famous monument, the red-and-black-striped **Parque de Bombas,** or fire station. Built for an agricultural fair in 1882, it only later became the city's fire station. It seems a strange juxtaposition, with the gaudy building abutting the classical cathedral. The church authorities tried to have this colorful structure moved, but the people of Ponce had become so attached to it they refused to do so. Inside, a **museum** contains antique fire-fighting tools, uniforms, and a splendid old fire engine.

The story of the city is well documented in the nearby **Museo de la Historia de Ponce.** An exhaustive but rewarding tour of the ten exhibition halls embraces the ecology, economy, architecture, politics, and daily life of Ponce over the centuries. It ends with a 35-minute documentary about the city.

Ponce
Map 126 C1
Visitor information
www.ponceweb.org
291 Los Cosbos Ave. Valles Torres Sector
787/843-0465

Parque de Bombas
Plaza las Delicias
787/284-4141, ext. 342
Closed Tues.

After leaving the museum, note the buildings on **Calle Isabel.** You can see houses built in the four different styles for which the city is famous—classical, Creole, Ponce Creole, and art deco. Note also the chamfered pavements on each street corner. These facilitated the easier passage of horse-drawn carriages allowing the wheels to ride smoothly up on a turn, thus avoiding an uncomfortable jolt for passengers.

On the other side of Calle Isabel from the museum is the **Casa Wiechers Villalonga.** Now fully restored, this interesting building was constructed in 1911 and is notable for its many adaptations to the tropical climate—underfloor ventilation, louvered fretwork windows, stained-glass panels to filter the sunlight, and the pressed tin ceilings that are a hallmark of Ponce architecture. One of its peculiarities is a *mirador,* an outdoor observatory on the roof, supported by columns. The dining room contains some outstanding examples of art deco furniture, ceiling lights, and glass, all of which were imported from Spain.

The city is extremely proud of its **Museo del Arte,** which was designed by Edward Durell Stone, the architect of the Museum of Modern Art in New York. Noted for its elegant interior, the museum claims to hold the largest collection of art in the Caribbean—more than 850 paintings, 800 sculptures, and 500 prints spanning more than five centuries of Western art. It is particularly strong on the Pre-Raphaelites, the baroque period, and contemporary Latin American works. One of its most famous paintings is "Flaming June," by the

Museo de la Historia de Ponce
- 51–53 Calle Isabel
- 787/844-7071
- Closed Tues.
- $$

Casa Wiechers Villalonga
- 106 Calle Reina & Calle Menendez
- 787/843-3363
- Closed Mon.–Tues.
- $

Museo del Arte
- Ave. las Américas
- 787/848-0505
- $$

"Flaming June," in the Museo del Arte

Pre-Raphaelite Frederick, Lord Leighton. The museum also stages frequent special exhibits.

Perched high above the town is the **Museo Castillo Serrallés.** Built in the 1930s in Spanish revival style, the mansion was originally the home of the Serrallés family, owners of the Dom Q rum distillery. This airy, multilevel house combines Spanish and Moorish elements; the interior features period furnishings and a beautiful inner courtyard.

The fascinating tour includes the history of the oldest rum-making family on the island, permanent and temporary exhibits, and a short film on the sugar and rum industries. The site also has a gift shop and an excellent café with views over Ponce.

Museo Castillo Serrallés
www.castilloserralles.org
- 17 El Vigia
- 787/259-1774
- Closed Mon.
- $$$

PARQUE CEREMONIAL TIBES

This intriguing Taino site, located just outside of Ponce, is said to be the oldest cemetery in the Caribbean, with burials dating back to A.D. 700. Two dance grounds and seven ball courts (one in the form of a star) have been discovered here, underlining its importance as a major ceremonial center. It is assumed that there is a correlation between the positions of these constructions and solstices or equinoxes.

The largest court, measuring about 110 yards (100 m), is the longest in the Caribbean; 187 skeletons have been unearthed here, some showing evidence of human sacrifice. A re-creation of a Taino village and a small museum display Indian ceremonial objects, pottery, and jewelry. The bilingual guides give informative tours about this particular site and about the pre-Columbian Taino culture generally. They shed light on similarities between Taino culture and that of the Maya in Mexico.

Parque Ceremonial Tibes
- Rte. 503
- 787/840-2255
- Closed Mon.
- $

HACIENDA BUENA VISTA

Farther north of town, this wonderful old coffee plantation has been restored using 19th-century techniques and tools. Built in 1833, when the country's coffee production was at its peak, the whole estate is powered by an ingenious system of hydraulics. The original owners received permission to divert the Río Canas to provide power for their machinery if all the water was returned to its source—and this is how the system still works. Not a drop is wasted as the hydraulics power the depulping, husking, and polishing machines.

The manor house has also been fully restored, with the help of old photographs and family documents, to show how the hacienda was furnished and managed. The estate is set in a subtropical environment, home to the Puerto Rican screech owl, hummingbirds, and the mangrove cuckoo—among others. ■

Hacienda Buena Vista
- Rte. 10
- 787/722-5882
- Closed Mon.–Tues.; reservations essential
- $$

West of Ponce

THE SOUTHWESTERN CORNER OF THE ISLAND IS THE driest part of the country, especially in the 1,618-acre (655-ha) Bosque Estatal Guánica, just outside the port of Guánica. This dry forest is unique in Puerto Rico because it contains 700 plant species, 48 of which are endangered, and 16 of which exist nowhere else.

The **Bosque Estatal Guánica** (Guánica Forest Reserve) is also home to snakes, lizards, and endangered birds. About ten marked trails cross the arid scrub within the park, which also has a large, double bay, **Playa de Ventenas,** a popular beach with local surfers.

Guánica itself was the beachhead for 16,000 U.S. troops during the landings in July 1898 in the Spanish-American War. On the hill above town is an old fort, currently being restored.

Between Guánica and the forest is a beach with a big hotel, the Copamarina Beach Resort. Offshore is **Gilligan's Island,** a popular destination for day-trippers. You can also take excursions from the hotel into the coastal mangroves.

Farther west is **La Parguera,** which has grown from a fishing village into a popular resort area. It's a lively spot, particularly on weekends, and is also well known for the nearby **Phosphorescent Bay.** This lagoon amid the coastal mangrove swamps is similar to the bay on Vieques (see p. 136), although the latter seems to have more dinoflagellates in the water *(boats depart every 30 minutes from La Parguera between 7:30 a.m. and 10:30 p.m.).*

At the southwestern tip of the island is the **Cabo Rojo Lighthouse** *(Tel 787/851-7070),* from where you have views back down the coast. Five miles (8 km) inland from here is a wildfowl sanctuary, **Cabo Rojo Wildlife Refuge,** around the Boquerón Lagoon, near the resort of Boquerón. ■

Bosque Estatal Guánica
- 126 C1
- Rte. 116 to Rte. 334 and follow signs
- 787/821-5706

Cabo Rojo Wildlife Refuge
- 126 B1
- Rte. 301
- 787/851-7258
- Closed Sat.–Sun.

Boquerón, long a popular vacation spot, boasts some good beaches.

The Panoramic Route

Snaking its way through some of Puerto Rico's most fabulous scenery as it traverses the length of the island, the Panoramic Route is a classic drive, unlike any other in the Caribbean. It takes at least two days, but there are several mountain *paradores* (country inns) where you can stay. This description is from east to west. Many parts of the road are extremely narrow, so drive carefully. The route is marked at most junctions (brown signs with R.U.T.A. and symbols for mountains), but not all, so take care.

The route starts in the coastal town of **Maunabo,** heads inland to Yabucoa, and then crosses the Río Guayane before starting to climb into the foothills. Small settlements dot the ridge along which the road runs, with valleys and ravines on either side overflowing with clumps of bamboo, tree ferns, and banana plants. After about 6 miles (10 km), the road starts to climb even more steeply. At this elevation, small coffee plantations replace the cattle pastures of the lowlands.

The route then enters the **Reserva Forestal Carite ❶,** *(Tel 787/747-4545)* 6,000 acres (2,430 ha) of rain forest. The reserve is home to 50 species of birds and has several waterfalls and a blue pool known as the Charco Azul. Past here the views open up on both sides, with the sea and coastal plains visible to the south. Lagos Carite and Patillas can be seen, too.

The road continues along the ridgebacks of the Sierra de Cayey, bypassing the town of Cayey itself and rising again to a high point at the **Mirador Piedra Degetau ❷.** An observation tower, plus picnic and other

See area map pages 126–27
➤ Maunabo
120 miles
1.5–2 days
➤ Mayagüez

NOT TO BE MISSED
- Reserva Forestal Carite
- Cañon San Cristóbal
- Cerro Doña Juana

Bamboo shades the road toward the end of the drive.

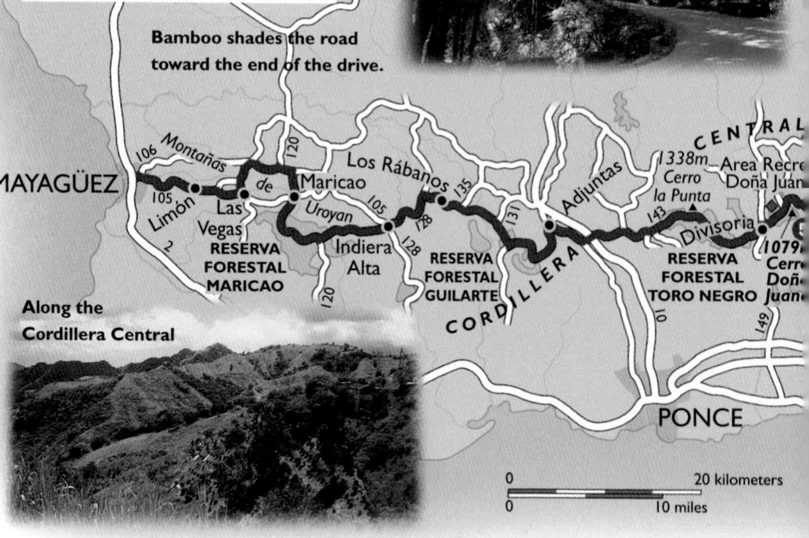

Along the Cordillera Central

facilities mark this summit, which is dedicated to the memory of Don Frederico Piedra Degetau y Gonzales (1862–1914), a distinguished writer and patriot who was inspired by this panorama.

Just to the north is the town of **Aibonito ❸,** once a retreat for the wealthy and still retaining some of its grandiose homes. It is also the highest town in Puerto Rico. Beyond Aibonito the **Cañón San Cristóbal** (San Cristóbal Canyon) ❹, the island's deepest gorge, plunges 700 feet (210 m) to the Río Usabon. The Conservation Trust of Puerto Rico *(P.O. Box 4747, San Juan, tel 787/722-5834)* is developing nature trails, but in the meantime only experienced hikers should attempt to descend its steep slopes.

The route twists and turns along the spine of the Cordillera Central, offering stunning panoramas across the whole island both to the north and south coasts. Beyond the Cerro El Malo (2,957 feet/902 m), the road enters another forest, the 7,000-acre (2,830-ha) **Reserva Forestal Toro Negro** (Toro Negro Forest Reserve). This is a particularly scenic area, with the road shrouded by a leafy canopy of bamboo.

Six miles (10 km) northeast of here is the **Area de Recreo Doña Juana** (Doña Juana Recreation Area). It's worth stopping and taking the path opposite, which leads to a huge swimming pool in the forest. The route beyond here leads upward to the **Cerro Doña Juana** ❺ at 3,538 feet (1,079 m). This is an easy path with no steep gradients and takes around 90 minutes for the return trip. At the top you can climb a small tower for a panorama of the mountains and the coastline. Beyond here you pass the **Cerro de Punta** (4,387 feet/1,338 m), the island's highest point and bristling with radio masts.

The road descends momentarily to the quiet little township of Adjuntas before climbing once more through the Cordillera Central, skirting the Montanas de Uroyan and finally ending on the west coast at **Mayagüez.** ■

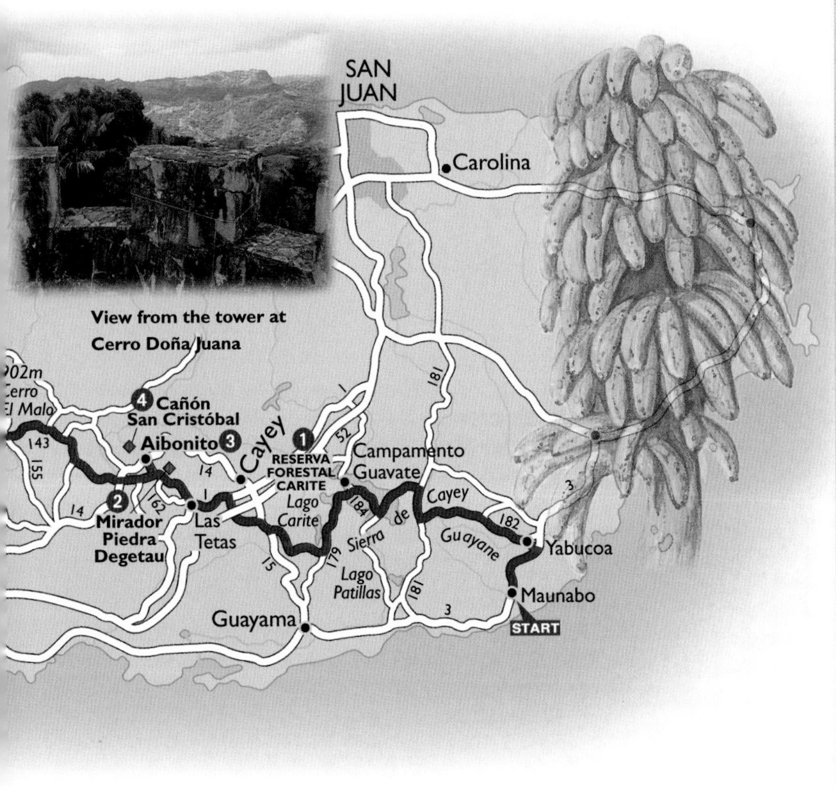

View from the tower at Cerro Doña Juana

The 706-acre (286 ha) Río Camuy Cave Park contains one of the most spectacular and complex cave systems in the world.

The northwest

NORTHWEST PUERTO RICO IS A LIMESTONE LABYRINTH laced with caves, underground rivers, and massive sinkholes. You can tour through the Río Camuy Cave Park, which takes in different caves and sinkholes, or visit the prehistoric Parque Ceremonial Caguana. The area also includes the fascinating Observatorio de Arecibo (see pp. 146–47).

Río Camuy Cave Park
- 126 C2
- Rte. 129, N of Lares
- 787/893-3100
- Closed Mon.–Tues.
- $$$$

RÍO CAMUY CAVE PARK

In the heart of the limestone karst country near Arecibo is the Río Camuy Cave Park. The caves have been carved out over the centuries by the Río Camuy as it carries the rainfall off the Cordillera Central down to the sea. Only two other rivers in the world (the Metali in Papua New Guinea and the Reha in Yugoslavia) are known to match this underground torrent.

Your guided exploration of this world of lofty caverns, mighty stalactites, and huge sinkholes begins at the visitor center, where there is a short audiovisual presentation on the cave system. You then board a motorized tram for the descent through a steep, winding ravine to the main cave, the **Cueva Clara de Empalme** (Clear Cave at the Crossroads). Sunlight filters through a natural entrance to the cave, and

pathways lead to the wonders beyond. The main cavern reaches some 200 feet (60 m) at its highest point, dwarfing the visitors walking around its perimeter. Stalactites hang from the ceiling in various strange shapes. Almost at the cave's center is an enormous stalagmite 17 feet (5.1 m) high and 30 feet (9 m) in diameter. Five different species of bats live in the caves, as well as crickets, guavas (a kind of tarantula), and microscopic shrimp that thrive in the pools of water within the caves. On one side of the Cueva Clara is a deep cleft, at the bottom of which the Río Camuy flows.

Alternatively, to the east, you emerge into a vast sinkhole (a collapsed cave) that is more than 150 feet (45 m) in diameter and 420 feet (128 m) deep. Lianas hang down from the uppermost cliffs, and water cascades down the sinkhole's moss-covered sides.

After the Cueva Clara, the tour continues to the **Sumidero Tres Pueblos** (Three Townships Sinkhole), so named because the borders of three local districts, Camuy, Hatillo, and Lares, coincide here. This measures some 400 feet (122 m) deep and 650 feet (198 m) in diameter: Its 6-acre (2.5-ha) base could hold all of San Juan's El Morro fortress. In one cave at the side of this sinkhole, artifacts have been discovered that show it was once occupied by the Taino.

The last sinkhole on the tour is the **Espiral,** which spirals downward toward the underground river. A series of 200 steps and walkways leads down to it.

To avoid the weekend crowds, visit on a Wednesday, Thursday, or Friday. Tours are available in Spanish or English.

PARQUE CEREMONIAL CAGUANA

South of Río Camuy Cave Park, between Utuado and Lares, is the Parque Ceremonial Caguana. Dating from A.D. 1200, Caguana is one of the largest and most important Taino ceremonial centers in the Caribbean. In addition to the large central court here, there are ten rectangular courtyards, as well as a circular one. Although permanently inhabited by very few people, the center attracted large crowds to religious ceremonies.

Circled by limestone hills, the setting is impressive. The grounds contain many plants, such as silk cottonwood, sapodilla, palms, and cedars, which were used for food and building materials. A small interpretive center has displays of ceramics, carvings, and other Taino artifacts. ■

Parque Ceremonial Caguana

- 9 miles (14.5 km) W of Utuado on Rte. 111
- 787/894-7325
- Closed Mon.–Tues.

A Taino carving on display at the Parque Ceremonial Caguana

Observatorio de Arecibo

Driving through the deeply cleft landscape of limestone karst to the south of Arecibo, the road switchbacks through deep ravines and up over ridges where cattle graze in small pastures. Eventually a slender concrete tower becomes visible, rising to an improbable height above the steep green hillsides: It is the first indication of what lies ahead, the extraordinary Observatorio de Arecibo (Arecibo Observatory)—the world's largest radio telescope.

This amazing observatory is set in a natural crater high in the mountains.

Even if you had no idea what this telescope is capable of doing, it would be impressive. The enormous central dish, which covers more than 20 acres (8 ha), is surmounted by a cat's cradle of wires suspended from three concrete pylons—and hanging like a giant spider in the middle is the receiver itself, weighing just under a thousand tons.

In fact, when it was built in 1963, no one knew for sure that this supersensitive receiver of cosmic radio signals would work at all. It is so big that of course it cannot move: The planet itself has to move for it to change direction. But Arecibo has paid off handsomely. It can examine weather patterns in the troposphere just 2 miles (3 km) above us, as well as probe the heart of quasars some 10 billion light years away. Major discoveries made here include the existence of pulsars (most of those known were mapped here), pulsars orbited by planets, ice in Mercury's polar regions, the rotational cycles of Venus and Mercury, and other productive astronomical information.

But Arecibo has also become associated with something that has more to do with the *X-Files* than radar astronomy—the search for extraterrestrial intelligence, or SETI. The telescope was featured in the film *Contact* (1995) and Dr. José Alonso, head of the visitor center, is quick to dismiss the notion that there has been a cover-up. "People are always very curious about the fact that this facility is capable of detecting signals from extraterrestrial civilizations," he says. "Many believe that we have in fact detected such signals and are keeping it quiet. The truth is that we do monitor a number of stars with surrounding planets that we believe could develop or have developed intelligence with whom we might be able to communicate. We look at them once in a while to see if there is any signal, but none has so far been received. People want to believe that it has happened, but it hasn't happened yet." The telescope collects a huge amount of data, all of which has to be analyzed, and there are so many billions of stars that the chances of pointing it at an area where there might be life are slim. Only around 5 percent of the telescope's work is devoted to SETI.

Inside the control room, banks of computer screens monitor the telescope, and arrays of fiber-optic cables feed the data into mainframes that send it to even bigger number crunchers at Cornell University; the observatory is part of the National Astronomy and Ionosphere Center operated by Cornell University and the National Science Foundation. Outside, a large container houses the research facility of Operation Phoenix, a privately funded foundation that is involved in the ongoing search for extraterrestrial intelligence.

The observatory welcomes visitors, who can tour an interpretive center, the Angel Ramos Foundation Visitor Center (*Tel 787/878-2612, www.naic.edu, closed Mon.–Tues., and Wed.–Fri. a.m., $$*). Located at the foot of one of the giant towers supporting the telescope, the center has some excellent and highly informative displays on science and astronomy.

Inspecting the illuminated platform above the reflector

The first floor houses exhibits on "The Earth and our Solar System, Stars, and Galaxies," and "Tools and Technologies," as well as an auditorium. The second floor concentrates on the work at Arecibo. ■

Mona Island

Mona Island
See inside back cover

SOMETIMES CALLED "THE GALÁPAGOS OF THE CARIBBEAN" because of its remoteness and abundance of wildlife, Mona Island is located 46 miles (74 km) off the western coast of Puerto Rico. Just under 7 miles (11 km) long and around 4.5 miles (7 km) wide, the island has a dry climate and is classified as a subtropical dry region.

Lying in the middle of the Mona Passage, the island was once inhabited by Taino Indians who left behind a series of hieroglyphics and rock paintings in the caves that dot the 200-foot-high (60 m) cliffs on the island's shoreline. Pirates and buccaneers later visited the island, and it's rumored that they may have left a different kind of treasure in these same caves.

In the 1880s a German entrepreneur, Anton Mobins, was granted a license to mine phosphate on Mona, and about 200 people lived on the island as a mining community. It was during this period that roads were built and the caves first explored. The mining company ceased trading in 1896 due to competition from Peru and the United States, and since then the island has been largely uninhabited.

This isolated island is renowned for its wildlife, which includes bats, seabirds, and iguanas that can be up to 3 feet (90 cm) long. It also boasts untouched coral reefs, particularly on its eastern and western coastlines, which are known for their prolific marine life.

Diving and ecotour operators organize tours to the island, which is accessed by private boat or airplane. Caves that can be visited to see Taino petroglyphs include **La Esperanza, El Gato,** and **La Negra.** Some of the more popular beaches frequented by visitors are **Playa Brava, Playa de la Mujeres, Playa del Uvero, Playa Sardineras,** and **Playa de Pajaros.** It's possible to camp on Playa Sardineras with prior permission from the Department of Natural Resources, which also maintains several cabins where you can stay. There are no shops or any other kind of facility, so you have to bring all the food and water you need. ■

The spiny epiphytic plant is found on Mona Island.

Mona Island

Permission to visit must be obtained from the Department of Natural Resources *(Tel 787/724-3724)*. Expeditions to the island are sometimes undertaken by ecotour operators such as Acampa *(Tel 787/706-0695, www.acampapr.com)* and Excursions Guariquén *(Tel 787/831-6447, www. guariquen.tk)* or check out others at *www .travelandsports.com.* ■

A jewel-like scattering of tiny volcanic islands, rocks, and reefs embedded in a turquoise sea, the Virgin Islands archipelago is the final link in the chain of Greater Antilles islands, and it is a magnet for sailors and sun lovers.

Virgin Islands

Colorful staircase Soper's Hole, Tortola

Virgin Islands

SPREADING OUT FROM THE VIRGIN PASSAGE, 50 MILES (80 KM) EAST OF Puerto Rico, the 100-plus Virgin Islands lay a ragged trail across 1,000 square miles (2,600 sq km) at the northeastern corner of the Caribbean Sea. Only a few of the greenest islands are inhabited; the rest are Robinson Crusoe islets and secretive cays once favored by pirates, rocky outcrops colonized by seabirds, and razor-sharp, wave-washed reefs.

At dawn and dusk, the hazy horizon of the Virgin Islands is a magical thing broken by layer upon layer of superimposed outlines: Unless you are a "belonger," as the local residents are called, or possess a cartographer's eye and a relief map, it is almost impossible to get your bearings.

Christopher Columbus first sailed into this nautical maze on his second voyage to the New World in 1493. Struck by their beauty (and profusion), he named the islands Las Once Mil Virgines, after the legend of St. Ursula and the 11,000 virgins (see below). The tiny islands held little attraction for the major European powers as they set about carving up the region, but their numerous secluded harbors and safe anchorages were a godsend for pirates, smugglers, and privateers such as Sir Francis Drake (1540–1596), who played hide-and-seek with the Spanish fleet and gave his name to the Sir Francis Drake Channel, one of the most picturesque maritime channels in the world.

The earliest European settlers were mid-17th-century Dutch *boucaniers*, who moved onto Tortola and raised cattle to supply passing ships with dried meat cured in smokehouses called *boucans*. The British snatched control of the island in 1672 and laid claim to the 60 or so cays and crags at the eastern end of the archipelago, now the British Virgin Islands (BVI). Meanwhile, the Danes secured the western islands of St. Thomas (1665) and St. John (1684) and purchased St. Croix from the French in 1733. St. Thomas they transformed into a flourishing free port; St. John and St. Croix were carpeted with sugarcane. In 1917, the Danish possessions were sold to the United States for 25 million dollars.

The legend of St. Ursula

The obscure and highly questionable legend of St. Ursula dates from the Dark Ages, when the Christian daughter of an English king sought to avoid marriage to a barbarian chief. Agreeing to the marriage on the condition she could undertake a visit to Rome in the company of virgins, she selected her retinue and sailed away. For three years she trained the women into a fighting force, hoping to overthrow her betrothed, but he discovered the ruse and had all 11,001 virgins massacred in the city of Cologne in Germany. ■

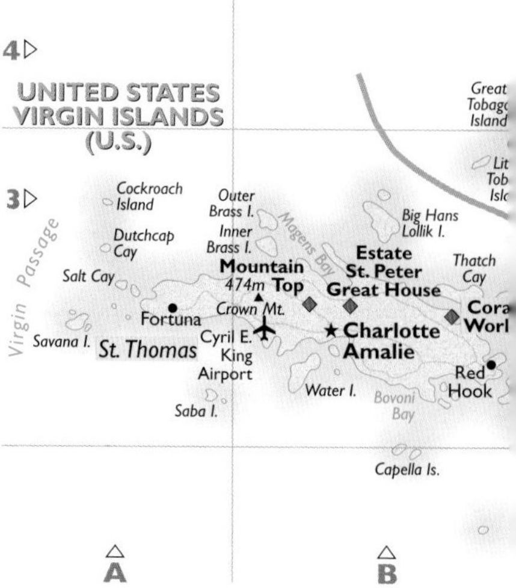

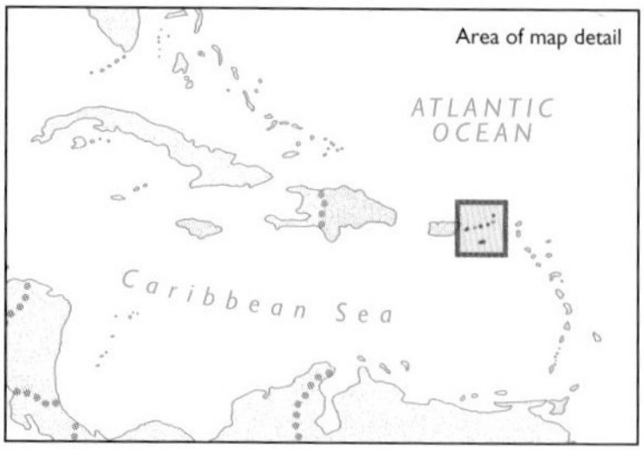

Today, together with 70 more rocks and reefs, they comprise the United States Virgin Islands (USVI).

Only 2 miles (3 km) separate the islands of St. John (USVI) and Tortola (BVI), but the U.S. and the British islands are light years apart in style. St. Thomas and St. Croix are indubitably American, upbeat and among the most developed and prosperous islands in the region. The American Paradise welcomes more than 1.5 million visitors a year and has fast-food franchises, icy air-conditioning, and standards of service rarely encountered elsewhere in the Caribbean. St. John is altogether quieter and boasts an unspoiled national park, which covers two-thirds of the island.

A 40-minute ferry ride away are the relaxed British Virgin Islands, laid back to the point of horizontal. With a population of around 21,500 compared to the 110,000 on the U.S. Virgin Islands, the islands have a more traditional rural West Indian feel, and local life proceeds at a distinctly leisurely pace. Here the tourism industry has been kept deliberately low key and pitched at an upscale but casual market. Yachting is a top attraction and many visitors simply use the islands as a jumping-off point for a sailing trip. ■

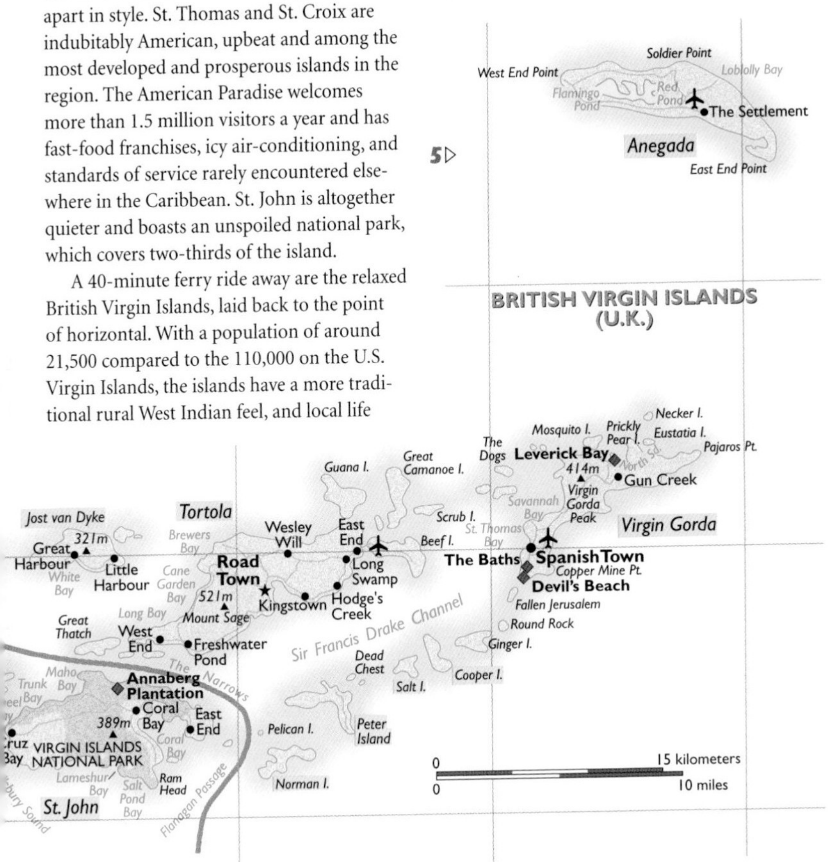

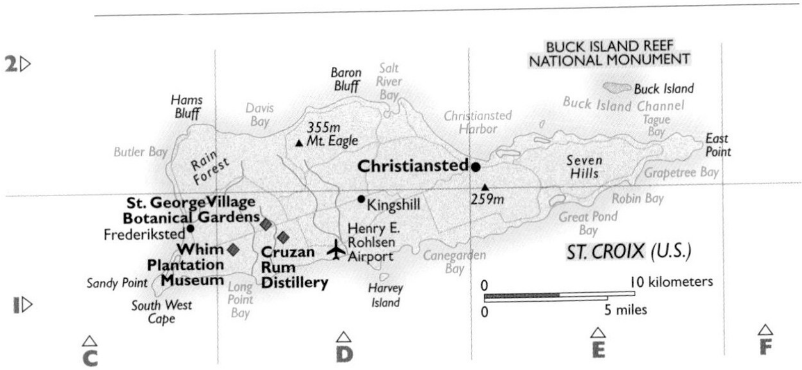

U.S. Virgin Islands

Three distinct identities, the islands of St. Thomas, St. John, and St. Croix (pronounced Croy) are linked by their common history. During the colonial era, the islands were Denmark's only Caribbean possessions, and both St. Thomas and St. Croix preserve attractive Danish colonial architecture in their main waterfront towns.

With the emancipation of slaves on the Danish islands in 1848 and the subsequent collapse of the sugar industry, the Caribbean colonies were on the wane by the 1860s when the strategic potential of the island group first attracted U.S. interest. The need to protect the Panama Canal (opened in 1914), coupled with German naval activity in the region during World War I, finally prompted the United States to purchase the islands from Denmark and place them under the administration of the U.S. Navy. The Department of the Interior took over in 1931, and self-government was introduced in 1936, but the islanders were not permitted to elect their own governor (previously selected by the President) until 1968. Today, Charlotte Amalie on St. Thomas is the capital of the U.S. Virgin Islands, which are unincorporated territories of the United States. The islanders are U.S. citizens and taxpayers, and their 15-member legislature is represented by a nonvoting delegate in the House of Representatives.

Cosmopolitan St. Thomas is the main gateway to the islands. It is a major cruise ship destination offering excellent duty-free

Above: Divers circling coral in the clear waters of the U.S. Virgin Islands
Right: Frederick Evangelical Church on Government Hill, Charlotte Amalie

shopping, fine dining and accommodations, several lovely beaches, and a few sightseeing attractions, all combining to make it an ideal choice for a short break. St. John is an easy day trip away, although for visitors in search of peace and quiet this tiny island could well be a better option. St. John is a leader in the sustainable tourism field and its national park is a major attraction. St. Croix is the least known of the USVI trio but well worth a visit. The island provides a good balance of pretty towns, shopping bargains to match St. Thomas, and more varied and interesting sightseeing opportunities. It is culturally distinct, too, celebrating a variety of musical and culinary traditions. ■

St. Thomas

THE FOUNDATIONS OF ST. THOMAS'S FORTUNES WERE laid in the 1670s by the traders of the Danish West India Company. The original settlement on the site of Charlotte Amalie provided a welcome watering hole for Caribbean merchants and pirates, including Edward Teach (died 1718), better known as Blackbeard. A certain raciness lingers on busy St. Thomas, as islanders offer cruise-ship passengers their first taste of the Caribbean.

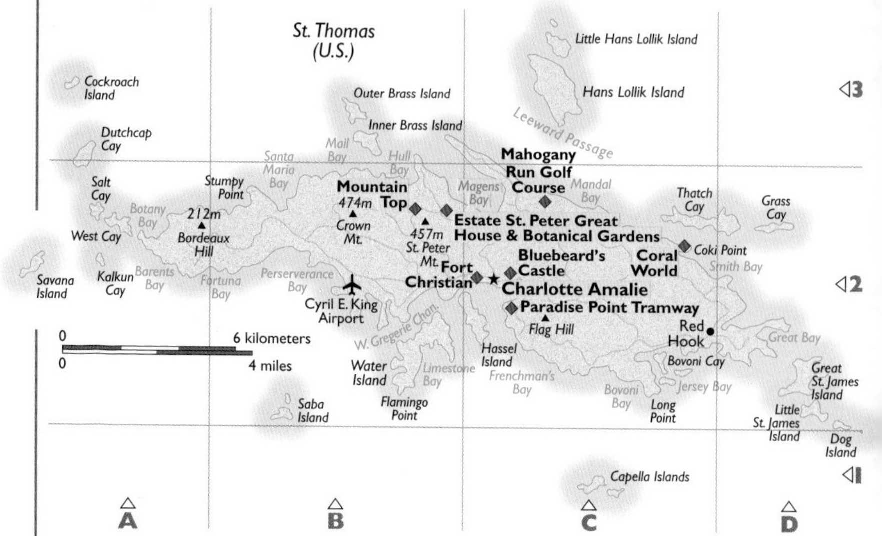

St. Thomas
150 A2
Visitor information
P.O. Box 6400, Charlotte Amalie, USVI 00804
340/774-8784

Above: A carved pirate recalls St. Thomas's early days. Opposite: The Paradise Point Tramway provides a bird's-eye view of St. Thomas Harbor and Charlotte Amalie.

As the town prospered, it was renamed Charlotte Amalie in honor of the Danish queen (wife of King Christian V) in 1691, and by the early 18th century its waterfront warehouses were crammed full of silks, guns, gold, and manufactured goods, which were traded for Caribbean sugar, rum, indigo, and cotton. While European conflicts were mirrored among the colonial powers of the Caribbean, St. Thomas continued to grow rich on the strength of Danish neutrality. The islanders also supplied arms to colonists fighting the American Revolution. For a time at the height of the plantation era, St. Croix eclipsed St. Thomas as the most important island in the group, and the capital was moved to Christiansted on St. Croix in 1775; it returned to Charlotte Amalie in 1871.

Bustling Charlotte Amalie (see p. 156) is the hub of the 12-by-3-mile (19-by-5-km) island. Beaches, bays, and hotels dot the island's ragged central and eastern shorelines (the western end is largely undeveloped), and the interior rises steeply to the 1,556-foot (474-m) peak of Crown Mountain, its ridges and crags peppered with houses and vacation homes. More than 50,000 people live here, making it one of the most populous islands in the region, and numbers

1
PARADISE
POINT
2
3

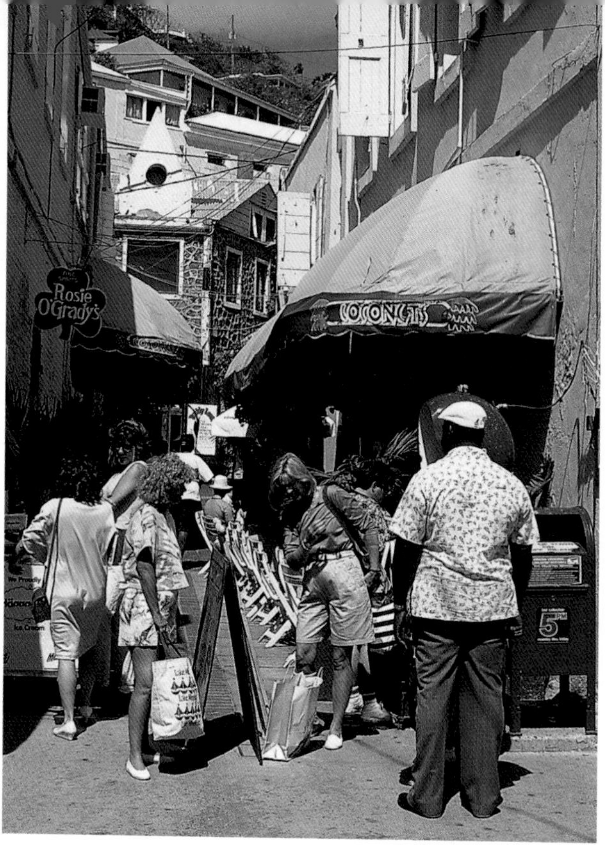

Above left: Walking tall at Carnival time
Above right: Shopping for bargains in the alleys off Main Street, Charlotte Amalie

are boosted daily by thousands of cruise-ship passengers who are shepherded to mountaintop observation points and spectacular Magens Bay (see p. 159). In St. Thomas you can find diving and water sports, deep-sea fishing, and the magnificent Mahogany Run golf course, but the island's chief sport is undoubtedly bargain hunting in Charlotte Amalie.

CHARLOTTE AMALIE

Radiating from its charming Danish colonial origins, Charlotte Amalie skirts the outline of St. Thomas Harbor, and clambers up into the amphitheater of surrounding hills. In the bay, giant cruise ships (up to ten at a time on a busy day) lie at anchor and disgorge their human cargo onto the waterfront, where the merchants of Main Street await, their mercantile instincts as finely honed as the 18th-century traders whose warehouses they now occupy.

Make an exploratory foray down **Dronningens Gade** (as Main Street is also known) and its warren of narrow alleys to discover a commercial kaleidoscope every bit as dazzling and cutthroat as it must have been 250 years ago, although the barrels and bales have been replaced with designer labels and electronic gadgets.

Main Street is at the heart of Charlotte Amalie's historic district, which stretches from Rothschild Francis Market Square in the west to Emancipation Park in the east. The park is a good place to begin a walkabout, with a visit to **Fort Christian.** The squat blood-red fort dates from 1672, and it now

Virgin Islands Museum
✉ Waterfront Hwy. Fort Christian
☎ 340/776-4566
🕒 Closed weekends

houses the **Virgin Islands Museum** and a local art gallery laid out in the former jail cells. Alongside detailed historical displays, small exhibits cover bush medicine and colonial furnishings, and pride of place in the central courtyard goes to an antique, animal-powered cane crusher. From the battlements, there is a view down to the 19th-century **Danish barracks building** near the waterfront, which has been spruced up with a lick of peppermint green paint to accommodate the Virgin Islands Legislature.

Above the park is **Government Hill,** crisscrossed with a grid of narrow streets and flights of steps lined with attractive private homes, public buildings, and monumental churches. Near **Government House,** a white neoclassic edifice on Kongens Gade, the **99 Steps** (actually 103) strike up toward **Blackbeard's Castle,** a stone watchtower with tremendous views. The bricks used to construct the steps and many local buildings were brought to the Caribbean as ballast carried from Denmark in the holds of ships.

Danish banker and merchant Hans Haagensen built a family home up here on the hill in the 1830s. Set in leafy terraced gardens, **Haagensen House** has been carefully restored and furnished with period art and antiques as one of a pair of 19-century townhouse museums together with neighboring **Villa Notman** *(Tel 340/774-9605, closed Sun. and afternoons, $$)*. On Crystal Gade near the junction with Raadets Gade, is **St. Thomas Synagogue,** flanked by palms and dating from 1833.

Fort Christian's clock tower was added in 1874 when the building became a police station, courthouse, and jail.

Atlantis Submarine
www.atlantisadventures.com
Havensight Mall, Suite L
340/776-5650
$$$$$

Skyride to Paradise Point
www.stthomasskyride.com
Long Bay Rd.
Info 340-777-4540, reservations 340/774-9809
$$$$

St. Thomas's first Jewish congregation were refugees from Dutch Sint Eustatius, exiled for their involvement in the arms trade during the American Revolution. Back down on the main drag, the Jewish Pissarro family once ran a trading store at **Dronningens Gade 14,** where Impressionist artist Camille Pissarro (1830–1903) was born. Four blocks west, between Store Strade and Strand Gade, is the **covered market,** which comes alive on Saturdays when farmers from the West End venture into town to sell their homegrown fruit and vegetables.

Around the harbor in the eastern suburbs, and fronted by Havensight Mall, is the **West Indian Company Dock,** Charlotte Amalie's main cruise-ship berth. It is also the shore base for the **Atlantis Submarine** *(Reservations advised).* The perfect solution to reef diving without getting wet, the tours begin with a harbor cruise; then passengers are ferried out to Buck Island and transferred to a miniature submarine for the reef tour. The one-hour narrated dives reach a depth of 90 feet (27 m) below the surface, where the reef is a mass of spectacular hard and soft corals regularly visited by colorful blue chromis, rock beauties, angelfish, moray eels, and sea turtles among others.

Across the street from Havensight is the **Skyride to Paradise Point,** which hoists a fleet of glass-enclosed cable cars to an observation deck 700 feet (210 m) above sea level (road access also). The deck provides splendid views of the harbor, sheltered by Hassel Island in the foreground, and Water Island beyond. On a clear day it is possible to spot St. Croix on the far horizon. There is also a short nature trail, a restaurant, shops, and a bar for sunset cocktails when the city turns into a blaze of twinkling lights encircling the bay. ■

ISLAND-HOPPING BY FERRY

Inter-island ferries are a great (and inexpensive) way to explore the Virgin Islands. Frequent daily services link St. Thomas and St. John. The crossing takes just 20 minutes from Red Hook on the east end of St. Thomas to Cruz Bay, St. John; or 45 minutes from Charlotte Amalie. There are also ferry services from St. Thomas and St. John to the British Virgin Islands of Tortola (daily), Virgin Gorda (several times weekly), and Jost van Dyke (weekends). Proof of citizenship is needed for travel between the USVI and BVI. ■

Sports & activities

Day sails: Boat trips with lunch, swimming, and snorkeling from Nightwind Charters *(Tel 340/775-4110)*; Heavenly Days Catamaran *(Tel 340/755-1800)*; Ike Witt Charters *(Tel 340/771-2600)*; or aboard the *Winifred,* maximum six guests *(Tel 340/775-7898)*. For a day trip to the BVI, contact *Stormy Petrel,* maximum 12 guests *(Tel 340/775-7990).*

Diving & snorkeling: Chris Sawyer Diving Center *(Red Hook, tel 340/777-7804 or 877/929-3483)*; Coki Beach Dive Centre *(Tel 340/775-4220 or 800/474-COKI)*; Underwater Safaris *(Havensight Mall, tel 340/774-3737, www.diveusvi.com).*

Golf: Mahogany Run Golf Course *(Mahogany Run Rd., North Coast, tel 340/777-6006, information and tee-times (48 hours in advance) or tel 800/253-7103, fax 340/ 777-6095, www.mahoganyrungolf.com).*

Kayaking: Nature tours with snorkeling in the Mangrove Lagoon marine sanctuary from Virgin Islands Ecotours *(Holmberg's Marina, East End, tel 340/779-2155, www.viecotours.com).*

Powerboat rentals: Nauti Nymph *(Red Hook, tel 340/775-5066)*; See and Ski *(American Yacht Harbor, tel 340/775-6265).*

Sportfishing: Several outfits operate out of the American Yacht Harbor at Red Hook, including Marlin Prince *(Tel 340/693-5929)* and Reel Therapy Sportfishing *(Tel 340/715-0472).* ■

Around St. Thomas

CORAL WORLD OCEAN PARK

An 80,000-gallon (363,000-liter) reef tank display, aquariums showcasing rare marine plant and animal life, a predator tank, and stingray pool are among the attractions at this popular marine park on St. Thomas's northeast coast. But the real showstopper lies beneath the waves, where the picture windows of the underwater observatory resemble a darkened marine theater in the round opening onto a 360-degree panorama of the ocean bed. A touch pool and the rescued baby turtle exhibit are particular hits with kids, and there are daily talks by marine experts as well as feeding sessions at the baby shark pool. The park is adjacent to busy Coki Beach, which has a dive and snorkel center.
154 C2 Coki Point 340/775-1555, www.coralworldvi.com $$$$$

ESTATE ST. PETER GREAT HOUSE & BOTANICAL GARDENS

Draped across the hillside 1,000 feet (305 m) above Magens Bay, these 5-acre (2-ha) botanical gardens have been laid out in the grounds of a former 19th-century plantation. You can tour the gardens on wooden boardwalk trails shaded by banana plants and breadfruit trees, tall stands of lobster-claw heliconias, and brilliant tropical gingers. Along the way, enjoy bird aviaries, fish ponds, waterfalls and more than 20 varieties of orchids. The great house has been reconstructed and furnished in contemporary style. A gallery sells Caribbean artworks, and there is a riveting series of photographs taken in the wake of Hugo, which destroyed the original great house in 1989. Viewing decks are equipped with orientation boards that point out local landmarks and more than 20 neighboring Virgin Islands.
154 B2 St. Peter Mountain Rd. 340/774-4999, www.greathouse-mountaintop.com $$$

MAGENS BAY

Over the mountain ridge from Charlotte Amalie, St. Thomas's most famous beach lines the base of a huge rectangular bay carved out of the north coast. Magens Bay's idyllic mile-long (1. 5 km) stretch of powder-soft sand fringed with palm trees is a prime contender in any list of the world's top beaches. It certainly gets busy, but on weekdays there is usually plenty of room for everyone. Several beach bars and restaurants cater to the crowds.
154 C2 Magens Road $

MOUNTAIN TOP

The top of St. Peter Mountain is the setting for yet more superb views over Magens Bay and off to St. John and the British Virgin Islands. This spot also claims to be the birthplace of the banana daiquiri; alcoholic and non-alcoholic versions are available at the viewing deck bar.
154 B2 Off Crown Mountain Rd. 340/774-2400 ■

The Coral World underwater observatory juts out from Coki Point above the sandy strip of Coki Beach.

Cruising

The Caribbean is the ultimate cruising destination, an idyllic combination of sun, sea, and varied landscapes, where it is possible to wake up every morning with a new island group on the bow and a different port at the foot of the gangplank. Christopher Columbus and Sir Francis Drake may have pioneered Caribbean cruising half a millennium ago, but the modern dictionary definition of cruising, "to make a trip by sea for pleasure, calling at a number of ports," reveals a leisure concept wildly at odds with those early seagoing missions of exploration and plunder.

More cruise ships ply Caribbean waters than any other place on Earth. There are more than a hundred vessels to choose from, and they vary considerably in terms of size, atmosphere, facilities, and itineraries. For first-time cruise passengers, selecting the perfect cruise can be a bewildering experience, but there are ways of narrowing down the field.

One of the first rules of cruising is that size does matter. Although no indicator of price or the vessel's position on the luxury scale, size does influence the type of cruising experience available. For instance, smaller ships catering for as many as 500 passengers can visit offbeat destinations inaccessible to larger vessels; they tend to allow their guests additional time ashore and to enjoy a more relaxed, intimate atmosphere. On the downside (although several smaller vessels offer a positively sybaritic degree of luxury), space is necessarily restricted.

The most common Caribbean cruising options are the medium (500- to 1,000-passenger) and large (1,000- to 2,000-passenger) cruise ships. They fall into three main categories: luxury-class vessels appealing to a sophisticated clientele with top-notch facilities from water sports and spa treatments to gourmet cuisine and spacious accommodations; premium class cruise ships offering good food, a high standard of service, and a broad spectrum of organized activities and entertainment; and standard class vessels aimed at a more casual crowd with fewer facilities, simpler menus, and limited cabin space. In a class of their own are the mega-ships, giant floating resorts with 2,000-plus passengers and a lifestyle that revolves around a range of shipboard activities and a wild nightlife, which rather precludes much in the way of sight-seeing.

The onboard activities package is a major consideration when planning a week or two afloat. Most medium to large cruise ships offer a day-long program of activities, which might include exercise classes, shore excursions, quiz competitions, cocktails to the accompaniment of a steel band, and an elaborate Las Vegas-style evening show, followed by a session in the discothèque. Mainstream vessels are all equipped with movie theaters, casinos, game rooms, and exercise facilities (worth remembering because the average cruise passenger gains around 4 pounds/2.2 kg during a week-long cruise). All these features and up to five meals a day (excluding alcoholic drinks) are included in the price of the cruise. Families should also check that the cruise line offers adequate children's facilities. Make sure that the supervised daytime activities programs cover the right age group(s), and ask about the availability of babysitters, kids' meals, cribs, high chairs, and other vital equipment.

The most popular cruise duration on the Caribbean run (excluding shorter trips to the Bahamas) is between one and two weeks. The majority of round-trip itineraries originate from the South Florida ports of Miami and Port Everglades in Fort Lauderdale, although some cruise lines operate out of San Juan, Puerto Rico. Most cruise itineraries feature a different port every day with two days at sea (sometimes three days on longer trips). High season (and high prices) is mid-December through April, but cruises are possible throughout the year and ships stay well clear of the Hurricane Belt from August through October. Cruises are rarely booked directly with the cruise line. For the best deals and expert advice consult a travel agent with membership of the Cruise Lines International Association (CLIA) or the National Association of Cruise-Oriented Agencies (NACOA). A wealth of cruising information is found on the Internet, too. ■

Above: Cruise passengers arrive at Heritage Quay in St. John's, the capital of Antigua.
Right: Gourmet buffets are a major attraction on board.
Below: Sailing into Great Bay and the famous duty-free port of Philipsburg, Sint Maarten.

St. John

St. John
151 C3
Visitor information
P.O. Box 200, Cruz Bay, USVI 00831
340/776-6450

A 2-MILE (3-KM) FERRY RIDE ACROSS THE PILLSBURY sound from St. Thomas, St. John is the unspoiled gem of the USVI. Two-thirds of it is Virgin Islands National Park, created with the help of Laurance Rockefeller, who donated the first chunk of land in 1956 (a cunning move to prevent anybody else building near his Caneel Bay resort), and much of the remaining third is untouched. Dense woodlands carpet the rolling hills of the interior, while sandy bays punctuate the irregular coastline.

Left: Beach vendor looking through window, surrounded by wares
Far left: St. John's forested hinterland slopes down to the north shore and a clutch of dazzling white sand beaches nestled in quiet coves.

During the colonial era, St. John was planted with sugarcane and cotton. One of the Caribbean's most successful slave revolts was staged on the island in 1733, when slaves armed with cane machetes massacred settlers and managed to hold the Danish garrison for nine months. The uprising was eventually quashed with the help of French troops, and the last rebels are believed to have leapt to their deaths at Mary's Point on the north coast. Things have been very quiet since, and the population of 5,000 mainly consists of incomers from down island and American expatriates lured by the serenity.

CRUZ BAY & AROUND THE ISLAND

Most visitors arrive in St. John at the **Cruz Bay ferry dock,** to be greeted by a coterie of taxi drivers and an engaging huddle of shops and restaurants set back from the waterfront. Over the hill south of town is **Great Cruz Bay,** the island's busiest resort area. But most set off on their round-island tour by taking the North Shore Road out of Cruz Bay, past the attractive Mongoose Junction mall, housed in a local plantation-style stone complex, and the informative **Virgin Islands National Park visitor center** *(Tel 340/776-6201, www.nps.gov/viis).*

St. John's best beaches rim the north coast from Honeymoon Beach on Caneel Bay, through Hawksnest Bay, famously gorgeous **Trunk Bay,** and Cinnamon Bay (backed by a campground) to Maho Bay. Beyond Maho, a side road heads off to the **Annaberg Plantation** (*Tel 340/776-6201*), where a self-guided

Sports & activities

Day sails: Fantasy *(Tel 340/775-5652)*; Hurricane Alley *(Tel 340/776-6256)*; Sail Safaris *(Tel 340/626-8181 or 866/820-6906)*.

Diving & snorkeling: See box opposite.

Horseback riding: Carolina Corral *(Coral Bay, tel 340/693-5778, www.st-john.com/trailrides)*.

Kayaking: Rentals and guided sea kayaking trips from Arawak Expeditions *(Tel 340/693-8312, www.arawakexp.com)*.

Water sports: Cruz Bay Watersports *(Tel 340/776-6234)* offers snorkeling, and wreck and reef dive trips with equipment rental, PADI and NAUI dive tuition, and powerboat outings to the BVI. ■

tour leads around the foundations of slave cabins, the old windmill, boiling room, and storehouse.

The North Shore Road then meets Centerline Road, which returns to Cruz Bay along a twisting mountain route with sensational views across to Drake's Passage. Its eastern arm continues to the quiet village of Coral Bay, St. John's original settlement.

Straddling the island around three 1,000-foot (300-m) peaks, culminating in Bordeaux Mountain (1,277 feet/389 m), the land-based portion of the **Virgin Islands National Park** is a subtropical tangle of forest greenery that has swallowed up all but the merest traces of the hundred-plus plantation estates that once carpeted the landscape. The visitor center provides a helpful introduction with maps, historical and natural history displays, and an activities program. A relief model graphically illustrates St. John's rugged terrain and details the park's 20-plus trails. These vary from short walks around Cruz Bay to more challenging hikes such as the Reef Bay Trail, which descends to the south coast from Centerline Road.

A smart way to avoid the strenuous return trip on this route is to take the park service guided tour (check schedules). Walkers are bused to the trailhead for the 2.5-mile (4 km) downhill hike through wet and dry forest to the Reef Bay sugar mill ruins. The trail detours to a petroglyph site decorated with rock carvings attributed to Arawak Indians. Take time to swim and snorkel before the boat trip back to Cruz Bay.

The park's 5,650-acre (2,287-ha) **marine preserve** offers excellent snorkeling in the calm, clear waters off the north coast beaches (see below) and the less accessible south coast around Saltpond and Lemeshur Bays. Parrotfish, angelfish, tangs, grunts, rays, snappers, jacks, and tarpon are frequent visitors to the reef areas and shallow sandy bays. One reason for the wealth of marine life is the mangrove nurseries where fish and marine species breed in the safe, nutrient-rich waters of the coastal swamp. The **Francis Bay Trail,** just around from Maho Bay, has a boardwalk section leading out into the mangroves where herons, Western Indian whistling ducks, pintails, teals, sandpipers, and other waterbirds come to feed. ■

Constructed on a hilltop to catch the breeze, the now ruined Annaberg Windmill dates from the late 18th century.

Beneath the waves

Snorkeling is something of a specialty in St. John; Trunk Bay even offers a 225-yard (205-m) self-guided trail with underwater signs indicating reef features. Snuba *(Tel 340/693-8063, www.visnuba.com)* is a cross between snorkeling and diving with air pumped from the surface. Slightly off the beaten track, there is snorkeling at Hawksnest Bay and Watermelon Cay in Leinster Bay. The best diving is farther offshore and in the BVIs. Contact Low Key Watersports *(Tel 340/693-8999)* or Cruz Bay Watersports *(Tel 340/776-6234).* ■

A welcome breeze sets the flags flying above the Christiansted waterfront as waves break against the distant reef.

St. Croix

THE LARGEST OF THE USVI AT 84 SQUARE MILES (217 SQ KM), St. Croix lies 40 miles (64 km) to the south of St. Thomas and the main body of the Virgin Islands. A former sugar island with mountains in the west and flat, fertile agricultural plains in the central district, St. Croix takes its history seriously. The St. Croix Heritage Trail, a self-guided driving tour, lists 200 sites of historic and cultural interest along its route. One popular stop is the Cruzan Rum Distillery.

St. Croix
151 E1
Visitor information
P.O. Box 4538, Christiansted
340/773-0495

Columbus made landfall at Salt River Bay on the north shore in 1493. He beat a hasty retreat on encountering the belligerent Carib but claimed the island for Spain and named it Santa Cruz (Holy Cross). Claimed by France in 1650, the island's name was translated to St. Croix, and it stuck when the Danes purchased the island in 1733.

The capital of St. Croix is Christiansted (see p. 167), a delightful little Danish-style town with a miniature fortress and shops tucked into a clutch of 18th- and 19th-century arcaded buildings. The island's main sight-seeing attractions lie off Centerline Road, heading west, although there are lovely drives along the North Shore

Road (Rte. 80) and on Mahogany Road (Rte. 76) through the rain forest.

On the west coast, Frederiksted (see p. 169) is where the cruise ships dock. It is another pretty town, splendidly renovated in 1998 to celebrate the 150th anniversary of the abolition of slavery in the Danish colonies. Denmark was the first nation to abolish the slave trade in 1803, although King Frederik VIII made no move toward emancipation until 1848, when he issued an edict stating that all slaves would be freed in 1859. The slaves on St. Croix and St. John rose up in revolt at the news, and the Danish governor, Peter von Scholten, taking the law into his own hands, declared the slaves free on July 3, 1848, at Fort Frederik.

CHRISTIANSTED

St. Croix's pint-size capital was laid out around a calm, reef-sheltered bay in 1733 and named in honor of the king of Denmark, Christian VI. Overlooking the waterfront in the **Christiansted National Historic Site,** spick-and-span **Fort Christiansvaern** looks like a child's toy carved out of yellow marzipan. It was built between 1738 and 1749, and its battlements are still guarded by neatly blacked cannon, which have never been fired in anger; there are historical displays on the upper level.

Around the small park in front of the fort are the **Old Danish Customs House** dating from 1751; the 19th-century **Scale House,** where ship's cargoes were inspected and weighed; the 1735 **Steeple Building,** a former Lutheran church housing a small museum; and the original **West Indies & Guinea Company Warehouse,** where slave auctions were once held in the courtyard. A short walk west down Company Street stands the 1832 Apothecary

Fort Christiansvaern has been restored to its appearance circa 1830–1840.

Christiansted National Historic Site
Steeple Bldg.
340/773-1460
$

Cruzan rum

The Cruzan Rum Distillery is the largest commercial rum-producer in the Virgin Islands and opens its doors for factory tours during working hours.

Visits to the rebuilt factory include a video presentation followed by a guided tour and explanation of the production process, tastings, and a chance to buy the award-winning finished article *(Rte. 64, off Centerline Rd., tel 340/692-2280, www.cruzanrum.com, closed Sat.–Sun., $$).* ■

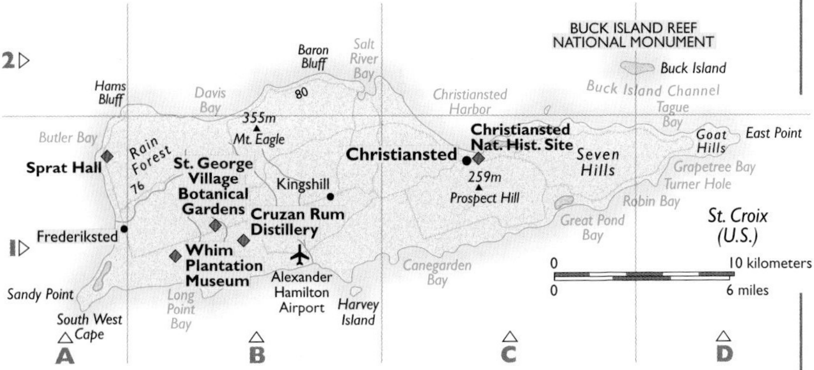

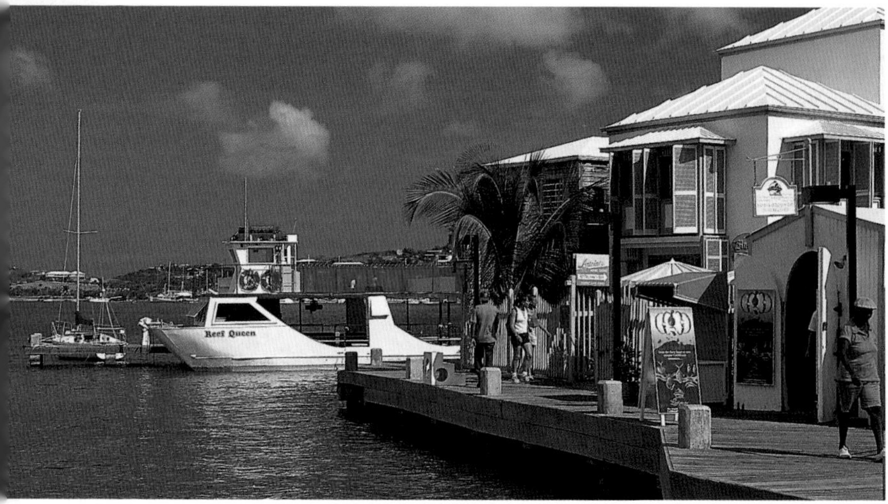

Strolling along the harborside boardwalk at Kings Wharf in downtown Christiansted

Hall that has been restored to display pre-Columbian artifacts discovered on the island. The **St. Croix Archaeology Museum** traces human habitation on St. Croix dating back more that 5,000 years before the arrival of Columbus. Ax heads, pottery, beads, and tools are among the finds.

One block north on King Street is **Government House,** which occupies two fine 18th-century town houses converted into a residence for Peter von Scholten in the 1830s.

Between King Street and the bay is the **Kings Wharf open-air mall**—a pleasant place to shop or find a café table in the sun before taking a stroll up Strand Street, past boutiques and shops squirreled away beneath picturesque, creeper-clad arcades. ■

St. Croix Archaeology Museum
- 6 Company Street
- 340/692-2365
- Open Sat. 10-12

Sports & activities

Day sails: Bilinda Charters *(Tel 340/773-1641)*; Capt. Francis' Diva *(Tel 340/778-4675)*.

Diving & Snorkeling: There is good diving for all skill levels. Anchor Dive Center *(Salt River, tel 340/778-1522 or 800/532-3483, www.anchordivestcroix.com)*; Cane Bay Dive Shop *(Tel 340/773-9913, www.canebayscuba.com)*. For something out of the ordinary, consider Homer's Incredible Night Snorkel Adventure *(Tel 340/774-7606, www.nightsnorkel.com)*.

Golf: Buccaneer Hotel *(18 holes; tel 340/712-2144, www.thebuccaneer.com)*; and the Robert Trent Jones-designed Carambola Golf Club *(Tel 340/778-5638, www.carambolabeach.com)*.

Horseback riding: Paul and Jill's Equestrian Stables *(Sprat Hall, tel 340/772-2880)*.

Sportfishing: Capt. Pete's Louie G *(Tel 340/773-1123)*; Lisa Ann Charters *(Tel 340/773-3712)*.

Tours: Minibuses from St. Croix Safari Tours *(Tel 340/773-6700)*. ■

Murals like these shopping and domestic scenes are a popular Caribbean art form, brightening up homes and public buildings throughout the region.

Around St. Croix

BUCK ISLAND REEF NATIONAL MONUMENT

Located 5 miles (8 km) off Christiansted (about an hour's sail), uninhabited Buck Island is renowned for its excellent reef snorkeling and diving. Here corals grow up to 30 feet (9 m) tall, and the reefs are home to a rich selection marine life. On land there are walking trails, sandy beaches, and picnic facilities.
167 C2 ☎ 340/773-1460, www.nps.gov/buis/ $ $$$$$ (includes transportation from Christiansted)

FREDERIKSTED

A 30-minute drive west of Christiansted, this sleepy small town is startled to life when the winter cruise ships arrive. Bloodred 1752 **Fort Frederik** *(closed weekends)* was named for King Frederik V. Governor von Scholten announced the slave emancipation in the courtyard, and several rooms contain island history and cultural displays. The town's center is worth exploring for its pretty Victorian gingerbread houses and the trim row of arcaded waterfront buildings. North of town, a sandy beach extends beyond the fort to the old Sprat Hall Plantation.
167 A1

ST. GEORGE VILLAGE BOTANICAL GARDEN

This 17-acre (6.8-ha) spread of lawned gardens and colorful plantings is set amid the ruins of a 19th-century sugar plantation built on the site of a pre-Columbian Amerindian settlement. The marked trail is lined with more than 1,500 native and exotic botanical species, and the site has a rain forest section and a cactus garden.
167 B1 ✉ Centerline Rd. ☎ 340/692-2874, www.sgrbg.org Closed Sun.–Mon. $ $$$

WHIM PLANTATION MUSEUM

St. Croix's Danish colonial past is on display at this restored 18th-century great house. The interior is kept remarkably cool by 3-foot-thick (90-cm) stone walls and an air moat. The rooms are furnished with antique mahogany pieces, including a splendid four-poster bed with typical pineapple carvings, the colonial symbol of hospitality. On the grounds are the remains of the old sugar mill.
167 B1 ✉ 52 Estate Whim, Frederiksted ☎ 340/772-0598, www.stcroixlandmarks.com Closed Sun.; also Sat. May–Oct. $ $$$

British Virgin Islands

Known locally as Nature's Little Secrets, these rugged small islands with amoebic outlines are scalloped into sheltered coves and bays. Once a haven for pirates and smugglers, the British Virgin Islands (BVI) now offer an escapist paradise for yachtsmen and a surprising choice of luxurious resorts for vacationers happy to venture off the beaten track and play at Robinson Crusoe with a gold credit card. Part of the charm of the British Virgin Islands, however, is to savor them as the islanders themselves do—island-hopping by ferry, snorkeling, or having a quiet drink in a harborside bar.

Most of the islands and islets of the BVI group, from the verdant heights of Tortola and Virgin Gorda to the rocky jumble of Fallen Jerusalem, are arranged in two irregular lines flanking the 3-mile-wide (5-km) Sir Francis Drake Channel. Only 15 of the 60 or so volcanic outcrops are inhabited, including Anegada, which is the only coral island in the group.

It took some time for the British to show a proper interest in their Virgin Island colonies and clear them of the piratical likes of Blackbeard, Henry Morgan (1635–1688), and Jost van Dyke (who has an island named after him). In the heyday of the 18th-century plantation era, settlers imported African slaves to plant and tend cotton and sugarcane on the challenging terrain, but their efforts were only

Above: From the hilltops to the crystal clear waters, the small British Virgins display their rich lushness.
Right: Tidal pools form around the huge Jurassic boulders of The Baths, Virgin Gorda.

moderately successful, and many planters sailed away, abandoning their slaves before emancipation in the 1830s. In order to survive, the freed slaves turned to small-scale farming. The BVI muddled along as part of the Leeward Islands federation of British colonies until independence. They toyed with the idea of political union with the USVI but opted to become a Crown Colony of Britain.

The BVI remain charmingly sleepy and friendlier than their better developed neighbors. But tourism and the financial services sector are bringing increased prosperity, and a mini-construction boom is under way. ■

Dockside at Soper's Hole attacts diners and boaters.

Tortola

TORTOLA WAS NAMED FOR ITS TURTLE DOVES, WHICH still outnumber the 14,000 inhabitants. It is the largest island in the BVI, measuring just 11 miles (18 km) east to west and 3 miles (5 km) north to south. To cross from the capital Road Town on the south coast to the beaches in the north, you have to tackle the central island ridge, where Mount Sage peaks at 1,708 feet (521 m), the highest point in the Virgin Islands archipelago.

Tortola
- Map: 151 C4

J.R. O'Neal Botanic Gardens
- Map: 173 C2
- Address: Botanic Rd.
- Phone: 284/494-4557
- Hours: Closed Sun.
- Admission: Donation

Most visitors use Tortola as a springboard for yacht charters and visits to the outer islands. However, it is a relaxing place to stay for a few days, soak up the sun, hop aboard a couple of ferries (see box p. 174), and generally unwind.

A handful of streets running parallel to the reclaimed waterfront, Road Town is the administrative and commercial center of the BVI, but it is somewhat short on charm. The harbor is usually a lively spot, with ferries coming and going, and yachts checking in and out of the busy marinas. Occasionally a moderate-size cruise ship drops off passengers for an island tour and a bit of shopping.

There is no need to allocate much sight-seeing time to the town itself, although one very pleasant stop is the small **J.R. O'Neal Botanic Gardens.** A short walk

from the town center, the lush palm-tree-shaded oasis of indigenous and exotic tropical plants is arranged around a water lily pond, orchid house, and pergola walk.

Another possible detour is the **V.I. Historical Society Folk Museum,** housed in a traditional West Indian house on Main Street *(hours vary)*. Among the exhibits are Amerindian relics and articles salvaged from the wreck of R.M.S. *Rhone* (see Salt Island p. 176).

AROUND THE ISLAND

Tortola's hotels and best beaches are strung out along the north coast. Starting in the west, secluded **Smuggler's Cove** is recommended for snorkeling and reached by a bumpy unpaved road from Long Bay. **Long Bay** itself is a mile-long (1.6-km) strip of blonde sand backed by palm trees and a hotel. **Apple Bay** is the surfers' favorite and home to Bomba's Surfside Shack, a great beach bar notorious for its full-moon parties. **Carrot Bay** has a couple of bars and a waterfront restaurant. Curving **Cane Garden Bay** is the island's best equipped beach, with windsurfing, waterskiing, and boating opportunities as well as beach restaurants and a few hotels. **Brewers Bay** is a good spot for snorkeling when the sea is quiet; the sandy beaches at **Trunk Bay, Josiah's Bay, Lambert Long Bay,** and **Elizabeth Beach** are good for

Golden trumpet flowers can be seen all over the island.

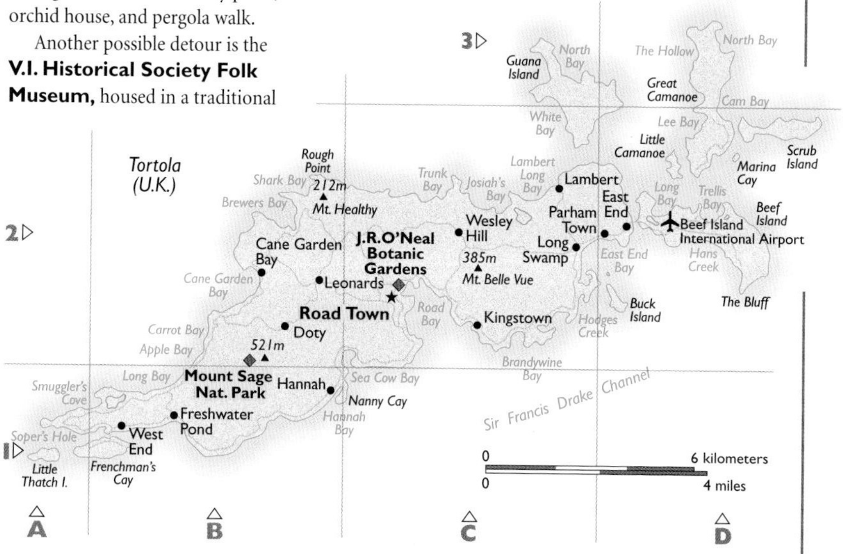

Sage Mountain National Park
www.bvinationalparkstrust.org
173 B2
Ridge Rd.

swimming. Attached to Tortola by a causeway is **Beef Island,** with fine beaches at **Trellis Bay** and **Long Bay.**

In the center of Tortola is the 92-acre (37 ha) **Sage Mountain National Park,** which was established in 1964 to protect the remnants of the native forest that once covered the whole of Tortola. The park's **Rainforest Trail** features many typical rain forest plants, such as giant elephant ear vines, tree ferns, bromeliads, and philodendrons flourishing beneath an umbrella of 100-foot-high (30-m) bulletwood trees and buttress-trunked ficus. The **Mahogany Forest Trail** leads off the main path up through white cedar, West Indian, and broadleaf mahogany plantations.

Ferries for Jost van Dyke and the U.S. Virgin Islands depart from **Soper's Hole** harbor on Tortola's West End. Across the bay on Frenchman's Cay is the **Soper's Hole marina,** which packs in private yachts and charter boats like sardines. On the dock, clapboard buildings house a few shops and restaurants. ■

Island-hopping by ferry

To see the Sir Francis Drake Channel, take one of the regular inter-island ferries between Tortola and neighboring Virgin Gorda. Contact Smith's Ferry Services *(Tel 284/495-4495)*; or Speedy's *(Tel 284/494-6154)*. Ferries make a number of daily round-trips to Jost van Dyke and St. John (USVI) from Tortola's West End dock; services for St. Thomas (USVI) generally originate in Road Town. Daytrip travel between the BVI and USVI requires proof of citizenship. ■

Balconies and hillsides around the island provide stunning views of neighboring islands.

Other British Virgin Islands

ANEGADA

North of Virgin Gorda—and accessible via flights from Tortola—lies Anegada, the second largest of the BVI at 15 square miles (39 sq km). Its name means "the drowned one" in Spanish, as the island barely reaches 28 feet (8.5 m) above sea level. Anegada's main attraction is its offshore **coral reefs—**which have snared literally hundreds of ships over the centuries—with their superb diving. The island has one small hotel with its own dive facilities, a couple of guesthouses, and campgrounds.
151 E5

COOPER ISLAND

Cooper Island's dinghy dock and bar-restaurant attract yachtsmen sailing the Sir Francis Drake Channel. Those who linger will find a good beach, dive shop, and a few cottages for rent around Manchioneel Bay.
151 D3

JOST VAN DYKE

A 4-mile (6.5 km) ferry hop across from Tortola's West End is the terminally laid-back

The ghostly relics of a copper mine tell of the mining history of these islands.

island of Jost van Dyke, which is a popular day trip for beach lovers. The details are sketchy, but local legend claims van Dyke was a 17th-century Dutch pirate, one of many who rampaged around the islands at the time. A notable historic figure who is definitely connected with the island is William Thornton (1759–1828), a physician and champion of the abolitionist movement, who won the competition to design the Capitol Building in Washington, D.C. He was born here; little appears to have happened since.

Jost van Dyke boasts several magnificent white sand beaches, although few visitors bother to venture beyond **Great Harbour,** where the ferry docks. Here there is a simple inn, a water-sports concession, and a couple of beach bars, which also serve West Indian food and snacks. **Foxy's,** at the east end of the beach, is the epicenter of one of the Caribbean's most excessive New Year's parties.
151 C4

NORMAN ISLAND

Uninhabited, save for a handful of goats, Norman Island is reputed to have been the setting for Robert Louis Stevenson's *Treasure Island.* Snorkeling is good around **The**

Indians (four jagged pinnacles accessible by yacht), and a floating restaurant is popular with the yachting crowd.
151 D3

PETER ISLAND

Just across the Sir Francis Drake Channel from Tortola is Peter Island, occupied by the exclusive **Peter Island Resort.** Even if you are not staying there, you can sample the luxury lifestyle on a day trip from Road Town by ferry.
151 D3

SALT ISLAND

Salt Island's three salt ponds once supplied passing ships with their vital salt rations, and in an appropriate variation of the traditional peppercorn (nominal) rent system, the island still pays an annual tax of one bag of salt to the British monarch. While the minuscule local populace (two at a recent count) still harvest salt in the old-fashioned way, the island is chiefly known for the wreck of R.M.S. *Rhone,* one of the best wreck diving sites in the Caribbean. The British royal mail ship went down with 300 crew during a hurricane in 1867, and it lies in 30–80 feet (9–24 m) of water on the reefs south of the island. Other notable local dive sites are **Blonde Rock** and **Painted Walls** to the west.
151 D3

VIRGIN GORDA

Christopher Columbus is to blame for Virgin Gorda's rather unflattering sobriquet, the "Fat Virgin." From the low and rock-strewn southern end, the island bulges up to a height of 1,359 feet (414 m) at **Virgin Gorda Peak** and is supposed to resemble a pregnant woman lying on her back. The majority of Virgin Gorda's 2,500 inhabitants live in **The Valley** (often marked as **Spanish Town** on maps), a meandering collection of old West Indian houses and more modern concrete villas on the southwest coast. Ferry passengers from Tortola disembark here, and there is also a small airstrip.

To the south of town is the island's chief sight-seeing attraction, **The Baths,** a bizarre jumble of monumental boulders piled along the shore. From the drop-off point (accessible by shared taxis from the dockside), a path leads 350 yards (320 m) downhill to the beach and the boulders. Turn left here and enter the caves for a ten-minute scramble up and down the giant rocks and across slapping, bubbling tidal pools to secluded **Devil's Beach,** which girdles an idyllic snorkeling spot.

Heading north from The Valley, the landscape becomes greener and more hilly. The road passes twin crescents of powdery white sand beach edging **Savannah Bay** on the west coast, and then it climbs toward Virgin Gorda Peak. (Hiking trails are signed from the roadside; the steep climb takes about 45 minutes round trip.) The views from the mountain road are fantastic, stretching down the Sir Francis Drake Channel to the south; and across the North Sound, a spectacular turquoise bay hemmed in by Mosquito and Prickly Pear Islands, with airline tycoon Richard Branson's private Necker Island in the background. When the road divides, the northern spur leads on to **Leverick Bay;** the other ends at **Gun Creek,** where small motorboats shuttle guests out to the Bitter End and Biras Creek resorts.
151 E4 ■

Sports & activities

Day sails: Day trips with lunch and snorkeling from *Patouche II (Tel 284/494-6300, www.patouche.com)* half days also available; *Silmaril (Tel 284/495-9225, www.charteraboat.com/silmaril); Tamarin II (Tel 284/495-9837).*

Diving: Blue Water Divers *(Tortola, tel 284/494-2847, www.bluewaterdiversvi.com);* Dive BVI *(Virgin Gorda, tel 284/495-5513); Sail Caribbean Divers (Tortola, tel 284/495-1675).*

Sportfishing: Pelican Charters *(Tortola, tel 284/496-7386).*

Water sports: Windsurfer rentals and tuition, and kayaks from Boardsailing BVI *(Tortola, tel 284/495-2447, www.windsurfing.vi);* kayaks, dinghies, waterskiing, and parasailing from Leverick Bay Watersports *(Virgin Gorda, tel 284/495-7376, fax 284/495-7014, www.watersportsbvi.com).* ■

The Dutch Caribbean islands are divided into two groups: one amid the northerly Leeward Islands; the other, off the coast of Venezuela. From these strategic bases, Dutch merchants once controlled the rich Caribbean trade.

Netherlands Antilles & Aruba

Colonial-gabled waterfront buildings, Willemstad, Curaçao

Netherlands Antilles & Aruba

MORE THAN 500 MILES (800 KM) SEPARATE THE TWO GROUPS OF ISLANDS that make up the Netherlands Antilles (Dutch Caribbean). To the north are the Dutch territories of Sint Maarten, Sint Eustatius, and Saba, and to the south are the islands of Aruba (autonomous since 1986), Bonaire, and Curaçao (commonly referred to as the ABCs). The northern group is known as the Dutch Windward Islands, which is rather perplexing, as their closest neighbors are the British and former British Leeward Islands.

The confusing terms date from the days of sail, when they described an island's geographical location in relation to its home country's preferred outbound and inbound Caribbean trading routes. The ABCs, lying within plain view (on a clear day) of South America, are the Dutch Leewards. From the early days of European exploration and settlement in the Caribbean, the Dutch were involved as brokers and traders. The extensive fleets of the Dutch West India Company looted the Spanish New World armadas with as much enthusiasm as the next man-of-war, and the emerging French and British colonies depended on Dutch ships for supplies and exports. Although the Dutch are credited with introducing the sugar industry to the region, they didn't choose their possessions with an eye to sugar growing but as trading posts. Hence, they took control of arid, mountainous Sint Maarten, two tiny volcanic blips known as Sint Eustatius (shortened to Statia in local parlance) and Saba, and the ABCs, three low, wind-blasted, cactus-strewn islets close to South America and the Dutch colonies in Brazil. Before long the calculated gamble paid off, and the islands of Sint Eustatius and Curaçao boasted two of the richest mercantile ports during the 17th and 18th centuries.

Like other Caribbean islands, the Netherlands Antilles changed hands on several occasions. The bulging warehouses of Sint Eustatius were ransacked almost two dozen times. In an unusually pragmatic arrangement the island of Sint Maarten/St.-Martin was divided between Dutch and French colonists in 1648. Despite frequent incursions by both sides and the occasional pesky British intervention, Dutch Sint Maarten and French St.-Martin continue to occupy the 37-square-mile (96 sq km) island, the smallest in the world shared by two sovereign states.

The Dutch secured the six Netherlands Antilles islands under the Treaty of Paris in 1816, but by then the sugar boom was over and by the mid-19th century the Caribbean trade had dried up. The discovery of oil in South America brought renewed prosperity to the ABCs in the 1920s, when North American and European oil companies built vast refineries on Aruba and Curaçao. The capital of Curaçao, Willemstad, became the administrative capital of the Netherlands Antilles and seat of the Staten (parliament), which was granted autonomy within the Kingdom of the Netherlands in 1954.

The collapse of the local oil industry in the mid-1980s was a time of major upheaval for the ABCs and forced the islands to rely on tourism. Aruba's festering resentment at

Curaçao's domination in the Staten hardened into demands for independence, and the island was granted autonomy in 1986. Although Aruba is no longer one of the Netherlands Antilles, it remains within the Kingdom of the Netherlands.

Aruba is now the tourism leader in the Dutch Leewards. Its hotel-lined shores, casinos, and busy cruise-ship terminal are the envy of the Curaçaoans, whose tourist industry is taking longer to develop. Quiet Bonaire has built up a reputation as one of the world's top diving destinations. Meanwhile, 500 miles (800 km) to the north, tourism is also the mainstay of the Dutch Windward Islands. Sint Maarten flourishes as a duty-free enclave in the old Dutch West India Company tradition. Sint Eustatius and Saba maintain a more low-key approach. With few beaches, their rustic charm endears them to visitors in search of peace and quiet. Although Dutch street names abound and the official currency of the Netherlands Antilles is the Netherlands Antilles guilder (Aruba has its own Aruban florin), English is the most widely spoken language in the Dutch Windwards. In the Dutch Leewards you'll hear Papiamento (see p. 201), a linguistic curiosity derived from Dutch, Spanish, French, Portuguese, African, and English tongues in the 17th century. Papiamento is unintelligible to all but the islanders. ■

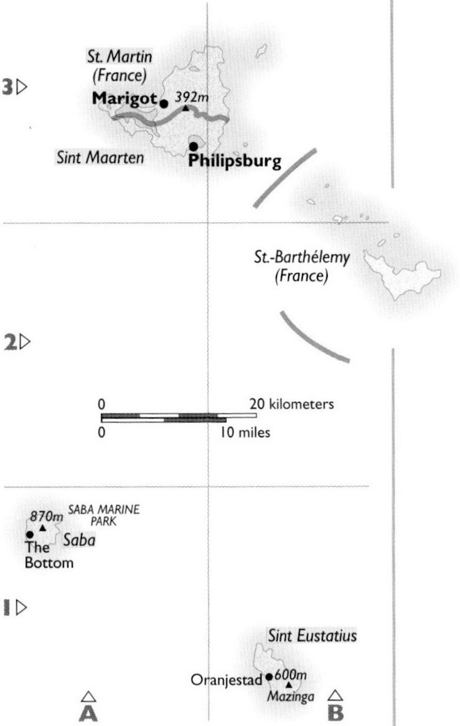

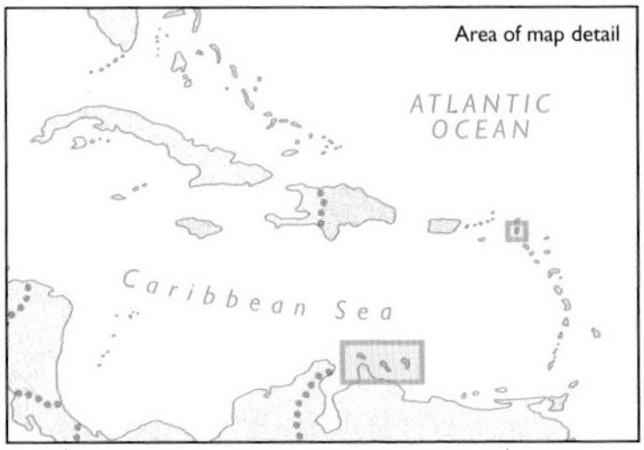

Sint Maarten/St.-Martin

SINT MAARTEN/ST.-MARTIN, ONE OF THE SMALLER ISLANDS in the region at just 37 square miles (96 sq km), celebrated 350 years of dual nationality in 1998. The French occupy the slightly larger northern portion. Although there are no border controls between the two sides of the island, local people are proud of their separate identities. This is particularly noticeable in French St.-Martin, which cultivates a distinctive Gallic air.

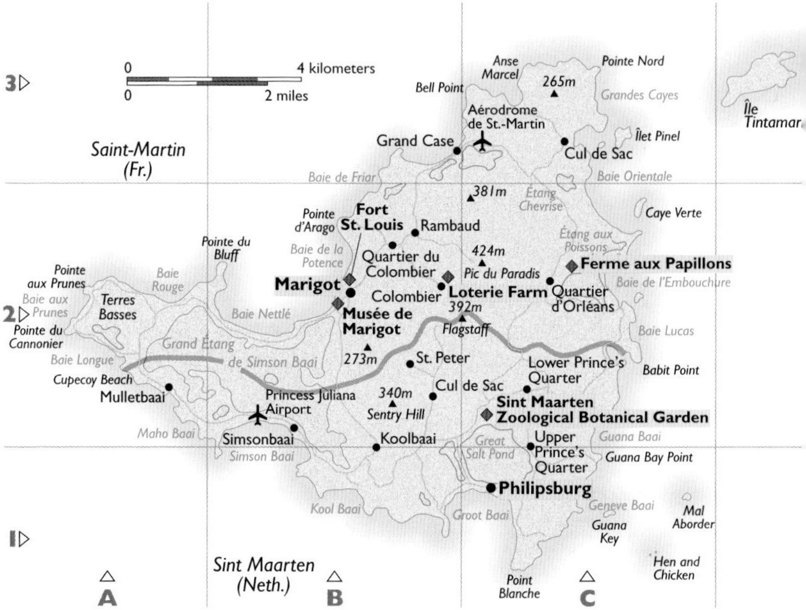

Philipsburg
180 C1
Visitor information
Wathey Sq.
599/542-2337

Sint Maarten Park
180 C2
Arch Rd.
Madame Estate
599/543-2030
$$

According to local legend, the division of the island was settled by a Frenchman and a Dutchman who set out to walk around the island in opposite directions, the former armed with a bottle of brandy, the latter with a bottle of gin. The Frenchman, refreshed by brandy, fared better and when the dividing line was drawn up between the point of their departure and the point where they met up, the French had secured a territory of 21 square miles (54 sq km), the Dutch only 16 square miles (41 sq km).

In spite of its diminutive proportions, Sint Maarten/St.-Martin attracts more than a million visitors a year. The Dutch capital of Philipsburg is the major gateway. This top Caribbean cruise-ship destination and duty-free port is well stocked with shopping bargains. The island is also famed for its beautiful beaches, which encircle the steep, scrub-covered hinterland. Most of the development is on the west coast between Philipsburg and the French capital, Marigot (St.-Martin), where hotels and time-share apartments jostle for space around the Simson Baai lagoon. You can travel between the two island capitals on minibuses, which depart regularly from early morning until late evening.

Modern gingerbread-style decoration featuring pineapple motifs

PHILIPSBURG

Squeezed onto a narrow sandbar between Grand Bay and the landlocked expanses of Great Salt Pond, Philipsburg unfurls along four long, parallel streets linked by alleys known as *steeges.* The heart of town is **de Ruyterplein,** or Wathey Square, where day-trippers arrive by boat from the cruise ships anchored in the bay. At the top of the square is the restored 19th-century **courthouse,** which has a carved pineapple topknot. To either side of the courthouse, bustling Front Street stretches off in a rich seam of duty-free shops, boutiques, and galleries. Follow the narrow steege down the right-hand side of the courthouse to a street market offering bargains on T-shirts, Haitian carvings, and beachwear.

A ten-minute walk east on Front Street will bring you to the **Guavaberry Factory Shop,** housed in a luridly painted gingerbread cottage on the sidewalk, dating from the 1830s. You can sample locally produced guavaberry liqueur (made from the fruit of *Eugenia floribunda,* not guavas).

A little farther up on the right, on an unnamed steege, is the **Sint Maarten Museum** *(7 Front St., tel 599/542-4917, closed Sat. p.m.-Sun.).* Laid out on the second floor, the tiny museum is a mine of local information. Geological displays include a relief map illustrating how the island was once linked to neighboring St. Barthélémy (St. Barts) and Anguilla. Check out the colonial artifacts, old musket balls, and other relics salvaged from the 1801 wreck of the frigate H.M.S. *Proselyte,* as well as a nostalgic collection of antique ice-cream makers, flatirons, and century-old photographs. More recent history is documented in the video of Hurricane Luis, which tore through the island on September 4, 1995.

Beyond the museum the steege ends at the sandy bayfront, a short walk from **Bobby's Marina,** with its pair of popular restaurants, daily ferries to Marigot, and boat trips to the islands of St. Barts and Saba. Minibuses depart for the French capital of Marigot from Back Street (one block behind Front Street).

AROUND SINT MAARTEN

The only sight-seeing attraction on the Dutch side is the **Sint Maarten Park,** a family-friendly zoological garden on the far side of Great Salt Pond. Caribbean birds are displayed in walk-through aviaries, and there's a small but interesting selection of South American reptiles and mammals such as capybaras (the world's largest living rodents), as well as a bat cave that's popular with children.

Beyond Philipsburg, Sint Maarten's chief lure is the beach. On the south side is **Simson Baai Beach,** which has good swimming and windsurfing, although it does lie in the flight path for Princess Juliana Airport. Head northwest along the coast for **Mulletbaai,** a

Rum and spices also flavor the local guavaberry liqueur.

Squashlike christophene, yams, eddoes, and plantains are staples of the Caribbean diet.

Marigot
180 B2
Visitor information
Marigot Pier
0590/87 57 21

tourist favorite with water sports concessions. For something quieter, try **Cupecoy Beach,** which is backed by low cliffs; nude bathing is permitted at the northern end.

MARIGOT

The appealing and unmistakably French capital of St.-Martin appears to have been plucked straight from the Côte d'Azur and grafted onto a Caribbean island. This is café-and-croissant country, where the sidewalk terraces blossom with bright umbrellas. The town center is laid out between the twin poles of the waterfront and the **Marina Port La Royale.** A craft market lines the waterfront, and the old warehouses along the boulevard de France have been converted into a string of restaurants and cafés.

The ruins of 18th-century **Fort St. Louis** survey the scene from the heights above the harbor, where the frequent daily ferry service to Anguilla and boat trips to St. Barts depart from the pier *(for information on services to St. Barts, contact* Voyager, *tel 0590/87 10 68).*

A grid of shopping streets leads back to rue de Hollande and the minibus pick-up/drop-off points for Philipsburg and Grand Case. To the west are the yacht-filled slips of the marina, edged by a collection of cafés and boutiques selling souvenirs and French fashions.

Currently closed and being relocated, the **Musée de Marigot** is well worth seeking out for its Amerindian section. This informative introduction to pre-Columbian culture is illustrated with artifacts including tools and shell ornaments.

AROUND ST.-MARTIN

The French side offers a further range of fine beaches (and topless bathing), starting with the alluring mile-long (1.6-km) expanse of **Baie Longue** on the southern tip of the Simson Baai lagoon peninsula. Around the corner is **Baie aux Prunes,** popular with surfers and snorkelers; **Baie Rouge,** where beachgoers can rent sun loungers and umbrellas or swim around the point at the eastern end to a secluded cove; and hotel-lined **Baie Nettlé,** which is good for water sports.

North of Marigot is **Grand Case,** its one pretty, sandy street lined with some of the island's best restaurants. Boats bob at anchor farther east in the well-protected harbor fronting **Anse Marcel,** which has safe swimming for children and water sports concessions. Off the east coast are glorious bayside beaches on the **Îlet Pinel,** accessible by ferry from Cul de Sac, and undeveloped **Île Tintamarre.** On the mainland is **Baie Orientale,** nicknamed "Le St.-Tropez des Antilles Françaises" for its sophisticated restaurants and shops.

Located in the lee of **Pic du Paradis**—at 1,390 feet (424 m) the island's highest peak—**Loterie Farm** is a secluded private forest reserve. Old mountainside slave trails have been restored for hikers; there's a zip wire; and a great little café for refueling afterward.

Another detour leads to the **Ferme des Papillons** (Butterfly Farm) at Baie de l'Embouchure. Hundreds of exotic butterflies flutter about the gardens, miniature waterfalls, and koi ponds inside a huge climate-controlled sphere, and tours provide an entertaining blend of butterfly fact and trivia. ■

Loterie Farm
180 B2
Colombier
0590/87 86 16
$$

Ferme des Papillons
180 C2
www.thebutterflyfarm.com
Rte. du Galion
0590/87 31 21
$$$

Sports & activities

Bicycling: Mountain bike rentals and guided tours from Tri Sports *(Simson Baai, Sint Maarten, tel 599/545-4384, www.trisportsxm.com,* and Authentic French Tours *(Marigot, St. Martin, tel 0590/87 05 11, e-mail froglegs@wanadoo.fr).*

Diving & snorkeling: Trips to dive sites, equipment rental, and instruction are available through Dive Safaris *(Simson Baai Beach, Sint Maarten, tel 599/545-2401, www.divestmaarten.com)* and Scuba-Fun *(Anse Marcel, St.-Martin, tel 0590/87 36 13, e-mail contact@scubafun.com, www.scubafun.com).*

Golf: The only 18-hole course is at the Mullet Bay Resort *(Sint Maarten, tel 599/545-2801).*

Horseback riding: Nature trails and beach rides from Caïd & Isa *(Anse Marcel, St.-Martin, tel 0590/87 45 70)* and Bayside Riding Club *(Rte. du Galion, St.-Martin, tel 0590/87 36 64).*

Kayaking: Kayak rental and tours from Tri Sports *(Simson Baai, Sint Maarten, tel 599/545-4384).* ■

Yachts gather in the inner harbor at Anse Marcel.

Sint Eustatius

Sint Eustatius
179 B1

Simon Doncker Museum
Wilhelminaweg, Oranjestad
599/318-2288
Closed Sat. p.m. and Sun. p.m.
$$

A SLEEPY CARIBBEAN BACKWATER SOME 35 MILES (56 KM) south of Sint Maarten, Sint Eustatius is the undeveloped Rip van Winkle of the Dutch Windwards, dozing quietly in the lee of its imposing volcanic cone, the Quill. Better known as Statia (pronounced STAY-sha), the island attracts a handful of curious visitors and a motley crew of American and European expatriates who revel in the absence of chic resorts, shopping malls, discos, and other manifestations of mass tourism.

There are no decent beaches on Sint Eustatius, but therein lies the island's quirky charm. Instead, Statia's glittering past looms from the history books out of all proportion to its modest physical dimensions. The island is just 2 miles (3 km) wide and 5 miles (8 km) long from its hilly northern tip through the low central plain to the southern slopes of the Quill. The 1,600 islanders live in the capital, Oranjestad, on the central west coast.

The Dutch West India Company set up shop in Oranjestad in 1636 and developed the port into such a phenomenally successful trading center and slave market that Statia was nicknamed the Golden Rock. Merchant vessels flying every conceivable national flag crowded the harbor, and as business expanded, land was reclaimed to build additional warehouses. On November 16, 1776, the cannon of Fort Oranje fired an 11-gun salute in reply to the merchant ship *Andrew Doria,* an American colonial brig flying the Stars and Stripes, and unwittingly Holland became the first nation to recognize the United States of America. This act earned the tiny island the sobriquet "America's Childhood Friend." In 1781, in retaliation, a British naval expedition under Adm. George Brydges Rodney (1718–1792) descended on Statia, taking possession of all the ships and goods in the port.

Statia never recovered, and her beachless shores have hampered the tourist industry. Today, the island is quietly developing a reputation as the new Saba for attracting divers in search of pristine dive sites. With good walks around the Quill (Mount Mazinga) and incredibly friendly local people, the island makes an interesting offbeat escape for visitors with a no-frills, no-problem attitude.

ORANJESTAD

A small cliff divides the villagey island capital into two parts. Hurricanes and Admiral Rodney's handiwork have all but destroyed the Lower Town around the harbor, so everybody lives in the **Upper Town,** perched on the clifftop guarded by 17th-century **Fort Oranje.** The Sint Eustatius Historical Foundation's **Simon Doncker Museum** is housed in a restored 18th-century brick home occupied by Rodney during his stay. Here pre-Columbian artifacts, blue glass trading beads used during the slave era, and porcelain from the Nanking cargo salvaged from the *South China Sea,* where it foundered in 1752 en route to Statia, can be seen alongside rooms furnished in colonial style. The foundation has ambitious plans for more museum exhibits.

The town has several historic

Opposite: Spreading buttress-type roots help anchor giant rain forest trees such as the santinay in thin rocky mountain soil.

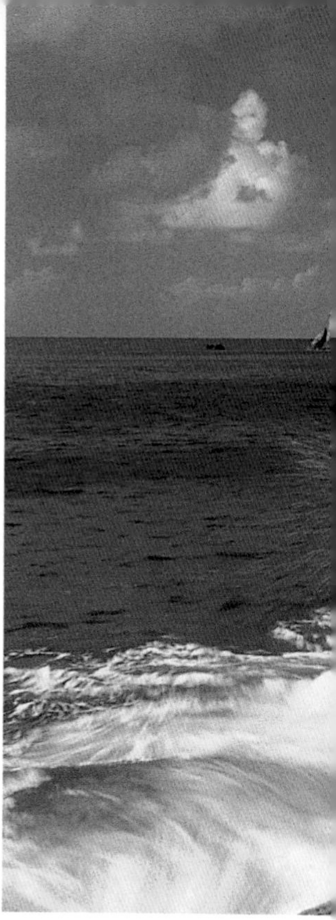

Canons atop Fort Oranje protect Oranjestad.

ruins, including the **Honen Dalim Synagogue,** the second oldest temple in the Western Hemisphere, dating from 1742. It fell into disrepair after Rodney took the Jewish community's money and then deported the people.

AROUND THE ISLAND

A trek up the Quill is a must during any visit to Sint Eustatius. Several routes go to the lip of the crater; the most direct follows a moderately steep path and takes about 45 minutes. Beneath the high point of **Mount Mazinga** (1,968 feet/ 600 m), the 550-foot-deep (168-m) crater is carpeted with lush vegetation. On the southwest coast are the ruins of **Fort de Windt,** which afford views across to St. Kitts. Even though fortresses once ringed Statia, the island still changed hands with monotonous regularity.

Statia does have a couple of beaches, but with grayish volcanic sand. Close to the Lower Town is **Oranje Beach,** popular with locals, and **Crooks Castle** is farther south. Because of dangerous currents, swimming is not safe in the bays on the Atlantic coast. Statia's underwater landscape—even more dramatic than its textbook-perfect volcano—is protected by a marine park opened in 1998. There are 30-plus official sites ranging from coral reefs and canyons to the ***Supermarket*** wreck site, where rare flying gurnards occasionally put in an appearance. The site is composed of two shipwrecks around a section of reef. The easily accessible **City Wall** site, just outside the harbor, was the original sea wall for the old Lower Town warehouse district. Contact local dive operators Dive Statia *(Tel 599/318-2435, www.divestatia.com),* Golden Rock Dive Center *(Tel/fax 599/318-2964, www.goldenrockdive.com),* or Scubaqua *(Tel/fax 599/318-5440, www.scubaqua.com).* ■

Cliffs frame Ladder Bay, where Saba's early settlers landed and carved a stone staircase into the rock face.

Saba

FROM A DISTANCE, TINY SABA (PRONOUNCED SAY-BA) RISES out of the sea like a witch's hat from its 5-square-mile (13-sq-km) base. On closer inspection, the dramatic outline of Mount Scenery (2,909 feet/870 m) doesn't stand alone but among a supporting cast of lesser peaks and ridges that make up the impressively rugged, green interior. The cliffs that edge the island drop away beneath the waves into an underwater world no less fantastically sheer and rated one of the top dive destinations in the Caribbean.

Life on Saba moves at a sedate pace. The 1,500 Sabans live in attractive villages where little white cottages with uniform red roofs perch precariously one above the other on steep hillsides. The capital of the island is The Bottom, but most visitors head up The Road (see p. 188) for the upland village of Windwardside.

Columbus sighted Saba in 1493, but it took a shipwreck to land the first Europeans on the island more than a century later. Dutch colonists from Sint Eustatius founded the first permanent settlement in the 1640s. In 1665 the infamous Welsh pirate Henry Morgan (1635–1688) captured Saba and banished all non-English speakers during his short stay. Thereafter the almost impregnable

Saba

179 A1

Visitor information

P.O. Box 527
Windwardside

599/416-2231
fax 599/416-2350

Saba Museum

✉ Windwardside

🕒 Closed weekends

$ $

THE ROAD

A minor miracle of engineering and a monument to Sabian stubbornness, The Road traverses Saba from Fort Bay in the southwest to Flat Point in the northeast. When the Sabians first investigated the possibility of a road to augment the old footpaths and donkey tracks in the 1930s, civil engineers from Holland said it couldn't be done. Josephus Hassell's response was to sign up for a correspondence course in civil engineering, and, utilizing his newly acquired knowledge, work began at Fort Bay in 1938. The Road reached The Bottom five years later, crept into Windwardside in 1951, and eventually arrived in Flat Point after carving a 19-mile (31-km) corkscrew passage across the island. ■

island changed hands by treaty rather than invasion, supported a few small sugar plantations, and lived very quietly.

AROUND THE ISLAND

Saba's capital, The Bottom, lies in a sloping valley and probably takes its name from the Dutch word *botte* (bowl). Among the traditional clapboard homes are several small businesses, shops, and bars and the **Lieutenant-Governor's Residence,** an attractive old Saban house with balconies and gingerbread decoration.

To the south for about a mile (1.5 km), The Road wriggles steeply down to **Fort Bay,** the main port. A leg-trembling flight of 500-plus steps descends to the harbor on **Ladder Bay.** In pre-Road days this was the only route on and off the island, and everything from a box of nails to a tin bathtub had to be carried up on somebody's back.

Tucked into the lee of Mount Scenery, with fantastic views down to the coast, **Windwardside** clings tenaciously to the slopes, its neat cottages linked by a cat's cradle of narrow alleys. Housed in a 19th-century Dutch sea captain's cottage, the **Saba Museum** serves up a modest history of the island.

Intricate hand-drawn lacework has been a cottage industry on Saba since the 19th century.

Although diving may be Saba's chief draw, hiking Mount Scenery is an excellent land-based diversion. The 1,064-step path to the summit passes through secondary rain forest to a gnarled and stunted world of elfin woodland carpeted with mosses and ferns and is frequently wreathed in mist. The tourist office and **Saba Trail Shop** *(Tel 599/416-2630)* in Windwardside have details of other trails and local guide services.

From Windwardside, The Road continues its serpentine way for just under a mile (1.5 km) to the settlement of **Hell's Gate** and on to the airport at Flat Point. ■

A tiger grouper and a scuba diver size each other up in the rich coastal waters of Saba.

Saba Marine Park

Established in 1987 to protect Saba's pristine marine environment, the park rings the island. Most of the dive sites are marked by permanent buoys off the west coast.

The astonishing diversity of the park's underwater landscapes is matched by vibrant marine life. Excellent visibility ranges upward from 125 feet (38 m) in winter. Varied, challenging diving is ensured by elkhorn forests, giant boulders encrusted with sponges, soft and hard corals, submerged pinnacles that attract big groupers, jacks, and rays, and walls dropping to depths of 1,000 feet (300 m) within half a mile (800 m) of the shore.

The park is partially funded by the small fee paid for each dive. Further information about dives can be obtained from Saba Marine Park *(P.O. Box 18, The Bottom, tel 599/416-3295, www.sabapark.org)* or by contacting local dive operators such as Saba Deep Dive *(Tel 599/416-3347, fax 599/416-3397, e-mail sabadeep@unspoiledqueen.com, www.sabadeep.com);* Saba Divers *(Tel 599/416-2740, fax 599/416-2741, e-mail info@scoutsplace.com, www.sabadivers.com);* and Sea Saba *(tel 599/ 416-2246 or 800/838-SABA, fax 599/416-2362, e-mail info@seasaba.com, www.seasaba.com).* ■

Curaçao

Curaçao
179 D1
Visitor information
Willemstad at Pietermaai 19
5999/434-8200

CURAÇAO HAS THE GREATEST LANDMASS OF THE DUTCH Leewards. These lie amid the larger group of Caribbean islands known as the Lesser Antilles, running parallel to the northern coastline of Venezuela. The ethnic mix of the islanders is as beguiling as Curaçao's beaches and limpid blue waters, and it seems fitting that the island should also be known for its vividly colored liqueurs.

The chief Dutch possession in the Caribbean since the 17th century, Curaçao is the largest of the five Netherlands Antilles islands at 38 miles (61 km) by 9 miles (14.5 km). It lies only 35 miles (56 km) off the coast of Venezuela. Curaçao's rocky shoreline, with its cliffs and coves, is indented with fingernail slivers of white sand beach and lapped by staggeringly blue waters. Inland, giant cactuses straight out of a cowboy movie lord it over the rugged *cunucu,* a scrub-covered landscape that receives less than 23 inches (580 mm) of rain a year.

The Spanish landed on Curaçao in 1499 and dubbed it the Isla de los Gigantes (Island of Giants) for the tall, seafaring Caquetio people they encountered. The native population was soon shipped off to work in the gold mines of Hispaniola, and the ABCs were declared *islas inútiles* (useless islands). In 1634 the Dutch West India Company spotted the potential of Sint Annabaai, Curaçao's huge natural harbor, the largest in the region and seventh largest in the world. The company ejected a handful of Spanish settlers and set about fortifying the harbor entrance

The Koningin Emmabrug pontoon bridge spans the Sint Annabaai channel to the Otrabanda district in Willemstad.

and constructing Willemstad within sturdy defensive walls.

Under the Dutch, Curaçao grew wealthy. A notable early governor of the island was Peter Stuyvesant (1592–1672), who lost his leg fighting the Spanish for possession of Sint Maarten in 1644 before sailing off to take up the governorship of Nieuw Amsterdam (New York). Willemstad's duty-free port handled all manner of goods from sugar to gold bullion; it also developed into the Caribbean's busiest slave market. A few plantations were established on the island, but the struggle with the arid climate and infertile soil was a difficult one. Their legacy is a collection of pretty Dutch colonial *landhuizen* (plantation houses) in the rolling hinterland.

The Dutch didn't abolish slavery until 1863, and Curaçao idled along until 1918, when construction of the world's largest oil refinery refueled the island's prosperity. Workers poured in from around the Caribbean, the Americas, and beyond creating a multiracial society. The present-day population of 130,000 is concentrated around Willemstad and the southwestern beaches. The northern part of the island contains Sint Christoffel National Park (see p. 194). This area is very quiet, with just a few small hotels, restaurants, and dive shops on the shore backed by acres of green-gray cunucu backcountry.

WILLEMSTAD

A little pocket of the Caribbean that will be forever Amsterdam, Willemstad's **Handelskade** waterfront is charming. Dutch gables and terra-cotta roof tiles adorn buildings painted pastel pink and pistachio, with a dash of citrus yellow here and curlicue white stucco plasterwork there. Though modern excrescences now outnumber historic buildings, the effect is still startlingly attractive and a favorite photo opportunity for the scores of visitors who arrive by cruise ship to plunder the capital's duty-free stores and explore its beautifully preserved streets.

Willemstad was recently added to the World Heritage List.

The city is divided by the Sint Annabaai channel, which leads into Schottegat Harbor. On the west side is the

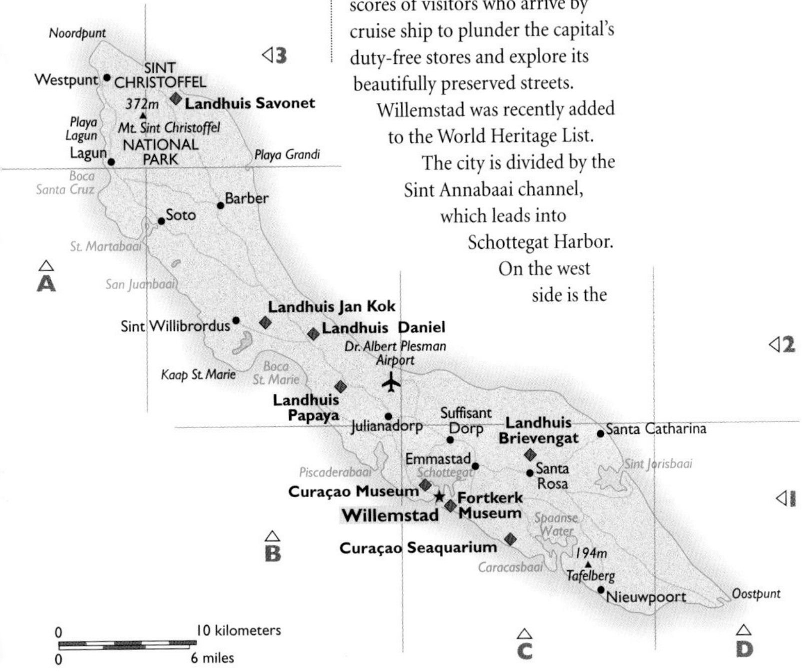

Otrabanda quarter, where the cruise ships dock; to the east Handelskade fronts the central **Punda district,** where the main shops and sights are found. One of the Punda's most popular attractions is the busy daily **Mercado Flotante** (Floating Market). Located around the corner from Handelskade, on the watery cul-de-sac of Waaigat, Venezuelan schooners line the **Sha Caprileskade** waterfront and goods spill out onto colorful market stalls arranged with fresh fruit and vegetables grown on the South American mainland.

A tour of historic Willemstad should begin on the waterfront along Handelskade at **Fort Amsterdam.** Government offices now occupy the former Dutch West India Company headquarters. There's free access to the courtyard and the 1769 fort church, which houses the small **Fortkerk Museum,** with its displays of antique silverware and maps. The church once doubled as a sail loft, and its rainwater cisterns were built of the tiny yellow and red bricks—used in many buildings around town—shipped from Holland as ballast.

Several years before Fortkerk was completed, Willemstad's Jewish community had begun to worship in the **Mikvé Israël-Emanuel Synagogue,** the oldest synagogue in continuous use in the Americas. Portuguese Jews arrived in Curaçao in the 1650s and founded the first synagogue in 1674; Mikvé Israël was dedicated in 1732. Located in the heart of Punda, the synagogue occupies an attractive courtyard complex alongside a museum displaying religious artifacts and memorabilia.

The old Jewish residential district of **Scharloo,** across Waaigat, is slowly being restored. In a reclaimed 18th-century waterfront mansion, the **Maritime Museum** displays collections of model ships, maps, and miniatures and offers ferry tours of the harbor. **Scharlooweg,** one block behind the waterfront, is lined with some of Willemstad's best preserved 18th- to 19th-century town houses.

The Otrabanda district is reached by the **Koningin Emmabrug** (Queen Emma Bridge) from Handelskade. The impressive swinging pontoon bridge was designed by U.S. consul Leonard B. Smith and installed

Sports & activities

Adventure tours: Various options (kayaking, snorkeling, biking, walking, etc.) from Dutch Daydream *(Tel 5999/461-9393, www.dutchdaydreamcuracao.com)*; Yellow Jeep Safaris *(Tel 5999/462-6262)*; and Wild Curaçao *(Tel 5999/561-0027)* who also arrange trips to the Hato Caves.

Day sails: Day sails and weekend trips to Bonaire and Venezuela with Insulinde *(Tel 5999/560-1340, www.insulinde.com)*; dive, snorkel, and sunbathe aboard *Bounty (Tel 5999/560-1887,www.bountyadventures.com)*.

Diving & snorkeling: Dive the leeward coast and visit the Banda Aboa Underwater Park. Dive Wederfoort *(Tel 5999/888-4414, www.divewederfoort.com)*; Ocean Encounters *(Tel 5999/461-8131, www.oceanencounters.com)*.

Hiking & horseback riding: See Sint Christoffel, p. 194. ■

Fortkerk Museum

Fort Amsterdam
Gouvernementsplein
5999/461-1139
Closed weekends
$

Mikvé Israël-Emanuel Synagogue & Jewish Museum

www.snoa.com/350/
Hanchi Snoa 29
5999/461-1633
Closed Sat. and Sun.
$

Maritime Museum

Van de Brandhofstraat 7
5999/465-2327
Closed Sun.
$$$

in 1888. (A free ferry operates when the bridge is opened to allow ships through.) Otrabanda is home to the cruise-ship terminal and the **Riffort,** a 19th-century fort that guards one side of the harbor. Also here is the excellent **Museum Kurá Hurlanda,** part of a beautifully restored complex of Dutch Colonial buildings, which houses one of the largest collections of African art and artifacts in the Caribbean. Exhibits range from art treasures of the West African empires to the re-created hold of a transatlantic slave ship.

One mile (1.5 km) north of the city center is the **Curaçao Museum,** located in a former seamen's hospital. The museum exhibits monumental colonial furniture, pre-Columbian relics, and works by local artists. ■

Curaçao cocktails

If the name Curaçao rings a bell but you know nothing about the island of the same name, think of bizarrely tinted cocktail additives. Bottles of vivid blue, red, orange, and green Curaçao liqueurs lurk behind cocktail bars the world over. Visitors to **Landhuis Chobolobo** *(Mercuriusstraat, Salinja, tel 5999/461-3526, closed Sat.–Sun.)* in the eastern suburbs of Willemstad, can sample the local brew, which is flavored with the sun-dried peel of a small bitter orange. The Curaçaoan soil and climate give the orange its distinctive flavor. ■

Elaborate stucco decorations on Handelskade are one of the highlights of Willemstad's Dutch colonial architecture.

Museum Kurá Hulanda

www.kurahulanda.com

✉ Klipstraat 9

☎ 5999/434-7765

$ $$$

Curaçao Museum

✉ Van Leeuwenhoekstraat

☎ 5999/462-3873

🕒 Closed Sat.

$ $$

Around Curaçao

SINT CHRISTOFFEL NATIONAL PARK

The 4,650-acre (1,880 ha) Sint Christoffel National Park, in the north of the island, is composed of three former plantations on the slopes of **Mount Sint Christoffel** (1,220 feet/372 m), the highest point in the Dutch Leewards.

The park center, on the grounds of **Landhuis Savonet** plantation, has a small museum describing the island's geology, flora, and fauna, and it is the starting point for a network of trails that strike off into the cunucu or down to the wave-lashed cliffs at **Playa Grandi.** There are fascinating guided walks daily *(Call for reservations)*, and special evening walks offer a chance to spot the rare Curaçaoan deer, a subspecies of the North American white-tailed deer introduced to the island in pre-Columbian times. Guides can also be arranged for private hikes and bird-watching. Horseback riding and mountain bike rental are available from the Rancho Alfin concession *(Tel 5999/864-0535)*.

191 B3 Savonet 5999/864-0363
$ $$$$

CURAÇAO SEA AQUARIUM

A marine life showcase with family appeal, the Sea Aquarium offers outdoor lagoons for sea lions and sharks, tanks housing toothsome eels and tropical fish, and touch tanks. More unusual aspects are an underwater observatory anchored to the shore and the Animal Encounters program *(Reservations required)*. The encounters take place in a natural reef pool, which is home to stingrays, sea turtles, jacks, tarpon, and sharks. After an introductory dive with a qualified instructor, participants can snorkel and scuba dive among the non-dangerous residents on one side of the pool and hand-feed the segregated lemon and nurse sharks through holes in a Plexiglass wall.

Adjacent **Sea Aquarium Beach** is one of the island's best, with access to the 12-mile-

A scuba diver feeds fresh fish to Caribbean reef sharks at the Curaçao Sea Aquarium.

Candle cactuses flourish in the scrublands around Mount Sint Christoffel.

long (19-km) **Curaçao Underwater Park,** a magnet for snorkelers and divers.
191 C1 Bapor Kibra, southeast of Willemstad 5999/461-6666, www.curacao-sea-aquarium.com $ $$$$

LANDHUIS BRIEVENGAT

The most interesting of Curaçao's historic *landhuizen*, Brievengat dates from the 1730s. The interior is furnished in a haphazard fashion with mahogany four-poster beds, and rocking chairs known as *ki-mi-ki-hasi* (what can I do about it?) in Papiamento. The pièce de résistance is the red-and-white spotted kitchen, a device to disorient evil spirits and flies. Bar and live music Friday nights; crafts and folkloric shows third Sunday of the month.
191 C1 Brievengat, northeast of Willemstad 5999/691-4961 $ $ ■

Landhuizen

About 300 country estates had spread across the island's interior by the early 19th century. Most of them had a modest little yellow-and-white Dutch colonial *landhuis* (plantation house) for the owner's family. A handful of these have been restored, notably **Landhuis Brievengat** (see left). You can also visit **Landhuis Jan Kok,** St. Willibrordus. **Landhuis Papaya,** which is painted bloodred (the rarer of the two traditional Curaçaoan color schemes), and **Landhuis Daniel,** both on the Westpunt road outside Willemstad, have been transformed into a bar-restaurant and a simple hotel with a good restaurant, respectively.

For information about all these sites, contact the Curaçao Tourism Development Bureau *(Tel 5999/434-8200).* ■

Bonaire

Bonaire
179 E1
Visitor information
Kaya Grandi 2, Kralendijk
599/717-8322 or fax 599/717-8408

SHAPED LIKE A DISTORTED BOOMERANG AND LYING 30 miles (48 km) east of Curaçao, Bonaire is a diver's paradise—and that's official, according to the legend adorning local car license plates. Along the sheltered leeward coast of the island and around the offshore islet of Klein (Little) Bonaire, more than 80 dive sites give access to some of the most spectacular and varied marine landscapes in the entire Caribbean.

Bonaire, a derivation of the Arawak word *bojnaj,* meaning "low country," was first noted by Italian explorer Amerigo Vespucci in 1499. When the Dutch wrested control of the island from Spain in 1634, they introduced slaves to harvest the salt pans in the flat southern portion of the island, and raised cattle on the scrub-covered cunucu backcountry to supply the burgeoning colony of Curaçao.

Activity on the island stuttered to an almost complete halt with the abolition of slavery in 1863, but after a century's break Bonaire's salt industry was revived in the 1960s. The decade also saw the first divers venturing to the out-of-the-way island, and Bonaire's special brand of low-key, dive-oriented tourism was born. Although the news about Bonaire's spectacular underwater world is well and truly out, and hotels are mushrooming, the island atmosphere is still quiet and definitely casual. Nondivers can find fantastic snorkeling from walk-in sites directly off the shore, as well as hiking, mountain biking, horseback riding, and bird-watching.

The modest capital of Bonaire is **Kralendijk** (Coral Dike), a small town of tidy yellow and gold Dutch Caribbean buildings, restaurants, and hotels facing the rounded outline of Klein Bonaire. From Kralendijk a road circles the southern portion of the island, passing the glittering white salt stacks awaiting shipment from the solar saltworks, which conceal flamingo nesting grounds.

Northwest of Kralendijk is Bonaire's oldest settlement, the sleepy inland village of **Rincon,** on the road to the national park. A short distance away on the Atlantic coast, at Boca Onima, Caquetio Indians left their marks scribbled in red dye on cave walls.

To the north of Rincon, and covering the northwestern portion of the island, is **Washington-Slagbaai National Park.** This 13,500-acre (5,463-ha) tract of land occupying one fifth of the island has

12 steps to heaven

The dramatically colored queen angelfish can be seen in the water around Bonaire.

Bonaire's Guided Snorkeling Program is a great way for nondivers to learn about the reefs and to get the best out of the marine park. Offered through dive shops and a dozen resorts, the program features 12 guided snorkel tours at selected sites around the island. Each tour is prefaced with a short slide show. There are snorkeling tips for beginners, safety checks, and a guide to reef etiquette to minimize damage to the delicate environment. Though transportation is included, you'll need to bring your own dive equipment or rent it. ■

operated as a wildlife preserve since the 1960s. It is crisscrossed by four-wheel-drive trails and hiking paths, one of which scales the high point of Mount Brandaris (784 feet/240 m). The park is home to most of Bonaire's 190 bird species, including parrots, hummingbirds, and a flamingo colony on the Gotomeer lagoon. Several snorkel and dive sites lie off the leeward coast, such as **Boca Slagbaai** (Slaughter Bay), where colonial ranchers killed their cattle before shipping the meat to Curaçao.

The island is surrounded by **Bonaire Marine Park.** Designated a marine preserve in 1971, the park rings the entire island and extends from the shore to the 200-foot-deep (60 m) contour through shallow, sloping terraces of fringe reefs to the drop-off. More than 80 species of corals have been identified, including elkhorn, staghorn, leaf, and brain corals, and the reefs are patrolled by a dazzling array of electric blue tangs, angelfish, parrotfish, grunts, and seahorses. All these delights are accessible to snorkelers. Simply locate one of the yellow dive markers and wade out. ■

Sports & activities

Diving & snorkeling: Buddy Dive Resort *(Tel 599/717-5080, www.buddydive.com);* Captain Don's Habitat Dive Center *(Tel 599/717-8290, www.habitatdiveresorts.com/bonaire);* and Bonaire Dive Adventure *(Tel 599/717-2227, www.discoverbonaire.com),* which can also arrange kayaking, landsailing, and a five-day Island Explorer package.

Horseback riding: Kunuku Warahama Ranch *(Tel 599/560-7949).*

Mountain biking: Cycle Bonaire *(Tel 599/717-7558).*

Windsurfing & kayaking: Jibe City *(Tel 599/717-5233, www.jibecity.com).* ■

Palm-thatched slave huts bake on the treeless shore.

Washington-Slagbaai National Park
www.washingtonparkbonaire.org
179 E1
599/785-0017
$

Bonaire Marine Park
www.bmp.org
179 E1
599/717-8444
$

Aruba

FIFTEEN MILES (24 KM) AS THE PELICAN FLIES FROM THE coast of Venezuela, with a population of 100,000, diminutive Aruba—20 by 6 miles (32 by 10 km)—is the one that got away. The island achieved *Status Aparte,* or independence, from the Netherlands Antilles in 1986 in the wake of the oil boom collapse and then turned wholeheartedly toward tourism. It is now one of the Caribbean's hottest vacation destinations, with a choice of luxurious hotels lining white sand beaches, 24-hour casino action, and duty-free shopping guaranteed to tempt even the most jaded cruise ship visitor.

Aruba
178 A2
Visitor information
L.G. Smith Blvd. 172, Eagle Beach
297/582-3777

Dismissed as an *isla inútil* (useless island) by its Spanish discoverers, Aruba was eventually used for ranching and developed something of a reputation for horse breeding. In 1824 gold was discovered, prompting a small-scale gold rush, but the mining became unprofitable and ceased altogether in 1914. Remains of the old mines and smelting works can be seen around Balashi and Bushiribana. Aloe vera plantations sprouted in the early 1900s, but oil refineries built in the mid-1920s made the island's fortunes, caused a population explosion, and gave Aruba one of the highest standards of living in the Caribbean region.

Arubans still live comfortably. They are ruled by a 21-member democratic parliament presided over by the prime minister. The Kingdom of the Netherlands, which handles defense and foreign affairs, is represented by a governor. Aruba has its own legal system, currency, and an excellent education system, which gives foreign languages a high priority. Most people speak English and Spanish as well as Papiamento (see p. 201). The islanders' Amerindian heritage is reflected in their looks, though there are now more than 40 nationalities bubbling in the Aruban melting pot.

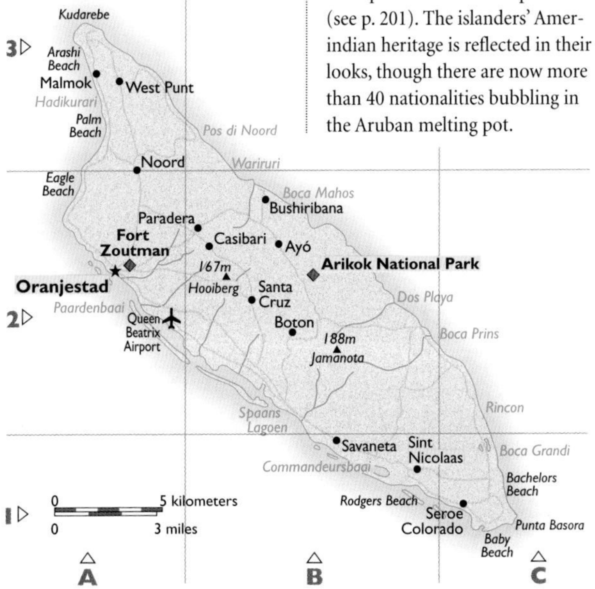

Sun worshippers head for the soft sands of Palm Beach.

Ornate gabled buildings proclaim Aruba's colonial heritage with a flourish in downtown Oranjestad.

ORANJESTAD

The island capital, Oranjestad was named in honor of the Dutch ruling family, the House of Orange. The town is a mixture of old Dutch Caribbean buildings and modern pastiches that house shops and busy malls. The oldest building on the island is **Fort Zoutman,** constructed on the waterfront in 1796. Now a short distance inland due to land reclamation, it still affords a good view over the yacht harbor. The Willem III Tower was added to the fort in 1868, doubling as a lighthouse and the island's first public clock. Every Tuesday evening year-round, the Bon Bini Festival, an entertaining folkloric show featuring local crafts, food stalls, music, and dancing, takes place in the fort precincts.

Oranjestad has three small museums. The **Numismatic Museum** boasts a collection of some 30,000 historic coins and banknotes from around the globe. The **Archaeological Museum** displays Amerindian tools, pottery, and 2,000-year-old skeletons unearthed from around the island. The Historical Museum, with its Spanish and Dutch Colonial artifacts, will reopen on Schelpstraat in early 2008.

Down on the waterfront, **Atlantis Submarines** offers a popular mini-submarine excursion to the Bacadera Reef. There's a motorboat transfer to the dive site before boarding the window-lined sub for a trip 150 feet (46 m) beneath the waves for a fish-eye view of the *Mi Dushi I* shipwreck or the *Sonesta* airplane wreck. The dives are narrated, and identification charts are good guides. ■

Numismatic Museum

www.museumaruba.org

✉ Weststraat (by Royal Plaza)

☎ 297/582-8831

🕒 Closed Fri. and Sat. p.m., all Sun.

De Olde Molen: This 19th-century windmill was brought to Aruba as a tourist attraction in 1961.

Papiamento

The mother tongue of the Dutch Leewards, Papiamento (from the Spanish *papia* meaning "talk" or "babble") emerged from the pidgin speech of the early colonists and their African slaves. Dutch merchants, Portuguese Jews, Spanish missionaries, South American traders, and local Indians all added to the vocabulary. The language is now spoken throughout the ABCs, with slight island variations (Aruban Papiamento is more Spanish sounding), and taught in schools. Islanders will be hugely entertained if you try a few words.

Welcome	*Bon bini*
Good morning	*Bon dia*
Good afternoon	*Bon tardi*
Good evening	*Bon nochi*
How are you?	*Con ta bai?*
I am fine	*Mi ta bon*
Good-bye	*Aye*
Thank you very much	*Masha danki*
Beautiful	*Bunita*
Very good	*Hopi bon* ■

Archaeological Museum

✉ Irausquinplein 2-A

☎ 297/582-8979

🕒 Closed weekends

Atlantis Submarines

✉ Renaissance Marina

☎ 297/583-6090

$ $$$$$

Park path passes candle cacti and divi divi tree in Arikok National Park.

Around Aruba

ARUBA'S BEACHES

Northwest of Oranjestad, Aruba's twin tourist poles are the magnificent sandy sweeps of **Eagle Beach** (the "low-rise strip") and **Palm Beach** (the "high-rise strip"). Both are busy and hotel lined, with water sports concessions.

Two smaller, less crowded beaches lie to the north—**Malmok Beach** (a windsurfers' favorite) and **Arashi Beach.**

Sports & activities

Diving and snorkeling: Aruba Pro Dive *(Tel 297/582-5520, www.arubaprodive.com)*; Red Sail Sports *(Tel 297/583-1603 or 877/REDSAIL, e-mail infoaruba@redsailaruba.com, www.redsailaruba.com).*

Golf: Aruba's best golfing is the 18-hole Tierra del Sol Golf Course on the northwest coast, designed by Robert Trent Jones *(Tel 297/586-4590, fax 297/586-4588).*

Horseback riding: Rancho Del Campo *(Tel 297/585-0290)*; Rancho Notorious *(Tel 297/586-0508).*

Touring: De Palm Tours *(Tel 297/582-4400, www.depalm.com)* offers everything from round-island bus and jeep excursions to sportfishing charters, cruises, and parasailing. ■

ALTO VISTA CHAPEL

On the remote northwest coast, this tiny mustard-colored chapel was built on the site of an 18th-century Spanish chapel. It is a spectacular spot hedged by cacti and sea.

199 B3

AYO

Inland, around the village of Ayo, giant boulders litter the dusty cunucu, and there are Amerindian rock paintings in the **Arikok National Park**. Nestled amid the wind-tortured divi-divi trees, Aruban farmsteads decorated with talismanic symbols crouch behind cactus fences.

199 B2

THE HOOIBERG

Located at the center of the island, the Hooiberg (541 feet/165 m) is a local landmark. Steps lead all the way to the hill's top, which does look a bit like its Dutch name suggests—a haystack. The view stretches across the island from coast to coast.

199 B2

SAN NICOLAAS

Aruba's largest settlement (population 25,000), located at the eastern end of the island, is undergoing a major facelift. A clutch of good beaches at the very tip of the island include palm-fringed **Rodgers Beach,** the quiet cove of **Baby Beach,** and the breezy strands of **Bachelors Beach** and **Boca Grandi.**

199 B1 ■

Bridging the gap between the Virgin Islands and the Windward Islands, the Leeward Islands of Antigua, Barbuda, and Anguilla are coral islands. St. Kitts, Nevis, and Montserrat are mountainous miniatures of the volcanic Windwards.

Leeward Islands

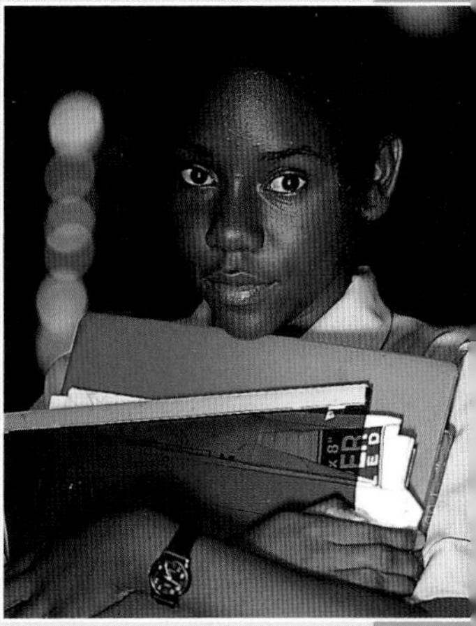

A Leeward Island student

Leeward Islands

THE SIX ENGLISH-SPEAKING LEEWARD ISLANDS HEAD UP THE CHAIN OF THE Lesser Antilles mingling with the Dutch Windward Islands and the French possessions of St. Martin and St.-Barthélemy (St. Barts). Antigua is the main gateway to this corner of the Caribbean, and it has been since the British established their chief Caribbean naval base here in the 18th century. The British influence lingers on throughout the region in a handful of notable historic sites, the occasional red mailbox, and, of course, the islanders' beloved sport of cricket.

The main European influence on the Leeward Islands might be British, but indigenous Caribbean culture is here, too, in the exuberant local carnivals, reggae, rasta, and the studied art of relaxation. There are beaches galore, water sports, and hiking, plus accommodations ranging from family-friendly resorts to state-of-the-art spas to gorgeous plantation hotel retreats.

England's first successful Caribbean colony was St. Kitts, settled in 1623. Nevis followed in 1628, and a decade later Antigua and Montserrat were added to a growing portfolio of Caribbean possessions. At first, English and French settlers agreed to share St. Kitts, banding together to rid the island of inhospitable Carib people. Once the Carib were defeated, the good neighbors soon fell out. And so began the battle for control of the eastern Caribbean islands, which would continue into the 19th century and cause the demise of the sugar industry.

While Antigua was systematically stripped of its native forest to make way for sugar plantations—and settlers did their best to plant cane wherever the topography allowed on St. Kitts, Nevis, and Montserrat—barren, low-lying Anguilla became a nest of pirates and smugglers. Slaves brought to the island by prospective planters were soon turned loose to scratch a living from the thin, sandy soil; they developed a local reputation for carpentry and boatbuilding. This early self-reliance fostered the Anguillans' fiercely independent spirit, typified by the bizarre circumstances of the Anguillan "revolution" (actually a reactionary desire to remain British and avoid independence as a satellite of St. Kitts) in the late 1960s.

Slavery was abolished throughout the British Caribbean in 1834, although a term of forced "apprenticeship" legally bound former slaves to their masters for a further period of years. In the end European sugar beets undermined the Caribbean trade to emancipate the slaves for good in the late 1830s. The islands sank into an impoverished backwater status, administered under the presidency of the Leeward Islands until 1967, when associated statehood brought a degree of autonomy. The twin-island nation of Antigua and Barbuda achieved independence in 1981, followed by St. Kitts and Nevis in 1983. Anguilla and Montserrat elected to remain British Crown Colonies.

Plantation hotels in beautifully restored colonial houses offer a relaxed and stylish alternative to beachfront accommodations.

Sugar continued to be grown in Antigua until the 1970s and still provides a modest income for St. Kitts, but for more than a century the Leeward Islands' precarious economies had been almost entirely dependent on remittances—money sent by islanders working overseas. In the last 40 years tourism has gradually injected new life into the region, and the top beach islands of Antigua and Anguilla, in particular, have seen considerable hotel development.

Although the Leewards share a common background, each island enjoys its own identity. For the ultimate laid-back Caribbean beach vacation, it would be hard to beat Anguilla, which focuses all the attention on its fabulous white sand strands and super-luxurious resorts. Very quiet and relatively undiscovered, Barbuda boasts a selection of delectable and often deserted beaches, where the only crowds are propelled by fins and inhabit magical coral reefs.

Antigua is altogether a more lively choice. In addition to claiming a beach for every day of the year (a wild but forgivable exaggeration), the island's historical sites make for interesting excursions, and friendly pubs provide live reggae and impromptu jump-ups at night. Lush St. Kitts and tiny Nevis combine colonial history with romantic plantation retreats and some fine upland hiking and riding country. Pint-sized and once lush and lovely Montserrat suffered a major setback to its quietly developing nature-tourism industry when the Soufrière Volcano erupted in 1995. However, the enterprising islanders have reopened for business and now welcome volcano-watching visitors. ■

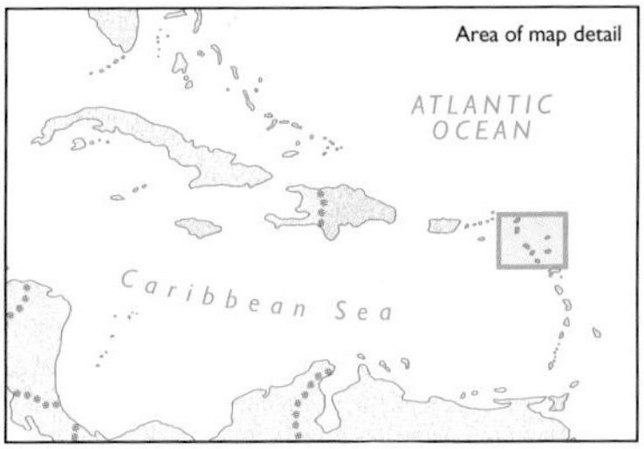

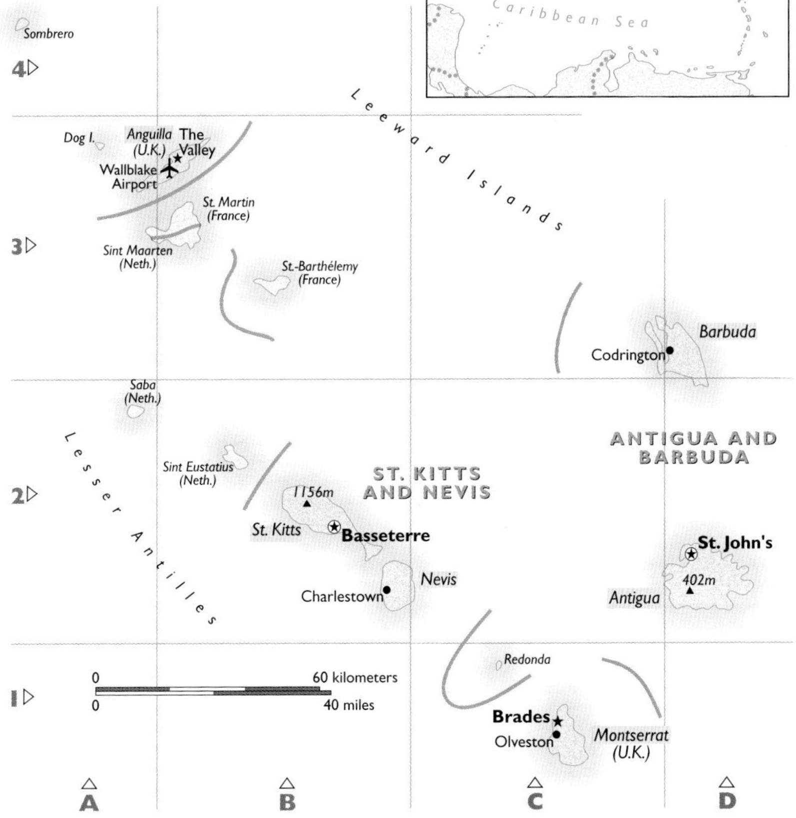

Sweeping beaches and bays fringe the coast of low-lying Antigua.

Antigua

AT 108 SQUARE MILES (280 SQ KM), ANTIGUA (PRONOUNCED An-TEE-gah) is the largest of the Leeward Islands. Its irregular coastline, resembling a ragged Rorschach inkblot, incorporates hundreds of scalloped inlets and bays. The locals boast there are 365 beaches to choose from, many of them secluded coves backed by sea grape trees and accessible only by boat.

Antigua
205 D2
Visitor information
P.O. Box 363, Nevis St., St. John's
268/462-0480

The interior of the island is rolling and dry. The lush carpet of sugarcane has disappeared and has been replaced by yellow-gray scrubland dotted with the shells of abandoned windmills. Small country villages provide brief bursts of color and greenery, painted wooden cottages and modern villas with flower gardens straggle along the roadside, and tethered goats and cattle graze in the dust. Antigua's coastal heights are generally topped with the remains of British ramparts; the most interesting is Shirley Heights (see p. 212), in Nelson's Dockyard National Park, overlooking the confines of English Harbour.

The first human traces on Antigua date back to the Stone Age Ciboney people, who migrated from South America to settle the island around 3000 B.C. Peaceable Arawak arrived on the scene about A.D. 100, and raiding parties of Windward Island Carib were moving up the island chain by the time Christopher Columbus sighted the island on his second voyage in 1493. He named it Santa Maria de la Antigua after a miraculous statue of the Virgin in Seville Cathedral. The Spanish and French showed little interest in the island, discouraged by its shortage of fresh water, but English colonists from St. Kitts established a base in 1632. Sugar was introduced in the 1650s, and by the height of the 18th-century plantation era, Antigua had more

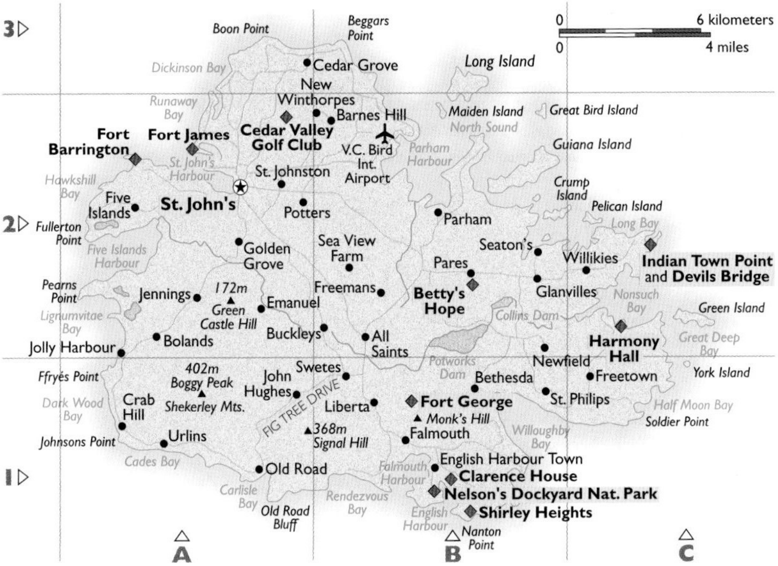

than 200 cane-crushing windmills, with African slaves forming 93 percent of the population.

Antigua's protected harbors (an important consideration in the Caribbean hurricane belt) and strategic position at the apex of a rough triangle between the major-league sugar colonies of Barbados and Jamaica made the island a natural choice for Britain's chief naval and military base in the Leewards. Fortresses sprang up along the coast, with the main defenses concentrated in the south around English and Falmouth Harbours. The result was so formidable that Britain's enemies gave the whole island a wide berth.

After British emancipation of the slaves in 1834, Antigua's fate mirrored that of other colonial possessions. The dockyard was closed, most of the plantations failed, and the islanders slipped into an unremitting pattern of subsistence agriculture. They were consequently largely ignored by Britain.

Appalling working conditions inspired the first organized labor movement in 1939. It gained strength during World War II, which heralded an influx of U.S. servicemen sent to man military bases on the island. The postwar Labour Party, under the leadership of Vere C. Bird, led Antigua and the sister island of Barbuda to self-governing associated statehood in 1967 and full independence in 1981.

Antigua and Barbuda's combined population numbers around 65,000, of which some 85 percent are of African descent. The capital of the twin-island nation is

Natty paintwork spruces up even the simplest wooden cottage in the countryside outside St. John's.

Sports & activities

Day sails: Sight-seeing and day trips with Adventure Antigua *(Tel 268/726-6355, www.adventureantigua.com)*; sail to Barbuda with Wadadli Cats *(Tel 268/462-4792, www.wadadlicats.com)*; or paddle your own canoe with Antigua Paddles Eco Kayak Tour *(Tel 268/463-1944, www.antiguapaddles.com)*.

Diving & snorkeling: Antigua's best reef sites are off the south and west coasts. Dive operators include Dive Antigua *(Dickenson Bay, tel 268/462-3483)*; Indigo Divers *(Jolly Harbour, tel 268/729-3483)*; and Ultramarine *(Hodges Bay, tel 268/463-3483)*.

Golf: Antigua's two 18-hole golf courses are the Cedar Valley Golf Club, near St. John's *(Tel 268/462-0161)*, and Jolly Harbour *(Tel 268/462-7771)*.

Horseback riding: Spring Hill Riding Club *(Falmouth, tel 268/460-7787)* and the St. James's Club *(Mamora Bay, tel 268/460-5000)*.

Sailing: Sailing is centered on English Harbour, Falmouth Harbour, and the Jolly Harbour complex. Charter companies supply yachts of all sizes, with or without crew, by the day, week, or longer. Contact Nicholson's Yacht Charters *(Tel 268/460-1530, e-mailnicholson@candw.ag)* or Sun Yacht Charters *(Tel 268/460-2615, e-mailcharterservices@candw.ag)*.

Windsurfing/Kitesurfing: From watersports specialists H2O Antigua *(Dutchman's Bay, tel 268/562-3933, www.h2oantigua.com)*. ■

The sturdy stone windmill tower at Betty's Hope plantation

St. John's, a bustling port city and cruise-ship destination on the west coast, well worth a visit. Antigua has several diversions for the inquisitive traveler who would like to get off the beach and have a look around. Renting a car is the best way to explore. Nelson's Dockyard National Park (see pp. 210–212) show-cases the finest surviving Georgian naval complex in the world, while the history of the island's sugar industry is explained at the restored Betty's Hope Museum (see p. 213) in the center of the island.

A favorite out-of-the-way detour on the southeast coast is a trip to Harmony Hall (see p. 213), a charming old sugar mill complex housing an arts-and-crafts gallery and an excellent Italian restaurant.

Tourists are generally welcomed wherever they go, and for a surefire conversational gambit try cricket or sailing, the islanders' twin passions. To capture Antiguans at their most spontaneous, join the regattas and riotous partying that accompany the annual **Antigua Sailing Week** at the end of the December-to-April yachting season. For a more modest hint of the local atmosphere, the Sunday afternoon jump-ups (impromptu dances) at Shirley Heights are entertaining rum-and-reggae-soaked affairs.

ST. JOHN'S & SURROUNDINGS

St. John's is an appealing West Indian town sloping gently back from the downtown waterfront in an orderly pattern of streets and narrow alleys, laid out in 1702. Old wooden buildings with drooping balconies cluster on the hill below the cathedral and its landmark silver cupolas. Charmingly time-worn, they appear anchored

together for support by a web of telephone wires above the road.

The sidewalks of St. John's are always crowded. More often than not during the winter high season, armies of day-tripping cruise passengers pile ashore intent on plundering the duty-free stores in the modern **Heritage Quay** mall at the foot of the pier.

The compact waterfront district remains the focal point of town. Next to Heritage Quay, there's a covered vendors' market full of souvenir stalls, and on its far side is **Redcliffe Quay,** a pretty shopping street lined with restored wood and stone town houses and warehouses now occupied by boutiques, galleries, and restaurants. The area behind the Quay was once part of a large barracoon, or dockside slave-holding compound, before emancipation.

It's a short walk up Long Street to the **Museum of Antigua and Barbuda,** housed in the neoclassic Old Court House, built in 1750 from stone quarried on Antigua's offshore islets. The fusty, old-fashioned layout conceals a remarkably informative introduction to the islands' history and geology. The archaeological finds are particularly interesting and include Stone Age Ciboney tools, an Arawak ax with a special hole designed to allow tree spirits to escape, and a collection of *zemi,* small stone or carved bone objects believed to attract benevolent powers.

At the top of the hill is the **Cathedral of St. John the Divine,** flanked by its twin towers and presiding over the town center. Constructed on the site of a previous stone church demolished by an earthquake in 1843, the cathedral has a cool, lofty interior clad in pitch pine to protect it against

The Cathedral of St. John the Divine rises over the capital's harbor.

Museum of Antigua & Barbuda

www.antiguamuseums.org/MuseumAntBar.htm

- Corner of Long & Market Sts. St. John's
- 268/462-1469
- Closed Sun.
- Donation

hurricane and earthquake damage. Take a little time to inspect the grand memorial plaques bedecked with coats-of-arms and flowery inscriptions. At the south gate of the tumble-down graveyard (a popular lunchtime picnic spot with local office workers) are the statues of St. John the Divine and St. John the Baptist, said to have been captured from an 18th-century French warship bound for Martinique.

A Rasta musician lets down his dreadlocks and entertains in a local restaurant.

The entrance to St. John's Harbour is overlooked by the ruins of two historic forts with good views. On the north side, reached by Fort Road, is **Fort James,** which was founded in 1706 shortly after the death of King James II. Continuing up the coast, there are a few hotels lining the beach at **Runaway Bay.** Just around a small headland is Antigua's most developed pocket of shoreline—**Dickenson Bay.** This is no Miami Beach high-rise strip but a mile-long (1.6 km) swath of fine, powdery white sand that turns the water a translucent opal. The beach is backed by just four low-rise hotels set in landscaped gardens. A good spot for active beachgoers, Dickenson Bay has several water sports concessions.

On the south side of St. John's Harbour is 17th-century **Fort Barrington,** one of Antigua's earliest (and most active) fortresses. The site was already fortified when it was named in honor of Admiral Barrington, who captured St. Lucia from the French in 1665, though most of the present defenses were constructed in 1779. From the fortress ruins there are views across to the neighboring islands of St. Kitts and Nevis on a clear day.

A handful of Antigua's best beaches are tucked into the bays and coves of the southwest coast. Out on the peninsula, near Fort Barrington, are **Deep Bay, Galley Bay,** and the assorted coves and hotel beaches of **Hawksbill Bay,** so named for the hawksbill turtle-shaped rock they overlook. The **Jolly Harbour** complex incorporates a busy marina, shops, and hotels, as well as a beach on Lignumvitae Bay. Farther south, **Dark Wood Bay** has a lovely strip of sand with a beach bar, and glorious views across to neighboring Montserrat. Busy at weekends, it is almost deserted on weekdays.

Nelson's Dockyard National Park
www.antiguamuseums.org/nelsonsdockyard.htm
207 B2
268/481-5021
$$$

NELSON'S DOCKYARD NATIONAL PARK

The national park covers 12 square miles (31 sq km) on the south coast around Falmouth Harbour, the original capital site of Antigua. A popular yachting center on its own sheltered bay, Falmouth is divided by a narrow isthmus from the virtually landlocked confines of English Harbour. English Harbour served as the British Royal Navy's eastern Caribbean headquarters during the 17th and 18th centuries.

Shirley Heights is the best place to begin a visit to the park. The sprawling 18th-century military complex was named for Gen. Sir Thomas Shirley, governor of the Leeward Islands between 1781 and

Hawksbill Rock stands silhouetted against the sunset off Antigua's southwest coast.

1791. It occupies a commanding position on the high ground above the dockyard, which is reached by a well-signed road from English Harbour. Make an initial stop at the **Dow Hill Interpretation Centre,** where a 15-minute multimedia presentation covers Antiguan history and culture from the Carib to cricket. The road continues to wind uphill, past the elegant stone colonnade of the officers' quarters, now open to the sky and studded with cactuses, until it reaches **Shirley Heights Lookout.** From here, eagle-eyed sentries could see all the way south to the French island of Guadeloupe, giving the British plenty of advance warning in the event of an attack. The French were never foolhardy enough to attempt it.

Down at sea level is **Nelson's**

Horatio Nelson

England's 18th-century naval hero spent a miserable posting in Antigua between 1784 and 1787. As captain of the 28-gun frigate H.M.S. *Boreas,* Nelson was dispatched to enforce the extremely unpopular Navigation Act, which banned planters and merchants from trading with the newly independent United States of America. At times his mission so incensed the islanders that he was afraid to put into shore and took refuge on Nevis, where he met and married Fanny Nisbet. "Woefully pinched by mosquitoes," Nelson felt so ill when he left for England that he ordered a barrel of rum be taken on board to preserve his body for a home burial if he died during the voyage. ■

Perched high above English Harbor, Fort Shirley's Georgian-era guardhouse dates from 1791.

Dockyard, which was considered a hardship posting and "an infernal hole" by its famous namesake, Admiral Lord Nelson (1758–1805). He was plain Captain Nelson in 1784, when he and his shipmates aboard H.M.S. *Boreas* arrived in the Leeward Islands for a three-year tour of duty (see p. 211). The dockyard was decommissioned in 1889 and fell into disrepair until the 1960s, when it was restored, renamed, and opened to the public as a national park. It is a delightful place for a stroll, guided by a series of signs that identify the various stores and workshop buildings. You can take a guided tour from the entrance gate. Top sights include the **Admiral's Inn,** housed in a former pitch and tar store, with the coral rock pillars of a sail loft in the gardens. Note the rounded water cisterns flanking the brick walls of the charming **Copper & Lumber Store Hotel,** and visit the **Dockyard Museum,** laid out in the Admiral's House, the last house to be completed in the dockyard, in 1855. There's a short walk out to **Fort Berkeley,** the dockyard's first line of defense, built on a rocky spit of land in 1704. The path starts by the dinghy dock in the marina, and there are grand views back across the harbor basin to waterfront **Clarence House.** ■

Exploring Shirley Heights

The military abandoned Shirley Heights in the 1850s, and since then many of its buildings have simply disappeared behind a screen of scrub. But signposts and footpaths still lead to an assortment of crumbling barracks and batteries, water cisterns, powder magazines, and the Military Cemetery, where the numerous victims of tropical fevers were laid to rest. The signals station at the highest point of the complex (490 feet/149 m) used flags to send messages to Fort George at Monk's Hill, above Falmouth, which were then relayed across a chain of hilltop signal-stations to St. John's. ■

Around Antigua

BETTY'S HOPE MUSEUM

Antigua's pioneer plantation, Betty's Hope was established during the 1650s. In 1668 it passed into the hands of the Codrington family of Barbados, who introduced sugar production to the island and for 250 years Betty's Hope was one of the island's most prosperous estates. Today, thorny acacia bushes and wild tamarind trees have swallowed up the former canefields, but one of two windmills has been carefully restored. Refitted with broad wooden sails and cane-crushing machinery, it is the only working sugar mill in the Caribbean.

Inside the small **visitor center** are exhibits explaining sugar processing and the work of the slave gangs; Betty's Hope employed about 310 West African slaves. There are also maps and drawings relating to the history of the plantation, as well as a detailed scale model of the now demolished great house, complete with machete-wielding cane cutters, farmyard animals, and smartly dressed Europeans strolling in the great house gardens, shaded from the sun by lacy parasols. In reality, most plantation owners preferred to live in Europe and leave their overseas estates in the hands of managers.

207 B2 Southeast of Pares 268/462-4930, www.antiguamuseums.org/bettyshope.htm Closed Sun.–Mon.

FIG TREE DRIVE

A rare pocket of lush natural vegetation in the southwest of the island, Fig Tree Drive runs 5 miles (8 km) from the inland village of **Swetes** down to **Old Road,** on the coast at Carlisle Bay. For a bird's eye view of the treetops, check out the **Antigua Rainforest Canopy Tour** *(Tel 268/562-6363, www.antiguacanopytour.com)*. An exhilarating combination of bridges, trails, and zip wires provides a rollercoaster forest ride. To the west is **Boggy Peak** (1,319 feet/402 m), Antigua's highest point, rising above the Shekerley Mountains, where escaped slaves once took refuge.

207 A1 St. Mary's Parish

FORT GEORGE

An easy hiking expedition for history buffs, Fort George perches on the modest heights of Monk's Hill, behind Falmouth Harbour. To reach the fort, turn off the main road at the village of **Liberta** (one of the first settlements founded by freed slaves) in the direction of Table Hill Gordon. The mile-long (1.5-km) marked track is on the right, navigable by four-wheel-drive vehicles or on foot. The fort, which dates from 1689, was intended as a stronghold for livestock, women, and children if Falmouth was attacked. Sections of the high defensive walls, water cisterns, powder magazines, and cannon emplacements have survived around the 8-acre (3-ha) site.

207 B1 Monk's Hill, near Liberta

HARMONY HALL

A delightful spot on the east coast, Harmony Hall is well worth a detour. The former great house of the Brown's Bay Mill sugar estate has been transformed into a gallery of Caribbean arts and crafts and a six-room B&B inn. The old windmill houses a bar overlooking **Nonsuch Bay,** and there is a restaurant serving lunch and afternoon tea. Call ahead, and they will even pack up a picnic and arrange a boat trip to a local beach from the dinghy dock. Visitors can also use the pool. A short drive (3 miles/5 km) southeast of Harmony Hall, beyond Freetown, is the alluring curve of **Half Moon Bay,** which is popular with swimmers, sunbathers, and bodysurfers.

207 C2 Brown's Bay (north of Freetown) 268/460-4120, www.harmonyhall.com Closed July to mid-Nov.

INDIAN TOWN POINT & DEVILS BRIDGE

Way out at the northeast tip of the island, a side road leads off 1 mile (1.6 km) to Indian Town Point and the site of Devils Bridge. On a blustery day the Atlantic surf crashes against the coastline, where it has hollowed out a natural limestone archway, and blasts through blowholes in the rock, creating fountains of windblown salt spray. Archaeologists have made several excavations in the Indian Town Point area, which was declared a national park in the 1950s. A short drive to the north is sandy **Long Bay.**

207 C2 East of Willikies ■

Magnificent frigatebirds roost in the coastal mangrove thickets of Codrington Lagoon.

Barbuda

A 28-MILE (45-KM) PUDDLE-JUMPER FLIGHT FROM Antigua, Barbuda bakes quietly in the sun and takes things very, very easy. The 14-by-8-mile (22.5-by-13-km) coral atoll is almost two-thirds the size of its more developed, upbeat sister, Antigua, but there are just 1,500 islanders, who live mainly by fishing, farming, and hunting. Barbuda's top attractions are mind-blowing, pinkish white sand beaches and superb snorkeling; ornithologists can also enjoy the frigatebird nesting grounds on Codrington Lagoon.

Any visit to Barbuda comes with an important caveat: Accommodations at the island's exclusive resorts are stratospherically expensive. If you've mislaid the number of your Swiss bank account, consider a day trip.

Barbuda's only settlement is **Codrington,** a handful of streets leading back from the saltwater lagoon. Both were named for Christopher Codrington, a 17th-century governor-general of the Leeward Islands who leased the whole island from the British crown in 1691. (It remained in the family's hands until 1872.) Poor soil and an annual rainfall of only about 38 inches (965 mm) meant sugar cultivation was impossible on Barbuda, but Codrington introduced deer, wild boar, and guinea fowl for hunting, raised cattle, and grew provisions to supply his five Antiguan estates. He also, so it was reported, used his private island to encourage slave breeding among his strongest and healthiest West African workers.

Barbuda is almost completely ringed by breathtaking beaches. One magnificent 14-mile (22.5-km) stretch starts at the southerly tip of **Cocoa Point** and sweeps up the west coast, past the landmark River Fort defensive tower to

BARBUDA CAVES

In the northern part of the island a low stone passage plumbs the depths of **Dark Cave,** where rare blind shrimp live in subterranean pools. **Darby Sink Cave,** in The Highlands region, reaches a modest 150 feet (45 m) above sea level. The 70-foot-deep (21-m) sinkhole harbors an unexpected flourish of palmetto palms and other greenery. ■

Redonda

An uninhabited volcanic rock 30 miles (48 km) southwest of Antigua, Redonda is the third territory of Antigua and Barbuda. It has a rather bizarre recent history. In the mid-19th century, some enterprising souls recognized there was money to be made from Redonda's guano deposits. Thousands of tons of bird droppings were shipped off the island for use as fertilizer. Subsequently, Britain annexed Redonda to its Leeward Island possessions. But an Irishman from Montserrat proclaimed himself King of Redonda, and the title has since passed to a succession of colorful (nonresident) literary types who have generously created Redondan peers out of any famous people who attract their attention, from Welsh writer and poet Dylan Thomas to British film actress Diana Dors. ■

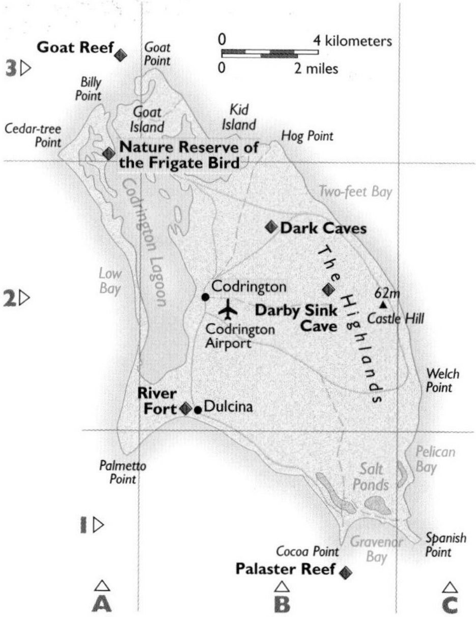

Palmetto Point, where it takes a sharp turn around the headland and continues on up the outer arm of **Codrington Lagoon.**

In the south, there's excellent snorkeling around **Gravenor Bay** and the 2-mile-long (3-km) **Palaster Reef,** a protected marine reserve off Cocoa Point. Goat Reef, in the north, is renowned for its wreck diving. As yet, Barbuda has no organized dive operation, so divers will need to bring all their equipment. Local fishing boats are available for charter.

Make it a point to take a boat trip out into the mangrove-lined **Frigate Bird Sanctuary** *(Map 215 A13)* at the north end of Codrington Lagoon. *(You pay the boatmen by the hour for the 1-2 hour trip. Visits are also included in day trip tours from Antigua.)* Here is the largest nesting colony of magnificent frigatebirds in the world, with an estimated 2,500 pairs. The glossy black birds have an 8-foot (2.5-m) wingspan and can soar at altitudes of up to 2,000 feet (600 m). During the mating season (Aug.–Nov.), male birds try to attract a female by puffing out their scarlet neck pouches like a huge balloon, trembling their outstretched wings, and emitting a strange drumming sound. A pair then builds a ragged, twig-lined nest and awaits the hatching of their ungainly, pure white young (Dec.–Feb.). More than 400 other bird species have been identified in the lagoon area. ■

Barbuda

205 D3

Visitor information

Codrington, Barbuda

268/460-0077

Anguilla
205 A3
Visitor information
P.O. Box 1388
The Valley
264/497-2759
fax 264/497-2710
Closed weekends

Anguilla

LONG BEFORE A WEALTH OF SUPERB SANDY BEACHES was considered an attraction, Spanish explorers took one look at the flat, desiccated, and most northerly of the Leeward Islands, christened it Anguilla, meaning "eel," and sailed on in search of richer, greener, and more promising territories. However, only 16 miles (25 km) long and 3 miles (5 km) wide at its broadest point, modern Anguilla's fortunes are founded on its 33 dazzling white beaches with sand so fine and deep that you have to wade rather than walk along them.

Forget rain forest hikes, historic forts, casinos, and duty-free shopping (although commercialized Sint Maarten/St.-Martin is only a 20-minute ferry ride away), and prepare to get horizontal. Anguilla has been neatly summed up in a one-line T-shirt slogan: "Life's a beach, and then you dine." And you can dine spectacularly well on Anguilla. The island may be lacking somewhat in the general interest department, but it does boast a selection of the Caribbean's most luxurious spas and architecturally striking hotels, with dining opportunities to match, several on the shore in earshot of gently lapping waves. This alluring combination draws an impressively star-studded A-list crowd.

To work up an appetite, wind-assisted water sports are available,

Many Anguillans build their own sleek, brightly painted fishing boats destined to ply the island's electric blue coastal waters.

St. Gerard's Catholic Church displays a certain individualistic take on island architecture.

and Anguilla boasts six marine parks, seven wreck dives, and terrific snorkeling. Most of the larger hotels have tennis courts and fitness centers, and the Greg Norman-designed Temenos Golf Course opened recently. Rental bikes (available from hotels) are a great way to explore the island.

AROUND THE ISLAND

Exploring Anguilla takes a day, but most visitors enjoy a change of scene, even if it's just swapping one beach for another. In the middle of the island is **The Valley,** the capital and administrative center. The settlement has no real focus, but there are some attractive shingled and shuttered traditional houses in jaunty poster-paint colors.

Set back from the main street is the **Anguilla National Museum** *(closed weekends, donations),* which presents changing exhibits on local themes, and is home to the **Anguilla National Trust.** The Trust *(Tel 264/497-5297)* organizes tours that include visits to Amerindian sites, birdwatching spots, and hawksbill turtle nesting grounds in summer. Near the airport is the 1787 **Wallblake House,** an annex of the museum and the island's only surviving plantation house complete with its old stable block and bakery *(tours Mon., Wed., Fri. 10-2; $$).*

Northeast of The Valley lies **Shoal Bay,** the island's liveliest beach, a broad belt of ankle-deep sand with a handful of beach bars, hotels, and water sports concessions renting out snorkeling gear, windsurfers, and dinghies.

Five miles (8 km) farther east by road, opposite the fishing village of

"The eel that squealed"

Laid-back Anguilla seems the last place on Earth to harbor revolutionary tendencies, but in the late 1960s it became the first British colony to stage a successful revolution against independence. In 1967, faced with the prospect of an unwanted union with St. Kitts and Nevis, the Anguillans rounded up and deported a detachment of Kittitian policemen, rolled an antique cannon onto the beach, and appealed to Britain for continued colonial status. Embarrassingly out of touch, the British government dispatched armed paratroopers to reestablish order two years later. They were greeted by cheering Anguillans waving Union Jacks and singing "God Save the Queen." The fiasco was dubbed Britain's Bay of Piglets. For an entertaining account of the whole saga, pick up a copy of Donald E. Westlake's *Under an English Heaven,* available on the island. ■

Island Harbour, is **Gorgeous Scilly Cay,** a tiny offshore islet with a palm-thatched restaurant and good snorkeling. If it's too far to swim, wave for the water taxi.

In the southeast corner of the island, seek out the **Heritage Collection** *(East End at Pond Ground, tel 264/497-4092),* a fascinating privately owned museum. The bulk of the exhibits are devoted to the revolution (box p. 218), with a detailed account of the proceedings and some entertaining photographs. There are also pieces of Amerindian pottery decorated with pelican heads and antique kitchen implements made out of coral.

You'll find other attractions to the west of The Valley. The island's deepwater port is located on the north coast at **Sandy Ground,** balanced on a curved spit of sand dividing the old salt pans from the ocean. The old salt factory is now a restaurant, and a ferry provides regular service to **Sandy Island,** another offshore beach and snorkeling spot with a snack bar. Continuing west, several hotels and good restaurants are gathered in the **Mead's Bay** and **Barnes Bay** area.

On the south coast, the futuristic apartments of Covecastles preside over **Lower Shoal Bay;** the Cap Juluca resort fronts **Maunday's Bay;** and Anguilla's longest beach, **Rendezvous Bay,** stretches out in a curving ribbon of dunes facing St.-Martin. ■

Sports & activities

Diving: Anguilla Divers Ltd. *(Tel 264/235-7742, www.anguilliandivers.com),* or Shoal Bay Scuba & Watersports *(Tel 264/ 487-4371, www.shoalbayscuba.ai).*

Hiking: Guided hikes with Oliver Hodge *(Tel 264/ 497-3696 or 264/ 772-3826).*

Horseback riding: El Rancho Del Blues *(Tel 264/ 497-6164).* ■

Boats or a cliff-hugging trail are the only way to reach secluded Little Bay on the central north coast.

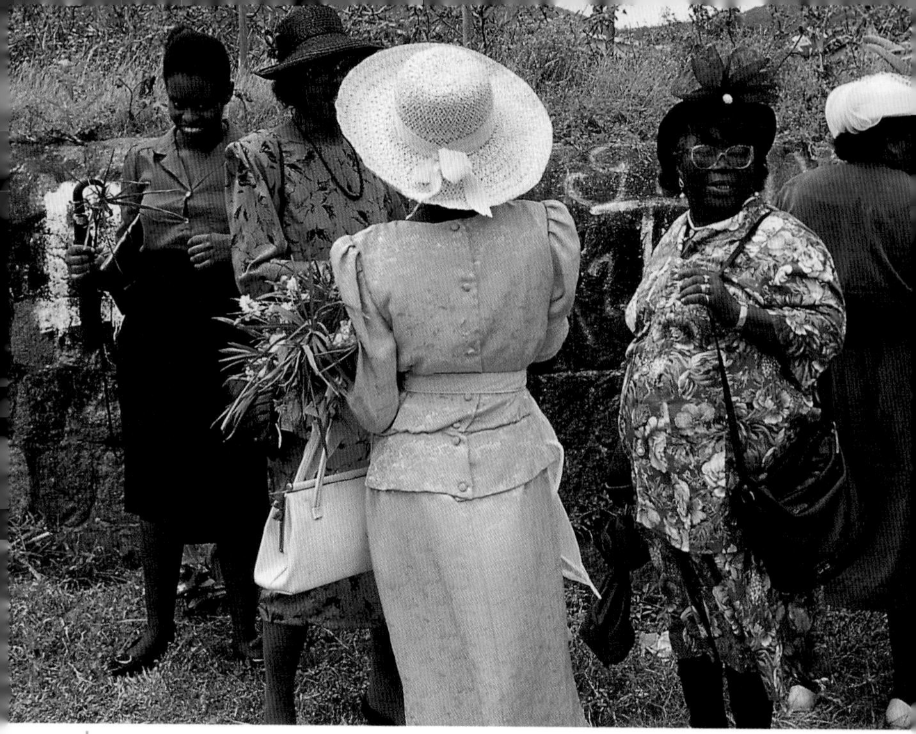

Kittitian churchgoers in their Sunday finery meet for a chat after the well-attended service.

St. Kitts

THE TWIN-ISLAND NATION OF ST. KITTS AND NEVIS LIES near the northern tip of a 500-mile-long (800-km) arc of volcanic peaks that stretches from Saba to Grenada along a curving submarine fault between the Atlantic Ocean and the Caribbean Sea. St. Kitts is the larger of the two islands at 68 square miles (176 sq km), with three distinct mountain ranges squeezed into its lush, green tadpole-shaped body. A spine of dry, rugged hills form the tail, which trails southeast toward Nevis.

St. Kitts
205 B2
Visitor information
Pelican Mall, Bay Rd., Basseterre
869/465-2620
Closed weekends

The best beaches and a small collection of hotels are gathered at the top of the tail section, close to the bustling island capital of Basseterre (see p. 222), on the south coast. To the north, the green-clad lower slopes of the ranges rise to a peak at Mount Liamuiga (3,792 feet/1,156 m), and a single perimeter road hugs the coast, linking quiet rural villages.

The Amerindian name for St. Kitts was Liamuiga (meaning fertile land), but when Christopher Columbus sailed by in 1493, he named it St. Christopher after his own patron saint and the patron saint of travelers. Just over a century later, British colonists, led by Sir Thomas Warner (1575–1649), settled on St. Kitts and set about cultivating tobacco. Having defeated the resident Carib population at Bloody Point in 1626, they ousted French colonists from the southern portion of the island, around Basseterre, and adopted St. Christopher as a base for colonizing the other Leeward Islands and Tortola in the Virgin Islands.

The island's Spanish name was Anglicized and shortened, and St. Kitts became known as the Mother Colony of the West Indies.

Naturally, the French refused to give up easily. The island and neighboring Nevis were important sugar producers, and St. Kitts, or parts of it, changed hands regularly despite the vast fortress built by the British at Brimstone Hill (see pp. 222–23), grandly but inaccurately touted as the Gibraltar of the West Indies. Britain finally secured sovereignty of the islands under the Treaty of Versailles in 1783. When the sugar bubble burst half a century later, the high-living plantocracy quit the islands in droves, and St. Kitts and Nevis shared the same dismal fate as other Caribbean sugar islands, largely ignored and left to fend for themselves by their uninterested colonial masters.

As Britain prepared to divest itself of its Leeward Island territories in the 1960s, plans were drawn up for a new tri-island state comprising St. Kitts, Nevis, and Anguilla. The Anguillans reacted immediately, staging a mini-revolution to avoid certain domination by larger and more populous St. Kitts. Despite similar reservations, Nevis entered into the state of St. Kitts and Nevis but inserted an escape clause in the constitution that would allow the smaller island to secede should the majority of Nevisians decide they would prefer to go it alone.

In recent years the Nevisian economy, boosted by offshore tax status, has outstripped that of St. Kitts, and traditional inter-island rivalries have been further exacerbated by what the Nevisians feel is undue Kittitian interference in their affairs. At present Nevis is limited to 3 representatives out of the 11-member Assembly of St. Kitts and Nevis, and the question of secession has been openly discussed. There is a very real prospect that Nevis will go solo in the near future.

While local politicians sharpen their rhetoric in the House of Assembly, island

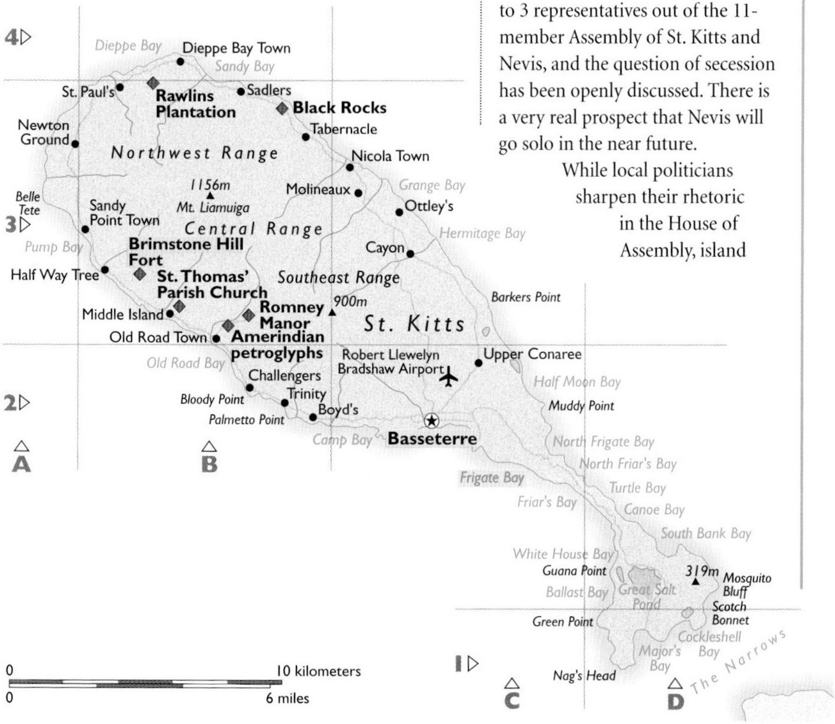

life moseys gently on. Almost two-thirds of St. Kitts' population of 35,500 live in and around Basseterre, with its boisterous street life and markets, restaurants tucked away in pretty stone courtyards, and harborfront cruise-ship pier. Beyond the town and the beach, rain forest hikes are popular. It takes a full day to hike the round-trip up to Mount Liamuiga's crater lip, but local guide companies offer several other less strenuous options, as well as jeep safaris to ruined plantation houses and sugar mills.

National Museum

- Bay Rd., Basseterre
- 869/466-9816
- Closed Mon. p.m., Sat. p.m.–Sun.

BASSETERRE

Originally settled by the French, as its name implies, Basseterre (low ground) skirts a broad bay at the foot of the Southeast Range. The British moved their capital here from Old Road in 1727, but most of the attractive skirt-and-blouse buildings (so-called for their stone ground floors and wooden uppers) postdate the major fire of 1867.

Local life revolves at a gentle pace around The Circus in downtown Basseterre.

The heart of town is arranged around the twin poles of **The Circus**—where the traffic makes its way around a fancy Victorian clock tower cum public seating area and meeting place—and **Independence Square.** The grassy square (a former slave market) has a gaudily painted fountain, a few palms, and a single poinciana, the national tree, which sports brilliant red blooms in summer. On the east side of the square the Roman Catholic church dates from 1670 but has been reconstructed several times. Behind a row of metal railings on the south side of the square stands the handsome **Old Georgian House,** looking as though it has been transplanted from a centuries-old market town in the English Cotswolds.

The Basseterre waterfront is undergoing a major facelift. An ambitious new marina, shopping area, and commercial development is planned for the area around the **Port Zante** cruise-ship pier. Meanwhile, the Old Treasury Building has been restored to house assorted island artifacts gathered in the **National Museum.** Follow Bay Road west, past fishing boats and old warehouse buildings, for ferry services to Nevis, which depart from behind the bus station.

BRIMSTONE HILL FORT & THE NORTH

A circumnavigation of northern St. Kitts makes a good day trip, with several historic sites, excellent scenery, and a choice of plantation house lunch stops along the way. You can hop aboard the **St. Kitts Scenic Railway** *(Tel 869/465-7263, www.stkittsscenicrailway.com)* and follow the old sugar train route, or hire a car and take the coast road northwest from Basseterre out along the Caribbean coast.

A local guide shares his knowledge of rain forest plants and wildlife on the slopes of Mount Liamuiga.

South (0.25 mile/0.4 km) of the village of Challengers is **Bloody Point,** the scene of the last pitched battle between St. Kitts' European settlers and Carib Indians. At **Old Road Town,** the first permanent British settlement and island capital for a century, there are **Amerindian petroglyphs** carved into a boulder on the side road leading up to **Romney Manor.** Badly damaged by fire, the partially rebuilt 17th-century manor houses the textile workshops of Caribelle Batik.

At Middle Island the tomb of Sir Thomas Warner lies in the overgrown graveyard of **St. Thomas' Parish Church.** Beyond the vil-

Romney Manor
- Map: 221 B2
- Address: Old Road Town
- Phone: 869/465-6253
- Hours: Closed Sat. p.m.–Sun.

Monkey business

The French legacy of St. Kitts extends beyond a couple of place-names, such as Basseterre and the quiet former sugar port of Dieppe Bay. The poinciana tree, with its flamboyant red blooms, is named after the first French governor of the island, Philippe de Poincy. The French also introduced green vervet monkeys, which were kept as pets. An estimated 50,000 descendants of the original monkeys are now living in colonies in the mountains. They feed off insects, berries, and fruit, and during summer (when food in the forest is more limited) they make forays to pillage small-scale farms on the edge of villages, where they are considered pests. ■

Close to the site of an old Carib Indian settlement, rock carvings of male and female figures adorn a volcanic stone outcrop.

Brimstone Hill Fortress
www.brimstonehillfortress.org
221 B2
Brimstone Hill
869/465-2609
$$$

lage the hulking volcanic outcrop of **Brimstone Hill** looms ahead enjoying commanding views across to the Dutch Windward Islands of Sint Eustatius and Saba.

A UNESCO World Heritage site, the colossal **Brimstone Hill Fortress National Park,** founded by the English in 1690, covers a 37-acre (15-ha) site 800 feet (240 m) above the coast. Built from blackened volcanic stone, the Gibraltar of the West Indies was considered impregnable until 8,000 French troops laid siege to it in 1782. It took a month of constant bombardment to destroy every building and breach the 7-foot-thick (2-m) walls, forcing the 1,000-strong garrison of defenders to surrender. The British regained control in 1794 and rebuilt the fortifications, crowned by **Fort George Citadel** which is once again bristling with cannon. A short information film is shown in the visitor's center.

As the main road rounds the north end of the island, it runs through the village of St. Paul's and

Sports & activities

Day sails: Blue Water Safaris *(Tel 869/466-4933, www.bluewatersafaris.com)* and Leeward Island Charters (*Tel 869/465-7474*) offer trips to Nevis.

Diving: Dive St. Kitts *(Tel 869/465-1189, www.divestkitts.com)* and Pro Divers, *(Frigate Bay, Tel 869/466-3483, fax 869/465-7808, www.prodiver@sisterisles.kn).*

Golf: There are 18 holes of golf at the St. Kitts Marriot in Frigate Bay *(Tel 869/466-2700).*

Hiking: It's best to join a guided walk as there are no marked trails. Recommended local guide services include Greg's Safaris *(Tel 869/465-4121, www.gregssafaris.com);* and Kriss Tours *(Tel 869/465-4042).*

Horseback riding: Rain forest trail rides and beach canters from Trinity Stables *(Tel 869/465-9603).* ■

past a bumpy track leading up to the lovely **Rawlins Plantation.**

Continuing down the east coast, make a stop at **Black Rocks.** These jagged volcanic formations were created by lava from Mount Liamuiga.

FRIGATE BAY & THE SOUTH

Just south of Basseterre lies **Frigate Bay,** St. Kitts' hotel enclave, with an 18-hole golf course and beaches on both sides of the isthmus. The broad, sandy beach on the more sheltered (southern) Caribbean coast is the island's busiest. It has a beach bar and several restaurants. On the Atlantic side of the isthmus the water is rougher, but there's good body-surfing and the swimming is safe. Swimming isn't recommended at **North Friar's Bay,** however, which has dangerous currents, but its opposite number, **South Friar's Bay,** is lovely, sandwiched between palm trees and glassy calm water.

A 10-mile (15-km) highway roller coasters down to the southern tip of the island, rounding the old salt ponds where several species of wading birds can be spotted, and egrets balance on the backs of well-fed cattle grazing by the roadside.

Facing Nevis across The Narrows are the small, undeveloped beaches on **Major's Bay, Banana Bay,** and **Cockleshell Bay; Turtle Bay** is served by a lively bar-restaurant. There's a dive operator here, snorkeling off the beach, and wind surfer and ocean kayak rental. ■

Fieldworkers wielding machetes harvest sugarcane in the old-fashioned way.

Nevis

Nevis

205 B2

Visitor information

Main St.
Charlestown

869/469-7550

DIVIDED FROM ST. KITTS BY A 2-MILE-WIDE (3-KM) CHANNEL known as The Narrows, Nevis rears up precipitously to an imposing volcanic cone. Columbus named the island Nuestra Señora de las Nieves (Our Lady of the Snows) in a rather fanciful allusion to the almost permanently cloud-capped heights of Nevis Peak (3,232 feet/985 m); his poetic name was later mangled by British settlers to less romantic but more serviceable Nevis (pronounced NEE-viss).

Colonists established a toehold on the island in 1627, and by the mid-18th century the planters of Nevis were so prosperous and fashionable that the pint-size island was hailed as the Queen of the Caribees, renowned for its grand plantation houses, fabulous parties, and the spa in Charlestown's Bath Hotel. Nevis was not immune to the French raiding parties that targeted St. Kitts, and suffered several attacks that destroyed buildings and crops. African slaves captured from the famed and highly profitable slave market on Nevis were regarded as an additional prize and were shipped away to work the cane fields of Guadeloupe and Martinique. A century and a half after the abolition of slavery, Nevis accepted independence from Britain as part of the Federation of St. Kitts and Nevis.

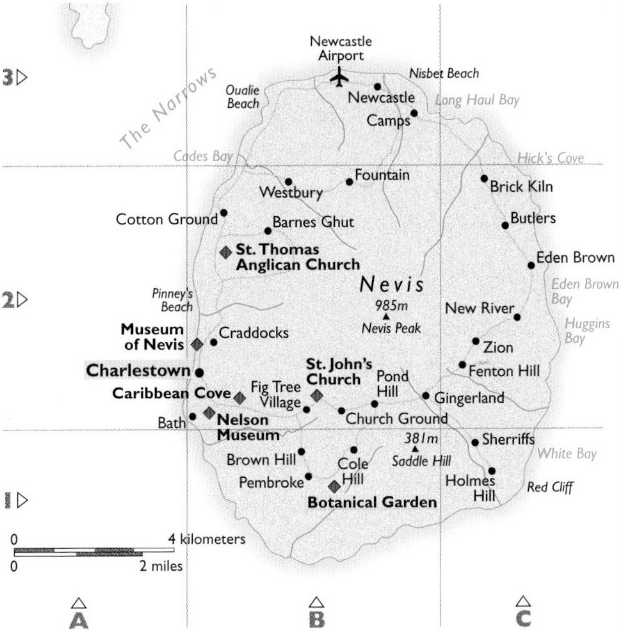

A dense mantle of rain forest greenery cloaks Nevis Peak, which dominates the interior of the island.

The smaller (36 square miles/93 sq km) and quieter partner in the two-island coalition, Nevis retains vestiges of its rich colonial past in a clutch of gracious plantation house hotels and the sturdy stone buildings of the main settlement, Charlestown.

The 10,000 Nevisians are among the most hospitable hosts in the Caribbean region, and the island's unhurried pace and gentle charm are soothing antidotes to world-weariness. Tourism Nevis-style is relatively upscale but determinedly low-key. Nevis has no casinos or air-conditioned malls, not even a major historical site, although Lord Nelson got married on the island, with a future king of England in attendance. Instead, guests at most of the plantation hotels have to journey to the beaches on the Caribbean (west) coast, work up an appetite horseback riding or hiking in the rain forest, and make a round-island tour that takes all of half a day.

CHARLESTOWN

Located two-thirds of the way down the Caribbean west coast, Charlestown is the capital of Nevis and the liveliest spot on the island. Founded about 1660 and named in honor of King Charles II in 1671, the town straggles along the main round-island road to its hub, a grassy triangle that doubles as a meeting place and minibus depot a short walk from the pier. Traditional two-story stone and wood colonial buildings with balconies and gingerbread trim line the street, and a selection of shops, cafés, and small businesses has moved into the alleys leading down to the rejuvenated waterfront, where ferries from St. Kitts unload passengers and provisions onto the dock.

At the north end of Main Street is the **Museum of Nevis,** housed in Alexander Hamilton House, birthplace of the American statesman (1757–1804) whose image graces the $10 bill (see p. 228). The one-room museum's modest

Museum of Nevis
- Low St., Charlestown
- 869/469-5786
- Closed Sat. p.m.–Sun.
- $$

Nelson Museum
Bath Rd.
Charlestown
869/469-0408
Closed Sat. p.m.–Sun.
$$

collections cover a broad spectrum of island history and culture, from Amerindian pottery shards to independence.

An early European visitor to Nevis was Capt. John Smith and a party of 144 Englishmen. They spent six days on Nevis in 1607 en route to found the colony at Jamestown, Virginia. The group were revived by a dip in the hot spring that would later feature as the centerpiece of the 18th-century **Bath Hotel** at the southern end of town. Today the hotel buildings are being gradually restored and visitors can once again take a dip in the steaming waters.

Just up from the hotel is the **Nelson Museum,** which examines the life and times of the great English naval hero. Horatio Nelson married local girl Fanny Nisbet at the Montpelier Estate in 1787, during an uncomfortable posting to Antigua (see p. 211). Exhibits include a plate from the wedding feast, a portion of the Union Jack flag under which Nelson stood when he was fatally wounded at the Battle of Trafalgar in 1805, and items from the mountain of Wedgwood, Staffordshire, and other memorabilia commissioned to commemorate his death.

AROUND THE ISLAND

Just north of Charlestown, parallel to the coast road, is **Pinney's Beach,** which unfurls in a 4-mile (6.5-km) reel of golden sand backed by palm trees. Along the way you'll pass **St. Thomas Anglican Church,** sitting on a small rise with views along the coast and across to St. Kitts. Founded in 1643, it is believed to be the oldest congregation on the island.

Farther north is **Oualie Beach,** which has good snorkeling and water sports. Beyond Newcastle Airport is the **Newcastle Pottery,** set in a small roadside workshop, where simple handmade bowls, candleholders, and jugs are fashioned from local red clay.

Alexander Hamilton

Born on Nevis on January 11, 1757, Alexander Hamilton served as aide-de-camp to Gen. George Washington during the American Revolution. He was nicknamed "the Little Lion" on account of his relatively diminutive stature (5 feet 7 inches/170 cm) and ferocious temper, which, it was said, turned his blue eyes to black when he was angry. Hamilton trained as a lawyer, and Washington appointed him the first secretary of the treasury. He died in a duel with Vice President Aaron Burr (1756–1836), his political rival, in 1804. ■

There is more reef snorkeling off the white coral sands of **Nisbet Beach** as the road circles around to the rougher Atlantic coast.

Four of Nevis' five plantation house hotels nestle beneath **Nevis Peak,** overlooking the south coast between Gingerland and Fig Tree Village. A glorious **Botanical Garden** has been established on the grounds of Montpelier Estate. The 8-acre (3-ha) site is ideal for a gentle stroll and offers plenty to interest the plant lover, from the fragrant rose and vine gardens to a rain forest conservatory, lily pools, a palm collection, and shady orchid terraces. Nelson and Fanny Nisbet's marriage at Montpelier Estate is recorded in a copy of the marriage register on display at **St. John's Church** in Fig Tree, on the road back to Charlestown. ■

Sports & activities

Diving: Scuba Safaris *(Oualie Beach, tel 869/469-9518).*

Golf: Excellent 18-hole Robert Trent Jones course at the Four Seasons Hotel *(Pinney's Beach, tel 869/469-1111).*

Hiking: Gentle rambles from Eco-Rambles *(Tel 869/469-2091, e-mail droll@caribsurf.com)* or challenging excursions, including treks to Nevis Peak, with Top to Bottom *(Tel 869/469-9080, e-mail info@walknevis.com).*

Horseback riding: Nevis Equestrian Centre *(Cades Bay, tel 869/469-8118)*; Hermitage Inn *(St. John's Parish, tel 469-3477).* ■

The register at St. John's Church, Fig Tree, records the marriage of Lord Nelson and Fanny Nisbet.

Botanical Garden

- Map: 227 B1
- Address: Montpelier Estate, St. John's Parish
- Tel: 869/469-3509
- Hours: Closed Sun.
- Price: $$$

Montserrat

Montserrat

205 CI

Visitor information

www.visitmontserrat.com

Montserrat Tourist Board
7 Farara Plaza, Brades
e-mail info@montserrattourism.ms

664/491-2230
fax 664/491-7430

THE MOST SOUTHERLY OUTPOST OF THE LEEWARD ISLAND group, Montserrat was long regarded as a haven of tranquility. A real slice of the old Caribbean with a smattering of beaches and hotels, and a lush, mountainous interior that invited exploration. The island's peaceful idyll was shattered by the devastating eruption of the Soufrière Volcano in 1995.

The island was named by Columbus for the famous Montserrate Abbey near Barcelona, Spain, and settled by Irish Catholics seeking refuge from Protestant persecution on St. Kitts in the 17th century. The Irish connection earned Montserrat its nickname, "the Emerald Isle," and today celebrate St. Patrick's Day as well as the Queen's birthday (the island is a British Crown Colony).

Life was a gentle round of fishing, farming, and a little low-key tourism until Montserrat's quiet repose was destroyed by ominous grumblings from the Soufrière Volcano in the summer of 1995. As ash, rocks, and lava rained down from the newly reactivated volcano, the southern portion of the island was evacuated and a safe zone established on the northern third. Increased volcanic activity in 1997 saw the abandoned capital, **Plymouth,** destroyed and at the present time volcanologists are unable to predict an end to Soufrière's volcanic activity.

However, this has not stopped the optimistic Montserratians from reinventing their island as a tourist destination with a difference. Forget your classic Caribbean beach holiday and visit Montserrat for rightup-close volcano-watching, which might feature spectacular dome collapses, massive ash clouds, and glowing nighttime lava flows. Overnight visitors will find several hotels keen to welcome intrepid travelers.

The top spot for volcano viewing is the **Montserrat Volcano Observatory** *(Tel 664/491-5647, www.mvo.ms),* which is manned by scientists monitoring volcanic activity and open for twice-weekly tours. Or take a picnic to the Jack Boy Hill viewing area. Other activities include hiking and bird watching in the verdant Silver and Centre Hills (both in the safe zone), mountain-biking, sea-kayaking, and diving (see below). ■

ISLAND ORIGINS

Montserrat is part of the volcanic Windward Island chain poised on Atlantic and Caribbean tectonic plates. As these plates grind slowly, magma escapes from the Earth's core. These eruptions have created a chain of peaks. All the major Windwards have an active volcano, called a *soufrière* (French for sulfur). In the Grenadines a new sea mount known as Kick 'em Jenny is gradually taking shape and promises to be the newest Caribbean island. ■

Information & transportation

The Montserrat Tourist Board's excellent website *(www.visitmontserrat.com)* provides visitor information. The new airport at Gerald's receives several flights daily from Antigua and Sint Maarten with Winair *(Tel 664/491-6988, www.fly-winair.com),* and Air Montserrat *(Tel 664/491-6728, www.airmontserrat.com).* For hotel information, see *www.montserrat-island-hotels.com.*

An unexpected benefit of the 2-mile marine exclusion zone around the island has been the creation of an underwater reserve abounding in diving opportunities. Contact local operators Green Monkey Dive Shop *(Tel 664/491-2960, www.divemontserrat.com),* or Sea Wolf Diving School *(Tel 664/491-7807, www.seawolfdivingschool.com).* ■

The French Caribbean islands of Guadeloupe and Martinique sashay to a vibrant Creole beat, while sybaritic St.-Barthélemy lends an unmistakable aura of European chic to the laid-back tropics.

French Antilles

Traditional Creole headdress

French Antilles

TWO OF THE LARGEST ISLANDS IN THE LESSER ANTILLES (AFTER TRINIDAD), Guadeloupe and Martinique flank Dominica midway down the chain of eastern Caribbean islands. These islands are the heart of the French Caribbean, exuding a zesty Creole atmosphere that permeates every aspect of daily life from the insistent rhythms of zouk music and the rapid-fire Creole language to local cuisine and the colorful checked madras cotton tucked into complicated women's headdresses. Some 150 miles (240 km) away among the Dutch islands and former British colonies of the Leewards, the smaller French territories of St.-Barthélemy (St. Barts) and St.-Martin (half an island shared with the Netherlands) stick to a more traditional French lifestyle modeled on that of *la métropole,* as mainland France is known.

The islets of Les Saintes are a popular destination for day-trippers

The first French colony in the Caribbean was founded on St. Kitts in 1624, the year after an English settlement was established on the island. A decade later, ambitious French colonists expanded their horizons and bravely tackled the Cannibal Isles, gaining a foothold on both Guadeloupe and Martinique between 1635 and 1636. The introduction of sugar cultivation in the latter part of the 17th century heralded *l'age d'or blanc* (the age of white gold) and the expansion of French influence down the eastern Caribbean chain and north to St. Domingue (present-day Haiti). As slave ships unloaded their human cargo to work the vast tracts of sugarcane, sizable fortunes flowed into the planters' coffers, and the town of St.-Pierre on Martinique developed into one of the most prosperous and fashionable cities in the West Indies.

Things did not always run smoothly, of course. Britain challenged France's authority at every turn and by a combination of treaties and brute force occupied virtually every French Caribbean territory during the 18th century. France did her best to return the compliment.

Ironically the supporters of the *ancien régime* of Martinique actually called the enemy in to assist when the French Revolution decreed the abolition of slavery. The British ruled the island for 20 years without liberating the slaves. Napoleon (whose wife came from a family of Martiniquan planters) reintroduced slavery in 1802, causing widespread chaos and slave rebellions in Haiti and Guadeloupe. The law was not repealed until 1848, when the plantations turned to East Indian indentured laborers to replace the freed slaves.

Unlike the British islands, which were gently but firmly urged down the road to independence in the 20th century, France has bound her Caribbean territories more closely. Guadeloupe and Martinique have been integrated into the republic's political mainstream as semiautonomous overseas *régions.* The islanders have the same rights as their mainland counterparts and elect representatives to the Assemblée Nationale in Paris, vote in French elections, and enjoy the benefits of substantial government subsidies that have elevated local standards of living way above average for the region.

Dramatic volcanic eruptions raised Guadeloupe and Martinique from the seabed, and both islands boast beautiful mountain ranges choked with rain forest greenery and encircled by cane fields and banana plantations. There are well-developed resorts on sandy beaches and upcountry hideaways, frenetic port cities and picturesque fishing harbors, where the catch of the day is flipped straight off the dock

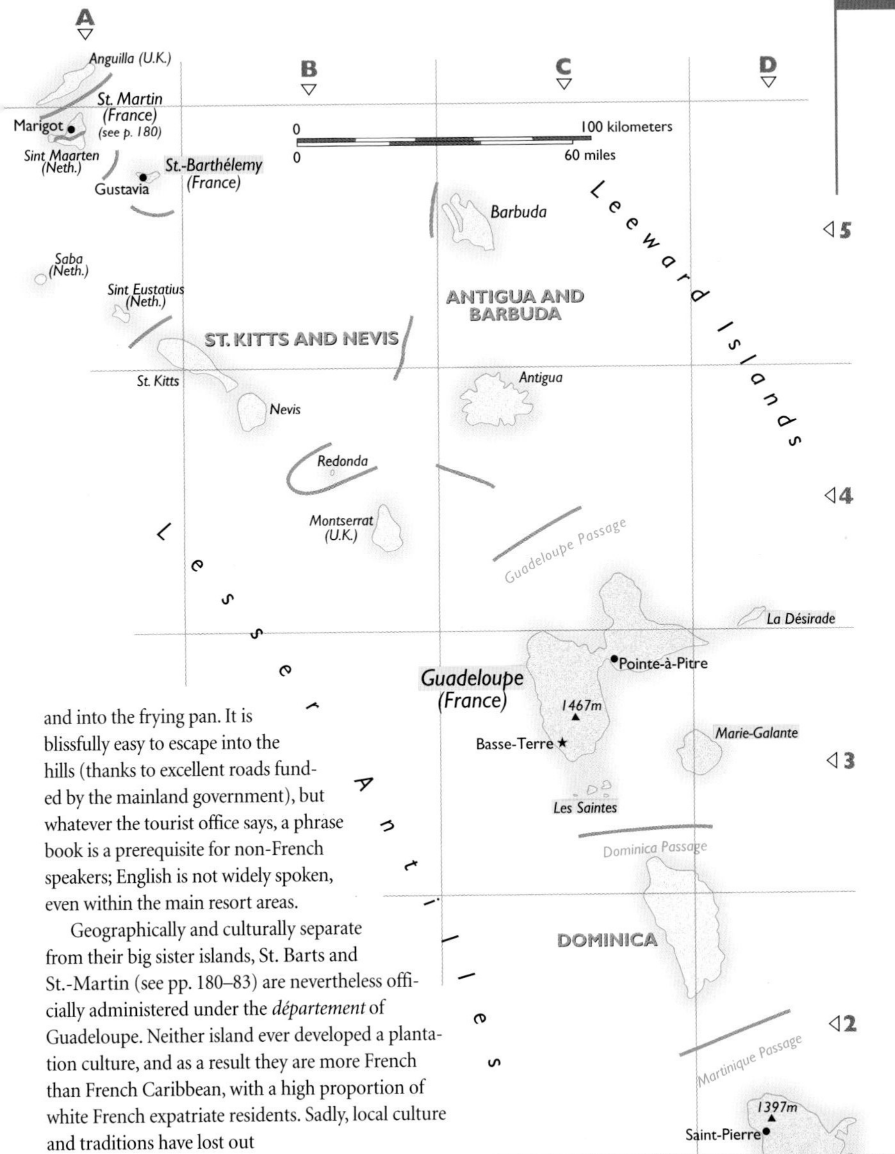

and into the frying pan. It is blissfully easy to escape into the hills (thanks to excellent roads funded by the mainland government), but whatever the tourist office says, a phrase book is a prerequisite for non-French speakers; English is not widely spoken, even within the main resort areas.

Geographically and culturally separate from their big sister islands, St. Barts and St.-Martin (see pp. 180–83) are nevertheless officially administered under the *département* of Guadeloupe. Neither island ever developed a plantation culture, and as a result they are more French than French Caribbean, with a high proportion of white French expatriate residents. Sadly, local culture and traditions have lost out to tourism, both the upscale and sophisticated model on St. Barts and the more accessible version peddled by St.-Martin, but excellent food, great beaches, and the prospect of fun in the sun with a French accent definitely has its charms. ■

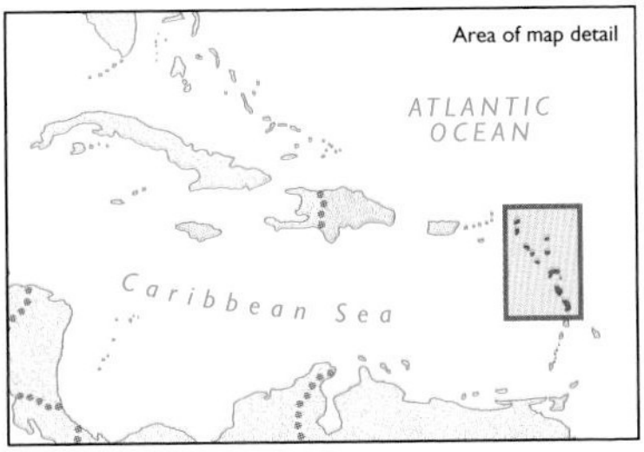

Hiking trails in the Parc National de la Guadeloupe traverse the challenging terrain of Basse-Terre's central highlands.

Guadeloupe

SHAPED LIKE A GIANT BUTTERFLY WITH MISMATCHED wings, Guadeloupe is in fact two separate islands crowded together by seismic upheavals and linked by a bridge over the Rivière Salée (Salt River). The western wing is Basse-Terre, its verdant and volcanic peaks marching south to the crater rim of smoldering Soufrière (4,815 feet/1,467 m). By contrast, the eastern wing of Grande-Terre is a rolling, dry limestone plateau fringed by beaches and coral reefs. Making up the Guadeloupean archipelago offshore are the islands of La Désirade, Marie-Galante, and the eight tiny islets of Les Saintes (see pp. 246–47). Guadeloupe is an inviting mixture of urban buzz and unspoiled scenery, suffused with an unmistakable Creole flavor.

Guadeloupe
233 C3
Visitor information
5 Square de la Banque, Pointe-à-Pitre
0590/82 09 30, fax 0590/83 89 22

Perhaps inspired by the dozens of streams and waterfalls that tumble down Basse-Terre's rain-forested flanks, the Carib people called the island Karukera (Island of Beautiful Waters). Christopher Columbus sailed past in 1493 and rechristened it Santa Maria de Guadalupe de Extremadura in honor of a famous Spanish monastery. A century and a half later the French colonized Guadeloupe with indentured settlers who worked for three years to pay off their sea passage. Unaccustomed to tropical conditions, they farmed with limited success until a four-year British occupation (1759–1763) turned the plantations around. The slow start meant Guadeloupe was administered from more successful Martinique and was forced to trade through the commercial port of St.-Pierre on Martinique, whose merchants paid artificially low prices for Guadeloupean sugar. As news of the French Revolution traveled across the Atlantic in 1789, it found the unhappy Guadeloupeans ripe for change.

Guadeloupe's settlers embraced the revolutionary regime with enthusiasm. Bands of armed *patriotes* (supporters of the revolution) overthrew the planters and installed a revolutionary government led by Victor Hugues (1770–1826). They erected the mandatory guillotine in Pointe-à-Pitre, where more than 300 enemies of the revolution lost their heads. The slaves were freed in 1794, but their freedom was short-lived. The old regime regained control, and slavery was bloodily reestablished; many former slaves preferred death to submission. The British came and went a couple more times before France secured the colony for good in 1815. The Guadeloupeans' independent cast of mind remains a force to be reckoned with today. There are occasional calls for independence from *la métropole,* but French cash is a powerful incentive to remain under the old colonial umbrella, particularly in view of the massive grants made available to help the island rebuild in the wake of hurricane damage.

Guadeloupe encompasses 530 square miles (1,372 sq km) and has a population of about 425,000. The contrasting island wings possess two equally diverse main cities. On the southwest coast of Basse-Terre is Basse-Terre town (see p. 242), the modest administrative capital tucked in the lee of La Soufrière. A circlet of small towns and villages, linked by a round-island road, ring the coast of Guadeloupe's west wing. Only one route, La Traversée, scales the central mountain range, clambering up into the Parc National de la Guadeloupe (see p. 243), a magnificent natural preserve with some of the best—and most challenging—hiking in the Caribbean.

In the southwest corner of Grande-Terre is Guadeloupe's biggest and busiest city—the sprawling commercial center and cruise ship port of Pointe-à-Pitre

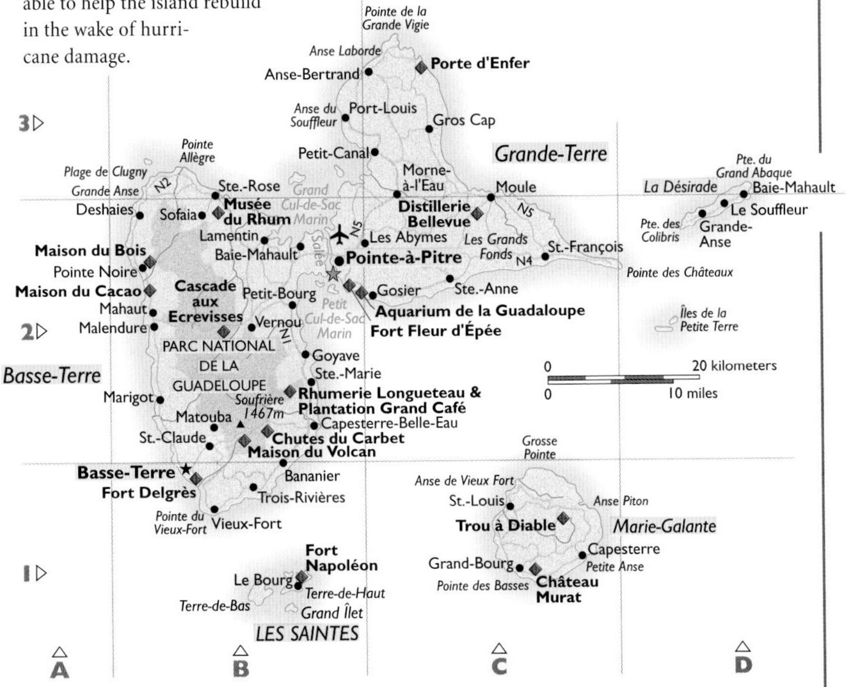

A rare open space shaded by stately palm trees provides a brief respite from the bustle of downtown Pointe-à-Pitre.

Opposite: Young Guadeloupean women dress in colorful costumes and gold jewelry for the annual pre-Lenten Carnival celebrations.

(see below). No great beauty, it has a frenetic pace at odds with the usual leisurely Caribbean tempo, but it's fun to explore the local markets, and ferries for the offshore islands leave from the waterfront. Dotted east along the coast from Pointe-à-Pitre are the seaside resort towns of Gosier, Ste.-Anne, and St.-François. Gosier is the most developed, with a wall of large, modern hotels fronting the shore and packed beaches. Ste.-Anne and St.-François have retained more of their local character. Here it is sometimes possible to catch a game of *boules* in progress on one of the dusty, tree-shaded squares before dining out stylishly *à la française* at an excellent (although not inexpensive) fish restaurant along the promenade.

Pointe-à-Pitre
235 B2

POINTE-À-PITRE

A teeming metropolis of 80,000 souls, Pointe-à-Pitre lies on a sheltered bay at the southern end of the Rivière Salée. Although the city dates from the 17th century, hurricanes, earthquakes, and fires have taken their toll, and modern concrete structures outnumber the few remaining colonial buildings.

With the sunlight blotted out by tall, thin buildings, downtown Pointe-à-Pitre is a maelstrom of traffic and pedestrians fighting for space on the narrow streets. At times it appears that there are more cars on the sidewalk than pedestrians, and jaywalking is obligatory. (Avoid driving in the downtown area at all costs.)

The focus of the old town is **La Darse,** the bustling waterfront area, with its ferry dock and jumble of street vendors' stalls selling anything from T-shirts and wood carvings to fresh produce and piping hot *accras* (see p. 238). Behind the dockside hubbub is **Place de la Victoire,** with its fringe of old colonial houses, their balconies full of flowers. A handful of sidewalk cafés provides a restful view of the city's green heart, planted with palm, mango, and African tulip trees.

Plunge into the grid of busy side streets west of the gardens to the **Cathédrale St.-Pierre et St.-Paul** *(place Gourbeyre).* Nicknamed *la cathédrale de fer* ("iron cathedral") for its elaborate

On rural Grande-Terre, a local farmer and his oxen pause to contemplate the antics of water-sport enthusiasts.

Creole cuisine & dining out

The Creole cuisine of Guadeloupe and Martinique is an inspired fusion of French culinary élan, traditional African cooking, and local Caribbean ingredients. Seafood is a mainstay of Creole menus and comes in a wide variety of guises, from simple *accras* (shredded salt-cod fritters) to *blaff* (a fish or shellfish stew cooked in a wine and herb court bouillon). Other specialties include *cirique* or *étrille* (little sea crabs), *chatrou* (octopus), *lambi* (conch tenderized with lime for salads), *langouste* (lobster), *ouassous* (crayfish), and *soudrons* (clams). *Crabes farcis* are stuffed land crabs, more meaty than sea crabs, and the locals are known to feed them with dried coconut and hot peppers to improve their flavor. Try *colombo,* a curried stew of chicken or goat *(cabri)* flavored with coriander, cumin, mustard, ginger, and pepper. Traditional accompaniments are *fruit à pain,* the rather tasteless fruit of the breadfruit tree, and *christophene,* a tropical squash served cooked or grated raw in salads.

Dining out can be expensive, but Creole food is generally cheaper than French. Limited-choice menus at a fixed price *(menu touristique)* are usually good value, and service is included *(compris).* It is de rigueur to round off a meal with a *digestif* from among the dozens of locally produced aged or fruit-flavored rums. ■

ironwork, the building was constructed in the early 19th century and has some fine stained glass.

Rue Frébault, the city's main shopping street, is lined with boutiques and stores full of French fashions and European imports. On the corner of Frébault and rue Peynier is the **Marché Couvert** (Covered Market), providing a boisterous slice of island life. Its maze of stalls is piled high with fruits and vegetables, bags of ground spices, and bunches of vanilla pods presided over by garrulous female vendors who giggle and haggle in a machine-gun patter of incomprehensible Creole.

West along rue Peynier is the **Musée Schoelcher,** devoted to the life and times of 19th-century abolitionist Victor Schoelcher (1804–1893), a leading light in the French antislavery movement. When emancipation finally reached the French Caribbean in 1848, Schoelcher was elected a deputy of Guadeloupe. The museum occupies a pretty pink town house with wrought iron decorations and a double staircase leading up to the entrance. Exhibits range from plantation-era artifacts and Schoelcher's campaigning pamphlets to African carved ivories, model ships, and other curios. The statue in front of the building depicts the revolutionary leader Victor Hugues.

AROUND GRANDE-TERRE

Though Grande-Terre's southern beaches act as a magnet for tourists, most of the island is undeveloped, a rural backwater where rolling limestone hills, known as Les Grands Fonds, shelter a smattering of small

Shoppers haggle and adopt a distinctly hands-on approach when selecting fresh local produce at street markets.

Musée Schoelcher

www.netgua.com.fr/musee Schoelcher

- 24 rue Peynier
- 0590/82 08 04
- Closed weekends
- $

Aquarium de la Guadeloupe
- 235 B2
- Place Créole-Marina
- 0590/90 92 38
- $$$

Fort Fleur d'Epée
- 235 B2
- 0590/90 94 61

Gosier
- 235 C2

farming hamlets, and the sugarcane harvest is still transported to the mill by ox-drawn carts.

Between Pointe-à-Pitre and Gosier is **Bas-du-Fort's** busy marina, which is a good place to stop off and sample the nautical atmosphere from a sunny café or to dine out in restaurants. Next to the marina is the **Aquarium de la Guadeloupe,** the biggest in the Caribbean. A showcase for tropical fish, it also has a mangrove section and a huge shark tank with a walk-through Plexiglas tunnel.

On a headland above Bas-du-Fort are the 18th-century coral rock ruins of **Fort Fleur d'Epée,** laid out on a hilltop site shaded by red-flowering flamboyant trees.

Across Grande Baie is the seaside town of **Gosier,** Guadeloupe's chief resort, taking its name from the brown pelican, a familiar sight throughout the Caribbean. The old town has been swamped by an avalanche of hotels, restaurants, cafés, and discos spilling downhill to the shore and stretching for several miles along the narrow sandy beaches. Hotels and concessions are well equipped for water sports, and small boats make the short voyage out to the tiny offshore pimple of **Îlet du Gosier,** where there's a lighthouse and another public beach (clothing optional).

Midway along the coast is **Ste.-Anne,** where long, sandy Caravelle beach offers water-sport activities and a Club Med resort to the west of town. Nearby is **Ste.-Anne Plage,** a lovely strip of fine white sand on a turquoise bay. It can get crowded, but plus points for families include shady trees, a row of café-restaurants across the street, and carts selling hot, sweet crêpes, and ice cream.

St.-François has a salty tang, with fishermen constructing traditional hexagonal fish traps from wooden battens and chicken wire on the waterfront. The closest beach is **Plage des Raisins Clair,** but to the east of town is the 7-mile (11-km) road out to Pointe des Châteaux, lined with beaches along the southern shore. **Plage Tarare,** on the north side, is a nudist haunt. At the tip of the headland is **Pointe des Châteaux,** with its own small beach cove where surfers ride the powerful Atlantic waves that have hollowed caves from the soft limestone. A rocky path scales the cliffs

Sports & activities

Bicycling *(cyclisme)*: Cycling is a hugely popular weekend sport when Guadeloupeans take to Basse-Terre's mountainous hinterland in a blur of Lycra. Grande-Terre offers gentler cycling. Rental details from local tourism offices.

Diving & snorkeling *(plongée sous-marine & plongée avec tuba)*: Best off Basse-Terre's west coast; also around Îlet du Gosier. Contact Les Heures Saines *(plage de Malendure, tel 0590/98 86 63, www.heuressaines.gp)*; Hotel Fleur d'Epée *(Gosier, tel 0590/90 85 11)*.

Golf: Golf de St. François *(Tel 0590/88 41 87)*, an 18-hole course.

Hiking *(randonnée)*: See p. 243.

Horseback riding *(équitation)*: Haras de St-François *(Grande-Terre, tel 0590/58 99 92)*; La Manade, St.-Claude *(Basse-Terre, tel 0590/81 52 21)*. ■

to an orientation table with blustery views to the out islands and peaks of Basse-Terre.

From St.-François, Rte. N5 runs north to **Moule,** once the capital of Guadeloupe. On a back road west of town is the **Distillerie Bellevue** *(open for visits),* the only rum distillery on Grande-Terre.

A country road continues up to the northern tip of the island, past a viewpoint at **Porte d'Enfer** (Gate of Hell), before reaching **Pointe de la Grande Vigie** (Grand Lookout), where French sentries once scanned the horizon for signs of British activity on Antigua.

Beach stops on the west coast include **Anse Laborde** (just north of Anse-Bertrand) and **Anse du Souffleur** (at Port-Louis). In the center of the island is **Morne-à-l'Eau,** famous for its classic French Caribbean cemetery. ■

Families flock to the shallow sheltered bay fronting Ste.-Anne.

Nature preserved

On the west coast of Grande-Terre is the **Réserve Naturelle du Grand Cul de Sac Marin,** an annex of the Guadeloupe national park. Its 9,000-acre (3,600-ha) territory encompasses mangrove swamps, coastal forest, and an adjacent marine preserve. The foreshore is a prime feeding ground for waterfowl and wading birds. The *bateau-mouche King Papyrus* offers trips to the marine preserve from the Marina de Pointe-à-Pitre *(Tel 0590/90 92 98).* ■

Distillerie Bellevue

- 235 C2
- Rte. D101, on the road from Moule to Les Abymes
- 0590/23 55 55

Around southern Basse-Terre

Basse-Terre
235 B1
Visitor information
Maison du Port, off blvd. du Général de Gaulle
0590/81 24 83

Rhumerie Longueteau
235 B2
0590/86 79 03
Closed Sat. and Sun. p.m.

Plantation Grand Café
235 B2
0590/86 33 06
Closed Sat. p.m.–Sun.
$$

Domaine de Valombreuse
235 B2
Cabout
0590/95 50 50

VIEWED FROM THE SUNNY BEACHES OF GRANDE-TERRE, the towering, luxuriantly green bulk of neighboring Basse-Terre appears to brood like some giant leviathan beneath a blanket of clouds. About two-thirds of the island is the unspoiled Parc National de la Guadeloupe with *traces* (walking trails) ranging from short, muddy scrabbles to waterfall beauty spots to serious long-distance hikes across the ridgeline or up to the Soufrière volcano. A fast modern road (Rte. N1) whisks you down the east coast from Pointe-à-Pitre to the capital of Basse-Terre in less than an hour, although there are several minor detours en route.

Inland from Petit-Bourg, the botanic gardens at **Domaine de Valombreuse** are laid out in the foothills. There are more than 1,000 species of plants, trails, bird life, and a children's play area. Just south of **Ste.-Marie,** a small coastal town where Christopher Columbus is thought to have come ashore and encountered his first Carib in 1493, there are signs off the main road to the **Rhumerie Longueteau** distillery and Plantation Grand Café, a banana plantation. Cane fields surround the modern Longueteau estate house and its tiny, old-fashioned steam mill. Informal tours operate year-round, but the mill is only working (and interesting) during the January-to-July harvest season. After the visit, you can sample straight rums and potent homemade rums spiked with tropical fruits such as guava, pineapple, carambola, or banana.

Just up the road is the **Plantation Grand Café,** which celebrates the not-so-humble banana. A banana garden displays different varieties from around the world—little plump pink velutinas from India, and crocodile's fingers from Indonesia, among others. The 30-minute tours rattle around the plantation in open-sided trucks.

On the southern edge of the town of Capesterre-Belle-Eau a side road leads up to the trailhead for the third and least spectacular of the **Chutes du Carbet,** a series of three waterfalls in the national park (see p. 243) fed by the Rivière Grand Carbe, which originates on La Soufrière. The third fall is a mere 65 feet (20 m) high, but it's a peaceful 45-minute trek into the rain forest beneath giant mahogany, gommier, and bois rouge trees. Although the path continues on to the two upper falls, the most popular access point is another side road about a mile (1.6 km) farther along Rte. N1, which takes a scenic route up to a parking area and collection of roadside barbecue stalls. It's a 20-minute uphill hike to the popular 360-foot-high (110-m) second fall. It takes two hours to reach the 410-foot-high (125-m) top fall and three hours to get up to **Soufrière.**

At the southern tip of the island is **Basse-Terre town,** which offers little to detain the dedicated sightseer, although it has a bustling provincial charm. Across the street from its French-style, palm-lined seafront esplanade, stalls are weighed down by succulent mangoes and pineapples, and teetering pyramids of fresh vegetables tumble out of the covered market. A tight grid of shopping streets squeezes in

between the Hôtel de Ville and the gray stone Catholic cathedral. To the south, **Fort Delgrès** stands guard over the harbor and houses a small history museum as well as the **Maison du Volcan,** with displays charting the origins of volcanoes and the history of La Soufrière above the city. Behind the city center are residential suburbs spreading up the hillsides to St.-Claude, where a few old Creole houses cling doggedly to slopes hedged in by exuberant gardens.

Above St.-Claude, Rte. D11 strikes on up through the encroaching rain forest, narrowing as it climbs toward **Savane à Mulets,** 1,000 feet (305 m) below the volcano's summit. From here the round-trip hike to the summit takes around two and a half hours along a well-marked trail past lava flows, boulders, and sludge deposited as recently as 1976, when Soufrière last erupted. The climb is generally accompanied by a steady drizzle and cool winds, so bring appropriate clothing. At the summit, not one crater but a chain of reeking, sulfur-spewing pits are staggered along the fault line, and heat radiates from the ground.

To complete a tour of southern Basse-Terre, the slow west coast road (Rte. N2) parallels the shore to **Mahaut,** where the Route de la Traversée (see p. 244) crosses back to the east coast for Pointe-à-Pitre. If you're in a hurry, however, it's quicker to return along the east coast. ■

Soufrière volcano dominates the southern half of Basse-Terre.

Fort Delgrès
235 B1
0590/81 37 48

Parc National de la Guadeloupe

For additional information about the national park in Guadeloupe, contact the park headquarters at Habitation Beausoleil *(Montéran, 97120 St.-Claude, tel 0590/80 86 00, www.guadeloupe-parcnational.com)*. The main access points to the park's trail network in Basse-Terre are along the Route de la Traversée (see p. 244) and around Soufrière. Guided hikes (some in English) can be arranged through the Bureau des Guides *(Tel 0590/80 56 48)*, or adventure tour operators such as Vert Intense *(Tel 0590/55 40 47)*. ■

A drive around northern Basse-Terre

This clockwise circuit of northern Basse-Terre begins with a spectacular rain forest drive along the Route de la Traversée before looping around the top half of the island. You can experience a variety of suggested diversions along the way, from a glass-bottomed boat trip to museums of cocoa, wood, and rum.

From **Pointe-à-Pitre** ❶ (see p. 236) follow signs for Basse-Terre west across the Rivière Salée, and south on the fast Rte. N1 to the exit for La Traversée (Rte. D23). The cross-island road skims west through the cane fields before ascending into the rain forest, where it enters the Parc National de la Guadeloupe (see p. 243).

Just inside the park boundary is the pretty **Cascade aux Écrevisses** (Crayfish Falls) ❷**,** a popular picnic spot at the foot of a scenic waterfall edged by dripping mosses and creepers. Beneath the forest canopy it's hard to resist scrambling around on the boulders that litter the stream like giant stepping-stones.

Just over a mile (1.6 km) on is the **Maison de la Forêt,** which provides an excellent introduction to the 74,000-acre (29,950 ha) park with exhibits covering geology, flora, and fauna (unfortunately only in French). Hiking maps are available giving details of the well-maintained, 190-mile (306 km) trail network within the park, and there are several round-trip walks from the maison.

One of the park's more challenging hikes is the **Trace des Crêtes,** which follows the mountain ridge above the west coast and crosses La Traversée at the **Col des Mamelles** ❸ (1,922 feet/586 m), a mountain pass between twin volcanic peaks. This is the highest point on the road, with fantastic views of the park on a clear day, although the vista is frequently obscured by cloud and rain (the annual rainfall here is about 250 inches/6,350 mm).

After the hairpin descent to the coast at **Mahaut,** there's an optional short (3 miles/5 km) detour south to **Plage de Malendure** ❹**,** where glass-bottomed boat trips depart for the marine preserve surrounding the tiny Îlet de Pigeon. The **Reserve du Commandant Cousteau** honors one of its early champions, oceanographer Jacques Cousteau (1910–1997), who helped introduce a fishing ban and named Pigeon Island one of the world's top ten dive sites (some considerable time ago). The coral reef site is rather crowded with divers and pleasure boats these days, but the visibility on a clear day (averaging 100 feet/30 m) ensures there's always something interesting to see.

One and a half miles (2.5 km) north

Ginger plant

of Mahaut on Rte. N2 is the **Maison du Cacao** ❺ *(Tel 0590/98 21 23)*, which delves into the history, cultivation, and manufacture of cocoa, introduced to Guadeloupe by Arawak Indians. The French went mad about the stuff in the 18th century, and drinking hot chocolate became a national obsession. Blocks of 100 percent natural cocoa are on sale.

It's worth stopping at **Maison du Bois** *(Tel 0590/98 16 90)*, a few minutes' drive up the coast. The House of Wood has built up an impressive collection of antique wooden tools and utensils. Among the coffee grinders, cassava root crushers, wicker lobster pots, and hand whisks are displays depicting boatbuilding and furniture-making.

The drive continues past the attractive fishing village of **Deshaies** ❻**,** with its pretty Jardin Botanique *(Tel 0590/28 43 02)* and the broad bay at **Grande Anse,** graced by one of Guadeloupe's finest beaches. The 2-mile-long (3-km) sweep of rosy gold sand is backed by palm trees, and there's a choice of snack bars or a Creole restaurant, Le Karacoli (see p. 377), which makes an inviting lunch break.

The road (Rte. N2) rounds the tip of the island and continues on to **Ste.-Rose;** follow signs for the **Musée du Rhum** ❼ *(Tel 0590/28 70 04, closed Sun.)* at nearby Bellevue. Exhaustive signboards and displays examine every last detail of three centuries of rum-making in the Caribbean along with such antique artifacts as an enormous cane juice vat hewn out of a single tree trunk. The interesting insect gallery displays some 5,000 butterflies, beetles, and bugs from around the world. After watching a short film (some showings in English), take a tour of the adjacent **Distillerie Reimonenq** *(Tel 0590/28 70 04)*.

Back on the main road (Rte. N2), it's a swift run back to Pointe-à-Pitre. ■

See area map page 235
- Pointe-à-Pitre
- 58 miles/88 km
- A full day with stops
- Pointe-à-Pitre

NOT TO BE MISSED
- Maison de la Forêt
- Col des Mamelles
- Musée du Rhum

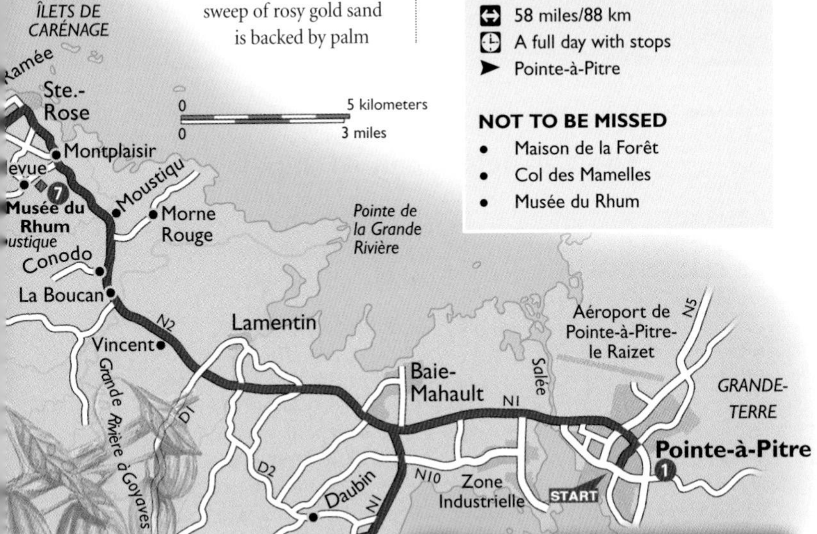

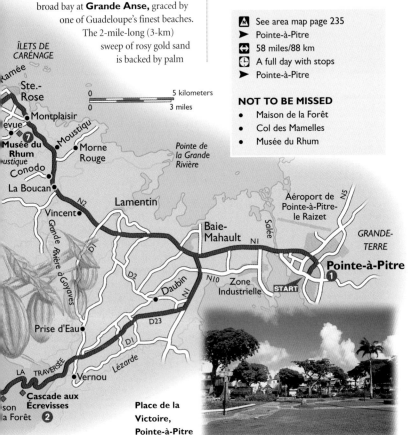

Place de la Victoire, Pointe-à-Pitre

Terre-de-Haut is the largest town in the Les Saintes island group.

The Guadeloupean Archipelago

LA DÉSIRADE

An arid, flat-topped table mountain 6 miles (10 km) off Pointe des Châteaux (the eastern tip of Guadeloupe), La Désirade was the first landfall sighted by Christopher Columbus on his second voyage to the New World in 1493. It signalled the end of the long Atlantic crossing, hence "The Desired One." Only 8 miles (13 km) long and one mile (1.6 km) wide, the island has a population of 1,700 mainly white inhabitants, several hundred sheep, and thousands of iguanas. The islanders lead a simple life farming or fishing. The main settlement is **Grande-Anse,** on the sheltered southern shore; farther up the coast, past the golden sands of Grande-Anse and **Le Souffleur,** you can see the ruins of an old leper colony at **Baie-Mahault.**

Daily ferry services *(Le Colibri, tel 0590/85 00 86)* depart from St.-François in Guadeloupe (one hour); you can also take scheduled flights (15 minutes). Car, scooter, and bicycle rentals are available through Jo Scooters *(Tel 0590/20 07 41)*. There are a few basic lodgings on the island, and locals offer B&Bs.

235 D1

MARIE-GALANTE

Twenty miles (32 km) south of Grande-Terre is the flat limestone island of Marie-Galante, which was named for Columbus's flagship, the *Santa Maria de Galante.* Shaped like a beech leaf, Marie-Galante was settled in 1648 and once carpeted with sugarcane. Dozens of old windmills dot the remaining cane fields that are still harvested to produce the island's famous rums.

Grand-Bourg *(Visitor information, tel 0590/97 56 51)* is Marie-Galante's main settlement. South of town is the 18th-century **Château Murat** *(see Grand-Bourg visitor information)* plantation house, which has a windmill and a museum illustrating local customs. Along the bottom of the island there is good swimming at **Petite Anse,** and water sports at **Pointe de la Feuillère,** near

Capesterre. Inland, a maze of country lanes burrows through tunnels of sugarcane; several rum distilleries offer tours and tastings. Another tourist stop is the **Trou à Diable** (Devil's Hole), an underground cavern that requires a flashlight and sturdy footwear to explore.

Fine beaches run the length of the northwest coast between **Vieux Fort** and the fishing village of **St.-Louis.** Daily ferry services *(Express des Iles, tel 0825-35 90 00 or Brudey 0590/90 04 48)* to Grand-Bourg and St.-Louis leave from Pointe-à-Pitre (one hour); scheduled flights are available (15 minutes). Cars and scooters are rented from Auto Moto *(St.-Louis, tel 0590/97 19 42)*. For hotel information contact the tourist office *(Tel 0590/97 56 51)*.

235 C1

LES SAINTES

A cluster of tiny islands 7 miles (11 km) south of Basse-Terre, Les Saintes were supposedly named for All Saints' Day (November 1) by Columbus. Only two of the jagged volcanic islets are inhabited. The quieter and less visited is **Terre-de-Bas,** a sleepy former plantation island with a couple of good beaches, one hotel, and rooms to rent. **Terre-de-Haut,** on the other hand, greets the daily invasion of day-trippers with equanimity and helps lighten their wallets in the welcoming restaurants and boutiques of **Le Bourg.** A fishing port, Le Bourg is set on a magnificent bay sheltered by the **Îlet à Cabrit** (Goat Island). Nowhere on the island is more than a 30-minute walk from Le Bourg, although it's a stiff uphill climb to **Fort Napoléon** *(Tel 0590/61 01 51, closed p.m.)*. The fortress houses a museum of local history, with a section devoted to the Battle of the Saints (see below).

Terre-de-Haut's best beach is the **Plage Pont Pierre,** in the east. Two quieter beaches are **Petite Anse Pain de Sucre,** west of Le Bourg, and **Anse du Figuier,** on the south coast (clothing optional). Daily ferry services *(Express des Iles, tel 0825-35 90 00 or Brudey 0590/90 04 48)* run to Terre-de-Haut and Terre-de-Bas from Pointe-à-Pitre (one hour) and Trois-Rivières (30 minutes). There are also daily sailings between Le Bourg and Terre-de-Bas, and flights from Guadeloupe. Scooters and bicycles can be rented in Le Bourg.

235 B1 ■

The Battle of the Saints

One of the most famous naval battles of the 18th century, the Battle of the Saints was the decisive factor in determining British supremacy in the Caribbean. In the spring of 1782, the French fleet was in Martinique, readying itself for an invasion of Jamaica calculated to destroy British credibility in the region. The preparations were being monitored by Adm. George Rodney (1718–1792) of the Royal Navy from his base on Pigeon Island, St. Lucia. On April 7, under Adm. François de Grasse, 33 French ships of the line set sail; Rodney gave chase, meeting the French off Les Saintes on the morning of April 12. In a surprise maneuver, which owed more to the weather conditions than design, Rodney broke the French line in not one but three places and carried the day. The tactic was later employed by Admiral Nelson at the Battle of Trafalgar. ■

Slavery

Sugar and slavery, the twin bastions of the West Indian colonial era, arrived in the New World with Columbus. Spanish conquistadores created the first Caribbean slaves when they put the native Amerindians to work on the plantations of Hispaniola (in the present-day Dominican Republic) and gold mines of South America. It took less than 20 years to decimate the indigenous population through disease and ill-treatment, prompting the Spanish to import African slaves to Hispaniola as early as 1511. (See pp. 308–309.)

The triangular trade

Portuguese merchants introduced the first African slaves to Europe in the 1450s, as exotic ornaments for the court. Domestic slavery of captured enemies was accepted practice among the tribes of the West African coast, and local traders were keen to exchange slaves for European manufactured goods such as textiles, glass, and weapons. The colonization of South America added a new dimension to this modest two-way traffic, bringing a steady trickle of African slaves across the Atlantic during the 16th century.

At first the British and French West Indian colonies relied on European laborers, but a combination of unaccustomed heat and tropical diseases killed as many as three out of four white settlers within two years of their arrival. When the sugar boom in the mid-1700s unleashed an urgent requirement for plentiful, cheap labor better prepared for the climate and backbreaking plantation work, the "triangular trade" was born. Ships from Europe headed to Africa where manufactured goods paid for African slaves. The slaves then embarked on the infamous Middle Passage to the New World, where the living cargo was exchanged for raw materials such as sugar, tobacco, cotton, and rum bound for Europe.

The Middle Passage

For the terrified slaves destined for the New World, their ordeal often began months ahead of transportation. Slavers selected their cargo from the vast barracoons (slave forts) that dotted the West African coast from Cape Verde to the Bight of Biafra, journeying from port to port until their vessels were filled to capacity. In preparation for the five- to eight-week voyage, food and water were taken on board and the cargo holds were subdivided into "slave decks," wooden shelves often no more than 2.5 feet (0.75 m) apart, where the slaves were packed in lying flat, the males shackled together left leg to right leg and wrist to wrist. Sickness, disease, and despair were rampant on the slave ships: One in eight slaves died on the Middle Passage. The survivors were oiled up to make them look healthier and auctioned off to the highest bidder in the slave markets of Curaçao, Nevis, Martinique, and Sint Eustatius, or on the wharf where the ship came into land.

It has been estimated that more than four million African slaves survived the journey to the West Indian colonies. British slave traders

Working patterns

West Indian planters devised two basic work regimes, the harshest of which was the "gang system" preferred on sugar estates. Slaves were divided into groups according to their strength, with the strongest first gang allocated the hardest manual tasks. Youths and old people in the second gang undertook lighter work, and the children in the third gang weeded and tidied. The gangs worked 10–12 hours a day, six days a week, and up to 18 hours during the harvest. The more liberal "task system" adopted on smaller farms and by slaves working as skilled craftsmen involved specific tasks that had to be completed in a given time. Slaves were then free to work their vegetable plots or undertake other jobs. ■

alone imported 2.5 million live slaves between 1690–1807, and the French added at least another million. By the 1750s, black slaves already represented 90 percent of the population on sugar-growing islands, though the proportion was much lower in the Bahamas, Cayman Islands, and Netherlands Antilles where plantations were impractical. The dramatic imbalance between black and white meant the planters lived in constant fear of slave rebellions and ruled their private fiefdoms with rods of iron. Ferocious slave drivers, armed with whips, disciplined the slave gangs in the fields and savage penalties were meted out for acts of disobedience or theft.

Opposite: A slave auction, from *The Negro's Complaint* (1826) by A. Opie
Top: The crossing, ca. 1840
Above: A sugar estate in Antigua, as depicted in 1823 by William Clark

Rebellion & emancipation

Despite the planters' best efforts to suppress their workforce, there were slave rebellions throughout the colonies in the 18th century. Most lasted no more than a couple of weeks or months before being ruthlessly crushed, though a successful revolt in the French colony of St. Domingue led to the creation of the black Republic of Haiti in 1804. In the 1780s, European intellectuals who had long opposed slavery on moral grounds were joined by churchmen, and the combined pressure of forceful pamphleteering campaigns and sermons caused widespread antislavery sentiment. The British outlawed the slave trade to their colonies in 1808, and decreed the abolition of slavery in 1834. Sweden (1846), France and Denmark (1848), and Holland (1863) followed suit, while the Spanish held out until 1873 in Puerto Rico. ■

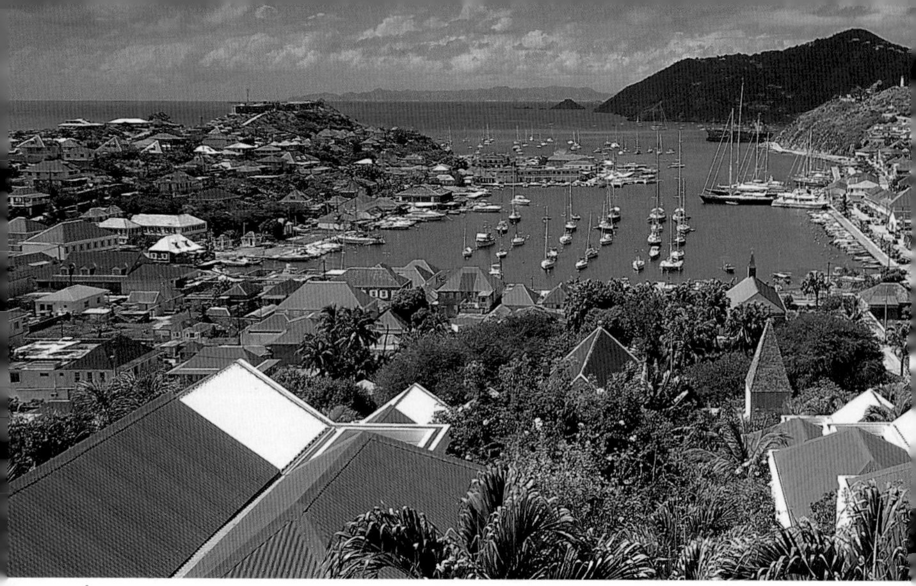

During the winter season, Gustavia harbor showcases the dizzy heights of luxurious yachting.

St.-Barthélemy

KNOWN AS MANHATTAN-SUR-MER TO THE COGNOSCENTI, St.-Barthélemy is the epitome of French Caribbean chic and arguably the most exclusive and expensive speck of volcanic rock in the region, give or take a private island or two. This is the winter playground of the super-rich and super-casual, where the shops overflow with Chanel and champagne, but dressing for dinner is frowned upon.

St.-Barthélemy
233 A5
Visitor information
www.st-barths.com
Quai du Général de Gaulle, Gustavia
0590/27 87 27, fax 0590/27 74 47

One of the first things to strike visitors to St. Barts (or Saint-Barth in French) is the paucity of black faces; almost all 6,000 permanent inhabitants are white, affluent, and of French descent. French culture defines every detail, from the humble baguette to the rarefied heights of gourmet cuisine, from designer labels to traditional *calèche* bonnets, the old-fashioned women's sun hats (now rarely seen except on high days and holidays) that recall St. Barts' pioneering colonists from Normandy and Brittany.

St. Barts was not born with a silver spoon in its mouth. The 8-square-mile (21-sq-km) island was named San Bartolomé for Columbus's brother and colonized by 60 French settlers from St. Kitts in 1648. The first colony was wiped out by a Carib raiding party, but the strategic position of St. Barts amid the English Leeward Island colonies prompted a second attempt by Protestant Huguenots in 1674. While other islands planted cotton and cane, St. Barts' stock in trade was piracy. Buccaneers frequently took refuge in its convenient coves.

In 1784 French King Louis XVI exchanged St. Barts for trading rights in the Baltic, and the island became Swedish for a century. The Swedes declared their sole Caribbean possession a free port, and for a while it profited handsomely, trading with the newly independent United States. When business tailed off, the island was sold back to France in 1878, and subsided into obscurity until quietly emerging as a stylish jet-set hideaway in the 1980s.

GUSTAVIA

Postcard-pretty Gustavia was named in honor of the Swedish King Gustav III and hems in three sides of its sheltered harbor, guarded by four hilltop forts. During the height of the winter season, splendiferous gin palaces line the docks, berthed sleek cheek-by-elegant jowl, and the boutiques, jewelers, and terrace cafés of the tiny town center are packed with serious shoppers and gawking day-trippers from Sint Maarten. The pointy-roofed **Swedish belfry** is a local landmark. On the western side of the harbor is the **Musée de Saint-Barth,** which provides a quick roundup of local history and customs. Its collections include Amerindian votive objects, colonial documents, fish traps, straw hats woven out of latanier palm fronds, and stiff-sided calèche bonnets, also known as *quichenottes* (or kiss-me-not) and once regarded as the best defense against amorous Englishmen and Swedes. The closest beach is **Shell Beach,** a ten-minute walk south of town at **Anse de Grand Galet.**

St. Barts peaks at less than 1,000 feet (300 m), but its tightly packed folds of perpendicular green hills make it seem much taller, while lovingly cultivated gardens create an impression of tropical lushness. The 18 small villages dotted about the island are linked by narrow roads that crawl doggedly up into the hills and then plummet back to the coast. At the bottom of a particularly vertiginous descent north of Gustavia is the charming fishing village of **Corossol.** Turn left at the waterfront for the **Inter-Oceans Museum,** an intriguing

Gustavia
251 A2

Musée de Saint-Barth
La Pointe
0590/29 71 55
Closed Wed. p.m., Sat. p.m.-Sun.
$

Inter-Oceans Museum
Corossol
0590/27 62 97
Closed weekends
$$

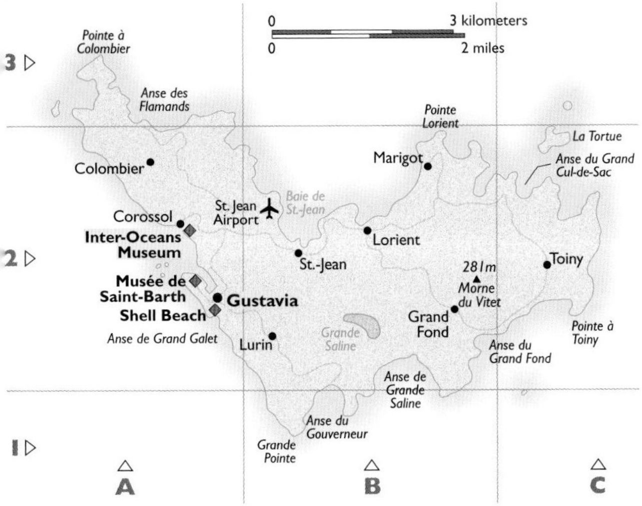

seashell collection said to be the second largest in the world, with several world-record-size exhibits. Basket-weaving is another specialty.

On the north coast is St. Barts' chief tourist hub, **St.-Jean,** where a small group of hotels, restaurants, and shops have sprung up along the roadside facing a glorious bay and busy beach.

A road circles the east end of the island, past the beach at Anse du Grand Cul-de-Sac and around **Morne du Vitet** (938 feet/281 m). The two best beaches are on the south coast: **Anse de Grande Saline,** reached via St.-Jean, and **Anse du Gouverneur,** south of Lurin. Both are undeveloped, with deep white sand and terrific views of Saba, Sint Eustatius, and St. Kitts in the distance. ■

Tall branches of torch cactus rise above the hardy scrub on the sunbaked hills surrounding Baie-de-St.-Jean.

Sports & activities

Day sails & water sports *(voile & activités nautique):* Marine Service *(Tel 0590/27 70 34, www.stbarths.com/marineservice)* can arrange anything from catamaran excursions with snorkeling to deep sea fishing; or Océan Must *(Tel 0590/27 62 25, fax 0590/27 95 17)* for boat rentals and scuba-diving.

Horseback riding *(équitation):* Saint Barth Equitation *(Tel 0590/62 99 30)*.

Tours: Contact Gustavia Office du Tourisme *(Tel 0590/27 87 27)*. ■

Mont Pelée looms above the ruined city of St.-Pierre, destroyed in the eruption of 1902.

Martinique

MARTINIQUE IS ONE OF THE MOST BEAUTIFUL OF ALL THE Caribbean islands. The Amerindians called it Madinina, the Island of Flowers, and Martinique is still celebrated for its glorious gardens and rampant rain forest, as well as its lovely women, fine beaches, and distinctive Creole culture. Measuring 50 miles (80 km) long and 22 miles (35.5 km) wide, it is flanked by the Windward Islands of Dominica to the north and St. Lucia to the south.

Martinique
233 D1
Visitor information
www.tourismefaf.com
76 rue Lazarre Carnot
0596/60 27 73, fax 0596/60 27 95

Northern Martinique is tall and explosively green, swathed in dense rain forest that swoops down from the heights of Mont Pelée, the island's only active volcano, through the lesser but still impressive peaks of the Pitons du Carbet (see p. 260) to a fringe of banana plantations clinging to the lower slopes. The central plain, stretching east from Fort-de-France (see p. 256), the island's capital on the west coast, is Martinique's sugarcane belt. The south of the island is characterized by the dry, hilly folds of the *mornes*, which back a scattered collection of beaches and small coastal resorts.

Columbus may have spotted Martinica, as he called it, on his second voyage, but he definitely stopped off here on his fourth expedition in 1502. He waxed lyrical about the beauty of the island and the Carib women who greeted his arrival with cries of "Madinina." It is uncertain whether Martinica is a corruption of Madinina or maybe a homage to St. Martin. The Carib were still in possession of the island when French settlers first came ashore near Le Carbet on the west coast in 1635. After a quarter of a century of violent skirmishes, a treaty ceded the Atlantic-facing east coast to the Carib, but before long the French had the whole island to themselves and proceeded to carpet it with sugarcane.

Martinique's administrative capital was established at Fort Royal (present-day Fort-de-France) in

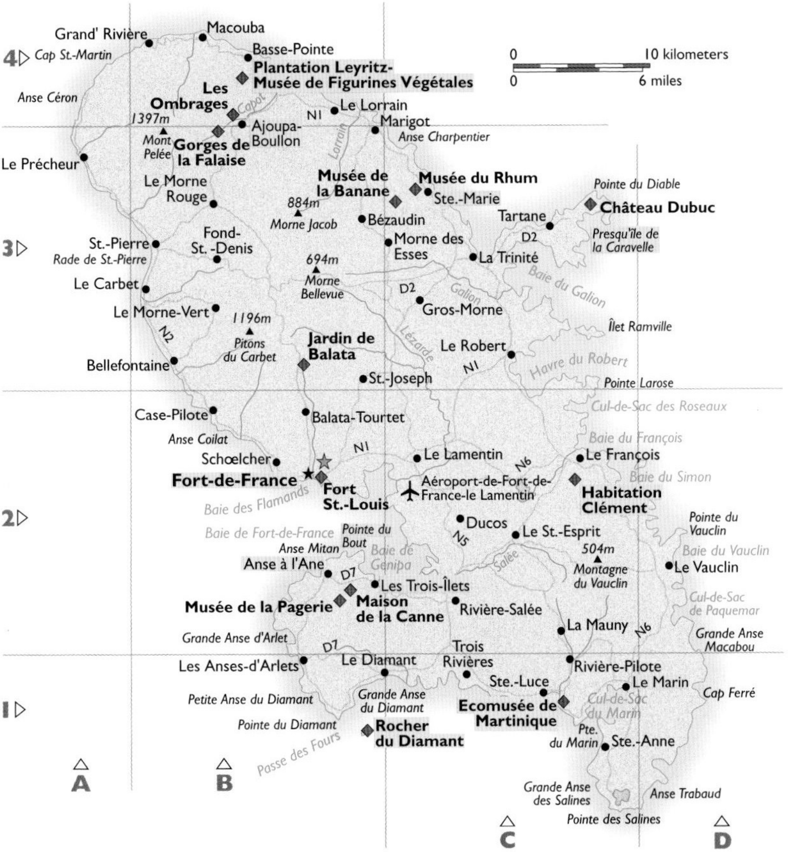

1681, but the real focus of the island was St.-Pierre, a gracious harbor city at the foot of Mont Pelée, which became the hub of French trade and culture in the region. The British captured the island in 1762 but returned it a year later (along with Guadeloupe) in exchange for Dominica, Grenada, St. Vincent, and Tobago, plus French territories in Senegal and North America. The extent of the French concessions reflected the importance they attached to their Caribbean possessions. In 1793 the French Revolution arrived in Martinique, and initially the republicans carried the day. But within a year the planters had restored the old regime, with the help of the British.

Although relatively stable, Martinique witnessed several slave uprisings before the abolition of slavery in 1848 and the subsequent decline in wealth and importance of the sugar economy. Yet the most devastating day in the island's history occurred 54 years later, on May 8, 1902, when Mont Pelée erupted, destroying the city of St.-Pierre and killing all but one of its 30,000 inhabitants.

While life has returned to St.-Pierre in a small way, it remains quite literally a shadow of its former self. In contrast, Fort-de-France has boomed. A big and bustling port city with more than 100,000 inhabitants, the capital is gobbling up the wooded hillsides behind the Baie des Flamands and spreading

The colorful bracts of the lobster claw are a familiar rain forest sight.

eastward to the industrial quarter of Le Lamentin and airport. Facing the city from across the broad mouth of the Baie de Fort-de-France are the well-developed hotel strip of Pointe du Bout and quieter Anse à l'Ane. The island's other two leading resort areas are the yachting center of Le Marin and Ste.-Anne, found down on the southeast peninsula close to Grande Anse des Salines, Martinique's best beach.

The Atlantic shore is rough and rocky, with another peninsula, the Presqu' île la Caravelle, about halfway up the coast, home to a few small hotels, sugar mill ruins, and a nature reserve.

The rain forest luxuriance of the north is dominated by the cloud-capped bulk of simmering Mont Pelée. It's not a particularly interesting volcano to climb, but there are several pretty walks out of the village of Ajoupa-Bouillon and a memorable drive north through the Pitons du Carbet from Fort-de-France (see pp. 260–61). Although distances are modest and the roads good, leave plenty of time to explore, and allow at least three or four days for a really good look around.

Fort-de-France
255 B2

FORT-DE-FRANCE

A vibrant and attractive city, Fort-de-France enjoys a splendid position on the Caribbean coast, set against a backdrop of dark green hills. Its compact heart is inviting and easy to explore on foot, with a busy shopping district and narrow streets of flat-fronted buildings adorned with elaborate ironwork balconies.

The original settlement grew up around Fort St.-Louis, founded by the French in 1639. The sturdy fortress has been considerably extended and sits on a headland

HARBOR FERRIES *(VEDETTES)*

Ferries make a neat way to pop into Fort-de-France from the beach resorts across the bay (or vice versa). There are frequent and inexpensive ferry services from the downtown waterfront near Fort St.-Louis to Plage du Bout, Anse Mitan, and Anse à l'Ane. Ferries operate from 6 a.m. until about midnight to the main resort of Pointe du Bout; the crossing takes 20 minutes. There are also services to Ste.-Anne on the far south of the island. ■

Sports & activities

Mountain biking *(VTT)*: Rentals from VT Tilt *(Pointe du Bout, tel 0596/66 01 01)*. Also see Tours, below.

Diving & snorkeling *(plongée sous-marine & plongée avec tuba)*: Martinique's best reef sites are off the south coast. There's good snorkeling at Les Anses d'Arlets. St.-Pierre's harbor offers wreck sites dating from the 1902 eruption of Mont Pelée. Planète Bleue *(Marina Pointe du Bout, tel 0596/66 08 79)*; Plongée Passion, *(Anses d'Arlet, tel 0596/68 72 52)*; Sub Diamond Rock *(Le Diamant, tel 0596/76 21 76)*; Tropicasub *(St.-Pierre, tel 0596/78 38 03)*.

Golf: The Martinique Golf & Country Club *(Les Trois-Îlets, tel 0596/68 32 81, fax 0596/68 38 97, www.golfmartinique.com)* has an 18-hole course designed by Robert Trent Jones.

Horseback riding *(équitation)*: Black Horse Ranch *(Les Trois-Îlets, tel 0596/68 37 80)*; Ranch Jack *(Les Anses d'Arlet, tel 0596/68 37 69)*.

Tours: Guided walking, kayaking, mountain biking, and 4x4 safaris from Adventures Tropicales *(Fort-de-France, tel 0596/64 58 49)*; Fort-de-France shopping and historical tours from Azimut *(Tel 0596/70 07 00)*.

Water sports *(activités nautiques)*: Hotels and concessions offer water sports in main tourist areas. Experienced wind- and kite-surfers will find more challenging conditions on the Atlantic side; contact Club Nautique de Vauclin *(Tel 0596/74 50 83)*. ■

jutting out into the water, where it guards the **Baie des Flamands** waterfront to the west and the yacht harbor to the east. There is always plenty of activity down on the wharf, where cruise-ship passengers arrive, ferries depart for the beaches across the **Baie de Fort-de-France** (see sidebar p. 256), and kids dive off the piers just for fun.

Across the street from the wharf is a colorful craft and souvenir market, which lays out its wares on the edge of **La Savane.** These 12-acre (4.5-ha) gardens are shaded by magnificent royal palms, and it's a pleasant place to take a stroll and admire the flowers or sit on a park bench and watch the world go by. Overlooking the gardens from rue de la Liberté is the **Musée Départemental d'Archéologie Précolumbienne et de Préhistoire de la Martinique,** where you can find displays of pottery and other Amerindian artifacts, as well as exhibits on slavery and colonial life illustrated with the help of period furnishings, crafts, and clothing.

Continue along the west side of the gardens to the fabulously eccentric **Bibliothèque Schoelcher,** a library named in honor of the great French abolitionist Victor Schoelcher and housed in an exotic Byzantine-Romanesque-art nouveau structure designed for the 1889 Paris Exhibition. When the show was over, the building was taken to pieces, shipped to Martinique, and reconstructed. Opposite the library is a headless statue of the Empress Joséphine (1763–1814). Once the pride of her Martiniquais compatriots, the empress was removed from her position at the center of La Savane, and beheaded in 1991, after a guidebook revealed her role in encouraging Napoleon to reintroduce slavery in 1802.

The interior of the Cathédrale de St.-Louis is illuminated by fine stained-glass windows.

For an insight into Martiniquan customs and traditions, take a detour to the **Musée Régional d'Histoire et d'Ethnographie** housed in a pretty 19th-century Créole villa, handsomely furnished in bourgeois period style.

Across the street from the library is rue Victor Sévère, which marks the top end of the main shopping district, bounded by rue de la Liberté, rue Victor Hugo, and rue de la République. The **Préfecture** is the first of several imposing colonial government buildings along this handsome street. Among the fashionable boutiques, patisseries, and stores chock-full of French luxury goods at the heart of the grid is the **Cathédrale de St.-Louis,** which stands on rue Victor Schoelcher. The brown-and-cream painted building, with its clock tower, steeple, and fancy ironwork, was erected on the foundations of six former churches in 1878.

AROUND SOUTHERN MARTINIQUE

Visible across the bay from Fort-de-France, Martinique's most

Musée Régional d'Histoire et d'Ethnographie

- 10 blvd. Général-de-Gaulle
- 0596/72 81 87
- Closed Tue. a.m., Sat. p.m.-Sun.
- $$

Musée Départemental

- 9 rue de la Liberté
- 0596/71 05 57
- Closed Mon. a.m., Sat. p.m.-Sun.
- $

Bibliothèque Schoelcher

- Corner of rue de la Liberté & rue Perrinon
- 0596/70 26 67

The stone cottage housing the Musée de la Pagerie was once a separate kitchen for the estate great house.

developed tourist enclave is the promontory of Pointe du Bout and the adjacent beach at Anse Mitan. This vacation center has a lively concentration of hotels, restaurants, beaches and water sports concessions frequented by day-tripping cruise passengers who hop across from the city by ferry (see p. 256).

Neighboring **Les Trois-Îlets** is an attractive little seaside village. A Saturday market is held on the square in front of the church where Napoleon's future empress was christened Marie-Rose Joséphine Tascher de la Pagerie in the summer of 1763. Just outside the village is the former family estate, now the home of the **Musée de la Pagerie,** which is laid out in a simple stone cottage among the ruins of the sugar mill. It houses collections of domestic utensils, period prints, and a few personal possessions of the empress, including letters from the emperor.

On the main road (Rte. D7) east of the village is the informative **Maison de la Canne,** occupying another restored old sugar mill. Exhibits cover the history of the early plantations and the slave trade amid a welter of antique paraphernalia, models, and bilingual signboards.

Heading counter clockwise around the coast from Trois-Îlets, you reach the narrow sandy beach at **Anse à l'Ane** and its popular beach bars. The lovely village of **Les Anses-d'Arlets** has several dark sand beaches nearby, including the tiny black sand strip of Petit Anse du Diamant, where dozens of traditional fishing boats painted orange, turquoise, and green ride the gentle swell in the bay. Around the headland there's a fine view of the **Rocher du Diamant,** an offshore islet shaped like a giant brioche with a slice carved out of it. In 1804 British troops from St. Lucia captured the rock to harass French shipping. It was "commissioned" into the British Navy, armed with cannon and nicknamed H.M.S. *Diamond Rock.* The British garrison held out for 18 months, hoisting provisions ashore from visiting ships until a concerted French bombardment forced the occupiers to withdraw.

East of Ste.-Luce, across the Rivière-Pilote, is the **Ecomusée**

Les Trois-Îlets
255 B2
Visitor information
www.trois-ilets.com
Place Gabriel Hayot
0596/68 47 63

Musée de la Pagerie
255 B2
Les Trois-Îlets
0596/68 38 34
Closed Mon.
$

Maison de la Canne
255 B2
Les Trois-Îlets
0596/68 32 04
Closed Mon.
$

de Martinique, providing a detailed and fascinating account of island history. Note, however, that the signs are all in French (although there's talk of providing English subtitles in the future). The excellent sections on Amerindian society and culture are accompanied by artifacts, models, and a list of common words derived from Amerindian languages, such as alligator, barbecue, and tobacco.

Continuing eastward, visit the yachting center of **Le Marin** at the foot of a deep, sheltered bay behind its packed marina. On the waterfront you can choose from a clutch of seafood restaurants serving up the catch of the day, accompanied by the creak of rigging in the breeze. Around the bay is the **Pointe du Marin** headland, with its crescent of sandy beach fringed by palms; a zigzagging hillside Calvary dominates the approach to the pretty resort town of **Ste.-Anne.** South of Ste.-Anne, the road passes the dry, sunbaked peninsula and salt ponds to **Grande Anse des Salines,** a refreshingly undeveloped curve of blonde sand. Palms, sea grape trees, and Australian pines provide a shady retreat, and there are snack wagons, vendors selling fresh pineapple, and a restaurant.

From Le Marin, Rte. N6 cuts across to the east coast town of **Le François.** In the rolling countryside just south of town is the old **Habitation Clément** sugar estate, which opens its doors to the public. Rum hasn't been distilled here since 1988, but the fully equipped distillery is on display, as are the *chais* (storehouses) where up to 1,400 barrels of Rhum Clément mature in oak imported from France. The highlight of the visit is the lovely 19th-century **plantation house.** In the dining room, carved colonial furniture is enhanced by oil lamps and antique silver. Go upstairs to see the embroidered coverlets on the four-poster beds. ■

Ecomusée de Martinique

255 C1
Anse Figuier
0596/62 79 14
Closed Mon.
$

Habitation Clément

255 C2
www.rhum-clement.com
Le François (2 mi/ 3 km from St.-François Rte. D18)
0596/54 62 07
Closed Sept.
$$

Seine fishermen check their nets at Bellefontaine. Nets are suspended vertically from floats and weighted.

A drive through the Pitons du Carbet to St.-Pierre

The first leg of this tour follows the historic inland trail to St.-Pierre, La Route de la Trace, carved through the highlands back in the 17th century. Martinique's tropical profusion is on display in the Jardin de Balata and in the untamed rain forest, while the grim but compelling story of St.-Pierre unfurls among century-old ruins.

From **Fort-de-France's** ❶ (see p. 256) inner city ring road, boulevard du Général de Gaulle, Rte. N3 follows the Rivière Madame north (toward Morne Rouge) and then climbs into the hillside suburbs. Stop off at the church of **Sacré Coeur** ❷ for a tremendous view over the capital. The domed "Montmartre Martiniquais" was inspired by its famous Parisian namesake and erected in 1923 as a memorial to the dead of World War I.

The air is noticeably cooler as the road winds on up to the **Jardin de Balata** ❸ *(Rte. de Balata, tel 0596/64 48 73)*, a gorgeous tropical garden laid out around a Creole home some 1,475 feet (450 m) above the coast. Meandering paths trail through flaming red-and-pink torch ginger, orchids, fruit trees, spice bushes, and swaths of leafy anthuriums gathered in the shade cast by palms, immortelles, and flamboyant trees.

The road begins to twist and turn in earnest as it passes through the Pitons (peaks) flanked by soft banks of ferns, 100-foot-high (30 m) stands of bamboo, and huge rain forest trees dangling ropes of twisted liana and festooned with bromeliads.

At the town of **Deux Choux** take Rte. D1 8 miles (13 km) west to **St.-Pierre** ❹ and the Caribbean coast, passing through the banana plantations. (See box for a possible detour.) Overlooking a handsome bay in the shadow of Mont Pelée, St.-Pierre was once the gracious Paris of the Antilles, a thriving colonial city renowned for the wealth of its merchants and the elegance of its buildings and inhabitants. Old photographs show the port filled with clipper ships waiting to load sugar and rum from the docks, and some private homes even boasted electricity in 1902. In the spring of that year, after centuries of inactivity, Mont Pelée rumbled. On May 5 the crater split, releasing a torrent of lava and mud, but local government officials in the crucial stages of an election campaign decided against evacuating the city. A warning was given on May 7, but only a thousand Pierrotins packed their bags and headed for Fort-de-France. A little before 8 a.m. on May 8, Mont Pelée erupted, sending a giant cloud of burning ash and poisonous gases into the sky. The pyroclastic flow, reaching temperatures of over 3,700°F (2,040°C), swept down over the town and caused the sea to boil.

St.-Pierre's present-day population of 6,000 lives among the gaunt ruins of the cataclysmic eruption. The **Cyparis Express** tourist train *(place des Ruines du Figuier, tel 0596/55 50 92)*, named for the only survivor, makes a narrated (in French) circuit, or visitors can roam freely around the shell of the old theater, inspect Cyparis's cell, and visit the cathedral rebuilt behind its surviving facade. The **Musée Vulcanologique** *(rue Victor Hugo, tel 0596/78 15 16)*, founded by U.S. volcanologist Franck Perret in 1932, displays photographs of the old city, melted glass bottles, fused nails, and other curios salvaged from the wreckage.

Take the Rte. N2 coast road a couple of miles (3 km) south of St.-Pierre to **Anse Turin** ❺, which once played host to Paul Gauguin (1848–1903). The celebrated French painter spent five months living by the beach in 1887 as he searched for a tropical isle where he could live like a "noble savage." Martinique

St.-Pierre on film

An interesting detour is a visit to **La Maison du Volcan** *(Tel 0596/52 45 45, closed Sun.)* in Morne Rouge. As well as information on volcanism (in French), this small museum on the main street provides a 45-minute video compiled from film footage of St.-Pierre before and after the 1902 eruption (English version on request). ■

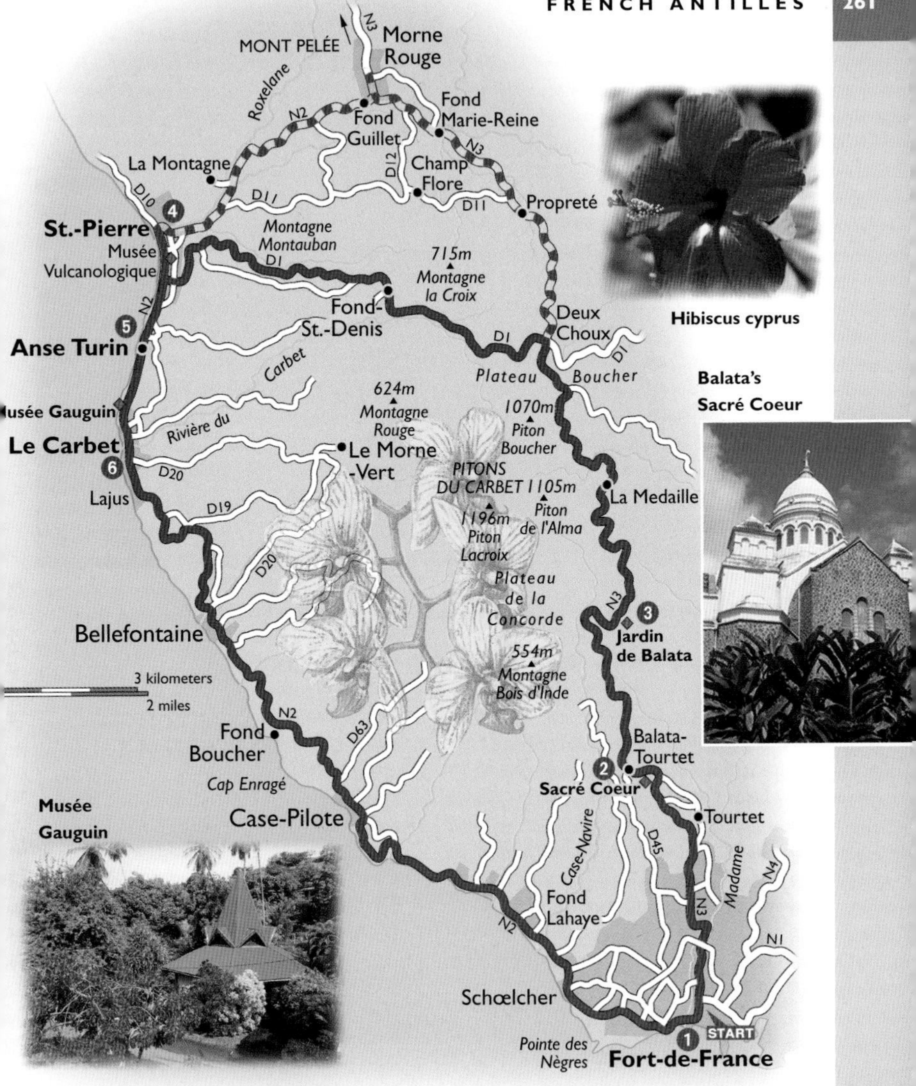

Hibiscus cyprus

Balata's Sacré Coeur

Musée Gauguin

was not a success, judging from letters home full of complaints and self-pity, and he wound up in Tahiti. Several of the letters and reproductions of his paintings are housed in the **Musée Gauguin** *(Anse Turin, tel 0596/78 22 66)*, which also exhibits local artwork.

Rte. N2 hugs the coast back to Fort-de-France, passing the village of **Le Carbet ❻**, where the founder of St.-Pierre, Pierre Belain d'Esnambuc, landed with a hundred Norman colonists to claim Martinique for France in 1635. ■

- See map page 255
- Fort-de-France
- 40 miles/65km
- An easy day trip with stops
- Fort-de-France

NOT TO BE MISSED

- Jardin de Balata
- St.-Pierre
- Musée Gauguin

The heavy purple-red flower of the banana plant hangs beneath a bunch of ripening fruit.

The north & northeast

AJOUPA-BOUILLON

This self-proclaimed *ville florale* displays its roadside banks of wild begonias, massed crotons, and shrimp plants with pride. Ajoupa is also home to **Les Ombrages** *(Tel 0596/53 31 90, $$)*, a lush botanical garden clambering up a rain forest ravine, and the village is the starting point for walks to the **Gorges de la Falaise** *(Tel 0596/52 55 09)*. The 30-minute trail starts just west of town and leads through the rain forest to a swimming hole fed by a waterfall.
255 B4 Immeuble Boulon, Quartier Racine 0596/53 32 87

CARAVELLE PENINSULA

From the main road follow signs for **Tartane** (Rte. D2), a small resort on the north coast of this wooded peninsula. At the end of the road a section of rough track leads to the ruins of 17th-century **Château Dubuc** *(Tel 0596/58 09 00, $$)*, which crown a rise overlooking a protected bay and the foundations of an old sugar mill. A quirky little museum houses old belt buckles, broken bottles, and clay pipe stems unearthed around the estate. From the parking lot, footpaths strike off into a natural reserve and to the cliffs and coves lining the shore.
255 C3

PLANTATION LEYRITZ-MUSÉE DE FIGURINES VÉGÉTALES

An attractive hotel-restaurant converted from an old sugar estate, this popular lunch stop is on the tour bus trail. It has a small museum of figurines in historical costume fashioned out of leaves, seeds, grasses, and other plant matter.
255 B4 Rte. D21 from Basse-Pointe 0596/78 53 92 $$

STE.-MARIE

Two of Martinique's most conspicuous products are showcased in museums just west and north of the town: rum and bananas. The **Musée de la Banane** *(Rte. de Bézaudin, tel 0596/69 45 52, $$$)* sits at the heart of a working banana plantation. Check out the history of the banana and amazing banana trivia (Germans devour more than 33 pounds/15 kg of bananas per person per year). Stroll along the banana walk and visit the packing houses on weekdays.

The **Musée du Rhum** *(Tel 0596/69 30 02)* also believes in transporting visitors to the business end of its operations with guided tours of the Distillerie Saint-James. The actual museum is an old plantation house with collections of antique tools and memorabilia.
255 C3 ■

Tethered in a row like giant green men-of-war, the Windward Islands of Dominica, St. Lucia, St. Vincent, and Grenada lie broadside to the rain-bearing Atlantic winds that feed their towering, forested peaks.

Windward Islands

Dressed for Carnival

Windward Islands

THE MAJESTIC QUARTET OF WINDWARD ISLANDS TAPERS OFF TOWARD THE tail end of the Lesser Antilles, rising sheer from the Atlantic surf on one side and the gentle wavelets of the Caribbean Sea on the other. The islands are the mere tips of a volcanic mountain range that has sprouted along a rift in the Earth's crust where the Atlantic and Caribbean tectonic plates collide. Three of the four main Windward Islands have an active *soufrière*, a sulfurous volcanic vent liable to erupt every hundred years or so (Grenada, the exception, has bubbling hot springs). Tall enough to create their own microclimates by trapping the winds off the Atlantic and converting them to rain clouds, the Windwards are fantastically fertile. Islanders grow bananas, coconuts, and spices for export, and farmers have their work cut out for them trying to keep the encroaching sea of green at bay. In the high country, rare parrots add a flash of brilliant color to the dense rain forest canopy towering above a steaming jungle of ferns, creepers, and twisted tree roots.

Today Dominica, St. Lucia, St. Vincent (with its chain of islands known as the Grenadines), and Grenada are independent nations, but their long association dates back to the days of sail when they fell to the windward side of the English colonial trading routes between Europe and the Caribbean. Later the term was adopted by 19th-century British administrators who governed the Windward Islands as a group distinct from British colonies in the Leeward Islands.

The earliest inhabitants of the Windward Islands were Arawak Indians, farmers and fishermen whose peaceful reign ended abruptly with the arrival of warlike Carib people (also known as Kalinago in Dominica today) about A.D. 1000. Spanish explorers gave the "Cannibal Isles" a wide berth, and they became the focus of Carib resistance in the region until the mid-17th century, when the sugar trade spurred French and English colonists into action. Initially the two most topographically challenging islands, Dominica and St. Vincent, were left to the Carib, who were joined by escaped African slaves. But a century later, white settlers had forced Dominica's few remaining Carib into exile on the Atlantic coast; on St. Vincent mixed-race black Carib took refuge in the hills and continued a dogged resistance until the early 19th century.

Throughout the plantation era Europe's conflicts were mirrored in the Caribbean arena, where Britain and France squabbled over the Windwards incessantly and won, lost, and regained territories with bewildering frequency. The islands inherited a confused legacy of French and English place-names, as well as the French-influenced Creole patois that is still widely spoken in Dominica and St. Lucia, although the islands have been officially English speaking for 200 years. When slavery was abolished in 1834, former slaves turned to the land and carved small-scale farms out of the rich soil. The islands slid into an agricultural backwater administered by a British governor based in Grenada. Several attempts to federate the British Caribbean territories came to nothing, and eventually the individual Windward Islands were granted self-government in the 1960s and full independence in the late 1970s. They are now members of the British Commonwealth.

Part of the Windward Islands' appeal is the coexistence of tourism and traditional island life. This is particularly true on Dominica, where vast tracts of primal rain forest and uplands remain in pristine condition, and fishing and farming still underpin the local economy. Also unspoiled and underappreciated, St. Vincent is another rain forest wilderness and tropical market garden but generally consigned to the role of steppingstone for yachtsmen heading for the Grenadines. The Grenadines are a yachting paradise, an alluring chain of minuscule islands with great beaches, some uninhabited, some harboring exclusive resorts. Others, such as pretty Bequai, fall somewhere between the two. To the south is charming Grenada. Easygoing and friendly, the Spice Island is

Spectacular waterfalls plummet hundreds of feet through a Dominican rain forest.

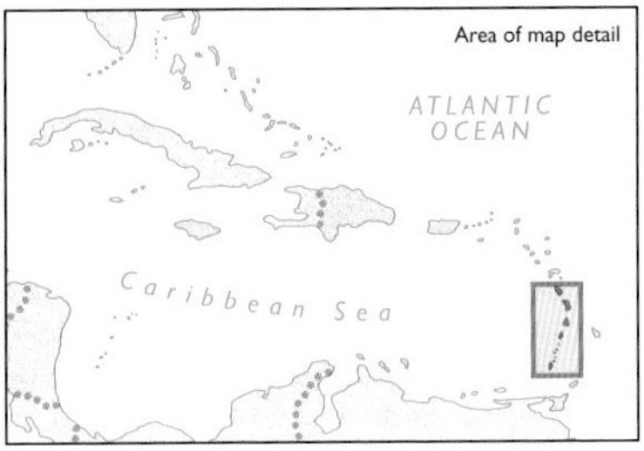

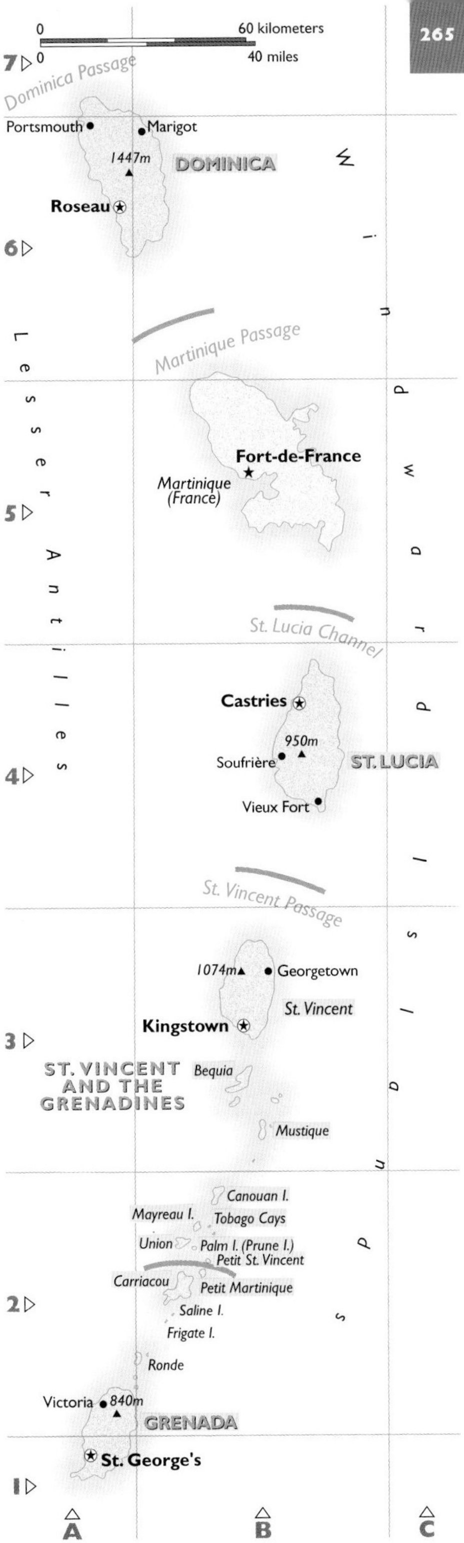

overloaded with natural beauties and ringed by sandy beaches, spice plantations, and pretty villages. St. Lucia is the most developed of the Windwards, but even here it's easy to escape the resort beaches of the northwest and take a trip to the mountains, where villages nestle amid fabulous tropical flowers and vegetable plots on the edge of the forest. ■

Dominica's Scotts Head/Soufrière Marine Park is a relatively recent addition to the list of top dive sites in the Caribbean.

Dominica

DOMINICA (PRONOUNCED DO-MIN-EE-KA) WAS KNOWN TO the Carib as Wai'tukubuli ("tall is her body"). From a 29-by-16-mile (47-by-26-km) base, the soaring interior peaks at Morne Diablotin (4,747 feet/1,447 m) within 5 miles (8 km) of the coast, and the jagged mountains of the central north-south spine average more than 3,000 feet (900 m). Dominica is generously endowed with natural wonders. The island is home to one of the world's last untouched rain forests, more than a thousand species of flowering plants, a boiling lake, 300-plus rivers, and almost as many waterfalls coursing down the mountainsides in a flash of shimmering silver and spray. Off the coast the underwater landscape is similarly breathtaking and has established quite a reputation as an exciting dive destination.

The population of about 71,000 is 98 percent black, mainly Roman Catholic, and most people still struggle to make a living from the land. Despite its undoubted beauty, Dominica is one of the Caribbean's poorest islands. Farming and fishing, augmented by traditional crafts, are the economic mainstays of one of the world's last surviving Carib, or Kalinago, communities, living on the Carib Territory in the

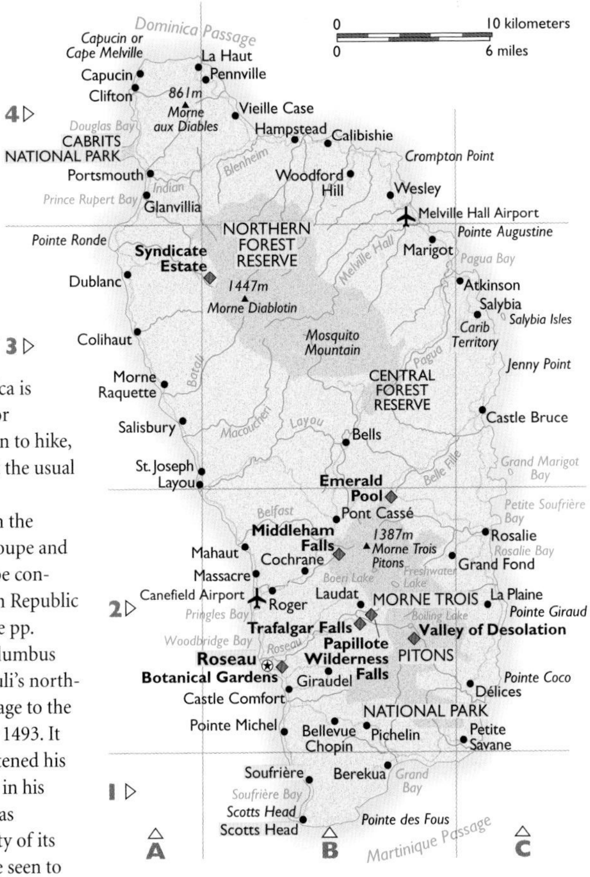

northeast. With few beaches (and those that exist tend toward narrow strips of gray volcanic sand), tourism is still in its infancy here. Dominica offers fairly low-key accommodations, and facilities are mostly modest and unsophisticated. On the plus side, Dominica is a rare Caribbean haven for adventurous travelers keen to hike, dive, and explore without the usual tourist distractions.

Dominica lies between the French islands of Guadeloupe and Martinique. (It is not to be confused with the Dominican Republic in the Greater Antilles, see pp. 95–124.) Christopher Columbus sailed around Wai'tukubuli's northern tip on his second voyage to the New World in November 1493. It was a Sunday, so he christened his find Dominica and noted in his logbook that the island was "remarkable for the beauty of its mountains...and must be seen to be believed." They say he would have little difficulty recognizing it today. French colonists laid claim to Dominica in the 1750s but ceded it to Britain under the Treaty of Paris in 1763. Despite a century of French raids, slave rebellions, and isolated attacks by bands of marauding Maroons (escaped slaves who hid in the near-impenetrable mountains), the British remained more or less in control. From the mid-19th century Dominica was administered with the Leeward Islands until 1939, when it was transferred to the Windward Islands. Independence arrived in 1978, and two years later the Dominicans elected the Caribbean's first woman prime minister, Dame Eugenia Charles, who served for almost 20 years.

The capital of the island, Roseau (see p. 268), is a small weather-beaten town and cruise-ship stopover with around 20,000 inhabitants. It lies at the mouth of the Roseau River on the southwest coast. Inland along the river lies the Trafalgar Falls (see p. 269), one of Dominica's most popular tourist attractions. The nearby village of Laudat is the main drop-off point for hikes in the Morne Trois Pitons National Park (see p. 270). South of Roseau there are several hotels and dive outfits on the water at Castle Comfort, and a narrow road hugs the shore to the southern tip of the

Dominica

265 B6

Visitor information

www.dominica.dm

Division of Tourism, National Development Corporation, Valley Road, P.O. Box 293, Roseau, Dominica

767/448-2045, fax 767/448-5840

Dominica Museum
- Bay St., Roseau
- 767/448-8932
- Closed Sat.–Sun. in the low season
- $$

Roseau Tourist Office
- Old Market Square
- 767/448-2045

island, home to the spectacular Scotts Head/Soufrière Bay Marine Park (see p. 273).

Dominica's second largest settlement is Portsmouth. Above the coast, endangered sisserou and jaco parrots are protected in the **Morne Diablotin National Park** on the slopes of Morne Diablotin, and a road crosses over to the Atlantic coast, past good swimming beaches at **Hampstead Estate** and **Hodges Bay.** There are a couple of beach bars and restaurants at **Calibishe,** and coconut plantations around Melville Hall Airport. South of Melville Hall the Transinsular Road carves a splendid route to Roseau through the Central Forest Reserve and the pretty mountain village of Bells. The drive takes 90 minutes and affords grand views of cloudy peaks and the rain forest. Remaining on the windward side, the coastal road runs through Carib Territory, passing roadside stalls selling traditional basketwork, to Castle Bruce and an alternative route back to the capital via the waterfall at Emerald Pool (see p. 271).

ROSEAU & THE ROSEAU VALLEY

Dominica's capital, which moved to Roseau (pronounced Row-SO) from Portsmouth in the late 18th century, is laid out in a neat grid between the banks of the Roseau River and Fort Young. Roseau has a certain dilapidated charm, with its motley collection of sturdy stone colonial buildings. Several historic gingerbread houses are being restored amongst the rather less appealing modern concrete structures. It's easy to explore on foot, and there are several small galleries, cafés, and craft shops around Cork Street.

Roseau's most animated corner is the local **produce market,** which spills out from the shade of its tin roof and onto the sidewalk at the river end of the waterfront.

The hub of colonial Roseau was the Old Market Place on **Dawbiney Square,** off King George V Street. Slave auctions were once held in the small cobbled, tree-shaded plaza, now annexed by a café and souvenir stalls squeezed in around a curious cast-iron centerpiece decorated with a regal crown. On one side of the square, facing the waterfront and downtown cruise-ship berth, is the **Dominica Museum,** which provides an interesting overview of island history and culture. Among the exhibits are Carib tools and a thatched *carbet* (hut), a section on Dominican writers, including Jean Rhys, and a series of fascinating 18th-century prints by Agostino Brunias, an Italian-born artist

Jean Rhys (1894–1979)

Writer Jean Rhys was born in Roseau in 1894; her mother's family were white Creole planters. Rhys traveled to Europe at age 16 and drew on her own experiences as a chorus girl, artist's model, and poet's wife for her first collection of short stories, *The Left Bank* (1927), which explores the role of women on the edge of bohemian society. After a checkered literary career, she returned to her Caribbean roots for *Wide Sargasso Sea* (1966). It recounts the imagined history of the first Mrs. Rochester, a white Creole heiress who became the mad wife of Charlotte Brontë's novel *Jane Eyre*. Set in Jamaica and Dominica in the early 1800s, it describes the decadence of a Caribbean lifestyle on the verge of extinction. ■

Tropical downpours are a frequent occurrence, but it is business as usual for the traders and shoppers in Roseau's waterfront market.

employed by Dominica's first British governor, Sir William Young, to record scenes of island life.

Sir William's name lives on at **Fort Young,** a short walk away along the seafront. Now a hotel (see p. 378), the fort was constructed of blackened volcanic stone in 1775. It retains few reminders of its military heyday, except for a couple of fancy brass cannon and workmanlike snipers' embrasures in the walls of the dining room.

Opposite the fort is the **Anglican Church,** which contains memorial tablets eulogizing 19th-century British colonial officials, and stained-glass windows behind the altar. The **Roman Catholic Cathedral,** on Turkey Lane, is in rather better shape, built of dark river rocks between 1800 and 1916. To the east are the green expanses of the **Botanical Gardens** *(Map 267 B2; off King George V St.)*, stretching over a 40-acre (16-ha) former cane field on the lower slopes of Morne Bruce. Teams play cricket in the large grassy park, and an aviary houses indigenous sisserou and jaco parrots. Among the botanical exhibits are flowering cannonball trees with their strange waxy blooms, teaks, flamboyants, and cassia trees. The Forestry Division Offices *(Tel 767/ 448-2401)* are a good source for information on hiking in the national parks, passes, maps, and experienced guides.

The **Trafalgar Falls** lie about 5 miles (8 km) east of town at the head of the Roseau Valley. *(Map 267 B2; take King George V St. out of central Roseau, in the direction of Laudat, and follow signs.)* Carving an imposing cleft deep into the green buttress of the Morne Trois Pitons highlands, the valley walls swoosh up to either side of the road, carpeted in a tangled mass of rain forest jungle and terraced vegetable plots grafted onto almost perpendicular slopes. The bumpy track runs out near the **Papillote Wilderness Retreat** (*Map 267 B2; tel 767/448-2287*), a delightful small hotel and restaurant set in pretty gardens, where guides offer their services. From here it's a steep 10- to 15-minute hike to the twin waterfalls, known as "mother" and "father." The father fall on the left is warm, while the mother is cold, and they plummet down the 200-foot

(60-m) cliff face in a roar of tumbling water and spray to a pool below, bouncing off giant boulders streaked orange with mineral deposits. Below the viewing platform are paths leading around to swimming areas.

MORNE TROIS PITONS NATIONAL PARK

Morne Trois Pitons National Park
267 B2
Forestry Division, Roseau
767/448-2401, ext. 3431
National Park Passes: One site pass $; day pass $$; one week pass $$$

Most of Dominica's best known natural attractions are found in the 17,000-acre (6,880-ha) national park, a UNESCO World Heritage site, stretching south of Morne Trois Pitons (4,550 feet/1,387 m). Sprinkled with mountain lakes, hissing volcanic fumeroles, sulfur springs, and an annual rainfall of almost 300 inches (7,600 mm), this is superb (if rather damp) upland hiking country. Together with Morne Diablotin National Park (see p. 271), the central highlands showcase the many different faces of the rain forest, from the grandeur of 100-foot-tall (30-m) secondary forest to stunted, high-altitude elfin woodlands, and a treasury of island plant life that numbers some 74 species of orchids and 22 kinds of fern.

Dominican wildlife is fairly difficult to spot, but there are occasional sightings of opossums, agoutis, iguanas, and five nonvenomous snakes, including elusive boa constrictors. More than 170 bird species have been identified. Locals catch freshwater shrimp, fish, crabs, and frogs for food. (Frog's legs are served up under the pseudonym "mountain chicken" in local restaurants.)

The easiest starting point for explorations in the park is the village of **Laudat,** east of Roseau. For a soft adventure into the rain forest canopy, an **aerial tram** *(Reservations, tel 767/448-8775)* skims the treetops over gorges and waterfalls, with commentary from an experienced guide. **Freshwater Lake,** 2,500 feet (760 m) above sea level, is accessible by car, and **Boeri Lake** is an attractive 40-minute walk farther on over two steep ridges cupped in a volcanic crater.

The park's best known and most challenging hike is the trail to **Boiling Lake,** a 200-foot-wide (60-m) flooded volcanic fumerole that bubbles and steams at 180° to 200°F (82–93°C). It's best to engage a qualified guide before undertaking the strenuous seven- to eight-hour round-trip trek. Local guides wait at the trail-

Sports & activities

Diving & whale-watching: Dominica's diving credentials are well established, but a lesser known fact is the island's excellent location for whale-watching. There are more sightings of sperm whales off Dominica's shores than anywhere else in the region (most common in Nov.–Mar.), as well as humpbacks and schools of spotted and spinner dolphins. The Anchorage Dive Center *(Tel 767/448-2638, www.anchoragehotel.dm)*, and Dive Dominica *(Tel 767/448-2188, www.divedominica.com)* offer both dive facilities and whale-watching trips.

Hiking & tours: Boiling Lake and Morne Diablotin hikes, and botany and bird-watching tours from Ken's Hinterland Adventure Tours *(Tel 767/448-4850, www.kenshinterlandtours.com)*. For mountain bike and sea kayak rentals and excursions (as well as diving), contact Nature Island Dive *(Tel 767/449-8181, www.natureislanddive.com)*. ■

head, or you can hook up with a reputable guide company (see p. 270). En route to Boiling Lake, the trail crosses the **Valley of Desolation,** a suitably hellish, barren landscape cluttered with huge boulders, where the fumes from noxious sulfur springs and sinister pools of bubbling gray mud have killed off all but the hardiest sprigs of vegetation.

At the western edge of the park are the **Middleham Trails** (3 hours round-trip), which strike out from Cochrane or Laudat for the dramatic 500-foot-high (150 m) **Middleham Falls** via the **Stinking Hole bat caves.**

A challenging 4- to 5-hour round-trip trail from Pont Cassé tackles **Morne Trois Pitons** itself, climbing into the eerily quiet world of elfin forest frosted with lichens and wrapped in mosses and mist.

A few miles farther east, outside the park and just off the Castle Bruce road, is **Emerald Pool.** The small green-blue swimming hole is fed by a waterfall and set in a fern-flanked rain forest grotto beneath lianas and elephant ears.

MORNE DIABLOTIN NATIONAL PARK

Larger than the neighboring Morne Trois Pitons National Park, this 22,000-acre (8,900-ha) forested preserve (*Map 267 B3; tel 767/448 2733*) on the slopes of Morne Diablotin is a refuge for Dominica's two endemic parrot species: sisserou and jaco. The green-and-brown sisserou is the national bird and the rarer of the two. Captive breeding programs have helped swell numbers in the wild to approximately 300. There are about a thousand of the more colorful jaco, or red-necked parrots.

A road from Dublanc, south of Portsmouth, clambers up to the park entrance at Syndicate Estate. At this former citrus and banana plantation 1,800 feet (550 m) above sea level, a short trail provides good bird-watching opportunities. The best way to see the birds is on a tour (see p. 270).

A guide is also recommended for a strenuous 6- to 7-hour round-trip ascent of **Morne Diablotin.** The mountain was named for the black-capped petrel that inhabited the forest before being hunted to extinction. ■

Hikers trek around the steaming cauldron of Boiling Lake high in Dominica's desolate central highlands.

Syndicate Estate

- Map: 267 B3
- Division of Tourism, Valley Rd., Roseau
- Tel: 767/448-2045

Wooden fishing boats drawn up on the volcanic shingle beach at Soufrière

Around Dominica

CARIB TERRITORY

Established in 1903, the 3,700-acre (1,500-ha) Carib Territory encompasses eight small villages along the Atlantic coast between Atkinson and Castle Bruce. Some 2,200 Kalinago (formerly Carib) people live in the territory, descendants of Amerindian migrants who paddled their dugout canoes from the Amazon Basin. Although most are now of mixed race, the Dominican Carib display their South American heritage in their facial features, bronze skin, and straight black hair.

Modern Carib have abandoned traditional thatched huts in favor of more comfortable wooden Creole homes balanced on stilts overlooking the sea. Basket-weaving is a local specialty on display at roadside stalls alongside model boats and other wood carvings. At the St. Marie of the Caribs Catholic Church, Salybia, there is an altar carved in the shape of a dugout canoe. A few ancient ceremonies and traditions such as boatbuilding survive, and there's an opportunity to see traditional crafts and practices in action at **Kalinago Barana Autê** (Carib Cultural Village by the Sea) on the Atlantic coast near Salybia *(Tel 767/445-7979, closed Mon in winter, Wed.–Thur. in summer, $$$).*

267 C3

PORTSMOUTH & CABRITS NATIONAL PARK

Portsmouth, once the island capital until malarial mosquitoes in the nearby swamps sent the British scurrying down to Roseau, is a scruffy little town of 5,000 souls set on the yachtsman's haven Prince Rupert Bay.

On the southern edge of town take a boat

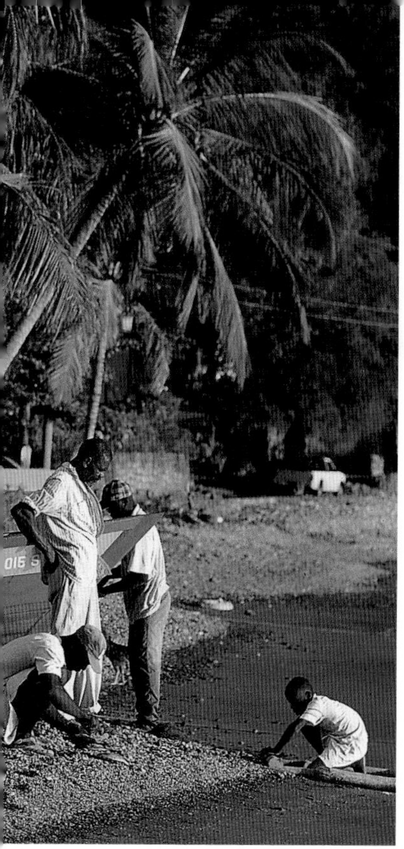

A Rasta oarsman paddles visitors up the Indian River near Portsmouth.

trip on the **Indian River**. You can paddle upstream through a tunnel of swamp ferns, bwa mang trees, wild hibiscus, and anthuriums. Herons and egrets stalk the shallows, and turquoise kingfishers flit past.

Just over a mile (1.5 km) north is **Cabrits National Park** *(Map 267 A4; tel 767/448-2401),* occupying the forested peninsula at the top of the bay. It's said that this sheltered anchorage attracted 16th-century explorers Sir Francis Drake (1540–1596) and Sir John Hawkins (1532–1595). They would stop off to resupply their ships, trading with the Carib and hunting goats (*cabrits*) left by previous expeditions for fresh meat. In 1765 the British founded **Fort Shirley** to defend the harbor. Its scattered remains, linked by footpaths, litter the hillside. Some of the old volcanic stone and redbrick buildings have been overtaken by jungle, but several others have been partially restored, and the former **Powder Magazine** houses a small museum.

Black sand beaches fringe Prince Rupert Bay, with several hotels and a dive shop at **Picard Beach.** The best snorkeling and coral reef and wall diving sites are located in **Douglas Bay,** north of Cabrits Peninsula.

SCOTTS HEAD & THE SOUTH

A half-hour drive from Roseau around the curve of Soufrière Bay, the narrow finger of Scotts Head Peninsula juts out from the Caribbean coast at the southern tip of the island. From the ruins of **Fort Cashacrou,** the view stretches off to the French island of Martinique 20 miles (32 km) to the south and back up the Dominican coast to the mountains.

Beneath the waters of the bay is a submerged volcanic caldera a mile (1.6 km) across and almost 1,000 feet (300 m) deep, forming the centerpiece of the **Scotts Head/Soufrière Bay Marine Park** *(Map 267 B1),* Dominica's top dive site. Around the crater rim lava pinnacles and reef sites are frequented by a kaleidoscope of marine species. Hard and soft corals and forests of sponges stud the walls of dramatic dropoffs. One site with particular appeal for snorkelers is **Champagne,** which lives up to its name in a cloud of tiny bubbles released from a volcanic vent in the seabed.

The fishing village of **Soufrière** takes its name from the hot sulfur springs reached by a winding road up into the hills. You can also reach the springs from the Tête Morne road above Berekua, on the shore at Grand Bay, near the Geneva Estate once owned by the family of writer Jean Rhys (see p. 268). ■

The twin volcanic peaks of the Pitons on the southwest coast are St. Lucia's most famous landmarks.

St. Lucia

LAVISHLY BESTOWED WITH DENSE GREEN RAIN FOREST, landmark peaks rising sheer from the sea, golden beaches, rare parrots, and a profusion of vivid tropical flowers, St. Lucia is a first-rank Caribbean beauty. The 27-by-14-mile (43-by-23-km) island is shaped like a pear and lies between Martinique to the north and St. Vincent in the south.

St. Lucia
265 B4
Visitor information
www.stlucia.org
Sureline Bldg., Vide Bouteille, Castries
e-mail slutour@candw.lc
758/452-4094, fax 758/453-1121

St. Lucia (pronounced LOO-sha) is the most developed and populous of the Windward Islands. Nevertheless, the entire central portion of the island is mountainous forest ringed by rolling acres of banana plantations, sugarcane, and coconut groves. Small fishing villages dot the coast, mountain hamlets cling perilously to absurdly verdant valleys, and most telltale signs of tourist development have been tucked neatly into the northwestern corner of the island above the capital, Castries (see p. 276), home to more than a third of St. Lucia's 156,000 inhabitants.

Christopher Columbus may have set foot on St. Lucia on his fourth voyage to the New World in 1502, but the island's earliest recorded European resident was one François Le Clerc, a 16th-century French pirate who established a base on Pigeon Island and attacked passing Spanish galleons. Also known as Jambe de Bois for his wooden leg, Le Clerc appears to have survived the attentions of the island's resident Carib people, who had already dispatched two attempted British settlements before the French finally established a colonial toehold in 1651.

St. Lucia was one of the most hotly contested plantation islands in the eastern Caribbean, nicknamed "the Fair Helen of the West Indies" for all the ships launched in the battle for her favors. Strategically placed next to the flourishing French sugar colony of Martinique and just as cultivable, the colony represented a considerable prize and changed hands 14 times, shuttling between her French founders and British usurpers. The British finally gained the upper hand after a fierce battle culminating on the slopes of Morne Fortune (see pp. 277–78) above Castries in 1796, although French revolutionaries continued a guerrilla war from hideouts in the mountains for some time afterward. St. Lucia was secured by Britain under the Treaty of Paris in 1814. The island, which became independent in 1979, remains part of the British Commonwealth.

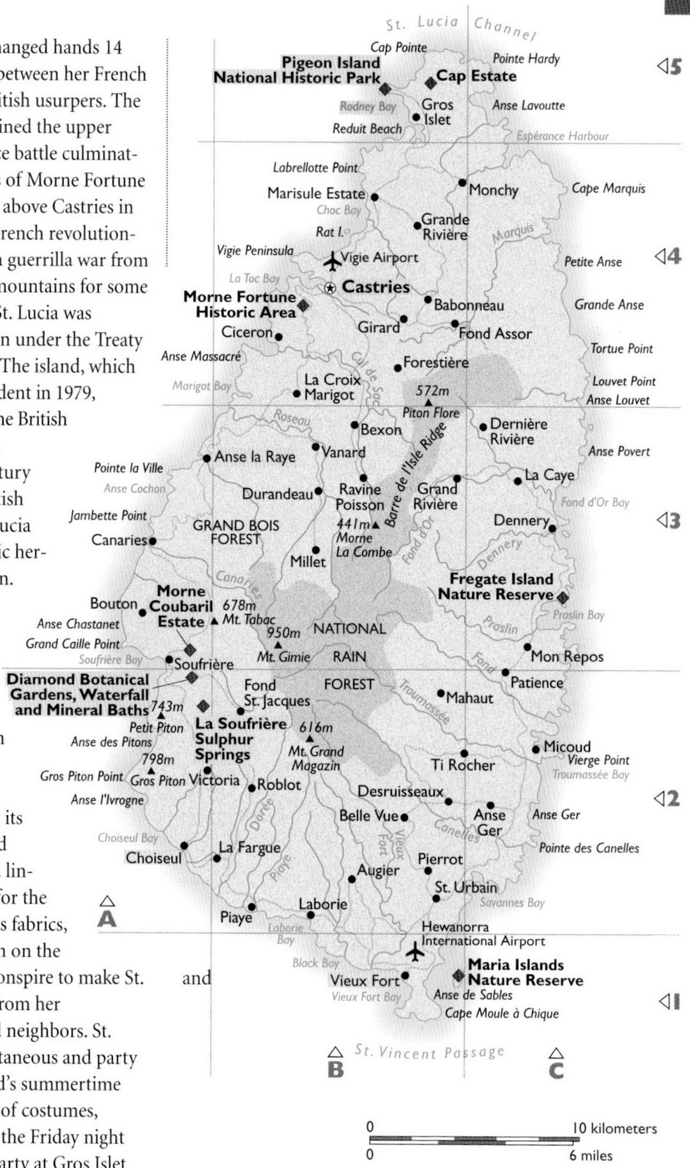

Despite a century and a half of British occupation, St. Lucia displays her Gallic heritage at every turn. French place-names are more common than English, and the local patois is based on Creole. Creole cooking, Creole architecture with its fancy gingerbread trimmings, and a lingering fondness for the checkered madras fabrics, more usually seen on the French islands, conspire to make St. Lucia stand out from her Windward Island neighbors. St. Lucians are spontaneous and party loving. The island's summertime Carnival is a riot of costumes, music, and food, the Friday night jump-up street party at Gros Islet (see p. 278) is an institution, which has inspired Anse-la-Raye's Friday seafood cookout, and Dennery's Saturday night Fish Fiesta, enjoyed by locals and visitors alike. Musical events are scheduled throughout the year, including a world-class summer Jazz Festival, and any number of fêtes, sailing regattas, and impromptu jump-ups.

African traditions also maintain a hold on the local imagination. Although the majority of the population is Roman Catholic (a French legacy), St. Lucia has a rich folkloric culture. Evil spirits are banished by the beating of drums, and houses are made safe by magical wreaths of thorny acacia and special herbs.

Although St. Lucia's traditional tourist heartland is the northwest, around the popular yachting center of Rodney Bay, most of the island's attractions are found south of Castries along the Caribbean coast and in the rain forest highlands. There has also been a recent flurry of luxury hotel developments, and a number of elegant spa resorts have opened their doors around Marigot, Soufrière, and even on the previously uncharted Atlantic coast.

Near the town of Soufrière are the Pitons ("peaks"), St. Lucia's most famous landmarks, which are depicted on the national flag. A brace of lofty volcanic plugs, they soar dramatically from the shore, upstaging the island's tallest peak, Mount Gimie (3,118 feet/950 m) a few miles inland. Close by are a marine park, a "drive-in" volcano, the gardens at Diamond, a working cocoa plantation, and the rain forest. Soufrière itself makes a good base for exploring the rain forest, diving, or enjoying the low-key atmosphere.

Castries

- 275 B4
- Visitor information, booth at Pointe Seraphine
- 758/452-7577

CASTRIES

St. Lucia's unremarkable capital lies at the foot of a sheltered inlet encircled by steep, forested hills. Castries was founded in the 1760s and named for the French Minister of the Marine, the Maréchal de Castries, who would have appreciated the well-protected natural harbor. But the city has a bad habit of burning down, and most of its uninspiring concrete architecture dates from the last conflagration, in 1948. St. Lucia is a regular feature

A bananaquit enjoys its leaf perch.

Rain forest birds

Of the 43 or so bird species that inhabit the St. Lucian rain forest, 33 are endemic, such as the rare white-breasted thrasher, St. Lucia oriole, St. Lucia wren, and the endangered St. Lucian parrot. Conservation measures established in the 1970s brought this last species back from the edge of extinction. Known as the *jacquot* locally, the 16- to 18-inch-tall (40- to 45-cm) parrot is one of the most colorful inhabitants of the rain forest. It has a green back, blue head, red throat patch, and flashes of yellow and red under its wings.

A good way to find the parrots is to look for a stand of towering santinay trees, where they like to nest and feed on the small pink fruits. Their raucous screech is another telltale sign. ■

on cruise-ship itineraries, and as the giant liners enter the harbor, they pass the old French battery at Vigie (Lookout) Point before berthing at the modern Pointe Seraphine cruise complex or right up against the downtown waterfront.

Set back from the waterfront is **Jeremie Street,** a bustle of market stalls, traffic, and pedestrians. T-shirt sellers and souvenir stalls perch on the dockside. Across the street the old covered market building has been hijacked by wood carvings, basketware, and beach bag vendors, while the produce market has been relegated to a concrete monstrosity with orange pyramid-shaped roofs. This is still the place to find a healthy dash of local color among the piles of citrus fruits and bananas, squashlike christophene, yams, ginger roots, and hot peppers.

A couple of blocks inland, past the Parliament and Court House on Laborie Street, lies the 19th-century **Cathedral of the Immaculate Conception.** The interior is painted from floor to ceiling with murals depicting biblical figures, African clerics, and pineapple motifs (the traditional Caribbean symbol for hospitality). Next to the cathedral is **Derek Walcott Square,** which honors the St. Lucian poet and playwright who won the Nobel Prize for Literature in 1992. There's a massive samaan tree on the square and a few old-style West Indian buildings around the edge.

Running south from the city center, Government House Road labors up Morne Fortune (pronounced For-TU-nay), past the Governor General's residence, and on to the **Morne Fortune Historic Area**

The brig *Unicorn* makes regular excursions along the west coast from Castries to Soufrière.

St. Lucians gather to chat along Rodney Bay, with the outline of Pigeon Island looming in the distance.

(at the top of the hill). In 1796, British soldiers of the 27th Inniskilling Regiment spent two days fighting their way to the summit of the morne, forcing the French to surrender. Their bravery is commemorated by the Inniskilling Memorial in the grounds of **Fort Charlotte**, where old military buildings have been restored and transformed into a college.

RODNEY BAY & THE NORTH

From Castries the main road north swings alongside the local airport, which is edged by 2-mile-long (3-km) **Vigie Beach,** and on past the Gablewoods Mall and Choc Bay hotel enclave to Rodney Bay, St. Lucia's busiest resort area. On the southern side of the bay, hotels line the soft white sands of Reduit Beach. At the head of the beach a narrow channel gives access to the yacht harbor and Rodney Bay Marina. This bustling Caribbean sailing center is bordered to the north by the waterfront village of **Gros Islet,** home to the famous Friday night jump-up.

The north shore of Rodney Bay curves around to **Pigeon Island,** the *gros islet* (big island) that gave the neighboring village its name. The former pirate lair of notorious Capitaine Jambe de Bois is now the **Pigeon Island National Park,** linked to the mainland by a sandy causeway. In 1778 Adm. George Rodney of the British Royal Navy set up a naval base in Gros Islet Bay (later renamed in his honor) and established a lookout post on the island. According to one story, the sentries on hilltop Fort Rodney used carrier pigeons to report sightings of passing vessels and developments on the French island of Martinique, clearly visible 20 miles (32 km) to the north. (A more prosaic explanation attributes the name to the quantities of red-necked pigeons that congregated here before the native forest was stripped away.) The ruins of Fort Rodney still afford spectacular views north to Martinique, and south down the serried peaks of St. Lucia's mountainous interior to the Pitons. A botanical trail meanders around the 40-acre (16-ha) island, and there are several old military

Pigeon Island National Park
- 275 B5
- Pigeon Point
- 758/452-5005
- $$

A guided walking tour picks up a trail into the St. Lucian rain forest.

ruins, such as barracks, powder magazines, and a sunken musket redoubt,to explore.

The restored 1824 Officers' Quarters contain an interpretive center with exhibits tracing Admiral Rodney's famous victory at the Battle of the Saints in 1782 (see p. 247). Look for the tavern under the arches of the cellars and bring beach towels for a swim.

To the east of Rodney Bay, the exclusive **Cap Estate** residential quarter occupies the hilly northern tip of the island. There are several stunning private houses, a golf course (see p. 280), and a lovely restaurant in the estate's original 250-year-old great house.

SOUTH TO SOUFRIÈRE

There are two ways to explore the sights of southern St. Lucia, and visitors staying in the north of the island should reckon on a full-day to visit the Soufrière area sights with a stop for lunch. A hassle-free option is to take a day sail from Castries or Rodney Bay, which includes a land tour of the attractions around Soufrière. On the other hand, you can rent a car and tackle the beautiful switchback road down the Caribbean coast, with the

Rain forest hikes & nature reserves

A number of trails carve their way through St. Lucia's 19,000-acre (7,700-ha) **National Rainforest.** From the lush lower slopes, some hikes strike up into areas of cloud forest and elfin woodland with fabulous views and bird-spotting opportunities. Walkers must obtain permission from the Forest & Lands Department *(Tel 758/450-2231/2078)*, which can supply information and guide services. They also provide tours of the **Fregate Island Nature Reserve's** frigatebird nesting grounds off the Atlantic Coast. Excursions to the southerly **Maria Islands Nature Reserve,** home to a rare harmless snake *(kuowess)*, lizards and seabirds, can be arranged through the National Trust's southern office *(Tel 758/453-7656)*. ■

VIEWS OF THE PITONS

Heading south from Castries, drivers have their work cut out on the stretch of serpentine road that drops briefly to sea level at Canaries, a small fishing community, before carving a path up through the rain forest and emerging above Soufrière. This is one of the best views of the Pitons, with the Petit Piton (2,461 feet/ 743 m) in the foreground and the Gros Piton (2,619 feet/ 798 m) 1.5 miles (2.5 km) behind. ■

option of continuing right around the island on a tour from the capital.

The road south to Soufrière starts from Morne Fortune, south of Castries, and swoops downhill into the banana plantations and cane fields of the Cul de Sac Valley. Across the ridge at the end of the valley, there is a turn on the right to **Marigot Bay,** an idyllic little hurricane hole surrounded by steep wooded hills where Rex Harrison talked to the animals during the filming of *Doctor Dolittle* in 1967.

The bay is currently being transformed from a sleepy yachting backwater into the setting for one of St. Lucia's newest and most luxurious hotel and villa resorts with an upscale marina village complete with shopping and dining opportunities. A regular miniature ferry shuttles across the mouth of the bay to the beach opposite.

A short run farther south is **Anse la Raye** (Skate Bay, named after the fish once caught here), a picturesque West Indian fishing village. Its narrow streets are lined with sun-bleached wooden cottages, and down on the waterfront you'll see a few fishing boats hollowed out of gommier trees. On Friday evenings, the village comes alive as crowds gather for the Fish Feast (from 6:30 p.m.). ■

Sports & activities

Day sails: Companies that offer sight-seeing tours to Soufrière and the Pitons from Castries or Pigeon Island include Brig Unicorn *(Tel 758/452-9842)* and Endless Summer *(Tel 758/450-8651)*. Whale-watching excursions from Hackshaw's Boat Charters *(Tel 758/453-0553)*.

Diving & snorkeling: St. Lucia's underwater scenery is every bit as impressive as its terrestrial landscape, promising excellent visibility, a diverse collection of corals and marine life in top condition, and wreck dive opportunities. For example, Soufrière Marine Park offers reef dives straight off the beach. Local dive operators include Buddies *(Water Side Landing, tel 758/450-8406)*; Dive Fair Helen *(Vigie Cove, tel 758/451-7716)*, and Scuba St. Lucia *(Anse Chastanet, tel 758/459-7755)*.

Golf: Attractive 18-hole course at the St. Lucia Golf & Country Club, Cap Estate *(Tel 758/450-8523, fax 758/450-0674)*.

Hiking: Permits are mandatory for hikes in the National Rain Forest and expert local guides a bonus. Contact the Forestry Department in advance *(Tel 758/450-2231, ext. 308)*.

Horseback riding: Ride estate and rain forest trails and take a tour of a working plantation at Morne Coubaril Estate *(Soufrière, tel 758/459-7340, fax 758/459-5759, e-mail coubaril@candw.lc)*. One or two hour and group coastal tours are available from Trim's National Riding Academy *(Gros Islet, tel 758/450-8273)*.

Sportfishing: Mako Watersports *(Rodney Bay Marina, tel 758/452-0412)*; Captain Mike's Watersports *(Vigie Marina, tel 758/452-7044)*.

Water sports: Reduit Beach, in Rodney Bay, is well supplied with hotel water-sports concessions. The best windsurfing is off the southern tip of the island; Club Mistral *(Anse des Sables, Vieux Fort, tel/fax 758/454-7400)*. ■

A single bell-ringer summons churchgoers in Vieux Fort.

Around Soufrière

AROUND TO THE ATLANTIC COAST

Not far beyond Soufrière, the round-island route exchanges its border of lush green forest for open countryside. The roadside **Livity Art Studio,** located in the village of Victoria, is worth a stop for souvenir hunting, as is the **Arts and Crafts Development Centre** in Choiseul. Down on **Choiseul Bay,** the village lines a crescent of sand where fishing boats unload their catches at the waterfront market and a stone church balances on a palm-fringed spit of land.

The town of **Vieux Fort** crouches at the neck of the Moule à Chique, St. Lucia's most southerly point, facing St. Vincent in the distance. Off the east coast is the **Maria Islands Nature Reserve** (see p. 279), harboring seabirds and several endemic wildlife species.

The relatively swift return route to Castries passes the hamlet of Micoud, the **Mamiku Gardens,** near Praslin *(Tel 758/452-8236)* with their lovely woodland trails and ocean views, and an observation point overlooking the **Fregate Island Nature Reserve** (see p. 279). At the banana town of Dennery, the road heads inland, crossing the Barre de l'Isle Ridge on its journey back to the island capital.

DIAMOND BOTANICAL GARDENS, MINERAL BATHS & WATERFALLS

Set in the hills above Soufrière, these lovely botanical gardens display a glorious profusion of tropical plants and trees crowding narrow pathways; the baths were built for French troops on the orders of Louis XVI.

275 A2 · East of Soufrière · $$

LA SOUFRIÈRE SULPHUR SPRINGS

Because you can drive to within a few yards of La Soufrière's sinister and smelly volcanic vent, this attraction has been billed as "the world's only drive-in volcano." At the heart of the 7-acre (3-ha) crater, pools of boiling mud belch in the chalky moonscape.

275 A2 · Southeast of Soufrière · $

FOND DOUX ESTATE

One of St. Lucia's oldest estates, Fond Doux was once at the thick of the fighting between French revolutionaries and the British. This plantation's handsome 19th-century estate house offers B&B, lunch, and trails through areas of citrus, cocoa, coconuts, coffee, cinnamon and nutmeg.

275 A2 · South of Soufrière, www.fonddouxestate.com · 758/459-7545 ■

St. Vincent & the Grenadines

St. Vincent
265 B3
Visitor information
www.svgtourism.com
Cruise Ship Terminal, Kingstown
e-mail tourism@caribsurf.com
784/457-1502, fax 784/451-2425

ST. VINCENT HEADS UP THE CHAIN OF THE GRENADINE Islands like an emerald green kite with a 75-mile-long (120-km) tail trailing down toward Grenada. At 18 by 11 miles (29 by 18 km), it's the smallest and probably the least discovered of the Windward Islands, with a slumbering volcano, and a nearly impenetrable jungle heart where generations of Carib once hid out and kept the Europeans at bay for more than two centuries.

ST. VINCENT

St. Vincent is still relatively overlooked today, outshone by the golden beaches and yachting havens of the Grenadines (see pp. 288–91) and the more widely publicized attractions of St. Lucia and Barbados. But while St. Vincent is no classic Caribbean idyll, all palm-fringed sands and rum punches (although the latter can be found), it does offer a quiet backwater charm, a miraculously undeveloped hinterland, and several hotels with discreet appeal for less hidebound travelers.

Successive waves of Ciboney, Arawak, and Carib settlers paddled their way from South America to Hairoun, as they called St. Vincent before Europeans added it to the New World map. But the island's rugged terrain and the prospect of ending up at the sharp end of a Carib barbecue curtailed further investigation, and St. Vincent became a refuge for Carib people forced from other islands. They were joined by escaped African slaves, some the survivors of shipwrecks off the coast, while others set sail on rafts from Barbados and were

Famous for its diving, the uninhabited Grenadine islands of Tobago Cays can only be reached by boat.

blown to St. Vincent by the westerly trade winds. Mixed Afro-Carib Black Carib soon outnumbered the original Yellow Carib and started to take their lands. In retaliation the Yellow Carib allowed the French to establish a small colony in 1719. The Black Carib took to the hills to continue their resistance, surviving the First Carib War, initiated by a British invasion in 1763—a Caribbean extension of Britain's and France's long-running European conflicts.

The French snatched the island back with embarrassing ease in 1779. When the challengers sailed in for the attack, the entire British garrison was away working the governor's plantation in the north of the island, and no one could locate the key to the gun battery. With the British reinstated by the Treaty of Versailles in 1783, the French switched allegiance to the Black Carib and backed the uprising that became known as the Second Carib War, or Brigands' War, lasting from 1795 to 1797. British plantations and settlements were torched and planters fed through the cane-crushing gear of their own sugar mills until the army regained control. The surviving 5,000 Black Carib were deported to British Honduras (present-day Belize). The last Yellow Carib retreated to the far north of St. Vincent, where their descendants still live today. The wars over, St. Vincent settled down to a quiet agrarian existence, growing a little sugar, Sea Island cotton, and arrowroot. It was granted independence from Britain in 1979, and it remains a member of the British Commonwealth.

Agriculture is still a mainstay of St. Vincent's economy, and the island is rampantly fertile. There's no escaping the evidence, from the stranglehold of its creeper-clad rain forest peaks to the vegetable plots and tropical fruit orchards clinging to steep-sided valleys. Jagged mountains rip the underbellies of lowering gray rain clouds, so it always appears to be raining somewhere on the island. Regular dustings of volcanic fertilizer from Soufrière, one of the Caribbean's most active volcanoes, further enrich the crumbling red earth. They say you could plant a pencil here, and it would take root.

The capital of St. Vincent and the Grenadines is Kingstown (see p. 284) on the south coast of St. Vincent, a 20-minute drive from the main tourist enclave at Villa. A busy working port, Kingstown is a transportation hub for the Grenadines and is served by regular ferries and small island-

Fresh produce spread on a Kingstown sidewalk

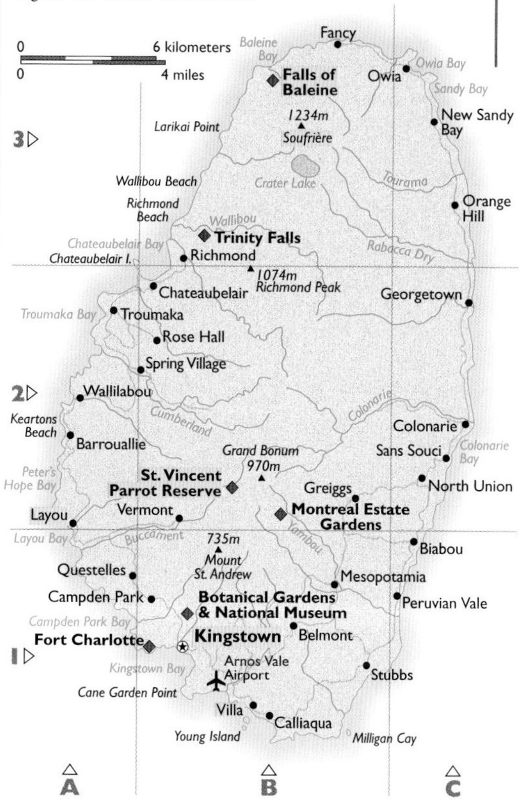

All manner of goods are loaded onto the inter-island ferry at Kingstown for transport down the Grenadines.

hopper aircraft. It's also a good place to begin any exploration of the island. Look to the west coast for quiet volcanic sand beaches and secluded coves only accessible by boat. Yachting is a major attraction, and day sails can be combined with diving and snorkeling. Hikers can plan some great days out around La Soufrière and the Buccament River Valley, where the beautiful, rare St. Vincent parrot makes its home.

Kingstown

Hemmed in by a crown of steep, wooded ridges, the capital of St. Vincent and the Grenadines hugs the mile-long (1.5-km) curve of Kingstown Bay and pushes back up the hillside. Down on the waterfront there's a lively bustle of cargo ships, ferries, and fishing boats, and the new cruise-ship and yachting complex sits smartly at the eastern end of the harbor. Behind the docks is Kingstown's pocket-size downtown district, which still has a few bumpy, old-fashioned cobbled streets and rows of arcaded shops sheltering the sidewalk from the sun and occasional cloudbursts.

Heading west on Halifax Street, take a detour down Hillsboro Street (by the Cenotaph) to investigate the **produce market.** The busiest days are Friday and Saturday, when farmers venture into town from all around the island. On the opposite side of Halifax Street, iron railings fence in the imposing gray stone **Law Courts,** where the St. Vincent Parliament meets. Pastel-painted **St. George's Anglican Cathedral,** founded in 1820, is just a little farther on. The interior of the church has an unusual stained-glass window depicting a red-robed angel. Supposedly commissioned by Queen Victoria to celebrate the birth of her first grandson, it was destined for St. Paul's Cathedral in London. But the monarch preferred her angels white, so the homeless window was presented to St. George's by the dean of St. Paul's. Among the many memorial plaques set in the walls of the cathedral, one commemorates Maj. Alexander Leith, a British war hero, who killed the Carib leader Chatoyer in a fencing duel on Dorsetshire Hill in 1795.

Across the way from the cathedral is Kingstown's most bizarre architectural monument, the 19th-century **St. Mary's Roman Catholic Church.** A riot of conflicting styles with a playful assortment of turrets, towers, pinnacles, and twisted barley-sugar columns, it was designed by a Belgian priest who drew his inspiration from pictures of famous European cathedrals.

Visitors with an interest in island history should check whether plans to relocate the small but fascinating **National Museum** and its collections of Amerindian artifacts to the Old Public Library have been completed.

On top of Berkshire Hill, at the western end of town, stands **Fort Charlotte,** which affords magnificent views down the Grenadines from its aerie 600 feet (180 m) above the bay. Named for George III's queen, the sprawling fortress was constructed in 1806 but never fired a shot in anger. A pictorial history of "St. Vincent and the Carib Wars" by William Linzee Prescott adorns the former cells.

Kingstown's pride and joy are the **Botanical Gardens,** set in the hills above the town center. The gardens are the oldest of their kind in the Western Hemisphere, founded in 1763. They were intended as a research and breeding station for useful tropical plants run as a distant adjunct of Kew Gardens in London. Their most

Kingstown
Map: 283 B1
Visitor information
Tel: 784/457-1502

Fort Charlotte
Address: 10 minutes' drive W of Kingstown
Tel: 784/456-1830

Botanical Gardens
Map: 283 B1
Address: Off Leeward Hwy.
Tel: 784/457-1003
Price: $$

famous success story concerns the breadfruit tree, introduced from the South Pacific to provide cheap, nutritious food for slaves working on the Caribbean plantations. Capt. William Bligh (1754–1817) set sail with the first consignment of saplings from Tahiti aboard H.M.S. *Bounty* in 1787, but the small matter of a mutiny delayed his arrival until 1793. At first the slaves refused to touch the bland, alien fruit, but now the breadfruit's starchy flesh is a staple vegetable dish.

Guides loiter near the entrance waiting to conduct tours, and their services certainly liven up a visit. They know all the good stories, such as how the traveler's palm tree automatically aligns itself east-west and contains a reservoir of water for the lost and thirsty adventurer.

There's no need to search for the aviary; the piercing screech of the St. Vincent parrot is guide enough. Predominantly yellow-gold with a glorious lilac head, these parrots are part of a captive breeding program.

Founded in 1823 and remodeled by Dom Charles Verbeke in the 1930s and '40s, St. Mary's Roman Catholic Church combines Romanesque and Moorish elements.

Sports & activities

Day sails: For sight-seeing and snorkeling trips on St. Vincent, contact Petit Byahaut *(Tel 784/ 457-7008)*; Fantasea Tours *(Tel 784/457-4477)*, also offer whale- and dolphin-watching trips; Sea Breeze Nature Tours *(Tel 784/458-4969)*. On Bequia, contact Sail Relax Explore *(Tel 784/495-0886)*.

Diving: Dive St. Vincent *(Tel 784/457-4928, www.divestvincent .com)*; Dive Bequia *(Tel 784/458-3504, www.dive-bequia.com)*; Dive Canouan *(Tel 784/458-8044 or 784/482-0820)*; Grenadines Dive, Union Island *(Tel 784/ 458-8138, www.grenadinesdive.com)*.

Hiking & island tours: See p. 286.

Sailing charters: Barefoot Yacht Charters *(Tel 784/456-9526, www.barefootyachts.com)*; The Moorings *(Tel 784/482-0653, www.moorings.com)*. ■

A short boat ride from Villa, Young Island was one of the region's first private island resorts.

Villa & the east coast

Most visitors will embark on their explorations from hotels in the small town of Villa, southeast along the coast from Kingstown. It makes an ideal starting point for touring the east coast of St. Vincent, along with its adjacent—and highly productive—agricultural hinterland.

Facing Villa's narrow sand beaches is the **Young Island resort,** which you can reach by water taxi from the waterfront. According to legend, the island was a gift from a Carib chief to Sir William Young, a British governor of St. Vincent who had presented the local leader with a horse. Behind Young Island are the ruins of **Fort Duvernette,** hugging another rocky islet. A staircase carved into the cliff leads to the 200-foot (60-m) summit, from which there are fine views.

North of Villa via the Vigie Highway, a panoramic vista extends over Kingstown to the Grenadines and inland to the misty mountains from a lookout point on the knife-edge ridge of **Ayri Hill.** The road continues to the fertile Marriaqua (or Mesopotamia) Valley, where much of the island's fresh produce is grown. A side road leads up to the gorgeous **Montreal Estate Gardens,** set in a circlet of cloudy peaks scoured by waterfalls. Giant orchids and tulip trees shade

Villa & Young Island resort
283 B1

Montreal Estate Gardens
283 B2
N of Mesopotamia
Closed Sept.–Nov., Sun.
$$

Hiking & island tours

You can undertake short walks such as the Vermont Nature Trails easily without a guide, but local knowledge adds greatly to the rain forest experience. Guides are recommended for volcano hikes. The Kingstown tourist office *(Tel 784/457-1502)* can assist, or contact Clint and Millie Hazell of HazECO Tours *(Tel 784/457-8634, fax 784/457-8105, www.hazecotours.com)* for excursions to Trinity Falls, Soufrière, and other hikes, island tours, and boat trips; Sailor's Wilderness Tours *(Tel 784/457-1721;* Petit Byahaut nature resort *(Tel/fax 784/457-7008, www.outahere.com/petitbyahaut).* ■

tropical flowers on terraces built of river rocks.

The Yambou River flows down from the village of Mesopotamia, past rocks carved with Arawak petroglyphs, and through the Yambou Gorge toward the Atlantic coast. Here the Windward Highway wriggles along the shore to Georgetown, through banana and coconut plantations, and continues around to the north of the island, dominated by the impressive bulk of the Soufrière volcano (4,048 feet/1,234 m). At **Rabacca Dry River,** just north of Georgetown, a four-wheel-drive track strikes up to the trailhead for the 3.5-mile (5.5-km) hike up the east side of Soufrière. It's a rewarding walk to the mile-wide (1.5-km) crater rim and back. A more challenging route sets out from Chateaubelair on the Caribbean side, and the two can be combined for a really strenuous expedition (see p. 286).

The west coast & Falls of Baleine

The Leeward Highway clambers north out of Kingstown and begins a roller-coaster journey past a series of small fishing villages to the beaches around Barrouallie and Richmond. Beyond these coastal attractions are a series of diverting stops, ranging from archaeological artifacts to exotic wildlife and scenery on a grand scale.

About 5 miles (8 km) from Kingstown, as the highway runs through the Buccament River Valley, a side road leads to the **Vermont Nature Trails.** The connecting trails are well marked and easy to follow, making a 2-mile (3-km) rain forest loop between the 1,000- to 2,000-foot (300- to 600-m) levels of Grand Bonhomme Mountain in the 10,870-acre (4,440-ha) **St. Vincent Parrot Reserve** *(Map 283 B2)*. One path follows the Dalaway River, which supplies 45 percent of St. Vincent's drinking water, and heads on through an area of Caribbean pine trees dripping with epiphytes. It continues into the rain forest proper, where giant buttressed santinay trees are a favorite parrot habitat. Between 500 and 700 parrots live in colonies spread about the preserve. It's usually easiest to spot them in the late afternoon at the **Parrot Lookout,** perched on the edge of a deep green wooded valley. Also keep an eye out for brilliantly colored hooded tanagers found only on St. Vincent and Grenada, several species of hummingbirds, and broad-winged and black hawks.

Back on the highway, at **Layou,** 1,300-year-old Arawak petroglyphs adorn a 20-foot (6-m) rock. *(The site is on private land, so call the Kingstown Tourist Office, tel 784/457-1502, in advance, or ask for permission to visit the site.)*

Peter's Hope Bay and **Keartons Beach,** lying on either side of the fishing village of Barrouallie, are good spots for a dip in the Caribbean Sea, and scenes from the movie *Pirates of the Caribbean* were filmed in lovely **Wallilabou Bay.** There's another beach near **Richmond** at the end of the highway. A popular excursion from here is the 45-minute hike to **Trinity Falls** *(Map 283 B3)*, which you can reach from a trail several miles north of town. The lovely rain forest walk emerges at a swimming hole fed by the waterfall.

At the north end of the island, accessible only by boat, are the Falls of Baleine, tumbling down from Soufrière in a 60-foot (18-m) cascade to a rock pool. Several vessels combine a visit to the falls with lunch and snorkeling (see p. 285). ■

Captain Bligh's bounty: Huge glossy-leaved breadfruit trees and their edible fruits are a familiar feature of many backyards.

Stunning a fish with rum

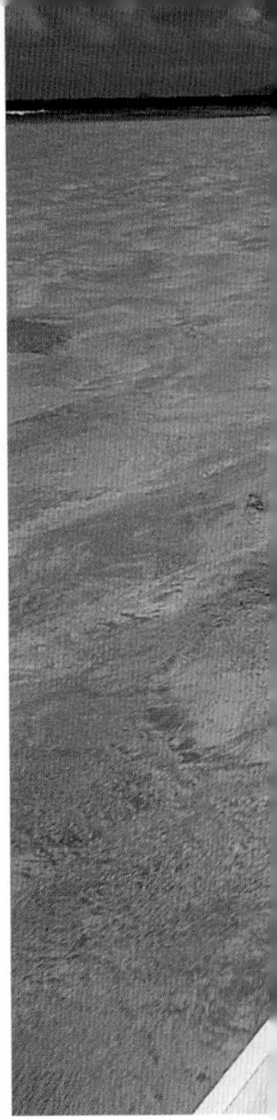

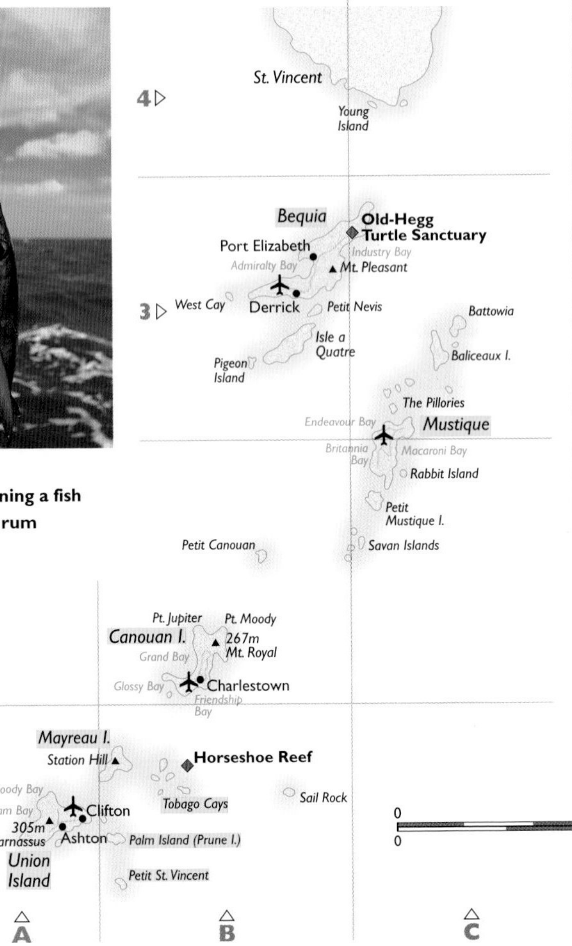

The Grenadines
265 B2
Visitor information
www.svgtourism.com
Cruise Ship Terminal, Kingstown, St. Vincent
e-mail tourism@ca rib surf.com
784/457-1502, fax 784/451-2425

THE GRENADINES

An irregular chain of 30-plus tiny islands and cays interspersed with a host of lesser sandbars and reefs, the Grenadines trail off from St. Vincent for about 35 miles (56 km) toward Grenada and the Grenadian Grenadine islands of Carriacou and Petit Martinique (see p. 300).

Fewer than a quarter of the islands are inhabited (part of their charm for yachtsmen), and while some welcome no-frills sailors and divers, others have been transformed into tiny oases of barefoot luxury.

It's not essential to be a yachtsman to see the Grenadines by boat. The M/V *Barracuda* mail boat *(Tel 784/456-5063)* sails from St. Vincent to Bequia and Canouan, Mayreau, and Union Islands on Mondays and Thursdays, returning Tuesdays and Fridays, and a round-trip minus Bequia on Saturday. The M/V *Gem Star (Tel 784-526-1158)* makes a weekly trip down island. The St. Vincent–Bequia run is served several times a day by the M/V *Admiral I* and *II (Tel 784/458-3348)*, and *Bequia Express (Tel 784/458-3472)*.

Bequia

An hour's ferry ride from St. Vincent is Bequia (BECK-way; *Map 288 C3*), the largest of the St. Vincent Grenadines at 6 square miles (15 sq km). The quaint settlement of Port Elizabeth *(Visitor information, tel 784/458-3286, e-mail info@bequiatourism.com, www.bequiatourism.com)* fringes Admiralty Bay, where the ferry docks within a stone's throw of shops and restaurants overlooked by the 18th-century Hamilton Battery. Water taxis shuttle around the bay to the palm-backed sands of Princess Margaret Beach and Lower Bay.

You can tour the island on foot or by taxi, or rent a scooter for a trip up to **Mount Pleasant,** with its view south to the tip of Grenada. Down on the windward side there's safe swimming and snorkeling at **Industry Bay,** and it's worth visiting the **Old/Hegg Turtle Sanctuary** *(Tel 784/458-3296)* at the end of the track to Park Beach.

Canouan Island

Midway down the Grenadines, dry and hilly Canouan Island (pronounced CAN-oo-ahn; *Map 288 B2)* has beautiful sandy beaches around the port settlement of **Charlestown** in the curve of Grand Bay. A popular yachting center, it also harbors the ultra-luxurious Raffles Resort *(Tel 784/458-8000)*.

Mayreau Island & Tobago Cays

Two fabulous beaches flank the 1.5-square-mile (4-sq-km) scrubby island of Mayreau (pronounced MY-row; *Map 288 B1)*. It's a steep climb from the makeshift dock to the village on **Station Hill** (population

Heading for a day on the beach away from it all in the Grenadines

Above: Carved wooden gingerbread decorations adorn porches and gables in Mustique.

Opposite: Yachtsmen play castaway for the day on Sandy Island at the tail end of the Grenadine chain.

fewer than 200). A couple of bar-restaurants cater to yachtsmen, and there are rooms to rent and a low-key resort on **Salt Whistle Bay.**

The four deserted Tobago Cays *(Map 288 B1)* lie east of Mayreau, surrounding **Horseshoe Reef,** a wildlife reserve and fabulous snorkeling spot accessible by day sails.

Mustique

The ultra-chic Caribbean hideaway of Mustique *(Map 288 C2)* offers money-is-no-object accommodations in 70 or so private villas, a 20-room hotel, and an upscale boutique hotel *(www.mustique-island.com).*

Yachts gather in **Britannia Bay,** and day-trippers are permitted ashore (no ferry service) to sample the gleaming white sands of **Macaroni Bay** or enjoy a drink at Basil's Bar. There are good walks around the 1,350-acre (546-ha) island and more swimming and snorkeling at secluded **Gallicaux Bay** and the hotel beach at **Endeavour Bay.**

Union Island

While not the most alluring Grenadine, Union *(Map 288 A1)* is certainly visually arresting, with a range of peaks culminating in Mount Parnassus (999 feet/305 m), the island chain's highest point. It's a busy transportation hub, with a lively yacht harbor and a couple of hotels at **Clifton,** the main town *(Visitor information, tel 784/458-8350).*

The best beaches are **Chatham Bay** on the west coast and **Bloody Bay** to the north, both only accessible on foot or by boat. ■

Palm Island & Petit St. Vincent

The Grenadine Islands make idyllic miniature resorts. Young Island, off the south coast of St. Vincent, is a prime example, and there are two more pint-size beach hideaways in the southern Grenadines. A mile off Union Island is Palm Island, which had to change its name from Prune Island after owners John and Mary Caldwell planted hundreds of coconut palms in their laid-back resort. Three miles farther south is Petit St. Vincent (better known as PSV; *Map 288 B1*), another barefoot paradise to welcome yachtsmen. ■

Room service local style on Petit St. Vincent

A picturesque huddle of West Indian houses is sandwiched between St. George's Anglican Church and the Carenage waterfront.

Grenada

TYPICALLY GREEN AND MOUNTAINOUS, GRENADA IS THE southernmost Windward Island, only 100 miles (150 km) or so from the coast of South America. Its smaller sister islands, Carriacou and Petit Martinique (see p. 300), are part of the Grenadines chain, which stretches north to St. Vincent. Grenada is wrapped in rain forest and sprinkled with sandy beaches. It's the Spice Island of the Caribbean, one of the world's top nutmeg producers (even the national flag incorporates a nutmeg). Visitors can hike and dive, bathe in rain forest waterfalls, stock up on spices from stalls run by pipe-chewing old biddies, and generally kick back and relax on one of the friendliest small islands (21 by 12 miles/34 by 19 km) in the region.

Grenada
265 A2
Visitor information
www.grenadagrenadines.com
S side of the Carenage (Burns Pont), St. George's
e-mail gbt@spiceisle.com
473/440-2001 or 473/440-2279, fax 473/440-6637

Christened Concepción by Columbus in 1498, Grenada (pronounced gren-AY-dah) was renamed by Spanish sailors homesick for the hills of southern Spain. French settlers from Martinique purchased the island from indigenous Carib for a handful of beads and tools in 1650, but the peace was short-lived and the French soon routed the opposition. The last Carib are said to have jumped to their deaths from the cliffs at La Morne des Sauteurs (Leapers' Hill) in 1651 (see p. 298). The French and English fought for control of the plantation island until it was ceded to Britain in 1783. During the French Revolution, Grenada was the scene of a bloody slave revolt led by Julien Fédon, a French planter, from his isolated coffee and cocoa estate at Belvidere. Arms were smuggled in from Guadeloupe, and the rebels overran most of the island, slaughtering British settlers, including the governor, during the 15-month insurrection. When the British finally regained control in June 1796, Fédon disappeared and the plantations were in ruins.

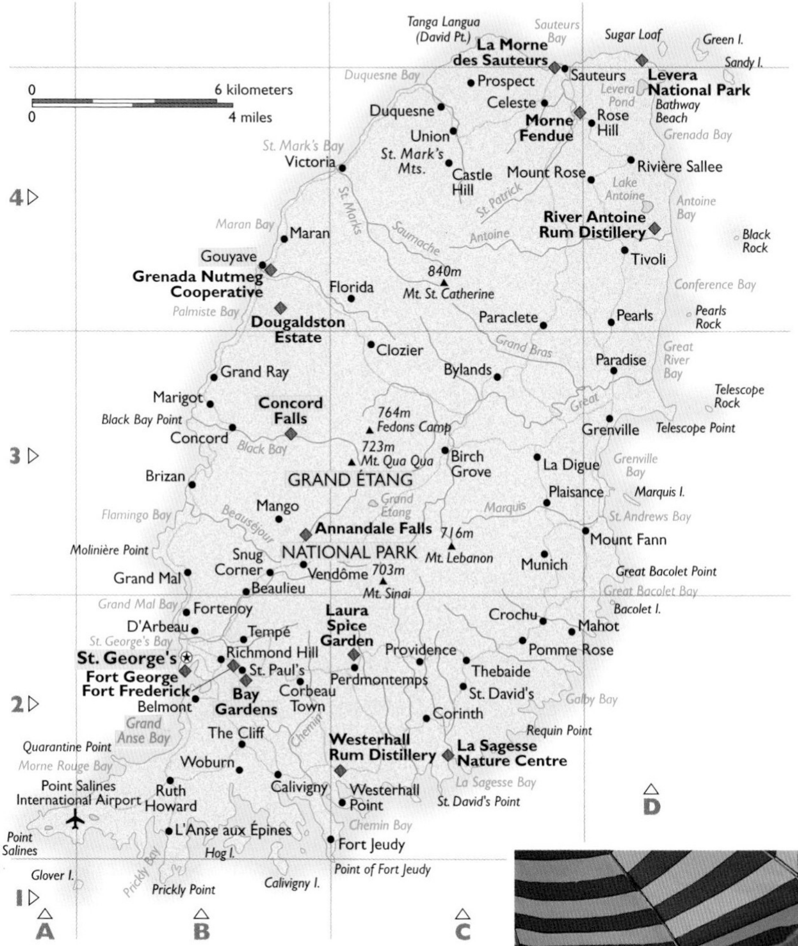

Grenada was rescued from the doldrums by the introduction of nutmeg in the 1830s. Popular legend has it that a doctor from the East Indies arrived with a couple of nutmeg trees in his baggage and jazzed up the local rum punch with a dusting of grated nutmeg. Grenada's nutmeg industry took off in the 1850s, and other spices were introduced. Thus the West Indies finally achieved a spice island by default, 400 years after Columbus had set out to find one.

Grenada took full independence from Britain in 1974, but freed from colonial restraints, the new regime became increasingly despotic. In March 1979 the opposition staged a bloodless coup led by Maurice Bishop, who initiated a program of socialist reforms that revitalized the economy, but soon he began to look equally repressive. Democratic elections were not called, ties with Cuba and the Eastern Bloc caused uneasiness abroad, and in October 1983 Bishop was ousted by a faction of his own party and executed in Fort George. Four days later, a joint U.S.-eastern Caribbean "friendly

Yachts lie at anchor in Mount Hartman Bay on Grenada's south coast.

Above: Costumed Carnival-goers wait to take their place in the main parade through St. George's.

Opposite: Two spices in one: Freshly opened nutmeg fruit show how strings of red mace enclose the nutmeg shell.

invasion" restored order.

Putting the episode behind them, the Grenadians set about building up a low key but very successful tourist infrastructure with a range of hotels concentrated in the south of the island, good roads and communications, and the national pride and joy, a brand new cricket stadium. On September 7, 2004, disaster struck. Historically considered below the Hurricane Belt, Grenada met the full force of Hurricane Ivan. Over night, 90 per cent of Grenada's housing was damaged or destroyed and 60,000 people were made homeless. The Parliament building and the stadium were in ruins. There was almost a billion U.S. dollars of damage.

The islanders began to rebuild immediately. Within a year almost 80 per cent of the island was back up and running. Today, give or take the odd nutmeg plantation and the absence of tall trees, it is hard to see anything but improvements. Hotels have been newly refurbished or completely rebuilt, the island is welcoming back visitors and the new stadium was completed just in time for the 2007 World Cup.

ST. GEORGE'S

There's no better introduction to Grenada than sailing into St. George's Harbour. It is one of the most picturesque ports in the Caribbean, nestled within the steep-sided walls of an extinct volcanic crater and guarded by a battery of old fortresses. St. George's was founded by the French but renamed in honor of England's King George III, and there are numerous examples of Georgian colonial architecture among the church steeples and neat rows of red-roofed homes that cling to the precipitous hillsides like contour lines.

A sharp ridge divides St. George's into two parts, which are linked by a Victorian tunnel bored through the rock in 1895. On the harbor side the horseshoe-shaped **Carenage** hugs the waterfront, edged by shops and restaurants. It is named for the wharves where ships were once careened (tipped on their sides to have their hulls cleaned), now a bustle of cargo boats and ferries, fishing sloops from nearby Carriacou, and tenders delivering cruise-ship passengers.

In the shadow of the ridge is the **Grenada National Museum,** housed in former French barracks dating from 1704. Island history and culture are explored in an assortment of Amerindian finds,

Grenada National Museum

- ✉ Monckton St. (off Long St.)
- ☎ 473/440-3725
- 🕒 Closed Sat. p.m.–Sun.
- $ $

Grenadian spices

Grenada is an olfactory banquet of spices redolent with the pungent tang of nutmeg, cloves, and sweet woody cinnamon. Nutmeg is the island's most important spice and easy to find by the roadside and in the hills. The nutmeg tree *(Myristica fragrans)* produces an apricot-like yellow fruit that splits when ripe to reveal a brown shell covered with a waxy red web of mace. The fruit is used to make preserves, the mace is processed as a separate spice, the inedible shell is recycled as a path-building material, and the inner kernel is the spice used in cooking and pharmaceuticals.

Like the nutmeg tree, cinnamon trees were imported from the East Indies. The bark is used as a food flavoring. Allspice *(Pimenta officinale)* originated in Jamaica. As its name implies, it tastes like nutmeg, cinnamon, and cloves all rolled into the one tiny unripe fruit. ■

Fort George
Church St.

colonial knickknacks, and a detailed, well-balanced account of the 1983 intervention.

Close to the museum is the 350-foot-long (107 m) **Sendall Tunnel,** which burrows beneath the ridge to the seafront **Esplanade** on the bay side of St. George's. Protecting the town from the headland at the harbor mouth is **Fort George,** which now serves as the police headquarters. It is open to the public, and there are great views over town from the 18th-century battlements.

A block back from the minibus depot on the bayfront is the **market square,** a hive of activity best visited on a Saturday morning. Women in headscarves and bright cotton dresses preside over an edible carpet of fresh fruit, vegetables, and spices spread out on the sidewalk as they banter with customers from the shady recesses of large, striped umbrellas.

A strenuous climb up Market Hill leads to **Church Street,** where several of St. George's finest Georgian buildings perched on the hillside. Hurricane Ivan caused considerable damage to historic **York House,** seat of the Grenadian Parliament and Supreme Court, also to **St. George's Anglican Church,** constructed in 1825. Both are undergoing major reconstruction and it is uncertain when they will reopen. Market Hill continues up to a busy junction orchestrated by a white-gloved traffic officer. Lucas Street heads past **Government House,** the governor-general's official residence guarded by pith-helmeted sentries, to tumble-down **Fort Matthew** and the rather better-preserved remains of **Fort Frederick.**

GRAND ANSE & THE SOUTH COAST

Lying just over 2 miles (3 km) south of St. George's is Grand Anse, Grenada's main tourist enclave. A clutch of low-rise hotels lines the 2-mile (3-km) stretch of white sand beach facing the Caribbean Sea. The swimming is safe, and water-

Sports & activities

Bicycling: Tours and rentals from Adventure Jeep Tours *(see Tours, below).*

Day sails & whale-watching: Carib Cats *(Tel/fax 473/444-3222).* Day and half-day sails, and four-hour whale-watching tours from First Impressions *(Tel/fax 473/440-3678, www.catamaranchartering.com).*

Diving & snorkeling: Aquanauts *(Tel 473/444-1126, e-mail aquanauts@spiceisle.com, www.aquanautgrenada.com).* Dive Grenada *(Tel 473/444-1092, e-mail info@divegrenada.com, www.divegrenada.com);* EcoDive *(Tel 473/444-7777, e-mail ecodive@ecodiveandtrek.com, www.ecodiveandtrek.com).*

Hiking: Expeditions from Henry's Safari Tours *(Tel 473/444-5313, fax 473/444-4460, e-mail safari@spiceisle.com, www.spiceisle.com/safari);* Telfor Hiking Tours *(Tel 473/442-6200).*

Tours: Minibus tours and boat trips from Henry's Safari Tours (see above); Adventure Jeep Tours *(Tel 473/444-5337, e-mail adventure@spiceisle.com, www.adventuregrenada.com).*

Sportfishing: True Blue Sportfishing *(Tel/fax 473/444-2048, www.yesaye.com).* ■

sports concessions rent windsurfers, dinghies, and kayaks. Waterskiing and parasailing are also available, and dive operators arrange trips to the reef sites off Molinière Point just north of St. George's, the Kick 'em Jenny submarine volcano, and the scuttled wreck of the *Bianca C*, a cruise ship that caught fire in St. George's Harbour in 1961.

West of Grand Anse, en route to the very tip of the island at Point Salines, is **Morne Rouge Beach,** set in a quiet cove. There are sandy crescents at **Dr. Grooms Beach, Magazine Beach,** and the deliciously named **Pink Gin Beach,** which nestles beneath a fashionable spa hotel. Tucked into the rocks at the end of **Tamarind Beach** is a great bar-restaurant with kayak rentals and snorkeling. On the southern shore of the peninsula is another handful of hotels, apartments, and private homes inhabiting the secluded coves of **Prickly Bay** and the narrow strip of sand beach at **L'Anse aux Épines.**

As the main road heads east from St. George's and the beaches, it swiftly runs into the countryside and cane fields growing at the foot of steep, forested hills. The **Bay Gardens,** set in the hills, make an interesting detour. More than 5,000 species of tropical plants display their finery along nutmeg shell paths winding around the site of an old sugar mill. You could also drop in at **Laura Herb & Spice Garden,** on the road to Windsor Castle, where top-quality herbs and spices are grown and packaged for export. At **Westerhall Rum Distillery,** they will probably provide an impromptu factory tour on weekdays. A few pieces of antique distilling equipment can still be seen.

Midway along the south coast, look for signs to **La Sagesse Nature Centre.** Follow the bumpy track to the beach, past a carefully tended checkerboard of vegetable gardens edged by banana plants and huge mango and soursop trees. The nature center is rather less official than it sounds. In reality it is a charming guesthouse and alfresco restaurant arranged around a little pink plantation house on a lovely beach.

A coconut seller offers fresh coconut milk straight from the shell in St. George's market.

AROUND NORTHERN & CENTRAL GRENADA

A clockwise circuit of northern Grenada, returning to St. George's via the central highlands, reveals a landscape of rich diversity from sea-level mangrove swamps to rain forest mountains, and scenes from island life in spice plantations, a nutmeg factory, and charming Creole villages.

Heading north of St. George's, the main road hugs the twisting coastline, edged by cliffs and the Caribbean Sea. At Concord,

Bay Gardens
- Map: 293 B2
- Address: Morne Delice, St. Paul's
- Tel: 473/435-4544

Laura Herb & Spice Garden
- Map: 293 C2
- Address: Perdmontemps, St. David's
- Tel: 473/443-2604
- Hours: Closed weekends
- Price: $$

follow signs for **Concord Falls** inland up into the hills through spice plantations and cocoa walks (cocoa tree groves) to the lowest of the three falls. It's an energetic 30-minute climb to the second fall and one and a half hours to the upper fall; both have swimming holes. The hike (4.5 hours) may be continued all the way to Grand Étang (see p. 299).

Back on the main road just south of the fishing village of Gouyave, look for the **Dougaldston Estate** on the right. In a sweet-smelling clapboard barn learn how nutmeg, mace, cloves, allspice, cinnamon, and cocoa are still harvested and processed in the old-fashioned (technology-free) way. In Gouyave (French for "guava"), you'll find the **Grenada Nutmeg Co-operative** processing station, which welcomes visitors interested in sniffing around its processing plant, stuffed full with sacks of nutmeg kernels ready for market. On the beach, brightly painted fishing boats are drawn up on the sand.

Beyond Gouyave the round-island road circles the St. Mark's Mountains and **Mount St. Catherine** (2,757 feet/840 m), Grenada's highest peak. The clifftop known as **La Morne des Sauteurs** (Leapers' Hill) on the north coast, is where, in 1651, the island's last Carib threw themselves to their deaths (see p. 292). A handful of Amerindian exhibits mark the spot. South of Sauteurs is the **Morne Fendue plantation house** *(Tel 473/442-9330)*, which makes a great lunch stop.

On the virgin northeast coast is **Levera National Park** *(Map 293 D5)*, with its mangrove swamp and fine stretch of golden sand where leatherback turtles come ashore to lay their eggs in summer (April–June). The swimming is safer, however, at nearby **Bathway Beach.** Bird-watching is good around **Levera Pond,** a wildfowl breeding and feeding ground where scarlet ibis are occasionally spotted. Nearby is the Rivière Sallee Boiling Spring, which provides Grenada's token volcanic activity.

The main road runs inland above the Atlantic coast, through the pretty country villages of Mt. Rose, Tivoli, and Paradise, past Creole cottages and colorful gardens, giant mango trees, wandering goats, and posses of giggling schoolchildren. From **Grenville,** Grenada's second-largest town, the cross-island road climbs into the rain forest and **Grand Étang** (Big Pond) **National Park.** Natural history displays at the park center detail local geology, flora, and

Barn doors flung open to catch the breeze, workers sort and prepare spices by hand.

Grenada Nutmeg Cooperative
- Map: 293 B4
- Address: Gouyave
- Hours: Closed Sun.
- Price: $

RIVER ANTOINE

On the coast road east of Tivoli, the River Antoine Rum Distillery is worth a detour on weekdays. One of the oldest working distilleries in the Caribbean, it uses antique cane-crushing equipment still powered by a water mill fed by Lake Antoine, a mile (1.6 km) away. The brave can sample the local brew. The 18-acre (72-ha) crater lake is another notable birding spot visited by snail kites, limpkins, and whistling ducks, among others. ■

fauna, and a 15-minute nature trail offers sweeping views off to the coast and a chance of spotting Mona monkeys, introduced to Grenada from Africa more than 300 years ago. Across the road a path leads to **Grand Étang,** a crater lake encircled by a 90-minute shoreline hike. The trailhead for longer hikes to Mount Qua Qua and Concord Falls is a short distance west of the park center.

On the road back to St. George's, **Annadale Falls** is a popular beauty spot with a swimming hole fed by the 30-foot (9 m) cascade. ■

Hiking in Grand Étang National Park

Grenada's best hiking opportunities lie within this national park in the central highlands. The **Mount Qua Qua Trail** is a moderately energetic, three-hour round-trip from the park center through elfin woodlands to the rocky summit of Mount Qua Qua. For a more challenging hike, take the Concord Trail, which continues from Mount Qua Qua for another three hours to the Concord Falls.

Other popular hiking destinations include the **Honeymoon Falls** and the **Seven Sisters Waterfalls,** both of which are best tackled with a guide (see p. 296). Birds of the rain forest include tanagers, doves, thrushes, and broad-winged hawks, while armadillos *(tatoo)* and opossums *(manicou)* live at ground level. ■

Grand Étang National Park Center

- 293 C3
- Grand Étang
- 473/440-6160
- $

Carriacou

Carriacou
265 B2
Visitor information
Main St.
Hillsborough
e-mail carrgbt
@spiceisle.com
473/443-7948,
fax 473/443-6127

Some 23 miles (37 km) north of Grenada (a three-hour ferry ride or 90 minutes by power catamaran), Carriacou (pronounced CARRI-ah-cou) is the largest of the Grenadines (8 by 5 miles/13 by 8 km), with a population of about 7,000.

The island is hilly and dry, largely undeveloped, and fringed by white sand strands. It takes its name from the Carib word for "land of reefs," and there's good snorkeling and diving offshore (see below). Carriacou was once planted with cotton and sugar, but when the plantations died out in the 19th century, the islanders turned to fishing, boatbuilding, and smuggling.

Hillsborough, the tiny capital, is built on a curving bay. Close by are several waterfront restaurants and the small **Carriacou Museum** *(Paterson St., closed weekends).* Its collections of Amerindian and colonial relics are laid out in a former cotton ginnery. There is also a collection of charming naïve-style paintings by local artist Canute Calliste (1914-2005).

Just north of town, the village of **Windward** is a good place to watch the local boatbuilders in action, working the white cedar wood grown on the island. Farther up the coast, **Anse la Roche** has a pretty and secluded beach.

South of Hillsborough, **Paradise Beach** boasts a lovely sweep of white sand with a beach bar facing a palm-shaded island.

Farther afield on the southwest shore is **Tyrrel Bay,** a popular yacht anchorage with a modest "restaurant row." ■

Sports & activities

Diving & snorkeling: Carriacou's best dive and snorkel sites are found around the offshore islets in Hillsborough Bay and uninhabited Saline and Frigate Islands to the south. Water taxis will ferry passengers out to Sandy Island from the Hillsborough waterfront. Sharks, rays, and eels are among the marine inhabitants of the Mabouya Island dive sites. Contact local operators Carriacou Silver Diving *(Tel/fax 473/443-7882, www.scubamax.com);* or Lumba Dive *(Tel 473/443-8566, www.lumbadive.com).* ■

Petit Martinique

Petit Martinique
265 B2

The diminutive island of Petit Martinique is a volcanic cone lying 2.5 miles (4 km) off the northeast coast of Carriacou.

Ferries from Hillsborough make the 20-minute crossing a couple of times daily during the week, less frequently at weekends. Petit (pronounced PETT-y) Martinique is pretty much a closed community of 900 or so islanders said to have one of the highest per capita incomes in the eastern Caribbean. As fishing and boatbuilding could hardly account for this, smuggling might hold the key. There are some fine beaches on the leeward side, but little to do unless you visit during the pre-Lenten Carnival. Tourist facilities are limited to one small guesthouse. ■

Once known as the Gateway to the West Indies, Barbados has welcomed travelers for centuries. The island's exquisite beaches, sophisticated lodgings, and a wealth of things to see and do add greatly to its present-day allure.

Barbados

Celebrating the Crop Over Festival

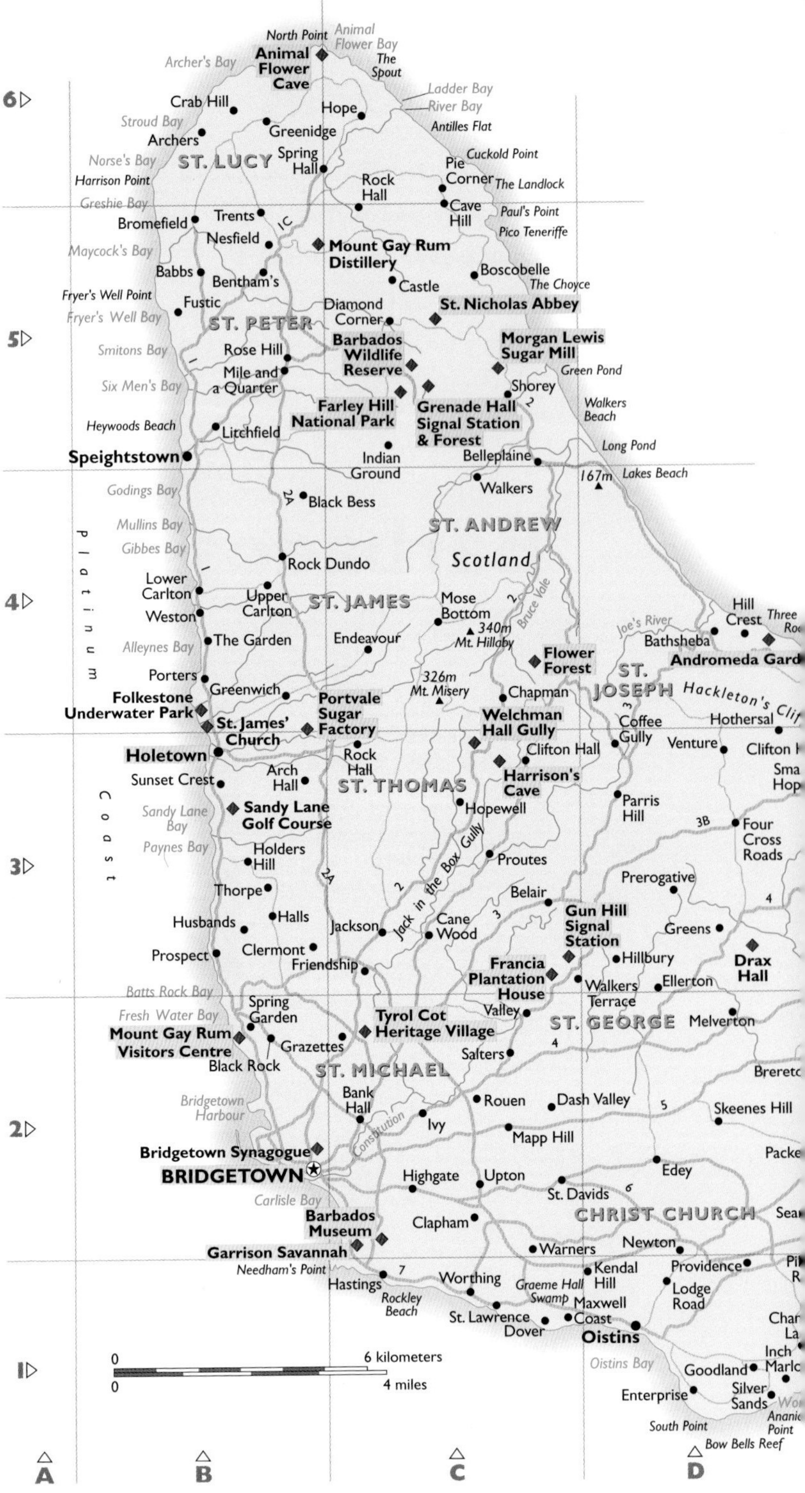
North Point
Animal Flower Bay
Animal Flower Cave
The Spout
Archer's Bay
Ladder Bay
River Bay
Antilles Flat
Crab Hill
Hope
Stroud Bay
Greenidge
Archers
Cuckold Point
Norse's Bay
ST. LUCY
Spring Hall
Pie Corner
The Landlock
Harrison Point
Rock Hall
Greshie Bay
Cave Hill
Paul's Point
Bromefield
Trents
1C
Pico Teneriffe
Nesfield
Mount Gay Rum Distillery
Maycock's Bay
Babbs
Bentham's
Castle
Boscobelle
The Choyce
Fryer's Well Point
Fustic
Diamond Corner
St. Nicholas Abbey
Fryer's Well Bay
ST. PETER
Smitons Bay
Rose Hill
Barbados Wildlife Reserve
Morgan Lewis Sugar Mill
Green Pond
Six Men's Bay
Mile and a Quarter
Shorey
Farley Hill National Park
Grenade Hall Signal Station & Forest
Walkers Beach
Heywoods Beach
Litchfield
Long Pond
Speightstown
Indian Ground
Belleplaine
167m
Lakes Beach
Godings Bay
Walkers
2A
Black Bess
Mullins Bay
ST. ANDREW
Gibbes Bay
Platinum Coast
Rock Dundo
Scotland
Lower Carlton
Upper Carlton
ST. JAMES
Mose Bottom
Bruce Vale
Weston
340m
Mt. Hillaby
Hill Crest
Three Ro
Joe's River
Bathsheba
Alleynes Bay
The Garden
Endeavour
Andromeda Gard
Flower Forest
Porters
326m
Mt. Misery
ST. JOSEPH
Hackleton's Cli
Folkestone Underwater Park
Greenwich
Portvale Sugar Factory
Chapman
St. James' Church
Welchman Hall Gully
Coffee Gully
Hothersal
Holetown
Rock Hall
Clifton Hall
Venture
Clifton H
Arch Hall
Sunset Crest
ST. THOMAS
Harrison's Cave
Sma Hop
Sandy Lane Bay
Sandy Lane Golf Course
Hopewell
Parris Hill
3B
Four Cross Roads
Paynes Bay
Holders Hill
Jack in the Box Gully
Proutes
Thorpe
Prerogative
Belair
Gun Hill Signal Station
Husbands
Halls
Jackson
Cane Wood
Greens
Prospect
Clermont
Hillbury
Drax Hall
Friendship
Francia Plantation House
Walkers Terrace
Ellerton
Batts Rock Bay
Fresh Water Bay
Spring Garden
Tyrol Cot Heritage Village
Valley
ST. GEORGE
Melverton
Mount Gay Rum Visitors Centre
Grazettes
Salters
Black Rock
ST. MICHAEL
Breret
Bridgetown Harbour
Bank Hall
Rouen
Dash Valley
Skeenes Hill
Constitution
Ivy
Mapp Hill
Bridgetown Synagogue
Packe
BRIDGETOWN
Highgate
Upton
Edey
Carlisle Bay
St. Davids
Barbados Museum
Clapham
CHRIST CHURCH
Sea
Garrison Savannah
Warners
Newton
Needham's Point
Hastings
Kendal Hill
Providence
Pi R
Worthing
Graeme Hall Swamp
Lodge Road
Rockley Beach
Maxwell
St. Lawrence
Coast
Dover
Oistins
Char La
Inch Marlo
0
6 kilometers
0
4 miles
Oistins Bay
Goodland
Silver Sands
Enterprise
Anani Point
South Point
Bow Bells Reef
6
5
4
3
2
1
A
B
C
D

Barbados

BARBADOS LIES 100 MILES (160 KM) EAST OF THE WINDWARD ISLANDS, surrounded by the Atlantic Ocean. Unlike its volcanic neighbors, the island is an undulating limestone massif. Its coral rock underpinnings are responsible for the famous Platinum Coast beaches, the island's upscale tourist heartland. The more informal (and affordable) side of Barbados is the south coast resort area, with a string of equally appealing beaches by day, some of the best dining on the island, and a lively nightlife after dark.

The British ruled Barbados for 340 uninterrupted years before independence and left an indelible, slightly formal imprint on this former sugar colony. There's considerable pride in the Barbados Parliament and more than a touch of Little England in the local passion for cricket, the ritual of afternoon tea, and dressing for dinner in some quarters.

Barbados takes its name from the huge, native bearded fig tree, also known as a banyan, which drops a curtain of aerial roots to the ground. Portuguese explorers called them *barbados* (bearded ones). Although Amerindian settlers discovered the island almost 4,000 years ago, it was uninhabited when English colonists landed near the site of Holetown on the west coast in 1627. Dutch settlers played a significant part in developing the early plantations, and they introduced sugarcane from Brazil in 1637. As the colony prospered, indentured laborers were shipped out from Britain, and soon African slaves were brought in to swell the plantation workforce.

With the abolition of slavery in 1834, the sugar industry lurched from virtual failure to moderate success in the early 20th century, but another downswing in the economy in 1937 led to rioting and the establishment of a strong labor union movement, which worked toward independence from Britain in 1966.

Beyond the sprawling capital city of Bridgetown, and the resort areas to either side, the landscape is remarkably rural. Cane fields and pockets of woodland roll back from the leeward coast, while Mount Hillaby (1,089 feet/340 m), and the 1,000-foot (300-m) crest of Hackleton's Cliff are poised dramatically above the Atlantic on the windward coast. The island is divided into 11 parishes (Christ Church and 10 named after saints), which are frequently given as an address rather than the name of a village. ■

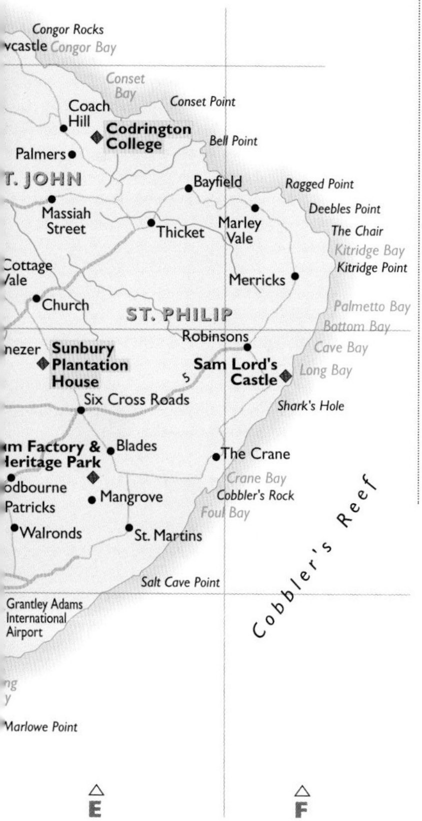

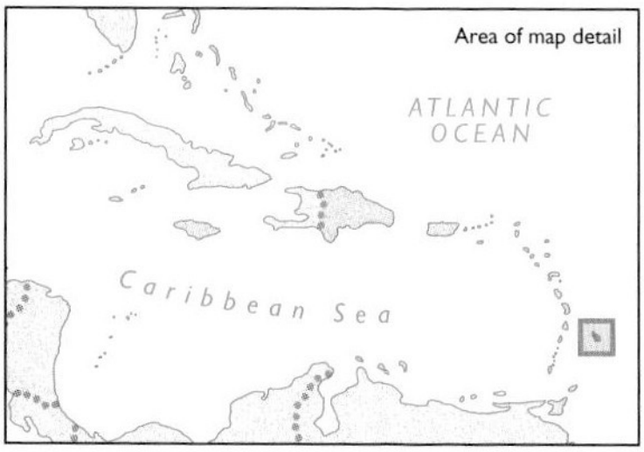

Bridgetown

Bridgetown
302 B2
Visitor information
Bridgetown Harbour
246/427-2623
Closed weekends

Bridgetown Synagogue
Magazine Lane
Closed Sat.–Sun.
$

BRIDGETOWN, THE ISLAND'S ENERGETIC CAPITAL CITY, IS an important Caribbean business center and home to about 100,000 residents. The heart of the city lies on the Careenage, a narrow inner harbor at the mouth of the Constitution River, where an English expedition discovered an Amerindian bridge in 1625. A few fishing boats and pleasure craft now tie up to the wharves, where ships were once tipped onto their sides to have their hulls cleaned and repaired (careened). A handful of waterfront cafés makes the Careenage a pleasant place to take a break and watch the world go by.

On the north bank of the inlet is **National Heroes Square,** known until recently as Trafalgar Square. Here the mellow complex of coral rock public buildings contains the House of Assembly, the seat of the Barbados Parliament where the island's legislators meet. Although the buildings only date from the 19th century, the historic assembly was first established in 1639.

A short walk east on St. Michael's Row leads you to **St. Michael's Cathedral,** which has been rebuilt several times (most recently in 1831) on the site of the original church, founded in 1625. George Washington (1732–1799) is said to have worshiped in one of its former incarnations in 1751, during his only trip outside what is now the United States. Washington was just age 19 when he sailed into Carlisle Bay on November 3. At that time Bridgetown was the biggest city in the English-speaking world outside Britain. George and his brother, Lawrence, stayed at Bush Hill House in Garrison Savannah (see pp. 305–306), which is currently being restored by the Barbados National Trust.

West of National Heroes is **Broad Street,** the city's main shopping and business district. Among modern offices and department stores are a number of fine old colonial buildings dressed up with fancy ironwork balconies. A few blocks away, off Magazine Lane, is the ice-cream pink-and-white **Bridgetown Synagogue.**

The first synagogue on the island was established by Jewish immigrants from Brazil and consecrated in 1654. Bridgetown's prosperous Jewish community acted as financial agents and export brokers for the fledgling colony, and it grew considerably in the mid-17th century, when the British islands offered freedom of religious practices under the direction of Oliver Cromwell (1599–1658). Largely destroyed by a hurricane in 1831, the present synagogue was reconsecrated in 1833, but many tombs in the cemetery date back much further.

From the city center the Princess Alice Highway heads west to **Bridgetown Harbour** and the cruiseship complex.

To the south, across the Careenage on the Chamberlain Bridge, Bay Street follows the curve of Carlisle Bay into the **Bayville** district, where a few pretty 19th-century town houses with gingerbread trimmings have survived on quiet back streets shaded by palm and mango trees.

A mile (1.5 km) south of Bridgetown is **Garrison Savannah,** once a British parade ground. The enclosure now doubles as a jogging track and a small racecourse where the Barbados Turf

Drinking in the view of downtown Bridgetown from a waterfront café on the Careenage

Barbados Museum
www.barbmuse.org.bb
✉ St. Anne's Garrison
St. Michael
☎ 246/427-0201
🕒 Closed Sun. a.m.
$ $$

The national flag flies over Bridgetown's Victorian coral rock parliament buildings.

Sports & activities

Day sails: Day sails or sunset cruises from Cool Runnings *(Tel 246/436-0911)*; Heatwave *(Tel 246/228-8142)*; Tiami Catamaran Cruises *(Tel 246/430-0900)*.

Diving & snorkeling: Reef diving and wrecks on the west coast, with good snorkeling at Paynes Bay and Folkstone. Contact PADI-registered operators Dive Pro Barbados *(Christ Church, tel 264/420-3337, e-mail info@diveprobarbados.com, www.diveprobarbados.com)*, or Lorenzo's Scuba Dreams *(St. James, tel 246/422-4414, e-mail bowlman@yahoo.com)*.

Golf: Eighteen championship holes at Sandy Lane Golf Club, Holetown *(Tel 246/444-2500)*; also at the public Barbados Golf Club, Christ Church *(Tel 246/428-8463)*.

Hiking: Barbados National Trust guided hikes on Sundays (6 a.m. or 3:30 p.m., *tel 246/426-2421; call the day before)*.

Horseback riding: Highland Adventure Centre, St. Thomas *(Tel 246/431-8928)*.

Kayaking: Coastal kayaking tours and swimming with turtles with Ocean Adventures *(Tel 246/438-2088)*.

Sportfishing: Billfisher II *(Tel 246/431-0741)*; Fishing Charters Barbados, Inc. *(Tel 246/429-2326)*.

Surfing: Dangerous swimming but excellent surfing on the east coast around Bathsheba. ■

Club hosts weekend races *(Tel 246/426-3980, www.barbadosturfclub.com)*. Nearby are several 19th-century buildings, including the distinctive **Main Guard** (also known as the Savannah Club), the former barracks and crumbling ramparts of 17th-century **Fort Charles,** and **St. Anne's Fort,** founded in 1704 but never completed.

The old military prison houses the excellent **Barbados Museum.** A circuit of the exhibits begins with an overview of the island's natural history and early Amerindian inhabitants accompanied by copious background notes.

In the plantation-era section, the Aall Gallery displays rare antique maps, including a second edition of Richard Ligon's original map of Barbados, published in 1657. It shows the island still partially

covered in native forest, with plantations blocked neatly along the leeward coast and wild boars rampaging about the interior. Prisoners once broke stones in the museum's lower courtyard and lived in cells around the leafy upper courtyard, now occupied by a series of rooms furnished in 19th-century style.

The Chancellor Gallery has a small selection of military memorabilia, and a fascinating collection of 17th- and 18th-century engravings is a highlight in the Cunard Gallery. Island views and studies of plantation great houses compete for attention with portraits of fashionable planters, dandies, dancers, and Rachel Pringle, Barbados's most famous 18th-century madame. ■

Bridge Gate spans the route south from the Careenage to Garrison Savannah.

Crop Over—Carnival Bajan-Style

The Bajan summer carnival dates back to the late 1700s, when Barbados was the world's largest sugar producer, and the island celebrated a successful harvest. Today, preparations begin far in advance with magnificent costumes sewn (constructed in some cases), dance routines practiced, and calypso acts honed. The five-week festival climaxes with the spectacular **Grand Kadooment** on the first Monday of August *(www.barbados.org/cropover.htm).* For a taste of the joie de vivre year-round, try the dinner show **Bajan Roots & Rhythms** at The Plantation, St. Lawrence *(Tel 246/428-5048).* ■

Sugar

At the height of the 17th- to 18th-century sugar era, Barbados was one of the most powerful islands in the Caribbean. For two centuries sugar was the backbone of the West Indies, the "white gold" that lined the planters' coffers, shaped the foreign policy of distant European countries, and instigated the largest forced transportation of human beings in history.

Sugar arrives in the New World

The Spanish conquest of the New World in the 16th century was fueled by South and Central American gold and precious gems. Lacking the mineral wealth of the mainland, the success of the West Indian colonies founded in the early 17th century depended on finding a profitable crop that could not be grown in Europe yet one that would survive the vagaries of transatlantic transportation. Cotton, indigo, and coffee were early contenders, but tobacco proved the most profitable option until new plantations in Virginia flooded the market with better quality tobacco, leaving the Caribbean settlers searching for an alternative.

Sugarcane was among a selection of experimental crops brought to the Spanish colony of Hispaniola by Christopher Columbus in 1493. Although the cane flourished, it was more than a century before Dutch planters from Brazil introduced sugarcane and their vital expertise to Barbados in the 1630s. By this time the new fashion for coffee and chocolate drinking in Europe provided a burgeoning home market, and the success of the first sugar crops ignited a planting frenzy that carpeted Barbados with cane by the 1650s and spread rapidly throughout the region.

Cultivation & processing

Compared with tobacco, which could be grown profitably on small holdings, sugar required larger plantations and extensive capital outlay for buildings and processing equipment. The labor force on the islands was also insufficient, so slaves were imported from West Africa to work the cane fields.

To prepare the land for sugar cultivation, the planter's first task was to clear native vegetation and divide his estate into large fields arranged around the central mill and processing facility. A crop grown from cane tops planted in well-prepared earth could be harvested after 18 months; but the Dutch introduced *ratooning*, a less expensive and faster method of propagation using shoots grown on cane roots left in the ground after the previous harvest and ripe for harvesting within a year.

The crop was cut by hand during the dry season (Jan.–May) and carried to the mill, which could be powered by wind, water, animal, or slave labor. Here the cane was crushed by rollers, the bagasse (trash) removed for fuel, and the cane juice diverted into a series of copper boiling pans. Lime water was added to assist clarification, and as the boiling syrup progressed through pans of ever decreasing size and increased temperature, it was skimmed to remove impurities. From the final pan, liquid sugar was poured into wooden cooling troughs where it separated into *muscovado* sugar crystals and molasses. The molasses was then drained off and distilled to make rum, and the semi-refined sugar was packed into hogsheads to await shipment overseas.

The origins of sugar

The recorded history of sugar begins in India, though how sugarcane reached the subcontinent from its probable origins in Polynesia is unknown. Discovered by Persian invaders circa 510 B.C., sugarcane and the secret of "honey without bees" traveled to the Middle East. A few centuries later, the ancient Greeks and Romans prized it as a luxury and a medicine, and during the Middle Ages small quantities of sugarcane were cultivated around the Mediterranean region. It was still regarded as a rare and expensive alternative to honey when crusaders returning from Syria introduced the "new spice" to England in 1099. ■

Boom & bust

Top: Farmers burn stubble on a Guadeloupe cane field. Above: Early 19th-century view of an Antiguan boiling house

At the beginning of the 18th century, the lucrative spoils of the booming Caribbean sugar trade were shared equally between Britain and France, and trade was at the core of a century of bitter rivalry between the two countries. European wars were an excuse to impose sanctions and mount invasion expeditions; peace treaties inevitably involved the transfer of colonial powers to the victors.

Peace with France in 1814 brought Britain a handful of former French West Indian colonies and a glut of sugar accompanied by a dramatic reduction in profits.

Across the Channel, the French turned to sugar beets, grown in Europe as a vegetable since Roman time, and a far cheaper and easier way of producing sugar since the discovery of a viable method of sugar extraction in 1812. The widespread cultivation of sugar beets in Europe, coupled with the emancipation of the slave workforce, spelled the end of the sugar industry in the smaller West Indian colonies in the 1840s. Only the big producers such as Barbados, Jamaica, and Trinidad survived by importing indentured labor from overseas. ■

Sunbury Plantation House recalls the elegant lifestyle enjoyed by plantation owners during the sugar boom.

Plantation houses & gardens

THE COLONIAL HERITAGE OF BARBADOS COMES ALIVE IN its wonderful plantation houses and lush tropical gardens. Plantation owners built gracious residences to reflect their exalted social standing. In doing so, they achieved a refinement that matches that of the sugar that underpinned their wealth. Lush gardens reinforce the notion of living in an island paradise.

Sunbury Plantation House
303 D2
www.barbadosgreathouse.com
St. Philip
246/423-6270
$$$

THE SOUTHERN HEARTLAND

The rolling countryside of southern Barbados cuts a swath eastward from Bridgetown and north of Grantley Adams Airport. The atmosphere here is redolent of two Barbadian mainstays: sugar-processing and rum. Set back from the coast amidst the undulating green carpet of cane fields that provided its wealth for centuries, the 300-year-old **Sunbury Plantation House** was a private home until the 1980s. This historic great house still retains charmingly homey touches such as fresh-cut flowers and potted plants dotted among the traditional Barbadian mahogany furniture and collections of antique china, glass, and silver. The bedrooms upstairs are open for inspection, with Victorian clothes laid out on capacious four-poster beds. The old yam cellar has been turned into a carriage museum and repository of old-fashioned agricultural and domestic implements. The Courtyard Restaurant in the garden serves lunch and afternoon tea. If the idea of a hurricane-lamp-lit dinner in the main house appeals, call and make a reservation for the five-course Plantation Dinner.

A short distance to the west, Drax Hall is one of the oldest houses in the region, dating from the mid-17th century. It is occasionally opened to the public under the Barbados National Trust's Open House Programme (see below).

HIGHLAND SITES

The central highlands of Barbados lie just to the east of the Platinum Coast. The terrain here was too hilly for large-scale plantations, so the landscape feels more unspoiled.

The first garden you come to is **Welchman Hall Gully,** located about 5 miles (8 km) due east from Holetown along the west coast. Originally laid out as a botanical walk in the 1860s, this fabulously lush mile-long (1.5-km) wooded gorge was created by the collapse of a limestone chamber in part of the Harrison's Cave underground cavern network (see pp. 315–16). Around the fantastical pinnacles and limestone rock formations, more than 200 species of exotic plants and flowers flourish in the cool shade of giant forest trees and towering stands of bamboo. A carpet of ferns and trailing lianas add to the jungle-like atmosphere, and you might hear vervet monkeys crashing about in the treetops in the early morning or late afternoon.

Another haven of exuberant tropical plant life, the 50-acre (20-ha) **Flower Forest** lies just 2 miles (3 km) northeast of Welchman Hall Gully. Flower Forest occupies a commanding position in the Scotland district with views across a ruffle of hills to the wide blue Atlantic. In the woodlands steep paths zigzag down through a forest of gingers, lobster claw heliconias, Chinese hat plants, and red hot cattails to a grassy lookout. A leisurely inspection of the orchid collection provides a welcome break on the trek back.

If orchids are your thing, then don't miss **Orchid World,** near Gun Hill. There are more than 20,000 orchids gathered here in a dazzling display of colors and varieties. Paths traverse the 6.5-acre landscaped gardens and there are five orchid houses to explore.

The views from Gun Hill Signal Station (see p. 315) nearby reach all the way to the coast. Just down the hill, the handsome early 20th-

Welchman Hall Gully
- 302 C3
- Welchman Hall, St. Thomas
- 246/438-6671
- $$$

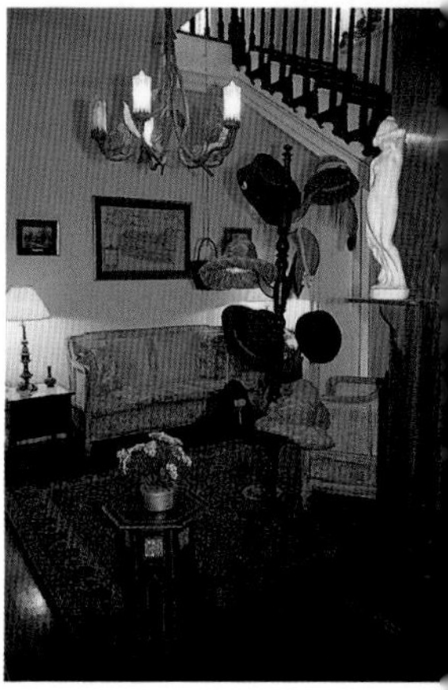

An elegant hat stand flanks a staircase at Sunbury Plantation House.

Flower Forest
- 302 C4
- St. Joseph
- 246/433-8152
- $$$

Orchid World
- 302 D3
- Groves, St. George
- 246/433-0306
- $$$ (discounted joint ticket with Flower Forest)

Barbados National Trust Open House Programme

Barbados' rich architectural history runs the gamut of styles from Jacobean gems and imposing contemporary mansions to wooden chattel houses. Most of these architectural treasures remain in private hands, unseen by locals and visitors alike. The popular annual Open House Programme (Jan.–Apr.) encourages owners to open their homes for a few hours once a year. In recent times, access has been given to the Prime Minister's official residence, as well as to a couple of stunning modern residences in exclusive Sandy Lane. Contact the National Trust (*Tel 246/426-2421, or www.barbados.org/openhse.htm*). ■

Above: Tropical palms add an unusual backdrop to the Jacobean-era St. Nicholas Abbey.

Right: The aptly named lobster-claw heliconia

Andromeda Gardens
- 302 D4
- Bathsheba St. Joseph
- 246/433-9261
- $$$

St. Nicholas Abbey
- 302 C5
- Cherry Tree Hill St. Peter
- 246/422-8725
- Closed weekends
- $$

century great house, Francia Plantation, is now a private school.

THE NORTHEAST COAST

The rolling uplands of the interior end abruptly in a series of dramatic coastal cliffs in the east. Although relatively unpopulated, the northeast coast of Barbados has a pair of memorable sites to visit.

The first is **Andromeda Gardens,** lying some 4 miles (6.5 km) east of Flower Forest. World-renowned for a fabulous collection of indigenous and exotic tropical flowers, these lovely gardens cling to the cliffs above the Atlantic coast like their namesake heroine in Greek mythology, who was chained to the rocks. The 6-acre (2.5-ha) gardens were established privately by Mrs. Iris Bannochie in 1954 and arranged in outdoor "rooms," where orchids, heliconias, hibiscus, and clouds of bougainvillea abound alongside fragrant bowers, water- lily ponds, and shady corners planted with ferns and striking ornamental foliage.

A shore road runs northward along the rocky eastern coast of Barbados, where there are few settlements but extensive beaches.

About 9 miles (14.5 km) north from Andromeda Botanic Gardens is **St. Nicholas Abbey.** A rare example of Jacobean architecture in the Caribbean, the "abbey" rejoices in a splendid gabled facade dating from around 1650-1660, but the building never had any religious connections. Tours with a local guide explore a handful of dark wood-paneled rooms containing colonial antiques, and there is a wonderful old home movie show depicting Bridgetown and plantation life in the 1930s. The abbey's new owner is currently restoring the property and has ambitious plans to bottle rum and sugar cane products in the old factory buildings in the grounds. ■

The south coast

AROUND THE SOUTHWEST TIP OF BARBADOS AT GARRISON Savannah (see p. 305), the main coastal highway runs into the Christ Church parish and a string of beachfront villages.

Heritage Park & Foursquare Rum Distillery

303 E2

Foursquare Plantation, St. Philip

246/420-1977

$$$

Sam Lord's Castle, built by one of Barbados's more colorful characters

Hastings, Worthing, and **Dover** back the best of the lovely south coast beaches, while **St. Lawrence** is a veritable restaurant row with the best nightlife on the island. At Worthing, the **Graeme Hall Bird Sanctuary** has a swamp boardwalk lookout on the island's largest expanse of inland water.

Beyond **Oistins,** a fishing center with a Friday night fish fry, is lively **Silver Sands Beach,** a favorite with windsurfers. Farther east you'll find secluded beach coves at Foul Bay, Crane Bay, and Long Bay, overlooked by **Sam Lord's Castle,** an 1820s mansion-turned hotel.

The interior of the south coast also has its share of attractions. Far and away the most popular is the unashamedly touristy **Heritage Park and Foursquare Rum Distillery** at Six Cross Roads. The south coast runs out at Ragged Point, where the rocks beneath the East Point Lighthouse are lashed by the Atlantic. ■

Rum punch

Rum is bottled as either clear white rum, or the slightly mellower gold rums colored with caramel and aged in wooden barrels. On the French islands the blending and aging of rums is a serious business, and the top producers even date their top of the range products to create vintages like wines. Rum punch was the planters' favorite tipple and a good way of transforming some of the rougher local brews into a palatable drink. The traditional recipe for rum punch calls for one measure of sour (lemon or lime), two of sweet (cane juice), three of strong (rum), and four of weak (water). ■

Rum punch can deliver a deceptive blow to the unwary.

Above left: This enlarged and creatively decorated chattel house has an air of permanence.
Above: A boatyard near Speightstown

More places to visit around Barbados

ANIMAL FLOWER CAVE

At the northern tip of the island, dozens of multicolored sea anemones flower in the rock pools of this subterranean cave hollowed out of the cliffs by wave action. Visitors can swim around with a guide, watch the "animal flowers" waving their tiny tentacles, and take a dip in one of the larger pools.
Map 302 B6 ✉ St. Lucy ☎ 246/439-8797
$ $$

BARBADOS WILDLIFE RESERVE & GRENADE HALL SIGNAL STATION & FOREST

The first of three attractions conveniently grouped in the same location, the Barbados Wildlife Reserve is a miniature animal kingdom set in a 4-acre (1.5-ha) pocket of mahogany forest. Vervet monkeys, shy Brocket deer, porcupines, and agoutis (tropical rodents) wander freely in the woodlands and provide real wildlife spotting opportunities that delight children. The reserve has an iguana sanctuary decorated with orchids, a walk-through aviary, and a secure caiman pool, as well as a caged python.

Across the parking lot is the Grenade Hall Signal Station, one of half a dozen lookout towers constructed in the early 1800s to keep a watch on slaves working on the plantations. Sentries used semaphore to relay news of disturbances or approaching ships at sea.

Nature trails in the adjacent Grenade Hall Forest offer a glimpse of how Barbados would have appeared to the first settlers. Native trees such as the whitewood, poison tree, and silk cotton tree are marked along the route.

Nearby, **Farley Hill Park** is a favorite picnic spot on the grounds of a ruined plantation house with an arboretum.
Map 302 C5 ✉ Farley Hill, St. Peter
☎ 246/422-8826 $ $$$$

CODRINGTON COLLEGE

A magnificent avenue of slender cabbage palms flanks the driveway leading to the imposing facade of this Anglican theological college. The college was founded in 1743 and financed by a bequest from Christopher Codrington (1668–1710), a one-time governor general of the Leeward Islands whose family was among the earliest settlers on Barbados. Access to the college buildings is limited, but visitors can view the outside of the Principal's Lodge (the original 17th-century estate house

where Codrington was brought up), stroll around the gardens that lead down to Consett Bay, and take a turn around the pretty water-lily pond. Codrington Woods offer a short nature trail through mature woodland, where native silk cotton trees, ironwood and white wood, and mahogany flourish.

303 E3 St. John 246/423-1166
$$

GUN HILL SIGNAL STATION

A strategic position 700 feet (213 m) above sea level gives this 1818 signal station unparalleled views across the island and off to the Atlantic. The site was first used as a lookout in 1697 and later became a convalescent station on account of the comfortably cool breezes. At the foot of the hill is the whitewashed Military Lion, carved from a single piece of rock by a convalescent British officer.

302 C3 Gun Hill, St. George
246/429-1358 Closed Sun. $$$

HARRISON'S CAVE

The island's top sight-seeing attraction is a miniature trolley ride around a subterranean cave carved out of the coral limestone by underground rivers. Passengers don hard hats and set off on a nearly mile-long (1.5 km) ride through a series of spooky, theatrically lit caverns festooned with dripping stalactites, rimstones, flowstones, and a spiky forest of stalagmites. The speleothems (cave formations) take approximately a hundred years to grow a single cubic inch of solid calcite, but eventually the stalactites and stalagmites can join up to create impressive pillars. There is an under-

Reef & wreck tours

Scuba diving is one way of seeing local marine life up close (see p. 306), or sign up for a guided snorkeling tour with Atlantis Submarines. For spectacular underwater views without getting wet, take the *Atlantis* minisub to reef and wreck sites at depths to 150 feet (46 m). The dive lasts about 45 minutes and there are day and nighttime excursions. *(Information and reservations, tel 246/436-8929, www.atlantis adventures.com).* ■

ground lake fed by a 40-foot (12-m) cascade. The cave lies at one end of the Welchman Hall Gully botanic walk (see p. 311).
302 C3 Welchman Hall, St. Thomas
246/438-6640 $$$$

MORGAN LEWIS SUGAR MILL

Hundreds of sugar-grinding mills once dotted the Barbadian landscape, and their crumbling ruins are a common sight along the tiny roads of the sugarcane belt today.

The 250-year-old Morgan Lewis Mill was the last old-style mill to close when it ceased operations in 1944. Placed on the List of 100 Most Endangered Sites in the World by the World Monuments Fund (1996), its weathered stone cone is the largest surviving windmill in the Caribbean. All its working parts are intact, and the old sails and wooden parts have been repaired with South American hardwoods. Climb up to the sail compartment for panoramic views of the surrounding Scotland district.
302 C5 Cherry Tree Hill, St. Andrew
246/422-7429 $$

MOUNT GAY RUM VISITORS CENTRE

Rum is synonymous with Barbados and has been produced on the island since the 1640s. The Mount Gay distillery is in the north of the island at St. Lucy, but here at the visitor center near Bridgetown Harbour *(Brandons, St. Michael)* the aging, blending, and bottling processes are on display, followed by tastings at the end of the tour.
302 B2 Spring Garden Hwy., Bridgetown 246/425-8757, www.mountgay.com Tours every 30 minutes (closed weekends) $$$

PLATINUM COAST

The focus of the famed Platinum Coast is **Holetown** *(Map 302 B3; 7 miles, 11 km N of Bridgetown on Rte. 1)*, where English settlers first disembarked in 1627 and established a small village they called Jamestown after King James I. The original name (it was changed to Holetown after a tidal hole close to the beach) is still preserved in the little coral rock church of St. James, founded in 1629 and originally built of wood, and in the surrounding district known as the Parish of St. James. Many of the island's most elegant hotels and private houses are located here. **Paynes Bay** is a particularly lively section of the beach, with beach bars and water-sports concessions.

Just north of Holetown there's snorkeling in the **Folkestone Underwater Park.**

Farther north along the coast is another busy beach strip at **Heyward's Bay,** north of Speightstown.

PORTVALE SUGAR FACTORY

The sugar factory produces about 14,500 tons of sugar a year. The spring harvest season (Feb. to May) is the best time to visit, when tours plunge into the ear-shattering, sweet and steamy atmosphere of the factory floor among the cane cutters, crushers, and boilers.

The informative **Sir Frank Hutson Sugar Machinery Museum,** adjacent to the factory, traces the history of the industry.
302 B4 St. James 246/425-1941
Closed Sun. Museum $$, including factory tour $$$

TYROL COT HERITAGE VILLAGE

A single-story stone house painted a jaunty white and orange with green louvered jalousies (shutters), Tyrol Cot was built by leading Barbadian architect William Farnum in 1854. The home of former prime minister Sir Grantley Adams (1898–1971) it is furnished with many family pieces, handcrafted mahogany furniture, paintings and photographs.

In the gardens the Heritage Village illustrates how the local architectural style developed from a basic slave hut thatched with bagasse to the first simple post-slavery wooden chattel house and its more elaborate gingerbread-trimmed descendants. After emancipation, workers were permitted to own houses but not land, so the original chattel house (from "goods and chattels") was a single unit easily dismantled and moved if the owner was evicted from a plantation site. As the homeowner prospered or the family grew, further units could be added, along with such refinements as jalousies and glass windows. The cottages now house artisans' workshops, and craft work is on sale. Drinks and snacks are available in the rum shop.
302 C2 Codrington Hill, St. Michael
246/424-2074 Closed weekends
$$$ ■

Though Trinidad and Tobago share a rich tapestry of natural delights, Trinidad's pulse races to the rhythms of steel pan, calypso and the urgent razzle-dazzle of Carnival, while life on Tobago beats to a more relaxed tempo.

Trinidad & Tobago

Topflight cricket

Trinidad

A TWIN-ISLAND NATION AT THE SOUTHERN EXTENT OF THE LESSER Antilles, Trinidad and Tobago make an odd couple. Boisterous, multicultural Trinidad is the larger of the two and home to the capital, Port of Spain. At 50-by-38 miles (80-by 61-km) it's also the largest of the eastern Caribbean islands, a chunk of South America severed from the Venezuelan coast just 7 miles (11 km) away as recently as 10,000 years ago. Trinidad breaks the traditional Caribbean mold with an industrialized, oil-based economy that has shunned tourism until recently. But for a lesson in how to develop, the Trinidadians need look no further than Tobago, a more typical West Indian escapist haven offering one of the warmest welcomes in the region (see p. 330).

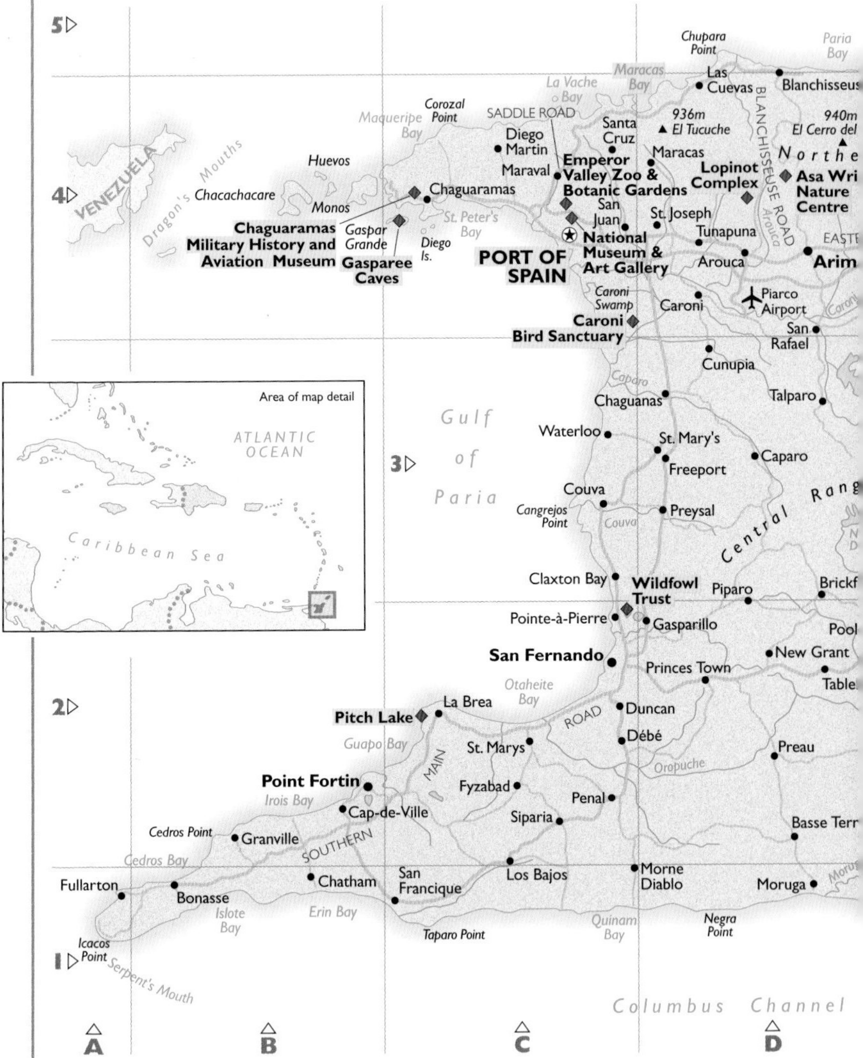

The Iere (Land of Hummingbirds) of the Arawak was rechristened Trinidad (Trinity) by Christopher Columbus, who sighted three peaks in the southeast of the island on his third voyage to the New World in 1498. Although the island was claimed for Spain, its Amerindian inhabitants kept settlers at bay until 1592, when the Spanish established a toehold, grew a little tobacco, and kept watch over their treasure fleets sailing home to Europe from South America. Trinidad was still a backwater by the late 18th century, when the Spanish king offered land grants to Roman Catholic settlers. An influx of French planters keen to escape the revolutionary guillotine on their own islands introduced sugar and cocoa plantations. But Spain never reaped the rewards because Britain snatched the island in 1797, later taking possession of neighboring Tobago in 1814.

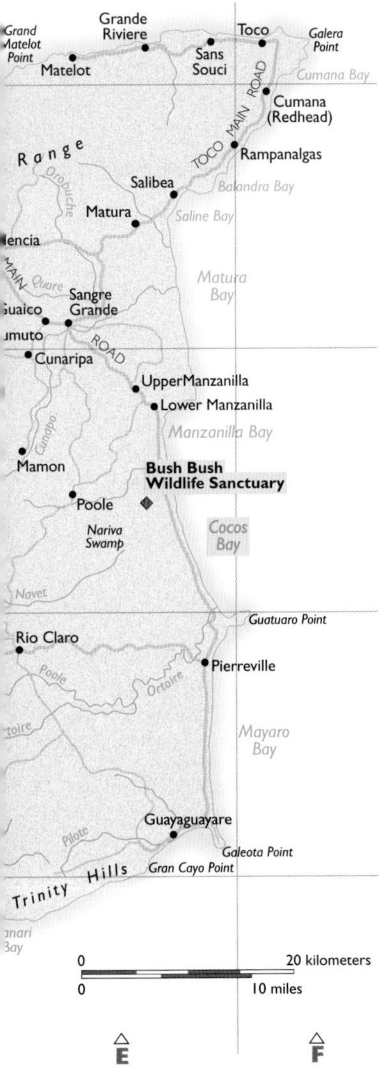

Trinidad's plantations foundered after emancipation in 1838, but once again the island found the solution by encouraging migration from abroad. This time the call was answered by East Indian indentured laborers, who were shipped to the Caribbean, worked a five-year term in the cane fields, and then chose between a return passage and a 5-acre (2-ha) plot of land. Many stayed, and their descendants now number 40 percent of the island's unusually diverse population of about 1.3 million. Another 40 percent of Trinidadians can trace their roots back to Africa, while the remaining 20 percent are of European, Chinese, Middle Eastern, and South American extraction.

World War II brought Americans to Trinidad in force. About 80,000 U.S. military personnel were stationed at 225 bases around the island. At about this time the first stirrings of steel-pan music were heard in the "panyards" of Port of Spain, as musical Trinidadians recycled old oil drums by beating out the steel surfaces until they could play a range of notes. The versatility of the steel drums (known as pans) added an extra dimension and sophistication to the traditional percussion bands, and the rippling rhythms of steel pan are the heartbeat of Trinidad's famous Carnival, alongside the raucous lyrics of calypso, soca (a fusion of soul music and calypso), and chutney (a fusion of calypso and traditional Indian music).

Trinidad and Tobago gained independence from Britain in 1962 and became a republic within the Commonwealth in 1976. Trinidad's oil wealth insulated the island from the tourism development that swept through other Caribbean islands in the 1960s and '70s, but the 1980s oil slump changed attitudes. Trinidad's tourist industry is still in its infancy (beach hotels are a novelty), but ecotourism is the island's trump card. ■

Art lovers mingle in a fashionable gallery in the heart of Port of Spain.

Port of Spain

TRINIDAD'S FRENETIC CAPITAL CITY, PORT OF SPAIN, reflects the island's multicultural heritage. Its teeming streets overflow with shoppers and market stalls, while pompous British colonial architecture rubs shoulders with Muslim mosques, West Indian gingerbread houses, and modern concrete office buildings. The heart of the city was laid out after a major fire in 1808, but Port of Spain now stretches for miles along the Gulf of Paria and back into the hills to sought-after residential suburbs such as Maraval.

Port of Spain

319 C4

Visitor information

www.visittnt.com

Trinidad & Tobago Tourism Development Company, 29 Tenth Ave., Barataria email info@td c.co.tt

868/675-7034, fax 868/675-7432

National Museum and Art Gallery

117 Frederick St.

868/623-5941

Closed Sun. a.m. and Mon.

Port of Spain's main downtown thoroughfare is **Frederick Street,** which links Brian Lara Promenade (named for a famous Trinidadian cricket player) with the grassy expanse of **Queen's Park Savannah.** The southern end of Frederick Street resembles an Eastern bazaar, with its Indian fabric shops and boutiques spilling out onto the sidewalk.

Midway up the street is **Woodford Square,** a small park bisected by paths where locals meet to "lime" (hang out and chat) on benches under the trees. The entire west side is flanked by the imposing bulk of the **Red House,** seat of the Trinidad and Tobago Parliament. On the south side is the mellow stone **Trinity Cathedral,** dating from the early 19th century. It's worth a visit for its soaring wooden ceiling and patchwork of stained glass (entrance on Queen Street).

A 15-minute walk north on Frederick Street takes you to the **National Museum and Art Gallery.** There's an interesting section on the famous Carnival, complete with sequined-and-plumed costumes, elaborate masks, and a photo montage of Carnival kings and queens dating back to the 1960s. Among the Trinidadian art on display, look for works by Michel Jean Cazabon, as well as

Jackie Hinkson's colorful depictions of Port of Spain in the 1940s.

Frederick Street ends at Queen's Park Savannah, a large open space with a circumference of 2.5 miles (4 km) proudly hailed by Trinidadians as the "largest traffic circle in the world." The Savannah plays a central role in the Carnival festivities and doubles as a sports field during the rest of the year. At one time Trinidad's premier racecourse was located in the park.

On the northwest side are seven grand old colonial mansions built in various styles around 1900. They have been nicknamed the **Magnificent Seven,** although several are now looking a little tired.

To the north is **Emperor Valley Zoo,** which showcases various South American mammals from capybaras and tapirs to the giant Brazilian otter. Here you can find deer, agoutis, and tree porcupines from Trinidad's forests, and aviaries for wetland birds *(Queen's Park Savannah, tel 868/622-3530, $).*

Next door to the zoo are the **Botanic Gardens** *(Queen's Park Savannah),* laid out in the 1820s by Sir Ralph Woodford. Although many of the magnificent tropical trees are carefully numbered, there are no names. At the far side of the gardens stands the President's House, a sturdy, L-shaped British colonial affair.

Southwest of the Savannah is the **Woodbrook district,** noted for its attractive gingerbread homes; there are also several good restaurants in the area.

Farther west is the **Western Main Road** in the St. James district. It's known as the "city that never sleeps," thanks to its lively nightlife, bars, ice-cream parlors, and street vendors selling rotis (Indian-style bread pockets stuffed with chicken, meat, or vegetables). ■

Carnival

Trinidad's famous Carnival originated in the late 18th century with French Roman Catholic settlers, who marked the approach of Lent with a series of elaborate feasts and parties or masquerades (which, shortened to "mas," is the traditional Trinidadian word for Carnival). The buildup to Carnival begins in the New Year with calypso and panorama (steel band) competitions around the island. The main event kicks off in Port of Spain the Friday before Lent and culminates on Shrove Tuesday as the Parade of Bands gathers on Queen's Park Savannah. Anyone can join in Carnival (or "play mas"), whether it's just dancing on the street or signing up with a mas camp and renting a fabulous Carnival costume. Check with the tourist office; you can even cruise the mas camps on the Internet (*www.visittnt.com*). ■

Above: Carnival costumes are often works of art and can take months to design and execute.

Cricket in the Caribbean

Cricket occupies a unique position in the Caribbean region. In many countries, particularly former British colonies such as Jamaica, Barbados, Antigua, and Trinidad, the sport is followed with a passion that verges on the religious. But, more importantly, it is one of the very few successful cooperative endeavors in a region where most other attempts at integration have failed. National rivalries are forgotten and the West Indies team presents a cohesive face as the ambassadors of the Caribbean on overseas tours.

One of contemporary cricket's greats, Trinidadian Brian Lara has captained the West Indies team.

The story of the development of West Indian cricket is a fascinating one, and it says much about the importance of the sport in the region that one of the best accounts of its development, *A History of West Indian Cricket* (1988) should have been written by no less a person than Michael Manley, former prime minister of Jamaica.

When cricket was introduced by the British, it was mostly played by army officers and plantation owners, but in the sweltering heat they preferred to bat rather than bowl (pitch), and it was the slaves and sons of slaves who were drafted in to bowl for them. After emancipation a network of cricket clubs sprang up, and it soon became clear that the descendants of the former slaves were incredibly good at cricket.

The first English team toured the West Indies in 1895, and in 1897 the first All-West Indies team was picked to play against another visiting English team. The first tour of England by a West Indies team took place in 1900, but the great turning point came in the 1920s, when the West Indies were granted Test status—that is, the right to compete on the international cricket circuit.

The West Indian team soon gained a reputation for stylish and exuberant playing, bringing a free-flowing athleticism and sense of humor to the game and earning them the nickname of the "calypso cricketers."

During the 1930s West Indian cricket was dominated by the presence of George Headley, judged to be the greatest West Indian batsman ever and globally among the six best of all time. He has a unique place in Caribbean history in that he personified black excellence in a white-dominated sport, a symbol of self-worth for the adoring crowds. During the postwar years the game was dominated by three Barbados players—Frank Worrell, Everton Weekes, and Clive Walcott. They were followed by one of the great West Indian stars of all time, the legendary Garfield (Gary) Sobers. The Sobers era, from 1960 to 1974, witnessed the highest level attained by the West Indies up to that date, during which they played 67 tests, of which they won 21, lost 16, drew 29, and tied 1.

The golden age of West Indies cricket, however, was yet to come. This was the decade, from 1976 to 1986, when they dominated the cricketing world. Out of 17 test matches they won 15, drew one, and lost one—a remarkable record of victories in any sport. They achieved a level of preeminence that was so great that opposing sides were almost beaten before the game began, so formidable was their reputation.

Since then the West Indies team has struggled to find its footing in a cricketing world dominated by the southern hemisphere nations.

Commentators believe that this malaise will pass, and that the region will continue to produce great cricketers such as Vivian Richards (from Antigua), Clive Lloyd (Guyana), and more recently Brian Lara, who comes from Trinidad. But others worry that the ascent of alternative sports will eclipse Caribbean cricket.

Top: The West Indies take on India in Gros Islet, Saint Lucia. Above: Any open space serves as a practice pitch for youngsters to hone their skills.

Soccer, basketball, and track and field are becoming increasingly popular among the younger generations. Baseball has long been the national sport of Cuba, the Dominican Republic, and Puerto Rico, with many Dominicans and Puerto Ricans playing major league baseball—and earning big money—in the United States. Nonetheless, the local fans were out in force for the 2007 World Cup, hosted by cricketing nations across the region. On many Caribbean islands an impromptu game of cricket will spring up anywhere that the youngsters can find a few sticks to act as stumps and a tennis ball to practice with, be it on the beach or the back streets. The aspirations and hopes of generations have become embedded in a game that symbolizes a rare sense of unity among Caribbean peoples. ■

Gasparee Caves

A group of five small islands lie off the tip of the Chaguaramas Peninsula, colonized by holiday homes and visited by yachtsmen. A 15-minute boat ride from the mainland, Gasparee Island is renowned for its caves. It's also a popular picnic spot, and you can ramble around its old military fortifications. Inexpensive water taxis depart from several marinas along Western Main Road (20 minutes from Port of Spain). Permission to visit the caves must be obtained from the Chaguaramas Development Authority *(Tel 868/634-4227).* ■

Around the north

The mountains of the Northern Range stretch right across the north of Trinidad, dividing the coast from the central plain. This is where you'll find the island's two highest peaks, **El Cerro del Aripo** (3,083 feet/940 m) and **El Tucuche** (3,075 feet/936 m). The range is cloaked in a lush tangle of rain forest that is home to many of Trinidad's 430 bird species, 630 species of butterflies, and 2,300 varieties of flowering plants. Two roads cross the mountains: the **Saddle Road,** which links Port of Spain and the beach at Maracas Bay; and the **Blanchisseuse Road** from Arima, which can also be accessed from Lopinot. The

Above: With eyes trained on the bird-feeding stations, guests identify winged visitors to Asa Wright Nature Center. Left: Rain forest retreat—relaxing on the veranda at Asa Wright

roads form the basis of a good circular day tour out of Port of Spain, heading counter-clockwise to Arima, then up to the Asa Wright Nature Centre, north to Blanchisseuse, and along the coast to Maracas before the return route over the Saddle Road.

West from Port of Spain is the **Chaguaramas Peninsula** *(Map 318 C3)*, which has a military history museum (see p. 328), marinas, and boat trips to a clutch of offshore islands, a man-made beach at Chagville, and Macqueripe Beach on the north coast.

Naturalists will want to make arrangements in advance to make a boat trip into the superb **Caroni Swamp—**a short drive south of the city (see Ecotours, p. 327).

ASA WRIGHT NATURE CENTRE

A visit here provides an unmissable opportunity to sample Trinidad's myriad and colorful birdlife and plant life; more than 170 species of birds have been recorded in the Arima Valley, where the nature center sits at a comfortable 1,200 feet (365 m) above sea level, hemmed in by the rain forest.

A series of trails explores the 200-acre (80-ha) estate, and guided walks provide a window on the rain forest, where leaf cutter ants share the paths and blue morpho butterflies flutter past like elegant turquoise magic carpets.

There's a ringside seat for the mating dance of the white-bearded manakin, accompanied by what sounds like a salvo of Chinese firecrackers as the male birds snap their wings with a loud popping noise.

Settle down on the veranda at the lodge to watch hummingbirds, honeycreepers, tanagers, and trogons drop in to snack on sugar water or fresh fruits. Guests staying a minimum of three nights at the center qualify for a visit to the world's most accessible colony of oilbirds. Known as guacharos ("one who wails" in Amerindian), these cave-dwelling birds feed

Above: The cooling swimming hole at Asa Wright. Above right: Scarlet ibis roosting in mangroves at Caroni Bird Sanctuary

their young on oily fruits such as palm, camphor, and laurels. Guacharos were prized for their fat, which was used for cooking and fueling oil lamps. They are now a protected species.

Bring sensible footwear as the trails can be very muddy and slippery, as well as a bathing suit for a dip in the swimming hole, and adequate supplies of mosquito repellent.

318 D4 · Arima Valley · Call in advance, 868/667-4655, www.asawright.org. Guided tours daily at 10:30 a.m. and 1:30 p.m. · $$$

CARONI BIRD SANCTUARY

This 40-acre (16-ha) wetlands preserve in the Caroni Swamp is renowned for the evening flight of the scarlet ibis returning to mangrove roosts just before sunset. Flat-bottomed boat tours leave from the dock (follow the signs from the highway) at about 4:30 p.m., puttering through tree-lined waterways to the heart of the swamp. Along the way you can spot caimans, four-eyed fish, mangrove roots festooned with oysters, maybe even a silky anteater, and 186 species of birds from the not-so-common common potoo, a nocturnal bird that is devilishly difficult to spot, to the egrets, herons, and scampering willets feeding on the mudbanks among a lunatic orchestra

of fiddler crabs sawing away with their outsize pincers.

About 10,000 scarlet ibis inhabit the sanctuary, nesting between March and September. Ibis chicks are black but develop a dark, silvery color at six to twelve months. The young birds don't achieve their brilliant red-orange adult plumage for another couple of years. Scarlet ibis are now protected from hunters, who once prized the feathers for carnival costumes. About half an hour before sunset the ibis begin to knife through the sky, iridescent red darts congregating in the dark mangrove greenery until it blazes like a Christmas tree caught in the last rays of the sun.

318 C4 ✉ Uriah Butler Hwy. $ $$$

Sports & activities

Ecotours: For hiking, biking and kayaking, contact The Pathmaster *(Tel/fax 868/621-0255, www.thepathmaster.com).* For trips in the Caroni Bird Sanctuary, Northern Range, and Nariva Swamp, contact Winston Nanan *(Tel/fax 868/645-1305)* at Caroni.

Golf: St. Andrew's Golf Club, Maraval *(Tel 868/629-0066, www.golftrinidad.com).*

Water sports: Windsurfer and kayak rentals at Chagville Beach, Chaguaramas Peninsula. ■

Sports-mad Trinidadians play soccer on the beach at Maracas Bay.

CHAGUARAMAS MILITARY HISTORY & AVIATION MUSEUM

A 20-minute drive west of Port of Spain, this rambling museum will appeal to military history buffs, especially Americans who served here in World War II. Much of the military hardware and memorabilia relate to the 1940s, but displays trace conflicts dating back to the native Amerindians and Spanish conquistadores, and up to Trinidad's short-lived coup by Muslim extremists in 1990.

Map 318 C4 · Address Chaguaramas · Phone 868/634-4391 · Price $

LOPINOT COMPLEX

A twisting scenic route leads up into the Northern Range, passing through small villages with burgeoning gardens and flapping Hindu prayer flags, to the settlement of Lopinot, founded by French cocoa planter Charles Joseph, Comte de Lopinot, in 1806. The count's simple wooden estate house contains a one-room museum surrounded by magnificent saaman trees, and there's a cocoa barn and old slave quarters.

Lopinot is one of the main centers of *parang*, the Spanish-based traditional music of Christmas in Trinidad. Introduced from Venezuela, parang is played on tiny, four-stringed *cuatro* guitars.

Map 318 D4 · Address Lopinot Valley

MARACAS BAY & THE NORTH COAST

Protected by steep wooded headlands and a stately border of palm trees, Maracas Bay *(Map 318 D4)* is Trinidad's most popular beach and attracts the crowds on weekends. This is the place to sample shark and bake, a seasoned fish sandwich served with hot pepper-and-tamarind sauce. This typically cheap and filling local culinary institution is served up from palm-thatched vendors' stalls.

Five miles (8 km) east of Maracas there's another curve of fine white sand at **Las Cuevas,** which takes its name from the caves (*cuevas* in Spanish) along the shore. Vacation homes dot the coast road to the fishing village of Blanchisseuse. Neighboring **Damier Beach** is a favorite with windsurfers. ■

Around the south

The Eastern Main Road from the town of Arima cuts across to Trinidad's Atlantic coast and a long palm-fringed sandy shore stretching down to the southeast tip of the island at Galeota Point. There are good beaches at **Manzanilla Bay** (named for the green, poisonous machineel trees behind the beach), **Cocos Bay,** and **Mayaro Bay.**

Inland is the 3,840-acre (1,554-ha) **Nariva Swamp,** home to a fantastic variety of wildlife. To visit the Nariva's **Bush Bush Wildlife Sanctuary,** get a permit from the Wildlife Section of the Ministry of Agriculture *(Tel 868/622-5114)* or approach an accredited tour operator (see p. 327).

On the west coast, just north of Trinidad's second largest city and oil center San Fernando, is the **Pointe-à-Pierre Wildfowl Trust** *(Map 318 C2; tel 868/658-4200, ext. 2512, $),* where wetlands and forest trails provide splendid bird-watching opportunities *(Call ahead for guided walks).*

PITCH LAKE

Around Otaheite Bay from San Fernando is the Pitch Lake at La Brea *(Map 318 C2),* one of Trinidad's most famous (but least exciting) sights. Probably the world's largest natural bitumen reservoir, the 100-acre (40-ha) "lake" looks like a massive parking lot, although predatory guides aim to liven up a visit with a fund of anecdotes (fix a fee in advance). The endless supply of gloopy black tar was used to caulk the hulls of conquistadores' galleons and to pave the streets of Paris and London, as well as Port of Spain, where it was also employed as fuel for 19th-century street lamps until residents complained about the appalling fumes. A small museum *(Tel 868/651-1232)* outlines the history of the lake. ■

Turtle watch

Endangered leatherback turtles lay their eggs on the beaches of northern and eastern Trinidad during the March-to-August breeding season. Beyond Arima and Valencia is the Toco Main Road, which heads out to the turtle beaches at Matura Bay and then rounds the tip of the island to the beautiful, undeveloped north coast beaches at Grande Rivière and Matelot. It is about a two-hour drive from Port of Spain to Toco. The Forestry Department can advise on the best beaches for turtle-watching *(Tel 868/622-5114),* or contact the Grande Rivière Visitor Facility *(Tel 868/670-4256).* ■

A hole in the Pitch Lake's soft, gray crust reveals the liquid bitumen beneath.

Tobago

TRINIDAD'S LITTLE SISTER ISLAND, TOBAGO, ALSO BROKE AWAY FROM SOUTH America (several million years ago in this case), but in look and feel it's more similar to the Windward Islands in the north. Just over 20 miles (32 km) from the hustle and bustle of Trinidad, Tobago is a mountainous green oasis of charm and calm, where the Trinidadians come to relax and the Tobagonians take pride in their easygoing hospitality and unspoiled natural surroundings.

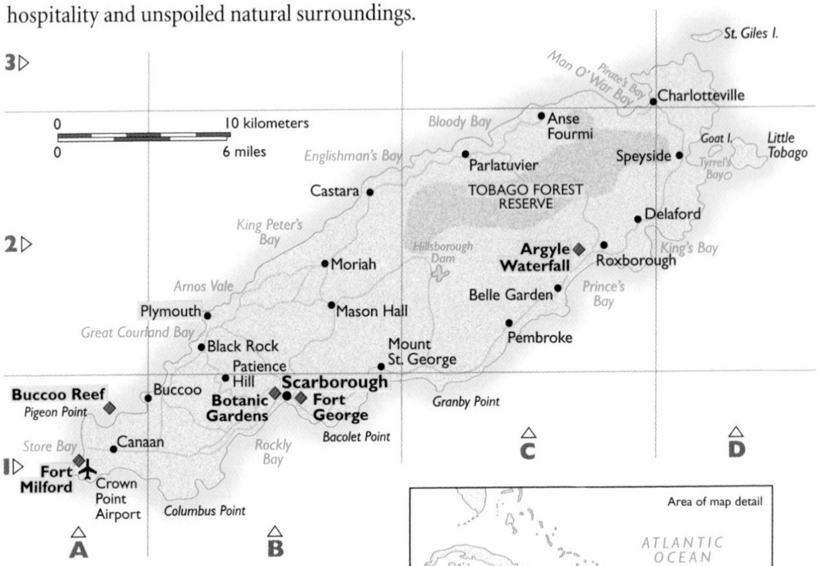

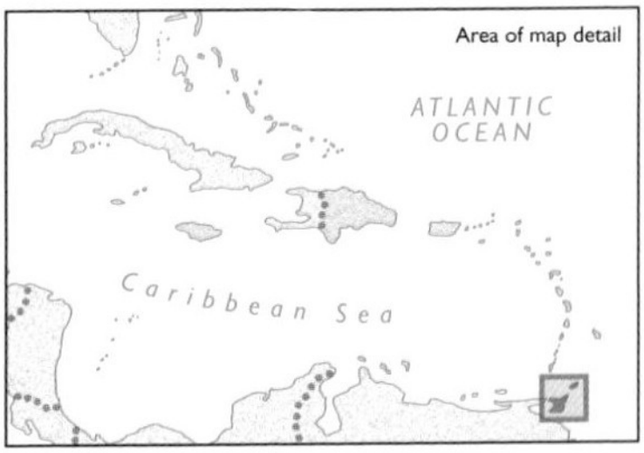

It's probable that Christopher Columbus sighted Tobago when he discovered Trinidad in 1498. He called it Bellaforma (Beautiful Form), although the original Amerindian name (derived from the word for "tobacco") has stuck. The Dutch, English, and French all laid claim to the island, which changed hands more than 20 times and developed into one of the richest sugar islands in the region. Secured by the British in 1814 and administered with the Windward Island group, Tobago found that its fortunes waned after emancipation in the 1830s. It was declared bankrupt in 1888 and appended to neighboring Trinidad. After a century as a poor rural backwater, Tobago now has a small but flourishing tourist industry, concentrated on the northwest coast between Crown Point Airport and Plymouth.

For a mere strip of an island at 20 by 5.5 miles (32 by 9 km), Tobago packs a lot. A central spine of mountains rises in the east and falls sharply through the rain forest to the broad bays of the southern windward coast and sheltered north shore. Here at the eastern end of the island, wooden pirogues from the villages of Speyside and Charlotteville ferry scuba enthusiasts out to Tobago's famous coral reefs. Enriched by nutrients swept along on the Guyana Current from Venezuela's Orinoco River, the reef sites contain 44 species of coral, including the world's biggest brain coral (12 feet by 16 feet/3.5 m by 5 m), a colony of giant manta rays, and occasional visitations by black-tipped, hammerhead, or huge plankton-eating whale sharks. The western end of the island is flat and covered in coconut palms, with stunning white sand beaches created by offshore reefs.

A pair of sculptured figures depicted in 19th-century costume dance the Tobago jig at Fort George.

SCARBOROUGH

The majority of the 50,000 Tobagonians (most of African descent) live in the island's west end and in the pint-size capital of Scarborough *(Map 330 B1; visitor information, Doretta's Court, 197 Mt. Marie, tel 868/639-2125, www.visittobago.gov.tt)* on the south coast.

This unpretentious town climbs steeply from Rockly Bay into a circlet of hills overlooked by **Fort George.** The Lower Town is a melee of fish sellers and noisy market stalls. Take a break in the charming **Botanic Gardens** *(Greenside St.)*, once part of a sugar estate, where the grassy slopes are planted with poinciana and poui trees, spreading Indian almonds, a mango grove, and a huge silk cotton tree near the gazebo.

Scarborough's few remaining colonial buildings are found in the Upper Town. On the way up to Fort George, look for **Gun Bridge,** with its black metal railings made out of old rifle barrels. The fort dates from the 1780s and affords a commanding view along the coast. The **Tobago Museum** *(84 Fort St., tel 868/639-3970, closed weekends)* is next door. It has a marvelous collection of Amerindian finds including tools, religious objects, and pottery adorned with animal motifs. ■

Around the island

TOBAGO IS AN IDEAL ISLAND TO EXPLORE IF YOU DON'T want to feel pressured to pack too much into a single excursion. The island's compact size ensures that no single trip is too long, and the laid-back atmosphere encourages you to linger along the way, pausing to admire the view, stop for a swim, or chat with local fishermen mending their nets on the shore.

The **Crown Point settlement** occupies the western tip of Tobago, with the airport and a handful of hotels and guesthouses set on Store Bay. Behind the scrap of beach, where fishing boats are drawn up on the sand, is a clutch of stands selling crafts and souvenirs. There are bars and snack shops. On Sandy Point you will find the low coral rock battlements of 18th-century **Fort Milford,** which now contain a small garden facing Pigeon Point, a classic Caribbean beach bordered by leaning palms. Offshore is **Buccoo Reef,** Tobago's most visited underwater attraction, although it has suffered somewhat from the glass-bottomed boat crowds.

Beach hotels are scattered along the road to **Plymouth** *(Map 330 B2),* where the ruins of Fort James are still guarded by antique cannon.

The sun sinks in the west behind the boat pier at Pigeon Point beach.

The drive through the hills behind the coast to **Parlatuvier** is charming, and you'll find fine secluded beaches down dirt tracks at King Peter's Bay, Englishman's Bay, and Bloody Bay before the road cuts up into the rain forest (see opposite) and down to the Atlantic coast at

Roxborough. Just short of Roxborough, a side road leads to **Argyle Waterfall** *(Map 330 C2)*. From the parking area in an old cocoa plantation, it's a shady 15-minute walk upriver to the falls, which bounce down a series of ledges on the cliff face to a swimming hole.

Speyside and Charlotteville flank the northeastern end of Tobago. Speyside borders Tyrrel's Bay along the Atlantic coast, overlooking Little Tobago (Map 330 D2) and Goat Island. **Little Tobago** is a seabird sanctuary and breeding ground for frigate-

Tobago Forest Reserve

The forest reserve was established back in 1764, making it the world's oldest legally protected forest. The dense rain forest heights of the Main Ridge remain almost untouched. The best way to visit the reserve without a guide is to take the **Gilpin Trace** marked off the Parlatuvier-Roxborough Road. It's a 2-mile (3-km) hike from the head of the trail down to The Hut. ■

A glass-bottomed boat hovers above touristy Buccoo Reef, but Tobago's best underwater scenery is in the north.

birds, boobies, and tropic birds. Boat trips run from the jetty, where dive operators and glass-bottomed boats depart for the offshore reefs.

Charlotteville, on the Caribbean side, is a sleepy little fishing village and dive center (see below) on the broad expanse of **Man O'War Bay.** Old wooden houses nestle beneath giant breadfruit trees, and the stone seawall is shaded by sea grape trees.

A 15-minute walk to the east of the village takes you to **Pirate's Bay,** a good beach. ■

Houses grafted onto the forested hillside behind the fishing village of Charlotteville

Sports & activities

Day sails: Catamaran cruises with snorkeling are available from Kalina Cats *(Tel 868/639-6306)* and Island Girl *(Tel 868/639-7245)*, also sunset and dinner cruises.

Diving & snorkeling: Tobago is encircled by excellent dive sites, from Buccoo Reef to the gorgeous Japanese Gardens and challenging Flying Manta. Local dive operators include Aquamarine Dive *(Blue Waters Inn, tel 868/639-5445, www.aquamarinedive.com)*; Man Friday Diving *(Tel/fax 868/660-4676)*; Undersea Tobago *(Manta Lodge, tel 868/631-2626, fax 868/639-7759, www.underseatobago.com)*.

Ecotours: Tobago's eastern highlands are cloaked in fabulously unspoiled rain forest, but unfortunately there are very few established trails that can be followed without a guide.

The Gilpin Trace loops off the Roxborough-Parlatuvier road (see p. 333). Otherwise you can hike with an experienced naturalist and arrange bird-watching trips to Little Tobago through David Rooks Nature Tours (*Tel 868/756-8594, e-mail rookstobago@yahoo.com*).

Golf: The Mount Irvine Bay Hotel (*Tel 868/639-8871*) has a lovely 18-hole course. ■

Travelwise

Green sea turtle

TRAVELWISE INFORMATION

GENERAL INFORMATION

Airlines
Although price is a factor in your choice of airline, check also on the safety record and frequency of flights. No-frills airlines usually have a limited number of flights, but often require no advance reservations. **Major airlines:** American Airlines, tel 800/433-7300, www.aa.com; Northwest Airlines, tel 800/225-2525, www.nwa.com; United Airlines, tel 800/538-2929, www.united.com; US Aiways, tel 800/428-4322, www. usairways.com
Smaller airlines: American Eagle, tel 800/433-7300, www.aa .com; BWIA,tel 800/538-2942, www.bwee .com; LIAT, tel 888/844-5428 or 268/480-5601, www.liatairline.com; Spirit Air, 800/772-7117, www.spiritair.com, and Winair, tel 866/466-0410, www.fly-winair.com.

Climate
Temperatures average 77°–86°F (25°–30°C) year-round. Northeasterly trade winds are fairly constant and provide some respite from the heat and humidity. The higher the latitude, the cooler the temperature, especially from November to January. May to October is the wettest period, and the hurricane season is July to October. The Weather Channel Connection gives up-to-date forecasts (Tel 900/932-8437).

Driving
Driving regulations vary, so consult the Getting Around section for each island. Current and former British dependencies drive on the left-hand side; French and Dutch on the right. Some islands require you to have a temporary visitor license (or local license). These are generally available from rental companies, or contact the local police station or tourist office. The state of main roads is good, although local roads can be poor. Take a road map with you.

Electricity
On most islands 110 and 120 volts AC supply is used, and outlets are identical to those in the United States. On the French and Dutch islands, and those with a British background, you may need an adapter for U.S. appliances. When making a reservation, ask your hotel which voltage is used. Most hotels have a supply of adapters.

Festivals & events
These are listed by island in this section. Contact local tourist offices and websites for more detailed festival information.

Insurance
A comprehensive travel insurance policy is a useful precaution and will include cancellation, interruption, default, trip delay, and full medical coverage.

Time zones
Most islands are on Atlantic Standard Time (AST), which is Eastern Standard Time (EST) plus one hour (GMT -4). AST is not affected by daylight saving time (DST). Jamaica and the Cayman Islands are on EST with no daylight saving, and the Turks and Caicos Islands are on EST with daylight saving.

Tipping
Rules for tipping vary, so check your bill for a service charge. If no service charge is included in the bill, leave a tip of 10 to 15 percent, depending on service. Tipping can be an important source of income.

Travelers with disabilities
The Caribbean travel industry is becoming more aware of the needs of travellers with disabilities, but the region can prove quite a challenging destination for those with mobility problems. One area where compliance with ADA (Americans with Disabilities Act) regulations is vastly improved is the cruise sector with wheelchair accessible cabins and facilities for assisted

Exchange rate March 2007

Country	Currency	Abbreviation	Value/US$1
Jamaica	Jamaican dollar	J$	J$ 65.24
Cayman Islands	Cayman Island dollar	CI$	CI$ 0.80
Turks and Caicos	US dollar	US$	
Dominican Republic	Dominican peso	RD$	RD$33.50
Puerto Rico	US dollar	US$	
Virgin Islands	US dollar	US$	
Netherlands Antilles (inc. Sint Maarten)	Netherlands Antilles florin or guilder	NAf	NAf 1.77
Aruba	Aruban florin	Afl	Afll 1.77
Leeward Islands	East Caribbean dollar	EC$	EC $2.70
French Antilles (inc. St.-Martin)	Euro	€	€ 1.31
Windward Islands	East Caribbean dollar	EC$	EC $2.70
Barbados	Barbados dollar	BD$	BD $1.99
Trinidad and Tobago	Trinidad and Tobago dollar	TT$	TT $6.25

embarkation/disembarkation. The U.S. Virgin Islands and Puerto Rico are also good destinations. When making reservations, ask specific questions concerning your needs and give airlines plenty of advance warning. Better still, consult a specialist agency such as Connie George (Tel 610/532-0989 or 888/532-0989, www.cgta.com).

JAMAICA

PLANNING YOUR TRIP

Arrival/departure

Most tourists heading for the resorts on the north coast arrive at the Donald Sangster International Airport, 2 miles (3 km) east of Montego Bay. However, those going south or east might do better to land at the Norman Manley International Airport, 13 miles (21 km) from Kingston.

Air Jamaica, tel 800/523-5585, www.airjamaica.com, as well as American Airlines, Northwest, US Airways, and Air Canada provide service from gateways such as New York, Los Angeles, Chicago, Miami, Atlanta, Baltimore, and Toronto. Most major airlines serve both airports. Numerous charter airlines also fly from the United States and Canada. Regional services are provided by Cayman Airways, British West Indian Airways (BWIA), and Antilles Luchtvaarkt Maatschappy (ALM). There are also small domestic airstrips in Negril, Ocho Rios, Port Antonio, and Tinson Pen (near the center of Kingston). They are served by Air Jamaica Express, tel 800/523-5585, with several flights each day between these points and the international airports. Many visitors find these short hops a convenient means of cutting down on transfer times to their hotels.

Departure tax is: J$100 (approx. US$27).

Entry requirements

A valid passport is required, along with onward or return ticket.

Festivals & events

January Accompong Maroon Festival; Air Jamaica Jazz and Blues Festival (Montego Bay)
February Bob Marley Week
March Fun in the Sun Gospel Festival (Ocho Rios)
April Yam Festival.
May Calabash International Literary Festival
June Ocho Rios Jazz Festival
July Reggae Sumfest (Montego Bay), Portland Jerk Festival
September International Marlin Tournament (Montego Bay)
October Port Royal Seafood Festival

National holidays include New Year's Day (Jan. 1), Ash Wednesday, Good Friday, Easter Monday, Labor Day (4th Mon. in May), Emancipation Day (Aug. 1), Independence Day (Aug. 6), National Heroes Day (3rd Mon. in Oct.), Christmas Day, and Boxing Day (Dec. 26).

GETTING AROUND

Car rental

Major companies include Budget, tel 876/924-8762; Island Car Rentals, tel 876/926-8012; Thrifty, tel 876/952-1126; and Hertz/Elite, tel 876/924-8028. To rent a car you must be 25 years old with a valid driver's license and major credit card. Driving is on the left.

Although major roads are generally good, you may encounter stray goats, dogs, and chickens, erratic cyclists, pedestrians —and potholes. At intersections, traffic coming from the right has priority, but don't rely on this. Always use your horn when passing, in case the driver in front suddenly swerves to avoid a pothole. There are few good signs, and you can only rely on major towns and resorts being shown. Road markings at junctions are almost nonexistent, except on new roads. In towns, watch out for No Entry signs, which are often below hood level where you can't see them.

Public transportation

Local bus timetables are erratic, and the buses are overcrowded. Minibuses travel on many of the same routes and may be slightly quicker, but equally overcrowded. Fares are inexpensive. Buses or minibuses can be flagged down anywhere along the roadside.

Taxis are widely available and most are unmetered: Agree on a fare before setting off (ask at your hotel for advice). Licensed taxis display red PPV (Public Passenger Vehicle) plates; avoid unlicensed cabs. Shared taxis (or route taxis) ply set routes around large towns or between towns and can be flagged down in the same way as buses or minibuses. The Jamaican Union of Travellers Association (JUTA) operates a fleet of tourist buses and taxis, and are often contracted for ground transfers.

PRACTICAL ADVICE

Emergencies

Ambulance or fire: tel 110.
Police: tel 119.

Telephones

The area code is 876.

Tourist information

Kingston: 64 Knutsford Blvd., tel 876/929-9200 or 800/233-4582 (U.S.), fax 876/929-9375, www.visitjamaica.com.

U.S. & Canada offices

Florida: 5201 Blue Lagoon Drive, Suite 670, Miami, FL 33126, tel 305/665-0557 or 800/233-4582, fax 305/666-7239.
Toronto: 303 Eglington Ave. East, Suite 200, Toronto, ON M4P IL3, tel 416/482-7850 or 800-465-2624, fax 416/482-1730.

CAYMAN ISLANDS

PLANNING YOUR TRIP

Arrival/departure

The Owen Roberts International Airport on Grand Cayman is the main point of entry, with direct flights every day from Miami. The national flag carrier is Cayman Airways, which has direct flights from Miami, Tampa, Fort Lauderdale, Chicago, Boston, Houston, and Havana (Cuba), Kingston and Montego Bay

(Jamaica). Other carriers include American Airlines, Delta, Northwest, and US Airways, with departures from Atlanta, Charlotte, Chicago, Detroit, Philadelphia, Miami and Tampa. Continental flies out of Newark. British Airways flies from the UK four times weekly, via Nassau (Bahamas).

Cayman Airways provides daily services to Cayman Brac and Little Cayman, while Island Air, tel 345/949-5252; www.islandaircayman.com, provides several flights daily to both islands from Grand Cayman.

Entry requirements

From January 23, 2007, all visitors including U.S. citizens require a valid passport and onward or return ticket.

Festivals & events

January Cayman Islands Tourism Association International Underwater Film Festival
February–March Cayman Classic—food and wine extravaganza
May Cayman Carnival Batabano
June/July Taste of Caymans Festival
August Annual Sand Sculpting Competition
October Pirates Week
December Jazz Fest

National holidays include New Year's Day (Jan. 1), Ash Wednesday (Feb. or March), Good Friday, Easter Monday (March or April), Discovery Day (mid-May), the Queen's Birthday (mid-June); Constitution Day (1st Mon. in July); Remembrance Day (2nd Mon. in Nov.); Christmas Day, and Boxing Day (Dec. 26).

GETTING AROUND

Car rental

Rental companies (or the police station) will issue a temporary driving permit (US$8.50) on production of a valid driver's license. Reputable companies include Avis, tel 345/949-2468, www.aviscayman.com; Budget Rent-A-Car, tel 345/949-5605, www.budgetcayman.com; Coconut Car Rentals, tel 345/949-4037, www.coconutcarrentals .com; Dollar Rent-A-Car, 345/949-4790, www.dollarlac.com; Thrifty Car Rental, tel 345/949-6640, www.cayman.com.ky/com/thrifty.

Driving is on the left. Speed limits of between 20 and 50 mph (30 and 80 kph) are strictly enforced. Seat belts are required. Avoid driving into George Town during rush hours.

On Little Cayman, hotels provide free bicycles for guests, and this is just about all you need to explore the western end of the island. Rental cars are available from McLaughlin Rentals, tel 345/948-1000, in Blossom Village if you want to reach the more remote beaches and snorkeling areas on the eastern end of the island, such as Point of Sands. Hotels also offer a drop-off/pickup service to Point of Sands.

On Cayman Brac, Brac Rent-A-Car, tel 345/948-1515, has cars and jeeps; B & S Motor Ventures, tel 345/948-1646, supplies cars, jeeps, scooters, and bicycles.

Public transportation

Grand Cayman: Minibus services operate from a terminal by the Public Library in downtown George Town. Routes include a service to Seven Mile Beach. Taxis are readily available from the airport, all resorts and the taxi stand by the cruise ship dock in George Town.

Little Cayman and Cayman Brac have no bus services, but taxis are available for transfers or sight-seeing tours.

PRACTICAL ADVICE

Emergencies

Grand Cayman
Police, fire, ambulance: tel 911. Royal Cayman Islands Police: tel 345/949-4222. George Town Hospital: tel 345/949-8600.
Little Cayman
Police: tel 345/926-0639. Clinic: tel 345/948-0072.
Cayman Brac
Emergency: tel 911. Hospital: tel 345/948-2225.

Media

The *Daily Caymanian Compass* (circulation 25,000) appears on weekdays. The complimentary monthly magazine *What's Hot* has good features on local life.

Telephones

The area code is 345.

Tourist information

Cayman Islands Department of Tourism, Regatta Office Park, Leeward Two, West Bay Road, PO Box 67 GT, George Town, Grand Cayman, tel 345/949-0623 fax 345/949-4053, www.caymanislands.ky.

U.S. & Canada offices
Chicago: One Lincoln Center, 18 W140 Butterfield Rd, Suite 920, Oakbrook Terrace, IL 60181, tel 630/705-0650, fax 630/705-1383.
Houston: Two Memorial City Plaza, 820 Gessner, Suite 1335, Houston, TX 77024, tel 713/461-1317, fax 713/461-7409.
Miami: 8300 NW 53rd Street, #103, Miami, FL 33166, tel 305/599-9033, fax 305/599-3766.
New York: 3 Park Avenue, 39th Floor, New York, NY 10016, tel 212/889-9009, fax 212/889-9125.
Toronto: 234 Eglington Ave. East, Suite 306, Toronto, ON M4P 1K5, tel 416/485-1550 or 800/263-5805, fax 416/485-7578; www.caymanislands.ky/canada.

TURKS & CAICOS

PLANNING YOUR TRIP

Arrival/departure

There are international airports on Providenciales, Grand Turk, and South Caicos. Providenciales is the main international gateway, served by daily from Miami by American Airlines. There are also scheduled services from Atlanta, Boston, Charlotte, New York, and Toronto, and regular services to Jamaica, Haiti, the Dominican Republic, and the Bahamas. Inter-island services are provided by Sky King Airways, tel 649/941-5464, and Air Turks &

Caicos, tel 649/946-4181, tel 649/941-5353.

Departure tax is US$35.

Entry requirements
Visitors require a valid passport and onward or return ticket.

Festivals & events
January Junkaroo Jump-Up (Jan. 1, most islands)
May Regatta Festival (South Caicos)
June Conch Carnival (Grand Turk); International Billfish Tournament (Providenciales)
July Summer Festival (Providenciales); Game Fishing Tournament (Grand Turk)

National holidays include New Year's Day (Jan. 1), Good Friday, Easter Monday, Commonwealth Day (spring), National Heroes Day (end May), Queen's Birthday (mid-June), Emancipation Day (1st Mon. in Aug.), Columbus Day (October), International Human Rights Day (Oct. 25), Christmas Day, and Boxing Day (Dec. 26).

GETTING AROUND
Car rental
Rental agencies on Providenciales include Avis, tel 649/946-4705; Budget, tel 649/946-4079; and Tropical Auto Rental, tel 649/946-5300. Foreign driver's licenses are valid; driving is on the left-hand side of the road.

Public transportation
Bus services on the islands are limited to Provo's Gecko Shuttle, which serves the Grace Bay area, and Grand Turk's Guana Shuttle, servicing the port and downtown district. Taxis are widely available and they can also be hired for island tours (always agree on the price beforehand).

PRACTICAL ADVICE
Emergencies
Call either 999 or 911.

Telephones
The area code is 649.

Tourist information
Grand Turk: Turks & Caicos Islands Tourist Board, Front St., Grand Turk, tel 649/946-2321, fax 649/946-2733,e-mail: tci.tourism@tciway.tc, www.turksandcaicostourism.com.
Providenciales: Stubbs Diamond Plaza, tel 649/946-4970, fax 649/941-5494.

U.S. office
New York: The Lincoln Building, 60 E. 42nd Street, NY 10165, tel 646/375-8830 or 800/241-0824, fax 646/375-8835.

DOMINICAN REPUBLIC

PLANNING YOUR TRIP
Arrival/departure
The main international gateway is Las Américas International Airport, 18 miles (29 km) to the east of Santo Domingo, which receives frequent scheduled services from North America. American Airlines, Continental, Delta, United and US Airways are among the many airlines offering flights either direct to the Dominican Republic or one-stop services via Miami or San Juan, Puerto Rico. In addition to Santo Domingo, there are international airports at Barahona (Maria Montez), Puerto Plata (Gregorio Luperon), Punta Cana, La Romana/Casa de Campo, Samana (El Catey and Arroyo Barril), and Santiago. Domestic flights are operated by Air Santo Domingo (tel 809/683-8006; www.airsantodomingo.com) and Caribair (tel 809/826-4441; www.caribair.com.do).

Departure tax is US$20.

Entry requirements
Visitors require a full valid passport and a Tourist Card (US$10). Tourist cards can be purchased on arrival (US$ cash only), and the receipt must be kept safely and shown on departure.

Festivals & events
January The festival of the patron saint of the Dominican people, Our Lady of Altagracia, is celebrated with all-night vigils, family visits, and singing and dancing.
July Merengue Festival (Santo Domingo)
October Jazz Festival (Puerto Plata)

National holidays include New Year's Day, the birthday of Juan P. Duarte (Jan. 26), Independence Day (Feb. 27), Good Friday, Easter Monday, Labor Day (May 1), Restoration Day (Aug. 16), Columbus Day (Oct. 12), and Christmas Day.

Each town also celebrates its own saint's day with a *fiesta patronal*, which starts with a Mass and then continues with races, sports, street games, and dancing.

GETTING AROUND
Car rental
Santo Domingo offices: Avis, tel 809/535-7191; Budget, tel 809/566-6666; Dollar, tel 809/221-7368; National-Alamo, tel 809/562-1444. Valid driver's license or international driver's license required, as well as a credit card. Driving is on the right; speed limits are 80-100 kph on highways, 40 kph in cities, unless otherwise indicated.

Public transportation
Taxis are available in all tourist areas and at the airports, but they are comparatively expensive; since they are unmetered, always agree on a price before setting off.

The country has a widespread network of public buses, with the better ones featuring air-conditioning and on-board snacks and videos on long-distance routes; it is advisable to reserve seats in advance. On lesser routes, privately operated minibuses known as *guaguas* operate between towns and villages, stopping to pick up or drop off passengers frequently.

Motorbike taxis (*motoconchos*) also operate between many villages and towns.

PRACTICAL ADVICE
Emergencies
Police, fire, ambulance: tel 911;

Tourism Police, tel 809/686-8639, or toll-free on island, tel 809/200-3500.

Telephones
The area code is 809.

Tourist information
Santo Domingo: Ministry of Tourism, Ave. México corner, 30 de Marzo, tel 809/221-4660, fax 809/682-3806, e-mail: info@godominicanrepublic.com, www.godominicanrepublic.com.

U.S. & Canada offices
Chicago: 561 W. Diversey Pkwy., Suite 214, Chicago, IL 60614, tel 773/529-1336 or 888-303-1336, fax 773/529-1338.
Miami: 848 Brickell Ave., Suite 405, Miami, FL 33131, tel 305/358-2899 or 888/358-9594, fax 305/358-4185.
New York: 136 E. 57th St., Suite 803, New York, NY 10022, tel 212/588-1012 or 888/374-6361, fax 212/588-1015.
Montréal: 2080 Rue Crescent, QC H3G 2B8, tel 514/499-1918 or 800-563-1611, fax 514/499-1393.
Toronto: 26 Wellington St. East, Suite 201, Toronto, ON M5E 1S2, tel 416/361-2126 or 888/494-5050, fax 416/361-2130.

PUERTO RICO

PLANNING YOUR TRIP
Arrival/departure
The main gateway is San Juan's Luis Muñoz Marín International Airport. There are also small regional airports at Aguadilla, Mayagüez, and Ponce. Most U.S. airlines offer direct flights to Puerto Rico from gateway cities across North America. American Airlines is the dominant carrier, with daily nonstop flights from Miami, Fort Lauderdale, Chicago, Dallas, New York, and Boston. Other regular scheduled services depart from Atlanta, Charlotte, Chicago, Detroit, Fort Lauderdale, Memphis, New Jersey, New York, Philadelphia, and Pittsburgh. There are frequent short-hop services to destinations throughout the region with local carriers including American Eagle, LIAT, and BWIA. Many shorter flights leave from Ribas Dominicci Airport in San Juan's Isla Grande district, which is more centrally located than the international airport.

Departure tax: None.

Entry requirements
Currently (2007) there is no requirement for U.S. citizens to present a passport on re-entry to the mainland United States from Puerto Rico. However, check updated travel news on www.travel.state.gov/travel. Other visitors will need to present a valid passport, visa and onward or return ticket in compliance with standard U.S. immigration procedures on arrival in Puerto Rico.

Festivals & events
March/April Carnival (Easter)
April/May Caribbean and Latin American Graphics, usually held in late spring (biennial)
May Heineken Jazz festival
June Celebrations of St. John the Baptist (June 23)
Casals Festival (music festival founded by famed cellist Pablo Casals)
December The Bacardí rum plant is host to the largest gathering of artisans and craftworkers on the island.
The Christmas season starts early in Dec. and lasts through Three Kings Day (Jan. 6).

National holidays All U.S. holidays are observed in Puerto Rico, and there are also nine local holidays honoring local leaders or events of the island's history.

GETTING AROUND
Car rental
Avis, tel 787/721-4499; Budget, tel 787/791-0600; Dollar, tel 787/791-5500; and National, tel 800/227-7368. Local rental companies are usually a better value; try Charlie Car Rental, tel 787/728-2418; Vias, tel 787/791-4120; or L&M Rental, tel 787/791-1160.

Public transportation
All taxis are metered, except when they are chartered for long-distance rides. In San Juan, *taxis turísticos* (white, with a logo on the door) operate with fixed rates between the airport, ports, and tourist areas (such as Condado or Old San Juan). City buses are a good way to get around in San Juan.

There are no scheduled bus services between cities, although you can catch shared taxis (known as *publicos*, they have yellow number plates with the letters P or PD at the end) that run to most parts of the island.

PRACTICAL ADVICE
Emergencies
Police, fire, and ambulance: tel 911.
Tourist Zone Police (Condado): tel 787/343-2020.

Telephones
The area code is 787.

Tourist information
San Juan: La Princesa Building, Old San Juan, tel 787/721-2400 or 800/866-7827, fax 787/722-5208; Luis Muñoz Marín Airport, tel 787/791-1014; in Old San Juan, tel 787/722-1709. www.gotopuertorico.com, or www.travelandsports.org.

U.S. & Canada offices
New York: 666 Fifth Avenue, 15th floor, New York, NY 10103, tel 212/586-6262 or 800/866-7827, fax 212/586-1212.
Florida: 901 Ponce de Léon Blvd., Suite 101, Coral Gables, FL 33134, tel 305/445-9112, fax 305/445-9450.
Los Angeles: 3575 W. Cahuenga Blvd., Suite 620, Los Angeles, CA 90068, tel 323/874-5991 or 800/866-7827, fax 323/874-7257.
Toronto: Sunny Montgomery & Kerry Richards, 6-295 Queen St. E., Suite 465, Brampton ON L6W 4S6, tel 416/580-6287.

VIRGIN ISLANDS

U.S. VIRGIN ISLANDS

Entry requirements

U.S. citizens do not require a passport to visit the USVI, but will need to provide Proof of Identity and a photo ID upon departure.

Telephone

The area code is 340.

National holidays

These include New Year's Day (Jan. 1), Martin Luther King Jr. Day (3rd Mon. in Jan.), President's Day (3rd Mon. in Feb.), Transfer Day (March 31), Good Friday, Easter Monday, USVI Emancipation Day (July 3), Independence Day (July 4), Labor Day (1st Mon. in Sept.), Columbus Day (2nd Mon. in Oct.), Thanksgiving Day (4th Thurs. in Nov.), Christmas Day, and Boxing Day (Dec. 26).

ST. CROIX

PLANNING YOUR TRIP

Arrival/departure

Several airlines fly daily to St. Croix from the U.S., including American Airlines (from Miami), Delta (from Atlanta), and US Airways (from Charlotte and Philadelphia), and there are many connections via Puerto Rico (see p. 340), and St. Thomas (see below) with American Eagle. Seaborne Airlines, tel 340/773-6442 or 888/359-8687, has frequent daily services between St. Croix and St. Thomas, as does Cape Air, tel 800/352-0714, with hourly services to St. Thomas, St. Croix, Tortola (BVI), and Puerto Rico.

Festivals & events

December–January The month-long Crucian Christmas Festival culminates in the Three Kings Day parade (Jan. 6).
March LPGA Tournament at the Carambola golf course
May St. Croix Half-Ironman Triathlon
November International Regatta
For a glimpse of the island's heritage catch a performance by Crucian quadrille dancers.

GETTING AROUND

Car rental

Avis, tel 340/778-9355; Budget Rent a Car, tel 888/264-8894; Judi of Croy, tel 340/773-2123; and Olympic Ace, tel 340/773-8000 can all arrange airport and hotel pickups and delivery. U.S. driver's licenses are valid on the island; driving is on the left in St. Croix.

Public transportation

It costs just a dollar to take the bus from Christiansted to Frederiksted; every 40 minutes 5:30 a.m.–9:30 p.m. Hourly on Sundays. Taxis are readily available at the airport and hotels or from taxi stands on King Street and at Market Square in Christiansted, or by Fort Frederik in Frederiksted. Taxis are not metered, but regulated by an official tariff carried by drivers. Check the fare in advance. Taxi vans offer cut-price transfers from the airport to island hotels.

PRACTICAL ADVICE

Emergencies

Police, fire, and ambulance: tel 911. St. Croix Hospital, tel 340/778-6311, has a 24-hour emergency room. Hotels have access to a 24-hour duty doctor.

Tourist information

Christiansted:
P.O. Box 4538, 41A Queen Cross St., tel 340/773-0495 or 800/372-8784, fax 340/773-5074, www.usvitourism.vi.

U.S. offices

New York: One Penn Plaza, Suite 3525, New York, NY 10119, tel 212/502-5300 or 888/273-4741, fax 212/332-2223.
Miami: 2655 South LeJeune Rd., Suite 907, Coral Gables, FL 33134, tel 305/442-7200, fax 305/445-9044.

ST. THOMAS & ST. JOHN

PLANNING YOUR TRIP

Arrival/departure

The major U.S. airlines provide daily direct flights to St. Thomas, and there are connections from numerous U.S. cities via Puerto Rico (see p. 340) on American Airlines. St. John does not have an airport, but it is a short ferry ride from St. Thomas. Regular services depart from St. Thomas, either Charlotte Amalie (45 minutes) or Red Hook (20 minutes), throughout the day. The Westin and Caneel Bay hotels provide a private boat service for guests.

Festivals & events

March–April International Rolex Cup Regatta (Easter weekend, St. Thomas)
April Virgin Islands Carnival (St. Thomas)
June–July St. John celebrates Carnival during the run-up to a big Independence Day party.
July Pillsbury Sound Race
August St. Thomas Open at Mahogany Run; Atlantic Open Blue Marlin Tournament

GETTING AROUND

Car rental

Avis, tel 340/774-1468 and Budget, tel 340/776-5774. Local operators, including Dependable, tel 340/774-2253, on St. Thomas, and St. John Car Rental, tel 340/776-6103, on St. John, can offer more competitive rates. U.S. driver's licenses are valid on the islands, but unlike the U.S. mainland driving is on the left in the USVI.

Public transportation

There is a local bus service on St. Thomas. On St. John, a regular bus shuttles between the ferry dock at Cruz Bay and Coral Bay on the east coast throughout the day. Taxis are readily available from St. Thomas's Airport and St. John's Cruz Bay ferry dock, as well as from hotels and taxi stands in tourist areas. They are not metered, but regulated by an official tariff carried by drivers. Check the fare in advance. Taxi vans offer cut-price transfers from the St. Thomas Airport to hotels around the island.

PRACTICAL ADVICE

Emergencies

Police, fire, and ambulance: tel

911. Roy Schneider Hospital, tel 340/776-8311, has a 24-hour emergency room. There are clinics in St. John, but medical emergencies will be transferred to St. Thomas. Hotels have access to a 24-hour duty doctor.

Tourist information

Charlotte Amalie: U.S. Virgin Island Department of Tourism, P.O. Box 6400, St. Thomas, USVI 00804, tel 340/774-8784, fax 340/774-4390, e-mail: info@usvi.tourism.vi, www.usvi.tourism.vi.

There are also offices at Emancipation Park (downtown Charlotte Amalie) and Havensight Mall in St. Thomas, and around the corner from the ferry dock in Cruz Bay, St. John.

U.S. offices:
See St. Croix, p. 341.

BRITISH VIRGIN ISLANDS

PLANNING YOUR TRIP

Arrival/departure

There are no direct flights to the British Virgin Islands from North America, but American Eagle and several local airline companies offer frequent short-hop services to Tortola from Puerto Rico (see p. 340), and from St. Thomas, USVI (see p. 341). Air St. Thomas flies to Virgin Gorda from Puerto Rico and St. Thomas. Clair Aero Services flies to Anegada from Tortola four times a week. With the exception of Anegada, the main BVIs are linked to each other, and St. Thomas and St. John in the USVI, by regular, inexpensive ferry services (see p. 158 and p. 174).

Departure tax is US$20 for air travelers, or US$5 for those leaving by sea.

Entry requirements

Visitors are required to produce a valid passport, together with a return or on-going ticket. A passport may not be necessary for U.S. citizens on day trips from the USVI, but check current U.S. re-entry requirements before departure.

Festivals & events

June–July HIHO windsurfing championships and regatta, conveniently timed to coincide with the Fourth of July
August BVI Festival (Tortola, 1st Mon., Tues., and Wed.)
December Foxy's famous New Year's Party (Jost van Dyke's Great Harbour, Dec. 31)

National holidays include New Year's Day, Commonwealth Day (2nd Mon. in March), Good Friday, Easter Monday, Whit Monday (May), Queen's Birthday (2nd Mon. in June), Territory Day (July 1), St. Ursula's Day (Oct. 21), Prince Charles's Birthday (Nov. 14), Christmas Day, Boxing Day (Dec. 26).

GETTING AROUND

Car Rental

On Tortola, Avis, tel 284/494-3322, Dollar, tel 284/494-6093, and Hertz, tel 284/495-6228, offer rental cars and 4WD vehicles.

On Virgin Gorda, contact L & S Jeep Rental, tel 284/495-5297, or Mahogany, tel 284/495-5469.

On Anegada, try Anegada Reef Hotel, tel 284/495-8002, or DW Jeep Rentals, tel 284/495-9677. Visitors are required to purchase a temporary license (US$10) in addition to a valid foreign driver's permit. Roads can be rough, and 4WD vehicles are good for negotiating bumpy tracks to the beach. Driving is on the left.

Public transportation

On Tortola, an irregular bus service operates out of Road Town to destinations along the south coast, but most visitors find taxis are a more reliable alternative.

On Virgin Gorda, day-trippers can take an island tour aboard an open truck with seats and an awning or hire a taxi.

There are frequent ferry services daily from Tortola to Virgin Gorda, Jost van Dyke, and the U.S. Virgin Islands of St. John and St. Thomas. Ferries also link Virgin Gorda with St. Thomas/St. John several times a week.

PRACTICAL ADVICE

Emergencies

Police, fire, and ambulance: tel 999 or 911. Peebles Hospital: Road Town, Tortola, tel 284/494-3497. Hotels can assist with locating a duty doctor. Serious medical emergencies are airlifted to St. Thomas, USVI, or San Juan, Puerto Rico.

Telephones

The area code is 284.

Tourist information

Tortola:
BVI Tourist Board, AKARA Bldg., 2nd floor, DeCastro Street, Road Town, tel 284/494-3134, fax 284/494-3866, e-mail: info@bvitourism.com, www.bvitourism.com. There is also a bureau in the Virgin Gorda Yacht Harbour, tel 284/495-5181.

U.S.:
New York: BVI Tourist Board, 1270 Broadway, Suite 705, New York, NY 10001, tel 212/696-0400 or 800/835-8530, fax 212/563-2263, e-mail: info@bvitourism.com.
Chicago: BVI Tourist Board, 401 N. Michigan Ave., Suite 1200, Chicago IL 60611, tel 312/836-3723, fax 312/836-3724.

NETHERLANDS ANTILLES & ARUBA

Entry requirements

For all islands in the group, U.S. citizens are required to produce a valid passport, together with a return or on-going ticket. On the Dutch/French island of Sint Maarten/St.-Martin, there are no passport controls between the two halves of the island.

National holidays

These include New Year's Day, Good Friday, Easter Monday, Queen's Birthday (April 30), Labor Day (May 1), Ascension Day (May), Christmas Day, and

Boxing Day (Dec. 26).
St.-Martin only: Whit Monday and All Saints Day (Nov. 1).

ARUBA

PLANNING YOUR TRIP

Arrival/departure

American Airlines flies direct to Aruba's Queen Beatrix International Airport, tel 297/582-4800, from Miami, Boston and New York, and also makes connections to other cities from Puerto Rico. United Airlines flies from Chicago; US Airways from Charlotte; and Delta from Atlanta. There are charter flights from many other U.S. cities.

Departure tax is US$35.

Festivals & events

January New Year celebrations
January-February Carnival Monday (early Jan.) marks the start of the month-long run-up to Carnival; National Anthem and Flag Day (March 18)
June Windsurfing Festival
October Aruba Music Festival
December Sint Nicolaas's (Santa Claus) Birthday (Dec. 5)

GETTING AROUND

Car rental

Avis, tel 297/582-7202; Budget, tel 297/582-8600; Optima Rent-A-Car, tel 297/582-4828; and Thrifty Car Rental, tel 297/585-5300, have offices at the airport and other useful tourist locations. Foreign driver's licenses held for a minimum of two years are valid on Aruba; driving is on the right.

Public transportation

Aruba has an inexpensive and reliable bus service that links the hotel areas with Oranjestad, the airport, and San Nicolas; private minibus services offer greater flexibility. Taxis are easy to find at the airport or hotel, or call the Oranjestad depot, tel 297/582-2116.

PRACTICAL ADVICE

Emergencies

All Emergencies: tel 911, Police: tel 911, Hospital: tel 297/587-4300. All hotels have a doctor on call 24 hours.

Telephones

The country code is 297.

Tourist information

On the island, contact the Aruba Tourism Authority, L.G. Smith Blvd., 172, Oranjestad, tel 297/582-3777, fax 297/583-4702, e-mail: ata.aruba@aruba.com, www.aruba.com.

U.S. office

New Jersey: Aruba Tourism Authority, 1200 Harbor Blvd., Weehawken, NJ 07087, tel 201/330-0800 or 800/TOA-RUBA, fax 201/330-8757.

BONAIRE

PLANNING YOUR TRIP

Arrival/departure

There are a number of one-stop flights from US gateway cities to Bonaire (via Puerto Rico, Aruba, Curaçao, and Montego Bay, Jamaica). American Eagle flies daily from San Juan, Puerto Rico to the island. Continental Airlines makes direct flights once a week from Newark and Houston. Direct flights into Curaçao and Aruba connect with local carriers Dutch Antilles Express, Insel Air, and Divi-Divi.

Departure tax is US$32 for international flights, or US$6 for trips within the Netherlands Antilles.

Festival & events

February Carnival
April Rincon Day
September Bonaire Day (Sept. 6)
October Annual Sailing Regatta

GETTING AROUND

Car rental

Avis, tel 599/717-5795; Budget, tel 599/717-4700; and Hertz, tel 599/717-7221, all have offices at the airport. Local operators include Lions Car Rental, tel 599/717-2222, and Island Rentals, tel 599/717-2100. Foreign driver's licenses are valid. Driving is on the right.

Public transportation

A few minibuses shuttle between Kralendijk and Rincon, and taxis are available at the airport and can be booked through hotels.

PRACTICAL ADVICE

Emergencies

Ambulance, tel 114. Police: tel 717-8000. St. Francis Hospital in Kralendijk, tel 599/717-8900, has a decompression chamber.

Telephones

The country code is 599.

Tourist information

Bonaire: Kaya Grandi 2, Kralendijk, tel 599/717-8322, fax 599/717-8408, e-mail: info@tourismbonaire.com, www.tourismbonaire.com.

U.S. office

New York: Tourism Corporation Bonaire, c/o Adams Unlimited, 80 Broad Street, Suite 3202, New York, NY 10004, tel 800/BONAIRE, fax 212/956-5913, e-mail: usa@tourismbonaire.com, www.adams-pr.com.

CURAÇAO

PLANNING YOUR TRIP

Arrival/departure

Hato International Airport receives daily direct flights from Miami with American Airlines, who also provide same-day connections from many U.S. gateway cities via Puerto Rico. Air Jamaica flies via Montego Bay, and there are regular services from Aruba.

Departure tax is US$32 for international flights, or US$6 for trips within the Netherlands Antilles.

Festivals & events

February/March Carnival
March Springtime fishing tournaments
April Celebration of the Queen's Birthday (April 30); Sailing Regatta
July Flag Day (July 2)
August Salsa Festival
October Jazz Festival

GETTING AROUND

Car rental

Avis, tel 5999/461-1255; Budget, tel 5999/868-3466; National, tel 5999/869-4433; and Thrifty, tel 5999/461-3089. Foreign driver's licenses are valid and driving is on the right.

Public transportation

Inexpensive public buses cover main routes around the island from Willemstad. Private minibuses offer a more flexible alternative. Taxis are unmetered.

PRACTICAL ADVICE

Emergencies

Police and fire: tel 911. Ambulance: tel 912. St. Elisabeth Hospital, Willemstad, tel 5999/462-4900; emergencies, tel 910.

Telephones

The country code is 5999.

Tourist information

Willemstad: Curaçao Tourist Board, P.O. Box 3266, Pietermaai 19, tel 5999/434-8200, fax 5999/461-5017, e-mail: ctdbcur@ctdb.net, www.curacao-tourism.com.

U.S. office

Miami: Curaçao Tourism Corp., 3361 SW Third Ave., Suite 201, Miami, FL 33145, tel 305/285-0511, fax 305/285-0535, e-mail: northamerica@curacao.com.

SABA

PLANNING YOUR TRIP

Arrival/departure

No direct flights from the United States, but Winair (tel 599/545-4237, www.fly-winair.com) makes the 15-minute hop from Sint Maarten to J.E. Yrausquin Airport several times a day. High-speed ferries from Sint Maarten with Saba-based Dawn II, tel 5999/416-3671, Tue., Thurs., Sat.; and Sint Maarten-based *The Edge*, tel 599/544-2640, Wed.–Sun., between Pelican Marina in Philipsburg and Saba's Fort Bay. Crossings take 75-90 minutes.

Departure tax is US$20 for flights connecting with a same-day international service; or US$5 for flights with a stopover in the Netherlands Antilles.

Festivals & events

April Celebration of the Queen's Birthday (April 30)
July–August Carnival
December Saba Day Festivities (1st weekend Dec.)

GETTING AROUND

Car rental

The island has just one car rental operator: Caja's Car Rental, The Bottom, tel 599/416-2388 or cell 522-7755, fax 599/416-3513.

Public transportation

Taxis are available at the airport or can be booked through hotels.

PRACTICAL ADVICE

Emergencies

Police: tel 599/416-3237. Medical Centre, The Bottom: tel 599/416-3288. Medical emergencies are generally flown to Sint Maarten.

Telephones

The country code is 599.

Tourist information

Windwardside: Saba Tourist Office, P.O. Box 527, tel 599/416-2231, fax 599/416-2350, e-mail: iluvsaba@unspoiledqueen.com, www.sabatourism.com.

SINT EUSTATIUS

PLANNING YOUR TRIP

Arrival/departure

There are no direct flights from the United States, but Winair operates several daily island-hopper services into F. D. Roosevelt Airport, tel 599/318-2887, from Sint Maarten (see p. 345); the flight takes 20 minutes. There are also connections to St. Kitts.

Departure tax is US$20 for flights connecting with a same-day international service; or US$5.65 for journeys including a stopover in the Netherlands Antilles.

Festivals & events

April Celebration of the Queen's Birthday (April 30)
July Carnival
October Antillean Day (Oct. 21)
November Statia/America Day (Nov. 16)

GETTING AROUND

Car rental

Browns, tel 599/318-2266 and Rainbow, tel 599/318-2811 are a couple of the dozen or so local rental operators. Foreign licenses are valid in Statia; driving is on the right.

Public transportation

With no buses on Statia, most visitors tend to walk or cycle. Taxis are available at the airport and can be ordered at hotels.

PRACTICAL ADVICE

Emergencies

Police: tel 111. Ambulance: tel 140. Queen Beatrix Medical Center, tel 599/318-2211. Medical emergencies are generally flown to Sint Maarten.

Telephones

The area code is 599.

Tourist information

Oranjestad: Sint Eustatius Tourism Development Foundation, Fort Oranje, 3 Fort Oranjestraat, tel/fax 599/318-2433, e-mail: euxtour@goldenrock.net

SINT MAARTEN/ST.-MARTIN

PLANNING YOUR TRIP

Arrival/departure

Princess Juliana Airport, tel 599/545-5757, in Sint Maarten is the main island gateway. American Airlines flies direct from New York and Miami and provides connections from other North American cities via Puerto Rico. Continental, Delta, United Airlines, and US Airways all offer services originating in the United States.

The island is a transportation hub for regional carriers Caribbean Star, LIAT, and Winair, providing air links to the Leeward Islands, Saba, Statia, St Barts, Tortola (BVI), and Puerto Rico. Dutch Antilles Express flies to the ABCs; while Air Caraïbes serves the French Antilles with smaller planes departing from St.-Martin's L'Espérance-Grand-Case regional airport.

Departure tax is US$30 for international flights or US$10 for trips within the Netherlands Antilles.

Festivals & events

January Epiphany (Jan. 6, St.-Martin)
February/March Carnival (St.-Martin)
March Heineken Regatta
April Queen's Birthday celebrations (Sint Maarten, April 30), Carnival (Sint Maarten)
June June Fest cultural events
July Bastille Day (St.-Martin, July 14); Schoelcher Day, marked with boat races in Grand Case (St.-Martin, July 21)
November Discovery Day (Nov. 11) unites the islanders to celebrate their dual heritage.

GETTING AROUND

Car rental

Avis, tel 599/545-2847, Budget, tel 599/545-4030, and Hertz, tel 599/545-4541, operate out of Princess Juliana Airport with local offices in St.-Martin. Foreign driver's licenses are valid on the island, and driving is on the right.

Public transportation

Frequent and inexpensive mini-bus services shuttle between Philipsburg and Marigot with connections to Grand Case. Taxis are plentiful, but quite expensive (rates are fixed in US$).

PRACTICAL ADVICE

Emergencies

Sint Maarten Police: tel 111. Fire: tel 120. Ambulance: tel 130. Hospital: tel 599/543-1111.
St.-Martin Police: tel 17. Fire: tel 18. Ambulance: tel 0590/29 29 34.

Telephones

The country code for Sint Maarten is 599, and 590 for St.-Martin. To make a local call on the Dutch side, simply dial the seven-digit local number; on the French side dial 0590 and the six-digit local number. Calls between the Dutch and French sides are international and rated accordingly. To call the French side from the Dutch side, dial 00 590 590 and the six-digit local number; to call the Dutch side from the French side, dial 00 599 and the seven-digit local number. When calling from the U.S., dial 011-590 590 and the number.

Tourist information

Sint Maarten

Philipsburg: W.G. Buncamper Rd. 33, tel 599/542-2337, fax 599/542-2734, www.st-maarten.com. Information kiosk by the Philipsburg pier.

U.S. office

New York: 675 3rd Ave., Suite 1807, New York, NY 10017, tel 212/953-2084 or 800/786-2278, fax 212/953-2145.

St.-Martin

Marigot: Office de Tourisme de St.-Martin, Route de Sandy Ground, 97150 St.-Martin, tel 0590/87 57 21, fax 0590/87 56 43, e-mail: info@st-martin.org, www.st-martin.org.

U.S. office

New York: St.-Martin Tourist Information Office, 675 3rd Ave., Suite 1807, New York, NY 10017, tel 646/227-9440 or 877/956-1234, fax 646/227-9448, e-mail: e-mail: nyoffice@st-martin.org.

LEEWARD ISLANDS

Entry requirements

For all islands in the group, U.S. citizens are required to produce a valid passport, together with a return or ongoing ticket.

National holidays

Holidays common to all islands include New Year's Day (Jan. 1), Good Friday, Easter Monday, Labour Day (1st Mon. in May), Christmas Day, and Boxing Day (Dec. 26).

ANGUILLA

PLANNING YOUR TRIP

Arrival/departure

There are no direct flights from the United States to Anguilla's Wallblake Airport, tel 264/497-5666. American Eagle operates daily services from Puerto Rico (see p. 340), and there are frequent connections from neighboring Sint Maarten/St.-Martin and Antigua.

A frequent (every 30 minutes from 7:30 a.m. to 6:15 p.m.) and inexpensive 20-minute ferry service operates between Blowing Point, Anguilla, and Marigot, the capital of French St.-Martin, tel 264/497-2231.

Departure tax is US$20 at the airport, or US$3 for the ferry crossing to St.-Martin.

Festivals & events

March Moonsplash Music Festival
May Anguilla Day
June Celebration of the Queen's Birthday
August Carnival
November Tranquility Jazz Festival

Anguillans are legendary boat-builders and like to celebrate holidays with regattas. The biggest sailing event of the year is the Anguilla Yachting Regatta in May.

National holidays include Whit Monday and Constitution Day (Aug. 6).

GETTING AROUND

Car rental

Apex/Avis, tel 264/497-2642; Island Car Rentals, tel 264/497-2723; Thrifty, tel 264/497-2656; and Triple K, tel 264/497-5934. Visitors must purchase a temporary license (US$20) in addition to presenting a valid overseas permit. Driving is on the left.

Bicycles

Bike rentals are available through all hotels.

Public transportation

There is no local bus service on Anguilla. Taxis are available at the airport, tel 264/497-5054, and ferry dock, tel 264/497-6089, or arranged through the hotel.

PRACTICAL ADVICE

Emergencies

All emergencies: tel 911. Police: tel 264/497-2333. Princess Alexandra Hospital, Stoney Ground: tel 264/497-2551. Serious medical cases are airlifted to Puerto Rico.

Telephones

The area code is 264.

Tourist information

The Valley: tel 264/497-2759 or 800/553-4939, fax 264/497-2710, e-mail: abtour@anguillanet.com, www.anguilla-vacation.com.

U.S. office

New York: Turnstyle Marketing Inc., 264 Central Ave., White Plains, NY 10606, tel 914/287-2400 or 877/4-ANGUILLA, fax 914/287-2404, e-mail: mwturnstyle@aol.com.

ANTIGUA & BARBUDA

PLANNING YOUR TRIP

Arrival/departure

Several carriers serve Antigua's V. C. Bird International Airport direct from the United States, including American Airlines out of New York and Miami, Continental, and BWIA. Antigua is also the hub for the local airlines Caribbean Star, Caribbean Sun, and LIAT, offering frequent connections to islands throughout the region.

Barbuda is served daily by Carib Aviation, tel 268/462-3147 from Antigua (10 minutes flight time); and the Barbuda Express ferry, tel 268/560-7989, a five-day a week 90-minute power catamaran service.

Departure tax from Antigua is US$20; there is no tax payable for trips between Antigua and Barbuda.

Festivals & events

April Antigua Sailing Week attracts a world-class field for five major races, smaller events and wild partying (for further information www.sailingweek.com).
July Carnival
National holidays include Good Friday, Easter Monday, Labor Day (1st Mon. in May), and Independence Day (Nov. 1).

GETTING AROUND

Car rental

Avis, tel 268/462-2840; Dollar Rent-A-Car, tel 268/462-0362; and Hertz, tel 268/462-4114 are found at Antigua's airport and other locations around the island. Visitors have to purchase a temporary driver's permit (US$20) in addition to presenting a valid overseas license.

On Barbuda there are no rental cars, but contact George Profit Burton, tel 268/460-0103; Eric Burton, tel 268/460-0465; or Nedds Tours, tel 268/460-0059 for taxi tours.

Public transportation

Antigua has an irregular daytime bus service geared to commuters heading into St. John's from around the island. Buses only leave when they are full; fares are inexpensive.

Taxis, bookable from the hotel, are not metered, but government fixed rates apply. Agree on the fee in advance. There is no public transportation on Barbuda.

PRACTICAL ADVICE

Emergencies

Police Headquarters in St. John's: tel 268/462-0125. Holberton Hospital: Queen Elizabeth Hwy., St. John's, tel 268/462-0251. Serious cases are airlifted to Puerto Rico or Miami. Most hotels are served by a 24-hour duty doctor.

Telephones

The area code for Antigua and Barbuda is 268.

Tourist information

St. John's: Antigua and Barbuda Department of Tourism, Nevis St. & Friendly Alley, tel 268/462-0480, fax 268/462-2483, e-mail: deptourism@candw.ag, www.antigua-barbuda.com.

U.S. offices:

New York: 305 E. 47th St., Suite 6A, New York, NY 10017, tel 212/541-4117, fax 212/541-4789, e-mail: info@antigua-barbuda.org.
Miami: 25 S.E. 2nd Ave., Suite 300, Miami, FL 33131, tel 305/381-6762, fax 305/381-7908.

ST. KITTS & NEVIS

PLANNING YOUR TRIP

Arrival/departure

American Airlines offers five direct flights a week from Miami to St. Kitts' Robert L. Bradshaw International Airport and US Airways operates from Philadelphia and Charlotte. There is easy access to both islands via regional gateways including Puerto Rico with American Eagle; Antigua with Caribbean Star and LIAT; and Sint Maarten with Winair. Regular flights also link St. Kitts and Newcastle Airport, Nevis. Ferries run several times a day between island capitals Basseterre and Charlestown.

Departure tax is US$22 from St. Kitts; US$20.50 from Nevis.

Festivals & events

June St. Kitts Music Festival
August Culturama, around Emancipation Day (1st Mon. in Aug. Nevis)
September Heritage Festival on Independence Day (St. Kitts and Nevis, Sept. 19)
December–January National Carnival kicks off on Dec. 26 and lasts into the New Year (St. Kitts).

National holidays include Whit Monday, the Queen's Birthday (2nd Sat. in June), and National Heroes Day (Sept. 16).

GETTING AROUND

Car rental

Car and jeep rentals are available through Avis: St. Kitts, tel 869/465-6507; and local operator TDC Rentals: St. Kitts, tel 869/465-2991; Nevis, tel 869/469-1005. TDC also offers an exchange rental arrangement between St. Kitts and Nevis (minimum three days). Visitors must obtain a temporary driver's permit (US$24) in addition to presenting a valid foreign license. Driving is on the left.

Public transportation

Inexpensive minibus services leave the ferry dock in Basseterre, and from Main Street Charlestown when they are full or the driver is ready. Taxis are readily available and fares are fixed by the government.

PRACTICAL ADVICE

Emergencies

Police: tel 911; or St. Kitts, tel 869/465-2241; Nevis, tel 869/469-5391. For medical problems, hotels can call for a doctor. The Joseph N. France Hospital in Basseterre, tel 869/465-2551, and Alexandra Hospital in Nevis, tel 869/469-5473, treat minor casualties. Serious medical emergencies are sent to Puerto Rico.

Telephones

The area code is 869.

Tourist information

St. Kitts: St. Kitts Tourism Authority, Pelican Mall, Bay Rd., Basseterre, tel 869/465-4040, fax 869/465-8794, www.stkittstourism.com.

Nevis: Nevis Tourism Authority, Main St., Charlestown, tel 869/469-7550, fax 869/469-7551, www.nevisisland.com.

U.S. office/New York: 414 E. 75th St., NY 10021, tel 212/535-1234 or 800/582-6208, fax 212/734-6511.

FRENCH ANTILLES

National Holidays

Holidays common to all islands include New Year's Day (Jan. 1), Shrove Tuesday, Ash Wednesday, Good Friday, Easter Monday, Labor Day (May 1), Victory Day 1945 (May 8), Ascension Day (May), Abolition of Slavery Day (May 22), Whit Monday, Bastille Day (July 14), Feast of the Assumption (Aug. 15), All Saints Day (Nov. 1), All Souls Day (Nov. 2), and Christmas Day.

GUADELOUPE

PLANNING YOUR TRIP

Arrival/departure

Air France operates direct services to Guadeloupe from Miami and Air Canada provides non-stop service from Montreal; while American Eagle flies daily from Puerto Rico (see p. 340). Pôle Caraïbes Airport lies just east of Pointe-à-Pitre, convenient for Gosier and other Grande-Terre coastal resorts. There are also regular services from regional transportation hubs such as Antigua (see p. 346) and Sint Maarten/ St.-Martin (see p. 345) with LIAT and Air Caraïbes, as well as short-hop flights to the islands of the Guadeloupean Archipelago.

Inexpensive daily ferry services link Guadeloupe with Martinique (3 hours 45 minutes), and the islands of the archipelago (see pp. 246–47). Ferries to Dominica and St. Lucia operate several times a week. For schedule information, contact L'Express des Îles, tel 0825/35 90 00, www.express-des-iles.com. Crossings can be rough; travelers might prefer a short plane ride.

Entry requirements

As for mainland France, visitors will need to produce a full valid passport and a return or ongoing ticket. Check visa requirements.

Festivals & events

January Carnival preparations begin early in the New Year and culminate in a giant three-day event running up to Ash Wednesday.

July Creole arts festival (Ste.-Anne)

August The annual Fête des Cuisinières is a gastronomic showcase for female chefs.

GETTING AROUND

Car rental

Avis, tel 0590-21 13 54; Budget, tel 0590-21 13 49; Europcar, tel 0590-21 13 52; and Hertz, tel 0590-21 13 46, are among the rental agencies at the airport and main tourist areas. Scooter rentals are also widely available. Overseas driver's licenses are valid for 20 days in Guadeloupe; driving is on the right.

Public transportation

Public buses serve most destinations around the island and operate from early morning until around 6–7 p.m. There is a useful service along the south coast of Grande-Terre to Pointe-à-Pitre with drop-off and pick-up points near the ferry terminal on La Darse. Carry small change for the fare. To stop the bus, shout "arrêt" or press a buzzer.

Taxi rates are fixed; agree on the price in advance.

PRACTICAL ADVICE

Emergencies

Police: tel 17. Fire: tel 18. Ambulance: tel 15 or SAMU 0590-89 11 00. There are hospitals in all major towns, and duty doctors can be summoned by hotels.

Telephones

The country code is 590. When making a local call in Guadeloupe, simply dial the six-digit local number. When calling from another French Antillean island, dial 0590 and the local number. When calling from the U.S., dial 011-590 590 and the number.

Tourist information

Pointe-à-Pitre: Comité du Tourisme des Îles de Guadeloupe, 5 Square de la Banque, 97110, tel 0590-82 09 30, fax 0590-83 89 22, e-mail: info@lesilesdeguadeloupe.com, www.lesilesdeguadeloupe.com.

U.S. office

New York: Maison de la France, 444 Madison Ave., 16th floor, New York, NY 10022-6903, tel 514/288-1904, fax 212/838-7855, e-mail: info.us@franceguide.com, www.francetourism.com.

ST.-BARTHÉLEMY

PLANNING YOUR TRIP

Arrival/departure

St. Barts' St. Jean Airport can only take small STOL (Short

Take-Off and Landing) aircraft, so the easiest access to St. Barts is from Sint Maarten (see p. 345), which is well served by direct flights from North America, and only a 10-minute hop away. St. Barth Commuter, Air Caraïbes, and Winair offer frequent daily services from Sint Maarten, and there are Winair connections to many other destinations in the Eastern Caribbean (often via Sint Maarten). Air Caraïbes also operates services to Guadeloupe. There are regular flights from St. Thomas and Puerto Rico.

Express ferries make the sea crossing daily from Sint Maarten/St.-Martin. Contact Voyager (St. Martin, tel 0590/17 10 68), or The Edge (Sint Maarten, tel 00 599/544-2640). The 90-minute trip can be quite rough, however fine the weather. Catamaran trips are slower but smoother.

Entry requirements

As for mainland France, visitors will need to produce a full valid passport and a return or ongoing ticket. Check visa requirements.

There is a departure tax payable of €4.50 (US$5.90).

Festivals & events

January Festival de Musique
March–April St. Barths' Bucket (mega-yacht regatta)
April–May Sailing regatta season
April Festival du Cinéma Caraïbe
July Deep Sea Fishing Tournament
November Swedish Marathon
December New Year's Eve Regatta

GETTING AROUND

Car rental

Avis, tel 0590/27 71 43; Budget, tel 0590/27 66 30; and Hertz, tel 0590/27 71 14. Open-top jeeps are popular. Motorbikes and scooters can be rented through Barth'loc, tel 0590/27 52 81, and Rent Some Fun, tel 0590/27 54 83, among others. Foreign driver's licenses are valid; driving is on the right. The gas station at St. Jean is closed Sun., and also Tue. p.m. in low season (Apr.–Nov.); the only other gas station is at Lorient and closes Thurs. p.m., Sat. p.m., and all day Sun.

Public transportation

There is no public bus service on the island. Taxis are available from the airport, and the taxi stand on Quai du Général de Gaulle in Gustavia, tel 0590/27 66 31. There is a flat rate for rides up to five minutes, and it goes up every three minutes thereafter.

PRACTICAL ADVICE

Emergencies

Police: tel 17. Ambulance and fire: tel 18. The Hôpital de Bruyn in Gustavia, tel 0590/27 60 35, can handle most casualties and hotels can help locate the duty doctor. Serious medical emergencies are taken to Sint Maarten or Puerto Rico.

Telephones

The country code is 590. When making a local call or calling from another French Antillean island, dial 0590 and the six-digit number. When calling from the U.S., dial 011-590 590 and the number.

Tourist information

Gustavia: Office du Tourisme, Quai du Général de Gaulle, 97133, tel 0590/27 87 27, fax 0590/27 74 47, www.st-barths.com or www.st-barth-wm.com.

U.S. office

See Guadeloupe, p. 347.

MARTINIQUE

PLANNING YOUR TRIP

Arrival/departure

Air France flies daily direct from Miami to Martinique's Lamentin Airport outside Fort-de-France. There are frequent services with Air France and American Eagle from Puerto Rico, and with Take Airlines from St Lucia, providing connections to a wide variety of US gateways. Local carriers serve other regional transportation hubs such as Antigua (see p. 346), Barbados (see p. 351), and Sint Maarten (see p. 345).

Inexpensive ferry services link Martinique to Guadeloupe (3 hours 45 minutes); to Dominica (1 hour 45 minutes); and St. Lucia (1 hour 20 minutes). For schedule information, contact L'Express des Îles (tel 0596/63 12 12, www.express-des-iles.com), or Brudey Frères (tel 0596/70 08 50, www.brudey-freres.fr). Crossings can be rough, so travelers might prefer a short-hop plane ride.

Entry requirements

As for mainland France, visitors will need to produce a full valid passport and a return or ongoing ticket. Check visa requirements.

No departure tax.

Festivals & events

January Pre-Carnival activities kick off in January and climax on Ash Wednesday.
April Martinique Food Show
July Fort-de-France Cultural Festival
August Round-island yawl (boat) race
December Winter music festival featuring jazz or guitar on alternate years

GETTING AROUND

Car rental

Avis, tel 0596/42 11 00; Budget, tel 0596/42 04 04; Europcar, tel 0596/42 16 88; and Thrifty agents Jumbo Car, tel 0596/42 22 22. Overseas driver's licenses are valid for 20 days and driving is on the right.

Public transportation

Public buses from Fort-de-France operate from early morning until around 7 p.m. They stop at designated bus stops; to get off shout "arrêt." Ferries from Fort-de-France serve local beaches and Ste.-Anne. Taxi rates are fixed; agree on the price in advance.

PRACTICAL ADVICE

Emergencies

Police: tel 17. Fire: tel 18. Medical emergencies and ambulance: tel 15 or SAMU

0596/75 15 75. There are well-equipped hospitals and local clinics. Hotels or the tourist office can assist with locating an English-speaking doctor.

Telephones
The country code is 596. When making a local call or calling from another French Antillean island, dial 0596 and the six-digit number. When calling from the U.S., dial 011-596 596 and the number.

Tourist information
Fort-de-France: Comité Martiniquais du Tourisme, Immeuble Le Beau Pré, Pointe de Jaham, 97233 Schoelcher, tel 0596/61 61 77, fax 0596/61 22 72, www.martiniquetourisme.com.

U.S. offices
See Guadeloupe, p. 347.
e-mail: info@martinique.org, www.martinique.org.

WINDWARD ISLANDS

National holidays
Holidays for the group include New Year's Day, Good Friday, Easter Monday, Whit Monday, Labour Day (1st Mon. in May) May Day, Dominica (May 1), Christmas Day, and Boxing Day (Dec. 26).

DOMINICA

PLANNING YOUR TRIP
Arrival/departure
There are no direct flights to Dominica from the U.S. mainland, but American Eagle has a daily service from Puerto Rico (see p. 340) to Dominica's Melville Hall Airport, in the north of the island (1 hour from Roseau). Local carriers LIAT and Caribbean Sun provide services from regional transportation hubs including Antigua (see p. 346), Barbados (see p. 351), Sint Maarten (see p. 345), and the French Antilles. Many smaller planes use Canefield Airport, just outside Roseau, a convenient option for most hotels.

Dominica can also be reached by scheduled high-speed ferry services from Guadeloupe (1 hour 45 minutes), Martinique (1 hour 30 minutes), and St. Lucia (3 hours 20 minutes); contact L'Express des Îles in Roseau, tel 767/448-2181, www.express-des-iles.com. The crossing can be rough.

Entry requirements
U.S. visitors require a valid passport and a return or ongoing ticket.

Departure tax is US$20.

Festivals & events
February–March Carnival (Mon. & Tues. before Lent)
June–July Domfesta (week-long celebration of island culture)
October-November Creole Music Festival
November Independence Day (Nov. 3);
Other holidays include 1st Mon. in Aug. and Community Day of Service (Nov. 4).

GETTING AROUND
Car rental
Bonus, tel 767/448-2650; Garraway, tel 767/448-2891; Island Car Rentals, tel 767/448-0737; and Valley Rent-A-Car, tel 767/448-3233. Drivers will need a temporary visitor's permit (US$ 12) in addition to their valid overseas license. Driving is on the left.

Public transportation
Irregular but frequent minibus services cover all the major island destinations from Roseau. Taxis are readily available from the airports and Roseau by day, or make an arrangement with your hotel. Reserve a taxi in advance for evening excursions. Government rates apply.

PRACTICAL ADVICE
Emergencies
Police, fire, and emergencies: tel 999. Princess Margaret Hospital in Roseau, tel 767/448-2231, and Portsmouth Hospital, tel 767/445-5237, are the island's main medical facilities. Serious medical emergencies are dispatched to Puerto Rico. Hotels can assist in locating a duty doctor.

Telephones
The area code is 767.

Tourist information
Roseau: Dominica Division of Tourism, NDC, Commonwealth of Dominica, tel 767/448-2045, fax 767/448-5840, e-mail: tourism@discoverdominica.com, www.dominica.dm. There are information offices at the airports.

U.S. office/New York:
Dominica Tourist Office, 110-64 Queens Blvd., P.O. Box 427, Forest Hills, NY 11375, tel 718/261-9615 or 888/645-5637, fax 718/261-0702, e-mail: dominicany@dominica.dm.

GRENADA, CARRIACOU, & PETIT MARTINIQUE

PLANNING YOUR TRIP
Arrival/departure
Grenada's Pointe Salines International Airport receives daily Air Jamaica flights from New York. BWIA flies daily from New York, Miami and Toronto to Trinidad for the short connecting flight to Grenada, and American Eagle offers daily services from Puerto Rico. US Airways flies direct weekly from Philadelphia. Otherwise, regional carriers LIAT and Caribbean Star provide connections from island gateways such as Antigua (see p. 346), Barbados (see p. 351), and St. Lucia (see p. 350).

Lauriston Airport on Carriacou is served by daily island-hopper flights from Grenada with St. Vincent Grenada Air.

Ferry services from Grenada to Carriacou take 3 hours on alternate days; daily express catamaran services with Osprey Shuttle, tel/fax 473/440-8126 cut the trip to 90 minutes, and continue on to Petit Martinique (Mon.–Fri., & Sun.). Petit Martinique can also be reached by water-taxi from Windward, on the northeast coast of Carriacou.

Entry requirements
Visitors will be required to produce a valid passport together with a return or ongoing ticket.

Departure tax from Grenada is US$19; from Lauriston Airport on Carriacou US$4.

Festivals & events

February–March Carnival (Carriacou, held before beginning of Lent); week-long St. Patrick's Day celebration (Sauteurs, Grenada)
May–June Fisherman's Birthday (Feast of St. Peter) in Gouyave (end June)
July–August Carriacou Regatta; Grenada Carnival (St. George's)
December Carriacou Parang Festival

National Holidays include Independence Day (Feb. 7), Corpus Christi (June), Emancipation Day (1st Mon. & Tues. in Aug.), and Thanksgiving Day (Oct. 25).

GETTING AROUND

Car rental

Archie Auto Rentals, tel 473/439-0086; David's Car Rental, tel 473/444-3399; Dollar, tel 473/444-4786; and Avis, tel 473/440-3936, operate in Grenada. For rentals in Carriacou, contact Martin Bullen, tel 473/443-7221, or John Gabriel, tel 473/443-7454. Drivers will require a temporary local driver's permit (US$12) plus a valid overseas license. Driving is on the left.

Public transportation

Private minibuses (dollar buses) cover virtually every corner of Grenada and Carriacou on an unscheduled though frequent basis from early morning until early evening. Visitors can flag them down and be squeezed in by the "put-man" who also collects the money. Rap hard on the roof to get off.

Taxis are available from the airport and main taxi stand on the Carenage in St. George's, by the ferry dock in Hillsborough, or make arrangements with your hotel. Always agree the price in advance.

For inter-island ferry information, see Arrival/Departure.

PRACTICAL ADVICE

Emergencies

Police and fire: tel 911.
Ambulance, St. George's: tel 434, St. Andrews: tel 724, Carriacou: tel 774. St. George's Hospital in Grenada, tel 473/440-2050, can cope with most sicknesses, though serious medical emergencies may be transferred to Puerto Rico. Hotels can contact the duty doctor. There is also a small private hospital facility, St. Augustine's, tel 473/ 440-6173, at Grand Anse, on the south of the island but it doesn't deal with emergencies.

Telephones

The area code for Grenada, Carriacou, and Petit Martinique is 473.

Tourist information

Grenada: Grenada Board of Tourism, P.O. Box 293, St. George's, tel 473/440-2279, fax 473/440-6637, e-mail: gbt@spiceisle.com, www.grenadines.com. There is also an information kiosk at the cruise ship dock on the Carenage in St. George's.
Carriacou: Main St., Hillsborough, tel 473/443-7948, e-mail: carrgbt@spiceisle.com.

U.S. office

Lake Worth: P.O. Box 1668, FL 33460, tel 561/588-8176 or 800/927-9554, fax 561/558-7267, e-mail: cnoel@grenadagrenadines.com

ST. LUCIA

PLANNING YOUR TRIP

Arrival/departure

Hewanorra Airport on the south of the island is St. Lucia's chief gateway for international jet flights, served by direct services from the United States with American Airlines from Miami, Air Jamaica from New York, Delta from Atlanta, and US Airways from Philadelphia and Charlotte. BWIA flies from New York and Miami via Barbados. It is a 90-minute transfer to hotels in the north of the island. George Charles Airport in Castries can only accept smaller planes, including American Eagle's daily services from Puerto Rico, and frequent LIAT and Caribbean Star services from local transportation hubs such as Antigua (see p. 346) and Barbados (see p. 351).

High-speed ferry services link St. Lucia with Martinique (1 hour 20 minutes). For information, contact Cox & Co., Castries, tel 758/456-5000, agents for Express des Iles (www.express-des-iles.com).

Entry requirements

Visitors are required to produce a valid passport and return or onward ticket.

Departure tax is US$25.

Festivals & events

May St. Lucia Jazz Festival (Pigeon Island & Castries)
July Carnival
September–October St. Lucia Billfishing Tournament (all welcome); Jounen Kweyol Entenasyonnal (International Creole Day)
November-December Atlantic Rally for Cruisers (Rodney Bay Marina)

National Holidays include Independence Day (Feb. 22), Corpus Christi (June), Emancipation Day (1st Mon. in Aug.), Thanksgiving Day (Oct. 4), and National Day (Dec. 13).

GETTING AROUND

Car rental

Avis, tel 758/452-2700; Budget, tel 758/452-8673; Cool Breeze Jeep Rentals, tel 758/458-2031; and Hertz agents Sun-Fun Car Rentals, tel 758/ 452-0679. A temporary visitor's permit (US$20) is required plus a valid overseas license. Driving is on the left.

Public transportation

Frequent and inexpensive minibus services run between Castries, Rodney Bay, and the north until about 10 p.m. (later on Fri. for visitors to the Gros Islet jump-up party). Less frequent services to Soufrière and the south depart from Bridge St.

Taxi rates are fixed by the government; always agree on the fare in advance.

PRACTICAL ADVICE
Emergencies
Police, fire, and ambulance: tel 911. St. Lucia's main hospitals are the Victoria Hospital in Castries, tel 758/452-2421, and St. Jude's in Vieux Fort, tel 758/454-6041. All hotels have a resident or on-call doctor.

Telephones
The area code is 758.

Tourist information
Castries: St. Lucia Tourist Board, Sureline Building, Vide Bouteille, P.O. Box 221, Castries, tel 758/452-4094, fax 758/453-1121, e-mail: slutour@candw.lc, www.stlucia.org.

U.S. office
New York: St. Lucia Tourist Board, 800 2nd Ave., 9th Floor, NY 10017, tel 212/697-9360, fax 212/697-4993, e-mail: slumission@aol.com.

ST. VINCENT & THE GRENADINES

PLANNING YOUR TRIP
Arrival/departure
Although there are no direct flights to St. Vincent and the Grenadines from the U.S. mainland, American Eagle and Caribbean Sun operate daily services to St. Vincent and Canouan from Puerto Rico (see p. 340), and there are easy connections from the neighboring islands of Barbados, Grenada, and St. Lucia, as well as Antigua, Martinique and Trinidad. St. Vincent's E.T. Joshua Airport, outside Kingstown, is a transportation hub for the Grenadine islands. These can also be reached by scheduled boat services originating from Kingstown (see p. 288).

Entry requirements
Visitors will be required to produce a valid passport and a return or onward ticket.

Departure tax is US$15.

Festivals & events
March–April Bequia Easter Regatta

June–July Carnival or Vincy Mas (Kingstown, St. Vincent)

December Nine Mornings marks the nine-day run-up to Christmas with arts and crafts exhibits, parades, carol singers, and night-time jump-ups.

National Holidays include St. Vincent and the Grenadines Day (Jan. 22), Caricom Day (July 5), Emancipation Day (Aug. 2), and Independence Day (Oct. 27).

GETTING AROUND
Car rental
On St. Vincent, Avis, tel 784/456-4389, has an office at the airport while Ben's Auto Rental, tel 784/456-2907; David's Auto Clinic, tel 784/456-4026, and Rent and Drive, tel 784/457-5601, will pick up from the airport. A temporary driving permit costs around US$18. You can find rental cars on the Grenadines, too. Driving is on the left.

Public transportation
Private minibuses (known as dollar buses) ply the south coast route between Kingstown and Villa/Calliaqua throughout the day, less frequently in the evening. To hail a bus anywhere along the route, point down at the road; to get off, rap on the roof or shout "driver, stop" over the music. There are services to Layou and the west coast from the waterfront depot in Kingstown. Taxis are available from the airport, downtown Kingstown, and through hotels. Fares are fixed by the government.

PRACTICAL ADVICE
Emergencies
Police, fire, coast guard: tel 911. Police HQ: tel 784/457-1211. Kingstown General Hospital, A&E: tel 784/456-1955; inquiries, tel 784/456-1185. Medical emergencies can be airlifted to Barbados or Puerto Rico. Hotels will contact a duty doctor.

Telephones
The area code for St. Vincent and the Grenadines is 784.

Tourist information
Kingstown: St. Vincent and the Grenadines Ministry of Tourism, Cruise Ship Terminal, tel 784/457-1502, fax 784/451-2425, e-mail: tourism@caribsurf.com, www.svgtourism.com.

U.S. office
New York: 801 2nd Ave., 21st Floor, New York, NY 10017, tel 212/687-4981 or 800/729-1726, fax 212/949-5946, e-mail: svgtony@aol.com.

BARBADOS

PLANNING YOUR TRIP
Arrival/departure
Barbados has good air connections with North America. American Airlines and BWIA both fly direct from New York and Miami to Grantley Adams International Airport; American also provides daily services from Puerto Rico. US Airways has flights from New York and Philadelphia; Air Jamaica has a direct flight from New York, and connecting services from their Jamaican hub at Montego Bay. LIAT, Caribbean Star, and other local airlines provide a network of inter-Caribbean links with the Leeward and Windward Islands, the French Antilles, Sint Maarten, and Trinidad and Tobago.

Entry requirements
U.S. visitors require a valid passport or proof of citizenship and photo ID, plus a return or ongoing ticket.

Departure tax is US$12.50.

Festivals & events
January Barbados Jazz Festival

March Holders Season, outdoor music theater and sports events on the grounds of Holder Plantation House

July–August Crop Over Festival, the Bajan Carnival

National Holidays include New Year's Day, Good Friday, Easter Monday, Labor Day (May 1), Whit Monday, Emancipation Day (July 31), U.N. Day (Oct. 6), Christmas Day, and Boxing Day (Dec. 26).

GETTING AROUND
Car rental
Local operators including Coconut Car Rentals, tel 246/437-0297; Courtesy Rent-A-Car, tel 246/431-4160; Drive-a-Matic, tel 246/422-3000; Stoutes Car Rental, tel 246/416-4456; and Sunny Isle/Sixt Rent A Car, tel 246/419-7498, Top Class can arrange airport and hotel pickup, and drop-off. In addition to a valid overseas license, drivers must purchase a temporary visitor's driving license (US$5). Driving is on the left.

Public transportation
Regular and inexpensive public bus and minibuses serve the coastal regions and Bridgetown from early morning until around midnight. Taxis are not metered, so agree on a price in advance.

PRACTICAL ADVICE
Emergencies
Police: tel 211. Fire: tel 311. Ambulance: tel 511. Queen Elizabeth Hospital, Bridgetown North: tel 246/436-6450. Hotels can contact a duty doctor.

Telephones
The area code is 246.

Tourist information
Bridgetown: Barbados Tourism Authority, P.O. Box 242, Harbour Rd., tel 246/467-3600, fax 246/426-4080, e-mail: btainfo@visitbarbados.org, www.barbados.org.

There are information kiosks at the airport and also at the cruise ship berth.

U.S. office
New York: Barbados Tourism Authority, 800 2nd Ave., New York, NY 10017, tel 212/986-6516 or 800/221-9831, fax 212/573-9850, e-mail: btany@visitbarbados.org.

TRINIDAD & TOBAGO

PLANNING YOUR TRIP
Arrival/departure
There are direct flights on American Airlines from Miami, and BWIA from Miami and New York to Trinidad's Piarco Airport, 30 miles east of Port of Spain. BWIA and LIAT also offer connections from Barbados, Grenada, and St. Lucia. BWIA flies direct to Crown Point Airport in Tobago from Washington, DC and American Eagle has a daily service from Puerto Rico, but most visitors fly to Trinidad and then hop to Tobago on Tobago Express (Tel 868/631-8015) air services (25 minutes), which operate up to eight times a day in both directions.

There is also a very inexpensive but slow (5 hours) ferry service between Port of Spain and Scarborough.

Departure tax is TT $100 (US$16), which must be paid in local currency.

Festivals & events
January–March Preparations for the famous Trinidad Carnival
March Phagwa (Hindu New Year)
June Muslim Hosay, a three-day event tied to the Islamic calendar
July Tobago Heritage Festival
August Steelband Week (Trinidad)
September Tobago Festival
October–November Divali (Hindu Festival of Light)

National Holidays include New Year's Day, Good Friday, Easter Monday, Labour Day (June 19), Emancipation Day (Aug. 1), Independence Day (Aug. 31), Christmas Day, and Boxing Day (Dec. 26).

GETTING AROUND
Car rental
Thrifty, tel 868/669-0602; local operators Auto Rentals, tel 868/675-7368, fax 868/675-2258, e-mail: morvant@autorentalstt.com; Econo-Car, tel/fax 868/622-8074, e-mail: econocar@trinidad.net. All three companies also have offices on Tobago: Thrifty, tel 868/639-8507; Auto Rentals, tel 868/639-0644.

U.S. and Canadian driver's licenses are valid on the islands. Driving is on the left. Gas stations are sparse, so fill up before setting off.

Public transportation
Inexpensive public buses cover most destinations on Trinidad, tel 868/624-9839, from the main depot at South Quay in Port of Spain. Tickets have to be purchased in advance.

Private minibuses, known as maxi-taxis, and shared taxis are a faster. The maxis are color coded by destination: yellow stripes for Port of Spain area; red for the east; green for the south. Taxis are readily available from the airport (fixed fares to Port of Spain and other popular destinations).

Tobago has public and private bus systems. Public buses depart from Gardenside Road, Scarborough, for Crown Point and other destinations. Maxi taxis (minibuses with a blue stripe) are often a better option and can be flagged down along any roadside.

Taxis wait at the airport and hover around some of the busier hotels. There are fixed rates from the airport to hotels.

PRACTICAL ADVICE
Emergencies
Police: tel 999. Fire: tel 990. Port of Spain General Hospital: tel 868/623-2951; ambulance, tel 868/624-4343. In Tobago, minor casualties are handled by Scarborough Hospital, tel 868/639-2551; ambulance, tel 868/639-4444. Emergencies may be airlifted to Trinidad.

Telephones
The area code for Trinidad and Tobago is 868.

Tourist information
Port of Spain: Trinidad and Tobago Tourism Development Company, Level 1, Maritime Centre, 29 10th Ave., Barataria, tel 868/675-7034, fax 868/624-8124, e-mail: info@tdc.co.tt.

U.S. office
Fort Lauderdale: Tourism Solutions, 2400 E Commercial Blvd., Suite 412, Fort Lauderdale FL 33308, tel 954/776-9595, fax 954/776-9581.

HOTELS & RESTAURANTS

Accommodations in the Caribbean are generally very expensive, although cheaper options are available. Prices drop dramatically in low season, sometimes by almost 50 percent, but you will be taking more chances with the weather. All-inclusive resorts can offer good value for money, although it is very easy to stay within the resort and not take the opportunity to explore the islands.

The standard of food is high, and there is a huge variety of styles, from street vendors selling jerk chicken to top-class French cuisine. Restaurants are run more informally here than elsewhere, so seating arrangements and closing times are flexible. Call ahead to check.

PRICES

HOTELS

An indication of the cost of a double room without breakfast is given by **$** signs.

$$$$$	Over $400
$$$$	$300–$400
$$$	$200–$300
$$	$100–$200
$	Under $100

RESTAURANTS

An indication of the cost of a three-course dinner without drinks is given by $ signs.

$$$$$	Over $80
$$$$	$50–$80
$$$	$35–$50
$$	$20–$35
$	Under $20

JAMAICA

KINGSTON

SOMETHING SPECIAL

STRAWBERRY HILL

Perched 3,000 feet (900 m) above Kingston in the Blue Mountains with fabulous views over the city, Strawberry Hill is an award-winning property owned by Island Records magnate Chris Blackwell. All villas have private verandas, kitchens, hand-crafted plantation-style furniture, four-poster mahogany beds with mosquito nets, and thick-louvered windows. The hotel also features a well-equipped Aveda spa.

$$$$$
IRISH TOWN
TEL 876/944-8400 or 800/OUTPOST
FAX 876/944-8408
www.islandoutpost.com
12 villas
All major cards

HILTON KINGSTON
$$$-$$$$
77 KNUTSFORD BOULEVARD
TEL 876/926-5430
FAX 876/929-7439
www.hilton.com

Centrally located in New Kingston, this landmark hotel is set on over 7 acres (2.8 ha) of tropical gardens and has an Olympic-size pool, health club & tennis courts, business center, gaming room, and a range of bars and restaurants.

303, 13 suites
All major cards

HOTEL FOUR SEASONS
$$-$$$
18 RUTHVEN RD.
TEL 876/926-8805
FAX 876/929-5964

Within walking distance of the uptown business/entertainment areas, the hotel has a section that was converted from an Edwardian house, and a new annex that surrounds one of Kingston's best hotel pools. The hotel has had the same hospitable management for the last 30 years.

76
All major cards

STRAWBERRY HILL
$$$$
IRISH TOWN
TEL 876/944-8400

High up in the Blue Mountains, the hotel's excellent restaurant specializes in "new Jamaican cuisine" with dishes such as dasheen and sweet potato gnocchi, yellowtail snapper with lemon butter sauce, and mouth-watering desserts. Salads, soups, and pasta are popular lunchtime choices, and the hotel is known for its Jamaican brunch.

All major cards

NORMA'S ON THE TERRACE
$$$
DEVON HOUSE
TEL 876/968-5488

One of Kingston's top restaurants, with considerable attention to detail in the sophisticated setting and creative menu—using mostly Jamaican ingredients, but with an international flavor. Excellent desserts.

All major cards

RED BONES BLUES CAFÉ
$$$
21 BRAEMER AVENUE
TEL 876/978-6091
www.redbonesbluescafe.com

Former Spanish colonial residence tastefully converted into a restaurant and live music venue, with an outdoor terrace and courtyard. Imaginative cuisine with a contemporary flavor, accompanied by international blues and jazz.

All major cards

THE GROG SHOPPE
$$
DEVON HOUSE
TEL 876/960-9730

The bar is housed in the former stables of Devon House and has a pleasant, shady courtyard with a light lunchtime menu, which includes soups, salads, quiche, and sandwiches.

Closed Sun. All major cards

MANDEVILLE

MANDEVILLE HOTEL
$-$$
4 HOTEL ST.
TEL 876/962-2138
FAX 876/962-0700
A venerable institution, tucked away on a quiet street off Mandeville's main square. The hotel has been in operation since the 19th century.
60 All major cards

MONTEGO BAY

ROUND HILL HOTEL & VILLAS
$$$$$
P.O. BOX 64, MONTEGO BAY
TEL 876/956-7050 or 800/972-2159
FAX 876/956-7505
www.roundhilljamaica.com
One of Jamaica's finest resorts—if not the Caribbean's—perched on a promontory 10 miles (16 km) west of Mo'Bay. The setting was once part of a sugar plantation, Round Hill Estate. Opened in 1953 as a hide-away for celebrities, the villas are privately owned—displaying personal touches; all have kitchens, and housekeepers to prepare your breakfast, and many have pools. The service is impeccable.
110 plus 27 villas All major cards

HALF MOON GOLF, TENNIS & BEACH CLUB
$$$$-$$$$$
TEL 876/953-2211 or 800/648-6951
FAX 876/953-2731
www.halfmoon-resort.com
Seven miles (12 km) east of Mo'Bay, the colonial-style resort is set on over 400 acres (162 ha). There are 11 bars and restaurants, an 18-hole Robert Trent Jones-designed golf course, 13 tennis courts, and almost every other type of recreational activity imaginable, including horseback riding, and a full range of water sports.
421 All major cards

SUGAR MILL AT HALF MOON GOLF CLUB
$$$
TEL 876/953-2314
Elegant terrace dining in the lee of the waterwheel of the namesake old sugar mill with views across the rolling golf course. Imaginative cuisine with a Caribbean flair shares the menu with classic seafood dishes and steaks. Good wine list.
All major cards

MARGARITAVILLE
$$
GLOUCESTER AVE.
TEL 876/952-4777
Wild and wacky bar with big-screen television, a 110-foot (33-m) waterslide into the ocean, a wide range of cocktails, and American and Jamaican food. Part of the same establishment is the Marguerites Restaurant next door, which has a pleasant ambience and fine sea views and specializes in seafood, pasta, and steaks.
All major cards

NEGRIL

SOMETHING SPECIAL

THE CAVES
Set above the honeycomb cliffs of Negril's West End, this beautiful property features hand-crafted thatched and wood cottages nestled in tropical gardens. A series of steps lead down to sundecks and hidden grottoes at sea level. All rooms have CD players and king- or queen-size beds, and there's an Aveda spa treatment center.
$$$$$
LIGHTHOUSE RD., WEST END
TEL 876/957-0270 or 800/OUTPOST
FAX 876/957-4930
www.islandoutpost.com
12 cottages All major cards

SUNSET AT THE PALMS
$$$-$$$$$
NORMAN MANLEY BLVD.
TEL 876/957-5350
FAX 876/957-5381
www.sunsetatthepalms.com
Attractive all-inclusive resort with impressive eco-friendly credentials. Natural wood cabins on stilts scattered among 10 acres (4 ha) of palm trees and tropical vegetation. Just a few minutes' walk away from Bloody Bay.
86, 3 suites All major cards

TENSING PEN
$$-$$$
P.O. BOX 3013
LIGHTHOUSE RD.
TEL 876/957-0387
FAX 876/957-0161
www.tensingpen.com
A collection of stylish, individually-designed bamboo and wood cottages set in lovely cliff-top gardens. A superb retreat.
All major cards

ROCKHOUSE HOTEL
$$
LIGHTHOUSE RD.
TEL 876/957-4373
FAX 876/957-0557
www.rockhousehotel.com
The resort's thatched-roof, octagonal beehive huts overlook Pristine Cove on the West End's foreshore. Connected by wooden walkways, the huts have four-poster beds and ceiling fans. There is a stunning pool on the shore.
28 rooms

LE VENDÔME
$$$$
CHARELA INN, NEGRIL BEACH
TEL 876/957-4648
Spicy Jamaican cuisine with a French twist, a choice of either the à la carte menu or a five-course table d'hôte.

Good selection of imported French wines. Folklore shows Thursday and Saturday.
Closed L daily All major cards

NORMA'S
$$-$$$
SEA SPLASH HOTEL, NORMAN MANLEY BLVD.
TEL 876/957-4041
Don't let the modest setting fool you, leading Jamaican chef Norma Shirley cooks up a storm delivering an often surprising and always delicious take on traditional local fare.
All major cards

RICK'S CAFÉ
$$
WEST END RD.
TEL 876/957-4335
A Negril institution, swamped at dusk by hundreds of sunset-watchers crowding the bar, but the terrace restaurant is also very popular. Specialties include seafood pasta dishes, broiled lobster, and enticing desserts. The fresh fruit daiquiris are also winners.
All major cards

SWEET SPICE
$
WHITE HALL RD.
TEL 876/957-4621
Honest local cooking all day long, with specialties that include curried chicken, and fresh-caught fish.
All major cards

OCHO RIOS

SOMETHING SPECIAL

JAMAICA INN
Undoubtedly one of Jamaica's top properties, the hotel exudes a sense of civilized elegance. Its rooms are impeccably furnished, each with a private balcony overlooking the sea complete. The hotel has one of the best beaches in Ocho Rios, with excellent swimming in its sheltered cove.

$$$$$
NORTH COAST HWY.,
TEL 876/974-2514 or 877/470-6975
FAX 876/974-2449
www.jamaicainn.com
49 rooms, 4 suites
All major cards

HIBISCUS LODGE
$$-$$$
87 MAIN STREET
TEL 876/974-2676
FAX 876/974-1874
Small, friendly hotel set in pretty gardens on the cliff-side with pool and tennis courts. Pleasant rooms.
26 rooms
All major cards

ALMOND TREE
$$$
HIBISCUS LODGE HOTEL
TEL 876/974-2813
Popular restaurant with an extensive à la carte menu featuring Jamaican specialties as well as seafood and steaks. At night dinner is served by candlelight on a terrace overlooking the sea.
All major cards

EVITA'S
$–$$
EDEN BOWER RD.
TEL 876/974-2333
Set on the hillside above town, this cheerful Italian-owned restaurant serves authentic homemade pasta (albeit with a Jamaican twist), salads, soups, and a wide range of desserts in an elegant setting overlooking the bay.
All major cards

PORT ANTONIO

TRIDENT VILLAS & HOTEL
$$$$
ANCHOVY
TEL 876/993-2602
FAX 876/993-2590
Long-established hotel spread across 14 acres (6 ha) of the shoreline, with rooms and villas furnished in antique style.
27 rooms/villas/suites
All major cards

MOCKING BIRD HILL
$$$-$$$$
SAN SAN
TEL 876/993-7267
FAX 876/993-7133
www.hotelmockingbirdhill.com
Charming and comfortable little eco-resort in the hills above San San. The light, airy rooms feature bamboo furniture, ocean-view balconies, and works by the artist-owner.
10 rooms
All major cards

JAMAICA PALACE
$$$
P.O. BOX 277
TEL 876/993-7720
FAX 876/993-7759
www.jamaicapalace.com
Lavish, château-style hotel with a beach and watersports set on 5 acres (2 ha) of grounds in the foothills of the Blue Mountains. Well-equipped rooms, business center.
65 rooms
All major cards

BLUE LAGOON
$–$$
FAIRY HILL
TEL 876/993-8491
This famous waterfront bar has a spectacular setting on the Blue Lagoon itself and serves top-quality jerk chicken, pork, and fish, as well as crayfish and pizzas. A beautiful spot for either lunch or dinner. Live music weekends.
All major cards

SOUTH COAST

JAKE'S
$$
TREASURE BEACH, CALABASH BAY, ST. ELIZABETH
TEL 876/965-0635
FAX 876/965-0552
www.islandoutpost.com
Superb collection of cottages designed in an mix of Jamaican, Mexican, and Catalan styles. Simplicity is the key: Cooled by sea breezes and

ceiling fans, the cottages have private outdoor showers, no phones or television (CD players are provided).
14 cottages All major cards

JAKE'S
$
TREASURE BEACH
CALABASH BAY, ST. ELIZABETH
TEL 876/965-0635
Well-prepared and reasonably priced dishes including local staples such as Escovitch fish, rice 'n' peas, and saltfish 'n' ackee.
All major cards

CAYMAN ISLANDS

CAYMAN BRAC

BRAC REEF RESORT
$$
WEST END
TEL 345/948-1323 or 800/594-0843
FAX 345/948-1207
www.bracreef.com
Relaxing and friendly property on the white sand shore. All rooms feature TV, fans, and balcony or patio. The hotel has a good beach and a full service on-site dive shop.
40
All major cards

LA ESPERANZA
$-$$
STAKE BAY
TEL 345/948-0591
FAX 345/948-0525
www.laesperanza.net
Small, friendly self-catering option: Four two-bedroom apartments and two three-bedroom houses, plus restaurant, bar, and oceanview terrace. Fishing and snorkeling by arrangement.
11 All major cards

WALTON'S MANGO MANOR
$
STAKE BAY
TEL 345/948-2551
FAX 345/948-0518
www.waltonsmangomanor.com
Quaint bed-and-breakfast in an old house with beach access, and fruit trees and parrots in the garden. Five spotlessly clean rooms and a two-bed villa ($$).
6
All major cards

GRAND CAYMAN

GRAND CAYMAN MARRIOTT BEACH RESORT
$$$$-$$$$$
WEST BAY ROAD, SEVEN MILE BEACH
TEL 345/949-0088 or 800/228-9290
FAX 345/949-0288
www.marriottgrandcayman.com
Deluxe oceanfront resort with a full range of facilities (including diving and water sports). The beach, however, is very popular and can get crowded.
309 rooms, 4 suites
All major cards

SOMETHING SPECIAL

RITZ-CARLTON GRAND CAYMAN

This fabulous beachfront behemoth has set a new gold standard for luxury in the region. Facilities include the Caribbean's first La Prairie Spa, a Nick Bollettieri tennis school, Greg Norman-designed golf course, gourmet dining and so much more.
$$$-$$$$$
SEVEN MILE BEACH
TEL 345/815-6851
FAX 345/815-6855
www.ritzcarlton.com
365
All major cards

WESTIN CASUARINA RESORT
$$$-$$$$
WEST BAY ROAD, SEVEN MILE BEACH
TEL 345/945-3800 or 800/WESTIN-1
FAX 345/945-3804
www.westincasurina.net
One of the smarter resorts along Seven Mile Beach, with rooms equipped with TV, minibar, and marble bathroom. Round-the-clock room service. Two swimming pools, swim-up pool bar, and spa.
343
All major cards

COLBALT COAST
$$$
SEAFAN DRIVE, P.O. BOX 159H
TEL 345/946-5656 or 888/946-5656
FAX 345/946-5657
www.cobaltcoast.com
Designed in the style of a Caribbean Great House, this comfortable and welcoming hotel is well away from the bustle of Seven Mile Beach and has 120 ft (37 m) jetty with access to great shore diving.
18
All major cards

THE REEF RESORT
$$-$$$
EAST END, P.O. BOX 30865 SMB
TEL 345/947-3100 or 888/232-0541
FAX 345/947-3191
www.thereef.com.ky

PRICES

HOTELS
An indication of the cost of a double room without breakfast is given by $ signs.

$$$$$	Over $400
$$$$	$300–$400
$$$	$200–$300
$$	$100–$200
$	Under $100

RESTAURANTS
An indication of the cost of a three-course dinner without drinks is given by $ signs.

$$$$$	Over $80
$$$$	$50–$80
$$$	$35–$50
$$	$20–$35
$	Under $20

Good value beachfront resort, 20 miles from George Town at the quieter east end of the island. Generous condo-sized suites ideal for families. Close to first-rate diving and snorkeling.
110 All major cards

SUNSET HOUSE
$$
S. CHURCH ST., GEORGE TOWN
TEL 345/949-7111 or 800/854-4767
FAX 345/949-7101
www.sunsethouse.com
A popular budget choice for dedicated divers, Sunset has a fully equipped dive school, underwater photo school, and good shore diving. Deluxe rooms have ocean views.
57 All major cards

TURTLE NEST INN
$$
BODDEN TOWN
TEL 345/947-8665
FAX 345/947-6379
www.turtlenestinn.com
Spacious and attractive one-bedroom apartments in a genuinely friendly and intimate seaside inn 10 miles from George Town. Patios/verandas with barbecues; good snorkeling off a quiet sandy beach.
7 All major cards

LIGHTHOUSE RESTAURANT
$$$
BREAKERS
TEL 345/947-2047
A Cayman landmark for the last 30 years, this never was a real lighthouse. The very popular restaurant has a terrace overlooking the seashore on the south side of the island. Specialties include seafood salads, pasta, fish, and mixed seafood grills. Excellent, if a bit high-priced.
All major cards

CRACKED CONCH BY THE SEA
$$$
WEST BAY
TEL 345/945-5217
A long-standing institution, the Cracked Conch specializes in local cuisine (including conch steak, fritters, and chowder), as well as grills, pasta, and chicken dishes. Very popular for its Sunday Caribbean brunch. Pleasant bar overlooking the ironshore.
All major cards

RISTORANTE PAPPAGALLO
$$$
CONCH POINT RD.
TEL 345/949-1119
Atmospheric restaurant housed in a large thatched building overlooking a natural lagoon. One of Grand Cayman's top restaurants, it specializes in northern Italian cuisine and seafood.
Closed L daily All major cards

LITTLE CAYMAN

PIRATES POINT RESORT
$$$
PRESTON BAY
TEL 345/948-1010
FAX 345/948-1011
www.piratespointresort.com
One of the island's older resorts, with simple but charming bungalows set on a small beach among palms and seagrapes. The resort has a reputation for gourmet cooking. Two scheduled boat dives daily.
10 All major cards

LITTLE CAYMAN BEACH RESORT
$$
BLOSSOM VILLAGE
TEL 345/948-1033 or 800/327-3835
www.littlecayman.com
Modern resort with good facilities, set out around a small pool. All rooms have color TVs, balconies, and ceiling fans. Fully equipped dive center.
40 All major cards

SOUTHERN CROSS CLUB
$$
SOUTH HOLE SOUND
TEL 345/948-1099 or 800/899-2582
FAX 345/948-1098
www.southerncrossclub.com
Chalets are spaced out across a white sandy beach around a central dining/bar area. Small pool and sundeck. Fully equipped dive center.
11 chalets All major cards

HUNGRY IGUANA
$$
SOUTH HOLE SOUND
TEL 345/948-0007
Next door to the airport at Paradise Villas, the restaurant is a popular meeting place with ocean views. Local and international cuisine.
All major cards

TURKS & CAICOS

GRAND TURK

ISLAND HOUSE
$$-$$$
COCKBURN TOWN
TEL 649/946-1519
FAX 649/946-2646
E-MAIL ishouse@tciway.tc
www.islandhouse-tci.com
A few minutes outside of town, overlooking North Creek, this newly refurbished complex features spacious and well-equipped suites.
8 All major cards

OSPREY BEACH HOTEL
$$
DUKE ST., COCKBURN TOWN
TEL 649/946-2666
FAX 649/946-2817
www.ospreybeachhotel.com

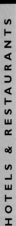

Attractive beachfront rooms/suites with cool, crisp décor and patio/balcony; some four-posters (atrium rooms face inner courtyard). Bar, restaurant, scuba packages.
27 rooms · All major cards

SALT RAKER INN
$-$$
DUKE ST., COCKBURN TOWN
TEL 649/946-2260
FAX 649/946-2817
E-MAIL sraker@tciway.tc
Dating from the 1840s, this charming old inn (once a Bermudian shipwright's home) has a hospitable atmosphere and lovely shady garden. The best rooms are those on the first floor, with balconies overlooking the sea.
13 · All major cards

MICHAEL'S ATRIUM
$$
OSPREY BEACH HOTEL
DUKE ST., COCKBURN TOWN
TEL 649/946-2666
Tapas menu, local and Jamaican specialties, but the real key to Michael's success is the twice-weekly barbecue nights (Wed. and Sun.). Great atmosphere, live music, and the grills laden with delicious ribs, lobster, the catch of the day, and more.
MC, V

THE SECRET GARDEN
$$
SALT RAKER INN
DUKE ST., COCKBURN TOWN
TEL 649/946-2260
Tucked away in a leafy courtyard at the back of the hotel, this pleasant restaurant is good value. There is a popular weekly barbecue and sing-along.
All major cards

NORTH CAICOS

OCEAN BEACH HOTEL & CONDOMINIUMS
$$
WHITBY
TEL 649/946-7113 or 800/710-5204
FAX 649/946-7386
E-MAIL oceanbeachhotel@aol.com
www.turksandcaicos.tc/oceanbeach
One- and two-bed ocean view suites with kitchens and living areas decorated in island prints. Families welcome; bike and kayak rentals; bar and restaurant.
10 suites · All major cards

PELICAN BEACH HOTEL
$$
WHITBY
TEL 649/946-7112
FAX 649/946-7139
E-MAIL pelicanbeach@tciway.tc
www.tcimau.tc/pelicanbeach/
This property was the first locally owned hotel on the island and has a friendly, laid-back atmosphere. Rooms are showing their age but charming nonetheless.
16 · All major cards

MIDDLE CAICOS

BLUE HORIZON RESORT
$$–$$$
CONCH BAR
TEL 649/946-6141
FAX 649/946-6139
E-MAIL bhresort@tciway.tc
www.bhresort.com
Beachfront cottages and villas sporting bright blue tin roofs. Kitchens, screened porches, bicycles available.
5 · All major cards

PROVIDENCIALES

GRACE BAY CLUB AND VILLAS
$$$$
GRACE BAY ROAD
TEL 649/946-5050 or 800/946-5757
FAX 649/946-5758
E-MAIL info@gracebayclub.com
www.gracebayclub.com
Intimate, all suites hotel with excellent resort facilities featuring stylishly equipped ocean-facing accommodations with kitchens and terraces (no children under 12 in hotel). Families can opt for the stunning new villa complex equipped with health club, spa and kids' club.
21 suites · All major cards

OCEAN CLUB
$$$
GRACE BAY RD.
TEL 649/946-5880 or 800/457-8787
FAX 649/946-5845
www.oceanclubresorts.com
Well-designed and efficiently managed condominium complex on Grace Bay. The fully equipped and tastefully furnished studios and suites are set in a lush garden with two small pools. Excellent restaurant (see Gecko Grille p. 359).
191 · All major cards

COMFORT SUITES
$$
TEL 649/946-8888 or 888-678-DIVE
FAX 649/946-5444
E-MAIL comfort@tciway.tc
www.comfortsuitestci.com
Comfortable, affordable, and conveniently located close to the beach, plus all the amenities of the Comfort Suites chain.
108 · All major cards

TURTLE COVE INN
$$
GRACE BAY RD., TURTLE COVE
TEL 649/946-4203 or 800/887-0477
FAX 649/946-4141
E-MAIL info@turtlecoveinn.com
www.turtlecoveinn.com
Conveniently located on Turtle Cove, within walking distance of several restaurants, shops, and dive facilities. Small pool, lively poolside grill and bar, gourmet restaurant. Comfortable and good value.
30 · All major cards

SOMETHING SPECIAL

ANACAONA

A-serious contender for the island's finest dining experience, this gourmet restaurant has a romantic setting on the beachfront beneath a circular thatched roof. The Caribbean/ Mediterranean-inspired cuisine is light and assured and features fresh island seafood. Dress code elegant, no children under 12. Live music some evenings.
$$$$
GRACE BAY CLUB
TEL 649/946-5050
All major cards

GECKO GRILLE

$$$-$$$$
OCEAN CLUB, GRACE BAY
TEL 649/946-5885
Well-established restaurant with a reputation for innovative cuisine. Specialties include "ocean escargot" (tender young conch from the island's farm, in a garlicky herb butter), and blackened wahoo salad. Attractive courtyard; live music.
Closed L & Mon. All major cards

AQUA BAR & TERRACE

$$-$$$
TURTLE COVE INN, TURTLE COVE
TEL 649/946-4763
On the waterfront at Turtle Cove, this popular meeting spot serves breakfast from 7a.m., a wide range of sandwiches, wraps, soups and salads throughout the day, and a variety of evening meals that include sushi nights, seafood specials, burgers, and home-made desserts.
All major cards

GILLEY'S AT LEEWARD

$$
LEEWARD MARINA
TEL 649/946-5094
Overlooking the Leeward Channel, Gilley's is well known for its fresh local seafood and extensive wine list. Good soups and salads at lunchtime.
All major cards

BUGALOO'S CONCH SHACK

$-$$
BLUE HILLS
NO PHONE
There's probably no better place to go native and sample the best fresh conch in the islands. Conch every which way from spiced to salad via cracked and fritters, plus the catch of the day and chilled rum punch in an eye-catching beachside shack.
Closed D No credit cards

DOMINICAN REPUBLIC

CABARETE

NATURA CABINS

$$
PLAYA PERLA MARINA
TEL/FAX 809/571-1507
www.naturacabana.com
Eco-sensitive, upscale Robinson Crusoe thatched roof cabanas and rustic stone bungalows shaded by palms and almond trees on the beachfront just outside Cabarete. Loll about in a hammock. Take a yoga class, relax with a spa therapy. Family-run and kid-friendly; healthy eating.
10 MC, V

WINDSURF APARTMENT HOTEL

$$
TEL 809/571-0718
FAX 809/571-0710
www.surfcabarete.com
A useful budget option in this busy international resort area. Spic-and-span apartments (some with air conditioning) in a modern complex with on-site restaurant.
60
All major cards

CENTRAL HIGHLANDS

RANCHO BAIGUATE

$$
JARABACOA
TEL 809/574-4940
FAX 809/574-6890
www.ranchobaiguate.com
The country's only dedicated adventure sports center, set on extensive grounds bordered by the Baiguate and Jimenoa Rivers just outside Jarabacoa. Activities include trekking, mountain biking, quad-biking, canyoning, paragliding, rafting, plus expeditions to Pico Duarte. The center has a large pool, restaurant, and bar. Accommodations are clean and simple, and will appeal to those seeking peace and quiet after a full day's activities in the mountains.
27
All major cards

SANTO DOMINGO

RENAISSANCE JARAGUA HOTEL & CASINO

$$$-$$$$$
367 AVE. GEORGE WASHINGTON
TEL 809/221-2222
FAX 809/221-8271
www.renaissancehotels.com
On the Malecón, this well-managed hotel has a gym, tennis facilities, a free-form swimming pool, meetings facilities, and four restaurants.
300
All major cards

SOFITEL NICOLAS OVANDO

$$$-$$$$$
CALLE LAS DAMAS
TEL 809/685-9955
FAX 809/686-6590
www.sofitel.com
A luxurious landmark hotel carved out of the historic 16th-century residence of the First Governor of the Americas in the heart of the Zona Colonial. The elegant conversion is a chic modern take on colonial style with

high ceilings, exposed stonework, and spacious bedrooms featuring minimalist four-posters and rattan furniture. Fine dining; cigar club. Sofitel also operates a similarly refined boutique hotel, the **Francés Santo Domingo** *(Tel 809/685-9331)*, in a former convent nearby.
107 All major cards

BARCELÓ GRAN HOTEL LINA
$$-$$$
AVES. MAXIMO GOMEZ & 27 DE FEBRERO
TEL 809/563-5000
FAX 809/686-5521
www.barcelolina.com
Very comfortable five-star hotel with well-equipped rooms and efficient service. It has a great swimming pool, and there's also a casino.
217 All major cards

VESUVIO TIRADENTES
$$$$
AV. TIRADENTES 17
TEL 809/562-6060
Considered to be one of the city's top restaurants, the Vesuvio specializes in gourmet international and Caribbean dishes, and homemade pasta.
All major cards

CANTABRICO
$$$
54 AVE. INDEPENDENCIA
TEL 809/687-5101
Formal restaurant with a wood-panel dining room well-known for its fish and seafood as well as Segovian suckling pig and other meat dishes.
All major cards

MESON DE LA CAVA
$$$
1 AVE. MIRADOR DEL SUR
TEL 809/533-2818
Funky restaurant, set in a natural cave 50 feet (15 m) below ground and reached via a spiral staircase. Renowned for its steaks and seafood. Live music and dancing in the evening.
All major cards

SPAGUETTISSIMO
$$-$$$$
PASEO DE LOS LOCUTORES 13
TEL 809/227-4455
A sophisticated setting in a former private house with poolside terrace for contemporary Italian cuisine with an element of Asian fusion. Good value light lunches and salads.
Closed Sun. D All major cards

SCHEREZADE
$$–$$$
AVE. ROBERTO PASTORIZA 226, ENSANCHE NACHO
TEL 809/227-2323
Located in a lavish Moorish-style building, this atmospheric restaurant specializes in Mediterranean and Middle Eastern food, plus fish and seafood.
All major cards

EL CONUCO
$–$$
152 CALLE CASIMRO DE MOYA
TEL 809/686-0129
Highly atmospheric restaurant with an entryway and rustic thatch roof reflecting its country theme. The food is excellent, and at lunchtime there is a popular buffet. When the waiters and waitresses are finished serving they perform a song-and-dance routine.
All major cards

EAST OF SANTO DOMINGO

CASA DE CAMPO
$$$$$
LA ROMANA
TEL 809/523-5405 or 800/877-3643
FAX 809/523-8548
www.casadecampo.com
The only hotel complex in the region with its own international airport (with daily American Airlines 727 service from Miami), Casa de Campo claims to be the Caribbean's most complete resort. Accommodations comprise luxury villas and spacious rooms, all equipped to a high standard. Its four golf courses are world famous, and it also features a shooting center, polo stables, its own beach and marina, dive shop, 10 restaurants, and 13 tennis courts.
350 plus 150 villas All major cards

PRICES

HOTELS
An indication of the cost of a double room without breakfast is given by **$** signs.

$$$$$	Over $400
$$$$	$300–$400
$$$	$200–$300
$$	$100–$200
$	Under $100

RESTAURANTS
An indication of the cost of a three-course dinner without drinks is given by $ signs.

$$$$$	Over $80
$$$$	$50–$80
$$$	$35–$50
$$	$20–$35
$	Under $20

IBEROSTAR PUNTA CANA
$$$
PLAYA BAVARO, HIGÜEY
TEL 809/221-6500
FAX 809/688-9888
www.iberostar.com
Spacious and comfortable all-inclusive resort on a good stretch of Punta Cana's beach. Diving, water sports.
346 All major cards

PUNTA CANA RESORT AND CLUB
$$-$$$$$
PUNTA CANA, HIGÜEY
TEL 809/959-2262 OR 888/442-2262
FAX 809/959-4650
Attractive suites and two- and three-bedroom beach or garden casita cottages well

spread out over a 105-acre site. Excellent facilities include tennis, dive center, water sports, and horseback riding.
418 All major cards

NORTH COAST

PLAYA DORADA

CASA COLONIAL BEACH & SPA
$$$-$$$$$
PUERTO PLATA
TEL 809/320-3232 OR 866/376-7831
FAX 809/320-3131
www.casacolonialhotel.com
First impressions are formed by the stunning colonial-contemporary lobby-lounge and it just gets better at this delectable boutique hotel. Impeccably tasteful from the rooftop infinity pool to the wine cellar via spacious suites with Roman tubs in the bathroom, Asian-Mediterranean fusion cuisine, and a Bagua spa.
52 All major cards

OCCIDENTAL GRAND PUERTO PLATA
$$$
TEL 809/320-5084
FAX 809/320-6319
www.occidentalhotels.com
Well-managed hotel, within the Playa Dorada complex. The decor is Spanish in style. Two pools, water sports, tennis, and an extensive activities program.
582 All major cards

PLAYA NACO RESORT & SPA
$$$
TEL 809/320-6226
FAX 809/320-6225
www.naco.com.do
All-inclusive beachfront property offering every conceivable facility. Large pool, pool bar, tennis, horse riding, water sports, beach sports, kid club, sports, nighttime entertainment, disco, five bars, choice of cafés and restaurants.
418 All major cards

AGUACEROS
$-$$
EL MALÉCON 32
TEL 809/586-2796
An opportunity to dine out Mexican-style across from the seafront. All the usual suspects (burritos, fajitas) washed down with rum punch, plus barbecued fish, lobster and burgers.
Closed L All major cards

SANTIAGO

PEZ DORADO
$
43 CALLE DEL SOL, PARQUE COLÓN
TEL 809/582-2518
Fish, fish, and Oriental cuisine are the staples of this long-standing and well-regarded restaurant in the center of the city.

SOSÚA

PIERGIORGIO PALACE HOTEL
$$-$$$
CALLE LA PUNTILLA 1, EL BATEY
TEL 809/571-2626
FAX 809/571-2786
www.piergiorgiopalacehotel.com
Terrific location on the Sosúa cliff tops with views out to the Atlantic. Romantic Victorian décor and ocean-facing rooms with billowing curved balconies. Also two-bedroom penthouses with kitchens and private terraces. No beach, but motorized water sports and scuba diving off the rocks. Italian restaurant and an excellent pizzeria with wood-fired oven.
51 rooms/suites All major cards

ON THE WATERFRONT
$-$$
CALLE DR ROSEN 1, EL BATEY 36
TEL 809/571-2670
You can eat your way from breakfast through dinner at this excellent spot with its waterfront deck. It's so popular, reservations are advised in the evening. Locally caught fish and seafood are specialties, but the imported steaks are good, too.
All major cards

PUERTO RICO

CENTRAL HIGHLANDS

HOTEL CASA GRANDE
$
RTE. 612, KM 0.3, UTUADO
TEL 787/894-3939 OR 888/343-2272
FAX 787/894-3900
www.hotelcasagrande.com
Set high up in the mountains of the Cordillera Central, with stunning views across an unspoiled valley, this peaceful, small hotel has simple rooms equipped with balcony and hammock. Once a coffee plantation, the house is surrounded by 107 acres (43 ha). There are several hiking trails in the surrounding hills. It also has its own café with a veranda.
20 All major cards

DORADO

EMBASSY SUITES HOTEL DORADO DEL MAR
$$$-$$$$
201 DORADO DEL MAR BLVD.
TEL 787/796-6125 OR 800/362-2779
FAX 787/796-6145
www.embassysuitesdorado.com
An all-suites hotel fronting Dorado Beach 25 miles from San Juan, this is a good location and excellent family option. Water sports, tennis, spa, shopping, restaurants with ocean views, and live entertainment at weekends.
174 All major cards

FAJARDO

WYNDHAM EL CONQUISTADOR RESORT & SPA
$$$$$
AVE. EL CONQUISTADOR
TEL 787/863-1000
FAX 787/863-6500
www.wyndham.com
This enormous complex occupies a commanding position above the point where the Atlantic and Caribbean meet. The resort comprises four separate hotels, each with a different style, one is located on the marina at the base of the cliff; the main hotel is linked to the marina by an automatic cable car. There is no beach, but the hotel boasts it's own offshore island, with regular shuttle service from the marina. There is also an 18-hole Arthur Hills' champion-ship golf course, and the resort has 10 restaurants, 5 pools, and 7 tennis courts. The immaculate rooms all have VCRs and music systems.
918
All major cards

GUANICA

COPAMARINA BEACH RESORT
$$$–$$$$
KM 6.5, RTE. 333, CANA GORDA
TEL 787/821-0505 or 800/468-4553
FAX 787/821-0070
www.copamarina.com
On 20 acres (8 ha) of lush gardens at the water's edge, this resort offers a full range of facilities including water sports, diving, tennis, mountain biking, and ecotours in the neighboring Guanica Biosphere Reserve. The hotel has two pools, a spa and fitness center. The comfortable rooms are decorated in bright tropical colors and equipped with all amenities. The restaurant is excellent.
106
All major cards

PONCE

HOLIDAY INN & TROPICAL CASINO
$$
PLAYA PONCE
TEL 787/844-1200 or 800/465-4329
FAX 787/841-8683
Efficiently managed and pleasant hotel just outside of Ponce, with views of the city and the ocean from its hilltop position. The comfortable rooms all have balconies and cable TV. The casino and nightclub are popular with locals on the weekends.
116
All major cards

PITO'S SEAFOOD
$$$
LAS CUCHARAS
TEL 787/852-1784
With a large terrace overlooking the ocean just outside Ponce, Pito's is a great place for a long, indulgent lunch. Specialties include plantain stuffed with shrimp and lobster, stuffed clams, grilled mahi mahi, and red snapper in Creole sauce.
All major cards

RINCON

SOMETHING SPECIAL

HORNED DORSET PRIMAVERA
Undoubtedly the island's most chic and exclusive hotel, this Mediterranean-style resort is impeccably run and caters to a discerning clientele seeking absolute tranquility and relaxation—there are no TVs, radios, or telephones (or children under 12) in the hotel. The rooms, furnished in antiques, are immaculate. Set on its own beach, the hotel has won numerous awards. It is also a member of the prestigious Relais & Château group and has a superb restaurant.
$$$$$
KM.3, ROAD 409
TEL 787/823-4030 or 800/633-1857
FAX 787/823-5580
www.horneddorset.com
30
All major cards

HORNED DORSET PRIMAVERA
$$$$$
KM.3, ROAD 409
TEL 787/823-4030
One of the island's top restaurants outside of the capital, the Horned Dorset's sophisticated setting and imaginative cuisine have won it many admirers in foodie circles. French food with Caribbean accents, the repertoire includes dishes such as shrimp and fennel bisque, grilled tuna with mango salad, seared breast of duck with caramelized pineapple, and grilled marlin with fresh herbs and lemon.
Closed L All major cards

RIO GRANDE

WESTIN RIO MAR BEACH RESORT & GOLF CLUB
$$$$-$$$$$
6000 RIO MAR BLVD.
TEL 787/888-6000 OR 888/627-8556
FAX 787/888-6320
www.westinriomar.com
Well-run property on its own beach, handy for El Yunque National Park. The hotel's impressive range of facilities includes spa and fitness center, a tennis center, restaurants, casino, shops, a full range of water sports, and swimming pools. The 481-acre complex also includes two world-class golf courses (the River Course and the Ocean Course).
600, 72 suites, 59 villas
All major cards

PALIO AT THE WESTIN RIO MAR
$$$$
6000 RIO MAR BLVD.
TEL 787/888-6000
The resort's top restaurant offers a wonderfully tempting array of dishes styled with Italian flair. Specialties include fish baked in a banana leaf, with tomatoes, fresh peppers, and onions.
All major cards

SAN JUAN

HOTEL EL CONVENTO
$$$$-$$$$$
100 CALLE CRISTO, OLD SAN JUAN
TEL 787/723-9020 or 800/468-2779
FAX 787/721-2877
www.elconvento.com
This small, deluxe hotel occupies the top floors of a historic building (once a convent) in the heart of the old town; the inner courtyard features cafés, restaurants, galleries, and shops. Each of the rooms has its own distinctive character and all have views over San Juan and the sea. Shops, business services, and casino.
54 rooms, 4 suites All major cards

SHERATON OLD SAN JUAN HOTEL & CASINO
$$$$-$$$$$
100 CALLE BRUMBAUGH, OLD SAN JUAN
TEL 787/721-5100 or 866/376-7577
FAX 787/721-1111
Located in the heart of the old city on the waterfront and overlooking the cruise ship piers, this comfortable, well-run hotel is a popular choice with cruise passengers stopping over.
240 rooms All major cards

GALLERY INN
$$-$$$$
NORZAGARAY 204, OLD SAN JUAN
TEL 787/722-1808
FAX 787/977-3929
www.thegalleryinn.com
Charming and idiosyncratic hostelry in an old rambling building, stuffed full of artworks and curiosities, with great views from its vantage point atop the old city.
13 rooms, 10 suites
All major cards

AJILI MOJILI
$$$$
1052 ASHFORD AVE., CONDADO
TEL 787/725-9195
This is a very popular restaurant (reservations recommended) specializing in local Puerto Rican cuisine. Most people start with the excellent assorted fritters (pumpkin, white yam and cheese, plantain, chicken, and corn) followed by skewered pork, chicken, beef, or swordfish served with their richly flavored trademark Ajilli-Mojili sauce.
Closed L. Sat.–Sun.
All major cards

PIKAYO
$$$$
299 DE DIEGO AVE
TEL 787/751-1124
Chef Wilo Benet is one of the rising stars in the island's culinary world, and his restaurant is one of the most celebrated in the city. His perfectionist attitude to the presentation of food and the combining of flavors ensures a steady stream of repeat customers to this stylish, contemporary restaurant.
Closed Sun.
All major cards

RAMIRO'S
$$$$
1106 MAGDALENA AVE., CONDADO
TEL 787/721-9049
One of the city's top restaurants, Ramiro's delivers creative Castilian cuisine from the kitchen of renowned chef Luis Ramiro.
Closed L Sat.
All major cards

IL PERUGINO
$$$
105 CALLE CRISTO, OLD SAN JUAN
TEL 787/722-5481
Set in a beautifully restored house in the old city, this intimate restaurant has won many awards for its excellent Italian cuisine. Specialties include *pasta a la vongole, carpaccio,* rack of lamb, and marinated salmon. Extensive wine list.
Closed L Sun.–Wed.
All major cards

AMADEUS
$$–$$$
106 CALLE SAN SEBASTIAN, OLD SAN JUAN
TEL 787/722-8635
This relaxed and charming restaurant attracts a trendy crowd drawn to its nouvelle Caribbean menu, which includes chicken breast stuffed with escargots and mushrooms, fresh salads, and plantain mousse with shrimp.
Closed L Mon. All major cards

DRAGONFLY
$-$$
364 FORTALEZA ST.
TEL 787/977-3886
In the heart of the hip SOFO (South Flortaleza) sector of Old San Juan, Dragonfly is a popular eaterie with a difference, offering Latin-Asian cuisine dishes such as pork and amarillo dumplings and peking duck nachos.
Closed L & Sun. All major cards

PAMELA'S CARIBBEAN CUISINE
$-$$
1 SANTA ANNA ST., OCEAN PARK
TEL 787/726-5010
On the beach with indoor

and outdoor dining, Pamela's has a relaxed atmosphere with first-class service that matches the culinary creations emerging from chef Esteban Torres' kitchen. Fresh seafood is the mainstay, accompanied by an extensive wine list and some delectable desserts.
All major cards

YABUCOA

PALMAS DE LUCIA
$$-$$$
RTE. 901, SECTOR PLAYA LUCIA
TEL 787/ 893-4423 or 800/981-7575
FAX 787/893-00291
www.palmasdelucia.com
This small, friendly hotel is part of the government-run parador scheme. Near the beach and handy for the start of the Ruta Panoramica.
25
All major cards

VIRGIN ISLANDS

U.S. VIRGIN ISLANDS

ST. CROIX

BUCCANEER HOTEL
$$$$-$$$$$
GALLOWS BAY
TEL 340/712-2100 or 800/255-3881
E-MAIL mango@thebuccaneer.com
www.thebucaneer.com
Luxurious family-run resort with secluded beaches, water sports, golf, tennis, kids' club, and eco-packages. Spacious accommodations (all with private balconies) in the attractive hilltop main building or nearer the beach, also family villas and deluxe suites.
138
All major cards

CARAMBOLA BEACH RESORT
$$$
KINGSHILL
TEL 340/778-3800 or 888/503-8760
www.carambolabeach.com
Elegant former Rockresort spread across 28 beachfront acres (12 ha) with a Trent Jones-designed golf course and excellent sports facilities. Generous suite-style rooms with Mexican tiles in the showers, screened porches, and fully equipped kitchenettes.
151
All major cards

HIBISCUS BEACH RESORT
$$$
4131 LA GRANDE PRINCESSE
TEL 340/773-4042 or 800/442-0121
FAX 340/773-7668
Small, relaxing resort arranged in two-story blocks with gingerbread decoration near a lovely beach 2 miles (3 km) west of Christiansted. Well-equipped rooms all with balcony or patio; hammocks under the palm trees.
37 All major cards

WAVES AT CANE BAY
$$
CANE BAY
TEL 340/778-1805 or 800/545-0603
FAX 340/778-4945
There are 11 airy and comfortable housekeeping studios and a villa on the waterfront a couple of minutes' walk from the beach. Low-key and friendly; good snorkeling and diving; on-site dive shop.
11 studios, 1 villa
Some rooms
All major cards

MT. VICTORY CAMP
$
CREQUE DAM RD.
P.O. BOX 696
FREDERIKSTED
TEL 340/772-1651 or 866/772-1651
FAX 340/719-3222
www.mtvictorycamp.com
Small, friendly eco-camp in a valley enfolded in the green hills west of Frederiksted. Three tented platforms and two two-story bungalows (sleeping up to 6) are fashioned from local hardwoods. All have kitchenette, linen, cold water. Hot water bathhouse.
5 units None

PRICES

HOTELS
An indication of the cost of a double room without breakfast is given by **$** signs.

$$$$$	Over $400
$$$$	$300–$400
$$$	$200–$300
$$	$100–$200
$	Under $100

RESTAURANTS
An indication of the cost of a three-course dinner without drinks is given by **$** signs.

$$$$$	Over $80
$$$$	$50–$80
$$$	$35–$50
$$	$20–$35
$	Under $20

BLUE MOON
$$$
17 STRAND ST., FREDERIKSTED
TEL 340/772-2222
Bistro-cum-jazz spot (live music Fri. night and Sun. brunch) facing the waterfront with a garden patio and eclectic menu—Cajun shrimp, Luna Pie (cheese and vegetable phyllo pastry parcel), and hot, hot, hot Creole chicken.
Closed Mon. All major cards

LE ST. TROPEZ
$$$
67 KING ST., FREDERIKSTED
TEL 340/772-3000
French restaurant in an old gingerbread house opening onto a leafy courtyard. Salade Niçoise and croque monsieur (toasted cheese sandwiches) at lunch; homemade pâtés, frog's legs, and lobster for dinner.
Closed all Sun., & L Sat.
All major cards

TUTTO BENE
$$$
BOARDWALK BUILDING, HOSPITAL STREET, CHRISTIANSTED
TEL 340/773-5229
Italian bistro serving great food with great atmosphere. Drop in for a chicken pesto sandwich at lunchtime, have an evening drink at the bar, or settle in for hearty seafood and impeccable pasta dishes. Reservations recommended.
All major cards

KENDRICKS
$$-$$$
21-32 COMPANY STREET CHRISTIANSTED
TEL 340/773-9199
Take your place amongst the locals dining out at this popular downtown eaterie. The menu is eclectic with myriad influences. The chef's signature dish is roast pecan-encrusted loin of pork.
Closed L & Sun.

RUM RUNNERS
$$-$$$
HOTEL CARAVELLE, BOARDWALK CHRISTIANSTED
TEL 340/773-6585
Location, location, location is a clue to Rum Runners' success. This local favorite enjoys a wonderful harborfront position in the center of town and serves up a pretty good burger, too. Ribs, steaks, pick-your-own lobster salad.
All major cards

OFF THE WALL
$-$$
NORTH SHORE (RTE. 80)
TEL 340/778-4771
An all day beach bar and restaurant that can offer anything from eggs Benedict for breakfast to spectacular sunsets and a hammock for a postprandial nap. Burgers, pizzas, nachos, "melt-in-the-mouth" Philly sandwiches and seafood, plus jazz on weekends.
All major cards

ST. JOHN

SOMETHING SPECIAL

CANEEL BAY RESORT

Classic Laurance Rockefeller-built luxury resort on a stunning 170-acre (68 ha) peninsula site with seven beaches. Rooms in two-story blocks or stone-walled cottages strung along the shore (no phone, TV, or air-conditioning); tennis, water sports, children's activities.

$$$$$
CANEEL BAY
TEL 340/776-6111 or 800/928-8887
E-MAIL caneelres@rosewoodhotels.com
www.caneelbay.com
166 P All major cards

GALLOWS POINT SUITE RESORT
$$$$-$$$$$
CRUZ BAY
TEL 340/776-6434 or 800/323-7229
FAX 340/776-6520
E-MAIL gallows@islands.vi
www.gallowspointresort.com
Very comfortable rental suites (individually decorated) in two-story units amid gardens, five minutes' walk from Cruz Bay town. Swimming and snorkeling from the shore.
52 P All major cards

MAHO BAY CAMPS
$-$$
MAHO BAY
TEL 340/776-6226 or 800/392-9004
E-MAIL mahobay@maho.org
www.maho.org
Screened tent-style cottages grafted onto the steep forested hillside above Maho Bay in the national park. Communal bathhouses, basic cooking facilities, and eco-conscious ethos. Also more luxurious solar-powered Harmony Studios constructed from recycled materials.
114 P All major cards

ASOLARE
$$$$
NORTH SHORE RD.
TEL 340/779-4747
Gorgeous views overlooking Cruz Bay and St. Thomas, and a dynamic fusion of Asian and Pacific Rim cuisine make this one of St. John's hottest dining experiences. There are a few classical French dishes among the Thai beef salads and specialty seafood dishes. Reservations advised.
Closed L All major cards

CHATEAU BORDEAUX
$$$$
CENTERLINE RD. BORDEAUX MOUNTAIN
TEL 340/776-6611
Cozy and romantic small dining room with a terrace overlooking the surrounding hills. An eclectic international menu equally at home with shrimp green curry and roast rack of lamb or wild game. Wine lovers will find Bordeaux well represented.
Closed L All major cards

FISH TRAP
$$$
RAINTREE INN, CRUZ BAY
TEL 340/693-9994
Locals recommend this casual al fresco restaurant for its fresh fish specialties, grilled steaks, pasta dishes, and diet-breaking homemade desserts.
Closed L & Mon.
All major cards

MORGAN'S MANGO
$$
CRUZ BAY
TEL 340/693-8141
Lively dinner spot and bar with a lamp-lit wooden deck opposite the national park dock. International influences range from the Caribbean and South America to Asia; also a long cocktail menu and live

music on Thursdays.
Closed L
All major cards

ST. THOMAS

RITZ-CARLTON
$$$$$
6900 GREAT BAY
TEL 340/775-3333 or
800/241-3333
www.ritzcarlton.com
Sybaritic luxury in elegant faux-Italianate surroundings with gardens and tinkling fountains. All the balconied rooms have sea views. Excellent facilities include fine dining, tennis, boat trips, water sports, and a beach.
228
All major cards

BOLONGO BAY BEACH RESORT
$$$$
7150 BOLONGO BAY
TEL 340/775-1800 or
800/524-4746
E-MAIL info@bolongo.com
www.bolongobay.com
Lively family-run beach resort property offering extensive water sports facilities, tennis, beach volleyball, and basketball courts.
65
All major cards

POINT PLEASANT RESORT
$$$
ESTATE SMITH BAY
TEL 340/775-7200 OR
800/524-2300
FAX 340/776-5694
www.pointpleasantresort.com
Spacious suites in a series of red-roofed villas spread across the hillside (kitchens, cable, balconies). Snorkeling from the beach; dive packages; tennis; trails through 15 acres of tropical greenery.
128 suites
All major cards

SECRET HARBOUR BEACH RESORT
$$-$$$
6250 ESTATE NAZARETH
TEL 340/775-6550 or
800/223-6510
FAX 340/775-1501
www.secretharbourvi.com
Spacious studios and one- and two-bedroom housekeeping condos with tropical decor in a AAA 3-diamond property. Palm-lined beach, water sports center, tennis.
64
All major cards

HOTEL 1829
$$-$$$
GOVERNMENT HILL
CHARLOTTE AMALIE
TEL 340/776-1829 or
800/524-2002
E-MAIL info@hotel1829.com
www.hotel1829.com
A national historic site, the atmospheric inn is furnished with antiques, painted tiles, and Tiffany glass. The rooms vary in size (the best are in the original building). Splendid bar; tiny courtyard pool.
14
All major cards

OLD STONE FARM HOUSE
$$$$$
MAHOGANY RUN GOLF COURSE
TEL 340/777-6277
Fine dining amid the 200-year-old brick arches and wooden beams of a former sugar estate building. Sample a light garden vegetable strudel, Caribbean crab cakes, flash grilled tuna, or pan-seared potato-crusted pork loin with Calvados brandy sauce.
Closed L & all Mon.
All major cards

HERVÉ
$$$$
GOVERNMENT HILL,
CHARLOTTE AMALIE
TEL 340/777-9703
Panoramic views over the harbor and a stylish French-American menu with a Caribbean twist. Lunches such as salade Niçoise and crêpes, and dinner favorites including pistachio-crusted brie, *moules marinière*, steaks, seafood, and crème brûlée. Reservations recommended.
Closed Sun. L All major cards

AGAVÉ TERRACE
$$$-$$$$
POINT PLEASANT RESORT
ESTATE SMITH BAY
TEL 340/775-4142
Head out to the East End for this excellent seafood restaurant with stunning views across to St. John from the namesake terrace. Lobster is a specialty, also pasta dishes and steak. Live entertainment nightly.
Closed L All major cards

CUZZINS' CARIBBEAN RESTAURANT & BAR
$$
7 BACK ST.,
CHARLOTTE AMALIE
TEL 340/777-4711
Delicious local cooking in an attractive downtown brick dining room decorated with carnival props and local art. Mutton stew, curried chicken, shrimp creole, and a host of tasty local side dishes.
Closed all Sun. & D Tues.
All major cards

VICTOR'S NEW HIDEOUT
$$
103 SUBMARINE BASE
(OFF RTE. SR30W)
TEL 340/776-9379
Good views from this hilltop hideout close to the airport. Caribbean curries and specialty lobster Montserrat with fruits as well as seafood and a few continental dishes.
Closed L Sun. All major cards

DUFFY'S LOVE SHACK
$-$$
RED HOOK PLAZA,
EAST END
TEL 340/779-2080
It's loud, it's fun—that applies to the décor, the waitstaff, the music, and the outrageous

cocktails. Classic burgers and wings, plus coconut-smoked New York Strip and tamarind-honey ribs.
None

BRITISH VIRGIN ISLANDS

ANEGADA

ANEGADA REEF HOTEL
$$-$$$
SETTING POINT
TEL 284/495-8002
FAX 284/495-9362
www.anegadareef.com
Total peace and quiet in simple but charming rooms (oceanfront or garden); rates include three meals a day. Fishing and diving from the hotel boat; jeep rentals.
20 P All major cards

TORTOLA

LONG BAY RESORT
$$$$-$$$$$
LONG BAY, ROAD TOWN
TEL 284/495-4252
FAX 284/495-4677
E-MAIL longbay@eliteislandresorts.com, www.eliteislandresorts.com
Very comfortable and well equipped rooms, studios, and one- to three-bedroom villas on the hillside, and waterfront cabanas on the beach. All boast generous decks. Pool rooms (recommended for families); tennis; water sports.
155 P All major cards

SUGAR MILL HOTEL
$$$–$$$$$
APPLE BAY, ROAD TOWN
TEL 284/495-4355
FAX 284/495-4696
www.sugarmillhotel.com
Quiet hideaway attached to a notable restaurant. There are comfortable modern rooms and family suites, a two-bedroom villa, and two simple rooms in a wooden cottage set in rampant garden foliage.
23 P Some rooms All major cards

LIGHTHOUSE VILLAS
$$
CANE GARDEN BAY
TEL 284/494-5482
FAX 284/495-9101
E-MAIL bvilighthouse@surfbvi.com
Spacious, bright efficiencies, crisp blue and white decor, and balconies overlooking the glorious bay. A minute's walk down to the beach.
6 P All major cards

SOMETHING SPECIAL

MRS. SCATLIFFE'S

Reservations are a must for Mrs. Una Scatliffe's West Indian restaurant, which she operates out of her own home. The veranda serves as the dining room, and the four-course set menu features traditional soups, home-baked bread, pot roasts, and fruit and vegetables from the garden.
$$$
CARROT BAY
TEL 284/495-4556
All major cards

BRANDYWINE BAY
$$$$
BRANDYWINE BAY
TEL 284/495-2301
Tortola's most elegant dining room with a terrace overlooking the Sir Francis Drake Channel. Florentine specialties grilled over charcoal, homemade pasta and sauces with fresh garden herbs, plenty of Italian wines on the wine list, and superb attention to detail.
Closed L, Mon., & Aug.–Oct. All major cards

SUGAR MILL
$$$
APPLE BAY
TEL 284/495-4355
Lovely setting in the former boiling house of an old sugar mill decorated with Haitian paintings. Cookbook writers Jinx and Jefferson Morgan offer a small but delicious daily menu: Caribbean sweet potato soup with gingered shrimp, tropical game hen with orange curry butter, and fresh garden vegetables.
All major cards

PUSSER'S LANDING
$$
SOPER'S HOLE MARINA, WEST END
TEL 284/495-4554
English-style pub grub at lunchtime replaced by a more refined and international menu in the evening, although beef Wellington still lurks among the Maryland crab cakes and pasta dishes. The decor and diners have a nautical air.
All major cards

QUITO'S GAZEBO
$–$$
CANE GARDEN BAY
TEL 284/495-4837
Bar/restaurant with a covered deck overhanging the beach. Burgers and sandwiches, fettuccine Alfredo, or grilled kingfish followed by homemade brownies or pecan pie. Quito himself leads the live music on Fri. and Sat. nights.
All major cards

VIRGIN GORDA

BITTER END YACHT CLUB
$$$$$
NORTH SOUND
TEL 284/494-2745 or 800/872-2392
FAX 284/494-4756
www.beyc.com
Friendly yacht club ambience, excellent sailing school, and a selection of dinghies, windsurfers, dinghies, and yachts. Hillside villas (good for families) or romantic thatched huts on stilts with wooden decks.
85 All major cards

LITTLE DIX BAY
$$$$$
LITTLE DIX BAY
TEL 284/495-5555 or 800/928-3000
FAX 284/495-5661
www.littledixbay.com

Sister to Caneel Bay on St. John (USVI), casually elegant Little Dix bears the inimitable Rockefeller stamp. Hexagonal and stilted rooms catch the breeze, though a/c (and phone) is an option here. Hiking, tennis, water sports, boat trips, children's program.
98 All major cards

LEVERICK BAY HOTEL
$$
LEVERICK BAY
TEL 284/495-7421 or 800/848-7081
FAX 284/495-7367
www.leverickbay.com

Brightly painted villas with sea views and amazingly affordable rates for hotel rooms and one- and two-bedroom suites with kitchen. Tennis, spa, water sports, and dive shop.
18 All major cards

GIORGIO'S TABLE
$$$
MAHOE BAY
TEL 284/495-5684

A water's edge restaurant and bar on the west coast in the lee of Gorda Peak. Feast on the wonderful selection of authentic Italian hors d'oeuvres followed by veal, beef, or a mountain of fresh pasta.
All major cards

TOP OF THE BATHS
$$
THE BATHS
TEL 284/495-5497

A terrific position above The Baths augments the all-day menu with views over the Sir Francis Drake Channel. Tables are out on the deck and an air-conditioned dining room. Salads, sandwiches, and burgers at lunch; dinner entrées might include filet mignon and fresh lobster.
All major cards

NETHERLANDS ANTILLES & ARUBA

ARUBA

HYATT REGENCY RESORT & CASINO
$$$$-$$$$$
J.E. IRAUSQUIN BLVD. 85
PALM BEACH
TEL 297/586-1234 or 800/554-9288
FAX 297/586-1682
www.aruba.hyatt.com

Luxurious resort complex on 12 acres (5 ha) of beachfront. Attractive, well-equipped rooms and suites; spectacular pool area, tennis, golf, water sports, and Camp Hyatt offering kids' activities.
360 All major cards

PLAYA LINDA BEACH RESORT
$$$-$$$$
J.E. IRAUSQUIN BLVD.
PALM BEACH
TEL 297/586-1000
FAX 297/586-5210
www.playalinda.com

Fully equipped one- and two-bedroom condos with balconies in a smart beachfront development. Tennis, water sports, shopping, and pool featuring a waterfall.
198 All major cards

AMSTERDAM MANOR BEACH RESORT
$$
J.E. IRAUSQUIN BLVD. 252
EAGLE BEACH
TEL 297/587-1492 or 800/766-6016
FAX 297/587-1463
www.amsterdammanor.com

Pretty Dutch colonial-style all-suite resort. Studios and two-bedroom apartments with kitchens and sea views across from the beach. On-site mini market; water sports nearby.
72 All major cards

PRICES

HOTELS
An indication of the cost of a double room without breakfast is given by $ signs.

$$$$$	Over $400
$$$$	$300–$400
$$$	$200–$300
$$	$100–$200
$	Under $100

RESTAURANTS
An indication of the cost of a three-course dinner without drinks is given by $ signs.

$$$$$	Over $80
$$$$	$50–$80
$$$	$35–$50
$$	$20–$35
$	Under $20

PAPIAMENTO
$$$$
WASHINGTON 61
NOORD
TEL 297/586-4544

Utterly charming family restaurant set in the gardens of a 150-year-old manor house. The Ellis parents occupy the front of the house, while the children cook award-winning seafood, steaks, and special healthy and vegetarian dishes.
Closed L & Sun. All major cards

GASPARITO
$$$
GASPARITO 3, NOORD
TEL 297/586-7044

Combination restaurant and Aruban art gallery specializing in local cuisine and international dishes. Try barracuda-stuffed ravioli, shrimp in coconut milk and brandy, or a typical *stoba* (stew).
Closed L & all Sun. All major cards

RUMBA BAR & GRILL
$$-$$$
HAVENSTRAAT 4
ORANJESTAD
TEL 297/588-7900

An intimate little downtown eaterie with terracotta walls,

banquettes, polished wood and rush-backed chairs. The open kitchen's charcoal grill cooks up everything from hearty breakfasts to scallops, coconut shrimp, rack of lamb and steaks. Good salads, too.
All major cards

BRISAS DEL MAR
$$
SAVANETA 222, SAVANETA
TEL 297/584-7718
Small and casual open-air seafood restaurant run out of a waterfront fisherman's hut. The daily catch might include lobster or baby shark, plus a selection of local side dishes.
Closed Mon. All major cards

BONAIRE

HARBOUR VILLAGE BEACH RESORT
$$$$-$$$$$
PLAYA PABAO
TEL 599/717-7500 or 800/424-0004
FAX 599/717-7507
www.harbourvillage.com
Bonaire's top hotel boasts a palm-fringed beach and attractive rooms or housekeeping condos in Mediterranean-style villas. Also tennis, diving, a full-service marina, and shopping.
64 P All major cards

CAPTAIN DON'S HABITAT
$$$
PLAYA PABAO
TEL 599/717-8290 or 800/327-6709
FAX 599/717-8240
www.habitatbonaire.com
Captain Don is Bonaire's dive supremo, and his Habitat offers casual, comfortable suites, villas, and two-bedroom cottages, plus diving, water sports, a minuscule beach, and Captain Don's weekly dive chats on Tuesdays.
93 P All major cards

SAND DOLLAR CONDOMINIUM RESORT
$$-$$$
PLAYA PABAO
TEL 599/717-8738 or 800/288-4773
FAX 599/717-8760
www.divesanddollar.com
Studio, one-, two-, and three-bedroom individually furnished apartments with full kitchens and balconies over-looking the waterfront. Top-rated dive operation, tennis, grocery store, and high season kids' activities program.
76 P All major cards

DIVI FLAMINGO BEACH RESORT
$$
PLAYA PARIBA
TEL 599/717-8285 OR 800/367-3484
FAX 599/717-8238
www.divibonaire.com
Low-rise hotel and a clutch of brightly-painted studio suites set in tropical waterfront gardens. A friendly atmosphere, tennis, a casino, and entertainment. Dive programs include special facilities for the disabled.
145 P All major cards

LA GUERNICA FISH & TAPAS
$$$
KAYA BONAIRE 4C
KRALENDIJK
TEL 599/717-5022
Fine boardwalk location overlooking the harbor with a terrace and distinctly laidback dining room featuring soft seating lounge areas and Spanish-style tiles to compliment the tapas menu. Also good seafood, some Japanese dishes and cocktails.
Closed L, Wed. All major cards

RICHARD'S WATERFRONT
$$$
J.A. ABRAHAM BLVD.
60 PLAYA PARIBA
TEL 599/717-5263
Romantic waterfront setting and a relaxed welcome from Bostonian owner, Richard Beaty. Daily blackboard menus feature plenty of fresh local seafood, filet mignon, and signature chicken Benito with chopped spinach and Dutch cheese.
Closed L & all Mon.
All major cards

CASABLANCA
$$-$$$
ABRAHAM BLVD. 6
KRALENDIJK
TEL 599/717-4433
Lively Argentinian grill just south of the town center. Gargantuan portions—the mixed grill could comfortably feed a small family on steak, ribs, chicken, pork loin, sausages and seafood. Add lashings of chimichurri for a spice K.O.
Closed L Sun. & Mon.
All major cards

ZEEZICHT BONAIRE
$$
KAYA J. N. E. CRAANE 12
KRALENDIJK PLAYA
TEL 599/717-8434
Overlooking the downtown waterfront, Zeezicht kicks off the day with an American breakfast, moves on to grilled fish and conch sandwiches for lunch, and produces a flavorful international dinner menu with a few Indonesian specialties.
All major cards

CURAÇAO

CURAÇAO MARRIOTT BEACH RESORT & CASINO
$$$$
PISCADERA BAAI
TEL 5999/736-8800
FAX 5999/462-7502
E-MAIL curmc.reservations@marriotthotels.com
Elegant and very upscale resort with a contemporary colonial-style motif. Very comfortable accommodations with balcony or terrace set in landscaped

gardens. Excellent water sports facilities and dive shop, tennis, kids' program, full casino.
247 P All major cards

LODGE KURÁ HULANDA & BEACH CLUB
$$$-$$$$$
WESTPUNT
TEL 5999/839-3600 OR 877/264-3106
FAX 5999/839-3601
www.kurahulanda.com
Gorgeous new upscale beach hotel featuring spacious rooms/suites, tropical chic décor, a range of water sports, an on-site dive shop, tennis, spa, and fine dining. Complimentary shuttle to boutique sister hotel in Willemstad.
74 P All major cards

AVILA BEACH HOTEL
$$–$$$
PENSTRAAT 130–134
WILLEMSTAD
TEL 5999/461-4377
FAX 5999/461-1493
www.avilahotel.com
The heart of this waterfront complex is a charming historic hotel ($$), now flanked by tasteful modern wings. The nicest is the wood-built Blues Wing; the newest, the Octagon Wing, boasts a spa and pool.
182 P All major cards

ALL WEST APARTMENTS & DIVING
$
BANDA ABAO, WESTPUNT
TEL 5999/461-2310
FAX 5999/461-2315
www.allwestcuracao.com
Simple, bright, and attractive studios and apartments (sleep four) with kitchenettes, balconies/terraces, and sea views. Quiet location; dive packages and PADI courses.
7 P All major cards

SOMETHING SPECIAL

BISTRO LE CLOCHARD
Cozy dining room in the former fortress jail with a waterfront terrace. Delectable Swiss-French cuisine includes fondues, beef and shrimp cooked on a heated stone slab brought to the table, and rich chocolate desserts.
$$$$
RIFFORT, WILLEMSTAD
TEL 5999/462-5666
All major cards

LA PERGOLA
$$$$
WATERFORT ARCHES 12
WILLEMSTAD
TEL 5999/461-3482
Cozy, quiet dining room tucked into the brick arches of the old waterfort in Willemstad's miniature restaurant row. Tables on the terrace and a northern Italian menu featuring pasta and risotto dishes, veal, and snapper fillets cooked in Pinot Grigio.
Closed Sun. lunch All major cards

LANDHUIS DANIEL
$$
WEG NAAR WESTPUNT
TEL 5999/864-8400
Great setting on the shady, breeze-cooled veranda of an historic plantation house hotel set back from the sea. The imaginative menu is full of unusual ideas, and the chef prepares a weekly changing menu surprise. Authentic Dutch pancakes, seasonal local game dishes, French-Italian-Mediterranean influences with a Caribbean twist.
All major cards

JAANCHIE'S
$
WESTPUNT 15
TEL 5999/864-0126
Great spot for a lazy lunch. Outdoor tables shaded by greenery. Seafood and local dishes such as goat stew, or iguana for the adventurous.
Closed D All major cards

SABA

WILLARD'S OF SABA
$$$$-$$$$$
BOOBY HILL
TEL 599/416-2498
FAX 599/416-2482
www.willardsofsaba.com
A small, upscale retreat boasting a fabulous setting in the hills south of Windwardside. Accommodations in the main building and bright, spacious bungalows. Cliff-top jacuzzi, tennis. No children under 14.
7 P All major cards

JULIANA'S
$$
WINDWARDSIDE
TEL 599/416-2269
FAX 599/416-2389
www.julianas-hotel.com
A cute and cozy small hotel set in gardens bursting with colorful tropical plants. There are studio-style rooms, a two-and-a-half room apartment, and two two-bedroom modern cottages, all simply but comfortably decorated.
9, 1 apt. & 2 cottages P All major cards

SCOUT'S PLACE
$$$
WINDWARDSIDE
TEL 599/416-2740
Scout's Place is a country inn and local institution just above the village. The lively bar is a popular hangout, there is a snack shop for takeout and ice creams, and the veranda restaurant serves plenty of fresh seafood and local dishes.
All major cards

BRIGADOON
$$
WINDWARDSIDE
TEL 599/416-2380
The dining area is hemmed in by trellises, and the menu is long on seafood. Try the local bouillabaisse-style fish soup,

Creole shrimp, or fresh lobster. Closed L All major cards

SINT EUSTATIUS

OLD GIN HOUSE
$-$$
ORANJE BAAI
TEL 599/318-2319 or 800/634-4907
FAX 599/318-2135
www.oldginhouse.com
This historic inn set in an 18th-century cotton gin is one of the island's most appealing addresses. Colonial-style rooms with tiled floors and dark wood furnishings over-look a pool. Good restaurant; also a grill and four ocean-facing rooms over the road.
18 All major cards

KING'S WELL RESTAURANT
$$
ORANJE BAAI
TEL 599/318-2538
Friendly spot with lovely sea views from the terrace, and a German-Continental-American menu that reflects the owners. Imported U.S. beef, tasty schnitzels, and local seafood.
MC, V

SINT MAARTEN

DIVI LITTLE BAY BEACH RESORT
$$$
LITTLE BAY
PHILIPSBURG
TEL 599/542-2333 or 800/367-3484
FAX 599/542-4336
www.divilittlebay.com
An appealing jumble of red roofs, whitewashed buildings, and palm trees balanced on a narrow peninsula just outside Philipsburg. Good value rooms and suites with floral fabrics and wooden latticework. Water sports, tennis, dive shop, spa, and children's programs.
159 All major cards

MARY'S BOON BEACH PLANTATION
$$-$$$
SIMSON BAAI 117
TEL 599/545-7000
FAX 599/545-3403
www.marysboon.com
Relaxed, friendly inn on a three-mile stretch of white sand beach close to shops and restaurants. Colorful studios with Indonesian furnishings. Charming staff. Restaurant; honor bar.
32 All major cards

PASANGGRAHAN ROYAL INN
$$
FRONT ST. 19, PHILIPSBURG
TEL 599/542-3588
FAX 599/542-2885
www.pasanhotel.com
Bayfront, 19th-century former governor's residence who's once honored guests included Queen Wilhelmina,. The old fashioned charm extends to afternoon tea. Town center location, but quiet, stylishly refurbished rooms with pretty fabrics, colonial-style furnish-ings, and balconies.
30 All major cards

ANTOINE'S
$$$
119 FRONT ST., PHILIPSBURG
TEL 599/542-2964
Pretty blue-and-white terrace dining room with a view across the bay. Classical French menu featuring chilled vichyssoise, scallops Nantaise, veal Dijonnaise, Montmorency duck with cherry brandy, plus a few Italian pasta dishes and an occasional dash of Creole.
All major cards

THE GREEN HOUSE
$$
BOBBY'S MARINA
PHILIPSBURG
TEL 599/542-2941
A restaurant, bar, and nightclub rolled into one, this island institution has been packing them in since 1986. Happy hour is a 150-minute marathon complete with reduced price appetizers. The official menu offers steak, ribs, lobster, and fresh Caribbean fish.
All major cards

WAJANG DOLL
$$
ROYAL VILLAGE, COLE BAY
TEL 599/544-2255
Traditional Indonesian fare from the Dutch East Indies makes for a delicious and unusual treat. Wildly generous set-price 14- or 19-dish *rijsttafel* feasts, or go à la carte with *nasi goreng Jawa* (rice platter with shrimp, pork satay, egg, and spicy red pepper sambal).
Closed Sat. L, Sun. All major cards

KANGAROO COURT CAFFE
$
HENDRIK GEVANGENISTEEG
TEL 599/542-4278
Tucked down the side of the courthouse, this is a great place for breakfast, coffee and pastries, light lunches (deli sandwiches, pasta, salads), or a refreshing afternoon iced tea in the leafy court-yard shaded by Indian almond trees.
Closed D Sun.

ST.-MARTIN

CAPTAIN OLIVER'S
$$$$
OYSTER POND
TEL 0590/87 40 26
FAX 0590/87 40 84
www.captainolivers.com
Comfortable efficiency bungalows decorated in pastel shades and set on landscaped grounds beside a lagoon. The complex includes a marina, dive shop, and bar frequented by yachting types. Water taxi service to Dawn Beach.
50 All major cards

HÉVÉA
$$$
163 BLVD. DE GRAND CASE
GRAND CASE

TEL 0590/87 56 85
FAX 0590/87 83 88
www.hotel-hevea.com
Small and charming Creole inn just across from the beach. A choice of rooms, studios, and apartments (some with a/c); the nicest have colonial-style mahogany beds draped with mosquito nets.
10 All major cards

FISH POT
$$$$
82 BLVD. DE GRAND CASE
GRAND CASE
TEL 0590/87 50 88
Arguably the highlight of Grand Case's beach-facing restaurant row. Lantern-lit terrace dining, rather formal service, and classic French-Caribbean dishes such as *bouillabaisse des caraïbes* and duck breast cooked in aged rum flavored with paprika, plus a thoughtful selection of vegetarian options.
Closed L All major cards

SOMETHING SPECIAL

LA SAMANNA

Gorgeous super-luxurious enclave with a Moorish-Mediterranean theme set in tropical gardens above the beach. Elegant accommodations in rooms, suites, and villas. Gourmet restaurant, superb service, tennis, and water sports.

$$$$$
BAIE LONGUE
TEL 0590/87 64 00 or 800/854-2252
FAX 0590/87 87 86
www.lasamanna.com
82 All major cards

THE RAINBOW
$$$
176 BOULEVARD DE GRAND CASE, GRAND CASE
TEL 0590/87 55 80
The fresh blue-and-white decor lends an appropriately nautical air to this jolly little seaside restaurant, where the menu encompasses French and Caribbean dishes. The best tables are on the airy breezeway above the beach.
Closed Sun. All major cards

BISTRO NU
$$-$$$
ALLÉE DE L'ANCIENNE GEÔLE
MARIGOT
TEL 0590/87 97 09
Cozy dining room tucked away in an alley off rue de Hollande. Generous traditional brasserie-style cuisine (snails, steak-frîtes) and very popular.
Closed L, Sun. MC, V

CLAUDE MINI-CLUB
$$-$$$
FRONT DE MER
MARIGOT
TEL 0590/87 50 69
Lovely views of Marigot harbor and bright checked madras cotton providing a splash of traditional color to go with the Creole/French menu specialties. Plenty of seafood and great value barbecue buffets on Wed. and Sat. nights.
Closed Sun. p.m. All major cards

SHANTY TOWN
$
BLVD. DE GRAND CASE, GRAND CASE
This handful of open-air barbecue kitchens *(lolos)* overlooks the beach between the two piers. Ribs, chicken, shrimp kebabs, stuffed crab backs, and *accra* (Creole fish cakes) served up with macaroni salad and coleslaw.
Closed D None

LEEWARD ISLANDS

ANGUILLA

CAP JULUCA
$$$$$
MAUNDAY'S BAY
TEL 264/497-6666 or 888/852-5822
FAX 264/497-6617
www.capjuluca.com
Gorgeous Moorish-style oasis set on a curving white sand beach surrounded by lush gardens. Huge rooms decorated in restful beige and white, monumental double tubs in the suites, a tented restaurant, babysitting, and top-notch sports facilities.
98 rooms, 18 villas
All major cards

MALLIOUHANA
$$$$$
MEAD'S BAY
TEL 264/497-6111 or 800/835-0796
FAX 264/497-6011
www.malliouhana.com
One of the Caribbean's very finest establishments. Chic Mediterranean-monastic-meets-Asian colonial amid Haitian art and vanilla-scented candles. Guest rooms range from a beach villa to suites or huge and lovely marble-tiled rooms. Excellent facilities and luxurious spa, kids' programs, gourmet dining.
54 rooms & suites, 1 villa

PRICES

HOTELS
An indication of the cost of a double room without breakfast is given by $ signs.

$$$$$	Over $400
$$$$	$300–$400
$$$	$200–$300
$$	$100–$200
$	Under $100

RESTAURANTS
An indication of the cost of a three-course dinner without drinks is given by $ signs.

$$$$$	Over $80
$$$$	$50–$80
$$$	$35–$50
$$	$20–$35
$	Under $20

All major cards

ANGUILLA GREAT HOUSE
$$$
RENDEZVOUS BAY
TEL 264/497-6061 or 800/583-9247
FAX 264/497-6019
www.anguillagreathouse.com
Friendly, unpretentious spot on a fabulous beach. Simple, spacious gingerbread cottages with tin roofs, shutters, and mahogany furnishings. Beach bar and restaurant. (See more small properties at www .anguillacharmingescapes.com.)
31 Some
All major cards

BLANCHARD'S
$$$$$
MEAD'S BAY
TEL 264/497-6100
Candle-lit tropical elegance on Mead's Bay. Melinda Blanchard's cuisine incorporates New American and Asian flavors with specialties such as lemon-glazed lobster dumplings and Japanese-inspired tuna fillet. Award-winning wine list. Reservations advised.
Closed L & all Sun. All major cards

MANGO'S SEASIDE GRILL
$$$$
BARNES BAY
TEL 264/497-6479
Casual beachfront setting with a canvas awning over the wooden deck and back wall adorned with tropical murals. Homemade bread, "famous" Barnes Bay lobster cakes, sesame-crusted snapper fillet marinated in soy, mouthwatering cakes and pies (coconut cheesecake to die for), and an extensive wine list.
Closed L & Tues. All major cards

TASTY'S
$$-$$$
SOUTH HILL
TEL 264/497-2737
Malliouhana-trained chef Dale Carty's upscale diner combines great island cuisine with a distinctly funky paint job. Traditional Johnny cakes for breakfast, knockout lobster salad for lunch, and delicious dinners.
Closed Thur. All major cards

JACQUIE'S RIPPLES
$$
SANDY GROUND
TEL 264/497-3380
A great place to hang out with a cozy indoor dining room and tables on the veranda (reserve ahead). The broad-ranging menu features grilled fish, Thai salads, pasta, crispy coconut chicken, and the like. The bar gets buzzy in the evening.
All major cards

ANTIGUA

CARLISLE BAY
$$$$$
ST MARY'S
TEL 268/484-0000
FAX 268/484-0001
www.carlisle-bay.com
Luxurious all sea-facing suites in a fabulous contemporary hotel on the south coast. Cool, minimalist décor marries white linen and dark mahogany; beachside and Asian restaurants; spa; complimentary Kids' Club.
80
All major cards

CURTAIN BLUFF
$$$$$
MORRIS BAY
TEL 268/462-8400 or 888/289-9898
FAX 268/462-8409
www.curtainbluff.com
Antigua's most famous and elegant hotel perched on a steep bluff winding down to the beach. Excellent all-inclusive sports facilities and gourmet dining (jackets for gents after 7 p.m.).
61 All major cards

HAWKSBILL BEACH RESORT
$$$$
FIVE ISLANDS
TEL 268/462-0301
FAX 268/462-1515
www.rexcaribbean.com
Bright and comfy rooms and cottage-style accommodations strung out along the shore (access to four beaches including one "clothing optional"). Deluxe club cottages for romantics; beach cottages with connecting doors for families. Water sports, tennis, kids' activities.
113 All major cards

SIBONEY BEACH CLUB
$$-$$$
DICKENSON BAY
TEL 268/462-0806
FAX 268/462-3356
www.siboneybeachclub.com
Delightful small property at the quiet end of Antigua's busiest beach. Twelve one-bed suites with kitchenettes and balconies overlooking tropical gardens. The restaurant is a big plus (see Coconut Grove, below). Water sports nearby.
12 All major cards

ADMIRAL'S INN
$$
ENGLISH HARBOUR
TEL 268/460-1027
FAX 268/460-1534
www.admiralsantigua.com
Charming historic inn and waterfront garden in Nelson's Dockyard. Simple rooms with antique furnishings in both the main building and an annex (rather dark). Free transportation to the beach.
14 Some All major cards

CHEZ PASCAL
$$$$
GALLEY BAY HILL, FIVE ISLANDS
TEL 268/462-3232
Sympathetic French hosts and traditional French cooking served on the pool terrace

or in a long, low-ceilinged dining room. Escargots in basil butter, rack of lamb with Provençal herbs, and melt-in-the-mouth *tarte tatin*.
All major cards

ALBERTO'S
$$$
WILLOUGHBY BAY
TEL 268/460-3007
Pretty Italian restaurant and local hideaway from the tourist hoards northeast of English Harbour, with decking and lots of greenery. Asparagus and shrimp ravioli, osso buco, and an ebullient patron.
Closed L & all Mon.
All major cards

COCONUT GROVE
$$$
SIBONEY BEACH CLUB
DICKENSON BAY
TEL 268/462-1538
Romantic lantern-lit beach-front setting with smoochy music. Offerings include fresh swordfish and salmon carpaccio, seared mahi-mahi with Antiguan herbs, and Jamaican jerk chicken with banana-guava marmalade. Good wine and brandy list.
All major cards

CATHERINE'S CAFÉ
$$
ENGLISH HARBOUR
TEL 268/460-5050
Cracking little dockside café with marina views and a French-inspired menu served with authentic Gallic flair. Lunchtime crêpes, quiches, salads; moules marinières for dinner.
Closed Mon. D–Tues.
MC, V

SOMETHING SPECIAL

JULIAN'S ALFRESCO
A tropical garden set back from the beach provides the perfect setting for alfresco dining and Julian Waterer's inspired Asian-European-Caribbean cuisine. Top choice: the jerk-spiced chicken with lobster medallions and a guava beurre blanc.
$$$$
BARRYMORE BEACH CLUB
RUNWAY BAY
TEL 268/562-1545
Closed Sun. L & Mon.
All major cards

BIG BANANA-PIZZAS IN PARADISE
$$
REDCLIFFE QUAY, ST. JOHN'S
TEL 268/462-5387
A handy refueling stop in an old brick warehouse in the shopping district. Pizzas, sub sandwiches, salads, espressos, capuccinos, and cold drinks.
Closed Sun.
All major cards

BARBUDA

K CLUB
$$$$$
SPANISH WELLS POINT
TEL 268/460-0300
FAX 268/460-0305
www.kclubbarbuda.com
Italian fashion designer Krizia's exclusive and stratospherically expensive Caribbean hideaway. Spacious and beautifully decorated villas and cottages. All-inclusive rates include water sports, sportfishing, tennis, nine holes of golf, and gourmet Italian meals in the main house.
39
All major cards

ST. KITTS

GOLDEN LEMON INN & VILLAS
$$$$-$$$$$
DIEPPE BAY
TEL 869/465-7260 or 800/633-7441
FAX 869/465-4019
E-MAIL info@goldenlemon.com
Lovingly restored and antique-filled 17th-century great house facing a strip of volcanic sand beach. Six "Old World" rooms in the house and 18 very comfy and chic one- and two-bedroom modern villas with private plunge pools.
26
All major cards

OTTLEY'S PLANTATION INN
$$$$-$$$$$
OTTLEY'S
TEL 869/465-7234 or 800/772-3039
FAX 869/465-4760
www.ottleys.com
Splendid 18th-century plantation great house set in lawned gardens surrounded by cane fields. Huge, pretty rooms in the main house with its antique furnishings and breezy verandas, plus two- or three-bedroom cottages on the grounds. Shuttle to the beach.
23
All major cards

SUGAR BAY CLUB
$$$-$$$$
FRIGATE BAY
TEL 869/465-8037 or 800/345-0356
FAX 869/465-6745
E-MAIL sugarbayclub@caribsurf.com
www.eliteislandresorts.com
Attractive resort complex on the Atlantic side of the island offering garden and poolside rooms, suites, and two-bedroom cottages on the beachfront. Tennis, children's club, grocery, golf nearby.
100 All major cards

TIMOTHY BEACH RESORT
$$-$$$
FRIGATE BAY
TEL 869/465-8597 or 800/288-7991 (Canada)
FAX 869/466-7085
www.timothybeach.com
The only property on the Caribbean beachfront in Frigate Bay. Good value accommodations, all with balconies or patios. Versatile layout, excellent for groups/families. On-site restaurant; shops and tennis nearby.
60
All major cards

RAWLINS PLANTATION INN
$$$$ (Lunch $$)
MOUNT PLEASANT
TEL 869/465-6221
Elegant plantation inn (with 10 rooms $$$$$) serving a superb West Indian buffet lunch—curries, fish dishes, herb-flavored rice, and homemade chutneys—and set four-course dinners. Dinner reservations essential.
All major cards

FISHERMAN'S WHARF
$$$
FORTLANDS, BASSETERRE
TEL 869/465-2754
Something of an island institution with sweeping views of the harbor (and its twinkling lights at night) from a big wooden deck. Steak and seafood cooked on an open charcoal grill, good and spicy jerk chicken, lobster, excellent chowder.
All major cards

BALLAHOO
$$
THE CIRCUS, BASSETERRE
TEL 869/465-4197
Popular downtown meeting place. Tuna melt subs, sandwiches, and burgers for lunch, hot chili shrimp, mahimahi steaks with basil-mustard butter, chicken, pasta, and vegetarian options in the evening.
Closed Sun.
All major cards

STONEWALLS
$-$$
5 PRINCES ST., BASSETERRE
TEL 869/465-5248
An exuberant tropical garden greets visitors to this friendly bar-restaurant set in a stone-walled courtyard. The constantly changing menu runs the gamut from mega-spicy jerk pork to pasta or roast beef and Yorkshire pudding.
Closed L, Sun.
All major cards

NEVIS

FOUR SEASONS RESORT
$$$$$
PINNEY'S BEACH
TEL 869/469-1111 or 800/819-5053
FAX 869/469-1040
www.fourseasons.com
Terrific position on Nevis's main beach for this sprawling property. Large rooms and suites with oversize baths and private patios by the waterfront or golf course. Sports packages, excellent children's facilities, polished service.
196
All major cards

MONTPELIER PLANTATION INN
$$$$$
FIG TREE
TEL 869/469-3462
FAX 869/469-2932
www.montpeliernevis.com
Glorious old stone plantation house on a former sugar estate. Airy, elegant rooms in cottages set in the 10-acre landscaped grounds. Meals served in the main building English country house-style. Tennis, beach shuttle.
17
All major cards

SOMETHING SPECIAL

HERMITAGE

Enchanting plantation inn with rooms in gingerbread cottages dotted about the flower-filled gardens of the oldest wooden house in the Caribbean (circa 1680–1740). Romantic four-posters, hammocks on the veranda, horseback riding, peace and quiet.

$$$$-$$$$$
GINGERLAND
TEL 869/469-3477 or 800/682-4025
FAX 869/469-2481
www.hermitagenevis.com
15 All major cards

OUALIE BEACH HOTEL
$$$
OUALIE BEACH
TEL 869/469-9735 or 800/682-5431
FAX 869/469-9176
www.ouaiiebeach.com
Small and informal beachfront property with well-priced rooms and studios in wooden cottages with screened porches overlooking the beach. Diving and windsurfing packages; mountain bikes.
32 All major cards

MISS JUNE'S
$$$$$
JONES BAY
TEL 869/469-5330
A local institution, Miss June Meister cooks a grand Caribbean-Asian-European buffet in her home about three times a week (reservations essential). Guests meet for cocktails at 7:30, before being unleashed on the two dozen gourmet dishes.
Call ahead for schedule
All major cards

UNELLA'S BY THE SEA
$
CHARLESTOWN
TEL 869/469-5574
A breezy upstairs terrace by the dock and budget menu offering fish burgers with tartar sauce, crabmeat-shrimp-salad stuffed pita pockets, beef stir fry, chicken and fries, and local dishes.
Closed L Sun. All major cards

FRENCH ANTILLES

GUADELOUPE

LE JARDIN MALANGA
$$$-$$$$
TROIS RIVIÈRES, BASSE-TERRE
TEL 590/92 67 57
FAX 590/92 67 58
www.jardinmalanga.com
Fabulous hillside setting with views of the Îles des Saintes

from the deck of this low-key hideaway. Minimalist chic rooms in 1920s plantation house or superb cottages.
9 P All major cards

LA TOUBANA
$$$
STE.-ANNE, GRANDE-TERRE
TEL 590/88 07 74
FAX 590/88 38 90
www.toubana.com
Lovely sea views and quaint one- and two-bedroom cottages *(toubanas)* with kitchenettes on the hill leading down to a small beach cove with water sports. Tennis; some evening entertainment.
33 P All major cards

AUBERGE LES PETITS SAINTS AUX ANARCADIERS
$$-$$$
TERRE-DE-HAUT, LES SAINTES
TEL 590/99 50 99
FAX 590/99 54 51
www.petitssaints.com
Pretty Creole home overflowing with antiques and kitsch collectibles amassed by the delightfully eccentric artist owners. Ten comfortable rooms five minutes from the town center; good restaurant.
11 All major cards

HÔTEL-RÉSIDENCE CANELLA BEACH
$$-$$$
POINTE DE LA VERDURE, GOSIER, GRANDE-TERRE
TEL 590/90 44 00
FAX 590/90 44 44
www.canellabeach.fr
Well-equipped studios and duplex apartments on a beachfront property in Gosier's resort area. This is a good option for families, with a children's pool and range of water-sports activities.
145 units P All major cards

LE VERGER DE STE.-ANNE
$
5 LOT. MARGUERITE
STE.-ANNE
TEL 590/88 27 56
FAX 590/88 21 45
E-MAIL verger@guadeloupe-hebergement.com
www.guadeloupe-hebergement.com
Six delightful Creole cottages dotted around the gardens. Verandas with sea views, fully-equipped kitchenettes, rattan furnishings, and inside and outside showers. A genuinely warm welcome from Danièle Granger, who can arrange rental cars, organize itineraries and, serves a mean ti-punch!
6 P All major cards

LA VIEILLE TOUR
$$$$
AUBERGE DE LA VIEILLE TOUR
GOSIER, GRANDE-TERRE
TEL 590/84 23 23
Elegant hotel dining room with sea views (reserve a window seat) and a classic French-Creole menu. Crayfish tartare, fresh fish with lobster butter, beef Creole, and magnificent desserts.
Closed L
All major cards

LA PORTE DES INDES
$$$-$$$$
DEVARIEUX, SAINT-FRANÇOIS
TEL 590/21 30 87
Connoisseurs of Indian cuisine cannot praise this delightful *temple de la gastronomie* highly enough. A statue of the elephant god Ganesh presides over the dining pavilion and a classic and creative Indian menu. Excellent wine list.
Closed Sun. D–Mon. V

IGUANE CAFÉ
$$$
RTE. DE LA POINTE DES CHÂTEAUX, ST.-FRANÇOIS
GRANDE-TERRE
TEL 590/88 61 37
Bright and funky café on the beach road serving a creative menu strong on local ingredients. Marble of foie gras and lobster with dark rum and shellfish aspic, crispy saffron conch and christophine gratin, five-spice fish.
Closed L Mon.–Sat., & Tues. mid-Sept.–mid-Oct.
All major cards

LE KARACOLI
$$-$$$
GRANDE ANSE, BASSE-TERRE
TEL 590/28 41 17
Popular beach restaurant offering fixed price menus and slightly more expensive à la carte options. Classic Creole cuisine with plenty of seafood including conch, scallops, stuffed crab, and lobster.
Closed D
All major cards

LE VIEUX PORT
$$
ST.-FRANÇOIS, GRANDE-TERRE
TEL 590/88 46 60
Tiny wooden house facing the seafront with a minuscule veranda and cozy atmosphere. *Soupe de poissons,* crayfish with ginger and coconut, curried fish and fresh pineapple in flaky pastry, menu langouste (lobster) for two ($$$$).
All major cards

PRICES

HOTELS
An indication of the cost of a double room without breakfast is given by $ signs.

$$$$$	Over $400
$$$$	$300–$400
$$$	$200–$300
$$	$100–$200
$	Under $100

RESTAURANTS
An indication of the cost of a three-course dinner without drinks is given by $ signs.

$$$$$	Over $80
$$$$	$50–$80
$$$	$35–$50
$$	$20–$35
$	Under $20

MARTINIQUE

SOMETHING SPECIAL

HABITATION LAGRANGE

Lovely 1850s Creole plantation house in a remote forest clearing. Elegant antique furnishings and large rooms in the main house; smaller versions in garden outbuildings around the pool (30 minutes from the beach). Tennis, good food, and charming hosts; a great choice for a romantic hideaway.

$$$$$
LE MARIGOT
TEL 0596/53 60 60
FAX 0596/53 50 58
www.habitationlagrange.com
18 P
All major cards

SOFITEL BAKOUA

$$$$
POINTE DU BOUT, TROIS ILETS
TEL 0596/66 02 02 or 800/221-4542
FAX 0596/66 00 41
www.sofitel.com

Attractive and well-equipped resort set on a bluff above a private beach. Comfortably appointed rooms with views. Tennis, water sports, helpful tour desk, golf nearby.

139 P
All major cards

LEYRITZ PLANTATION

$$
BASSE-POINTE
TEL 0596/78 53 92
FAX 0596/78 92 44
www.plantationleyritz.com

This old sugar estate is a busy tourist attraction by day, but peaceful retreat by late afternoon. Comfy and antique-filled accommodations in the plantation house, slave quarters, and stone cottages around the grounds. Tennis; 30 minutes from the beach.

56 P
All major cards

MANOIR DE BEAUREGARD

$-$$$
CHEMIN DES SALINES, STE.-ANNE
TEL 0596/76 73 40
FAX 0596/76 93 24
www.manoirdebeauregard.com

Stylish 18th-century manor house with marble floors, wooden beams, and open, stone archways. A few lovely rooms with traditional Creole furnishings in the house and simpler accommodations in the garden.

11 P
All major cards

DIAMANT LES BAINS

$
BOURG DU DIAMANT
TEL 0596/76 40 14
FAX 0596/76 27 00

Small and welcoming family-run hotel on the beach with seven bright and simple rooms in the main building (where the restaurant is located) and garden bungalows. Diving, water sports, tennis, and horseback riding nearby.

27 P
All major cards

LE FROMAGER

$$$
QUARTIER ST. JAMES
MORNE ABEL
TEL 0596/78 19 07

Fabulous views over St. Pierre from the veranda of this Creole dining room on the Fond St. Denis Road. Notable specialties include *feroce* (avocado, saltfish, and ferociously hot peppers), crayfish colombo (curry), and *blanc mangé* (coconut custard).

Closed D & Oct. All major cards

POÏ ET VIRGINIE

$$-$$$
10 AVENUE JEAN-MARIE TCHIBAOU, STE.-ANNE
TEL 0596/76 72 22

Pretty, bamboo-lined dining room with a waterfront terrace. The seafood platter for two is legendary (crab, oysters, prawn, shrimp, clams and more). There's a delicious fish tartare with basil or tasty octopus fricassee.

Closed Tue.
All major cards

TI SABLE

$$-$$$
GRAND ANSE, ANSES D'ARLET
TEL 0596/68 62 44

Enviable sand-between-the-toes beachfront location and a French-Creole menu offering tuna carpaccio, grilled shrimp, yummy salads, and delicious desserts. Sunday buffet with live music.

Closed D Mon.–Fri.
All major cards

AU POISSON D'OR

$$
ANSE MITAN, TROIS ILETS
TEL 0596/66 01 80

Popular Creole restaurant on the Pointe du Bout road. Lots of bamboo, greenery, and waitresses in traditional costume. Specialties include lime-marinated conch, spicy shark, and grilled lobster Creole.

Closed all Mon., L (low season only), & July All major cards

LA DUNETTE

$$
HOTEL LA DUNETTE
STE.-ANNE
TEL 0596/76 73 90

Seaside views in the heart of the village and a largely seafood menu featuring local delicacies such as smoked fish, snapper stuffed with sea urchins in a curry sauce, and killer chocolate gâteau.

Closed mid-June–mid-July
All major cards

ST.-BARTHÉLEMY

EDEN ROCK

$$$$$
ST. JEAN
TEL 0590/29 79 99
FAX 0590/27 88 37
www.edenrockhotel.com

St. Barts' first hotel has been stylishly rebuilt. The new buildings seem to grow organically from a rocky promontory above the beach. Cool classic suites featuring natural wood or colorful silks, romantic boudoirs, and delectable cottages. Good restaurants; intimate atmosphere.
36 P
All major cards

FRANÇOIS PLANTATION
$$$$$
COLOMBIER
TEL 0590/29 80 22
FAX 0590/27 61 26
www.francoisplantation.com
A dozen clapboard Creole cottages with crisp blue and white decor and old colonial furnishings buried in heavenly hillside gardens. Stunning views; excellent restaurant in the elegant estate house (see Le Domaine, right).
12 P
All major cards

LE TOINY
$$$$$
ANSE DE TOINY
TEL 0590/27 88 88 or 800/LET-OINY
FAX 0590/27 89 30
www.hotelletoiny.com
Superbly elegant and secluded Relais & Châteaux property, with a dozen spacious and beautifully decorated cottages boasting private pools, kitchenettes, and fitness equipment. Excellent restaurant (see Le Gaïac, below).
15 P
All major cards

LES ILETS FLEURIS
$$
HAUTS DE LORIENT
TEL 0590/27 64 22
FAX 0590/27 69 72
E-MAIL caraibes@outremer.com
Simple and pretty one-bedroom cottages (some canopy beds for romantics) with kitchenettes perched on a hilltop. Affordable rates include rental car (5 minutes to the beach); sea views add to the price ($$$).
9 P
All major cards

LE GAÏAC
$$$$$
LE TOINY, ANSE DE TOINY
TEL 0590/27 88 88
Small and chic with sea views, Le Gaïac delivers top-notch French-Caribbean cuisine. Chilled spicy mango soup, foie gras terrine, lamb chops with sweet potato and plantain pie, conch ravioli. Reservations recommended.
Closed Mon., Sept.–Oct.
All major cards

FRANÇOIS PLANTATION
$$$$-$$$$$
COLOMBIER
TEL 0590/29 80 22
Romantic open dining room framed by gardens, and sophisticated French cooking accompanied by an excellent international wine list. Gazpacho of marinated scallops and skewer of roasted duck magret and pineapple highly recommended.
Closed L, and Mon.; Sept. to mid-Oct. All major cards

EDDY'S
$$$$
RUE DU CENTENAIRE
GUSTAVIA
TEL 0590/27 54 17
Balinese teak, bamboo, and an explosion of greenery lend a Southeast Asian note to the decor, further reflected in the French-Caribbean-Asian menu. Fashionable spot for shrimp green curry, Creole colombo, and grilled fish.
Closed L & all Sun.
All major cards

LE SÉLECT
$
RUE DE LA FRANCE, GUSTAVIA
TEL 0590/27 86 87
Hip downtown bar with bustling garden patio and pumping reggae, zouk, and live music in the old brick warehouse at night. Cheeseburgers and cocktails are the highlights.
All major cards

WINDWARD ISLANDS

CARRIACOU

GREEN ROOF INN
$-$$
HILLSBOROUGH
TEL/FAX 473/443-6399
www.greenroofinn.com
This unpretentious little Scandinavian-owned guesthouse is an absolute charmer. Clean pastel shades and white linen in the guest rooms and a romantic white clapboard cottage hideaway with its own kitchenette. Fabulous views, beach access, friendly bar and veranda restaurant.
5 rooms, 1 cottage P
MC, V

DOMINICA

FORT YOUNG
$-$$$
ROSEAU
TEL 767/448-5000 or 800/581-2035
FAX 767/448-5006
www.fortyoung.com
Attractive rooms and spacious suites built around a pool deck nestled in the remains of a historic seafront fortress, plus a smart new ocean view block down on the water. Good location, in-house tour desk.
70 P
All major cards

PICARD BEACH COTTAGE RESORT
$-$$
PICARD BEACH, PORTSMOUTH
TEL 767/445-5131
FAX 767/445-5599
www.avirtualdominica.com/picard
Simple rooms in quiet Creole cottages on one of Dominica's better black sand beaches. Private verandas and

kitchenettes; lovely gardens on an old coconut plantation.
18 P Some
All major cards

SOMETHING SPECIAL

ZANDOLI INN

A lovely little country inn balanced on cliffs 80 feet above the ocean in the south of the island. Fabulous views, delightful gardens with a plunge pool, and pretty guest rooms decked out in soothing blues and greens. Good food (and company) in the restaurant. Walking trails nearby. No children under 12.

$$
ROCHE CASSÉE – STOWE
TEL 767/446-3161
FAX 767/446-3344
www.zandoli.com
5 P
All major cards

ANCHORAGE HOTEL & DIVE CENTRE

$-$$
CASTLE COMFORT
TEL 767/448-2638
FAX 767/448-5680
www.anchoragehotel.com
Small block of modern units with a splash of Creole color and balconies overlooking the sea just south of Roseau. This is a great base for activities, with a PADI dive center and hiking trips, a squash court, plus helpful and friendly staff.
32
All major cards

DE BOUILLE

$$$
FORT YOUNG HOTEL, ROSEAU
TEL 767/448-2930
The island's smartest restaurant enclosed by rough-hewn stone walls decorated with local art. Baked crab with parmesan, grilled tuna in a creamy watercress sauce, conch Creole served with ground provisions and fresh garden vegetables.
All major cards

LA ROBE CREOLE

$$$
3 VICTORIA ST., ROSEAU
TEL 767/448-2896
Renowned restaurant in a cozy old stone town house promising Dominican specialties such as mountain chicken (frog's legs) crêpe, lobster and spicy stuffed land crabs in season. Waitresses wear the traditional Madras *robe créole*.
Closed Sun.
All major cards

PAPILLOTE WILDERNESS RETREAT

$$
TRAFALGAR VALLEY
TEL 767/448-2287
Neat rain-forest inn (8 simple rooms, $) with tables on a leafy terrace hemmed in by greenery. The unpretentious menu is packed with favorite Caribbean staples, seasonal fruits, and vegetables. Reservations recommended for dinner.
All major cards

COCORICO CAFÉ

$-$$$
BAYFRONT (AT KENNEDY AVE.), ROSEAU
TEL 767/449-8686
A French café set in a jauntily painted Creole house, and a great spot in front of the ferry terminal to hang out and watch the world go by. The day starts with breakfast, moves on to stuffed baguettes and savory croissants for lunch, cocktails at sunset, then dinner.
Closed D, Sun. MC, V

GRENADA

CALABASH HOTEL & VILLAS

$$$$$
L'ANSE AUX EPINES
TEL 473/444-4334
FAX 473/444-5050
www.calabashhotel.com
Sedate and charming beachfront hotel with very comfortable suites (some with small private pools) arranged in an arc of two-story garden cottages. Caring service includes breakfast prepared in your suite by the maid. Tennis and non-motorized water sports; good food (see p. 380). A small and exclusive development of architect-designed villas is taking shape.
30 rooms, 2 villas P
All major cards

LA SOURCE

$$$$$
PINK GIN BEACH
TEL 473/444-2556 or 888/527-0044
FAX 473/444-2561
www.theamazingholiday.com
This luxurious, all-inclusive spa has undergone a major post-hurricane rejuvenation and is due to reopen in autumn 2007 with improved facilities and activities opportunities.
100 P
All major cards

SPICE ISLAND BEACH RESORT

$$$$$
GRAND ANSE
TEL 473/444-4258
FAX 473/444-4807
www.spicebeachresort.com
All-suite property stretching along Grenada's largest beach. Pastel colors, wicker furnishings, and whirlpools (some units have private pools and exercise facilities). Tennis and nonmotorized water sports.
66 P
All major cards

FLAMBOYANT

$$-$$$
GRAND ANSE
TEL 473/444-4247
FAX 473/444-1234
www.flamboyant.com
A steep (but mercifully short) hike up from the beach, great views across to St. George's, and a selection of comfy rooms, self-catering one- or two-bedroom suites and studios, all with balconies.
67 P Some
All major cards

LA SAGESSE NATURE CENTRE
$$
LA SAGESSE, ST. DAVID'S
TEL/FAX 473/444-6458
www.lasagesse.com
An off-the-beaten-track beach hideaway with simple, spacious rooms in a 1920s estate house, an oceanfront annex (including a suite and two duplexes), and two rooms in a cottage. Ceiling fans, verandas, good food.
12 P MC, V

RHODES RESTAURANT
$$$$
CALABASH HOTEL, L'ANSE AUX EPINES, GRENADA
TEL 473/444-4334
This elegant and pretty terrace dining room is a Caribbean outpost for acclaimed British chef, Gary Rhodes. The seasonally inspired menu features local produce from jerk chicken with sweet pawpaw salad to Grenadian fish stew flavored with saffron and orange. Reservations.
Closed L All major cards

COCONUTS' BEACH RESTAURANT
$$$
GRAND ANSE
TEL 473/444-4644
Dine on the sand or inside the old wooden house. French Creole specialties such as conch curry, lobster, or catch of the day in a variety of sauces.
Closed Tue. All major cards

AQUARIUM BEACH CLUB & RESTAURANT
$$
TAMARIND BEACH POINT SALINES
TEL 473/444-1410
Woodsy, open-air beach restaurant. Well-prepared world food from satay or pumpkin and ginger soup to snapper with a coriander-herb crust, oven-baked Cornish hen, New Zealand lamb, and U.S. steaks. Sunday barbecues.
All major cards

MORNE FENDUE
$
NEAR SAUTEURS, ST. PATRICK'S DISTRICT
TEL 473/442-9330
This small plantation home is renowned for its West Indian lunch buffet. A groaning table of local fish, meat, rice 'n' peas, and vegetable dishes including pepperpot stew.
Closed D All major cards

THE NUTMEG
$
THE CARENAGE, ST. GEORGE'S
TEL 473/440-2539
Casual local meeting place with harbor views, a lively bar, and a simple menu of soups, sandwiches, roti, and fruit or rum punches with a generous sprinkling of nutmeg.
Closed B & L Sun. All major cards

ST. LUCIA

ANSE CHASTANET RESORT
$$$$$
SOUFRIÈRE
TEL 758/459-7000 or 800/223-1108
FAX 758/459-7700
www.ansechastanet.com
Set in a steep-sided beach cove down a bumpy track, this delightful small spa resort is wonderfully relaxing and a good dive center. Lovely rooms in octagonal gazebos with wraparound balconies, hillside or beachside suites, great views, tennis, attentive service.
49 P All major cards

TI KAYE VILLAGE
$$$-$$$$
ANSE COCHON
TEL 758/456-8101
FAX 758/456-8105
www.tikaye.com
Grafted onto a wooded bluff above the beach between Castries and Soufrière, charming cottages and duplexes (great for families) in landscaped grounds. Hammocks on the balcony, net-draped beds, some private plunge pools. Super restaurant, beach bar-grill, diving.
33
All major cards

PRICES

HOTELS
An indication of the cost of a double room without breakfast is given by **$** signs.

$$$$$	Over $400
$$$$	$300–$400
$$$	$200–$300
$$	$100–$200
$	Under $100

RESTAURANTS
An indication of the cost of a three-course dinner without drinks is given by $ signs.

$$$$$	Over $80
$$$$	$50–$80
$$$	$35–$50
$$	$20–$35
$	Under $20

SOMETHING SPECIAL

RAINFOREST HIDEAWAY
Imagine a rustic-chic waterfront dock set with tables, a champagne bar amongst the mangroves, and gentle jazz. The fusion dinner menu combines Caribbean, Asian and Oriental flavors (ravioli stuffed with ginger and coconut crab); lighter and simpler lunches.
$$$$-$$$$$
MARIGOT BAY
TEL 758/451-4485
Closed Tue. All major cards

MARIGOT BEACH CLUB
$$-$$$
MARIGOT BAY
TEL 758/451-4974

KEY Hotel Restaurant No. of bedrooms Parking Closed Elevator

FAX 758/451-4973
www.marigotdiveresort.com
Delightful inn with a selection of comfortable rental studios and two- and three-bedroom villas above Marigot Bay. Tiny beach, water sports, dive shop, sailing packages.
25 P
All major cards

HARMONY MARINA SUITES
$$
RODNEY BAY
TEL 758/452-8756
FAX 758/452-8677
www.harmonysuites.com
Small and friendly complex on the water minutes from Reduit Beach. Well-equipped standard suites and deluxe units, some kitchenettes. On-site restaurant, mini-mart, and beauty salon.
30 P
All major cards

GREAT HOUSE
$$$$
CAP ESTATE
TEL 758/450-0450
Elegant dining in a re-created plantation great house adorned with chandeliers and spreading tropical flower arrangements. Specialties include seafood casserole, beef tenderloin with wild mushrooms, and iced coconut nougat for dessert.
Closed L & all Mon.
All major cards

JACQUES' WATERFRONT DINING
$$
VIGIE MARINA, CASTRIES
TEL 758/458-1900
Popular bar and terrace dining area in a harborside cove behind Pointe Seraphine. French patron-chef Jacky Rioux's specialty is fish and seafood including favorites such as octopus and conch in a curried coconut sauce.
Closed Sun.
All major cards

HUMMINGBIRD
$$
HUMMINGBIRD BEACH RESORT, SOUFRIÈRE
TEL 758/459-7232
Delightful garden restaurant with views of the Pitons and a well-earned reputation for fine French and Creole cuisine. The signature seafood dish is marinated and stuffed dorado with local herbs, and the vegetables are homegrown.
All major cards

THE LIME
$$
RODNEY BAY
TEL 758/452-0761
A longstanding favorite with visitors and locals alike. Tables inside and out, and a menu that opens with breakfast and fills out to include Caribbean and international dishes from steaks and seafood to Jamaican jerk.
All major cards

ST. VINCENT

YOUNG ISLAND
$$$-$$$$$
OPPOSITE VILLA
TEL 784/458-4826 or 800/223-1108 (U.S.)
FAX 784/457-4567
www.youngisland.com
A private island resort with pretty wood and stone cottages enfolded in tropical greenery. Patios and sea views, some small swimming pools. Tennis, water sports, yachting excursions, spa treatments.
30 P
All major cards

GRAND VIEW BEACH HOTEL
$$
VILLA POINT
TEL 784/458-4811 or 800/223-6510 (U.S.)
FAX 784/457-4174
www.grandviewhotel.com
Suitably grand views and very comfortable rooms in a turn-of-the-20th-century plantation house with a bright and airy modern wing on a cliff top promontory. Steps down to the beach, tennis, squash; friendly and helpful staff.
19 P
All major cards

FRENCH VERANDAH RESTAURANT
$$$$
MARINERS HOTEL, VILLA BEACH
TEL 784/457-4000
Charming hotel-restaurant on the waterfront facing the twinkly lights of Young Island at night. The menu is long on fish and seafood, some local flavors such as *calaloo* and conch soup and stuffed crab backs, and indubitably French garlic snails and steak frîtes. Good French wines.
All major cards

LIME 'N' PUB
$$
VILLA
TEL 784/458-4227
Jolly pub with a terrace, dining room, and bar decorated with fishing nets and colored lights. Huge choice of British-style pub grub, sandwiches, and burgers, plus a more formal dinner menu offering plenty of seafood.
All major cards

BEQUIA

FRIENDSHIP BAY BEACH RESORT
$$$-$$$$$
FRIENDSHIP BAY
TEL 784/458-3222
FAX 784/458-3840
www.friendshipbayhotel.com
Casual and friendly small resort with cute rooms and beach cottages featuring hand-painted decorations and ocean views from private terraces. Tennis, sailing, water sports, dive packages.
28 All major cards

GINGERBREAD
$-$$
PORT ELIZABETH
TEL 784/458-3800
Three dining options in one: The daytime Gingerbread

Café does a great line in coffees, juices, and homemade cakes. Fresh seafood kebabs and chicken end up on the Gingerbread BBQ at lunch. Or there is the Gingerbread Restaurant, with bay views from the veranda and a lunch menu of pasta, salads, omelets. Callaloo and shrimp soup and curries in the evening.
All major cards

CANOUAN

RAFFLES RESORT
$$$$$
SALT WHISTLE BAY
TEL 784/458-8000
FAX 784/458-8885
www.canouan.raffles.com
Peerless luxury resort set amphitheater-style around a pristine bay. Huge and elegant accommodations in single- and double-story villas, every amenity from personal golf carts and Fazio-designed golf course to Amrita spa and European-style casino.
156 All major cards

MAYREAU

SALT WHISTLE BAY CLUB
$$$$$
SALT WHISTLE BAY
TEL 784/458-8444
FAX 784/458-8944
Barefoot island escape with a handful of simple but appealing stone cottages set amid tropical gardens by a fabulous beach. Hammocks, windsurfers, snorkeling, dive packages.
8 All major cards

MUSTIQUE

MUSTIQUE VILLA RENTALS
$$$$$
TEL 784/488-8000
FAX 784/488-9000
E-MAIL villarentals@mustique.vc
There are about 50 sumptuous two- to seven-bedroom villa rentals on the island. All come with cook and maid.
50 villas All major cards

BARBADOS

ALMOND BEACH VILLAGE
$$$$$
HEYWOODS, ST. PETER
TEL 246/422-4900 or 800/425-6663
FAX 246/422-0617
www.almondresorts.com
Large and attractive all-inclusive property on a fine beach. Wide range of accommodations and facilities ranging from golf, water sports, tennis, and squash to well-designed children's programs.
330 P
All major cards

COBBLERS COVE
$$$$$
SPEIGHTSTOWN, ST. PETER
TEL 246/422-2291 or 800/890-6060
FAX 246/422-1460
www.cobblerscove.com
Small and elegant all-suite hotel. Lovely accommodations with balcony or terrace overlooking the tropical gardens, plus two fabulous luxury suites. Tennis, water sports, notable restaurant.
40 P
All major cards

CORAL REEF CLUB
$$$$$
HOLETOWN, ST. JAMES
TEL 246/422-2372 or 800/223-1108
FAX 246/422-1776
www.coralreefbarbados.com
Gracious family-owned operation with a faithful clientele. Accommodations in attractive and thoughtfully appointed garden cottages and more luxurious suites. Lovely grounds, tennis, water sports, good food.
64 P
All major cards

BOUGAINVILLEA BEACH RESORT
$$$-$$$$
MAXWELL, CHRIST CHURCH
TEL 246/418-0990 or 800/988-6904
FAX 246/428-2524
www.bougainvillearesort.com
Very spacious and comfortable studios and one- or two-bedroom suites with kitchenettes and waterfront balconies or terraces. Dining, tennis, and water sports are all available.
138 P
All major cards

ALLAMANDA BEACH HOTEL
$$
HASTINGS, CHRIST CHURCH
TEL 246/438-1000
FAX 246/435-9211
E-MAIL vacation@allamanda beach.com
Large and comfortable bedroom units with kitchenettes on the waterfront a short walk from Rockley Beach. Friendly family management.
50 P Some
All major cards

PEACH AND QUIET
$-$$
INCH MARLOW, CHRIST CHURCH
TEL 246/428-5682
FAX 246/428-2467
www.peachandquiet.com
This really is a peachy little spot. An affordable ocean front all-suites guesthouse with charming Brit owners, a restaurant, and peace and quiet virtually guaranteed (no kids under 16). All suites have balcony /terrace. Snorkeling; hiking.
22 P MC, V

THE CLIFF
$$$$$
DERRICKS, ST. JAMES
TEL 246/432-1922
A brace of theatrically lit terraces carved into the limestone sea cliffs and clientele poised to sample some of the finest cuisine in the region. Combinations such as lightly char-grilled tuna with corian-

der cream sauce; impressive wines. Reservations.
Closed L
All major cards

DAPHNE'S
$$$$$
PAYNE'S BAY, ST. JAMES
TEL 264/432-2731
A Caribbean outpost for one of London's exclusive restaurants. Flaming torches in the courtyard, beachside dining, and stylish modern Italian cuisine that's both delicious and beautifully-presented. Reservations advised.
All major cards

DAVID'S PLACE
$$$$
ST. LAWRENCE MAIN RD., WORTHING, CHRIST CHURCH
TEL 246/435-9755
The setting in a wooden cottage overlooking St. Lawrence Bay is perfect for fine Bajan cuisine. Lots of fresh fish, and signature dishes such as Arawak pepperpot stew, and simple but delicious, cheddar cheese bread.
Closed L, & Mon.
All major cards

PISCES
$$$
ST. LAWRENCE GAP
CHRIST CHURCH
TEL 246/435-6564
Split-level dining room with trellises, clambering plants, and terra-cotta lanterns on the water's edge. Seafood specialties include shrimp and tomato stuffed snapper in a parsley-lime sauce or pasta and chicken dishes. Delicious desserts—rum-raisin ice cream.
Closed L All major cards

RAGAMUFFINS
$$$
1ST ST., HOLETOWN, ST. JAMES
TEL 246/432-1295
Jaunty green and blue chattel house with a lively bar and cozy-casual atmosphere. West Indian curries, blackened shrimp, grilled kingfish, T-bone steaks, and vegetarian options.
Closed L All major cards

ATLANTIS HOTEL
$$
BATHSHEBA, ST. JOSEPH
TEL 246/433-9445
The set-price buffet here is a lunchtime institution on the tourist circuit, and Sunday's West Indian buffet brunch (reservations) is a veritable feast. Cliff-top terrace and dining room.
Closed D Sun.
All major cards

WATERFRONT CAFÉ
$$
THE CAREENAGE, BRIDGETOWN
TEL 246/427-0093
Handy downtown café on the south bank of the Careenage. Broad menu from Bajan fishcakes, smoked flying fish, and salads to jerk pork and pasta. Music nightly.
Closed Sun.
All major cards

TRINIDAD & TOBAGO

TRINIDAD

TRINIDAD HILTON
$$$
LADY YOUNG RD.
PORT OF SPAIN
TEL 868/624-3211
FAX 868/625-9710
www.hiltoncaribbean.com/trinidad
A reliable option on Queen's Park Savannah, the Hilton makes up for its somewhat bland profile with polished service and good facilities. Well-appointed rooms, tennis, and entertainment.
394 P
All major cards

ASA WRIGHT NATURE CENTRE & LODGE
$$
ARIMA
TEL 868/667-4655 or 800/426-7781
FAX 868/667-4540
www.asawright.org
Simple lodgings at the famous rain forest nature center (see p. 325). Rooms with screened verandas in garden cottages, a two-bed cottage, or two large, airy rooms in the Colonial-style main building. All meals included; field trips extra.
25 P All major cards

KAPOK
$$
16–18 COTTON HILL,
ST. CLAIR, PORT OF SPAIN
TEL 868/622-5765
FAX 868/622-9677
www.kapokhotel.com
Pleasant businessmen's hotel on the northwest corner of Queen's Park Savannah. Comfortable rooms with tropical fabrics and wicker furnishings; good restaurant.
94 P
All major cards

MT PLAISIR ESTATE
$
GRANDE RIVIÈRE
TEL 818/670-2216
FAX 868/670-0057
www.mtplaisir.com
Simple but seductive remote beach getaway with a rainforest backdrop and sea views. Rooms furnished by local craftsmen (sleep 4-6); turtle-watching and eco excursions; restaurant serves local items including lobster, fruit and vegetables from the estate and homemade bread.
13 All major cards

APSARA
$$$
LEVEL 1, 13 QUEENS PARK EAST, BELMONT,
PORT OF SPAIN
TEL 868/623-7959
A handsomely renovated colonial house is the setting for impeccably authentic Northern Indian food (not the Trinidadian version) in stagy Indian surroundings. Sample specialities from the

tandoori ovens including locally-caught lobster tails. Closed Sat. L, Sun. All major cards

SOLIMAR
$$$
6 NOOK AVE., ST. ANN'S
PORT OF SPAIN
TEL 868/624-6267
Pretty veranda setting with meandering greenery and an international menu. Duck with couscous, crab ragout, spicy beef with lemon grass, swordfish gravlax with a saffron-mustard. Reservations. Closed Sun. All major cards

TIKI VILLAGE
$$$
KAPOK HOTEL (8TH FLOOR)
16-18 COTTON HILL
PORT OF SPAIN
TEL 868/622-5765
The great Trinidadian culinary melting pot continues with this popular Chinese and Polynesian restaurant perched above Queen's Park Savannah with views over the city lights at night. Lunchtime dim sum buffet, and dinner specialties include walnut-shrimp firepot. All major cards

VENI MANGÉ
$-$$
67A ARIAPITA AVE.
WOODBROOK
PORT OF SPAIN
TEL 868/624-4597
Funky lunch spot run by local chat show hostess Allyson Hennessy and her sister Roses. Nouvelle Caribbean dining adds up to great soups, creative seafood, and vegetarian options such as black-eyed pea croquettes. Closed D Mon., Tue., Thur. & Sat.–Sun. all day All major cards

TOBAGO

COCO REEF RESORT
$$$$
COCONUT BAY
TEL 868/639-8571
FAX 868/639-8574
www.cocoreef.com
Contemporary plantation-style with a grand foyer opening onto a man-made beachfront lagoon. Rooms, suites, and villas with terra-cotta tiles and white wicker furnishings. Tennis, water sports, spa, golf nearby. Walking distance to shops and restaurants.
135 All major cards

SOMETHING SPECIAL

FOOTPRINTS ECO RESORT

Hammocks and solar jacuzzis for latter-day Robinson Crusoes. Rooms, suites, and villas built of teak and recycled hardwoods, thatched, and perched on stilts like tree houses. Spa, hiking, snorkeling, organic produce in the restaurant.
$$-$$$
CULLODEN BAY
TEL 868/660-0118
FAX 868/660-0416
www.footprintseco-resort.com
15 All major cards

KARIWAK VILLAGE
$$
CROWN POINT
TEL 868/639-8442
FAX 868/639-8441
www.kariwak.com
A "holistic haven and hotel," Kariwak nurtures guests with yoga, relaxation sessions, massage, and healthy food. Accommodations in garden rooms or pool cabanas a 10-minute walk from the beach. Daily shuttle to Pigeon Point.
24 All major cards

LA TARTARUGA
$$$$
BUCCOO BAY ROAD
BUCCOO
TEL 868/639-0940
Italian restaurant named after the leatherback turtles that nest nearby. Homemade pasta, pizzas, authentic antipasto, fish and rock lobsters, and scrumptious desserts served inside or out on the terrace. Over 200 Italian wines in the cellar, plus a deli selling olives, cheese, salami and home baked bread. Closed Sun. All major cards

SHIRVAN WATERMILL
$$$
MOUNT PLEASANT
TEL 868/639-0000
Pretty circular pavilion framed with tropical plants by an old stone mill. Fish salad with tomato vinaigrette, seafood crêpe, grilled freshwater crayfish, char-broiled lamb with rosemary sauce. L All major cards

KARIWAK VILLAGE
$$
KARIWAK VILLAGE
CROWN POINT
TEL 868/639-8442
Alfresco dining in a nest of palm-thatched tiki huts. Home-cooking flavored with garden herbs. Seafood soup with cumin and basil, green fig (banana) salad with chives and parsley, scrumptious nutmeg ice cream. Buffet and band Friday and Saturday. All major cards

CIAO CAFÉ
$
20 BURNETT STREET
SCARBOROUGH
TEL 868/639-3001
A handy Italian café and gelateria in downtown Scarborough. Enjoy a break with a real cappuccino or espresso and a slice of cheesecake, or choose from 20 different flavors of ice cream. More substantial offerings include lasagne al forno and freshly made pizzas. Closed Sun. L No credit cards

SHOPPING

JAMAICA

Jamaica offers something for everyone, from hand-rolled cigars to elaborate wood carvings or duty-free goods. The roadside stalls and crafts markets' best sellers are wood carvings, T-shirts, hammocks, shell craft, straw hats, bamboo items, and alabaster sculptures.

Almost every town has a market, usually with some craft items. However, for the widest range of straw goods, hats and similar items the best place to go is the **Craft Market** in Kingston (Ocean Boulevard, Mon.-Sat.). Bargaining over the price (or "haggling") is the norm—never pay the first asking price. Avoid items made using "tortoiseshell" (from the endangered hawksbill turtle), black coral, or crocodile skins: Importing these into the United States is illegal.

Another great buy is reggae music: there are good music outlets in most towns and resorts, although the best are in Kingston and the **Island Village Complex** in Ocho Rios.

Essential oils and bodycare products from the Blue Mountain Aromatics and Starfish Aromatherapy also make excellent souvenirs. Local spices are always a good buy, particularly food seasonings such as the spicy Pickapeppa sauces or "jerk" sauces. Blue Mountain coffee, either pre-ground or as beans is another good souvenir. Premium Jamaican rums are also widely available, as is the superb locally made Tia Maria coffee liqueur.

Jamaica has a strong tradition of fine art, spanning many different contemporary forms. In Kingston try the **Grosvenor Galleries** (1 Grosvenor Terrace, tel 876/924-6684), or the **Contemporary Art Gallery** (1 Liguanea Ave., tel 876/927-9958). Upmarket arts and crafts are also available in the shops at **Devon House**.

Duty-free or "in bond" shops carry items such as silverware, crystal, china, watches, jewelry, linens, and perfumes. Savings can be made, but check the purchase price at home before leaving. All goods must be paid for in U.S. currency; you will need your travel documents (airline/cruise ticket and identification). Alcohol and tobacco purchases are delivered to airports/cruise ship piers before you leave.

CAYMAN ISLANDS

On duty-free Grand Cayman discounts of between 20–50 percent on U.S. prices are promised, particularly on items such as linen, leather goods, designer clothes, crystal, porcelain, perfumes, watches, and camera equipment. Most shops are in George Town, but several malls have sprung up on the West Bay Road, including the **Westshore Plaza, Galleria Plaza, Coconut Place, the Strand,** and **Cayman Falls.** In George Town itself, the **Anchorage Shopping Center, Duty Free Center,** and **Kirk Freeport Center** are some of the main outlets. (To avoid the cruise ship crowds, go on Fridays and Saturdays.) Grand Cayman also has some excellent diving equipment shops with a good range of the latest gear.

Local arts and crafts are worth seeking out in galleries such as **Pure Art** (S. Church St., tel 345/949-9133) and the **Kennedy Gallery** (West Shore Center, tel 345/949-8077). Sea-salvaged coins from Spanish or Dutch treasure ships can be bought at **Artifacts** (Harbour Dr., tel 345/949-2442), and similar numismatic items are also available at **24 K-Mon Jewelers** (several locations including Cayman Falls Plaza, tel 345/949-1499). For an unusual underwater souvenir, take home a stunning print by world famous under-water photographer Cathy Church (Sunset House, tel 345/949-7415).

The islands' biggest selling export item is rum cake. Made from a recipe reputedly over 100 years old, this cake features as its chief ingredient five-year-old Tortuga Gold rum. Buy it at any one of the many outlets of the **Tortuga Rum Company**, which can be found in the island's major shopping centers.

TURKS & CAICOS ISLANDS

If you are planning to go shopping in TCI, then head for the gateway island of Providenciales. Most of the shops here are in small malls along the Leeward Highway on Providenciales, such as **Ports of Call, Arch Plaza, Central Square, Market Place,** and **Caicos Cafe Plaza.**

With no sales tax on the islands, you can buy duty-free goods such as jewelry, watches, perfumes, crystal, cameras, cigars, and liquor. Duty-free outlets include **Royal Jewels** (several locations), **The Goldsmith** (Central Sq.), and **Carib West** (downtown, liquor and tobacco products only).

One of the island's best-known galleries, the **Bamboo Gallery** (Market Place), features paintings by local and Haitian artists, as well as beaded jewelry, wooden masks, ceramics, and soapstone and granite sculpture.

Other craft and art outlets include **Anna's Art Gallery & Studio** (Saltmills), the **Tourist Shoppe** and **Greensleeves** (Central Sq.), and **Maison Creole** (next to Ports of Call).

DOMINICAN REPUBLIC

Duty-free goods are available at **Centro de Los Héroes** and **Las Atarazanas** in Santo Domingo. (Purchases are delivered to airport departure gates.)

One of the main shopping streets in Santo Domingo is **Calle el Conde**—now pedestrianized. Most major resorts have shops selling summer attire, T-shirts, and swimwear. Crafts can be found in the main markets in every town (the biggest is the **Mercado Modelo** on Ave. Esquina Santomé in

Santo Domingo), although the products tend to be production-line straw hats, wooden boxes, and animal sculptures. Naïve Haitian art is also on sale almost everywhere. The Dominican Republic produces reasonably priced rum and cigars.

PUERTO RICO

Puerto Rico is not a duty-free island but has no sales tax (except on jewelry). There is no duty on items taken into the U.S., so you can good prices on china, crystal, fashions find, and crafts. All prices are in US$. Old San Juan offers a variety of shops, especially for jewelry, leather, and clothes. (Retailers include Tommy Hilfiger, Coach, and Polo/Ralph Lauren.) There are also some fine art galleries.

Condado is known for its exclusive boutiques and fashion designer shops such as Louis Vuitton, Cartier, Mercier, Jacardi, La Favorita, and Oggetti.

In the heart of the San Juan metropolitan area is **Plaza Las Américas,** the largest shopping center in the Caribbean, with over 200 stores.

Old San Juan has a number of souvenir and handicraft shops. For local arts and crafts buys, check out the excellent **Centro Nacional de Artes Populares y Artesanias** (Calle Cristo 253).

Popular gifts include *santos* (small carved saint figures), carnival masks, and *mundillo*, handmade bobbin lace. Fine hammocks are still made here, and, of course, Puerto Rico is a major producer of rum and cigars.

U.S. VIRGIN ISLANDS

ST. CROIX

Downtown **Christiansted** offers the best shopping on the island, centered on Strand, King, and Company Streets, and King's Alley Walk. The walk offers boutiques and galleries, craft stalls selling coconut shell carvings, and jewelry stores, where the turquoise-colored gemstone larimar (found exclusively in the Caribbean) has been incorporated in pendants, rings and bracelets. The **Caribbean Bracelet Company** specializes in Cruzan Hook bracelets: You wear the hook facing your heart if it is taken, away from the heart if you are available. And on the first Thursday of every month local galleries stay open late for **Art Thursday.**

Frederiksted's main shopping area is clustered near the cruise ship pier, and offers a selection of specialty shops and art galleries displaying works by local artists.

You can watch artists work in the **St. Croix LEAP** woodwork studio (Mahogany Rd. Rte. 76), north of Frederiksted, and buy carvings on island hardwoods. The **Whim Museum** gift shop has a good range of local crafts, condiments, books, and maps.

ST. JOHN

Shopping on St. John is low-key. There are a few small boutiques and jewelers in **Wharfside Village,** close to the ferry dock. For more of a selection, head to **Mongoose Junction** (North Shore Rd.)—an open-air complex in the local plantation house style. **R. & I. Patton Goldsmithing** sell Rudy and Irene's island-inspired designs in 14- to 18-carat gold and sterling silver, as well as authenticated antique Spanish coins set in rings and pendants. **Big Planet Adventurer Outfitters** can outfit hikers and offers colorful swimwear and resortwear. **Fabric Mill** specializes in table and bed linens, batik, and hand-painted cotton T-shirts and sweaters in fabulous aquamarines and sunset oranges by local designer Sloop Jones.

ST. THOMAS

U.S. visitors can take advantage of a $1,600 duty-free allowance on returning home, and families can pool their allowances for larger purchases. Any items actually made in the USVI do not count toward the duty-free exemption. Popular buys are fine crystal and china, electronics, jewelry, and perfume, sold in large stores on Dronningens Gade/Main Street and the Havensight Mall. Stores are generally open Monday to Saturday 9 a.m. to 5 p.m. If a cruise ship calls on a Sunday, some stores will open for at least part of the day.

In Charlotte Amalie, a slew of boutiques is tucked in the narrow alleys leading down to the Waterfront, where the eye-catching boutique. **Local Color** does a fun line in pretty Jams World uncrushable sundresses and other cotton prints, straw hats, hand-painted T-shirts, and silver jewelry.

For great Caribbean crafts and souvenirs, check out the **Native Arts and Crafts Cooperative,** bottom of Tolbod Gade, piled high with locally produced items including woodcarvings, costume dolls, and Taste of Paradise sauces and jellies. Also the **Caribbean Marketplace** in Havensight Mall. Duty-free stores, here, sell jewelry, cameras and electronics, liquor, and tobacco.

Outside Charlotte Amalie, **Tillett Gardens** is an artisans' enclave with galleries, craft studios, a restaurant, and pet iguanas basking in the shade.

BRITISH VIRGIN ISLANDS

TORTOLA

Road Town's top souvenir stop has to be the **Sunny Caribbee Spice Co.** on Main Street. This is condiment city, piled high with exotic fruit teas and liqueurs, preserves made from guava, papaya, and passionfruit, tamarind chutney, jerk seasonings, love potions, and hangover cures. The art gallery next door showcases Caribbean paintings, affordable prints, Haitian voodoo flags, and pottery. You can purchase Pusser's rum and yachting-style casualwear at **Pusser's Company Store;** or T-shirts and other small souvenirs at the colorful pastel-painted stalls behind the waterfront.

Shopaholics will also find assorted boutiques and souvenir outlets at the **Soper's Hole Marina** in the West End.

NETHERLANDS ANTILLES & ARUBA

ARUBA

Duty-free bargain hunters will find most of the big stores in Oranjestad's Ports of Call Marketplace, Renaissance Marketplace & Mall, Royal Plaza, Sun Plaza Mall, and Wharfside Mall, also along the main street, Caya G.F. Croes. China, linens, electronic goods, perfumes, and designer clothes are all good buys at around 20–30 percent below U.S. prices.

Jewelry is a popular buy, and **Gandelmen Jewelers** outlets around town stock precious and semi-precious jewelry items, designer watches, Montblanc pens, Baccarat crystal, china, and leather accessories.

For arts and crafts, check out **Artesania Arubiano**, L.G. Smith Boulevard 178, for paintings, pottery and other handcrafted local goods. Also, the **Bonbini Festival** at Fort Zoutman every Tuesday evening.

CURAÇAO

Willemstad offers good deals on perfume, jewelry, china, cameras, and electronic goods. The major stores and boutiques are crowded into the Punda district around Breedestraat. On the Otrabanda side, close to the cruise terminal, **Kas Di Alma Blou** (the Blue House), is a popular stop with art lovers. A small and well-stocked gallery, it showcases local artwork, photographs, and a few antique maps and prints.

Out in the countryside, several landhuisen, including **Landhuis Jan Nok** and **Landhuis Bloemhof,** house arts and crafts galleries.

SABA

Mary Gertrude Johnson introduced the art of drawn threadwork, or Saban lace, to the island in the 1870s, and intricately embroidered linen tableware is sold in several **Windwardside** craft shops. Another local specialty is Saba Spice, a 75.5-proof rum flavored with cinnamon, cloves, nutmeg, orange peel, and brown sugar. For local artworks, look in at potter Judy Stewart's **Peanut Gallery,** Lambee Plaza, for ceramics, woodcarvings and colorful paintings.

SINT MAARTEN/ ST.- MARTIN

Both Dutch and French sides of the island offer duty-free shopping and deals worth 25–50 percent on perfumes, electronic goods, jewelry, china, crystal, linen, and fashions.

Philipsburg's **Front Street** shopping district boasts the widest array of goods, and even a New World outlet for classic Dutch ceramics. The **Dutch Delft Blue Gallery** imports blue and white Delftware, and also rare green and Japanese Imari-style Delft designs from Holland.

For locally-made souvenirs, check out the open-air **Philipsburg Market Place,** on Back Street. Also the boutiques, stores and sidewalk cafés on Old Street.

Marigot is the island's fashion capital. The small mall by the marina is brimful with boutiques selling designer labels, and the fashion-conscious can take their pick from racks of elegant apparel from the high priests of the fashion scene, including Dior, Gaultier, Gallino and Lacroix. Around the dock, **Gingerbread Mahogany** is one of the best Haitian art galleries in the Caribbean.

Down by the waterfront in the West Indies Mall, there is an outpost of **Hédiard,** the famous Parisian delicatessen, well-stocked with foie gras, fine wines, caviar, and confits.

LEEWARD ISLANDS

ANGUILLA

Black-belt shopaholics may suffer withdrawal symptoms on Anguilla. However, it does offer a couple of interesting arts and crafts outlets. The **Savannah Gallery** in The Valley specializes in Haitian paintings, tin carvings, fabulous sequined voodoo flags, and works by local photographers.

On Main Road West, look for **Cheddie's Carving Studio,** where Cheddie Richardson exhibits his driftwood sculptures and limited edition bronzes. Also Fabiana Liburd's **Why Knot** boutique selling lovely lightweight and versatile cotton fashions.

ANTIGUA

Downtown **St. John's** is this island's chief shopping district. **Heritage Quay** is packed with duty-free stores selling jewelry, designer fashions, perfumes, and gifts. On **Redcliffe Quay,** there are boutiques stocked with colorful island fashions; Hans Smit sells his innovative and temptingly affordable jewelry at The **Goldsmitty;** and **Kate Design,** in a shady square marked by signs off the main drag, is a showcase for St. Kitts-based artist Kate Spencer's limited edition prints, greeting cards, table mats, and T-shirts, as well as a small line of stunning printed silk scarves and shirts.

Outside St. John's, **Harmony Hall** on the east coast is a great place to check out local arts and crafts (see p. 213). Also **Rhythm of Blue,** English Harbour, where potter Nancy Nicholson and scrimshaw artist Michael

Strzalkowski showcase their work alongside other local and regional artists.

ST. KITTS

The **Caribelle Batik factory** at Old Road Town is a favorite stop on the St. Kitts shopping trail; also the **Plantation Picture House,** painter Kate Spencer's gallery-cum-studio at the Rawlins Plantation Inn in Mount Pleasant. **Island Hopper,** on The Circus in downtown Basseterre, stocks colorful beachwear and souvenirs. Down Bank Street, Kate Spencer strikes again with **Kate Design,** and a collection of prints and greeting cards of local scenes, as well as lovely printed silks.

On Independence Square at the **Spencer Cameron Gallery** you'll find both originals and prints, from Gloria Lynn's market ladies and Donald Dahlke's fishwives to Rosie Cameron Smith's carnival dancers and tropical fruits.

Glass Island (4–5 Princes St.) is chock-full of fused glass plates, picture frames, Christmas tree decorations, and colored glass earrings with silver fittings.

NEVIS

Charlestown's restored waterfront district boasts a few small boutiques and souvenir outlets, as does the Cotton Ginnery building nearby. **Island Hopper,** on Main Street, carries Caribelle Batik's bright, casual clothing from St. Kitts.

St. Kitts artist Kate Spencer's watercolor prints, silk scarves, and Caribbean-style table accessories are on sale at the **Café des Arts** gallery, on the waterfront. Café owners Gillian Smith and Ceri Whitfield offer half-day gallery tours to meet local artists and crafts people with lunch afterwards (information, tel 869/469-7098).

Stamp collectors can capture a little local color at the **Nevis Philatelic Bureau,** in Lower Happy Hill Alley between the ferry berth and Main Street.

FRENCH ANTILLES

GUADELOUPE

Shopping is not a high priority in Guadeloupe, though French luxury goods at mainland prices can be tempting. Some **Pointe-à-Pitre** stores offer an extra 20 percent discount on purchases made with a credit card or traveler's checks.

The capital's main shopping streets are **rue Frébault, rue Schoelcher,** and **rue de Noziers,** and there are small, upscale boutiques in the **Centre St.-John Perse** mall by the cruise-ship terminal.

Rum is available from supermarkets, the airport duty-free, or the Musée du Rhum in Bellevue. Gosier, Ste.-Anne, and St.-François all have handicrafts shops and stalls specializing in Caribbean arts and crafts, and souvenirs such as costume dolls dressed in bright Madras cotton.

MARTINIQUE

Fort-de-France is the style capital of the French Antilles, offering French luxury goods from designer fashions and perfumes to china and glass at prices lower than in mainland France. Some stores give an additional 20 percent discount for purchases made with U.S. traveler's checks (always ask).

The best selection of boutiques is found along **rue Victor Hugo** and the grid of streets between **rue de la République** and **rue de la Liberté.** Jewelers on rue Lamartine and rue Isambert are an excellent hunting ground for Baccarat crystal, Limoges porcelain, and jewelry including the *chaîne forçat,* a gold "slave chain" necklace that puts the finishing touch to traditional Creole costume. Madras cotton traditional costumes and frilly white shirts are sold at market stalls in most towns.

Martiniquan rum is among the Caribbean's finest, and the island's basketware, pottery, shell art, and patchwork can be found at the **Centre des Métiers d'Art,** rue Ernest Deproge.

ST.- BARTHÉLEMY

St. Barts' duty-free status is a good excuse to indulge in some seriously upscale retail therapy. Cartier, Gucci, and Hermès all maintain outposts in **Gustavia,** alongside duty-free emporiums such as **Carat,** on rue de la République, **Goldfinger,** on rue de la France, and **Oro de Sol** at Le Carré d'Or, quai de la République. French perfumes and cosmetics, jewelry, watches, and crystal are all popular buys.

Wine buffs can check out the impressive vintage selection at **Cellier du Gouverneur,** quai de la République.

For the best French and Italian designer fashions, try **Stéphane & Bernard** at Gallerie Gréaux. **Villa Créole mall** in St. Jean has more boutiques, and **La Boutique Made in St.-Barth** carries souvenir T-shirts, paintings, and handcrafted works of art produced on the island.

WINDWARD ISLANDS

DOMINICA

The island's Carib craftsmen are famous for their basketware made from l'arouma reeds. The intricate designs are fashioned in a combination of natural, brown, and black, and can be bought from roadside stalls in **Carib Territory,** or from one of Roseau's many crafts shops. The **Iris Dangleben Gallery** (31 Cork St.) exhibits works by many of Dominica's leading artists. Names to look out for include Darius David and Arnold Toulon (painters), and Carl Winston (woodcarver). Another good gallery and source of local handicrafts is **Butterfly Boutique** at Papillote Wilderness Retreat.

There is a **Craft Market,** behind the Dominican Museum, which combines local crafts with a raft of souvenirs. Dominican products to look out for include the island's 100 percent Arabica coffee, Café Sisserou, bay rum rum and colognes from Dominica Essential Oils & Spices, and Bello's pepper sauces, fruit syrups, and marmalades.

GRENADA

Spices are a great buy on Grenada. Mixed baskets of nutmeg, cinnamon, cloves, and bay rum leaves make great gifts for cooks, or as souvenir potpourri.

The **Carenage** boasts several small galleries and craft shops. Check out **Yellow Poui Art Galleries (**Cross St.) for local art, photography, crafts, and antique map prints. In the **Art Fabrik** boutique you can see the batik process in the courtyard factory (9 Young St.), opposite **Tikal,** another crafts store.

Convenient for the southern beach hotels, **Grand Anse Shopping Centre** has a good selection of gift shops and galleries selling Caribbean arts and crafts, and boutiques stocking island fashions. There is a local spice market, too, located between the main road and the beach.

ST. LUCIA

The waterfront **Castries craft market,** and the vendors' market across the street, offer T-shirts, hand-woven straw goods, local pottery, and woodcarvings.

Another mini magnet for shoppers is the attractive open-air mall at **Pointe Seraphine.** Among the duty-free stores and boutiques, **St. Lucia Fine Art** sells antique prints of Caribbean flora and fauna and works by contemporary local artists including Llewellyn Xavier (studio visits by arrangement with the gallery). Local cottage industries include **Bagshaw Studios,** which sells their colorful hand-printed clothing and tableware in Pointe Seraphine, and from a factory shop at La Toc, just outside Castries. On Morne Fortune, **Eudovic's Studio** specializes in woodcarvings. A supermarket, post office, banks and boutiques gather at Gablewoods Mall (on the road to Rodney Bay), where **Sunshine Books** features West Indian literature and works by St. Lucian Nobel Prize winner Derek Walcott.

At Victoria in the south, the **Livity Art Studio** is crammed with local earthenware pottery, woodcarvings, and shell jewelry; also the **Choiseul Arts and Crafts Centre** at La Fargue Choiseul (see p. 281).

ST. VINCENT & THE GRENADINES

There is duty-free shopping at the new cruise berth in **Kingstown,** as well as boutiques and souvenir outlets offering a selection of Caribbean crafts, spices, and gift ideas.

On Bequia, there is an outpost of **Noah's Arkade** at the Frangipani Hotel in Port Elizabeth, and a **waterfront craft market** selling beachwraps, T-shirts, and bead jewelry. Bequia's boat-building heritage is celebrated in miniature at **Sargeant Brothers,** and slightly more affordably at **Whitfield Sails & Model Boats,** both on Front Street. Further afield, check out the artists' studios at **The Boathouse,** Friendship Bay; **The Banana Patch,** Paget Farm; and **Spring Pottery & Art Gallery,** in an old sugar mill at Spring.

BARBADOS

Bridgetown is a duty-free port offering savings of up to 30–50 percent off European and U.S. retail prices. The best of the tax-free action is on Broad Street, where the **Cave Shepherd, Harrisons** department stores, and the **DaCostas Mall** offer the widest selection of jewelry and watches, cameras, electronic goods, china, crystal, perfumes, and cosmetics. To make a duty-free purchase, take the immigration slip issued on arrival in Barbados; most stores will deliver to the airport or hotel.

For Caribbean crafts and island fashions, check out the **Pelican Craft Centre,** near Bridgetown Harbour, and colorful **Chattel Village** shopping complexes in Holetown and St. Lawrence Gap. Holetown also boasts the **West Coast Mall,** while Speightstown has a duo of art galleries **Mango's** and the **Gallery of Caribbean Art.**

On the south coast, shoppers head for **Hastings Plaza** and the **Quayside Centre** in Rockley. The **Best of Barbados** boutiques around the island are a good source of quality local crafts and gifts.

TRINIDAD & TOBAGO

The lower end of **Frederick Street** in Port of Spain resembles a hectic international bazaar. Indian sari shops and boutiques spill out onto the sidewalk, street vendors hawk jewelry, leather goods, and the latest calypso, soca, and chutney tapes and CDs, and **Selection House** (Woodford Sq.) stocks souvenirs and kitsch from costume dolls and mini steel pans to crafts and beachwear.

For a more upscale goods, take a trip to the **Ellerslie Court shopping center** in Maraval, and the **Market Shoppes,** with its boutiques, galleries and craft shops attached to the Normandie Hotel (Nook Ave., St. Ann).

Tobago is somewhat limited on mainstream shopping, but there are no shortage of arts and crafts. The small shopping village at **Store Bay** offers a colorful array of batik and tie-dye beachwear, T-shirts, straw hats, bead jewelry, pottery, and other crafts. Check out local galleries and studios as you tour the island.

INDEX

Bold page numbers indicate illustrations

A

B